D0578484

# Human Rights Innovators

# Human Rights Innovators

## Volume 2
## M-Z

SALEM PRESS
A Division of EBSCO Information Services, Inc.
Ipswich, Massachusetts

**GREY HOUSE PUBLISHING**

Cover photo: Leymah Gbowee

Copyright ©2016, by Salem Press, A Division of EBSCO Information Services, Inc., and Grey House Publishing, Inc.

All rights reserved. No part of this work may be used or reproduced in any manner whatsoever or transmitted in any form or by any means, electronic or mechanical, including photocopy, recording, or any information storage and retrieval system, without written permission from the copyright owner. For information contact Grey House Publishing/ Salem Press, 4919 Route 22, PO Box 56, Amenia, NY 12501

Human Rights Innovators, 2016, published by Grey House Publishing, Inc., Amenia, NY, under exclusive license from EBSCO Publishing, Inc.

∞ The paper used in these volumes conforms to the American National Standard for Permanence of Paper for Printed Library Materials, Z39.48 1992 (R2009).


Publisher's Cataloging-In-Publication Data
(Prepared by The Donohue Group, Inc.)

Names: Salem Press.
Title: Human rights innovators / [edited by] Salem Press.
Description: [First edition]. | Ipswich, Massachusetts : Salem Press, a division of EBSCO Information Services ; Amenia, NY : Grey House Publishing, [2016] | Includes bibliographical references and index.
Identifiers: ISBN 978-1-68217-157-8 (set) | ISBN 978-1-68217-159-2 (vol. 1) | ISBN 978-1-68217-160-8 (vol. 2)
Subjects: LCSH: Human rights workers--Biography. | Human rights--History--20th century. | Human rights--History--21st century.
Classification: LCC JC571 .H86 2016 | DDC 323.092/2--dc23

PRINTED IN THE UNITED STATES OF AMERICA

# CONTENTS

## VOLUME 1

# VOLUME 2

**Appendixes**

**Indexes**

# PUBLISHER'S NOTE

*Human Rights Innovators* profiles some of the most innovative human rights leaders from around the world. The individuals we have selected dedicated their work, and sometimes their entire life, to promote and protect a human rights initiative that they believed should be inherent to all individuals. By studying the lives of these influential individuals, researchers will gain new points of reference and a deeper understanding for how each of them changed history.

## SCOPE OF COVERAGE

*Human Rights Innovators* features 208 biographies of activists, writers, environmentalists, lawyers, philosophers, political leaders, scientists, and Nobel Prize recipients who have had an impact on human rights initiatives since the 1960s. Biographies represent a strong multi-ethnic, cross-gender focus. In addition to including the individual's historical significance and leadership skills, you will discover that many of the profiled human rights innovators demonstrated new and different ways of thinking for the time in which they lived, often impacting the social and political events of today. Our criteria also included the individual's appeal to high school and undergraduate students, as well as to general readers.

## ESSAY LENGTH AND FORMAT

Each biographical essay averages 4,000 words in length and offers standard reference top matter:

- The name by which the individual is best known;
- Birth and death dates, followed by locations of those events as available;
- Primary Field that the individual is most associated with;
- Synopsis of the individual's historical importance, and why he or she should be studied today.

The text of the essays is divided into the following:

- **Early Life** provides facts about the individual's upbringing and historical context;
- **Life's Work**, the heart of the article, consists of a straightforward, generally chronological account of how the individual gained recognition, emphasizing their most significant endeavors and achievements;
- **Sidebars** explore significant developments in a specific organization or group that the individual was most affiliated with;
- **Personal Life** includes post-achievement activities or positions, family life, and topics of general interest;
- **A Further Reading** section accompanies each essay providing a starting point for additional research.

## SPECIAL FEATURES

Several features distinguish this series from other biographical reference works. The back matter includes the following valuable elements:

- **Annotated Timeline** presents a comprehensive list of milestone events in the evolution of human rights;
- **Website Directory** for major human rights organizations and movements;
- **Category Index** lists human rights innovators by the field in which they had the most impact;
- **Index** includes figures, organizations, groups, and events.

## CONTRIBUTORS

Salem Press would like to extend its appreciation to all involved in the development and production of this work.

# KEY TO ABBREVIATIONS USED IN FURTHER READING

| | | | | |
|---|---|---|---|---|
| Ag | August | My | May |
| Ap | April | N | November |
| A.P. | Associate Press | nd | no date |
| D | December | no | number |
| ed | edited, edition, editor | O | October |
| F | February | p | page |
| il | illustrated | pam | pamphlet |
| J | Journal | por | portrait, -s |
| Ja | January | S | September |
| Je | June | sup | supplement |
| Jl | July | tr | translated, translation, translator |
| mag | magazine | v | volume |
| Mr | March | w | weekly |

# Human Rights Innovators

# M

## MA JUN

### Environmentalist

**Born:** 1968; Qingdao, China
**Primary Field:** Environmentalism
**Affiliation:** Institute of Public and Environmental Affairs (IPE)

#### INTRODUCTION

*Ma Jun is the founding director of the Institute of Public and Environmental Affairs (IPE), an independent research organization in China. A former journalist, he is the author of the book* China's Water Crisis *(1999), Ma is considered one of China's foremost environmental activists, known for combining old-fashioned detective work and digital media to pressure multinational corporations and state-owned enterprises to reform their business practices. Though IPE has no official regulatory authority, Ma and his team have been able to affect change through the distribution of information. This in itself is revolutionary in China, where the government often obscures or censors information about issues it views to be politically sensitive. According to Chi-Chu Tschang for the blog* Business of Water *(2 Apr. 2011), "[the] Chinese government actually generates voluminous amounts of data [on the environment]," However, "no one had collected the data and put it into a database for everyone to access until the IPE came along."*

*The IPE's air and water pollution maps have helped to increase public awareness about environmental issues in China, "When 1 look at China's environmental problems, the real barrier is not lack of technology or money," Ma told Christina Larson for* Fast Company *(27 Apr. 2012). "It's lack of motivation. The motivation should come from regulatory enforcement, but enforce-*

*ment is weak and environmental litigation is near to impossible, so there's an urgent need for extensive public participation to generate another land of motivation."*

*In 2006, Ma was listed in the Time 100, Time magazine's list of the world's one hundred most influential people. For his innovative brand of grassroots environmentalism, Ma was awarded the Goldman Prize for Asia—often described as the "Green Nobel Prize"—in 2012.*

#### EARLY LIFE

Ma was born in Qingdao, a large city in China's Shandong province, in 1968. His mother was an administrator and his father was an engineer. They raised Ma in Beijing. "[It] was such a different city/" Ma told Larson, recalling the capital's lack of cars and the variety of bugs "swirling" around the city streetlamps. He learned the poems of Chinas great ancient poets, such as Li Bai and Du Fu, who revered the country's rivers and wildlife. "I also have a vivid memory of dazzling sunlight coming out of the sky," he told Larson. Now, Beijing's skies are clouded with smog from cars, burning coal, construction, and factories. In an article for the bilingual environmental news website *China Dialogue* (13 Mar. 2012), Ma wrote that the city's lung cancer rates have risen by 60 percent over the last ten years. He imagines a day in Beijing without pollution, stating, "On the morning of that day, you won't wake up with a sore throat [and] in the dazzling sunlight of an afternoon, even very ordinary buildings will look beautiful against the blue backdrop of the sky."

After graduating with a degree in journalism from the University of International Relations in Beijing, Ma joined the Beijing staff of the *South China Morning Post*

## Affiliation: Institute of Public and Environmental Affairs (IPE)

Ma founded the Institute of Public and Environmental Affairs (IPE) in 2006, and the group's first project, the China Water Pollution Map, was launched in September. Ma told Haffner that the IPE and its databases were founded on the idea that "participation requires information." The IPE began with Ma, two staffers, and a network of volunteers rooting out company violations from a mass of records. In 2007, the IPE joined a coalition of NGOs to launch the Green Choice Alliance, a database that allows consumers and companies to search for records of a supplier's violations within the previous nine years. In 2008, the IPE's job got a little easier after the Chinese government passed a law requiring local governments to release pollution data. The same year, Walmart used the database to identify factories within their supply chain that were in violation of China's green laws and worked with the IPE to make changes in those factories. Other international brands like Panasonic, Coca-Cola, GE, Levi's, and Microsoft followed suit—citing the database as evidence for changes in their supply chains.

In 2009, the IPE uncovered a plethora of reports of heavy metal pollution causing health problems, though the source surprised them. "To our surprise, the source wasn't mines or government-operated smelters," Ma told Larson, "but factories manufacturing global IT equipment." As it turned out, IT companies were responsible for several other public health violations. Factory workers in at least one plant were exposed to a chemical called n-hexane, used to clean touch screens, and were suffering from nerve damage. After undertaking an investigation that sought to match the offending factories with the international companies that employed them, the IPE found that Wintek, the company operating the factory where there had been reports of exposure to n-hexane and a subcontractor of the company Foxconn, was a supplier for Apple.

that the book could be considered "for China, what Rachel Carson's *Silent Spring* was for the U.S.—the country's first great environmental call to arms."

## LIFE'S WORK

In 2000, Ma became the chief representative of the *South China Morning Post* website. Two years later, he joined China's Sinosphere Corporation as an environmental consultant. In this role, he made a startling realization when he was tasked with preparing a corporate social responsibility (CSR) program for the supply chain of a major company. The company was reviewing the practices of its supply chain under pressure from labor and environmental groups, and Ma was surprised by the company's decision to change its business practices in light of public discontent. "When we first identified gaps, and made clear that if [the suppliers] didn't change they were going to lose their business, they changed, their behavior in just a few months," Ma told John Haffner for Carnegie Councils online magazine, *Policy Innovations* (11 Feb. 2013). "When you put a multimillion dollar contract at stake, it has big leverage."

Ma was invited to Yale University in New Haven, Connecticut, as a visiting World Fellow in 2004. At Yale, he compared environmental management laws and systems in China with those of the United States. Ma observed that successful environmental agencies in the West took violators to court. However, he knew that in China'—where courts were often beholden to local officials sympathetic to polluters—such a route would not be effective. Instead, Ma realized that if he put the information in the hands of the people (or from a business perspective, the customers) they might be motivated to act as a unit, putting pressure on the Chinese government as well as shaming offending companies into cleaning up their act. After struggling to find a publisher for his next book upon returning to China in 2005, Ma decided to use his writing as a guide for establishing an organization devoted to environmental issues.

as a researcher and translator in 1993. Travelling for his job, Ma was shocked by the environmental impact of the Three Gorges Dam project and the dried up remains of Dongting Lake; it was not the landscape he remembered from the poems of his childhood, Ma wanted to write a story about water pollution and ill-advised engineering projects like the Yellow River Commission, but realized that he had compiled too much information for just a single news article. Using the archives that were available to him as a journalist, Ma wrote a book called *China's Water Crisis,* which published in 2004. It took a while for the book to find its audience, but later, the actor and environmentalist Ed Norton (whose father oversaw the Nature Conservancy's Yunnan Great Rivers project in China) mote in *Time* magazine (8 May 2006)

In 2010, the IPE and the Green Alliance contacted Apple's CEO Steve Jobs, as well as the CEOs of twenty-eight other tech companies to report their findings. Siemens, the German electronics conglomerate, was among a number of companies that agreed to work with the IPE. Apple did not. The tech giant refused to confirm its relationship to any of the factories—arguing that, as Gies put it, releasing such information would 'Jeopardize trade secrets." Though this response was clearly a dismissal, Ma assured Apple that the IPE was not interested in smearing the company, only in improving environmental and working conditions.

This shrewd approach has set Ma apart from other activists. He seeks to work with companies to make a change, appearing to operate under the premise that, if companies only knew-what was happening within their supply chain they would work to make it right. "He's naturally cooperative, more of a Paul Newman-style activist than Ralph Nader," Larson wrote of Ma. Still, Ma's attempts to reach out to Apple were met with silence. The same year, Ma sent a letter to Jobs, written with a factory worker named Jia Jing-chuan who was hospitalized for n-hexane poisoning. Alter the letter went unanswered, Ma took a more public tack. What followed is an excellent example of Mas own efficient use of informed public participation as a tool for activism.

Ma launched a social media "Poison Apple" campaign protesting Apple's lack of oversight. In January 2011, Ma wrote a report called "The Other Side of Apple" that was published widely on the Internet. It chronicles Apple's digressions and subsequent denial of any wrongdoing. It also includes information on twelve employee suicides that occurred at Foxconn in 2010. Ma also produced a video that intercuts footage of factory workers suffering from n-hexane poisoning with images from Apple's celebrated launch events.

Soon after, Apple released its own progress report. The paper confirms reports of n-hexane poisoning in its factories, but fails to address any of the larger issues raised by the IPE. The IPE launched a full investigation into Apple's supply chain, which culminated in a forty-six-page report called "The Other Side of Apple II," published in September 2011, Its release coincided with Tim Cooks official promotion to CEO at Apple, following the death of Jobs in October 2011Within a week of Cook's tenure, the company contacted the IPE to set up a meeting to discuss issues related to n-hexane exposure. In 2012, Apple issued a supplier-responsibility progress report, citing environmental audits on fourteen of the company's suppliers.

According to a January 2013 report from the IPE, Apple has made significant strides since 2010. Most notably, the company has allowed third-party audits of some of its business practices, overseen by the IPE and the Green Alliance. "Apple and the NGOs [IPE, Friends of Nature, Envirofriends, and Nanjing Greenstone], in a step-by-step process, gradually came to a common understanding to push highly polluting materials suppliers to make real changes," the IPE wrote in a January 29, 2013, press release. Ma has expressed the hope that the IPE's success with Apple will encourage other companies to self-regulate.

In 2013, Ma and the IPE launched a social media campaign called "Take a Picture to Locate a Polluter," in which citizens and activists are encouraged to post photos of environmental pollution and offending factories. After a photo is posted, the IPE investigates and verifies the claim. The value of the project is two-fold: the crowd sourcing improves the accuracy of the IPE pollution maps, and it gives the amateur photographer a sense of affectivity—a sense of being a part of something larger.

The availability of clean water in China is an issue that has continued to plague the country, According to a report in the *Economist* in October 2013, the situation has become increasingly dire in the years after Ma's book was first published. China is facing a dangerous water shortage due to the country's unsustainable levels of consumption. In addition, there are significant regional disparities pertaining to water resources—most of China's water is in the south, but half of its population and most of its farmland are in the north. Additionally, pollution from farms and factories present additional environmental problems, making what little water remains largely unusable. According to the *Economist* (12 Oct, 2013), only half of the water sources in Chinese cities are fit to drink: "More than half the groundwater in the north China plain, according to the land ministry, cannot be used for industry, while seven- tenths is unfit for human contact, i.e., even for washing."

To rectify the problem, the Chinese government proposed the South-North Water Diversion Project, a vast linkage of canals and tunnels connecting the Yangzi River in the south with the Yellow River in the north. China has accomplished several large-scale water infrastructure projects—the best known being the Three Gorges Dam on the Yangzi Riven Nevertheless, many environmentalists'—including Ma—have argued that the water diversion project will do more harm than good. Environmentalists argue that rather than looking for ways to conserve water and ways to crack down on polluters, the Chinese government has focused on increasing water supply in the short term, wreaking more environmental havoc in the process. Ma told Naomi Li for *China Dialogue* (21 Sept. 2006) that local government officials are all too willing to sacrifice clean water for the revenue that regulation-flouting companies bring to the provinces. "Water issues present a dichotomy between development and environmental protection. The central government has adjusted some of its strategies and policies, but at a local level, officials still place too great an emphasis on economic development."

The Chinese government has become more responsive to the pleas of environmentalists, in part a result of work conducted by organizations like the IPE. The Chinese media has begun to issue more reports on pollution and the environment, and some local authorities are beginning to warm to the idea of tougher regulations. Mere generally, enthusiasm for environmental action in China has been spurred by abysmal conditions in the country. On October 25, 2013, Edward Wong for the *New York Times* reported that the northeastern city of Harbin was shut down by dangerous smog conditions. The emergency terrified residents who wondered what the coming months might bring. "With winter approaching, cities north of the Huai River are turning on their coal-fired municipal heating systems, whose emissions were found in one study to shorten residents' life spans by an average of five years," Wong wrote.

The city has undertaken an emergency program aimed at decreasing air pollution, but Ma, who was interviewed by Wong for the article, said the program is not enough. "I think people won't be satisfied with just knowing which day to put on face masks or not go to school or keep their children indoors. They really want blue-sky days."

## PERSONAL LIFE

Ma lives in Beijing.

## FURTHER READING

*Gies, Erica. "Advocate Helps Track Polluters on Supply Chain." New York Times. New York Times, 22 Apr. 2012. Web. 18 Dec. 2013. Haffner, John, and Ma Jun. "Ma Jun: Information Empowers." Policy Innovations. Policy Innovations, 11 Feb. 2013. Web. 18 Dec. 2013; Larson, Christina. "Most Creative People of 2012: 1. Ma Jun." Fast Company. Mansueto Ventures, 27 Apr. 2012. Web. 18 Dec. 2013; Ma Jun. "Tackling China's Water Crisis Online." Interview by Naomi Li. China Dialogue. China Dialogue, 21 Sept. 2006. Web. 18 Dec. 2013; "Water: All Dried Up." Economist. Economist Newspaper, 12 Oct. 2013. Web. 18 Dec. 2013; Wong, Edward. "Response to a City's Smog Points to a Change in Chinese Attitude." New York Times 25 Oct. 2013: A12. Print.*

---

# CATHARINE A. MACKINNON

## Professor; Writer; Political Activist

**Born:** October 7, 1946; Minneapolis, Minnesota
**Primary Field:** Feminism

## INTRODUCTION

*In the late 1970s and early 1980s, the pivotal work of the controversial lawyer, professor, and feminist activist Catharine A. MacKinnon convinced the United States federal courts that sexual harassment is a form of sex discrimination and, therefore, illegal according to existing civil rights statutes. Her more than twenty-year legal battle against sexual harassment and pornography prompted Fred Strebeigh to describe her as "the law's most prominent feminist legal theorist" in his profile of her in the* New York Times Magazine *(October 6, 1991), in which he asserted that during the 1980s "MacKinnon may have had as much effect on American law as any professor in the country." Laurence H. Tribe, a professor at Harvard Law School, told Strebeigh that "feminist legal theory is likely to be the most fertile source of important insights in the law" of the future, superseding the two most important recent trends in legal thought: critical legal studies, which are concerned with the status quo, and economics and the law, whose main architect, Richard A. Posner, studies the economic consequences of legal decisions.*

## EARLY LIFE

Catharine Alice MacKinnon was born in 1946 to George E. MacKinnon, a federal appellate judge, and Elizabeth V. (Davis) MacKinnon. A Republican nominee for governor of Minnesota and a one- term congressman from that state, MacKinnon's father was an adviser to the presidential campaigns of both Dwight D. Eisenhower and Richard Nixon. "That politics was about change is—to put it mildly—not what I was brought up with," MacKinnon told Strebeigh. Like her mother and her grandmother before her, MacKinnon attended Smith College, in Northampton, Massachusetts, graduating magna cum laude with a B.A. degree in government in 1969. She received a J.D. from Yale University, in New Haven, Connecticut, in 1977 and a Ph.D. in political science from the same institution in 1987. A hotbed of political activism and "consciousness-raising," Yale Law School was not unlike many other institutions of higher learning during the 1970s. As a graduate student, MacKinnon protested against the Vietnam War, learned martial arts, and worked with the radical activist group the Black Panthers. During that time, she also cofounded a lawyers' collective, became involved with the burgeoning women's movement, and created the first course to be included in Yale's women's studies program.

## LIFE'S WORK

MacKinnon's involvement with the issue of sexual harassment began in 1974, when she learned of the case of Carmita Wood, an administrative assistant who had resigned from her job after being sexually harassed by her supervisor. Because Wood was presumed to have left her position for "personal" reasons, she was denied unemployment benefits. Although MacKinnon, who did not become a lawyer until 1978, when she was admitted to the Connecticut state bar, was not able to help Wood, whose claim had been rejected in 1975 by an unemployment appeals board, she redefined sexual harassment as a form of sex discrimination in her thesis. "I felt this is about everything the situation of women is really about," MacKinnon told Fred Strebeigh, "everything that the law of sex discrimination made it so difficult if not impossible to address. So I decided I would just design something." Her thesis eventually became part of her first book, *Sexual Harassment of Working Women: A Case of Sex Discrimination* (1979).

Until 1977 no court had ruled that sexual harassment was discriminatory. Previous judicial decisions had deemed harassment a "private" or "personal" harm

but not a form of actionable discrimination. It was not until July of that year that the United States Court of Appeals for the District of Columbia ruled in *Barnes v. Costle* that a woman who was sexually harassed was discriminated against solely because of "her womanhood" and, therefore, illegally. One of the judges concurring in that ruling reminded the court that to some extent, the behavior it was now defining as harassment had until then been perceived as a "normal and expectable" component of private deportment. The author of that narrowing opinion was MacKinnon's father.

In 1986 the United States Supreme Court heard its first sexual harassment case, *Meritor Savings Bank v. Vinson*, with Catharine MacKinnon serving as co-counsel for Vinson. Previously, sexual harassment had been typically defined as quid pro quo—that is, sexual favors in exchange for continued employment. In this case, Mechelle Vinson, an employee at the bank, complained that her supervisor's almost constant harassment, which allegedly included forced sex, fondling in front of other employees, and following her into the women's rest room, had created working conditions so difficult that she would have eventually been compelled to quit. (Vinson had successfully sued the bank after being fired for taking excessive leave, and the bank had subsequently appealed.) MacKinnon defined this form of harassment as constituting a "hostile environment." In its groundbreaking ruling, the Supreme Court unanimously agreed that both types of sexual harassment, quid pro quo and hostile environment, were forms of sex discrimination that were illegal under Title VII of the Civil Rights Act of 1964. (In 1993 the United States Supreme Court further refined the "hostile environment" concept, ruling in *Harris v. Forklift Systems, Inc.* that employees need not prove that their sexual harassment had resulted in severe psychological damage, as several lower courts had ruled in the wake of the *Meritor decision;* an employer's harassing behavior need only "detract from employees' job performance" in order to bring Title VII into play.)

By the mid-1980s sexual harassment had been displaced as the main focus of MacKinnon's work by her involvement in a campaign against pornography, which she labeled a form of sex discrimination that harms women by creating and reinforcing misogynist attitudes that, in turn, contribute to a social climate in which violence against women becomes more likely. MacKinnon joined the feminist antipornography movement in the early 1980s, partly as an outgrowth of her friendship with Andrea Dworkin, a radical feminist writer who had been deconstructing various cultural forms of "woman hating" in her writings. Dworkin advised MacKinnon to meet Linda Marchiano, a victim and survivor of one of the more gruesome publicized cases of pornographic abuse. In her book *Ordeal*, Marchiano, who was previously known as Linda Lovelace, alleged that she was imprisoned, tortured, and coerced into making pornographic movies, the most famous of which was *Deep Throat*. Contending that each time someone watched that movie, which was released in the early 1970s, the viewer was watching Marchiano being raped (sometimes at gunpoint), MacKinnon and Marchiano sought to stop the showing of that film. (The statute of limitations had run out before MacKinnon was able to make a legal claim on Marchiano's behalf, but the lawyer nonetheless did what she could to publicize Marchiano's case.)

Arguing that pornography, which they defined as the "graphic, sexually explicit subordination" of women, was a form of sex discrimination and a violation of women's civil rights, MacKinnon and Dworkin drafted and backed antipornography legislation in Massachusetts and Florida and crafted a local ordinance, versions of which were proposed in cities across the United States, including Minneapolis, Indianapolis, Los Angeles, and Bellingham, Washington. The laws would have provided women with the legal means to sue producers, distributors, and "perpetrators" for damages if they could prove that they had been harmed as a direct result of a specific piece of pornography. So far, these laws, bills, and ordinances either have failed to win approval by local governments or have been rejected on appeal.

Many people, both in and out of the legal profession, have expressed mixed feelings about MacKinnon's attempts to "legislate morality," as some put it, because of its possible interference with First Amendment rights. MacKinnon defended her views on the issue to Tamar Lewin for the *New York Times Book Review* (May 3, 1987): "Pornography isn't protected by the First Amendment any more than sexual harassment is. It's not a question of free speech or ideas. Pornography is a form of action, requiring the submission of women. . . . Women's experience and empirical research show the same thing: the more pornography men see, the more they enjoy it and the less sensitive they become to violence against women. A rape stops being a rape, the woman stops being a person. It's a terrifying,

escalating dynamic, and the prognostication for women is grim."

More than fifty prominent feminists signed a legal brief submitted by the Feminist Anti-Censorship Task Force (FACT), in which MacKinnon's and Dworkin's civil rights ordinance was attacked for "reinforcing] rather than undercutting] central sexist stereotypes in our society" and for containing dangerously vague definitions that might eventually be used against feminists. Accusing the members of FACT of "fronting for male supremacy," MacKinnon said, as quoted by Strebeigh, "The black movement has Uncle Toms and Oreo cookies. The women's movement has FACT." But even staunch opponents of the ordinance, such as Burt Neuborne, then the legal director of the American Civil Liberties Union, have acknowledged that MacKinnon's work had irrevocably altered the terms of debate. Neuborne told a reporter for Newsweek (March 18, 1985) that "she's changed the way people think about a problem.

She's telling people that porn is not cute, it has social ramifications, it's a symbol of a serious social malaise in the country. What racist speech was to racism, pornography is to sex discrimination."

MacKinnon had published her ideas on pornography and the law and refuted her critics in two books: *Pornography and Civil Rights: A New Day for Women's Equality,* cowritten with Andrea Dworkin and published in 1988 by the Minneapolis-based Organizing Against Pornography, and *Feminism Unmodified: Discourses on Life and Law* (1987), a collection of speeches given by MacKinnon from 1981 to 1986 on such subjects as abortion rights, rape, women's athletics, sexual harassment, and the rights of Native American women. Much of the material in *Feminism Unmodified* centers on MacKinnon's views on gender, which she has defined not in terms of natural differences between the sexes but as "an inequality of power, a social status based on who is permitted to do what to whom."

Critics of *Feminism Unmodified* took MacKinnon to task for her sometimes inscrutable style as well as for her unorthodox ideas. Maureen Mullarkey, writing in the *Nation* (May 30, 1987), charged that MacKinnon's arguments depend too heavily "on slogans, false premises, half-information, sinister innuendo, and ad hoc reasoning." Reviewing the book for *Psychology Today* (September 1987), Joanne B. Ciulla maintained that "MacKinnon's brand of radical feminism does more to alienate people from feminism than win converts.

It takes either a disciple or a charitable reader to dig through MacKinnon's circuitous reasoning and angry rhetoric for the nuggets of truth." In a mostly favorable evaluation for the *New York Times Book Review* (May 3, 1987), the political philosopher Alison M. Jaggar noted that MacKinnon's work "is not without elitist elements. For instance, she does not hesitate to reinterpret women's accounts of their own experience when those accounts conflict with her assertions." Nonetheless, Jaggar concluded, "to readers who can grapple with her style, Ms. MacKinnon offers a systematic and persuasive perspective on issues that are central not only to feminism but to social theory in general."

A watershed in MacKinnon's academic career came in 1989, when she was offered a tenured position at the University of Michigan Law School, in Ann Arbor. For much of the preceding decade, MacKinnon had been a visiting professor at such prestigious institutions as Yale University, Harvard University, Stanford University, the University of California at Los Angeles, and the University of Chicago. She was an assistant professor of law at the University of Minnesota from 1982 to 1984 and a professor of law at York University, in Toronto, from 1988 until she accepted the position at Michigan. Even her appointments for visiting professorships did not come easily. She was widely criticized for her views, and her scholarship was called into question. As MacKinnon told at an audience at Stanford in 1982, "My work is considered not law by lawyers, not scholarship by academics, too practical by intellectuals, too intellectual by practitioners, and neither politics nor science by political scientists."

Explaining why MacKinnon's acceptance by the mainstream may have taken so long, Lee Bollinger, the dean of the Michigan Law School, told Tamar Lewin of the *New York Times* (February 24, 1989), "I think a lot of people initially feel threatened by her ideas. . . . But as you look at what she's written, the force of her scholarship and the quality of her mind becomes more and more apparent." Joseph Weiler, the head of the law school's appointment committee, told Lewin that he considered MacKinnon to be "the leading figure" in the field of feminist jurisprudence, and he called her "a major scholar" and a "major social theorist." Thrilled with her new post, MacKinnon said, in an interview with Lewin, that being asked to join the faculty at Michigan was "like being called to the priesthood," and she added, "I take it as a victory for women, in that you can hold out for the integrity of your work and still survive.

I understand it as an expression of the seriousness with which they take the kind of work I do, and their willingness to recognize other models of scholarship than the traditional one."

MacKinnon continued to publish the results of her scholarly research and to address feminist issues in her book *Toward a Feminist Theory of the State* (1989). Written over a period of eighteen years, the book constitutes MacKinnon's attempt to analyze politics, sexuality, and the law from women's perspective. Assessing the book for the *Nation* (January 8-15, 1990), Wendy Brown wrote, "MacKinnon's persistent endeavor to codify the feminist analysis and the feminist method is emblematic of a profoundly static world view and an undemocratic, perhaps even antidemocratic, political sensibility. This political and intellectual rigidity, with its attendant defensiveness and dismissiveness toward others toiling in similar fields, profoundly subverts her wide erudition, searing critical faculties, sagacity about the pernicious ways of liberal jurisprudence, and passion for feminist justice."

*Toward a Feminist Theory of the State* contains further elucidation of MacKinnon's stance on pornography, which she defined as "the technologically sophisticated traffic in women that expropriates, exploits, uses, and abuses women." She argued that "pornography sets the public standard for the treatment of women in private and the limits of tolerance for what can be permitted in public. ... It engenders rape, sexual abuse of children, battery, forced prostitution, and sexual murder. In liberal legalism, pornography is said to be a form of freedom of speech. . . . Women's speech is silenced by pornography and the abuse that is integral to it. . . . Once this is exposed, the urgent issue of freedom of speech for women is not primarily the avoidance of state intervention as such, but getting equal access to speech for those to whom it has been denied. First the abuse must be stopped."

Although laws upholding MacKinnon's point of view have been consistently struck down in the United States, in February 1992 the Supreme Court of Canada upheld the obscenity provision of its criminal code. In a unanimous decision, the court ruled in *R. v. Butler* that it is legitimate to suppress materials that harm women; the court also redefined obscenity to include materials that subordinate, degrade, or dehumanize women. The opinion said, in part, "If true equality between male and female persons is to be achieved, we cannot ignore the threat to equality resulting from exposure to audiences of certain types of violent and degrading material. Materials portraying women as a class as objects for sexual exploitation and abuse have a negative impact on the individual's sense of self- worth and acceptance."

"This makes Canada the first place in the world that says what is obscene is what harms women, not what offends our values," MacKinnon, who helped write the brief, told Tamar Lewin of the *New York Times* (February 28, 1992). "In the United States the obscenity laws are all about not liking to see naked bodies, or homosexual activity, in public. Our laws don't consider the harm to women." It was the Canadian court's decision that the materials' potential for harm to women justifies the law's limitations on freedom of expression guaranteed in the Canadian Charter of Rights and Freedoms, which is similar to the United States Bill of Rights. The court determined that the "community as a whole" is the arbiter of what materials contain "undue exploitation of sex," adding that "the portrayal of sex coupled with violence will almost always constitute the undue exploitation of sex." (Some exceptions were made for explicit sexual materials used for artistic purposes.)

In her book, *Only Words* (1993), MacKinnon went beyond the rallying cry coined years ago by the writer Robin Morgan: "Pornography is the theory and rape the practice." In *Only Words* pornography itself is described as the practice, indistinguishable from action. "In terms of what the men are doing sexually," she wrote, "an audience watching a gang rape in a movie is no different from an audience watching a gang rape that is re-enacting a gang rape from a movie, or an audience watching any gang rape." Most reviewers found her prose hyperbolic and condemned as totalitarian her ideas about using state power to ensure women's equality. To show that there is a difference between thought and deed, Carlin Romano took her argument that "unwelcomed sex talk is an unwelcome sex act [and] to say it is to do it and to do it is to say it" to its logical extreme and described the rape of MacKinnon in print, in his review of *Only Words* for the *Nation* (November 15, 1993). Analyzing the controversial review in the *Village Voice* (January 4, 1994), Nat Hentoff concluded that "Romano deliberately, cruelly, set out to debase Catharine MacKinnon's person, along with her ideas. It was not a rape that will land him in a cell, but his name will be connected with it for a long time."

One notable exception to the tenor of most critics' evaluations of *Only Words* was that of Charlotte Allen's review for the *Washington Post* (November 28, 1993).

Observing that "MacKinnon does paint a melodramatic tableau in Only Words of omnipresent rape, abuse, and sexual harassment, even in the home," Allen found such overstatement useful, because "MacKinnon forces us to face the unpleasant fact that although we have created a fiction of gender-blind egalitarianism, biology—along with the palpable differences between the sexes it entails—remains intractable.... In her clumsy, exaggerated, even demented way, MacKinnon sees the real harm of pornography: that it expresses and encourages the breakdown of the customary restraints on the libido that make up the social fabric in general and regulate relations between men and women in particular.... In short, she shows the dark side, the true side, of male-female relations."

## PERSONAL LIFE

Known as Kitty to her friends and family, Catharine MacKinnon was described by Fred Strebeigh as being "among the most dynamic legal lecturers in the country, a speaker so forceful that her entire body seems intellectually engaged. Her eyes seem to flash, her shoulders to broaden. Even her hair seems implicated: it begins most classes piled high in an abundant Gibson, but as her lecture unfolds, it does also, ending in a cascade down her shoulders." Paul Brest, the dean of Stanford Law School, told Strebeigh, "Nobody who has ever had her as a teacher is not affected in a significant way."

Perhaps because of all the hostility her work has engendered, MacKinnon has been rather guarded in discussing her private life with reporters, often refusing to cater to what she perceives as the public's unwillingness to listen to a woman without first ascertaining her marital or sexual status. "There is this urgent need," she explained to Strebeigh, "to define women by whom they have sex with—without [knowing] that, people don't seem to know how to read." Nevertheless, Dinitia Smith revealed in *New York* (March 22, 1993) that MacKinnon was engaged to the psychoanalyst and writer Jeffrey Moussaieff Masson. When asked by Smith how she could justify marriage given her views, MacKinnon replied, "Does one not have any relations simply because society is hierarchical? We do our best. He's not not a man, and I'm not not a woman."

## FURTHER READING
*N Y Times Mag p28+ O 6 '91 pors; New York 26:36+ Mr 22 '93 pors; Contemporary Authors vol 132 (1991); Who's Who of American Women, 1993-94*

# THULI MADONSELA

## Public Protector of South Africa

**Born:** September 28, 1962
**Primary Field:** Social Justice
**Affiliation:** The Nkandla Report

### INTRODUCTION

*Thuli Madonsela is South Africa's public protector. As described by Alexis Okeowo for the* New York Times Magazine *(16 June 2015), Madonsela's role "falls somewhere between a government watchdog and a public prosecutor." Her office, which was created to investigate and report on government corruption, was established in the 1996 post-apartheid South African constitution. She is the third person and the first woman to hold the post. She was appointed by South African president Jacob Zuma after he was elected in 2009. The year before she came on the job, the office of the public protector handled almost nineteen thousand cases; under Madonsela, within five years the office was handling double that number.*

### EARLY LIFE

Thulisile Nomkhosi Madonsela was born on September 28, 1962, in Soweto, a township in the sprawling city of Johannesburg. (Mandela lived in Soweto until his arrest the same year Madonsela was born.) Her mother worked as a maid. Her father was an electrician who later started a taxi business. She has two sisters and one brother. Madonsela was a bright student and attended school in the neighboring country of Swaziland because her parents did not want her to study at the apartheid-era schools for black children. She loved comic books and, as a student at Evelyn Baring High School, aspired to be a lawyer. Her father, who wanted her to be a nurse, refused to pay for her higher education. Still, as Madonsela revealed in a letter to her sixteen-year-old self for *Oprah Magazine South Africa* (26 Apr. 2012), academics buoyed her self-esteem and engendered pride in her family members, friends, and church: "I know you are socially awkward, plagued by a nagging feeling of being unloved and ugly," she wrote, but "you will excel, academically, throughout your life and this will bring you to where you are right now."

Madonsela's good grades earned her a scholarship to the University of Swaziland, where she began working with the black trade union movement. Her brother,

*Thuli Madonsela.*

Musa, was an anti-apartheid activist, and their work often brought police officers knocking on the door of their family home. Madonsela earned her bachelor's degree in 1987 and graduated with a law degree from the University of the Witwatersrand (Wits) in Johannesburg in 1990. The ban on the ANC was lifted—and Mandela was freed—the same year. Mandela was elected president of the ANC in 1991. During this historic moment in South Africa's history, Madonsela served as a legal advisor for the ANC and helped draft the country's new constitution. "It was once-in-a-lifetime," she recalled to Okeowo.

### LIFE'S WORK

In the early 1990s, along with her role in the new government, Madonsela was a research fellow and part-time lecturer at Wits Law School, and she continued her work with trade unions. For about a decade starting in 1994, she moved through positions of increasing responsibility with the Independent Electoral Commission and the Department of Justice. She was working for the South African Law Reform Commission, an independent organization that works with the South African Parliament

481

and local legislatures, when President Zuma appointed her public protector in 2009. (Candidates for the job are culled from public nominations. Finalists are interviewed by members of Parliament, who then recommend one finalist to the president.)

Madonsela approached her job with a zeal the office had not seen before. Her first major case came in 2011, when she issued a report on the national commissioner of the South African Police Service, Bheki Cele. Madonsela and her team alleged that Cele had made unlawful deals with a well-connected property company to secure sites for police headquarters in Pretoria and Durban, on the eastern coast. Cele and the government agreed to a highly inflated rate on ten-year leases for the buildings, without putting the project out to bid. While Madonsela found no evidence of criminality, in her report she said that Cele's conduct was "improper, unlawful, and amounted to maladministration." A week after releasing the report, police raided her office, looking, Aislinn Laing reported for the *Telegraph* (28 July 2012), "for documents Miss Madonsela had refused to allow Mr. Cele to see." Newspapers reported rumors that Madonsela was under investigation for corruption

---

## Affiliation: The Nkandla Report

In 2014, the same year she was named to Time magazine's list of the world's "100 Most Influential People," Madonsela presented the findings of an eighteen-month investigation of Zuma. In what would come to be called the Nkandla report, Madonsela revealed that the president had used over $20 million in taxpayer funds to renovate his sprawling estate near the town of Nkandla in the province of KwaZulu-Natal.

The report spawned a backlash from Zuma's powerful political party, the African National Congress (ANC). For South Africans, the ANC is a "democratic beacon," Okeowo wrote—the party that shaped post-apartheid South Africa, led for years by the late Nelson Mandela. The ANC has been in power in South Africa for more than two decades. Under the party's leadership, the country has made significant strides. "The lives of the bottom 20 percent have changed since apartheid," Jonny Steinberg, a South African professor at Oxford, told Okeowo. "And all of these changes have been delivered directly by the state." Still, in recent years, the country has suffered from sluggish economic growth, chronic electricity blackouts, local corruption, and a national unemployment rate of 25 percent—50 percent for young people. Accusations of cronyism and, as Okeowo reported, a mishandling of the AIDS crisis have further contributed to the party's declining public favor under the Zuma administration. But Madonsela's work illustrates the difficulty of reforming the ANC or removing it from power. In many ways, her continuing struggle with Zuma—and what it says about the power and perceived importance of her office—is the story of a country still reckoning with its past. "The work here has exposed fault lines in our democracy," Madonsela told Okeowo of her report. "It's got people talking about what kind of democracy we have—and what kind of democracy we deserve."

---

herself, but she refused to succumb to public pressure and held a press conference to announce that she was continuing her investigation. Cele was a powerful ally of Zuma's, but in 2012 Zuma, in what many viewed then as the biggest scandal of his presidency, sided with Madonsela and fired Cele. In 2014, Cele was appointed minister of agriculture, forestry, and fisheries. After the release of the Nkandla report, he criticized Madonsela in *Beel*d, an Afrikaans daily, as quoted by the South African *City Press* (7 Apr. 2014), saying, "She must stop acting like she is God."

The Cele investigation won Madonsela many supporters in South Africa and abroad; in 2011, the South African newspaper the *Daily Maverick* named Madonsela "South African Person of the Year." Liang reported that about a quarter of annual state spending (around

$3.5 billion) is wasted in kickbacks and maladministration. In South Africa, the term for this kind of corruption is "tenderpreneurship," or the practice of awarding government contracts to companies owned by government officials or their families or friends. In 2012, the BBC followed Madonsela as she investigated one case involving a primary school on the rural Eastern Cape. The school opened in 2008, but in 2012, the school had still not received money for desks or chairs. The case is indicative of the kind of work Madonsela does on a daily basis. "I was particularly concerned about the ordinary administrative wrongs against ordinary people," she told Okeowo of her attitude upon taking the job. "I wanted to position the office so that any *gogo dlamini,* any old lady, in the middle of nowhere in South Africa knows where to go when they feel they've been wronged by the state."

In March 2014, less than two months before national elections, Madonsela released the Nkandla report—culled from nearly two years of investigation and formally titled *Secure in Comfort*—regarding the financing of President Zuma's sprawling estate in the KwaZulu-Natal Province. Madonsela reported, as quoted by Alan Cowell for the *New York Times* (19 Mar. 2014), that Zuma "benefitted unduly" from state-funded improvements to his home made for the stated purpose of improving security. These improvements included an amphitheater, a helipad, a cattle enclosure, and a visitor center; a swimming pool was officially described as "firefighting equipment," Cowell reported, "to justify the cost." (Madonsela officially released the report in 2014, but a draft of it was leaked to South Africa's *Mail and Guardian* newspaper in late 2013.) Madonsela called on the president to return the money.

She faced swift retribution for her report from politicians, church leaders, and anti-apartheid organizations, some of whom went so far as to accuse her of being racist toward ANC voters. The deputy minister of defense, Kebby Maphatsoe, even accused her of being a CIA agent. "I was sad that people would stoop that low," she told Okeowo of Maphatsoe's comments. "It was the saddest moment of my career. That is the ANC that I grew up loving." The report hurt Zuma's public image, but he has yet to address it in any serious way, though he made jokes about it in Parliament in May 2015. He was elected to a second term in 2014.

In March 2015, the State Security Agency announced that it was conducting an investigation into accusations that Madonsela is a CIA agent. In April, Parliament denied her request for an expanded budget—according to Okeowo, Madonsela's office had settled some twenty-one thousand of twenty-nine thousand of its most recent cases but required a larger staff to complete the rest. Her request was denied, and Mathole Motshekga, the ANC chair of a parliamentary justice committee, accused her of wasting taxpayer money. Her race, gender, and age have made her job more difficult, she told Okeowo. Parliament has criticized her high salary—though her male predecessor was paid the same amount. After the release of the Nkandla report, she faced a barrage of criticism, including insults about her physical appearance. "I have felt the way some of the people talk down to me," she said. "There's internalized racism by black people themselves, who would feel, 'I can take an order from a white person, I can take orders from a male, but really I'm not used to taking orders from a black woman.'"

However, Madonsela has never shown any signs of backing down from her commitment to responsible government, writing to her sixteen-year-old self for *Oprah Magazine*: "Today, you are the nation's Public Protector—a very responsible position that helps curb excesses in the exercise of public power while enabling the people to exact justice for state wrongs. You had the privilege of playing some role in bringing about change in this country. . . . Above all, remember that love is everything and don't forget to forgive yourself and others."

## PERSONAL LIFE

She has two children, a daughter named Wenzile Una and a son named Mbusowabantu "Wantu" Fidel.

## FURTHER READING

Cowell, Alan. "Report Faults South African Leader for State-Funded Work on Home." *New York Times. New York Times*, 19 Mar. 2014. Web. 2 Aug. 2015. Laing, Aislinn. "Thuli Madonsela: South Africa's Anti-Corruption Watchdog Raises the Nation's Hopes." *Telegraph. Telegraph Media Group*, 28 July 2012. Web. 2 Aug. 2015. Okeowo, Alexis. "Can Thulisile Madonsela Save South Africa from Itself?" *New York Times. New York Times*, 16 June 2015. Web. 30 July 2015. Page, Samantha. "Thuli Madonsela's Letter to Her 16-Year-Old Self." *Oprah Magazine South Africa. Associated Media*, 26 Apr. 2012. Web. 30 July 2015. "South Africa Police Chief Bheki Cele in 'Unlawful Deal.'" *BBC News. BBC*, 14 July 2011. Web. 2 Aug. 2015. "Thuli Madonsela Must Stop Acting Like She Is God—Bheki Cele." *News24. 24.com*, 7 Apr. 2014. Web. 2 Aug. 2015.

# Ellen R. Malcolm

## Political Activist

**Born:** February 2, 1947; Hackensack, New Jersey
**Primary Field:** Pro-Choice Abortion Rights
**Affiliation:** EMILY's List

## Introduction

*In 1985, when 25 women gathered in Ellen Malcolm's home to start the organization EMILY's List, no Democratic woman had been elected to the U.S. Senate in her own right (although a handful had Ellen R. Malcolm been appointed to fill seats left vacant by the deaths of their husbands). Additionally, no woman had been elected governor of a large state, and the number of female members of the U.S. House of Representatives was in decline. The founders of EMILY's List, a donor network and political action committee (PAC), saw that promising pro-choice female candidates often struggled to obtain sufficient campaign money in the male-dominated political arena, and they wanted to devise an efficient way to offer financial assistance. (The acronym "EMILY" stands for "Early Money Is Like Yeast," because "It helps the dough rise," according to the organization's Web site.)*

## Early Life

Malcolm was born Ellen Reighley on February 2, 1947 in Hackensack, New Jersey. She was raised in the nearby suburb of Montclair. Her parents met while working for the International Business Machines (IBM) Corp; her father, William Reighley, was employed as a salesman, and her mother, Barbara, as an assistant in the sales department.

When Malcolm was six months old, her father died of cancer. As a result, Malcolm became the sole heir to her paternal great-grandfather's fortune, to which she was granted access when she turned 21. Her great-grandfather, A. Ward Ford, was one of the founding partners of the Bundy Manufacturing Co., which eventually became part of IBM. Although Malcolm has never publicly revealed exactly how much she inherited, Laurie Kretchmar wrote for *Fortune* (April 6, 1992, online) that the heiress once admitted to having "millions upon millions upon millions."

When Malcolm was three her mother married Peter Malcolm, another IBM salesman. Her half-brothers, Doug and Andy, were born soon afterward. Despite the

money she stood to inherit when she was older, Malcolm recalled to Spake that her family had a modest lifestyle. "We were not a jet-setter family," she said. "We had a station wagon and two golden retrievers."

When Malcolm, who was raised in a Republican household, was encouraged by her mother to hone her typing skills so that she could one day become an executive secretary, she chafed at the idea. In an opinion piece she wrote for the *Washington Post* (May 10, 2008, online) in support of Hillary Clinton's 2008 presidential campaign, Malcolm recalled, "When I was growing up in the 1960s, I wanted to play basketball. In those days, the rules said girls could dribble only three steps and then had to pass the ball. To make sure we didn't overexert ourselves, we weren't allowed to cross the half-court line. It's a wonder our fans (our mothers) could stay awake when a typical game's final score was 14-10." She continued, "It's remarkable that my generation of women entered the workforce and began to compete in business, politics and the hurly-burly of life outside the home. How did we ever learn to locate, much less channel, our competitive instincts in a world that made us play halfcourt and assumed that we would be content staying home to iron the shirts? It's a tremendous tribute to women of my generation that we sucked it up and learned to compete in the toughest environments."

## Life's Work

Malcolm attended Hollins College, a women's school in Virginia that had a reputable experimental-psychology program. (The institution has since been renamed Hollins University.) While she initially hoped to become a clinical psychologist, Malcolm disliked many of the required lab courses. Although she earned a bachelor's degree in psychology in 1969, Malcolm—inspired by the liberal Mends and professors she had met in college—decided instead to pursue a career in political activism. (In 1968 she had worked on the unsuccessful presidential campaign of the Democrat Eugene McCarthy.)

In 1970 Malcolm moved to Washington, D.C., and began working with Common Cause, a nonprofit advocacy group that encourages open government and political accountability. Volunteering at first, she was soon offered a post as a salaried field coordinator. By 1976, however, she had become "completely burned out," as she told Spake. After working briefly on the failed presidential campaign of the Democrat Morris "Mo" Udall, she found herself with little direction or ambition. "I think when you have enough money that you don't have to work for a living, in some kind of backward way, it makes the choices very difficult," she told Spake. "It did for me. I didn't want having wealth to define who I was." Malcolm bought a home and earned a real-estate license, which she did not use. "Like a clock spring, I unwound until the most exciting thing in life was being able to go out and get the groceries," she recalled to Spake.

In 1977 a bored and dispirited Malcolm decided to return to political activism and found a position as a project director with the National Women's Political Caucus (NWPC), a nonpartisan grassroots organization dedicated to increasing women's involvement in politics. There she met Lael Stegall, then the organization's director of development. Until then Malcolm had not disclosed information about her fortune to anyone outside her family or her group of financial advisers, but after hearing that Stegall was looking for a way to branch out on her own and fund progressive women's organizations, Malcolm revealed her wealth.

Together, Stegall and Malcolm devised a way to channel Malcolm's money to various advocacy groups anonymously. They set up the Windom Fund (named after the street on which Malcolm lived) and moved their operation to an office in the Dupont Circle section of Washington, D.C The fund easily found progressive organizations to back, and operations proceeded smoothly—until some groups began to ask who was responsible for the largesse. Malcolm responded to the inquiries by naming an imaginary philanthropist, Henrietta C. Windom. Meanwhile, she kept busy as a speech-writer for Esther Peterson, the special assistant for consumer affairs in the administration of President Jimmy Carter. By 1980 Malcolm had begun to realize that if she were better able to channel and invest her money, she could wield considerable political influence. She entered the M.B.A. program at George Washington University, in Washington, D.C., graduating in 1984. "I ended up loving business, understanding how to make money and being successful at it," she told Spake.

In 1985 Malcolm and Stegall convened a meeting of women with whom they had worked at the NWPC. They discussed forming an organization to help pro-choice female Democrats adequately fund their campaigns early in the election process. The idea for the organization was largely inspired by the 1982 defeat of U.S. Senate candidate Harriett Woods, who lost partly because she ran out of campaign money before the election. Several of the women at the meeting, including Malcolm, had participated in Woods's campaign, and they understood that the key to keeping female candidates competitive was to donate money to them at the start. The late Ann Richards, a founding member of the group and an EMILY's List-endorsed candidate who was elected governor of Texas in 1990, told Connie Koenenn for the *Los Angeles Times* (October 9, 1991), "Women's races are lost early. You have to be a player early on. Texas has 19 major media markets and you have to make media buys early. It takes sophisticated crafting and planning. We needed money for focus groups, for polling necessary to shape the message. It takes early money to do all that." "You see, what happens to women is that people say they can't win," Joan Mondale, the wife of former U.S. vice president Walter Mondale and an EMILY's List advisory-board member, told Spake. "So they won't give them money. Then they can't raise money. And then they can't win. It's a vicious cycle."

Other prominent founding members of EMILY's List include the late Anne Wexler, a former aide to Carter and founder of a major lobbying firm; Barbara Boxer, now a Democratic U.S. senator from California; and Donna Shalala, the secretary of health and human services under President Bill Clinton and now president of the University of Miami. Journalists have sometimes commented on the perceived whimsicality of the group's name; Koenenn wrote, "[It] might sound like a tea party invitation, but the cuteness is deceptive." Malcolm explained to Spake, "If we had decided to become the Democratic Women's Early Money Fund, we probably would have raised $1.98 by now."

To build the organization's membership, Malcolm and the other founding women sent out personal letters to potential donors, and Malcolm visited 30 cities, talking to gatherings of women at events jokingly referred to as "the ultimate Tupperware parties," according to Koenenn.

EMILY's List was registered as a PAC because any organization or group that donates more than $1,000 to a political candidate must register as such. However, EMILY's List does not function in the same way as many other PACs. A typical PAC collects fees from members and then sends a single check to each candidate. (A PAC, according to law, can donate no more than $5,000 to a candidate in a federal race.) EMILY's List, on the other hand, endorses several candidates and asks each member to write a check for at least $100 each to at least two of the candidates. The organization then bundles the checks and sends them to the candidates. (There is no law limiting how many individual contributions can be made through an organization, as long as the checks are not written to the organization or cashed by it.)

By the 1986 elections, a year after the founding of EMILY's List, the organization had raised $545,000 to fund the campaigns of two Senate candidates and pay its own operating expenses. One of the organization's candidates, Barbara Mikulski of Maryland, became the first female Democrat elected to the U.S. Senate in her own right. In 1988 the organization recommended nine congressional candidates to members and raised more than $900,000. EMILY's List members donated to the successful campaigns of Nita Lowey of New York and Jolene Unsoeld of Washington State; the two victories reversed the long decline in the number of Democratic women serving in the House. (The pair boosted the number of female representatives to 14, the most since 1972.) In 1990 the organization claimed more than 3,500 members and broke the million-dollar mark for the first time, with members contributing $2.7 million. That year two governors and seven members of Congress who had been endorsed by EMILY's List won office. Two years later 20 new congresswomen and four new pro-choice female U.S. senators endorsed by EMILY's List were elected to office. Membership reached more than 23,000 members that year, and contributions totaled $10.2 million.

EMILY's List soon became, according its Web site, "a full-service political organization that raises money for women candidates, helps them build strong campaigns, and mobilizes women voters." In 2000, with the election of four new Senate members and four new House members, EMILY's List helped produce a record

---

## Affiliation: EMILY's List

EMILY's List has grown into one of the nation's biggest PACs, boasting more than 100,000 members. Since its inception the group has helped elect almost 100 women to Congress and numerous others to state and local offices. Malcolm, a founder of the organization and for 25 years its president and public face, is widely credited for her pioneering work in organizing on behalf of female political candidates. Amanda Spake wrote for the Washington Post (June 5, 1988), "Malcolm was really the first person to believe it could happen, that women like herself—who came of age in the late '60s and early '70s, who went to work and who now have both money and a mission—would organize and ante up to elect other like-minded women."

The success of EMILY's List stems in part from its unique approach to fundraising. As a donor network, it provides members with information about candidates it has endorsed and encourages members to write checks directly to those running for office. The organization then bundles the members' checks and sends them to the individual candidates. Each member of EMILY's List is asked to contribute $100 to the group itself and to pledge $100 each to at least two endorsed politicians. That successful fund-raising model has made EMILY's List one of the Democratic Party's main allies. In 2008 alone, for example, the organization and its members contributed more than $9 million to candidates for fed-

eral and gubernatorial office. Bara Vaida and Jennifer Skalka wrote for the National Journal (June 28, 2009), "EMILY's List has won wide praise over the years for leveraging the power of women at the polls and building an unprecedented network of progressive female donors." As quoted on the group's Web site, Jennifer Granholm, then running for governor of Michigan, once stated in a speech: "EMILY is every working mom who's managed to balance a checkbook, who's managed a clean house, a corporate budget and a 12-year-old's basketball tournament in one day. . . . She's every candidate who's ever been asked how she can run for office and have a family at the same time. She is every African American woman who has had to work three times as hard to be considered as good as her white male colleague. She is every Jewish woman who has ever been called a princess. She is every Hispanic woman who has been asked how long her family has been in this country. She is every woman who has been called too soft or too strong or too aggressive or too nice or too ambitious to get the job done. She is every woman who has ever been measured against a glossy picture in a magazine. . . . She is you. . . . And EMILY doesn't get mad—she gets elected!"

Malcolm stepped down as president of EMILY's List at the end of January 2010. She has continued to chair its board of directors.

10 female senators and 41 House members, and two years later the group helped to elect three new governors and two new House members. Every incumbent it supported also won reelection.

In 2006, however, EMILY's List suffered several losses. The group endorsed 31 House and Senate candidates, but only eight won office. Some political analysts believed that the influence of EMILY's List had waned because reproductive rights remained the group's main issue. They argued that the organization, in order to stay viable, should endorse women who were moderate on abortion rights but progressive on other issues. Marcy Kaptur, a Democratic U.S. representative from Ohio, told Vaida and Skalka in 2009 that the organization's focus was "too narrow." "I represent women who organize unions, carry mail on their backs, raise children, fight harassment in the workplace," she said. "They love their husbands and their sons. And with EMILY's List, I always felt there was a class-based, gender-based divide."

In 2008 EMILY's list rebounded somewhat, raising more than $43 million and contributing to the successful elections of 12 new female House members and two senators. It also played a role in the victory of the first female governor of North Carolina, and all the incumbents up for reelection remained in office. The group faced criticism from some progressives, however, for its ardent support of Hillary Clinton during the 2008 Democratic primaries. As a popular pro-choice Democratic senator from New York, Clinton was a fitting candidate for EMILY's List. Malcolm co-chaired Clinton's campaign and stumped for the candidate, and EMILY's List was one of the top five donors to the campaign, bundling roughly $850,000 and spending another $1.5 million on efforts to mobilize voters. However, a rift between the organization and its political allies was revealed when Malcolm announced that EMILY's List might not donate to those running for other offices if they supported Clinton's chief opponent for the Democratic nomination, Barack Obama. According to Vaida and Skalka, Malcolm's proclamation "incensed many in progressive Democratic circles, who viewed it as a threat." Malcolm later said to the *National Journal* that she had meant only to convey that EMILY's List donors who were unhappy with a List-backed candidate's support for Obama might cease making donations to that candidate.

Tensions were also exacerbated when EMILY's List questioned Obama's commitment to the pro-choice cause and criticized abortion-rights groups, such as NARAL Pro-Choice America, for endorsing him. The political pollster Celinda Lake told Vaida and Skalka, "I think one thing that EMILY's List has demonstrated is that they can play as bare-knuckles as the boys." Despite the organization's skepticism about Obama, it threw support behind the future president after he triumphed over Clinton for the Democratic Party nomination.

According to Vaida and Skalka, among other observers, the tension caused by EMILY's List's ardent support for Clinton reflected a large generational gap. The authors noted that during the primaries, "Baby Boomer moms continually resuscitated Clinton's candidacy while their daughters backed the more youthful Obama." That clash of values between younger female voters, who have typically faced less sex discrimination and have always had choice with regard to reproduction, and those who recall a less-tolerant era, is one that the group will have to contend with as it continues to expand. Nonetheless, Malcolm told Vaida and Skalka that younger voters are not her "market segment." "People who are donors to politics across the board are older, because they have the wherewithal to do it," she said. "Am I going to craft a message for 18-year-olds right now and try to raise money from them? No."

In November 2009, when the U.S. House passed a health-care reform bill that included the Stupak-Pitts Amendment, which prohibits taxpayer funding for abortions, many pro-choice groups, including EMILY's List, voiced frustration. "The assault on women's reproductive rights continues with a vengeance," Malcolm said, as quoted by Phillip Klein for the *American Spectator* (November 9, 2009). A petition to stop the amendment was made available on the EMILY's List Web site.

The end of January 2010 marked the end of Malcolm's service as president of EMILY's List; she has retained her post as chairwoman of its board of directors. Her successor as president, Stephanie Schriock, has a great deal of hands-on political experience, most recently as the chief of staff for Democratic U.S. senator Jon Tester of Montana and as the campaign manager for Al Franken's successful run for the U.S. Senate in Minnesota. "We've set the stage for history," Malcolm said a few weeks before she stepped down, as quoted by Philip Rucker in the *Washington Post* (January 7, 2010). "We've had astonishing victories. The U.S. House is a very different place today than it was when we began. The world has changed." Noting one major change, Malcolm said of Schriock, "She views politics through the lens of the Internet, which is what we will need going forward,"

Malcolm has often been sought out for commentary related to political campaigns and has appeared on CBS's *60 Minutes* and NBC's *Today Show*, among other TV programs. She has been featured in such magazines as *People* and *Fortune*, and her opinion pieces have been published in the *Washington Post*, the *Los Angeles Times*, the *New York Times*, the *Chicago Sun-Times*, and other newspapers. She was named one of America's most influential women in a 1998 issue of *Vanity Fair*, and the following year she was selected as one of the 100 most important women in the nation by *Ladies' Home Journal*.

In 2003 Malcolm co-founded America Coming Together (ACT), a national organization devoted to voter mobilization. She was also involved in the creation of America Votes, a coalition of progressive organizations—including ACT and EMILY's List—that works to energize voters.

## FURTHER READING

*Los Angeles Times E pi Oct. 9, 1991; National Journal (on-line) June 28, 2008; Washington Post A pi Dec. 25, 1984, (on-line) May 10, 2008; Washington Post Magazine W p32 June 5, 1988*

---

# SOMALY MAM

## Social Activist

**Born:** 1970 or 1971; Cambodia
**Primary Field:** Anti-Sex Trafficking Advocate
**Affiliation:** Somaly Mam Foundation

## INTRODUCTION

*Somaly Mam is an advocate for victims of sex trafficking, the worldwide, illegal industry that reaps billions of dollars for exploiters who force men, women, and children to perform sex acts for very little or no money. The sex-trafficking industry thrives in impoverished cities, where job opportunities are scarce and government and many law-enforcement officials are corrupt; it is most common in Southeast Asian countries, particularly Cambodia, Vietnam, Laos, and Thailand. Mam is the co-founder of the organization Agir pour les Femmes en Situation Precaire (AFESIP), which translates as Acting for Women in Distressing Circumstances, based in Phnom Penh, Cambodia; she also founded the United States-based Somaly Mam Foundation. Both organizations aim to rescue and rehabilitate victims of human trafficking and raise awareness of the growing global problem of sexual slavery. Mam, a former sex worker herself, was born into a rural tribe in Cambodia in the early 1970s, during the height of the oppressive Khmer Rouge regime, led by the violent dictator Pol Pot. The regime imposed a radical form of agrarian communism under which the population was forced to work on collective farms and elsewhere; the Khmer Rouge*

*tried systematically to eliminate every person thought to be involved in free-market activities, including professionals, college graduates, urban residents, and many others. Mam wrote in her memoir,* The Road of Lost Innocence, *that during that brutal period in Cambodia's history, children were "a kind of domestic livestock," and there was "only one law for women: silence before rape and silence after." Abandoned at a young age, Mam was raised by a cruel man who sold her when she was 14 years old to an abusive husband, who in turn sold her to a brothel in Phnom Penh when she was 16. There, she was forced to have sex with numerous men each night and was beaten if she resisted. After escaping from the brothel four years later, she married a French aid worker and moved to France. She later returned to Cambodia and, in 1996, founded AFESIP, which has rescued and rehabilitated more than 4,000 former sex-trafficking victims. Mam, who has put herself in great danger for her cause, and whose 14-year-old daughter was briefly kidnapped by traffickers in 2006 in retaliation for her work, has received many international awards, including the Roland Berger Human Dignity Award, presented to her in November 2008. Mam wrote in her memoir, as quoted by Claire Armitstead in the* London Guardian *(February 9, 2008): "People ask me how I can bear to keep doing what I do. I'll tell you. It's the evil that was done to me that propels me on. Is there any other way to exorcise it?"*

## EARLY LIFE

Somaly Mam does not know exactly how old she is but estimates her birth year to be 1970 or 1971. She was born a member of the Phnong tribe, in Mondulkiri, a province in eastern Cambodia known for its mountains, dense forests, and waterfalls. The farming-based tribe was so remote that it had no schools or doctors and did not even use money. Because the tribe seemed to live collectively and was untouched by Western habits, it was not targeted by Pol Pot's regime. Mam lived with her parents and grandmother before she was abandoned at a young age. In her book Mam pondered the possible reasons for her parents' absence, taking into account the violence and chaos that ravaged the country during the Pol Pot regime: "Perhaps they were seeking a better life, or perhaps they were forced to leave. . . . There are many reasons why my parents might have left the forest." She spent years living on her own, foraging for wild fruits in the forest and seeking shelter with neighbors. When Mam was about 10 years old, a man claiming to be her grandfather took her in. He forced her to become his servant, regularly beat her, and, when she was 12 years old, accepted money from an older man in exchange for permitting the man to have sex with her. During that time Mam met and befriended a local teacher, who tried to offer the young girl comfort but was powerless to protect her. Mam, having no name that she was aware of, took the woman's name, Somaly Mam, as her own. When Mam was 14 years old, the man who claimed to be her grandfather sold her to another man, who married her. He too was cruel; he would get drunk, then beat and rape her. Sometimes he fired bullets at her, narrowly missing her head and feet.

When Mam was 16 years old, her husband sold her to a brothel in the Cambodian capital, Phnom Penh. Told by her captors that she needed to work to pay off her "grandfather's debts," Mam was sometimes forced to have sex with a half-dozen men in one night. Today, although prostitution is officially illegal in Cambodia—one of Southeast Asia's poorest countries—most brothels in Phnom Penh, a center of trafficking activity, operate in the open. The sex industry is generally tolerated by government and law-enforcement officials, in part because of the perceived economic benefits reaped from "sex tourism," which include bribes of local authorities. Many sex workers are sold into slavery by their husbands or parents for the equivalent of as little as $10; others join the brothels with the false hope that they might earn enough money to escape their impoverished surroundings. Their pimps—who are often women—take most of their earnings, leaving them with a meager salary of about $15 per month. Women are often beaten, tortured, or even murdered if they refuse customers. Brothel owners often give the women amphetamines or other drugs, so that they will form addictions, making them less likely to try to leave their circumstances. There is high demand for young girls (some are as young as five years old) in part because of a cultural belief that sex with a virgin is beneficial; many people even believe that the act destroys HIV, the virus that causes AIDS. Sexually transmitted diseases are rampant in brothels; an estimated 29 percent of sex workers have HIV.

If Mam refused to have sex, she was beaten or subjected to torture that involved such things as snakes or maggots. "I never thought, just lived hour by hour," Mam said to Bruce Finley for the Denver Post (April 6, 2008), describing her psychological state in the brothel. "I played with nothing. In my head: nothing. It was dark, dark, dark. I never trusted people. ... I was dead." Mam remained at the brothel for four years. Over that time she felt her spirit break and even tried to commit suicide. A turning point in her life came when she saw the pimp who ran the brothel murder one of Mam's best friends, a woman named Srymom, for refusing a customer. Realizing that she needed to escape and help others, too, Mam stole the keys to the brothel door and helped two newcomers to get away. (For that she was beaten and her skin was burned with a car battery.) Mam befriended one of her customers (or "Johns"), a European aid worker named Dietrich, who was not violent with her and eventually gave her enough money to buy her way out of slavery. (According to some sources, Mam was set free when she became too old to attract customers as a prostitute.) In her memoir Mam recalled showering for the first time in her life, in Dietrich's hotel room. "He . . . turned on a shiny thing, like a snake, and it flashed to life, spitting at me," she wrote, as quoted by Paula Bock for the Seattle Times (September 16, 2008). "That was the first time I ever used proper soap, and I remember how good it smelled, like a flower."

## LIFE'S WORK

After escaping the brothel, in 1991, Mam worked as a midwife at Cambodia's Choup District Hospital. That year she began dating a French relief worker, Pierre Legros. The two married in 1993 and moved to France. Mam recalled in her book being initially terrified by aspects of the modern world, such as airplanes and the tall buildings in cities. She was also surprised by the love and respect she received from her husband and was perplexed when he encouraged her to spend her time doing whatever she wanted. Mam attended school and earned money by cleaning houses and hotels. She later worked as the director of personnel at a restaurant and as a social worker at a retirement home. During that time Mam and Legros had three children. In 1995 Mam returned to Cambodia with her husband and began working for the Swedish nongovernmental organization (NGO) Medecins Sans Frontieres (Doctors without Borders), a group that provides medical care to people in war-torn regions of developing countries.

In 1996 Mam and Legros founded *Agir pour les Femmes en Situationb* to help prostitutes and other trafficking victims escape brothels and make the transition to self-sufficiency. The organization also works to improve the conditions in brothels. Mam became the group's president and worked at its headquarters, in Phnom Penh. At its main refuge, located in the countryside about three hours outside the city, Mam provides girls and women who have been rescued from brothels with free medical care and access to education. Many of the rescued girls have undergone such intense physical and psychological trauma that they require extensive medical and psychiatric care; for the many infected with HIV, Mam tries to make their lives as comfortable as possible. The refuge also provides the women with training, in weaving, sewing, and hairdressing, in an effort to build their confidence and skills. "If girls have financial independence, they can say no to the brothels," Mam explained to Susan Dominus for *Glamour* (December 2008). "So we have a hairdressing shop and sewing machines for them to learn skills." After the girls and women are rehabilitated, Mam and her colleagues typically return them to their families—but only if it appears that they will not be sold back to the brothels or return there on their own. Mam explained that many women return to brothels because they do not feel that they have other options. "Sometimes the women themselves, they think that it is normal that they have been sold in a brothel," she told David Montgomery for the *Washington Post* (September 22, 2008). "It's like me. Before, I think it's normal that I have been sold.... I never knew that I had rights." The brothel owners allow Mam's staff to visit the brothels because they bring condoms, soap, toothpaste, and other supplies related to hygiene; they also teach the women safe-sex practices.

As the organization's mission became known, its reach expanded to Laos, Vietnam, and Thailand. In 1998 Mam founded AFESIP International, with additional bureaus in France and Switzerland. Also in 1998 she was made a member of the jury that judged performers at the First International Festival of Solidarity of the European Commission, held in Spain. That year, in addition, she was given Spain's Prince of Asturias Award as well as the Premio Principe de Asturias-Cooperacion Internacional, which honors contributions to mutual understanding or fraternity among peoples. In 1999 she was elected president of the Confederation of Women's Organizations in the Association of Southeast Asian Nations (ASEAN).

Mam's work is dangerous, and it is not unusual for her and her staff to receive death threats. In 2004 Mam worked with police to launch a raid of a hotel that ran one of Phnom Penh's biggest brothels, where about 200 women were held. A few days later a mob of men broke into Mam's refuge and took away 90 of the women and girls who were staying there; Mam never saw any of them again. Around that time a friend in France telephoned Mam and urged her to flee Cambodia, because of the danger she was clearly in, but she refused to leave. Instead, Mam spent three days recording her life's story on cassettes, to ensure that someone would know about it in the event that she was silenced. She sent the tapes to a friend in France, who passed them on to a ghostwriter. Mam's story was thus published in France in 2005 under the title *Le Silence de l'innocence*, which was translated into English by Lisa Appignanesi as *The Road of Lost Innocence* (2008). The book's first half is devoted to the story of Mam's life; the second half focuses on the women and girls she cares for and the broader issues of sexual slavery and human trafficking. One of her observations is that the "moral bankruptcy" that exists within present-day Cambodia is linked to the violence and chaos the country experienced under Pol Pot. During the Khmer Rouge regime, she wrote, "people detached themselves from all kind of human feeling, because feeling meant pain. They learned not to trust their neighbors, their family, their own children." The memoir, which has appeared in many languages, was acclaimed by reviewers for its "matter-of-fact storytelling, which is strengthened by Mam's detachment and humility," as Charmaine Chan wrote for the *South China Morning Post* (September 28, 2008). A reviewer for the *Irish Sunday Business Post* (January 27, 2008) wrote that although Mam "is not a naturally gifted writer," the memoir "is a corrective for anybody who might somehow think there is anything consensual about foreign prostitution."

Mam's work received mainstream attention in August 2006, when the French journalist Marianne Pearl published an article in *Glamour*, as part of a year-long series dedicated to discovering "who changes the world and how." (Pearl is the widow of the journalist Daniel Pearl, who was kidnapped, held captive, and killed by Islamic militants in Pakistan in 2002.) When Pearl met with Mam in Cambodia, in May 2006, Mam's 14-year-old daughter, Ning, had been missing for 24 hours. Two days later police discovered Ning in Battambang, a province near the border of Thailand, known as a human-trafficking hub. She had been kidnapped, drugged, and raped, likely in retaliation for Mam's work. Pearl's article, which included painful stories of women in brothels and in Mam's refuge, shone a media spotlight on the atrocities of sexual slavery in Southeast Asia. Mam was named one of *Glamour's* 2006 Women of the Year and was honored at a ceremony held at New York City's Carnegie Hall. During that visit Mam met with philanthropy-minded celebrities, including the actress Susan Sarandon, to seek help with fund-raising. (In October 2009 Sarandon received the first Somaly Mam Voices for Change Award, for her advocacy work on behalf of victims of human trafficking. The advisory board for the Somaly Mam Foundation also includes the actor Ron Livingston, the actresses Daryl Hannah and Laurie Holden, and the model Petra Nemcova.)

In 2008 Mam was contacted by two U.S. Air Force Academy cadets, Nic Lumpp and Jared Greenberg, who, after learning about human trafficking, had resolved to fight it. After visiting Mam's operation in Cambodia, they worked with her to found a U.S.-based group to stop human trafficking. The Somaly Mam Foundation, located in Denver, Colorado, is a nonprofit organization that raises money to dissuade foreign "sex tourists" from entering Southeast Asia and to fund continued rescue-and-rehabilitation efforts for girls and women at shelters in Cambodia and neighboring countries. The organization's current goals for Mam's three centers in Cambodia include providing micro-financing opportunities to newly released victims who want to start their own businesses and, in collaboration with Regis University in Denver, Colorado, creating a program to teach English as a second language. As of April 2009 the organization's Tom Dy Center contained a childcare house, to provide care for the young children of residents who

were taking part in rehabilitation and vocational training. As of April 2008 the group had raised $400,000 from celebrities and corporations, including LexisNexis, which has taken up Mam's cause as part of its philanthropic support of "rule-of-law" projects. "We need the United States. Americans are more active," Mam told Finley. "Cambodia's own efforts to combat the sex trade have been crippled by corruption of police and courts." In March 2009 a group of 25 took part in Futures '09 Cycling Challenge, a 500-kilometer bike tour through Cambodia, to raise awareness and money for the Somaly Mam Foundation. According to the group's Web site, the event succeeded in raising $79,562. In June 2009 the Somaly Mam Foundation graduated its first class from its Voices for Change program, which trains survivors of slavery to become activists for the foundation. That same month the AFESIP Cambodia welcomed Carol Rodley, the U.S. ambassador to Cambodia, who visited the Siam Reap center. In August 2009 the Siem Reap center also hosted a U.S. delegation, which included Robin J. Lerner, the counsel to the Senate Committee on Foreign Relations, and Janice V. Kaguyutan, the senior counsel to the Senate Committee on Health, Education, Labor and Pensions, among others.

Mam continues to be honored for her work. In April 2008 she received the World's Children's Prize, established by the Swedish NGO Children's World and awarded by a jury of former child soldiers, street children, bonded workers, and refugees from 17 countries. Mam was also the winner of the 2008 Global Friends' Award, which is determined by a worldwide vote among some 6.6 million children. In November 2008 Mam was the recipient of the first Roland Berger Human Dignity Award, from the Munich, Germany-based Roland Berger Foundation, which documents human trafficking and slavery around the world. That award included a grant worth 1 million euros (the equivalent of about $1.3 million). For years Mam has lobbied U.S. lawmakers to pass stronger legislation against human trafficking. President George W. Bush signed such a bill—sponsored by New York congresswoman Carolyn B. Maloney, who chairs the Congressional Human Trafficking Caucus—into law. Among other functions, it increases penalties against traffickers, expands protections for trafficking victims and their families, requires that the Department of Justice develop a new state-level law to investigate and prosecute cases of human trafficking, authorizes increased assistance for victims, and establishes a presidential award for extraordinary anti-trafficking efforts. In December 2008 Mam was named one of *Time* magazine's people of the year, and in April 2009 the editors included her on the magazine's list of the 100 most influential people.

## PERSONAL LIFE

Mam is still haunted by memories of her past. She has difficulty sleeping, showers repeatedly every day, and wears copious amounts of perfume in an effort to forget the smells of the brothel. Though many have called her beautiful—"outshining] supermodels at foundation fundraisers," according to Paula Bock—Mam wrote in her book, "I still feel that I'm dirty and that I carry bad luck." She finds solace in her ability to help and comfort the girls and women at her refuges. "I'm not sure what being happy really means," Mam told Pearl. "But when I cuddle with the girls, giving them the love I never received, then I do feel happy." Mam is constantly in danger of retaliation from the powerful forces she is fighting. Though she has been offered safe haven in other countries, Mam has refused to leave Cambodia. She wrote in her book, as quoted by Catherine Price for *Salon.com* (September 23, 2008): "I don't feel like I can change the world.... I don't even try. I only want to change this small life that I see standing in front of me, which is suffering. I want to change this small real thing that is the destiny of one little girl. And then another, and another, because if I didn't, I wouldn't be able to live with myself or sleep at night." Mam and Legros divorced several years ago.

## FURTHER READING

*Denver Post B p3 Apr. 6, 2008; Glamour (on-line) Aug. 1, 2006; (London) Guardian p9 Feb. 9, 2008; Salon. com Sep. 23, 2008; Seattle Times D p3 Sep. 16, 2008; Washington Post Cp1 Sep. 22, 2008; The Road of Lost Innocence, 2008*

---

# MAHMOOD MAMDANI

## Expert on African Affairs; Writer; Educator

**Born:** April 23, 1946; Kampala, Uganda
**Primary Field:** Social Justice

## INTRODUCTION

*Mahmood Mamdani is one of the world's most prominent social critics and scholars on Africa, particularly with regard to that continent's history and politics and the legacies of colonialism. Born in the African nation of Uganda, of Indian descent, Mamdani is probably best known for his provocative explanations of regional conflicts in Africa and elsewhere and his ability to frame such issues in historical context, in ways that lead even his critics to reexamine their views. Mamdani's ability to describe the forces behind developments, often challenging conventional wisdom (and, he would argue, politically expedient explanations), has earned him the label of dissident. Frequently involved in controversial debates over the causes of and solutions to many of the region's biggest challenges, Mamdani has been dismissed by some as a dogmatic leftist; but in the eyes of admirers his skill in drawing connections from colonial institutions to contemporary wars, and from Cold War policies to present-day crises, has made his work an indispensable guide to understanding the how and why of conflicts in regions from Darfur to Iraq. Mamdani's work is not seen as merely critical: his nuanced views on past and present circumstances have also been helpful in finding constructive ways to move forward—for instance, in seeking to effect reconciliation between rival groups after civil wars—and he has served on several important advisory boards in Africa. Mamdani, who in 2008 was called one of the leading public intellectuals in the world by both* Prospect *and* Foreign Policy *magazines, is the author of books including* Citizen and Subject: Contemporary Africa and the Legacy of Late Colonialism *(1996);* When Victims Become Killers: Colonialism, Nativism, and the Genocide in Rwanda *(2001);* Good Muslim, Bad Muslim: America, the Cold War, and the Roots of Terror *(2004); and* Saviors and Survivors: Darfur, Politics, and the War on Terror *(2009). The director of Columbia University's Institute of African Studies from 1999 to 2004, he is currently professor of government in the university's Department of Anthropology and Political Science and the School of International and Public Affairs; he has held several top teaching posts at universities in Uganda, Tanzania, and South Africa. Mamdani told Bernard Tabaire for* Africa News *(August 12, 2004), "I have been pre-oc-*

*cupied with the institutional legacy of previous eras of the colonial world, of empires and how they tend to treat people as insiders or outsiders." In that regard, Mamdani has sometimes been compared to his colleague, friend, and mentor at Columbia, the late Palestinian intellectual and activist Edward Said.*

## EARLY LIFE

A third-generation East African, Mahmood Mamdani was born on April 23, 1946 in Kampala, Uganda. Many of the Indians who made up the minority entrepreneurial classes in East Africa had arrived under British colonialism, a system that manipulated various race and class cleavages in order to function effectively. Upon finishing his O-level examinations at Senior Secondary School, in the Old Kampala district, in 1962—the year Uganda won its independence from Great Britain—Mamdani was one of a handful of students there offered scholarships to study in the U.S. "The scholarships were part of America's independence gift to Uganda. . . . Certainly, without a successful struggle for independence, I would not have got the higher education that I did," Mamdani wrote for the Uganda publication *New Vision* (April 28, 2007). During his years as a student at the University of Pittsburgh, in Pennsylvania, in the 1960s, Mamdani was a debater and a participant in the American civil rights movement, then at its height. He wrote for the *New Vision* article, "In less than a year, I was among busloads of students going from northern universities to march in Birmingham, Alabama, in the south. ... I and scores of other students were thrown in jail. Allowed to make one phone call from jail, I called the Uganda ambassador in Washington DC. 'What are you doing interfering in the internal affairs of a foreign country?' he asked. 'This is not an internal affair. This is a freedom struggle. How can you forget? We just got our freedom last year,' was my response."

## LIFE'S WORK

Mamdani received a B.A. degree in 1967, then earned an M.A. and an M.A.L.D. (master of arts in law and diplomacy) from the Fletcher School of Law and Diplomacy at Tufts University, in Medford, Massachusetts, in 1969. Staying in the Boston area, Mamdani then pursued a Ph.D. in government at Harvard University, where he led a student strike to protest increases in tuition. He earned his doctorate in 1974.

Meanwhile, Mamdani had returned to Uganda in early 1972, to work as a teaching assistant at Makerere University, in Kampala. By the end of that year, he had become one of the 70,000 Ugandans of South Asian descent deported and dispossessed by the country's leader, Idi Amin; having mounted a successful military coup the previous year against the dictatorship of President Milton Obote, Amin claimed with the deportations to be finishing the work of independence by empowering black Africans. "I returned home . . . as a convinced Pan-African nationalist, but was thrown out later in the year as an Asian," Mamdani wrote for *New Vision*. In November 1972 he fled the country and was admitted to a refugee camp in London, England. "The British press was full of stories about Amin and the Asian expulsion," he wrote. "Every story talked of Amin not as a dictator, but as a black dictator. With few exceptions, the British press racialised Amin. His blackness was offered as the primary explanation for his brutality. Fresh from civil rights struggles in the American south, and anti-Vietnam war struggles in the American north, I had seen brutality in the white and was unwilling to accept this explanation." Nine months after he had arrived in England, a disillusioned Mamdani left for Tanzania to begin a teaching job at the University of Dares Salaam, then a fertile environment for leftist and radical African activism; some of his colleagues and students there would go on to join anticolonial guerrilla groups around Africa, and some went on to become presidents and rebel leaders, among them Yoweri Museveni, who became Uganda's president in 1986; Laurent Kabila, who assumed power in the Congo (formerly Zaire) in 1997; and Ernest Wamba dia Wamba, who went on to become a member of the Congo Senate.

"Although my physical being was in Dares Salaam where both my parents had been born," Mamdani wrote, "my mind was preoccupied with Uganda: Why Amin? Why the support for Amin?"

While he found black Africans' support for Amin painful on a personal level, Mamdani attempted to understand it. He has said that he fully understood the dynamics of the political situation in Uganda only after he returned there from exile, in 1979, following Amin's ouster. "Every Ugandan understood in his or her guts that the secret of Asian business success lay not just in hard work, but also in a racially unjust colonial system which made it difficult for black people to enter trade, thereby confirming Asian dominance in trade . . . ," Mamdani wrote for *New Vision*. "The demand for political independence went alongside another— that for social justice for those who had been the victims of colonial racial discrimination." Even after independence, elites—many of them Asian— had maintained their positions in Uganda by entering into lucrative alliances with bureaucrats. "Pointing to this informal apartheid in a complacent post-Independence Uganda, Amin asked uncomfortable questions, even if in a coarse and racist language. ... I realized that Amin spoke the language of justice, however crudely, and that was the reason he was able to ride the crest of a historic wave of popular protest." In a controversial article for the *London Review of Books* (December 4, 2008) in which Mamdani tried to contextualize the recent policies of forcible land redistribution (in which land was taken from white farmers and given to blacks) carried out by Robert Mugabe in Zimbabwe, he wrote: "What distinguishes Mugabe and Amin from other authoritarian rulers is not their demagoguery but the fact that they projected themselves as champions of mass justice and successfully rallied those to whom justice had been denied by the colonial system. Not surprisingly, the justice dispensed by these demagogues mirrored the racialised injustice of the colonial system. In 1979 I began to realize that whatever they made of Amin's brutality, the Ugandan people experienced the Asian expulsion of 1972—and not the formal handover in 1962—as the dawn of true independence. The people of Zimbabwe are likely to remember 2000-3 as the end of the settler colonial era. Any assessment of contemporary Zimbabwe needs to begin with this sobering fact."

In 1979, as Obote and others were preparing a violent campaign to regain power from Amin, Mamdani left the University of Dares Salaam and returned to teach political science at Makerere University, where he would remain until 1993. In the *New Vision* article, he recalled the decade after 1979 as "one of coming to political age for a second time." At Makerere Mamdani became a leading expert on the rural-urban divide in postcolonial Uganda as well as on agrarian policies and their relation to unrest in the nation. He also became an outspoken critic of Uganda's government and participated in literacy programs and campaigns for workers' rights. In 1985, in the midst of another civil war—which would bring Museveni to power—Mamdani was once again exiled for his criticisms of the government. Returning to teach at Makerere in 1986, Mamdani was made chair of the Ugandan Commission of Inquiry into Local Government, a post he occupied until 1988, and was also the founding director of the Center for Basic Research in Kampala, where he served from 1987 to

1996. In the latter year he moved to postapartheid South Africa, where he was made director of the Center for African Studies at the University of Cape Town. He remained in the position until 1999, when he was made director of the Institute of African Studies at Columbia University in New York. There, he taught courses in the school's Anthropology and Political Science Departments and in its School of International and Public Affairs. Mamdani was also the president of the Council for the Development of Social Research in Africa, the continent's most important social-science body, based in Dakar, Senegal, from 1999 to 2002. From 2005 to 2006 Mamdani was a chief adviser to the U.N. High Level Group of the Alliance of Civilizations.

Mamdani is a prolific writer whose works have become staples in the field of postcolonial and African studies. His early works include *From Citizen to Refugee* (1973), *Politics and Class Formation in Uganda* (1976), and *Imperialism and Fascism in Uganda* (1983). The book that first brought him widespread attention, *Citizen and Subject: Contemporary Africa and the Legacy of Late Colonialism* (1996), is regarded as a seminal work in both African and postcolonial studies; it won several awards and was named by a jury in Ghana in 2002 as one of the 20th century's most important books on Africa. In the book Mamdani offered a new perspective on what he saw as the failures of postcolonial states in Africa. He described the newly independent countries as being incapable of reforming the old colonial system of rule through that system's methods, or via elites and tribal structures. During colonialism, while elites became the citizens through whom the ruling country could exercise direct control, the indigenous and rural masses became subjects, to be ruled indirectly via decentralized despotism—that is, through tribal structures managed from the outside. Mamdani referred to that arrangement as the bifurcated state. Its legacy, in the era of independence, is either centralized despotism (one-party or military) or states in which there is a massive and disastrous disconnect between urban and rural life. The book also examines the nature of resistance movements, particularly in South Africa.

Mamdani's book *When Victims Become Killers: Colonialism, Nativism*, and the *Genocide in Rwanda* (2001) traces the root causes of the 1994 genocide in the African nation of Rwanda by viewing it in the contexts of colonialism and regional conditions. Mamdani argued that the Belgian colonial authorities, acting through a divide-and-conquer policy, had defined the

Tutsi minority as a privileged alien population through which they could rule the indigenous Hutu majority. The revolution of 1959, through which the Hutus overthrew the

Tutsi monarchy, sending thousands of Tutsis into exile, reproduced and ossified those colonial identities. When the exiled Tutsis, who felt like foreigners in Uganda, repatriated to Rwanda in 1990, the Hutu fear of a Tutsi return to power sparked in 1994 a state-sanctioned policy of genocide. Mamdani wrote, "In its motivation and construction, I argue that the Rwandan genocide needs to be understood as a natives' genocide. It was a genocide by those who saw themselves as sons—and daughters—of the soil, and their mission as one of clearing the soil of a threatening alien presence. This was not an 'ethnic' but a 'racial' cleansing, not a violence against one who is seen as a neighbor but against one who is seen as a foreigner; not a violence that targets a transgression across a boundary into home but one that seeks to eliminate a foreign presence from home soil, literally and physically." Mamdani made the point that the atrocities in Rwanda were not the results of inherent tribal conflict but arose from specific historical contexts.

Similarly, in *Good Muslim, Bad Muslim: America, the Cold War, and the Roots of Terror* (2004), Mamdani tried to debunk the notion that Islam was at the root of much of contemporary nonstate-sponsored terrorism, including the 9/11 attacks; he identified the source instead as the Cold War. "However awful, unpleasant and tragic 9/11 was, I hoped some good [would] come out of [discussions about it]," Mamdani told Arthur Pais for *India Abroad* (May 14, 2004). "But the lid over the debate was put back in no time and amnesia has been created about American responsibilities for creating terrorism. I used to think before 9/11 tragedies could bring people together in a way prosperity does not. Prosperity could isolate people but tragedy could connect. I was proved wrong by the American response to 9/11." In a direct attack on the notion of a "clash of civilizations" advanced by the scholars Samuel Huntington, Bernard Lewis, and others, according to which "good Muslims" are pro-American and "bad Muslims" are anti- American, Mamdani argued that religion had little to do with terrorism. Looking at what he called the late Cold War, which began after the U.S. defeat in Vietnam, in 1975, Mamdani argued that the U.S.— unable any longer to get citizens' support or financial backing for more overseas military interventions—decided to back proxies to

fight the Cold War on its behalf. As the theater of the Cold War shifted from Asia to Africa with the fall of the Portuguese empire in Africa, in 1975, the U.S. began supporting nonstate, privatized combatants (financed, Mamdani wrote, through underground economies such as the drug trade, since Congress would not approve payments for wars that had not been officially declared). "The simple fact the government had to face was that if you decide to wage war without legislative consent, then you are likely to be short of funds," Mamdani wrote in *Good Muslim, Bad Muslim*. "Time and again, the agencies pursuing covert wars seemed to arrive at the same solution to their financial problems: collude with drug lords." In Angola, Mozambique, and later Nicaragua, the U.S. backed nonstate groups against leftist governments. (Mamdani pointed to the neoconservative U.S. diplomat Jeane Kirkpatrick's notion that there were two types of dictatorships in the Third World—left-wing totalitarian and right- wing authoritarian. "The difference, she argued, was that totalitarian dictatorships were incapable of reforming from within and so needed to be overthrown forcibly from without, whereas authoritarian dictatorships were open to internal reform, which could be tapped through constructive engagement," Mamdani wrote for the February 17, 2004 issue of the Nigerian newspaper *This Day*. "The political importance of Kirkpatrick's argument cannot be overstated. By giving a rationale for why it is fine to make friends with dictators while doing everything to overthrow left-wing governments, she solved the moral problem with [President Ronald] Reagan's foreign policy.") According to Mamdani, the lessons learned from taking that approach in Africa and Central America were later applied to Afghanistan, whose population the U.S. armed to fight the Soviets—then abandoned after the fight was won; Afghanistan became a base of operations for the terrorist group Al Qaeda, which was responsible for the 9/11 attacks. "Official America learned to distinguish between two types of terrorism—'theirs' and 'ours'— and cultivated an increasingly benign attitude to ours," Mamdani wrote in Good Muslim, Bad Muslim. "But then it turned out that their terrorism was born of ours." He told Nermeen Shaikh of the Asia Society (May 5, 2004, on-line), "The point of the book is that terror is a strategy to which the US turned to win the Cold War, that non-state terror was born of state terror, and that Islamist terror represents only the final and concluding outcome in this relationship, that its earlier outcomes, whether with [the armed conservative political group]

Renamo in Mozambique or the Contras in Nicaragua, have little if anything to do with Islamist terror." With the help of Edward Said, Mamdani's book was picked up by a division of Random House and sold well in 2004, as the anti-Iraq war movement grew in force and a significant number of people began to question the official rhetoric of the "war on terrorism." Mamdani joked to Andrew Rice for the *New York Observer* (April 4, 2005) that the book sold well because people misunderstood the title, taking it to be "a directory of good Muslims and bad Muslims—you know, which ones to avoid." The book was criticized by some for downplaying the economic goals of Cold War geopolitics, notably the opening of markets.

In *Saviors and Survivors: Darfur, Politics, and the War on Terror*, Mamdani examined the conflict in the Darfur province of Sudan, in Africa, in the context of colonial history. He argued that, contrary to most Western accounts of the conflict— which he dismissed as dangerously simplistic— the genocide in Darfur was not a race-based conflict but a war over land, climate change, and desertification. As with the Belgians in Rwanda, the British colonial tactic in Sudan was to divide the region into tribal homelands, assigning the label "native" to the groups given rights to the land, while outsiders, often nomads, were forced to pay tribute. "The British engineered the grand narrative . . . ," Mamdani told Joel Whitney for *Guernica* magazine (May 2009). "Tribe became the basis of systematic discrimination. So you got settler and native as a tribal distinction." Decades of severe drought drove nomads from the previously fertile lands in the north to Darfur, making the colonial-land rights an even more contentious issue. In addition, neighboring Chad became the site of a proxy Cold War fight that supplied the region with guns. That combination of factors, Mamdani wrote, led to a civil war in Sudan in the late 1980s, which intensified in the following decades with the government attempting unsuccessfully to create new tribal homelands and then engaging in a brutal counterinsurgency against rebel tribes. Mamdani also strongly criticized the "Save Darfur" campaign in the West as embracing a misguided, historical account of events that relied on stereotypes of Arabs reinforced by the "war on terrorism." The assumption that one set of evil people, Arabs— somehow "less African"—were committing genocide against another, native blacks, was, according to Mamdani, an attempt to simplify a complex problem. In his view, the crisis was less a genocide than the story of a civil war, or, more specifically,

an insurgency and a counterinsurgency, with killing on both sides. "I need to convince [supporters of the Save Darfur movement] that there is a politics around this—not simply good intentions and moralism and a fight against evil," Mamdani told Christopher Lydon, as broadcast on Radio *Open Source* (April 2, 2009). "I need to tell them that there is no such thing as a transhistorical evil in the world in which we live; that, in fact, all violence without exception has causes, and the causes are historical. And if you want to do something about the violence, we need to do something about the causes. The idea that violence is its own explanation is an idea which will take us nowhere except into a cycle of violence." Mamdani told Peter Hart and Steve Rendall on the radio show *Counter- Spin* (March 16, 2007) that the Western media, "because of the way they have reported Darfur," have "obscured the fact that there is a civil war going on. They have obscured the fact that the only way to stop the violence against the civilians is to settle this civil war. Instead, they have promoted the idea of an external military intervention as a possible solution. And the very prospect of an external military intervention has given hopes to the rebels that they may in fact end up with the entire cake, and instilled fears among the government that they may end up with no power whatsoever. So on both sides, it has reinforced those who think military and violence is the only way for them to safeguard their own position.

Mamdani argued that the words "humanitarian" and "genocide" have political meanings of their own— that the former, once used to protect victims now serves the goals of foreign intervention; that the latter is used to demonize enemies of the West, particularly in the "war on terrorism"; and that its use aggravates conflicts by marginalizing key groups from peace talks. The solution, according to Mamdani, is not to call for the one-sided enforcement of criminal justice but to reform the colonial land-rights system. "The only conflicts in Africa that we have managed to resolve successfully are those conflicts where criminal justice took a second seat to political reform," he told Cheryl Chorley for the National Public Radio program *Tell Me More* (March 5, 2009). "I think the turnaround was in South Africa with the end of apartheid. The end of apartheid was predicated on an agreement between the ANC [African National Congress] and the apartheid government, whereby the apartheid government agreed to political reforms in return for impunity."

## PERSONAL LIFE

Mamdani, who speaks nine languages, is married to the Indian filmmaker Mira Nair, whose movies include *Salaam Bombay!*, *Mississippi Masala*, *Monsoon Wedding*, and *Amelia*. The two met when Nair interviewed him in 1989 in Uganda as part of her research for *Mississippi Masala*, about a romance between an Indian-American woman and an African-American man from the South. Mamdani and Nair live in Kampala and New York and have a son, Zohran.

## FURTHER READING

*Boston Globe* p7 Mar. 22, 2009; *Guernica* May 2009; *India Abroad* p22 May 14, 2004; *London Review of Books* (on-line) Mar. 8, 2007; *New York Observer* pi Apr. 4, 2005; *New Yorker* plOO Dec. 9, 2002; *(Uganda) New Vision* Apr. 28, 2007; *From Citizen to Refugee,* 1973; *Politics and Class Formation in Uganda,* 1976; *Imperialism and Fascism in Uganda,* 1983; *Citizen and Subject: Contemporary Africa and the Legacy of Late Colonialism,* 1996; *When Victims Become Killers: Colonialism, Nativism, and the Genocide in Rwanda,* 2001; *Good Muslim, Bad Muslim: America, the Cold War, and the Roots of Terror,* 2004; *Saviors and Survivors: Darfur, Politics, and the War on Terror,* 2009

# NELSON MANDELA

## President of South Africa

**Born:** July 18, 1918; Mvezo, Cape Province, South Africa
**Died:** December 5, 2013; Johannesburg, South Africa
**Primary Field:** Anti-Apartheid

## INTRODUCTION

*In August 1962 Nelson Mandela, who not long before had emerged as a leading member of the African National Congress (ANC), South Africa's oldest civil rights organization, was arrested on charges of inciting workers to strike and leaving the country without valid travel documents. When he appeared in court for a formal remand, which was attended by a number of white attorneys who knew him personally, Mandela had a revelation of sorts. He sensed that on some level the spectators knew that he had committed no crime and that he was simply, in his words, "an ordinary man being punished for his beliefs." "In a way I had never quite comprehended before," Mandela wrote in his autobiography* Long Walk to Freedom *(1994), "I realized the role I could play in court and the possibilities before me as a defendant. I was the symbol of justice in the court of the oppressor, the representative of the great ideals of freedom, fairness, and democracy in a society that dishonored those virtues. I realized then and there that I could carry on the fight even within the fortress of the enemy."*

*Mandela went on to do just that, not only in the 1962 trial and in the famous Rivonia Trial of 1963-64, in*

Nelson Mandela.

*which he was convicted of treason and sentenced to life in prison, but also throughout the twenty-seven years of his incarceration. Mandela has continued to fight for the creation of a truly democratic society in South Africa since his dramatic release from prison in 1990, first as the guiding force in the ANC's negotiations with the white- minority government to end apartheid and to replace it with a multiracial government of national unity and then, since 1994, as South Africa's first freely elected president. Yet as far as Mandela is concerned, the challenge of transforming South Africa into a non-racial society has only begun. "I have walked that long road to freedom . . . ," Mandela wrote in his autobiography. "But I can rest only for a moment, for with freedom comes responsibility, and I dare not linger, for my long walk is not yet ended." For his efforts, in 1993 Mandela won the Nobel Peace Prize, which he shared with his predecessor, F. W. de Klerk, the former president of South Africa.*

## EARLY LIFE

Nelson Mandela was born Rolihlahla Dalibhunga Mandela on July 18, 1918 in the village of Mvezo, in the Transkei, a region on South Africa's southeastern coast. His father, Gadla Henry Mphakanyiswa, was the chief of Mvezo and a member of the royal house of the Thembu tribe, and his mother, Nosekeni Fanny Mandela, was one of his father's four wives. Following his father's death, when he was nine, Mandela came under the guardianship of Jongintaba Dalindyebo, the powerful regent of the Thembu people, who groomed him for tribal duties as counselor to the chief and whom he came to admire greatly. In fact, Mandela's mature ideas about leadership, especially his belief in the importance of leading by consensus, were inspired by the example set by the regent, as Mandela revealed in his autobiography: "I always remember the regent's axiom: A leader, he said, is like a shepherd. He stays behind the flock, letting the most nimble go out ahead, whereupon the others follow, not realizing that all along they are being directed from behind."

As a youth Mandela was also influenced by certain Western cultural values that prevailed at the Methodist primary and secondary schools he attended. The schools were modeled after British schools, and as a result Mandela and his classmates were taught to aspire to be "black Englishmen," he has recalled somewhat ruefully. Mandela's identification with British interests remained strong at the University College of Fort Hare, in Alice, which he entered at the age of twenty-one at the urging of his guardian. Indeed, when the South African government entered World War II on the side of the Allies to help liberate Europe from German domination, Mandela and his classmates heartily supported

the move—"forgetting," he has written, "that we did not have that freedom here in our own land."

Mandela's exposure to Western culture also distanced him from Thembu traditions, to the extent that he could not bring himself to submit to his guardian's wish that he marry a woman of the guardian's choosing, in accordance with Thembu custom. To avoid marrying the woman, in 1941 Mandela fled to Johannesburg, where, with the help of Walter Sisulu, a prominent black businessman from the Transkei, he soon got a job as a law clerk in the office of a liberal Jewish law firm. Concurrently, he began a correspondence course from the University of South Africa, which awarded him a B.A. degree in 1942.

## LIFE'S WORK

During his early years in Johannesburg, Mandela was surrounded by people of all political persuasions, but he did not allow himself to feel pressured to embrace any one particular philosophy. Instead, he carefully considered all points of view, including not only those of friends who belonged to the Communist Party and the African National Congress (many of whose members were students at the University of the Witwatersrand, which Mandela entered in 1943 with the aim of obtaining a bachelor of law degree) but also those of his white employers, who did their best to discourage him from pursuing a career in politics.

After much thought, Mandela found that he had the greatest affinity for ideas promoted by the ANC, whose principal goal was the liberation of black South Africans from the shackles of racism. "I had no epiphany, no singular revelation, no moment of truth, but a steady accumulation of a thousand slights, a thousand indignities, a thousand unremembered moments, produced in me an anger, a rebelliousness, a desire to fight the system that imprisoned my people," Mandela wrote in his memoir. "There was no particular day on which I said, From henceforth I will devote myself to the liberation of my people; instead, I simply found myself doing so, and could not do otherwise."

Mandela joined the ANC in 1944, and shortly after that he and others helped establish the ANC Youth League, which eventually came to dominate the ANC and whose aims were nothing less than "the overthrow of white supremacy and the establishment of a truly democratic form of government," as Mandela has described them. Those goals became more elusive than ever after the Afrikaner-dominated National Party came to power in 1948. In the following years the Nationalists passed a series of sweeping laws that transformed from custom into law the system of racial segregation known as apartheid. In addition to requiring each of South Africa's racial groups to live in separate, designated areas, the laws prohibited marriage between people of different races, mandated that all South Africans be registered according to their race, and outlawed the Communist Party in terms so broad that almost anyone could be considered a member.

In response to the new measures, the ANC leadership felt compelled to rethink its strategy to protest the oppression of black South Africans. That rethinking ultimately prompted the ANC to demand, in a letter to the prime minister in 1952, that the government repeal the discriminatory laws. When the demand was rebuffed, as expected, the ANC launched the Campaign for the Defiance of Unjust Laws, which Mandela helped organize. Those involved in the campaign committed such nonviolent—and, according to the new laws, illegal—acts as entering proscribed areas without permission, using "whites only" facilities, including toilets and railway station entrances, and taking part in strikes. Because of his role in the campaign, Mandela, along with many others, was found guilty of "statutory communism," despite the fact that he did not even belong to the party. As a punishment, he was "banned," which meant that he was prohibited from attending rallies or other gatherings (even nonpolitical ones) for several months. (In 1952 Mandela, having already qualified to practice law, established the first black-run law practice in South Africa, with his friend Oliver Tambo.) Mandela was later banned again, and as a result he did not return to the public eye until 1955.

On December 5, 1956 Mandela was among 156 resistance leaders charged with high treason— specifically, committing acts aimed at toppling the government and replacing it with a Communist regime—an offense punishable by death. The acts in question included the Defiance Campaign of 1952 and similar challenges to the government's legitimacy. In the trial, which did not begin until 1959 (Mandela was free on bail during the interim), the government was unable to show that Mandela or the ANC had plotted any sort of violent revolution, and on March 29, 1961 he and his comrades were acquitted. Mandela was pleased by the verdict, though he regarded it not "as a vindication of the legal system or evidence that a black man could get a fair trial in a white man's court," as he wrote in *Long Walk to Freedom*, but rather as "a result of a superior defense team and the fair-mindedness of the panel of these particular judges." His circumspection proved to be well founded, for not long after his acquittal a warrant for his arrest was issued, the ANC having been banned by the government in 1960. In the following months Mandela thus lived as a fugitive, posing variously as a chauffeur, cook, or gardener.

Throughout his years of involvement with the ANC, Mandela was committed to fighting to end apartheid through nonviolent means. By the early 1960s, however, he, along with other ANC leaders, began to question the effectiveness of this approach, for increasingly the government was responding to the ANC's actions with violence. One of the more infamous instances in which the government resorted to violence occurred in the town of Sharpville in 1960, when sixty-nine protesters were killed by police. Whether or not to launch an armed struggle subsequently became the subject of heated debate, especially at an ANC meeting in June 1961. For his part, Mandela, having become convinced that "it was wrong and immoral to subject [his] people to armed attacks by the state without offering them some kind of alternative," argued that the ANC had no choice but to take up an armed struggle against the state. Notwithstanding his lack of military experience, Mandela was given the task of organizing an armed wing of the ANC, Umkhonto we Sizwe (Spear of the Nation), whose mission was to organize acts of sabotage against the state with the aim of overthrowing the white- minority government. Mandela now had more reason than ever to be mindful of his movements around the country. His uncanny luck and success in evading capture earned him the nickname "the Black Pimpernel," after the Scarlet Pimpernel, the title character of a book by Emmuska Orczy who eludes capture during the French Revolution.

Mandela's underground existence came to an end on August 5, 1962, when he was arrested on charges of inciting workers to strike and leaving the country without valid travel documents. In the trial that followed, in which he conducted his own defense, he never denied the government's charges, for he had indeed organized workers to strike and left the country without proper papers. Instead, he argued that the state had no jurisdiction over his activities since its laws had been made by a government in which he had no representation, and that it was merely his natural desire to live as a free man in a state that denied him freedom that had put him on the wrong side of the law. "There comes a time," he declared to the court at the trial's conclusion, "as it came in my life, when a man is denied the right to live a normal life, when he can only live the life of an outlaw because the government has so decreed to use the law to impose a state of outlawry upon him." On November 7, 1962 he was sentenced to five years in prison with no chance of parole.

Eight months later South African authorities raided the ANC's headquarters at a farm in Rivonia and seized documents outlining the organization's plans to wage guerrilla warfare in South Africa. That discovery enabled the state to try Mandela, along with several other top ANC officials, on new and more serious charges. The Rivonia Trial, as it became known, ended with the defendants being convicted of treason, Although their crime was punishable by death—an outcome that Mandela fully expected—the court sentenced them to life in prison, with no chance of parole, on June 12, 1964. The trial was the subject of considerable media attention around the world, and appeals for clemency were received in South Africa from abroad. An editorial writer for the *New York Times* predicted that history would judge that "the ultimate guilty party is the government in power— and that is already the verdict of world opinion."

For the next eighteen years, Mandela was confined to the maximum-security prison on Robben Island, off South Africa's coast. His first cell there was seven feet square, with a single light bulb and a mat on the floor for sleeping. He had the right to receive only one brief letter and one visitor every six months. But in spite of the harsh conditions, Mandela was determined not to surrender to despair. Indeed, he has said he never seriously considered the possibility that he would not one day walk on South African soil as a free man.

Within a year or two, conditions at Robben Island improved somewhat, in part through the efforts of the International Red Cross. Mandela was permitted to take correspondence courses from the University of London, and he and the other prisoners were eventually provided with desks and, later, stools. Still, virtually all conversation among the prisoners was forbidden, and they were not allowed to read newspapers, which they nevertheless felt duty-bound to try to do (and which they succeeded in doing), so as to keep abreast of political developments in South Africa. Beginning in the 1970s, as conditions permitted, Mandela and his ANC comrade Walter Sisulu led political study groups. Mandela also drafted judicial appeals for other inmates, often piecing together the details of a case as information slowly came to him through the prison grapevine.

In 1980, at the urging of several top ANC officials, the *Johannesburg Sunday Post* launched a campaign to free Mandela by printing a petition that readers could sign to demand that he and other political prisoners be released. Although it met strong resistance from the government—newspapers had long been barred from printing Mandela's photograph or citing his words—the campaign established him more firmly as the embodiment of black South Africans' fight for freedom.

In 1982 Mandela was transferred to Pollsmoor Maximum Security Prison. By then the effort to end apartheid had taken on greater urgency among the younger generation of black South Africans and as a result was gaining attention and sympathy abroad. There were also signs that the South African government was not impervious to the mounting international criticism of its policies, and that, more important, it realized it might eventually have to accommodate at least some of the concerns of the country's increasingly militant black majority-

One such sign came in 1985, when President P. W. Botha offered to free Mandela and all other political prisoners if they agreed to "unconditionally" repudiate violence. Mandela refused, for the same reason that he had committed himself to the armed struggle against apartheid more than two decades before—namely, that the government, by resorting to violent means itself, had left the ANC with no other course of action. But he saw in Botha's offer a change in attitude and decided to take a chance. Later that year, on his own initiative, he began exploring the possibility of conducting secret talks with the government. Such an effort, not coincidentally, had only then become logistically feasible, because in that year Mandela was moved to a cell where he had little contact with his colleagues and could thus speak with government officials privately.

Mandela at first told no one about his plan. "There are times when a leader must move ahead of the flock, go off in a new direction, confident that he is leading his people the right way," he wrote in his memoir. He took some consolation in the fact that his "isolation furnished [his] organization with an excuse in case matters went awry: the old man was alone and completely cut off, and his actions were taken by him as an individual, not as a representative of the ANC."

By 1987 Mandela had had several secret discussions with the minister of justice, Kobie Coetsee, the upshot of which was that the government appeared to be interested in reaching some sort of compromise with the ANC. In late 1988 Mandela was transferred to Victor Verster Prison, also near Cape Town, where he was provided with a cottage with a swimming pool and allowed to keep his own schedule. There, the talks continued.

In 1989 Botha stepped down both as head of the National Party and as president; he was succeeded by F. W. de Klerk. At first Mandela, like most political observers both within and outside South Africa, viewed de Klerk as simply a party man, but he soon came to see the new president as "a man who saw change as necessary and inevitable." And as it turned out, change was not long in coming. Shortly after taking office, de Klerk overturned many of the laws that constituted petty apartheid (such as those segregating parks and restaurants and other public facilities), released a number of black leaders from prison, and met personally with Mandela. Then, in a speech before parliament on February 2, 1990, de Klerk lifted the ban on the ANC as well as on other opposition organizations, declaring, "The time for negotiations has arrived." The following week he told Mandela that his release was imminent.

Mandela's release from prison, on February 11, 1990, was one of the most dramatic news events of the year. A few months later Mandela embarked on a world tour, making stops in major cities throughout North America and Europe, where he was welcomed as a hero and a world leader. In Great Britain he met with Prime Minister Margaret Thatcher. In the United States he addressed a joint session of Congress and conferred with President George Bush. After his meeting with Bush, the two men held a press conference on the White House lawn.

The task of establishing a truly democratic, nonracial government in South Africa fell to the multiparty Convention for a Democratic South Africa, which began in December 1991. The negotiations that ensued, led by Mandela and de Klerk, were by no means without conflict and were broken off at various points. A major hurdle was crossed on September 26, 1992, when Mandela and de Klerk signed the Record of Understanding, which formalized their agreement that a single, freely elected constitutional assembly would both serve as the transitional legislature and draft a new constitution. Another milestone was reached on June 3, 1993, when it was agreed that the first elections open to all South

African citizens would be held on April 27, 1994. For their efforts to bring South Africa to that point, Mandela and de Klerk were awarded the 1993 Nobel Peace Prize.

Few were surprised when Mandela became a candidate for president in those elections. As expected, the ANC won handily, capturing 62.6 percent of the popular vote. "The images of South Africans going to the polls that day are burned in my memory," he recalled in his autobiography. "Great lines of patient people snaking through the dirt roads and streets of towns and cities; old women who had waited half a century to cast their first vote saying that they felt like human beings for the first time in their lives; white men and women saying they were proud to live in a free country at last. The mood of the nation during those days of voting was buoyant. The violence and bombings ceased, and it was as if we were a nation reborn."

In the months that followed his inauguration, on May 12, 1994, Mandela and the government of national unity began to draft a program of reconstruction and development aimed at both satisfying the demands of long-disenfranchised blacks and attracting new investments from abroad. While it remains to be seen how successful the new government will be in achieving those goals, Mandela has already been credited with one major accomplishment: significantly advancing the cause of mutual understanding and tolerance among his country's diverse ethnic and political groups. He has done so by including in his cabinet not only members of the ANC but also members of the Inkatha Freedom Party, with which the ANC has long been in conflict, and of the National Party. He also led discussions with members of the right-wing Conservative Party, while one of his ministers held similar talks with the neo-fascist Afrikaner Resistance Movement. As a result, he has succeeded in gaining the confidence of the more conservative elements of South Africa's electorate. "Even if Mandela achieves little more before he retires, he will have won a special niche in South African history as the dignified, white-haired patriarch who won the respect of his political enemies," Patrick Laurence wrote in *Africa Report* (November/December 1994).

## PERSONAL LIFE

From his marriage to Evelyn Mase, a nurse, which lasted from 1944 until 1956, Nelson Mandela has three children (a fourth died in infancy). In 1958 he married Nomzamo Winnie Madikizela, then a young social worker. The couple had two daughters in the four years they lived together before Mandela's imprisonment. Winnie Mandela became her husband's principal supporter and spokesperson during his years in prison, and she ultimately developed a political power base of her own. Her reputation was later marred by charges of criminal behavior. Following Mandela's release, the couple became estranged, and they separated in April 1992.

In addition to the Nobel Prize, over the years Mandela has received numerous honors and awards. He won the Bruno Kreisky Prize for Human Rights in 1982, and he was named an Honorary Citizen of Rome in 1983. He received the Sakharov Prize in 1988 and the Gaddaff Human Rights Prize in 1989 and shared the Houphouet Prize in 1991. He has received a great number of honorary doctorates, including a joint honorary degree from thirty-eight traditionally black American universities, which he received in 1990 during a ceremony at Morehouse College, in Atlanta.

"The policy of apartheid created a deep and lasting wound in my country and my people," Nelson Mandela concluded in his autobiography. "All of us will spend many years, if not generations, recovering from that profound hurt." Mandela nevertheless remains full of

hope that such a recovery will eventually take place. "My country is rich in the minerals and gems that lie beneath its soil, but I have always known that its greatest wealth is its people, finer and truer than the purest diamonds."

In June 2004, amid failing health, Mandela announced that he was "retiring from retirement" and retreating from public life. Although continuing to meet with close friends and family, the Foundation discouraged invitations for him to appear at public events and denied most interview requests. When Mandela died in 2013, Zuma proclaimed a national mourning period of ten days, with December 8 a national day of prayer and reflection. Mandela is often cited alongside Gandhi and Martin Luther King, Jr. as one of the 20th century's exemplary anti-racist and anti-colonial leaders.

## FURTHER READING

*Ebony p40+ Ag '94 por; Benson, Mary. Nelson Mandela: The Man and the Movement (1986); Mandela, Nelson. Long Walk to Freedom (1994); Meer, Fatima. Higher Than Hope (1990); International Who's Who, 1994-95*

---

# WILMA P. MANKILLER

## Principal Chief, Cherokee Nation of Oklahoma

**Born:** November 18, 1945; Tahlequah, Oklahoma
**Died:** April 6, 2010; Adair County, Oklahoma
**Primary Field:** Native American Activism

### INTRODUCTION

*When Wilma Mankiller was sworn in as principal chief of the Cherokee Nation in December 1985, succeeding Ross O. Swimmer, who had been appointed assistant secretary of the interior for Indian affairs, she became the first woman ever to serve as chief of a major North American Indian tribe. The Cherokee, with 92,000 members, are second in size only to the Navajo. Two years later, in July 1987, Wilma Mankiller reaffirmed her mandate when she defeated her opponent, Perry Wheeler, in a closely contested election. Stressing economic self-sufficiency as well as pride in Cherokee culture, Wilma Mankiller, in her unique position, brought*

*nationwide attention to the plight of the American Indian, and she served as a role model for her people, demonstrating how they can overcome adversity to lead productive lives.*

*To reach her position, Wilma Mankiller surmounted considerable personal hardship. Her family was relocated from their land in Oklahoma to San Francisco, California in the 1950s, after their farm failed, and they had to adapt to a radically different way of life. Wilma Mankiller first became involved in the American Native Rights movement in 1969, when she helped to raise funds for the Indians who occupied the prison on Alcatraz Island in protest of the plight of American Indians. After becoming a social worker, she returned to her family's land in Oklahoma and started working for the Cherokee Nation, most of whose members subsist at the poverty level. There, she implemented several innovative rural-development projects that brought her nationwide attention and so impressed Chief Swimmer that he asked her to be his running mate in 1983. Wilma*

*Mankiller saw her main purpose as helping her people become self-sufficient, and she wanted others to "see the tremendous strength and beauty and creativity that [she] see[s] in Indian people in this country, and the tremendous potential for people to solve their own problems, given half a chance."*

## EARLY LIFE

Wilma P. Mankiller was born on November 18, 1945 to Irene and Charlie Mankiller in Tahlequah, Oklahoma. Her mother is Caucasian; her father, a full-blooded Cherokee. The surname Mankiller comes from a high Cherokee military rank that a male ancestor adopted. Wilma Mankiller spent her early childhood on a 160-acre tract of land, known as Mankiller Flats, in Adair County, Oklahoma. The land was given to her grandfather by the United States government as part of the settlement the government made with the Cherokee after they were forced, in 1838, to relocate from their traditional lands in the Southeastern United States to "Indian territory" in Oklahoma. Several thousand Indians died en route, along the so-called Trail of Tears, while another thousand escaped into the Great Smoky Mountains, where they lived as fugitives. Further hardship followed when the federal government dismantled the Cherokee tribal government in 1907 and reapportioned their lands. The Cherokee Nation was legally reconstituted in 1971, on 7,000 square miles in northeastern Oklahoma.

Like the majority of American Indians, Wilma Mankiller's family, which included eleven children, lived in abject poverty, and such amenities as indoor plumbing and electricity were almost unheard of. When the family farm was ruined by two years of drought, Wilma, at the age of twelve, and her family were forced to move to San Francisco, under the Bureau of Indian Affairs's relocation program, which was designed to "mainstream" rural Indians into American cities. "Relocation was yet another answer from the federal government to the continuing dilemma of what to do with us," Wilma Mankiller later told Michele Wallace in an interview for *Ms.* (January 1988) magazine. "We are a people with many, many social indicators of decline and an awful lot of problems, so in the fifties they decided to mainstream us, to try to take us away from the tribal land base and the tribal culture, get us into the cities. It was supposed to be a better life."

The Mankillers had a hard time adjusting to modern city life. "One day I was here and the next day I was trying to deal with the mysteries of television, indoor plumbing, neon lights and elevators," she later recalled to a reporter for *People* (December 2, 1985). "I guess they thought we would open a liquor store." Wilma Mankiller's father became a warehouse worker and a union activist. He was "the only full-blooded Indian union organizer I ever ran into," she said in the *People* magazine interview.

## LIFE'S WORK

During the 1960s, Wilma Mankiller studied sociology, worked as a social worker, married a wealthy Ecuadoran accountant, and gave birth to two daughters. It was in 1969 that she became active in the American Native Rights movement, after a group of young Indian demonstrators took over the property and building that once housed Alcatraz prison, in San Francisco Bay, to bring to the public's attention the deplorable treatment of American Indians. During the prison occupation, which lasted eighteen months, Wilma Mankiller helped to raise funds for the protestors. "Those college students who participated in Alcatraz articulated a lot of feelings I had that I'd never been able to express," she told John Hughes in an interview for the *Chicago Tribune* (May 14, 1986). "I was a mother, so I couldn't join them, but I did fundraising and got involved in the activist movement."

The Alcatraz experience changed her life. Wilma Mankiller began attending college at night and worked as the Native American programs coordinator for the Oakland, California public school system. In the mid-1970s Wilma Mankiller divorced her husband after ten years of marriage and returned to Oklahoma to claim her grandfather's land. "I wanted my children to experience the rural life," she told John Hughes, "and I thought some of the skills I'd learned out there (in San Francisco), I could practice here." She built a small wooden house on her property, Mankiller Flats, and, in 1977, landed a job as economic stimulus coordinator for the Cherokee Nation. In the meantime, she continued her studies, earning a B.A. degree in social science from Flaming Rainbow University in Stilwell, Oklahoma and later, in 1979, took graduate courses in community planning from the University of Arkansas.

Using her skills in social work, Wilma Mankiller set out to instill in the Cherokee the precept that self-help is a source of self-esteem. "My goal has always been for Indians to solve their own economic problems," she once said, as quoted in *Fortune* (October 12, 1987) magazine. In 1979 she became program development specialist for the Cherokee Nation, and in 1981 she founded the

Community Development Department of the Cherokee Nation and became its director, after raising the funds necessary to establish the department.

As director, she instituted several innovative programs—stressing community self-help—that included the development of rural water systems and the rehabilitation of housing. One successfully completed project that has received national attention and has served as a model for other Indian tribes was the Bell Community Project, which entailed laying out sixteen miles of water lines and rehabilitating several homes within the community of Bell, Oklahoma. Capitalizing on her talent for writing grant proposals, Wilma Mankiller obtained a number of grants for community development projects, including funding for the Cherokee Gardens, a successful commercial horticultural operation, and for social services.

It was Wilma Mankiller's involvement in and successful implementation of these types of projects that led Ross Swimmer, the principal chief of the Cherokee Nation, to select her as his running mate for deputy principal chief in the tribal elections in 1983. Swimmer and Wilma Mankiller had considerable philosophical differences: he was a conservative Republican banker, while she characterized herself as a liberal Democrat. But Swimmer has said about Wilma Mankiller, as quoted in the *People* magazine story: "She knows her strengths and her weaknesses, and she is one sharp businesswoman." With the Swimmer-Mankiller ticket winning the election, Wilma Mankiller became the first woman to serve as deputy chief of the Cherokee people. And when Swimmer was appointed head of the Bureau of Indian Affairs in Washington, D.C., in 1985, Wilma Mankiller was sworn in as principal chief of the Cherokee on December 15, 1985, becoming the first woman to hold that position as well.

In spite of their ideological differences, Wilma Mankiller made clear at the time of her swearing-in ceremony that she would "stay on the same path" that her predecessor had taken. Swimmer had worked on making the Cherokee Nation less dependent on handouts from the federal government. Under his leadership, the tribe opened a number of businesses, including a motel, a restaurant, an electronics manufacturing firm, and a cattle and poultry ranch. Swimmer and Wilma Mankiller also worked together on reducing stress within the tribe, brought about by tensions between full-blooded and mixed-blooded members.

Although the Cherokee, like many North American Indian tribes, were originally matrilineal in descent, their contact with the white men resulted in their adopting a male-oriented system of government. "Early historians referred to our government as a petticoat government because of the strong role of the women in the tribe," Wilma Mankiller told *Ms.* magazine. "Then we adopted a lot of ugly things that were part of the non-Indian world and one of those things was sexism. This whole system of tribal government was designed by men. So in 1687 women enjoyed a prominent role, but in 1987 we found people questioning whether women should be in leadership positions anywhere in the tribe. So my election was a step forward and a step backward at the same time." In spite of resentment toward Wilma Mankiller among some Cherokee members, she stressed that immediate economic and social concerns overrode the issue of the sex of the principal chief of the Cherokee Nation. Her people, she told Robert Reinhold of the *New York Times* (December 15, 1985), "are worried about jobs and education, not whether the tribe is run by a woman or not." But Wilma Mankiller has acknowledged that she is conscious of the pressure to perform that her position as the first female principal chief of the Cherokee has put on her. "I'm conscious of the fact that I'm the first female chief," she told John Hughes, "and people are watching me, and I want to make sure I do a good job. So I feel like I have to do a little extra."

When Wilma Mankiller ran for election as principal chief of the Cherokee Nation in her own right in 1987, for a four-year term, she campaigned with the pledge to improve the tribe's economic interests. Her second husband, Charlie Soap, a Cherokee who is involved in rural development work, helped to convince the male members of the tribe that Wilma Mankiller was "safe" to run the Cherokee Nation. His fluency in Cherokee also proved useful. Wilma Mankiller's extensive experience in rural development and the resulting contact she had maintained with members of her tribe enabled her to defeat her opponent, Perry Wheeler, a funeral director and former deputy chief who had unsuccessfully run against Swimmer in 1983. In the July 20, 1987 election, in a four-way race, Wilma Mankiller received 45 percent of the vote, compared to Wheeler's 29 percent. Because tribal law requires that a candidate must receive more than 50 percent of the vote to be elected, a runoff election was held in July 1987, in which Wilma Mankiller received 5,914 votes compared to Wheeler's 4, 670 votes.

Wilma Mankiller has concentrated on such basic issues as the Cherokee Nation's 50 percent unemployment rate, low educational levels, and inferior quality of health care, as well as on the economic development of northeastern Oklahoma. She recently founded the Cherokee Nation's Chamber of Commerce, which combines the tribe's business ventures with a project to use the rocky Cherokee lands. One projected plan is the building of a hydroelectric plant. "I'd like to see whole healthy communities again," Wilma Mankiller remarked in the Ms. magazine interview, "communities in which tribe members would have access to adequate health care, higher education if they want it, a decent place to live and a decent place to work, and a strong commitment to tribal language and culture." The Institute for Cherokee Literacy is one way the Cherokee Nation is ensuring the promulgation of its language and culture. Operating during the summer, the institute teaches students how to read and write the Cherokee language. In exchange, the students return to their communities and pass on what they have learned.

The Cherokee Nation, headquartered in Tahlequah, Oklahoma, has an operating budget of $48 million and approximately 1,000 tribal government employees. It administers social welfare programs and its tribal business enterprises. To achieve ultimate independence from reliance on the federal government, Wilma Mankiller emphasizes the "empowerment of the people on a local level," encouraging members of her tribe to become more self-reliant in their outlook. "One of the biggest problems is that we need to really trust our own selves and our own thinking, and not allow others to convince us that our thoughts, ideas and plans and visions aren't valid," Wilma Mankiller explained to Catherine C. Robbins for the New York Times (May 28, 1987).

The novelty of Mankiller's status has brought nationwide attention to the Cherokee Nation—a situation that she has capitalized on as an opportunity to expose the plight of the American Indian, as well as to dispel popular misconceptions about her people. "There are so many forces working against Indian tribes," she explained during the interview with Ms. magazine. "There are people in Tulsa and Oklahoma City who don't realize our communities exist as they do today, that we have a language that is alive, that we have a tribal government that is thriving. Most people like to deal with us as though we were in a museum or a history book." On the contrary, Wilma Mankiller has asserted: "We are a revitalized tribe, we have kept the best of our old ways

of life and incorporated the sounder elements of today's non-Indian world."

One other experience has dramatically affected Wilma Mankiller's life. In 1979 the car she was driving crashed head-on into another car that was driven by a friend. The friend was killed, and Wilma Mankiller was badly injured. "Everyone kept looking at the car, and looking at me and saying 'I don't know how you could have survived this,'" she recounted to John Hughes in the Chicago Tribune article. Following the accident, Wilma Mankiller underwent seventeen operations to correct physical problems caused by the crash. In addition, during the course of treatment, she discovered that she had muscular dystrophy and was forced to endure a series of chemotherapy treatments. Today, the muscular dystrophy is in remission. "Everything has been up from that point on," she told Hughes. "In a way it seems it was a test of perseverance or something that I went through. It was a maturing kind of process. It was a definite preparation."

In 1987 Wilma Mankiller was named Woman of the Year by Ms. magazine. She is the recipient of numerous other awards and honors, including the John W. Gardner Leadership Award in 1988 and a Citation for Outstanding Contributions to American Leadership and Native American Culture, bestowed by the Harvard Foundation in 1986. She also serves on a number of boards, including the Council of Energy Resource Tribes, the Cherokee Nation Industries, Inc., the Cherokee National Historical Society, the Indian Law Resource Center, the Ms. Foundation for Women, and the Oklahoma Academy of State Goals.

## PERSONAL LIFE

A small, stocky woman with coal-black hair and a deep voice, Wilma Mankiller lived in the small wooden house that she built on her Mankiller Flats land. Her bookshelves featured works by Plato, Chaucer, Tolstoy, and Kant. She married Charlie Soap in October 1986, but she continued to use her maiden name. Wilma Mankiller has two daughters: Gina and Felicia, and one grandson. Asked by John Hughes what she would like to be remembered for, Wilma Mankiller replied: "I want to be remembered as the person who helped us restore faith in ourselves."

**FURTHER READING**
*Chicago Tribune V pl+ My 14 '86, V pi fa 20 '88; N Y Times p30 D 15 '85, C pi My 28 '87; Ms 16:68+ fa '88; People 24:91+ D 2 '85*

---

# THURGOOD MARSHALL

## Associate Justice of the United States Supreme Court

**Born:** July 2, 1908; Baltimore, Maryland
**Died:** January 24, 1994; Bethesda, Maryland
**Primary Field:** Civil Rights
**Affiliation:** U.S. Supreme Court

### INTRODUCTION

*In 1939 Thurgood Marshall was at the forefront of the civil rights movement, arguing cases before the United States Supreme Court in his capacity as chief counsel for the National Association for the Advancement of Colored People Legal Defense and Educational Fund. Fifty years later, as the only black member of the Supreme Court since his appointment in 1967, he continues to act upon his longstanding commitment to the constitutionally protected rights of the individual by opposing capital punishment, racial discrimination, and the encroachment of the state upon First Amendment freedoms.*

*Marshall made his best-known contribution to progress in civil rights while he was still a lawyer for the NAACP, when, in 1954, he persuaded the Supreme Court that "separate but equal" public school systems violated the Fourteenth Amendment's guarantee of equal protection of the laws. After hearing Marshall's argument, the Court unanimously declared that segregation was unconstitutional in the landmark decision Brown v. Board of Education. Marshall continued to litigate desegregation cases until 1961, when he was appointed a federal appellate judge by President John F. Kennedy. Four years later, he became President Lyndon B. Johnson's solicitor general. He served in that capacity until his appointment to the Supreme Court.*

*When Marshall joined the Court, then under the leadership of Chief Justice Earl Warren, he replaced a centrist justice whose vote often created a five-to-four conservative majority. Marshall tipped the balance in favor of a liberal, or activist, majority, but before long*

*he found himself increasingly in the minority. The two chief justices since 1969, Warren E. Burger arid William H. Rehnquist, were both appointed to the Court by President Richard M. Nixon. Three additional Nixon appointees were joined by one Gerald R. Ford appointee in the 1970s and by three Ronald Reagan appointees (one of whom replaced a Nixon appointee) in the 1980s. The resulting conservative revanchism has placed Marshall in the position of frequently dissenting—along with the last remaining Dwight D. Eisenhower appointee, William J. Brennan Jr.—from decisions that would, in his view, lead to the erosion of hard-won civil rights gains.*

### EARLY LIFE

Thurgood Marshall was born on July 2, 1908, the younger of the two sons of William Canfield Marshall and Norma A. (Williams) Marshall in Baltimore, Maryland. His mother was an elementary school teacher, and his father was a Pullman car waiter before becoming a steward at an all-white yacht club on Chesapeake Bay. He was named after his paternal grandfather, who assumed the name Thoroughgood in compliance with Union Army regulations during the Civil War that required every soldier to record both a first and a last name. His great-grandfather was captured in Africa and brought as a slave to Maryland's eastern shore. Speaking of his great-grandfather, Marshall once said: "His more polite descendants like to think he came from the cultured tribes in Sierra Leone. But we all know that he really came from the toughest part of the Congo." His rebellious nature, according to Marshall, won him his freedom. William Marshall carried on the tradition by advising his son to fight his own battles. Marshall has quoted his father as telling him, "Son, if anyone ever calls you a nigger, you not only got my permission to fight him—you got my orders to fight him."

After graduating with honors from Douglas High School in Baltimore, Marshall enrolled at Lincoln University, an all-black college in Oxford, Pennsylvania.

His mother pawned her wedding and engagement rings to help pay his expenses, and he worked part-time as, at different times, a busboy, waiter, baker, and grocery clerk during his college years. Marshall had originally intended to study dentistry, according to his mother's wishes, but because he excelled on the debating team he switched his major to pre-law. "My father turned me into a lawyer without ever telling me what he wanted me to be," Marshall once said, as quoted in the *New York Times* (October 22, 1964). "In a way, he was the most insidious of my family rebels. He taught me how to argue, challenged my logic on every point, even if we were discussing the weather." Marshall graduated with honors in 1929.

## Life's Work

After his application to the all-white University of Maryland Law School was rejected on the basis of race, Marshall enrolled at Howard University Law School in Washington, D.C. He was awarded an LL.B. degree, magna cum laude, in 1933. Employing his newly attained knowledge of the law as counsel to the Baltimore chapter of the NAACP, he compelled the law school that had rejected him to admit its first black student in 1935. The student, Donald Murray, was also the first black student admitted to any state law school south of the Mason-Dixon line.

In addition to his work with the NAACP, Marshall maintained a private practice in Baltimore from 1933 to 1937. Specializing in civil rights and criminal law, he often represented clients who could not afford to pay him for his services. The NAACP did not pay well either, and, even after he moved to the organization's headquarters in New York City to become the assistant to Charles H. Houston, the national counsel for the NAACP, in 1936, he was paid only a modest annual salary. When Houston resigned in 1938 to resume private practice, Marshall was elevated to his post. The following year he helped to found the NAACP Legal Defense and Educational Fund (LDF) to mount a legal assault on segregation. (Since the mid-1950s the LDF has functioned independently of the NAACP.)

As director and chief counsel of the LDF, Marshall was the chief strategist in the campaign to desegregate America's school systems. Much of his time was spent traveling throughout the South, creating a network of sympathetic lawyers to handle civil rights cases and instigating local challenges to segregated education. Although segregation was consistently upheld by the lower courts, Marshall coordinated appeals to the higher courts, and he himself argued the cases before the Supreme Court, having been admitted to practice before that body in 1939. Of the thirty-two cases he argued on behalf of the NAACP, he won twenty-nine.

Marshall's most important victory occurred on May 17, 1954, when the Warren Court ruled unanimously in *Brown v. Board of Education* that "separate educational facilities are inherently unequal," overturning the "separate but equal" doctrine laid down in *Plessy v. Ferguson* (1896). Racial segregation was held, in two separate rulings in Brown, to deprive blacks of both equal protection of the laws and due process of law, under the Fourteenth and Fifth amendments, respectively. Much of Marshall's remaining work with the LDF consisted of litigating compliance with the decision on a case-by-case basis. He also worked to eliminate racial discrimination in voting, housing, public accommodations, and the disciplining of black American soldiers stationed in Korea and Japan, countries to which Marshall traveled in 1951 in order to gather firsthand information. He eventually obtained reduced sentences for twenty-two of the forty black soldiers who alleged that they had received unfair trials.

On September 23, 1961 President Kennedy appointed Thurgood Marshall to the United States Court of Appeals for the Second Circuit, which comprises New York, Vermont, and Connecticut. Despite an increase in salary that would nearly double his annual income, it was a tough decision for Marshall to leave the civil rights battle. "I had to fight it out with myself," he said, as quoted in the *New York Times* (October 22, 1964), "but by then I had built up a staff—a damned good staff—an excellent board, and the backing that would let them go ahead. And when one has the opportunity to serve his government, he should think twice before passing it up." In a subsequent interview for the Washington Post (December 26, 1965), Marshall told Joseph E. Mohbat: "I've always felt the assault troops never occupy the town. I figured after the school decisions, the assault was over for me. It was time to let newer minds take over."

As an indication of the struggles that still lay ahead for the civil rights movement, Marshall's confirmation was stalled for nearly one year by segregationist senators. He was finally confirmed on September 11, 1962 by a vote of fifty-four to sixteen. During his tenure as a federal appellate judge, he wrote more than 150 decisions. According to Fred P. Graham of the *New York*

*Times* (June 14, 1965), Marshall "tended to tackle tough issues, even when they could be avoided on procedural grounds." Among other things, he ruled that the loyalty oaths required of New York teachers were unconstitutional; curbed the power of immigration authorities to expel aliens summarily; and strengthened the protective powers of the Fourth and Fifth amendments in cases dealing with illegal searches and seizures and double jeopardy.

Marshall took a pay cut and gave up lifetime tenure as a federal judge in order to accept the position of solicitor general, the third-highest post in the Justice Department. In contrast to the year-long delay in his confirmation process four years earlier, he was confirmed by voice vote on August 11, 1965—less than one month after President Johnson offered him the job. Since Johnson had indicated his intention to appoint a black person or a woman to the Supreme Court during his tenure, Marshall's appointment to the Justice Department was widely viewed as a steppingstone to the High Court.

When Marshall succeeded Archibald Cox as solicitor general, Attorney General Nicholas Katzenbach described him as "one of the greatest Americans alive today." "It's no exaggeration to say that a good measure of the civil rights progress we've made is built on what this fellow has done over the years," Katzenbach told Joseph Mohbat. That progress included the Voting Rights Act of 1965, which was signed into law just days before Marshall assumed the job of the nation's chief prosecuting attorney. Authorized by the new voting rights legislation to abolish literacy requirements and other voter qualification tests, including poll taxes, Marshall argued the government's case on appeal before the Supreme Court, thereby dismantling such discriminatory obstacles to full voter participation.

Of the nineteen cases he argued before the Supreme Court as solicitor general, Marshall won fourteen. He also argued, in an amicus brief filed with the California Supreme Court, that the court should declare unconstitutional Proposition 14, an anti-fair housing amendment to the state constitution that was passed in 1964. He contended that popular initiatives were unconstitutional if they furthered racial discrimination—not only despite popular support, but also because of it. "Everybody knows minority groups do not have the strength to win a popular statewide vote," he wrote. One of the few cases Marshall lost for the government was one of the confession cases collected under *Miranda v. Arizona* (1966), in which he argued that criminal suspects unable to

afford a lawyer did not have the right to court-appointed counsel. As a Supreme Court justice, however, Marshall has consistently supported the *Miranda* doctrine of right to counsel, beginning with his first major opinion as a member of the High Court.

Few political observers were surprised when President Johnson appointed Marshall to the Supreme Court on June 13,1967, most recognizing not only Marshall's eminent qualifications, but also the political expediency of appointing the first black Supreme Court justice in an era of acute racial tensions. Marshall was confirmed by the Senate on August 30, by a vote of sixty-nine to eleven. The vacancy on the Court that Marshall filled had been created by the retirement of Justice Tom C. Clark, who had stepped down in order to avoid the appearance of conflict of interest after his son, Ramsey Clark, became Johnson's attorney general. Ramsey Clark, in his chapter of a book on Supreme Court justices edited by Leon Friedman, remarked upon the progress in civil rights symbolized by the replacement of Tom Clark, the grandson of a Confederate soldier, by Thurgood Marshall, the grandson of a Union soldier and great-grandson of a slave.

To the syndicated columnist Joseph Kraft, however, Marshall's appointment symbolized only "the outmoded principle of ethnic representation, and for years to come his seat on the Court will probably be a Negro seat." Calling Marshall's appointment "an unhappily fit climax to a term that has shown the Court to be hung up on outworn liberal and moralistic doctrines of the past," Kraft contended, in a column that appeared in the *Washington Post* on June 15, 1967, that, despite Marshall's "generous sympathies, common sense, and ... feel for the political issues that bulk largely in the work of the Court," he "will not bring to the Court penetrating analysis or distinction of mind."

In his chapter of the book *The Justices of the Supreme Court, 1789-1978* (1980), Ramsey Clark wrote, "Thurgood Marshall adjusted easily, quietly, almost comfortably to the work of the Supreme Court while its majority possessed an expanding vision of justice." As a civil rights lawyer, Marshall had attempted to expand the Court's definition of equality, but as a member of the liberal majority on the Warren Court, he eschewed ringing constitutional declarations, preferring to use his negotiating skills to encourage unanimity among the justices so that their decisions would carry more weight. This strategy was consistent with Marshall's behavior as a lawyer for the NAACP, according to a longtime friend, who told a reporter for Newsweek (June 26, 1967): "He always looked at the big picture. He never wanted to win a battle if it would lose him the war."

The impending demise of the liberal majority signaled by Nixon's unsuccessful attempt to impeach Associate Justice William O. Douglas in 1970 prompted Douglas to wonder how the Court would retain what he saw as its independence, and what others saw as its liberal, activist tendencies. "Marshall's liberal vote] was weak," lamented Douglas, according to the paraphrasing of his thoughts by Bob Woodward and Scott Armstrong in their book *The Brethren* (1979). In Douglas's view, Marshall was "a correct vote, a follower, but no leader, no fighter. He was not one to speak up articulately or forcefully." But as the Court became more conservative, Marshall resumed the role of outspoken advocate, proving that Douglas's fears were unwarranted. In the words of Ramsey Clark, "Adversity challenged Thurgood Marshall. The people needed a champion again. His enormous passion rose, but a strong discipline directed it toward equal justice under law." According to Woodward and Armstrong, Marshall, a "plainspoken and direct" man, "saw his job as casting his vote and urging his colleagues to do what was right. On the Court, he had little interest in perfecting the finer points of the law."

Marshall expounded on his faith that justice could be achieved lawfully—without "violence for violence's sake," without black separatism—in a speech at Dillard University in New Orleans on May 4, 1969. Recalling that he was in Selma, Alabama a generation before the 1965 civil rights demonstrations, he explained: "I did that because I've never had to defend my country by lying about it. I can tell the truth about it and still be proud. [But] I'm not going to be completely satisfied. I'll be dead before I'll be satisfied." Marshall reiterated the need to avoid the complacency that often accompanies progress in a speech on the occasion of the dedication of a bronze statue in his honor in Baltimore on May 16, 1980. "Some Negroes feel we have arrived," he told the assembled crowd. "Others feel there is nothing more to do. I just want to be sure that when you see this statue, you won't think that's the end of it. I won't have it that way. There's too much work to be done."

Putting his philosophy into practice on the Supreme Court, Marshall often found himself dissenting from major decisions, especially in the area of criminal law, in his efforts to uphold the rights of the individual against preventive detention, illegal searches and surveillance, and improper methods of interrogation. Typical of his dissents was the one from the ruling in *United States v. Agurs* (1976): "One of the most basic elements of fairness in a criminal trial is that available evidence tending to show innocence, as well as that tending to show guilt, be fully aired before the jury; more particularly, it is that the State in its zeal to convict a defendant not suppress evidence that might exonerate him."

A staunch opponent of capital punishment, Marshall described it in his concurring opinion in *Furman v. Georgia* (1972) as "an excessive and unnecessary punishment that violates the Eighth Amendment." He continued: "Capital punishment is imposed discriminatorily against identifiable classes of people; there is evidence that innocent people have been executed before their innocence can be proved; and the death penalty wreaks havoc with our entire criminal justice system." In other opinions, Marshall has affirmed that the right of privacy is the basis for prohibiting states from infringing upon a woman's right to safe, legal, and affordable abortion; declared that the possession of obscene material is protected by the First Amendment; and cautioned that the police must work within the law in their apprehension of criminal suspects.

Rulings of the Rehnquist Court to limit affirmative action were accompanied by Marshall's blistering dissents. For example, he wrote that *Richmond v. Croson* (1989), which rendered Richmond, Virginia's affirmative-action program unconstitutional, represented "a full-scale retreat from the Court's longstanding solicitude to race conscious remedial efforts directed toward deliverance of the century-old promise of equality of economic opportunity." During the late 1970s and 1980s Marshall publicly denounced the conservative trend of the Court at judicial conferences and Bar Association meetings, and in a series of television interviews with the journalist Carl Rowan. Evaluating the records of American presidents on civil rights, Marshall placed Reagan at "the bottom" and gave high marks only to Johnson and Harry S. Truman.

## PERSONAL LIFE

Marshall's limited income during his long years with the NAACP resulted in his being the poorest justice on the Court, according to David O'Brien in *Storm Center* (1986). He lived in Falls Church, Virginia with his second wife, the former Cecelia S. Suyat, a former secretary for the NAACP whom he married on December 17, 1955. The couple have two sons: Thurgood Jr. and

John William. Marshall's first wife, Vivian G. (Burey) Marshall, died of cancer in February 1955 after twenty-five years of marriage.

Marshall died at the age of 84 in 1993. There are numerous memorials to Marshall, including an 8-foot statue that stands in Lawyers Mall adjacent to the Maryland State House.

## FURTHER READING

*Friedman, Leon, ed. The Justices of the Supreme Court, 1789-1978, vol 5 (1980); International Who's Who, 1989-90; O'Brien, David M. Storm Center: The Supreme Court in American Politics (1986); Who's Who among Black Americans, 1988; Who's Who in America, 1988-89; Woodward, Bob and Scott Armstrong. The Brethren (1979)*

# RUEBEN MARTINEZ

## Bookseller; Literacy Advocate

**Born:** April 19, 1940; Miami, Arizona
**Primary Field:** Literacy Reform

## INTRODUCTION

*"We come into this world with nothing and leave with nothing," Rueben Martinez said to Justino Aguila for the* Orange County (California) Register *(September 28, 2004). "So why not do something with this life? I tell students, teachers and parents to take advantage of this time on earth. That's the kind of energy I like to spread." Rueben Martinez is one of 23 recipients of the 2004 Mac Arthur Fellowship, awarded to individuals on the basis of demonstrated creativity and intended as an investment in their future contributions to society. Such contributions have long been a priority for Martinez, the owner of Libreria Martinez Books and Art Gallery in Santa Ana, California, which had an unusual beginning: it originated on the premises of Martinez's barbershop. The store now serves as a major supplier of literature for the United States' highest concentration of urban Spanish-speaking people. (In over 66 percent of Santa Ana households, no one over 14 speaks English.) Through his visits to local schools and his work with a number of organizations, Martinez combats illiteracy and growing high-school dropout rates, seeking in particular to reach Latinos, at least one in three of whom nationwide, it has been predicted, will not complete high school. Martinez helped to establish the El Sol Science and Arts Academy of Santa Ana; with the actor Edward James Olmos, he founded the Latino Book and Family Festival, which has grown into the country's largest Spanish-language book expo. He has served as an executive board member of the California Democratic Party and treasurer of the Orange County Democratic Party and has twice been a delegate to the Democratic National Convention. "I found out my heart was in a political party that was a party of the people, for the people," Martinez said to Dennis McLellan for the* Los Angeles Times *(March 31, 1996).*

## EARLY LIFE

A son of Mexican immigrants, Rueben R. Martinez was born on April 19, 1940 in Miami, Arizona, a mining town of 3,000 people, 80 miles east of Phoenix. His father mined copper while his mother stayed at home to take care of the couple's eight children. Martinez grew up in an environment with very few books, as there were no bookstores or libraries in Miami. The only books he had were given to him by his teachers; he eagerly accepted them. While Miami had good schools, there were not many job opportunities in the small mountainside town. "There was no future there," Martinez said to Dennis McLellan. "I had to go out and see if there was anything on the other side of that mountain."

After he graduated from Miami High School, in 1957, Martinez and two friends drove to California in a 1949 Ford. "I've been here ever since. California has been very good to me," he said to Dennis McLellan. After settling in East Los Angeles, Martinez worked in a supermarket, starting as a box boy and working his way up to a position with more responsibility in the produce section. He later held jobs at firms including McDonnell Douglas and the Ford Motor Co. For a year he worked nights as a crane operator at Bethlehem Steel and spent his days learning to cut hair at Hill Street Barbers in Los Angeles. Martinez cut hair full-time for two years before opening his own shop, in 1974. In the following year he moved his business to Santa Ana.

While cutting hair, Martinez became known for inspiring his customers to keep up with current events through his discussions of news and politics. He kept newspapers and magazines at the shop for his customers to read and began lending them books written in English or Spanish. (Most of the books were not returned to the shop.) By the early 1990s Martinez had progressed to selling books that he owned between haircuts, and soon afterward, as demand grew and he began buying additional books, there were volumes spread all over the barbershop. According to Dennis McLellan, the message on the shop's answering machine announced, "The best in books and hair." David N. Ream, Santa Ana's city manager and a longtime customer of Martinez's, described Martinez as one of the most positive influences on the residents in Santa Ana, telling Dennis McLellan in 1996, "He not only knows everybody in town and keeps up with what's going on—which is always interesting and entertaining—but he's not just a lot of talk. He's a lot of action. He really puts the efforts behind his words and ideas." Conversation is an important part of Martinez's barbering process. "Sometimes I talk too much," Martinez said to McLellan. "Some barber customers get a kick out of it, and some of them don't. They say 'Rueben, I've got to go. Please hurry.' But they know what to expect." In the mid-1990s Martinez still made most of his income from haircuts. That did not stop him from inviting authors to speak at his 320-square- foot shop. On one occasion Isabel Allende, the famous Chilean author of novels including *The House of the Spirits* and *Daughter of Fortune*, agreed to hold a book signing at Martinez's establishment. Martinez recalled that Allende seemed surprised when she saw that the bookstore was also a barbershop. A thousand people showed up there to see her.

## LIFE'S WORK

Martinez's book-selling business soon grew to such an extent that he moved his bookstore into a larger space, 2,800 square feet on the ground floor of a law office on Main Street. At the new site, haircutting is relegated to a back room, where there is a single chair. "I've always had that feeling that if you don't grow, you die, and the opportunity was there," Martinez said to McLellan. Twenty young volunteers from the Boys and Girls Club of Santa Ana helped Martinez to transfer his books to their new location. The new Libreria Martinez Books and Art Gallery (where new exhibits are mounted every so often) quickly became one of the largest sellers of Spanish-language books in the country. In 2000 Martinez opened a children's bookstore next door, and a third

store opened in Lynwood, California, in 2003. "Every opportunity I get, I go out there and tell people buy books, rent books," Martinez said to Ben Fox for the *San Diego Union-Tribune* (October 3, 2004, on-line), "and not only will you notice growth within yourself, everyone else will, too."

Meanwhile, Martinez continued the community activity that has always been a priority for him. "You're here; you have to do something," he explained to Dennis McLellan. "I've always been this way. Some of my friends say I'm all over the place, they wonder how I get things done. I'm used to it. As far as being involved, it's just like getting a driver's license. It's a privilege to drive. It's an honor to be active, to do things. I chose a long time ago to be a giver rather than a taker." In 2001 Martinez co-founded the El Sol Science and Arts Academy of Santa Ana, a charter school for kindergarteners through eighth graders located two blocks from his bookstore. Martinez has held fund-raising events for the academy and sponsored hearing and vision clinics at the bookstore. He is also co-founder of the nationally touring Latino Book and Family Festival and, for many years, on a volunteer basis, has visited classrooms to encourage children to stay in school, going on average to one school each week.

According to the *San Diego Union Tribune* (October 3, 2004), he has appeared on a weekly, nationally broadcast Spanish-language television program, encouraging children to learn to read. He has received the Giraffe Award from the Board of Education of the Santa Ana Unified School District in recognition of his efforts. Such work is "very important because a lot of the kids drop out," Martinez said to Dennis McLellan. "Without an education, it's going to be a tough future for them." "He's so inspirational," Delia Apodaca, a teacher at Cesar Chavez High School in Santa Ana, said to McLellan about Martinez. "The students love him. He treats them like his own kids. He goes over and he hugs them and he calls them 'mijito,' which means my little son, or 'mija,' my daughter. They like that, and he's funny and very outgoing. The fact that he's Hispanic just motivates the kids to do even better."

Motivating Spanish-speaking people to value literature has won Rueben Martinez acclaim from educators and librarians across the country and, in 2004, from the Mac Arthur Foundation, which awarded him a fellowship consisting of $500,000, to be given over a five-year period. Often called the "genius" grant, the award is presented to a variety of individuals on the basis of previous accomplishments and as an investment in the recipients' potential to benefit society. The fellowships are given to individuals rather than institutions so that each recipient can pursue goals as he or she chooses. "Certainly, what Rueben Martinez has done to date is important and creative," Daniel J. Socolow, director of the MacArthur Fellows Program, said to Justino Aguila. "We're betting he'll continue doing great things, maybe even greater things." "I'm still stunned," Martinez said to Justino Aguila. "I'm floating and scared at the same time. But deep down inside, I think it's good." Recipients of the grant are not informed in advance that they have been considered for it, and Martinez therefore did not expect the phone call that brought him the news of the award. "I thought it was a sales rep wanting something," Martinez said to Justino Aguila. "But there was a passion in his voice that kept me listening. One quarter

into the conversation he said, 'Mr. Martinez, don't hang up on me because this is the real stuff.'" In May 2005 the Latino Caucus of California's state Legislature honored Martinez in its annual tribute to people who strengthen their communities' "spirit."

## PERSONAL LIFE
Rueben Martinez has been described as gregarious and enthusiastic. He is divorced and has three adult children, all of whom have attended college. He enjoys bicycling, in-line skating, and running.

## FURTHER READING
*Los Angeles Times Life & Style E pi Mar. 31, 1996; Orange County (California) Register Sep. 28, 2004; Orange County (California) Weekly (on-line) Oct. 1-7, 2004; San Diego Union Tribune (on-line) Oct. 3, 2004*

---

# VILMA MARTINEZ

## Lawyer; Social Activist; Diplomat

**Born:** October 17, 1943; San Antonio, Texas
**Primary Field:** Civil Rights
**Affiliation:** Mexican American Legal Defense Fund (MALDEF)

## INTRODUCTION
*Vilma Martinez—a former president and general counsel of the Mexican American Legal Defense Fund (MALDEF)—grew up in an impoverished, predominantly Mexican-American neighborhood of San Antonio, Texas, where she witnessed firsthand the de facto segregation that seemed designed to make Chicanos a permanent underclass. Symptomatic of this discrimination, Martinez, though she earned near-perfect marks in school, was encouraged by teachers and guidance counselors to attend a vocational institution rather than an academic high school, "because to become a secretary was the highest thing a girl like me could aspire to," as she explained to Grace Lichtenstein for Quest (February/March 1980). Refusing to succumb to such low expectations, Martinez gained entry into not only an academic high school but, subsequently, the University of Texas at Austin and Columbia Law School, in New York City, before embarking on her prestigious career at MALDEF and beyond. During her time as MALDEF's*

*president, from 1973 to 1981, Martinez struggled to rectify the injustices suffered by the millions of Latinos living in the United States— injustices she experienced as a child growing up in Texas. Though Martinez has accomplished much since her tenure at MALDEF, her successful stewardship of the civil rights organization remains her principal accomplishment: at MALDEF, as Lichtenstein stated, Martinez "built a bridge from the rural and urban barrios of the Southwest to various enclaves of American wealth and conscience—an achievement that many compare with the early career of Cesar Chavez as leader of the Mexican- American farmworkers."*

## EARLY LIFE
The eldest of five children, Vilma Martinez was born on October 17, 1943 in San Antonio, Texas, to a Spanish-speaking family of limited means. Describing the segregation that existed in Texas at the time, Martinez remarked, according to a profile posted on the American Bar Association (ABA) Web site, "We [Latinos] weren't allowed to go into some of the parks. When we went to the movies, we had to sit in the back of the theater." Given her gender as well as her ethnic heritage, Martinez found little support for her interest in attending college. When her guidance counselor sent her records to a local trade school, telling her that she would be more

comfortable in that environment, Martinez demanded that her transcript be sent to an academic high school, where she was subsequently accepted. The determination she showed in pursuit of her early education became a hallmark of her later career. She has credited her maternal grandmother with instilling this drive in her: "She was forthright," Martinez told Lichtenstein, "she was a coper and a woman of action." Martinez excelled in high school. When she was 15 she volunteered during the summer at the law firm of Alonso Perales, a Latino civil rights attorney; the experience left a lasting impression, and she soon began planning a career as an attorney. Martinez was determined to attend the University of Texas at Austin, but her high-school counselor, as shortsighted as her earlier advisers, refused to help her with the application process. Martinez's father, a carpenter, offered to pay for her education only if she agreed to attend a nearby Roman Catholic college. Again she refused to accede to what others expected of her; she applied to and was accepted at the University of Texas at Austin. "What pushed me," she told Lichtenstein, "was that Mexican-Americans weren't treated on the basis of merit. I was impelled to show them that I could speak English without an accent." To help finance her education, Martinez earned money by cleaning a school science lab and lived frugally in a campus co-op. She completed college in less than three years, graduating with a B.A. degree in 1964. Since her time at Perales's law practice, though many had tried to dissuade her, Martinez had remained intent on becoming an attorney. She wanted to attend the University of Texas law school, but again her gender and race made this an unlikely prospect: "My counselors kept telling me not to get my hopes up," Martinez explained to Lichtenstein. "They finally said, 'Why don't you try those Eastern liberal schools?' So I did." Accepted by Columbia Law School, Martinez headed to New York City. She graduated in 1967.

## LIFE'S WORK

Martinez initially applied for jobs at several Texas law firms, but was told that many clients were not comfortable with the idea of a female or a Mexican being their legal counsel. So she began her career at the National Association for the Advancement of Colored People (NAACP) Legal Defense Fund, where she worked primarily on cases involving job discrimination and equal employment.

In 1973, not quite 30 years old, Martinez was named president and general counsel of MALDEF. "Getting that job wasn't easy," Martinez stated in a lecture given at Stanford University, as quoted by Marisa Cigarroa in the *Stanford Online Report* (April 29, 1998). Many associates dissuaded her from lobbying for the post, telling her the organization was not ready for a female president— especially one so young—and that the conservative judicial climate created by President Richard Nixon's appointments would make it difficult for MALDEF to achieve any of its goals in the courts. Martinez, as she had in the past, refused to heed these doubters.

When Martinez first took over, the organization had an inexperienced staff and was in difficult financial straits: close to insolvency, MALDEF depended almost entirely on monetary grants from the Ford Foundation. Martinez tirelessly traversed the nation seeking money and increasing support; in so doing she helped transform MALDEF from a disorganized, poorly financed operation into what Lichtenstein described as "a broadly funded enterprise with savvy lawyers, five offices

---

### Affiliation: Mexican American Legal Defense Fund (MALDEF)

In 1968, a year after Martinez received her law degree and joined the NAACP, MALDEF was founded. The group is often seen as a Chicano parallel to the NAACP; its mission "is to foster sound public policies, laws and programs to safeguard the civil rights of the 40 million Latinos living in the United States and to empower the Latino community to fully participate in our society," its Web site states. Martinez was one of the first women to join MALDEF's board of directors, and she acted as a liaison between MALDEF and the NAACP. MALDEF's mission in promoting Chicano rights, as Martinez later explained to Bill Curry for the *Washington Post* (March 28, 1978), was analogous to the movement in the 1950s and 1960s for African-American civil rights: "The issues are the same. The denial of an, equal education opportunity, the denial of jobs, the denial of effective participation in the voting process and police brutality." In 1970 Martinez left the NAACP Legal Defense Fund to become the Equal Employment Opportunity Counsel for the New York State Division of Human Rights. The next year she entered private practice, serving as a litigation associate at the New York firm of Cahill, Gordon and Reindel, though she continued her involvement with MALDEF.

around the country, and a new grass roots organization as well."

In addition to improving MALDEF on an organizational and financial level, Martinez aggressively promoted the group's agenda in the courts. In 1974 she persuaded a United States appeals court to guarantee the right of bilingual education to non- English-speaking students in public schools. In 1975, in what many regard as the organization's— and Martinez's—greatest achievement, MALDEF successfully lobbied Congress to add amendments to the 1965 Voting Rights Act that extended the law's protections to Latinos and required that voting ballots be printed in Spanish as well as English in districts with high concentrations of Latinos. MALDEF also helped delay proposals to punish employers who hired undocumented workers; after these proposals passed, MALDEF strove to lessen their impact on Latinos through legal action and organized studies that demonstrated that the punitive measures had no impact in dissuading employers from hiring undocumented workers, but served rather to promote xenophobia. Under Martinez, MALDEF won lawsuits against the school boards of El Paso and Uvalde, Texas, paving the way for the desegregation of students by ethnicity; the group also defeated the U.S. Border Patrol in court, proving that the organization's height and weight requirements excluded many Latinos. In 1982, Martinez's last year as head of MALDEF, the organization scored another major legal victory when the U.S. Supreme Court ruled (in Plyer v. Doe) that undocumented children were entitled to a public education.

Disseminating information about public policy to Latinos was another vital aspect of MALDEF's strategy under Martinez. In 1980, for example, many Latinos were leery of participating in that year's census, fearing that the information might be used by the government as a means of discrimination. However, an undercount of Latinos would diminish their total impact on congressional redistricting and adversely affect their political influence. Consequently, MALDEF teamed up with the Roman Catholic Church to inform Latinos about the census and encourage them to participate.

Describing Martinez's bearing as president of MALDEF, Lichtenstein observed, "[She] at first gives the impression of a mild-mannered, smiling schoolmarm, but one encounter is usually enough to dispel that impression. She is an operator—in the best sense of the word—who brings to her work considerable charm and poise supported by a backbone of steel." Martinez's

soft-spoken intensity was often remarked upon by observers; recalling an encounter with her, Carol Lawson wrote for the *New York Times* (May 19, 1978) that Martinez "talked in a bold and blunt manner about how the country's eight million Mexican-Americans [the number has since greatly increased] have been 'oppressed and discriminated against' and had their 'rights trampled upon,' and how 'the country is not honoring its Constitutional commitment to this group of people.' But instead of sounding shrill or even impassioned, her tone was soft and gentle."

Martinez's success at MALDEF raised her profile nationally, and government officials soon began requesting her counsel. President Jimmy Carter named her to his Advisory Board on Ambassadorial Appointments, and in 1976 California governor Jerry Brown selected her to serve on the University of California Board of Regents. U.S. senator Alan Cranston of California then tapped her for the state's Judiciary Selection Committee. "These are all interesting, yet difficult roles," Martinez told Lawson. "I'm chosen because I'm an advocate of Mexican-Americans and women's rights. So I do battle with [diplomats] Averell Harriman and Dean Rusk, trying to convince them that there are qualified Hispanics who could be ambassadors to Europe." In 1976, during Martinez's tenure on the University of California Board of Regents, the board voted on whether to divest the school's portfolio of stock in companies involved in South Africa, a country then in the grip of racial apartheid. Surprisingly to many, Martinez voted in opposition to divestment. She explained to Lawson that her decision was made with the interests of the university in mind: "I thought it would be too costly to sell so much stock, and I wasn't sure that this would be an effective way of remedying the apartheid situation in South Africa."

Martinez continued to serve on the board of regents after leaving MALDEF, in 1982, to become a partner at the Los Angeles law firm Munger, Tolies & Olson. In 1984 she began her term as chairwoman of the board of regents, a post she held until 1986. During Martinez's tenure as chairwoman, the issue of South African divestment reemerged. In June 1985 the board instituted a plan in which a committee reviewed each of the university's stock holdings to ascertain whether the particular companies doing business in South Africa were also helping to promote racial equality in the divided nation. If the companies were not, the panel could recommend that the specific stocks be divested. Not long after this policy was adopted, however, recession and violence erupted in South Africa, and calls for full divestment resurfaced. Nevertheless, Martinez refused to change course, telling David G. Savage for the *Los Angeles Times* (August 28, 1985), "This was a very difficult issue. We gave it careful consideration and a resolution was reached. And I suspect most of us [on the board of regents] will want to give it a chance to work." Controversy over a job-discrimination lawsuit in Texas engulfed both MAL-DEF and Martinez in February 1987. Three Latinos, former employees of the H. E. Butt Grocery Co., sued the company for discrimination. MALDEF offered its services on behalf of the plaintiffs, while Martinez, now in private practice, was retained by the grocery-store chain. Subsequently MALDEF's board fired Antonia Hernandez, then the head of MALDEF, for bungling the case. Hernandez's critics claimed that the suit fell apart as a result of her friendship with Martinez, and some felt that Martinez's involvement constituted a conflict of interest. (Legal experts have ruled that Martinez was within her rights to accept the case.) Martinez defended herself in a letter to MALDEF's board, but her missive did little to appease her detractors, who maintained that although she did nothing legally wrong, her judgment in choosing to represent a client taking on MALDEF in court left much to be desired.

The retirement of U.S. Supreme Court justice Harry A. Blackmun, in 1994, led to rampant speculation about his possible replacements. Many felt that President Bill Clinton should nominate a Latino for the position as none had ever before served on the court. Martinez was among those mentioned as a potential candidate, along with Secretary of Transportation Federico Pena and U.S. District Judge Jose A. Cabranes of Connecticut. (President Clinton eventually tapped Stephen Breyer, a native Californian with a long history of judicial appointments, for the post.) Martinez's name was in the running for another judicial appointment in June 2001, following the death of California Supreme Court justice Stanley Mosk, but she did not get that appointment, either. Most pundits attribute Martinez's failure to receive a high-court nomination to her lack of experience as a judge; most nominees have served in some capacity on the judicial bench in lower courts, something Martinez has yet to do.

Martinez has received numerous accolades for her civic achievements over the years. In 1978 she was honored with Columbia Law School's Medal for Excellence; she later received a Medal for Excellence from Columbia University as well. The University of Texas gave Martinez its Distinguished Alumnus Award, and the American Institute for Public Service bestowed its Jefferson Award on her. In recognition of her contributions to the organization, MALDEF honored Martinez with the Valerie Kantor Award for Extraordinary Achievement. She has also received the John D. Rockefeller III Youth Award from the Rockefeller Foundation, the Maynard Toll Award for Distinguished Public Service from the Legal Aid Foundation of Los Angeles, and the Lex Award from the Mexican American Bar Association. Martinez holds honorary doctorates from Amherst College, in Massachusetts, and the California School of Professional Psychology. In 2003 she and seven other successful women founded the Directors' Council, an executive-search firm whose purpose is to locate qualified women to serve on corporate boards. Martinez is currently a member of the advisory boards of the Asian Pacific American Legal Center of Southern California and of Columbia Law School. She is the chairwoman of the Pacific Council's Study Group on Mexico and serves on the boards of the Los Angeles Philharmonic Association, as well as those of Anheuser-Busch and Sanwa Bank California.

## PERSONAL LIFE

Martinez met her husband, Stuart Singer, a tax lawyer, in a prep course for the New York bar exam. Together they have two children and currently make their home in Los Angeles. Summing up Martinez's legacy, the profile posted on the ABA Web site states, "[Her] steadfast determination to oppose discrimination and injustice presents an inspiring role model to all. Her life reaffirms that hope and perseverance can create exciting and unimagined possibilities."

## FURTHER READING

*American Bar Association Web site, with photo; Columbia Law School Web site, with photo; Los Angeles Times p3 Aug. 28, 1985, II pi Feb. 17, 1987, II p5 Feb. 19, 1987, NT p8 Feb. 9, 1989, with photo, A pi Apr. 13, 1994; MALDEF Web site; Metropolitan News-Enterprise pi Sep. 19, 2003; New York Times A pl4 May 19, 1978, with photo; Quest p28 Feb./Mar. 1980, with photo; San Diego Union Tribune A p3 June 21, 2001; Stanford Online Report Apr. 29, 1998; Washington Post A pi Mar. 28, 1978*

# CAROLYN MCCARTHY

## U.S. Representative from New York

**Born:** January 5, 1944; Brooklyn, New York
**Primary Field:** Gun Control
**Affiliation:** Democratic Party; U.S. House of Representatives

### INTRODUCTION

*Carolyn McCarthy became the focus of national attention in December 1993, after a crazed gunman killed her husband and critically wounded her only child in what was dubbed the Long Island Rail Road massacre. Before that tragedy, McCarthy was a suburban homemaker, avocational gardener, and onetime nurse who described herself as "the quietest woman in the world." In the months immediately afterward, she became an ardent spokesperson for gun control while devoting most of her time to her son's care and rehabilitation.*

*In March 1996, Daniel Frisa, the congressman from her district (New York's Fourth Congressional District), voted to repeal a ban on certain types of assault weapons. McCarthy, who had fought for passage of the 1994 legislation that instituted the ban, was outraged, and she announced her candidacy for his seat in the U.S. House of Representatives. Denied the endorsement of local Republican officials, McCarthy, a longtime registered Republican, ran on the Democratic and Independent lines, and she won a resounding victory. The first woman to represent any part of Long Island, New York, in the House, she was sworn in as a member of the 105th Congress on January 1, 1997, a few days before her 53rd birthday. On November 3, 1998, she was reelected to a second term. She served until 2015. Her top priority, however, is reducing what is often called "gun violence." "If we [in Congress] don't try to end gun violence, who will?" she wrote in a column for McCall's (September 1997). "That's the question that keeps me going."*

### EARLY LIFE

Carolyn McCarthy was born Carolyn Cook on January 5, 1944, in the New York City borough of Brooklyn. Her father, Thomas Cook, was a boilermaker, and her mother, Irene Cook, was a homemaker who also worked for a while as a salesperson in a five-and-dime store. With her three siblings, McCarthy grew up in the suburban town of Mineola, on Long Island, in the house where she later spent her married life and which remains her primary residence. As a youngster, she was an excellent athlete, and she dreamed of becoming a gym teacher. Although she applied herself diligently to her schoolwork, she had difficulty reading, and she felt very fearful whenever a teacher would call on her to read aloud in class. Years later, she learned that she suffered from dyslexia. The disorder still plagues her, Dan Barry reported in the *New York Times Magazine* (June 22, 1997), and when preparing a speech to be presented on the floor of Congress, she practices by repeating proper names and other words that she finds particularly troublesome. When giving speeches in less formal environments, she generally speaks extemporaneously.

Sometime during her high school years, McCarthy's boyfriend at the time was badly hurt in a car accident. With the encouragement of the nurse that his family hired to tend to him, McCarthy assisted in his care. After several days, the teenager died of his injuries. That experience led McCarthy to change her career goal, and after graduating from high school, she attended nursing school and became a licensed practical nurse. In 1966, she married Dennis McCarthy; their son, Kevin, was born the following year. At some point, the McCarthys got divorced. They remarried after Dennis overcame his dependency on alcohol. According to McCarthy, erroneous accounts of their breakup and remarriage have been spread about, and she plans someday to write an autobiography in which she will describe what really happened during her marriage.

### LIFE'S WORK

Father and son commuted to and from Prudential together on the Long Island Rail Road, and they were seated side by side when, on December 7, 1993, another passenger on their late-afternoon train—a man named Colin Ferguson—took out a 9-millimeter semiautomatic pistol and, while walking through two cars, shot 25 people. Dennis McCarthy and five other people were killed. Ferguson was eventually convicted of the six murders and, in 1995, received the maximum sentence—six consecutive life terms in prison.

The most seriously hurt among the 19 injured passengers was Kevin McCarthy, who was then 26; nearly a seventh of his brain was destroyed, one of his hands was shattered, and he had sunk into a coma. Doctors at the hospital to which he was brought gave him only a 10 percent chance of survival; if he did pull through, they cautioned, he would most likely spend the rest of his life paralyzed and in a vegetative state. At a press conference held at the hospital on December 9 that Carolyn McCarthy attended, the doctors voiced that grim prognosis. "Excuse me, you're wrong," McCarthy suddenly blurted out, as she recalled to Jonathan Mandell for *Good Housekeeping* (September 1996). "He will live. And he will move." Determined to make that prediction come true, McCarthy concentrated on talking to Kevin and touching him in an attempt to awaken him from his coma. Within a week, he did so, and he began speaking. McCarthy's widely publicized efforts to help her son recover captured the attention and sympathy of countless people around the nation.

After the shootings, McCarthy pondered the question "Could this have been prevented?" "I thought a lot about the people who made and sold those weapons without any sense of where they would end up . . . ," she recalled to Bruce Shapiro for the *Nation* (November 11, 1996). "I am at the point where I hold the manufacturers more responsible than the person who did the act." McCarthy sued the company that produced Colin Ferguson's gun, but the suit was dismissed.

Media interest in McCarthy intensified when, at the request of Mario Cuomo, who was then the governor of New York, she joined the fight for a state ban on assault weapons and then the campaign for a federal ban. At first, she did not realize that such a ban was highly controversial. "I was pretty naive," she admitted to Bruce Shapiro. Much to her surprise, her public appearances and speeches soon made her a target of the National Rifle Association (NRA), members of which would call her late at night. "It was always male voices, and would follow a pat line, beginning with 'I'm sorry for your grief and loss' but then becoming quite harassing . . . ," she told Shapiro. "The sheer audacity [of the NRA] is something I never get used to. When the NRA tries to shut down the Centers for Disease Control [CDC] because the CDC is tracking gun deaths as a health issue, something is clearly wrong." In the summer of 1994, the U.S. House and Senate passed, and President Bill Clinton signed into law, major anti-crime legislation that included a ban on the manufacture, sale, and possession of 19 types of assault weapons, as well as bans on guns with various features associated with assault weapons and on gun clips that hold more than 10 rounds of ammunition.

Early in 1995, anti-gun-control legislators in Congress began mounting a campaign to repeal the 1994 assault-weapons ban. The repeal came up for a vote in the House of Representatives on March 22, 1996. (The vote did not take place in 1995 only because legislators opposing the ban feared that, in the wake of the April 1995 bombing of the Alfred P. Murrah Federal Building, in Oklahoma City, a repeal might provoke a nationwide public outcry.) That day, McCarthy stationed herself in the Capitol building and spoke briefly to members of Congress as they arrived to cast their votes, in an attempt to persuade them to vote against the repeal. But the measure passed, with 239 in favor and 173 opposed. (Ultimately, though, the measure failed.)

One of the "yes" votes came from Daniel Frisa, a freshman congressman who represented the southwestern part of Nassau County, on Long Island. Earlier, McCarthy had declared publicly that if Frisa carried out his stated intention to vote for repeal, she would do everything she could to make sure that he did not win reelection. In the weeks following the vote, McCarthy made up her mind to run against Frisa herself in the Republican primary. After local Republican officials turned down her request for their support, she turned to their Democratic counterparts, and she received their enthusiastic backing. (She later received help—in the form of both funds and advisers—from the national Democratic Party.) By running as a Democrat, she avoided a primary contest, because no registered Democrat entered the race.

During the campaign, Frisa (and many people in the media) repeatedly dismissed McCarthy as a "one-issue candidate," that single issue being gun violence. McCarthy strongly rejected that charge. "I do not pretend to be an expert on policy, but I understand what the people of our district want and need," she told Clyde Haberman of the *New York Times* (May 29, 1996). As Bruce Shapiro noted, through her experiences as the mother of someone needing long-term medical care, as a working nurse, as the daughter and sister of staunch union members, and as a lifelong resident of an area that had become heavily polluted from industrial waste, among other roles, she had become familiar first-hand with a number of current issues and problems. "On crime itself, McCarthy's view is far broader than the conventional stereotype of the victim activist," Shapiro reported. "She'd like to see more treatment and less jail time for drug offenders. The death penalty offers 'nothing but a false sense of security. It's a political ploy, as far as I'm concerned'—though in a campaign in which she's been incessantly liberal-baited, McCarthy said she'd support legislation incorporating capital punishment if her constituents demanded it."

Unlike her opponent, who relied primarily on direct mailings to gain voter support and who, according to *Congressional Quarterly* (January 4, 1997), "virtually disappeared] in the final days of the campaign, shunning public appearances and interviews," McCarthy gave speeches and stumped throughout her district in what has been described as an "emotionally charged race." She appeared on national television on August 27, 1996, when she gave a speech during prime time at the Democratic National Convention, in Chicago—a signal honor for a political newcomer. Shortly before the election, Bruce Shapiro reported, polls showed that she was "narrowly ahead of Frisa." But on November 5, Election Day, McCarthy captured 57 percent of the total votes cast (some 220,000); Frisa trailed with 41 percent, and another candidate, Vincent P. Garbitelli, who ran on the Right-to-Life ticket, came in a very distant third. On the night of the election, the Nassau County Republican chairman, Joseph N. Mondello, applauded McCarthy's victory before introducing his own party's winners. "Mrs. McCarthy has shown great courage, grit, and determination," he declared. "Not: only in this political campaign but throughout the tragic circumstances that led her to this day." "All we wanted to do was make something good come out of a horrible situation," McCarthy told supporters that night. "Well, we did that." According to *Congressional Quarterly*, McCarthy visited her husband's grave shortly after the election and exclaimed, "Hey Den! My God, Dennis. Look at me now. Who would've ever thought?"

As the congresswoman from New York's Fourth Congressional District, McCarthy represents a significant number of working-class people as well as upper-middle-class and upper-class suburbanites. Nearly a quarter of her constituents are African- American or Hispanic. Most of the residents of her district commute to jobs in New York City.

McCarthy did not succeed in getting the committee assignments of her choice—seats on the House Commerce, Judiciary, Ways and Means, or Appropriations committees. Instead, she was assigned to the House Education and Workforce Committee, which focuses on education for people of all ages and safety in the workplace, and the House Small Business Committee, which assists and protects small businesses. More than half of all employees in the private sector work in small businesses.

Since coming to Congress, McCarthy has cosponsored, with her fellow New York State legislators Senator Alfonse M. D'Amato and Representative Peter T. King, a bill to help legal immigrants. Although she is personally against abortion, she supports reproductive rights for women, and, after many hours of anguished deliberation, she voted against the proposed ban on a specific type of late- term abortion. "I started to think about all the things I've been trying to do," she told Dan Barry. "I started to think about gun violence—all this stuff came into play. If we don't back the mothers, what are we doing? The mothers who are having children. And having women have children who don't want to have children—that's the cycle of violence, which contributes to child abuse and all the other things that go with it."

In the area of gun control, McCarthy has fought—in vain, so far—for a measure that would make child-proof safety locks mandatory on all handguns. "It is a simple safety lock," she declared on the floor of the House in May 1997, shortly before Congress ruled out the inclusion of her lock provision in a juvenile-justice legislative package. "We have bills that make it impossible for children to get into an aspirin bottle. Do my colleagues not think we should do the same thing with a gun?" McCarthy has received so many threats on her life because of her continued support for gun-control laws that she has arranged to have police escorts at most of her public appearances.

## PERSONAL LIFE
On January 8, 2014, McCarthy announced that she would not run for re-election that November, citing her poor health; she retired in January 2015 and was replaced by fellow Democrat Kathleen Rice. She still lives on Long Island.

## FURTHER READING
*Biography p58+ May 1997, with photos; Congressional Quarterly p75 Jan. 4, 1997, with photo; Good Housekeeping p64+ Sept. 1996, with photos; McCall's p83 Sept. 1997, with photo; Ms. pi9 Sept./Oct. 1996, with photo; Nation pl5+ Nov. 11, 1996; New York p36+ Oct. 28, 1996, with photos; New York Times A pl+ Aug. 8, 1994, with photo, B p6 Apr. 12, 1996, with photo, B pi May 29, 1996, p25 Oct. 12, 1996, with photo, A pl+ and B pl5 Nov. 7, 1996, with photo, B p6 Jan. 8, 1997, with*

*photo; New York Times Magazine p20+ June 22, 1997, with photos; People p75+ Sept. 9, 1996, with photos,* *p96 Dec. 30, 1996-Jan 6, 1997, with photo; Washington Post pBl+ Aug. 27, 1996, with photos*

# RIGOBERTA MENCHU

## Guatemalan Human Rights Activist

**Born:** 1959; Chimel, Guatemala
**Primary Field:** Social Justice & Equality –
    Guatemala's Indigenous People
**Affiliation:** Nobel Peace Prize

### INTRODUCTION

*"My country has two faces,"* the Guatemalan human rights activist Rigoberta Menchu has said. *"There is the ugly face of blood and violence, and there is another face which is silent now, silent and unseen."* For the past twelve years, Menchu has labored tirelessly to increase international awareness of the plight of Guatemala's indigenous people, who have been persecuted by the landowning classes and the military during a thirty-three-year civil war, the longest-running conflict in Central America. The death toll, according to human rights organizations, has reached 150,000 people, not including 50,000 who have been categorized as "disappeared." In addition, 100,000 people have been widowed, 250,000 have been orphaned, and one million have been displaced, or "resettled" in "model" villages. Among those tortured and killed by Guatemalan security forces were Menchu's father, mother, and a younger brother, in separate incidents in 1979 and 1980. In 1981 Menchu herself escaped to Mexico, where she has lived in self-imposed exile ever since. From listening to the tales of woe told by each successive wave of Guatemalan refugees, 43,000 of whom have officially registered as such (the actual number is thought to be twice as high), Menchu came to understand the political dimensions of the problems they faced and vowed to dedicate her life to the preservation of their cultural heritage and to the restoration of their basic rights to land, health, and education.

In recognition of her efforts to bring about an enduring reconciliation among all parties in Guatemala, whose human rights record is considered to be the worst in the Western Hemisphere, Menchu was awarded the Nobel Peace Prize in 1992. She took the opportunity afforded by the attendant flurry of publicity to focus the lens of the international media not on her personal achievements, which have included organizing and educating other Maya, but on the history of Guatemala, where the Maya have been systematically subjugated by colonial settlers and their descendants ever since the Spanish conquest, in the early sixteenth century. Like other Latin American countries whose independence from European powers and adoption of Western-style constitutions have masked widespread oppression of the native populations, Guatemala has experienced decades of right-wing dictatorship, with the ten-year exception of the consecutive administrations of Juan Jose Arevalo and Jacobo Arbenz Guzman, the latter of whom was overthrown in a CIA-backed coup in 1954. Although civilians have governed the country since 1986, military officers remain the primary behind-the-scenes power brokers because of their immunity from prosecution for alleged human rights violations. Contending that no peace agreement between the government and the guerrillas will succeed unless it addresses the causes of the Indians' discontent, Menchu helped found, in 1987, the National Committee for Reconciliation, which has advocated a negotiated settlement with the government. Peace talks between government representatives and the Guatemalan National Revolutionary Union, which comprises three rebel armies, have been initiated, disrupted, and resumed repeatedly since 1991. Hope for a resolution of the conflict was rekindled in June 1993, with the election of President Ramiro de Leon Carpio, the government's former attorney general for human rights.

### EARLY LIFE

Rigoberta Menchu is a member of the Quiche, one of twenty-two groups of Mayan Indians who constitute 60 percent to 80 percent of Guatemala's population of ten million. (Another indigenous Guatemalan ethnic group is the mestizos, also known as ladinos—those of mixed Spanish and Indian heritage.) The sixth of the nine children of Vicente Menchu, a catechist and community leader, and Juana Menchu, a midwife and traditional healer, Rigoberta Menchu was born in 1959 in the village of Chimel, near San Miguel de Uspantan, the capital of the northwestern province of El Quiche, Guatemala. Like many other families of the altiplano, a mountainous region in northern Guatemala, where farmers subsist on the beans and corn that they grow on small plots of land, the Menchus spent the months of October to February picking coffee beans or cotton on the fincas, or plantations, on the south coast. From the age of two, Rigoberta Menchu made the annual trip with her family in a covered truck, which was so crowded with humans and animals that the smell was, in her word, "unbearable." By the age of eight, she was toiling in the fields from 3:00 a.m. until dusk alongside her mother for subsistence wages.

Working conditions on the coffee plantations approximated those of slavery. Menchu's eldest brother, Felipe, whom she never knew, died from inhaling fumes from the pesticides that were sprayed on the coffee crops while the family was working. When she was eight, her youngest brother, Nicolas, died of malnutrition. The family was not allowed to bury him, and Menchu, her mother, and another brother, who had been looking after Nicolas, were evicted from the plantation without being paid for the previous fifteen days of work. "From that moment, I was both angry with life and afraid of it, because I told myself: 'This is the life I will lead, too; having many children, and having them die,'" Menchu said in her autobiography, *I, Rigoberta Menchu* (1983), which was recorded, transcribed, edited, and introduced by Elisabeth Burgos-Debray, a Venezuelan-born anthropologist. "It's not easy for a mother to watch her child die, and have nothing to cure him with or help him live. Those fifteen days working in the finca was one of my earliest experiences and I remember it with enormous hatred. That hatred has stayed with me until today."

At the age of twelve Menchu went to Guatemala City to work as a maid for a landowning family. As she recounted in her autobiography, she slept on a straw mat next to the family dog, which was treated better than she was. After four months of back-breaking labor and humiliation, Menchu returned to her home village in the altiplano, only to learn that her father had been imprisoned for organizing the resistance to the government-sanctioned effort to oust the Maya from their homelands. For years Vicente Menchu had been trying to prevent the appropriation of Indian farms by wealthy landowners, who hired soldiers to mount raids on Chimel and other villages, apparently with the cooperation and approval of governmental authorities. Again and again,

armed men destroyed the Indians' homes and their few belongings, raped their young women, and killed their dogs, which in the Mayan faith is tantamount to murdering human beings. At first, Vicente Menchu had sought to redress the Indians' grievances legally, but after exhausting all his options, he and his neighbors resorted to guerilla tactics. Retreating farther into the mountains, the peasants used every available resource--machetes, stones, chile, salt, and hot water--and their knowledge of the terrain to defend themselves, set booby traps, and ambush soldiers who tried to enter their villages. Despite their efforts, the village of Chimel was virtually eradicated, its population reduced from 400 to twelve by 1992.

## LIFE'S WORK

It took Rigoberta Menchu and her family more than a year to obtain Vicente's freedom. Three months later, he was kidnapped near his home by the landowners' guards, who tortured him and left him for dead in the road. As soon as he recovered, he resumed his organizing activities, this time with Rigoberta in tow. She traveled everywhere with him, learning some Spanish and making contacts with Europeans and others who wanted to help. He often told Rigoberta, his favorite child, that she would have to carry on his work when he was no longer around. Both father and daughter were catechists whose Christian beliefs complemented, rather than supplanted, the tenets of the traditional Mayan faith. Inspired in part by the Biblical story of Judith, who had saved her town by killing the enemy general, Rigoberta Menchu helped to instill in the villagers the will to prevail against their enemies.

In 1977 Vicente Menchu was incarcerated again and sentenced to life imprisonment for Communist subversion. In response to community protests, he was released after fifteen days, but not without threats from the authorities that he or one of his children would be assassinated. In prison, Vicente had encountered another political prisoner, who spurred him to found, with others, the Committee of Peasant Unity, which is known by its Spanish abbreviation, CUC. Going into hiding in 1977 to protect his family, Vicente Menchu returned sporadically to teach them and others in the community about the political aspects of their struggle for land rights, which until then had remained obscure to him, as Rigoberta reported in her autobiography: "We started thinking about the roots of the problem and came to the conclusion that everything stemmed from the ownership of land. The best land was not in our hands. It belonged to the big landowners. Every time they see that we have new land, they try to throw us off it or steal it from us in other ways." In 1979 Rigoberta and her brothers joined the CUC, which had emerged from underground activity in May 1978. It was around the same time that she decided to learn to speak, read, and write Spanish in order to break out of the cultural isolation that had simultaneously sheltered her and prevented her from exercising her legal rights. She also learned three other Indian dialects--Mam, Cakchiquel, and Tzutuhil--to facilitate her organizing work for the CUC in other communities.

With the entire Menchu family branded as Communists, none of them was safe. On September 9, 1979 Rigoberta's sixteen-year-old brother, Petrocinio, who had become a catechist and community leader, was turned in to the army by a villager. Literally dragged from the village, he was tortured for sixteen days before being flayed and burned alive with other prisoners in view of the entire community, including Rigoberta and her parents, who had been forced to watch. In January 1980 Vicente Menchu and other activists, among them Indian peasants, students, and trade unionists, took control of radio stations in El Quiche to broadcast the news of the human rights abuses. Then, on January 31, they occupied the Spanish Embassy in Guatemala City, where they thought the presence of high-ranking Spanish officials would ensure their safety. Ignoring the pleas of the Spanish ambassador, Guatemalan soldiers lobbed several hand grenades into the building. The explosions killed all thirty-nine people inside, including Vicente Menchu. Three months later, on April 19, 1980, Rigoberta's mother was kidnapped. After being repeatedly raped and tortured for many weeks, she was left to die on a hillside, where her body was eventually devoured by predators.

By the time of her mother's death, Rigoberta Menchu had broadened her organizing activities to include labor strikes. In February 1980 some 8,000 peasants went on strike on the sugar and cotton plantations on the southern coast of Guatemala. The strike drew as many as 80,000 supporters and lasted for fifteen days. In the following year Menchu's CUC led the peasants in forming the 31 January Popular Front, in memory of the massacre at the Spanish Embassy. Composed of many smaller organizations of students, peasants, and workers, the front carried out such actions as the Labor Day commemoration beginning on May 1, 1981, in which

demonstrators erected barricades, distributed leaflets, and delivered bomb threats to factories in order to force the owners to give workers some time off. Later in the summer, some priests and nuns who had sided with the protesters were kidnapped and tortured, prompting others to go into hiding.

From then on, Menchu was wanted by the government for her alleged subversive activities. Sheltered by her supporters, she managed to evade arrest until she ventured out on the street for the first time in weeks and was spotted by some soldiers. Knowing that she would meet the same fate as her parents and brother if she did not run, Menchu ducked into a nearby church and disguised herself, by letting her hair down, among the other kneeling worshipers. The soldiers searched the church but failed to recognize her. Even though the town was surrounded by security forces who had been alerted to her presence, she was able to escape and make her way to Guatemala City, where she went to work anonymously as a maid for some nuns. Three weeks later, upon learning that a young Nicaraguan the nuns were harboring worked for the Guatemalan secret police, Menchu was forced to find another hiding place. Shortly thereafter, she fled to Mexico, where she was protected by members of the Guatemalan Church in Exile, a liberal Roman Catholic group. There, through a chance encounter, she was briefly reunited with her two younger sisters, who had joined the guerrillas in the mountains a few years earlier. The three of them met Europeans who wanted to help them and who offered them the opportunity to live in Europe. Menchu and her sisters declined the offer, as she explained in her autobiography. "[My sisters] said: 'If you want to help us, send us help, but not for ourselves, for all the orphans who've been left.'"

It was during a trip to Europe in 1982 that Menchu recounted the story of her life to Elisabeth Burgos-Debray, while spending a week in Paris. Published in Spanish in 1983 and in English translation in 1984, I, Rigoberta Menchu has since been translated into twelve languages, including a pirated edition in Arabic, and it has become well known among American college students of multicultural literature. Menchu concluded her experiences with a justification of her role as a revolutionary leader: "The only road open to me is our struggle, the just war. The Bible taught me that....We have to defend ourselves against our enemy but, as Christians, we must also defend our faith within the revolutionary process."

Menchu's nomination for the 1992 Nobel Peace Prize was sponsored by two Nobel laureates, Adolfo Perez Esquivel of Argentina and Bishop Desmond Tutu of South Africa, who won the peace prize in 1980 and 1984, respectively. In protest, the Guatemalan government nominated its own candidate, Elisa Molina de Stahl, who works with the deaf and blind. Menchu's nomination was highly controversial not only because it coincided with the celebrations of the 500th anniversary of the "discovery" of the Americas by Christopher Columbus but also because she was accused of actively supporting violence. In an interview with Tim Golden of the *New York Times* (October 19, 1992), Menchu declared, "When there is already a war, when there is already a conflict, when there are two parties involved, the way to bring about a solution is not merely to condemn it. It is a matter of contributing so that the causes of the war are resolved."

On October 16, 1992, during a visit to the city of Quetzaltenango, in western Guatemala, Menchu was informed that she had been chosen from among a record 130 candidates to receive the Nobel Peace Prize. She accepted the award in Oslo, Norway, on December 10, 1992. In presenting the Nobel peace medal and diploma to her, Francis Sejersted, the chairman of the Norwegian Nobel Committee, said, "By maintaining a disarming humanity in a brutal world, Rigoberta Menchu appeals to the best in us. She stands as a uniquely potent symbol of a just struggle." Accepting the honor, Menchu replied, "I consider this prize not as an award to me personally, but rather as one of the greatest conquests in the struggle for peace, for human rights, and for the rights of indigenous people who, along all the 500 years, have been the victims of genocides, repression, and discrimination." Edmund Mulet, the president of Guatemala's National Congress and a supporter of indigenous peoples' rights, applauded the awarding of the Nobel Peace Prize to Menchu, calling it "a historic event that is going to change things in a most fundamental way."

Not everyone was pleased with the Norwegian Nobel Committee's decision. Although a spokesperson for the Guatemalan government was quoted by a Norwegian news agency as stating that "the government recognizes Menchu for her efforts and agrees with her that the prize is a recognition of the indigenous peoples and their efforts to achieve better economic and political conditions," Guatemala's chief military spokesman, Captain Julio Yon Rivera, had said, a few days before the announcement in October, "She has only defamed

the fatherland," and the Guatemalan foreign minister, Gonzalo Menendez Park, flatly declared that she should not have won the prize. Shortly after Menchu accepted her award, the Guatemalan army launched reprisals against leftist rebels in the northern regions of the country.

Displeasure with Menchu's recognition was not confined to the Guatemalan government, as Michael Reid reported in the *Guardian* (December 11, 1992). The elite citizens of Guatemala City, he noted, had begun to circulate a joke involving the creation of "Rigoberta dolls 'because Barbie needs a servant.'" Nor was hostility toward Menchu limited to Guatemalans. In an article for the conservative American Spectator (January 1993), Stephen Schwartz suggested that Menchu's autobiography reflected not her voice but the feminist and Socialist ideas of its transcriber and editor. Calling the book a "transparent...work of propaganda for armed revolution," Schwartz argued that "Menchu's cause is not that of peace and reconciliation, but of murder and subversion, as the Nordic snobs responsible for this ridiculous award know full well."

Menchu's reaction to the widespread opposition to her winning the award was philosophical. In her interview with Evelyn Blanck for Guatemala City's Cronica, which was reprinted in World Press Review (December 1992), she said, "Perhaps I would have been offended once, but now I understand that one must respect other people's opinions. Moreover, those criticisms are not personal but are addressed to an ideal that does not belong to me alone." She was nonetheless incensed when confronted with opinions such as Schwartz's. "The worst sin committed in this country," she told Evelyn Blanck, "is saying that the struggles of the Guatemalan people are the work of Communists. That crabbed, oversimplified, parochial view has led to people being killed here in the name of communism without anybody understanding what it is."

With her $1.2 million Nobel cash award, Menchu set up a foundation in memory of her father. Headquartered in Mexico City, with branch offices in Guatemala City and Berkeley, California, the Vicente Menchu Foundation works to ensure the human rights and education of indigenous peoples in Guatemala and throughout the Americas. In addition to her work with the Vicente Menchu Foundation, Rigoberta Menchu has continued her efforts on behalf of the Committee of Peasant Unity and the United Representation of the Guatemalan Opposition, a largely exile-based group that is allied with the guerrillas. She is also a member of the American Continent's Five Hundred Years of Resistance Campaign and the United Nations International Indian Treaty Council. In 1993 she served as the goodwill ambassador to the United Nations for the Year of Indigenous Peoples.

## PERSONAL LIFE

Rigoberta Menchu stands barely five feet tall. She customarily wears the richly embroidered and vibrantly colored traditional dress of the Maya. It remains too dangerous for Menchu to return to the land of her ancestors. Because of repeated death threats, international companions escort her whenever she leaves her communal residence in one of the poorest sections of Mexico City. "I would like to have a home, a family, and not be

a permanent traveler always hoping to return," she told Evelyn Blanck. "But that time never seems to come, and before you know it, one finds that one never had a normal life." Menchu writes poetry in the pockets of free time in between her far-flung speaking engagements.

## FURTHER READING

*Guardian p18 F 4 '92, p12 O 17 '92; People 38:87+ D 21 '92 pors; Progressive 57:28+ Ja '93 por; Time 140:61 O 26 '92 por; International Who's Who, 1993-94; Lazo, Caroline. Rigoberta Menchu (1994); Menchu, Rigoberta. I, Rigoberta Menchu: An Indian Woman in Guatemala (1983); Partnoy, Alicia, ed. You Can't Drown the Fire: Latin American Women Writing in Exile (1989)*

---

# ADAM MICHNIK

## Polish Historian; Journalist; Legislator

**Born:** 1946; Warsaw, Poland
**Primary Field:** Polish Political Dissident

## INTRODUCTION

*If Lech Walesa was the heart and soul of the Polish revolution against Communism, Adam Michnik can be said to have been its mind. Before Walesa emerged as the international symbol of Polish working-class concerns, Michnik provided the intellectual underpinning for the labor movement known as Solidarity, by means of his writings. It was Michnik, a Jew, who singled out the Roman Catholic church as a dependable champion of human rights in Communist Poland and fostered cooperation between the church and nonreligious dissidents. Michnik's concept of a "new evolution," in which dissidents doggedly pressed the Communist Polish government for basic rights without seeking to overthrow it, was a radical notion long before the wave of democratic reforms swept across Eastern Europe.*

*Michnik, now a member of the Sejm, or lower house of the Polish parliament, and the editor of the first independent daily newspaper in modern Poland, has paid a heavy price for his underground activities. Although he spent six years of his young life behind bars, he did not allow the experience to embitter him. Instead, he took advantage of the long hours of solitude to hone his writing skills and perfect his message of nonviolent pro-*

*test. "Michnik, in his long years of struggle, has found a voice that is not only brave but clear," Professor John Rensenbrink of Bowdoin College wrote in his book* Poland Challenges a Divided World *(1988). "There is no muddle in it, and no ideology. He speaks in the voice that most characterizes the stance of Solidarity: a constitutional voice, a voice beyond violence, beyond the Gnostic temptation to reconstruct the world, and beyond the foolishness of a politics-as-usual that denies and yet practices the one-sidedness of discriminatory power. It is a voice that affirms that the human being per se has dignity."*

## EARLY LIFE

Adam Michnik was born in 1946 in Warsaw, Poland to Jewish parents. Before World War II, his father spent eight years in jail for his activities as a Communist activist, and, after the war and the imposition of Communism in Poland, he helped to edit the authorized Polish edition of the writings of Karl Marx. Adam Michnik was thus raised in a fanatically Communist home, but in his early teens he began to question official dogma after he learned of a relative's banishment to Siberia and of other Soviet atrocities committed against the Poles. When he began to inquire about such matters openly in class, his startled teacher arranged his transfer to another school. Undaunted, at the age of fifteen Michnik organized the Seekers of Contradictions, a high school political-discussion group that drew the wrath of

Communist officials and was disbanded. When he was just sixteen, Michnik had the dubious distinction of being attacked personally as an enemy of socialism by the national party leader, Wladyslaw Gomulka.

## LIFE'S WORK

In 1964 Michnik enrolled as a history student at Warsaw University, where he fell under the influence of Jacek Kuron, who was a tutor there at the time. In that year Michnik was arrested for the first time for taking part in the writing and distribution of "An Open Letter to the Party," an antigovernment treatise signed by Kuron and Karol Modzelewski. Two years later he was suspended from the university for joining in an antigovernment discussion led by the philosopher Leszek Kolakowski. But it was 1968, the year of anti-Communist ferment in the Eastern bloc, that marked the real turning point in Michnik's life. "That was the year it turned out that everything had been nonsense," he recalled in an interview with Michael T. Kaufman, the Warsaw bureau chief of the *New York Times*, for a *New York Times Magazine* (April 26, 1987) profile. "The system that proclaimed freedom attacked defenseless students with inspired goons and vigilantes. The system that proclaimed liberty sent tanks into Czechoslovakia. The system that hung its slogans of universal brotherhood unleashed the most disgusting anti-Semitic campaign in Poland, the first in postwar Europe. This is the point where I said to myself, halt, stop, I do not want to have anything to do with the system....I cut my umbilical cord to Communism."

Later in the same year, Adam Michnik led a group of university students in an indirect, seemingly innocuous protest against government censorship by laying a wreath at the monument to the Polish poet Adam Mickiewicz, whose play Forefathers Eve had recently been closed down by authorities. Police promptly broke up the gathering and beat up several students. Michnik was expelled from the campus, imprisoned, and, on his release, ordered to work as a welder at the Rosa Luxemburg light-bulb factory in Warsaw, but in 1971 he was removed from the factory when authorities became aware that his anti-Communist views were beginning to "infect" his fellow workers. Hired as a secretary by the poet Antoni Slonimski, he resumed his study of history as an extension student at Poznan University, which gave him his master's degree in 1975.

In September 1976 Michnik, Kuron, and a dozen other intellectuals founded the *Committee for the Defense of Workers* (known by its Polish acronym KOR)

as a social support group to provide financial, legal, and medical aid to workers in the communities of Radom and Ursus who had been arrested, beaten, and otherwise punished for staging a strike to protest a sharp increase in food prices. To underscore their resolve to stand alongside the protesters in defiance of government intimidation, the founders not only signed their names to the KOR charter but provided their addresses and telephone numbers as well. At about that time, the French philosopher Jean-Paul Sartre intervened with Polish authorities to allow Michnik to visit him in Paris. From there, in October, Michnik published his critical essay "A New Evolutionism," in which he called on the Polish workers and intellectuals to join forces with the Roman Catholic church, not to overthrow Communism, an endeavor that he conceded was "unrealistic and dangerous," but rather to challenge the government to permit fundamental human rights and independent institutions. "New evolutionism," he wrote, "is based on faith in the power of the working class....There is no question that the power elite fears this social group most. Pressure from the working classes is a necessary condition for the evolution of public life toward a democracy. This evolution...requires that fear be constantly overcome and that new political consciousness be developed."

After spending eight months in France, Michnik returned to Poland in May 1977 to what he realized was certain arrest. After his release two months later, thanks largely to protests from other intellectuals, he set out to forge the links that would transform the theory of his "New Evolutionism" into the reality that would eventually be called Solidarity. As one of the founders of Nowa, an underground publisher of dissident literature, he quickly became adept at raising funds, acquiring scarce printing equipment and supplies, and establishing an underground distribution system. He lectured at so-called flying universities (impromptu classes held in private apartments), drafted and signed antigovernment petitions, and brought workers and intellectuals together. Michnik also smuggled out of Poland for publication in France in 1977 the manuscript of The Church, the Left, and Dialogue, in which he expanded what he had merely touched upon in "A New Evolutionism." Praising the Catholic church as a beacon of human and civil rights in Communist Poland, he set forth the basis for cooperation between the church and the anti-Communist intelligentsia.

In August 1980 Michnik and other dissident leaders were arrested, only to be released later in the month as part of the historic agreement between the Communist regime and striking shipyard workers in Gdansk, under the terms of which the labor movement Solidarity was legalized. Michnik has said that on that day he was transformed from a dissident in the old order to a political opponent in the new. "The 1980-81 events," he recalled in an interview with Erica Blair for the *London Times Literary Supplement* (February 19-25, 1988), "were a revolution for dignity, a celebration of the rights of the vertebrae, a permanent victory for the straightened spine." He added prophetically, "The downfall of the totalitarian Communist order began here in Poland. I am convinced that while the events of 1917 signaled the rise of the Communist system, the meeting at the Gdansk shipyards in August 1980 began its destruction."

During Solidarity's first period of legal existence--from August 1980 to December 1981--Michnik continued to nettle Communist leaders both at home and abroad with his bold writings. In January 1981 the Soviet paper Pravda weighed in with a vitriolic attack on Michnik, the first time a Polish dissident had been criticized by name in the Soviet media since the Gdansk accord, for his article "The Last Chance," in which he questioned the leading role of the Communist party in Poland. Pravda denounced him as an "antisocialist ringleader" and decried his "hostile and subversive outburst," but, no matter how subversive his writing may have seemed to the authorities, Michnik remained committed to his orderly, nonviolent pursuit of change. In May 1981, for example, he personally intervened to save the lives of police officers in Otwock, outside Warsaw, who had been surrounded by an angry mob of citizens.

By September 1981 Solidarity had taken over the function and responsibility of KOR, which was disbanded, and Michnik, the intellectual architect of the dissident movement, slipped comfortably into the role of adviser to Solidarity leader Lech Walesa. In the following months, the new government of General Wojciech Jaruzelski grew increasingly nervous over the behavior of the emboldened opposition forces, and on December 13, 1981 he declared martial law, ending Solidarity's sixteen months of legal existence. Some 10,000 Solidarity activists, including Michnik, were arrested. After spending nearly two years behind bars awaiting trial, Michnik was given a choice between exile to the West or indefinite imprisonment. He ridiculed his captors in an open letter to the interior minister, General Czeslaw Kiszczak, which was read by the Nobel laureate

Czeslaw Milosz in accepting an honorary doctorate for Michnik from the New School for Social Research in New York City in April 1984. "To offer a man imprisoned for two years the chance to go to the French Riviera in exchange for moral suicide, one must be a pig...," he wrote. "To believe I could accept such a deal one has to assume every man is no more than a police informer." Michnik was expected to go on trial during the summer of 1984, but at the last minute the government suddenly released him and other Solidarity leaders without explanation. His freedom was to last just six months.

On February 13, 1985 Michnik attended a Solidarity meeting called by Lech Walesa in a private apartment in Gdansk to consider the recent government announcement of another round of price increases. When the talk turned to the possibility of a fifteen-minute strike to protest the increases, Polish police raided the meeting and arrested everyone there. Although Walesa and most of the others were detained only briefly, Michnik and two other activists, Bogdan Lis and Wladyslaw Frasyniuk, were formally charged with inciting public unrest. At the trial in May 1985, Michnik was repeatedly removed from the courtroom for refusing to cooperate with what he denounced as a "classic example of police banditry." When Walesa stepped down from the witness stand, unwilling to offer incriminating testimony against his adviser, Michnik raised his fingers in a "V" sign and cried out, "Don't worry, Lech, Solidarity will win in the end!"

To no one's surprise, the three men were found guilty. Lis and Michnik, who despite his frequent periods of incarceration had never been formally convicted of a crime before, were sentenced to thirty months; Frasyniuk, a repeat offender, got an extra year. From his cell in Barczewa Prison in northern Poland and, later, in the Gdansk prison, Michnik continued to write. His incisive essays were smuggled out of the country and published in the West. An English translation of some of Michnik's writings was published in 1986 under the title Letters from Prison and Other Essays. In his Introduction to the book, Jonathan Schell noted that Michnik's writings are marked by a blend of gravity of purpose and lightness of style. He added: "Michnik is not a political philosopher--and certainly not a political scientist--nor is he a proponent of any ideology or system of political thought. His writings, like the Federalist papers of Madison and Hamilton, or the articles and letters of Gandhi, are not only reflections of action but a form of action themselves....Michnik's writings, then, both mirror and help to shape the new possibilities that have been and are being brought into existence by the Polish people."

Western leaders, particularly Italian prime minister Bettino Craxi, repeatedly urged the Polish government to release Michnik, and in August 1986 Jaruzelski freed him as part of a limited amnesty called for by the Tenth Congress of the Polish Communist party. While resting at the home of friends in the Baltic seaside resort of Sopot, he reflected on the value of imprisonment in the life of a dissident in another interview with Michael T. Kaufman of the *New York Times* (August 22, 1986). "A totalitarian civilization is a prison civilization," he observed, "and with the experience of prison you can better understand the mechanics of coercion that apply. For me the key to understanding our political authorities is to examine and analyze the conduct of the prison warden. The relationship between the warden, the guards, and the prisoners are the basic relationships in a totalitarian culture. What separates me now from General Jaruzelski is exactly what separated me from the warden of Barczewa Prison."

Two months after his release, Adam Michnik and another Solidarity leader, Zbigniew Bujak, were named recipients of the 1986 Robert F. Kennedy Human Rights Award. In May 1987 Senator Edward M. Kennedy of Massachusetts, who commended Michnik for "speaking truth to power," and other members of the Kennedy clan flew to Warsaw to present the award and the $40,000 prize to Michnik, who vowed to use the award money to aid the Polish underground press. He added in his acceptance remarks, "We can be free people even if our country is not free, and we can build a sovereign society in a country that is not sovereign."

At that point, not even Michnik, who had foreseen so presciently the form and direction of the Polish democratic movement, could have predicted the breathtaking pace at which reforms would sweep Eastern Europe over the next few years. With the tacit approval of Soviet leader Mikhail Gorbachev, the Jaruzelski government entered into an historic agreement with Solidarity, a legal organization once again, on April 5, 1989--an accord that paved the way for limited free elections and, ultimately, a Solidarity-led government. Under the terms of the agreement, which Michnik helped to hammer out as an adviser, all 100 seats of the newly created Senate were to be freely contested. In the Sejm, or lower house, two-thirds of the seats were to be reserved for the Communist party, with the remainder subject to free election.

On June 4, 1989 Solidarity-backed candidates swept virtually every contested parliamen-tary election, and Michnik was elected overwhelmingly to the Sejm from a working-class district in Silesia. Meanwhile, in a remarkable turn of events, the former dissident who had been jailed for his writings became the editor of the first uncensored daily newspaper in Poland in forty years. The first issue of *Gazeta wyborcza (The Election Gazette)* rolled off the presses on May 8, and, three months later, Michnik was named a contributing editor to the *New Republic*, the American weekly journal of opinion.

For all the recent advances in Eastern Europe, Michnik has warned that a dangerous new period lies ahead. In an article entitled "Notes on the Revolution" that appeared in the *New York Times Magazine* (March 11, 1990), he urged the emerging democracies to guard against a resurgence of the militant nationalism that had plunged the continent into war so many times before. "Among the many traps lying in wait," he cautioned, "nationalist conflict is especially dangerous....For now two roads [lie] open before my country, and to our newly freed neighbors: One road leads to border wars, the other to minimizing borders, reducing them to little more than road signs; one road leads to new barbed-wire fences, the other to a new order based on pluralism and tolerance; one road leads to nationalism and isolation, the other to a return to our 'native Europe.'"

## PERSONAL LIFE

Adam Michnik has been described as a rumpled, gregarious, at times playful figure whose only enduring mark of his years in prison is a tendency to pace up and down in a room while he talks. His speaking style, which is marred by a stammer, has been described by Timothy Garton Ash, the author of *The Polish Revolution* (1983), as "a brilliantly articulate sub-machine gun." Michnik's apartment reflects the paradox of his life: he displays a copy of the *New Testament* inscribed by Pope John Paul II near a bust of Karl Marx. He is married to a former state prosecutor in Gdansk. Their son is named for Antoni Slonimski, the poet who supported Michnik when he lost his job at the Rosa Luxemburg light-bulb factory.

## FURTHER READING

N Y Times Mag p38+ Ap 26 '87 por; New Yorker 61:47+ F 3 '86; Michnik, Adam. Letters from Prison and Other Essays (1985)

# MIHAJLOV, MIHAJLO

## Yugoslav Dissident; Writer; Teacher

**Born:** September 26, 1934; Pancevo, Yugoslavia, (now
Serbia) near Belgrade
**Died:** March 7, 2010; Belgrade, Serbia
**Primary Field:** Political Dissident

### INTRODUCTION

*Many people, when asked about the nation state of
Yugoslavia, would need to do a quick web search to
answer the question with any certainty. Yugoslavia no
longer exists because of ten years of sectarianism and
ethnic wars, ending in 2001. It has been replaced with
the countries of Bosnia-Herzegovina; Croatia; Kosovo;
Macedonia; Montenegro; Serbia; and, Slovenia. When
the carnage was over, which included acts of genocide
and other war crimes, Mihajlo Mihajlov, a Yugoslav
dissident of Russian ethnicity, and in exile since the
late 1970s (he received American citizenship in 1985),
finally was able to return to the land of his birth, to Belgrade, Serbia, in 2001.*

*Before he left, he spent most of early his adult years
in prison because of his writings exposing the seamy
side of the former U.S.S.R. (he had written that Stalin
had established the first "death camps") and his objections of the Communist, one-party, rule of Josip Broz
Tito in Yugoslavia. Tito, who was the most "liberal"
of the Communist dictators, took Mihajlov's criticisms
personally. In a web translation from Serbian-Croatian
to English, the Serbian paper (Vreme, Beograd [Bel-
grade]) in his obituary, stated: "On Sunday, March 7
[2010] in the morning, died in his apartment in Belgrade, Mihajlo Mihajlov, the only real dissident in Yugoslavia - except perhaps Milovan Djilas."*

*"Arrested, tried, and bounced around from prison
to prison," as he once summed up his 13-year ordeal,
the Yugoslav dissident and literary scholar Mihajlo
Mihajlov had been in and out of jail since 1965 and
was unable to publish his writing in his native country. The government had been particularly persistent
in suppressing him because, unlike most of the other
liberal critics of the Tito regime, Mihajlov had openly
denounced the nation's one-party system. Although he
acknowledged in the 1960s that Yugoslavia was less
repressive than the other Communist states, he had
consistently maintained that, so long as the Communist
Party possessed a monopoly of power, the country was
totalitarian and vulnerable to a revival of Stalinist tyranny. The blood bath after Tito's death in 1980 ushered
in many Stalinist war crimes, such as "ethnic cleansing" and systemic rapes.*

### EARLY LIFE

Mihajlo Mihajlov was born in Pancevo, Yugoslavia,
near Belgrade, on September 26, 1934. His parents were
Russian émigrés who met and married in Yugoslavia
after leaving the Soviet Union during the famine that
followed the Russian Revolution. Mihajlov's father was
an antifascist Partisan in World War II and, for some
years, a director of the Yugoslav Scientific Institute. His
mother, Vera Mihajlov, a former teacher, left Yugoslavia
in the 1970s and joined her daughter, Marija Mihajlov
Ivusic, in the United States, where they both spoke out
in Mihajlov s behalf.

### LIFE'S WORK

After completing his high school education in Sara-
jevo, Mihajlov studied comparative literature at the
philosophy faculty of Belgrade University and at the
philosophy faculty of Zagreb University, receiving his
degree from the latter institution in 1959. Following a
period of service in the army, he worked in Zagreb as
a translator, wrote for many Yugoslav periodicals, and
lectured over the radio. Through those activities, Mihajlov became known as an expert on Dostoyevsky and
post-Stalin Soviet literature. In December 1963, he was
appointed an Assistant Professor on the philosophy faculty of the Zadar branch of Zagreb University, where he
taught Russian Literature while working on his doctoral
dissertation.

A collection of Mihajlov's literary, political, and
philosophical essays, written over a period of five years,
beginning in 1961, and translated by his sister into English, was published in 1968 by Farrar, Straus & Giroux
under the title *Russian Themes*. In many of the essays,
Mihajlov used the works of Russian writers as spring-
boards for discussions of his own views on social and
political issues. Thomas Lask pointed out, in his review
in the *New York Times* (June 24, 1968), that the pages
of *Russian Themes* "are full of discerning summaries,
pithy evaluations and sensitive responses to style." The
essays of that collection, and other writings, of Mihajlov's contain allusions to non-Russian authors that

reveal his rather extensive reading in modern Western literature.

During the summer of 1964, Mihajlov spent five weeks in Moscow and Leningrad under a cultural exchange program between Yugoslavia and the Soviet Union. He recounted his conversations with Russian writers in an essay published in two installments under the title *Moscow Summer 1964* in the January and February 1965 issues of the Belgrade literary periodical *Delo*. Discussing Soviet concentration camp literature, he wrote that the first death camps were established, not by the Nazis, but by the Soviets, and, that, shortly before World War II, Stalin committed genocide against peoples in regions along the Turkish-Iranian border. Mihajlov furthermore asserted that the process of de-Stalinization in the Soviet Union was far from complete and quoted a Moscow University student as saying that only Stalin's victims within the Communist party had been rehabilitated.

Yugoslav President Josip Broz Tito had himself attacked the Soviet Union following his break with Stalin in 1948. But in the early 1960s, as relations between Yugoslavia and the U.S.S.R. improved, the Belgrade government no longer looked favorably upon anti-Soviet statements. At a meeting with public prosecutors, on February 11, 1965, Tito denounced Mihajlov as a "reactionary" and charged him with "defending Hitler's concentration camps." Although an injunction was issued to stop the sale of Delo, the Soviet ambassador to Yugoslavia formally protested the publication of the article, and soon afterward Mihajlov was arrested.

Accused of "damaging the reputation of a foreign state" and of mailing his banned article to a Rome publisher, Mihajlov went on trial on April 29, 1965, in the Zadar District Court. He argued that he had published only historical facts and that all forms of totalitarianism, such as death camps, whether Stalinist or fascist, were equally evil. On the following day, the court found the author guilty of both charges and sentenced him to nine months in jail. But, on June 23, the Supreme Court of Croatia, to which Mihajlov had appealed, dismissed his conviction on the charge of deriding the Soviet Union and suspended his sentence on the other charge. Some observers linked the reversal to the upcoming meeting in Yugoslavia of the International P.E.N. Club, a writers' organization.

His arrest, however, had cost Mihajlov his post on the Zadar faculty. He turned to writing full time, but could not get his articles published in Yugoslavia because their major thrust was a demand for the democratization of his country's politics. The Western press, however, welcomed his work. The American periodical, the *New Leader*, for example, published the *Delo* installments of "*Moscow Summer 1964*" in March 1965. In June, an additional segment, never published in Yugoslavia, appeared in that magazine (the essays were later consolidated into the book: *Moscow Summer in 1965*). Thereafter, he sent a stream of essays and open letters to Tito to the foreign press.

In "Why We Are Silent," an article published by the *New Leader* in August 1965 and reprinted in the *Washington Post* (September 5, 1965), Mihajlov presented his political views as those of a Democratic Socialist whose beliefs were based on Christian principles. He contended that true freedom existed neither in the West, with its private ownership of property, nor in the East, with its single-party regimes. He granted that Yugoslavia, where the Communist party had begun relaxing its controls over society in the 1950s, came closer than any other country to combining the political democracy of the West with the East's principle of material democracy. But Mihajlov warned that "every one-party system, whatever else may be said about it, is some kind of subspecies of Stalinism" and that a relapse into the worst excesses of totalitarianism was possible so long as the Communist party controlled all means of communication and barred non-Marxist ideas.

With the goal of breaking the Communist Party's monopoly, in December 1965, Mihajlov wrote a draft proposal for an independent Socialist magazine to serve as a nucleus for future opposition political groups. He circulated the manuscript among friends and, with about 20 supporters, planned to convene on August 10, 1966, an organizing conference for the magazine, to be called *Slobodni Glas (The Voice of Freedom)*. Two days before the meeting, he was arrested.

On September 22 and 23, Mihajlov was tried again in the Zadar District Court, for allegedly spreading false information about Yugoslavia in foreign publications, and for distributing his banned "Moscow Summer 1964" essay. No mention of the projected magazine was made in the indictment. In 1966, the government was allowing expanded freedom of discussion, particularly after the July purge of dogmatic, hard-line Vice-President and Police Chief Aleksandar Rankovic. Liberals were permitted to argue for greater democracy within the party and for a reduction of its role in society. The journal *Praxis* was conducting controversial philosophical debates on Marxism. But the crackdown on Mihajlov, as viewed in the Western press, indicated that the authorities drew the line for permissible dissent at any challenge to the party's monopoly of political power. Many dissidents also believed that Mihajlov had gone too far, and feared that he was jeopardizing recent gains by asking for more than could be expected. His reputation as an extremist limited his following.

However, there were groups of Mihajlov's supporters that were arrested in Yugoslavia in August and November 1966. But, as reported in the Western press, he has not attracted a substantial following in his native country, and according to the *New York Times* (April 23, 1967), his compatriots were troubled by what they felt was "an excess in his style, an overly frenetic quality, a mournful fanaticism akin to that of Dostoyevsky's underground man."

When the prosecutor charged at Mihajlov's September trial that his motive for publishing in the West was monetary, the tense but articulate defendant replied, as quoted in the *New York Times* (September 23, 1966), "My personal experience is that with political articles one earns prison more easily than money." In the courtroom, he also declared that only six or seven percent of the Yugoslav population, those belonging to the Communist Party, had rights, but he was not permitted to present to the court a written defense assailing totalitarianism. That statement was later published as "The Unspoken Defense" in *Russian Themes*.

While courtroom hecklers jeered him, Mihajlov was convicted of both formal charges and sentenced to one year in prison. Allowed to remain at liberty, while he was appealing to the Croatian Supreme Court, he reported receiving threatening phone calls and letters, and being followed through the streets by people who urged grocers not to sell him food. Having lost his appeal, he began serving his sentence on November 12 in the Sremska Mitrovca prison near Belgrade.

On April 17, 1967, Mihajlov was removed from jail and taken to the Belgrade District Court to face another trial. He was again accused of spreading false propaganda in the foreign press—the government simply chose a different group of articles from the one cited in his September 1966 indictment. Eric Bourne reported in the *Christian Science Monitor* (April 18, 1967) that even some official Communists regarded the new case as "stupid and unnecessary." Although Mihajlov was also accused of supporting émigrés favoring separatism for Yugoslavia's Republics, the prosecution's own

witnesses confirmed that he had little sympathy for separatism.

In his defense, Mihajlov told the court that nothing he had written violated his right of dissent as given by the Yugoslav Constitution and that he sent his articles abroad only because no one in Yugoslavia would publish them. Richard Eder of the *New York Times* (April 18, 1967) recorded that, when the judge asked the defendant why he did not go abroad to write, Mihajlov replied, "No, it would not be the same. When I write here in Yugoslavia, I am guaranteeing with my head everything that I write." The April trial brought Mihajlov a severe four-and-a-half year sentence minus time already served, a reduction in the number of visitors allowed him in prison, and a four-year ban on public activity following his release. Mihajlov appealed his conviction to the Serbian Supreme Court, which in October, as reported by the *Washington Post* (October 22, 1967), reduced his sentence by one year because two state psychiatrists found him "a psychopathic person not adequately prepared for social adaptation." The next month, he was placed in solitary confinement after refusing to engage in forced labor.

Released from prison on March 4, 1970, Mihajlov continued writing articles for foreign publications. He did not alter his fundamental political views in the 1970s, but devoted greater attention to the spiritual and religious aspects of freedom. In his essay "Two Convergences," published in 1971 and later reprinted in his *Underground Notes* (Sheed, Andrews & McMeel, 1976), he criticized Soviet physicist Andrei Sakharov's argument that the requirements of scientific-technical development would lead to democratization in the U.S.S.R. Mihajlov contended that freedom is an existential problem and that man opposes totalitarianism only when he "feels that by submitting to oppression he is losing his soul, his 'I' . . . And that feeling is a religious one."

The beleaguered dissident was arrested again, in October 1974. On February 25, 1975, during a year of severe repression in Yugoslavia that damaged its reputation as the most liberal Communist nation, he went on trial in Novi Sad on the usual charge of disseminating hostile propaganda in foreign publications. Three days later, he was sentenced to seven years at hard labor, and was again barred from public activity for four years following the completion of his sentence. In prison, he began protracted hunger strikes, in December 1975, and again in December 1976, to improve his living conditions. Meanwhile, human rights groups in the West petitioned Tito for his release.

To mark Yugoslavia's National Day, the state freed Mihajlov and a group of other prisoners in a November 1977 amnesty. "I do not intend to be quiet," he announced upon leaving jail. Mihajlov attributed his release to the fact that the East-West Commission on Security and Cooperation in Europe was meeting in Belgrade at the time to discuss, among other things, compliance with the human rights provisions of the Helsinki agreements of 1975. In early 1978, he urged the delegates to make reference to the human rights issue in the conference's final document, a plea that failed.

Even when he was not in prison, Mihajlov was unable to accept a standing offer, made in 1970, of an opportunity to carry on his academic work at Stanford University, because his government would not give him a passport. Early in 1974, he was also denied a passport to attend the annual meeting of the American Association for the Advancement of Science in San Francisco, to which he had been invited. The following August, he wrote a letter to Tito in which he appealed, "Either enable me to live normally in this country or enable me to leave the country." Eventually successful in obtaining a passport, he visited the United States in the summer of 1978 to arrange for the publication of an autobiographical and political book, and to collect material for another book, tentatively titled *American Summer*. During his stay, he wrote an article for the *New Leader* (July 31, 1978), "Notes of a Survivor: The Trials in That Other World" reflecting on the current wave of trials of dissidents in the Soviet Union, and a review for the *New York Review of Books* (October 26, 1978) of Dusko Doder's *The Yugoslavs*, calling attention to important Western misconceptions about Yugoslavia.

Because of an extensive crackdown on dissidents in Yugoslavia, Mihajlov prolonged his visit in the United States, where he lectured at dozens of universities, and, in 1979, began work on a new book, *Tyranny and Freedom*, to be published by Harper & Row. In August 1979, Yugoslav authorities issued an arrest warrant for him, in an attempt, as some observers interpreted it, to discourage his return.

According to the *New York Times* obituary of Mihajlov, "he resided in the United States, and, until 1985 taught Russian literature and philosophy courses at Yale, Ohio State University and the University of Virginia, as well as in Western Europe." He also worked as an analyst at the American-financed Radio Free Europe,

before returning to Serbia, in 2001, after the ouster of President Slobodan Milosevic." (Milosevic later stood trial for various war crimes at the Hague, including ethnic cleansing, and died in his jail cell before the conclusion of the trial of an heart attack. In many ways, he could be called Yugoslava's "Stalin.")

His sister, Maria, a Catholic who had immigrated to the U.S. in 1965, stated in another obituary in the *Washington Times*, regarding his return home to Serbia in 2001, "He was a celebrity in Yugoslavia." While he was in prison, Maria had tirelessly campaigned for his release. (See http://www.legacy.com/obituaries/washingtontimes/obituary.aspx?pid=140587864.) In this obituary, Mihajlov modestly downplayed the role that dissidents had in ending Communism in Eastern Europe. "I do not think that dissidents seriously affected the situation in Communist countries, especially Yugoslavia. Of course, it was important that they exist, but they did not overthrow one-party dictatorship. Western governments were more influential in such matters." Many others, however, disagree, stating that his writings were a pivotal force.

Mihajlov, who died in Belgrade of unknown causes on March 7, 2010, continued to campaign for the rights of dissidents. According to his biography in Alexandria Press's Biblioteka: "Since 1994 Mihajlov has been a Senior Associate with the Program on Transitions to Democracy, Elliot School of International Affairs, The George Washington University, Washington, D.C., Since 1999 he was also an Adjunct fellow of the Hudson Institute. In 2000, Mihajlov was a Visiting Professor at State University - Higher School of Economics in Moscow (Russia)." (See http://www.alexandria-press.com/Bio/mihajlo_mihajlov.htm.) The biography also stated that he was on the "editorial boards of several journals, and a member of the International P.E.N. Club, as well as an honorary member of many writers and human rights national and international organizations. He is also the Chairman of the Democracy International Committee to Aid Democratic Dissidents in (former) Yugoslavia (CADDY)."

According to *A Tribute to Mihajlo Mihajlov*, written after Mihajlov's death in *The St. Croix Review,* it was little known that Mihajlov was the founder of Democracy International Committee to Aid Democratic Dissidents in (former) Yugoslavia (CADDY). He and other members released the CADDY Bulletins publicizing the human rights violations of Yugoslavia.

Upon his return to Belgrade, Mihajlov continued to teach and lecture in Belgrade until his death. A funeral service was held in Belgrade on Saturday, March 13. His sister and a nephew were listed as his survivors in the the *Washington Times* obituary.

## PERSONAL LIFE

In 1978, Mihajlov received an annual award from the International League for Human Rights, and in 1980, he was the recipient of the Ford Foundation Award for Humanistic Perspectives on Contemporary Society. Yugoslavi's most famous dissident, Milovan Djilas, a former Vice-President who also spent many years in prison, had the highest praise for Mihajlov, when, in 1974, he credited the son of Russian émigrés with the best of Russian qualities—openness, sacrifice, and sensitivity—in an unalloyed form. Dedicated to his personal fight for freedom of speech and other human rights in Yugoslavia, Mihajlov never married.

## FURTHER READING

*Encounter 24:81+ Je '65; N Y Times p47 N 14 '74; New Leader 61:2 Jl 17 '78; Newsweek 68:42+ Ag 15 '66 por; Mihajlov, Mihajlo. Moscow Summer (1965), Underground Notes (1976)*

---

# W. DEEN MOHAMMED

## Islamic Scholar; Social Activist

**Born:** October 3, 1933; Hamtramck, Michigan
**Died:** September 9, 2008; Chicago, Illinois
**Primary Field:** Religious Freedom
**Affiliation:** American Society of Muslims

## INTRODUCTION

*The Islamic scholar Imam W. Deen Mohammed is the spiritual father of the American Society of Muslims, the predominately African-American organization that, with more than two million members, represents the largest Muslim community in the U.S. (Formerly known as the Bilallian Community, the World Community of Al-Islam in the West, and the American Muslim Mission, the current group has sometimes been referred to as the Muslim American Society. "Imam" is an Arabic title for a Muslim religious leader.) Mohammed's quiet style and inclusive, peaceful vision won him the respect of religious and political leaders worldwide. In an article posted on the New Africa Intelligentsia Web site, the humanitarian and former heavyweight boxing champion Muhammad Ali called Imam Mohammed, whom Ali has known since the mid-1960s, a "peaceful warrior, using his wisdom and kindness to fight for the betterment of all African Americans as well as Muslims."*

*Mohammed's father, Elijah Mohammed, was for over four decades the leader of the Nation of Islam (NOI), a black separatist religious movement begun in Detroit, Michigan, in 1930. Following the death of his father, in 1975, Mohammed assumed the leadership of the NOI. He subsequently changed the group's name, aligned its beliefs and practices with those of orthodox Sunni Islam, and opened its membership to individuals of all races. (In late 1977 Louis Farrakhan revived the NOI as a separate organization.) In addition to serving as the religious leader of many of America's Muslims, Mohammed is the international president of the World Conference on Religion and Peace and a member of the Peace Council and the World Supreme Council of Mosques. He has met with many world religious and political leaders, including the Dalai Lama and Pope John Paul II.*

*In 2003 Mohammed retired from his post as head of the American Society of Muslims, though he stated that he planned to remain active in the Muslim community and would continue to direct his ministry, the Mosque Cares. "His greatness came from the fact that he brought African American Muslims into a deeper understanding of mainstream Islam," Salam Al-Marayati, executive director of the Muslim Public Affairs Council, a Los Angeles, California-based advocacy group, said, as quoted by Rachel Zoll for the Associated Press (September 1, 2003). "His wealth of Islamic knowledge as well as his experience as an American has really cemented our understanding of what an American Muslim identity should be." Mohammed has written several books and contributes a weekly column to the Muslim Journal, the national newspaper of the American Society of Muslims. In addition, he has spread his ministry via a nationally syndicated radio program, Imam W. Deen Muhammad Speaks, which in the 1990s could be heard on more than 60 stations across the country. Ebony magazine named Mohammed one of the 100 most influential African-Americans in the world in both 2000 and 2001. In 2002 he received the Gandhi King Ikeda Award for Peace and was named one of the most influential people in the city of Chicago by the* Chicago Sun-Times *and the* Chicago Tribune.

## EARLY LIFE

The seventh of the eight children of Elijah and Clara Mohammed, Wallace D. Mohammed was born in Hamtramck, Michigan (some sources say Detroit), on October 30, 1933. (Variations of his name include W. D. Mohammed, Warith Deen Mohammed, Wallace Deen Mohammed, and Wallace Delaney Mohammed. As with his father, many sources print his last name "Muhammad.") Mohammed's father, who was born Elijah Poole, was the son of a Georgia sharecropper and a Baptist preacher. An unemployed migrant laborer, Elijah Mohammed moved his family to Michigan, where, in the early 1930s, he became a disciple of Wali Farad Mohammed, a mysterious Detroit clothing peddler and self-styled savior who claimed to have come from Mecca, Saudi Arabia—Islam's holiest city. (Farad, known to his followers as Master Farad or Master Fard, was reportedly born Wallace D. Fard.) Farad preached to underclass blacks that the time of white domination (he referred to whites as "devils") was coming to an end, and that African- Americans, the true children of God, should prepare themselves to inherit the new kingdom. Farad told his followers that Islam was their true religion, and Allah their God—though Farad's teachings deviated considerably from those of orthodox Islam. According to an article in *Cornerstone* magazine (Issue 111, 1997), as posted on the Answering Islam Web site, Farad transmitted his ideas not only through preaching, but also through a book, *The Teaching for the Lost-Found Nation of Islam,* as well as through a kind of oath of allegiance known as *"The Secret Ritual of the Nation of Islam."* Among Farad's (and later Elijah Mohammed's) more outlandish teachings were that blacks were exiled from the moon 66 trillion years ago; that white people were created by a mad black scientist named Yakub; and that a "mother ship," a large undetected aircraft built by black scientists in Japan thousands of years ago, still hovered over the globe, ready to defend the NOI against white America.

## LIFE'S WORK

Elijah Mohammed became one of Farad's most trusted followers; when Farad mysteriously disappeared in 1934, Elijah Mohammed proclaimed that Farad was God, or Allah, incarnate, and that he himself was Allah's messenger, the last prophet of God on Earth. (Both of these claims represent grave heresies in traditional Islam.) Elijah Mohammed worked to expand the NOI, which then had several thousand members, and continued to stress the group's teachings of racial separatism. According to *Cornerstone*, Elijah Mohammed moved his family to Washington, D.C., in around 1935; they then traveled the country, spreading the NOI message from city to city. Disenfranchised African- Americans were encouraged to transform their lives as black Muslims, to obey strict dietary laws, and to abstain from alcohol, tobacco, drugs, and frivolity. Under Elijah Mohammed the group moved its headquarters from Detroit to Chicago. It continued to expand during the 1950s and 1960s, when many impoverished and imprisoned African- Americans joined the NOI ranks. "Suddenly here were all these clean-cut, well-dressed young men and women—men mostly," Stanley Crouch wrote for the *Village Voice* (October 25, 1985). "You recognized them from the neighborhood. They had been pests or vandals, thieves or gangsters. Now they were back from jail or prison and their hair was cut close, their skin was smooth, they no longer cursed blue streaks, and the intensity in their eyes remade their faces. They were 'in the Nation' and that meant that new men were in front of you, men who greeted each other in Arabic, who were aloof, confident, and intent on living differently than they had." A major factor in the NOI's success during this period was Malcolm X, a brilliant and fiery young minister whose rousing orations regarding black power and the injustice of white supremacy galvanized many African-Americans. In an interview with April Witt for the *Miami Herald* (October 14,1997), W. D. Mohammed explained Islam's appeal: "African Americans have been disappointed so many times. Islam offers a new life. . . . Africa, during the slave trade to this country, was Islamic in some of its most civilized parts. So Islam is a way to connect with our past and have a comfortable sense of our worth, not just as individuals, but as a people."

According to the *Encyclopedia of American Religion and Politics* (2003), Farad foretold the birth of a favored son to Elijah Mohammed and predicted that the boy, whom he named Wallace Delaney Mohammed, would one day succeed his father as leader of the NOI. Even as a child, however, W. Deen Mohammed was skeptical of Farad and his father's teachings. "I remember I was about 7 years old, and I prayed, Dear Savior, excuse me if I'm not getting it right, but I don't understand," he recalled to Sally MacDonald for the *Seattle Times* (June 14, 1997). "I had common sense, and my common sense told me this was ridiculous, the idea that God is a God that wants one people to dominate others. [Farad] was not God, and I knew he was not God. Elijah Mohammed was not a prophet." Mohammed attended elementary and secondary school at the University of Islam in Chicago; he later studied at Wilson Junior College and Loop College (now Harold Washington College), both in Chicago. Elijah Mohammed hired a tutor from Jerusalem to teach his children Arabic, so that they could read the Koran, Islam's holy book, in the original language. However, reading the Koran only reinforced Mohammed's impression that the NOI's racial theology controverted the basic teachings of Islam. Despite those personal convictions, for many years Mohammed vacillated between acceptance and rejection of the NOI. "I shared something religious with my father. I didn't like his language, but I shared his love of God and his desire to see his people in better circumstances," he recalled to MacDonald. "He was innocent and naive. He was a spiritual man and a social reformer. But he was given a myth that he bought because he didn't know any better. He had only a third-grade education."

Mohammed became a minister in the NOI after completing high school. In 1961 he was drafted by the U.S. Army but refused to serve, and as a result spent the next three years in prison. While in prison he continued his study of mainstream Sunni Islam, and again took note of the considerable differences between it and the ideology promulgated by the NOI. Mohammed came to embrace an inclusive, non-radicalized version of Islam, which ultimately, in 1964, led to his expulsion from the NOI. That same year, Malcolm X was suspended from the organization after tension between him and Elijah Mohammed came to a boil. Like W. Deen Mohammed, Malcolm had come to the conclusion that Elijah was misrepresenting the Islamic faith and was guilty of sexual indiscretions. (In fact, Malcolm X had always felt a strong personal affinity for W. Deen Mohammed. In *The Autobiography of Malcolm X*, the charismatic NOI minister remarked: "I felt that Wallace was Mr. [Elijah] Muhammad's most strongly spiritual son, the son with the most objective outlook. Always, Wallace and I . .

. shared an exceptional closeness and trust.") Malcolm X's subsequent assassination, in 1965, served to divide the organization, in large part because NOI members loyal to Elijah Mohammed were suspected of having carried out the murder.

Elijah Mohammed reinstated his son just days after the death of Malcolm X, though later that year he expelled him once again for harboring dissident views. While Mohammed came to reject many of his father's beliefs, he nevertheless felt that the NOI, "with all its extremes, had some good," as he explained to April Witt. "Being self-supporting, being disciplined, believing that we should be constantly refining our own nature—those teachings were very strong." Mohammed was readmitted to the NOI in 1969 but was not allowed to resume his full duties as a minister until 1974.

Soon after Elijah Mohammed's death, in 1975, W. Deen Mohammed was elected supreme minister of the NOI, despite his turbulent relationship with the organization. He immediately set about downplaying the group's idiosyncratic doctrines and practices, and distanced himself from his father's black separatist teachings by welcoming white and other non-African-American Muslims into the group. Also in 1975 he renamed the organization the Bilalian Community, after an Ethiopian Muslim and companion to the Prophet Mohammed, and urged followers to learn Arabic, pray five times a day, and study the teachings of traditional Islam—just as Sunni Muslims around the world do. Mohammed established relationships with other Muslim organizations in the United States and abroad, meeting with the Egyptian president Anwar Sadat in Chicago in 1975 and receiving $16 million from Sheikh Ben Mohammed al-Qasmini of the United Arab Emirates for the purpose of building a mosque (an Islamic place of worship) and a school. Mohammed's Temple #7, the well-known community mosque in the Harlem section of New York City, was renamed Masjid (Arabic for "mosque") Malcolm Shabazz, in honor of Malcolm X, and Mohammed led a group of 400 Muslim African-Americans on a Hajj, or pilgrimage, to Mecca. (The Hajj is one of the five central precepts, or "pillars," of Islam.) In 1977 he changed the name of his organization to the World Community of Al-Islam in the West. He later renamed the group the American Muslim Mission, and still later, the American Society of Muslims.

Not everyone was happy with the direction in which Mohammed was leading his organization. In December 1977 Louis Farrakhan, a charismatic and outspoken minister who professed loyalty to the letter of Elijah Mohammed's teachings, publicly split with the World Community of Al-Islam in the West and reestablished the NOI. Whereas orthodox Sunni Islam avers that Mohammed, who founded the Islamic faith in what is now Saudi Arabia, in the seventh century, was the last of the prophets, Farrakhan, like Elijah Mohammed before him, taught that Elijah Mohammed was the final prophet—a belief that is considered heretical in orthodox Islam. Farrakhan's NOI also continued to teach that whites were "devils" and that African- Americans should establish their own culture and society apart from the white-dominated mainstream. Though the NOI's incendiary teachings gave the organization a certain dynamic appeal among young African-Americans, and despite the fact that the NOI is arguably the better known of the two groups, as of 2003 Farrakhan's NOI had fewer than 200,000 members, while Mohammed's American Society of Muslims had more than two million—more than half of them African-American. (Sources vary widely as to the NOI's total membership—estimates range from 20,000 to 200,000— and Farrakhan does not disclose exact figures. Estimates regarding the total number of Muslims in the United States also vary widely: many sources put the figure at around six or seven million.) Mohammed long considered Farrakhan's NOI misguided; he once called the group a "crippling force" for African-Americans, as quoted by MacDonald. Critics of the American Society of Muslims, on the other hand, argued that that organization focused disproportionately on religion while paying insufficient heed to social issues affecting African-Americans. "The main thing that separates Farrakhan from me," Mohammed told Neil Modie for the *Seattle Post-Intelligencer* (June 23,1997), "is that his idea of Islam, of the message, is that blacks are the only ones that are worthy of it, that we are not to take others seriously. . . . He's a radical and I'm not." "If [Farrakhan] would accept the religion and respect it," Mohammed told April Witt in 1997, "I would gladly stand by him as a social-reform leader or a leader for economic empowerment in depressed neighborhoods. I would even walk behind him if he would do that."

In 1978, wishing to assume a lower profile and to have fewer organizational ties, Mohammed changed his title from supreme minister to imam, a traditional Islamic designation, and adopted the name Warith Deen Mohammed. He retained his position as the group's spiritual guide. In 1985, dismayed by the resistance of some of the group's leaders to his inclusive teachings,

Mohammed dissolved the leadership council he had created in 1978. Most of the mosques that had been a part of the American Muslim Mission remained affiliated with Mohammed's ministry, and most of the organization's members continued to view Mohammed as their spiritual leader. "We shouldn't have so much organization in religion that we depend upon the minister or imam for overseeing our lives," Mohammed told Witt, "telling us when to go out and when to come in, what to wear, how to react. That should come from the word of God, from our own intellect and from the family. That's Islam." "[Mohammed] is shy, it seems, and soft- spoken," Herbert Berg, an associate professor of religion at the University of North Carolina, told Steven G. Vegh for the Norfolk, Virginia, *Virginian- Pilot* (October 10, 2002). "He's not a sound-bite guy. But the effect he has on some of his followers, it's incredibly strong."

In 1993, at the invitation of President Bill Clinton, Mohammed became the first imam to deliver the prayer and invocation on the floor of the United States Senate. That same year he served as the Muslim representative at President Clinton's inaugural interfaith breakfast, which brought together leaders from a variety of religious faiths. In 1995 he was elected a president of the World Conference on Religion and Peace (he later became international president); attended, along with Martin Luther King III and Rosa Parks, the Acts of Kindness Week held in Dallas, Texas; and gave an address titled "How Do We Save Our Youth?" at an event hosted by representatives from *Forbes* magazine in Naples, Florida. In 1996 Mohammed met with Pope John Paul II at the Vatican. (The two leaders, along with the Dalai Lama, the political and spiritual leader of the Tibetan people, met again in 1999, when Mohammed addressed 100,000 people gathered in St. Peter's Square at the Vatican.) In November 1996, as a member of the Peace Council, Mohammed traveled to Chiapas, Mexico, to support the human-rights work of Bishop Samuel Ruiz Garcia by listening to the concerns of Zapatista rebels who were fighting for the autonomy of the region's indigenous peoples. In December, at the invitation of the Palestinian leader Yasir Arafat, Mohammed led a delegation of Muslim Americans to Jerusalem and areas of Palestine. Around that time he also established the Collective Purchasing Conference (CPC), an economic plan to develop poor communities by working toward the establishment of new businesses, affordable housing, and cultural centers. In 1997 President Clinton invited Mohammed to read from the Koran at the

Presidential Inauguration Day National Prayer Service. The following year Mohammed participated in the Conference on Religion and Peace held in Auschwitz, Poland.

In the late 1990s Farrakhan began to lead the NOI toward mainstream Islam, and in 2000 Farrakhan and Mohammed publicly embraced, declaring an end to their longstanding dispute. (Farrakhan's battle with and recovery from prostate cancer in 1999 reportedly led him to place greater emphasis on unity and less on racial separatism.) Referring to previous disagreements between himself and Farrakhan, Mohammed said, as quoted by the BBC (February 27, 2000), "Whatever has troubled us in the past, I think we can bury it now and never look back at that grave." Despite the thaw in relations, the NOI and the American Society of Muslims remain mostly separate. In addition, serious differences remain between black Muslims and nonblack, immigrant Muslims. (African-Americans constitute roughly 30 percent of all Muslims in the United States, but more than 80 percent of nonimmigrant Muslims; many African-Americans have come to the Islamic faith through black nationalist movements such as the NOI.)

In the spring of 2001, Mohammed was a featured speaker at an event, held in South Africa, commemorating 1,400 years of Islamic history on the African continent. Following the September 11, 2001 terrorist attacks on the United States, which led to growing suspicion and resentment of Islam in America, Mohammed continued his efforts to present the peaceful and tolerant version of Islam he had long represented. "Terrorism has no place in Islam, just as it has no place in Christianity or Judaism," he told Stan Swofford and Aulica Rutland for the Greensboro, North Carolina, *News & Record* (November 2, 2001). Along with Farrakhan and the televangelist Reverend Robert Schuller, Mohammed participated in the October 29, 2001 "Evening of Religious Solidarity," an event meant to foster understanding between Christians and Muslims. That same year he served as a consultant to the actor Mario Van Peebles, who portrayed Malcolm X in the movie *Ali* (2001). In 2002 Mohammed served as a panel member on the televised program *Where Do We Go from Here? Chaos or Community?*, a group discussion on the future of the African-American community; opened an office of community relations in Washington, D.C.; and, as international president of the World Council on Religion and Peace, participated in the Conference of Religious Leaders, a meeting held in Nairobi, Kenya, to address the devastation caused in Africa by the HIV/AIDS epidemic. Also in 2002, Mohammed was elected a member of the Martin Luther King Jr. Initial Board of Preachers, and a member of the advisory council for the international Timbuktu Educational Foundation, based in Oakland, California. In 2003 Mohammed and his ministry helped to found Bridges Television, a network focusing on the American Muslim community. Mohammed's ministry has partnered with the Muhammad Ali Community and Economic Development Corporation, an organization dedicated to improving the lives of underprivileged Chicago residents.

After Mohammed retired as official head of the American Society of Muslims, in 2003, he expressed frustration with some of the group's imams. "I have tried over the last 10 or 12 years to encourage them to get more religious education, but I have made no progress," he told Salim Muwakkil for the *Chicago Tribune* (September 16, 2003). "They want their followers just to obey them, but not question them or right their wrong deeds." Muslim leaders and outside observers have expressed concern that Mohammed's retirement could lead to a leadership crisis within the American Society of Muslims. Nevertheless, many American Muslims continue to regard Mohammed as a spiritual guide, and in September 2004 the Mosque Cares held a convention in Chicago to connect with faithful Muslims.

Mohammed has authored a number of books, including *The Teachings of W. D. Muhammad* (1976); *Prayer and Al-Islam* (1982); *Religion on the Line* (1983); *An African American Genesis* (1986); *Al-Islam Unity and Leadership* (1991); *Islam's Climate for Business Success* (1994); and *The Champion We Have in Common: The Dynamic African American Soul* (2002). He has appeared on television programs such as *Larry King Live, Tony Brown's Journal*, and *Gil Noble's Like It Is*, and has hosted a weekly television program broadcast in the Chicago area, *W. Deen Muhammad and Guests*. He has lectured at many colleges and universities around the country, among them Morehouse, Yale, Georgetown, Howard, Harvard, Columbia, Ford- ham, and Duke, as well as at such venues as Radio City Music Hall, Lincoln Center, and the Jacob Javitz Center, all in New York City. In both 1992 and 1993 President Hosni Mubarak of Egypt honored Mohammed with a gold medal in recognition of his religious work in the U.S. In 1994 Mohammed received the Cup of Compassion from the Hartford Seminary, in Hartford, Connecticut. The mayor of Harvey, Illinois, presented Mohammed with a key to that city in 2000. That same year the city of Louisville, Kentucky, honored Mohammed's leadership with a three-day, 25th- anniversary tribute. The mayor of Augusta, Georgia, declared March 13, 2003 "Imam W. Deen Mohammed Day."

## PERSONAL LIFE

Mohammed, a short, balding man with a gray beard, an easy smile, and a booming laugh. He lived in Chicago until his death in 2008.

## FURTHER READING

*American Journal of Islamic Social Sciences p245+ vol. 2, 1985; BBC (on-line) Feb. 27, 2000, with photos;*

*Miami Herald C pi Oct. 14, 1997, with photos; Muslim Journal (online); Nation of Islam Web site; New Africa Radio Web site; Peace Council Web site; Seattle Times A pl2 June 14, 1997, with photos; Encyclopedia of American Religion and Politics, 2003; Marsh, Clifton E. From Black Muslims to Muslims: The Transition from Separatism to Islam, 1930-1980, 1984; The Teachings of W. D. Muhammad, 1976; Prayer and Al-Islam, 1982; Religion on the Line, 1983; An African American Genesis, 1986; Al-Islam Unity and Leadership, 1991; Islam's Climate for Business Success, 1994; The Champion We Have in Common: The Dynamic African American Soul, 2002*

---

# JAMES T. MORRIS

## Executive Director of the United Nations World Food Program

**Born:** April 18, 1943; Terre Haute, Indiana
**Primary Field:** Hunger Relief
**Affiliation:** United Nations World Food Program

## INTRODUCTION

*According to the World Food Program (WFP), the single largest agency under the umbrella of the United Nations, 10 million deaths each year result from hunger and malnutrition—that is, more than 27,000 people die every day from a basic lack of food. Described on its official Web site as the U.N.'s "frontline agency in the fight against global hunger," the WFP has been supplying food aid to the world's most desperate regions since 1962. In 2002 James T. Morris, a former businessman and public servant, took a lead role in that humanitarian fight, becoming the WFP's 10th executive director. Speaking to Scott Olsen for the* Indianapolis (Indiana) Business Journal *(March 24, 2004), Peter Beering, a former business colleague of Morris's, praised him for his "coalition-building skills" and his "overall knowledge and appreciation of the world in which we live. He views the World Food Program as a calling." An editorial in the* Indianapolis Star *(July 3, 2004) stated that Morris had seized his role at the WFP "with the zeal of an evangelist and has brought new visibility and stature to the office." Concurrently with his duties at the helm of the WFP, Morris has served as U.N. secretary gen-*

*eral Kofi Annan's special envoy for humanitarian needs in Africa since July 2002.*

## EARLY LIFE

The only child of Kathlyne (nee Gastes) and Howard James Morris, James T. Morris was born in Terre Haute, Indiana, on April 18, 1943. He received a B.A. in political science from Indiana University, in Bloomington, in 1965, and an M.B.A. from Butler University, in Indianapolis, in 1970. In 1968 he entered the public sector, becoming chief of staff to then-mayor of Indianapolis Richard Lugar, who is now a member of the U.S. Senate and the current chairman of the Senate Foreign Relations Committee.

## LIFE'S WORK

In 1973 Morris became the director of community development for the Lilly Endowment Inc., one of the largest charitable organizations in the world. The Lilly foundation was established by members of the Lilly family—known for the large pharmaceutical business Eli Lilly and Co.—as a private philanthropic foundation in Indianapolis in 1937. It is dedicated to fostering community development and to enriching the religious lives of Christians—mostly through the education and support of young pastors—in the city of Indianapolis and beyond. In the more than 15 years he spent with the foundation, Morris held a series of ascending positions, including vice president for community development, executive vice president, and president, in which capacity he served the Lilly Endowment from 1985 to 1989.

Morris then became chairman and chief executive officer of IWC Resources Corp., which is in the water-utility services industry, and their primary subsidiary, the Indianapolis Water Co. With Morris guiding it, the IWC grew into a multimillion-dollar holding company with 2,500 employees. He attempted to diversify the company's personnel and increase educational opportunities for employees. He stepped down from his position in 2002, the year he took over for Catherine Bertini as the executive director of the WFP. (The U.N. secretary general and the director general of the U.N. Food and Agricultural Organization [FAO] jointly appoint the WFP executive director to a term of five years. The executive director is the head of the secretariat of the agency.) The WFP is headquartered in Rome, Italy. As the WFP head, Morris has met with many foreign leaders and has often spoken to both houses of the U.S. Congress on issues relating to world hunger.

Established in 1961 as a limited-term experimental program scheduled to begin work in 1963, the WFP was thrown into humanitarian action in 1962, earlier than planned, by natural disasters in Thailand and Iran and by the plight of millions of refugees settling in Algeria after it had achieved independence from France. Among its other humanitarian achievements in recent history, the WFP helped to save the lives of 18 million people in southern Africa following terrible droughts in 1992; saved 19 million flood victims in Bangladesh in 1998; and delivered then-record amounts of food to Ethiopia, Sudan, and other East African nations suffering from the effects of a severe drought in 2000. For funding, the agency relies almost entirely on voluntary contributions of cash, food, and supplies for growing, storing, or preparing food. Dozens of governments give money to the WFP every year; the United States is by far the largest donor, regularly accounting for around half of the organization's total annual contributions. In 2004 the WFP employed almost 11,000 people, 90 percent of whom worked in the field, delivering food and monitoring its allocation and use. The WFP has the largest budget of any U.N. agency or program but the lowest operational overhead.

The official WFP Web site lists a series of "hunger facts," which include the following bleak statistics: despite global production of enough food to nourish the world's entire human population, more than 800 million people do not have enough to eat; one of every three people in sub-Saharan Africa is hungry; about 520 million of the world's hungry live in Asia and the South Pacific; while the average American family spends 10 percent of its income on food, poor people spend more than 70 percent; 54 countries do not produce enough food to feed their own people; and hunger and malnutrition are the biggest threats to global health— they kill more people every year than HIV, malaria, and tuberculosis combined.

As a result of the World Food Program's work in Iraq, which has been ravaged by the U.S.-led invasion, begun in March 2003, and the subsequent rebel insurgency, the agency's funding and operations expanded considerably. It mounted the largest humanitarian operation in history, feeding 26 million Iraqis by distributing more than two million tons of food over a seven-month period. Also in 2003, the WFP's aid program to North Korea—which has been in place since 1995, following a famine that killed an estimated two million people— was suspended due to the North Korean government's refusal to allow donor nations to monitor how the WFP food aid was being dispersed. In June 2004 Morris visited several African nations, including Malawi, Mozambique, and Namibia, where he witnessed firsthand the widespread deprivation of millions of Africans who lack sufficient food or money and suffer from HIV infection. "What is happening in southern Africa absolutely represents the most serious humanitarian crisis in the world today," Morris told Craig Timberg for the *Washington Post* (June 23, 2004). As a prime example of the obstacles Morris and the WFP often face in their attempts to feed needy populations, the government of the southern African nation of Zimbabwe, led by President Robert Mugabe, has declined to meet with Morris, refuses to acknowledge the country's worsening food shortage, and will not accept WFP assistance. In June 2004 Morris also visited the Sudan, where marauding Arab militias have been attacking black African populations in the western region of Darfur. It is estimated that more than 1.8 million people have been displaced within the Sudan, and that more than 200,000 Sudanese have fled across the border into neighboring Chad. The situation for these refugees and displaced Sudanese is dire, as disease, the elements, and food shortages have decimated their ranks. In October 2004 the World Health Organization estimated that more than 70,000 Sudanese had died, mostly through starvation and disease, between March and October 2004. To gather evidence of the wide-scale suffering, Morris kept a journal in Darfur; parts of it appeared in the *Indianapolis Star* (June 6, 2004). Morris wrote, "We had been just two brief days in Darfur, but it was more than enough to show us something was desperately wrong. . . . The need for an immediate and dramatic reinforcement of the humanitarian effort was as clear as the starlit desert sky. . . . We owe it to our humanity not to leave these people to the militias, to the elements, to what for many will be a death sentence. We must act, and fast." Though there has been some degree of outcry against what is occurring in Darfur, the plight of the refugees has continued and the international community has done comparatively little to alleviate it.

Food shortages in sub-Saharan Africa are also greatly affected by AIDS; the disease, which is rampant in the region, is killing off adult foodproviding members of society, leaving millions of hungry orphaned children. (Timberg reported that there are 11 million AIDS orphans in the region.) Morris has often addressed the links between disease and hunger and the need to combat the spread of HIV/AIDS in Africa—a continent of special concern to him because he also serves as the U.N. special envoy for humanitarian needs in Africa. "When you see a country in southern Africa where a third of the adult population is infected by HIV/AIDS, these are things you just don't forget," Morris told Scott Olsen. (As Morris told the *Washington Times* [January 12, 2004], there are approximately 30 million HIV/AIDS cases in Africa.)

The 2004 Indian Ocean earthquake, which struck off the coast of Aceh Province, on the Indonesian island of Sumatra, set off a series of tsunamis in the region that wreaked devastation on scores of Indian Ocean coastal communities; some tsunamis traveled as far as the eastern coast of Africa. The combined damage from the earthquake and tsunamis made the event one of the deadliest disasters in modern history. In the immediate aftermath of the disaster, the WFP was able to provide food from stocks already in place in Indonesia and Sri Lanka, as well as bring in new supplies by air, land, and sea. With help from governments, corporations, and individuals, the WFP distributed more than 4,000 metric tons (4,400 tons) of food within the first month—primarily rice, fortified biscuits, and noodles—in the hard-hit regions of Indonesia, the Maldives, and Sri Lanka, among others. The organization quickly drafted a six-month plan to bring aid to two million people, at a cost of $256 million. Early estimates held that some 169,0 metric tons (185,900 tons) of food would be needed for

crucial assistance. In a January 6, 2005, press release, Morris remarked, "WFP food will help with the immediate needs of those who have lost family members, houses and livelihoods. But as they gradually get back on their feet, this six- month operation will shift its focus from ending their immediate hunger to sustaining families while they revive their farmland, repair their fishing boats and communities. We can give them the chance to provide for their future once again."

In his speech at the World Conference on Disaster Reduction, Morris outlined the agency's plans to improve its emergency response system. About 80 percent of the WFP's efforts go to responding to emergencies; about half of that, or 40 percent of the total, go toward helping those affected by natural disasters. Morris took the opportunity to praise the generous outpouring of contributions from the international community after the tsunamis: "This tremendous disaster," he explained, "has ignited the single element that has been missing from past humanitarian relief efforts: empathy. For the first time, the mass media, international travel and the internet—three accessories of globalization— converged to make this a truly global crisis, in which we all shared." He added, however, that for the WFP, which plans to assist some 73 million people in 2005, the survivors of the terrible damage of the 2004 tsunami constitute only a portion of those in need. "Let me issue one word of warning. Emergencies seize our attention. We get swept up in the whirlwind of the media coverage. . . . But the truth is that those who die of hunger or HIV/AIDS rarely die in these kinds of emergencies. They die quietly in poor communities devastated by poverty in Bangladesh, Peru, and southern Africa. Every week, hunger claims as many lives as have been lost in the Indian Ocean tsunami. The chronic hunger and malnutrition that afflicts 300 million children worldwide does not create the dramatic media coverage of a tsunami, but it causes far greater suffering. We cannot afford to lose sight of that fact."

In the second half of 2005, the WFP was again grappling with a major food crisis brought on by a natural disaster, this time a massive earthquake in South Asia on October 8 that, as of a few weeks later, was estimated to have killed 78,000 people and to have left an estimated 3.3 million people homeless. Like the crisis that followed the tsunami, the earthquake crossed national borders, affecting parts of Pakistan, Afghanistan, India, and the disputed region of Kashmir; unlike the earlier disaster, the earthquake affected many areas that

---

## Affiliation: World Food Program (WFP)

The WFP is the largest humanitarian agency in the world. As reported on the program's Web site, on any given day the WFP has 20 planes in the air; 5,000 trucks on the road; and 40 ships at sea delivering food aid to the world's hungry and poor. (Common forms of WFP food aid are sugar, salt, bread, beans, wheat, and rice. Ninety percent of WFP food aid is delivered to target areas by ship.) In the last 40 years the program has fed more than 1.2 billion people. Following the U.S.-led invasion of Iraq in 2003, Morris helped coordinate the WFP's feeding of an estimated 26 million Iraqis, the largest humanitarian operation in history. Including its mission in Iraq, in 2004 the WFP fed more than 110 million people—mostly refugees and others displaced by war—in 80 countries by delivering 5.1 million metric tons (5.6 million tons, in U.S. measure) of food.

In late 2004 and into 2005 the WFP grappled with another humanitarian crisis of immense proportions—the December 26 Indian Ocean earthquake, which struck off the northwest coast of Sumatra and generated powerful tsunamis that inflicted devastation to numerous regions along the rim of the Indian Ocean. The disaster left an estimated 250,000 dead and more than one million displaced. The WFP has been one of the major suppliers of relief to the region. By July 2005 the organization had distributed 123,000 metric tons (136,000 U.S. tons) of food to more than two million people, and had begun a series of projects designed to help the many areas affected by the disaster to make a successful long-term recovery. As Morris pointed out not long after the disaster hit, the strength of the WFP's response was partially a result of how swiftly it was able to act. At the World Conference on Disaster Reduction in Kobe, Japan, on January 19, 2005, Morris told the audience, as reprinted on the WFP Web site, "We have already reached most of the people in the most critical need, giving them a ration sufficient for two weeks. No tsunami survivor should die from hunger or malnutrition. We can be proud of that."

A major difficulty facing Morris and the WFP is that world hunger cannot be eradicated simply with more food; it is inextricably tied to other scourges, such as poverty, disease, and political and economic despotism. Indeed, failed economic policies, natural disasters, political and ethnic violence, and AIDS and other diseases are continually creating new populations without enough to eat. Trying to battle such deleterious forces, the WFP finds itself underfunded and unable to help all those in need. "We are losing the battle against hunger," Morris stated in his testimony before the U.S. Senate Foreign Relations Committee on February 25, 2003. "Never before have we had to contend with potential starvation on the scale we face today. . . . The greatest threat to life remains what it was a hundred years ago, five hundred years ago, a thousand years ago—it is hunger."

---

were extremely remote, making the humanitarian relief efforts of the WFP and other organizations much more difficult. "We had never ever had [a] logistical challenge like this," Morris told a group of reporters, according to Chisaki Watanabe for the Associated Press (October 25, 2005). "People are so difficult to reach. People are so far away from accessibility."

In addition to his work with the WFP, Morris has volunteered his services as treasurer to the United States Olympic Committee and chairman of its audit and ethics committee, and as a member of the board of governors of the American Red Cross. Morris has worked with many other nonprofit and educational organizations and institutions, including Butler University; Christian Theological Seminary, in Indianapolis; the Haskell Indiana College Foundation; Indiana State University, in Terre Haute; the Indiana Pacer Foundation; the NCAA Foundation; the Rose Hulman Institute of Technology, in Terre Haute; and the United Way of Central Indiana. His considerable contributions and dedication to his home state include service as president of the board of trustees at Indiana University and co-chairman of the Indianapolis Campaign for Healthy Babies. Morris also founded the Indiana Sports Corporation and Youthlinks Indiana.

### PERSONAL LIFE
Morris and his wife, Jacqueline Harrell Morris, have three children and six grandchildren. After his first year with the WFP Morris told Olsen, "What I am doing right now is very fulfilling. I suspect I've had the greatest year of personal growth in my life."

**FURTHER READING**
*Indianapolis Star E p3 June 6, 2004, E p3 June 13, 2004; United Nations Web site; U.S. Senate Web site;* *Washington Post A pi7 June 23, 2004; Washington Times A pl9 Jan. 12, 2004; World Food Program Web site*

# GREG MORTENSON

## Humanitarian; Writer

**Born:** December 27, 1957; St. Cloud, Minnesota
**Primary Field:** Worldwide Education Reform
**Affiliation:** Central Asia Institute; Pennies for Peace

### INTRODUCTION

*A wrong turn that Greg Mortenson took in 1992, at the age of 34—while descending K2, the second-highest peak on Earth—led to a radical change in the direction of his life. Within months of his experience on the mountain, he had abandoned his career as an emergency-room nurse and taken the first steps toward what became his new profession—that of co-founder and director of the Central Asia Institute (CAI). Since 1996 the CAI has raised money for and/or completed the construction of approximately 130 schools serving tens of thousands of children, most of them in poverty-stricken Muslim villages in remote parts of northern Pakistan and Afghanistan. The CAI has also funded and overseen other community-based projects in those areas as well as in Kyrgyzstan and Mongolia, primarily with the aim of educating girls and women and shrinking the influence of the fundamentalist religious organization known as the Taliban.*

*For six years beginning in 1996, the Taliban, whose members belong to the Sunni branch of Islam, ruled most of Afghanistan, albeit unofficially; it was ousted from power by U.S.-led forces, who invaded in late 2001 in response to the September 11 terrorist attacks on the U.S. The Taliban has since regained strongholds in Afghanistan and taken over parts of Pakistan, all the while ruthlessly attempting to expunge Western culture from the region. One of the Taliban's principal beliefs is that no female should be formally educated; during the years that the group virtually ruled Afghanistan, it outlawed the schooling of girls and women, and in the past few years, members of the Taliban have destroyed hundreds of schools, including boys' schools that did not adhere to a strict Sunni Muslim curriculum. Mortenson firmly believes that the only way to defeat the Taliban in*

*the long run, and in the process change the societies in which it flourishes, is through the widespread education of girls in schools whose curricula include the promotion of basic human rights (as spelled out, for example, in the United Nations' Universal Declaration of Human Rights). Women educated along those lines, Mortenson contends, would not willingly agree to their sons' becoming suicide bombers, as the mothers of many Taliban bombers have, and they would not support their attacking others simply because of religious differences. Mortenson's ideas are based both on his observations during many visits to Afghanistan and Pakistan and on research showing that educating girls to at least the fifth-grade level leads to measurable improvements in the standard of living of the societies in which those girls become adults.*

*Mortenson's life and work are the subjects of the award-winning book* Three Cups of Tea *(2006), cowritten by David Oliver Relin, which as of October 25, 2009 had been on the* New York Times *paperbacks best-seller list for 141 weeks. Mortenson "has become a legend in the [Afghanistan-Pakistan border] region, his picture sometimes dangling like a talisman from rearview mirrors," and he "has done more to advance U.S. interests in the region than the entire military and foreign policy apparatus of the administration" of President George W. Bush, Nicholas Kristof wrote in his* New York Times *(July 13, 2008) column. "Mortenson's efforts remind us what the essence of the 'war on terrorism' is about," another* Times *columnist, Thomas L. Friedman, wrote for the July 19, 2009 edition of that paper, after witnessing Mortenson and Mike Mullen, the chairman of the Joint Chiefs of Staff, celebrate the opening of a new school in Afghanistan earlier that week. "It's about the war of ideas within Islam—a war between religious zealots who glorify martyrdom and want to keep Islam untouched by modernity and isolated from other faiths, with its women disempowered, and those who want to embrace modernity, open Islam to new ideas and empower Muslim women as much as men. America's invasions of Iraq and Afghanistan were, in part, an ef-*

*fort to create the space for the Muslim progressives to fight and win so that the real engine of change, something that takes nine months and 21 years to produce—a new generation—can be educated and raised differently."*

Mortenson's honors include the Golden Piton Award for humanitarian effort, from Climbing *magazine (2003), the Free Spirit Award, from the National Press Club (2004), and the Dayton Literary Peace Prize (2007). He has also received honorary doctoral degrees from 10 colleges and universities.*

---

## Affiliation: Pennies for Peace

Pennies for Peace is a program sponsored by Central Asia Institute, in which school children in the United States raise pennies to help fund CAI's educational projects. The program focuses on raising cross-cultural awareness through education to promote peace. Pennies for Peace was launched by CAI executive director Greg Mortenson to help broaden students' awareness of the developing world, and teach them about their capacities to be philanthropists by raising funds to cover costs of such as paper, pencils, books, uniforms and desks for students in remote northern Pakistan and Afghanistan. By 2012, Pennies for Peace had raised over 16 million pennies generated by more than 700 schools across the United States.

---

## EARLY LIFE

Of Norwegian ancestry, Greg Mortenson was born on December 27, 1957 in St. Cloud, Minnesota, the oldest child and only boy among the four children of Irvin "Dempsey" Mortenson and Jerene Mortenson. He has two married sisters, Kari and Sonja. His third sister, Christa, who was 11 years his junior, became mentally disabled and epileptic after she was stricken with meningitis in early childhood; a severe attack of epilepsy ended her life in 1992. When Greg was three months old, his parents settled in the part of East Africa now known as Tanzania, where they had taken teaching jobs. The family lived in a village on the remote Usambara Mountains and later in Moshi, a town at the base of Mount Kilimanjaro, Africa's tallest mountain. Mortenson's parents were Lutheran missionaries who "wore their faith lightly," in his words, and were more interested in helping to improve education and health care among the local people than in proselytizing. Mortenson's father spent a decade raising funds to establish the nation's first teaching hospital, the Kilimanjaro Christian Medical Centre, which opened in 1971. In 1969 Jerene Mortenson founded the Moshi International School, which currently has 300 students from more than 28 countries. Early on Greg Mortenson displayed sympathy for the poor and disadvantaged. His mother recalled to Karin Ronnow for the *Bozeman (Montana) Daily Chronicle* (October 7, 2007) that one day when Greg was a toddler, she found him outside their house, chatting with an old beggar and handing the man cookies from a jar. The little boy "didn't just give him something, they were talking," she said. "And that just sums

up how Greg has been all his life." Mortenson learned to speak Swahili and grew up without television.

At age 11 he climbed to the summit of Mount Kilimanjaro with his father. Though the exertion and thin air made him sick—"I was gagging and puking all the way to the top," he told Terry Gross for the National Public Radio series *Fresh Air* (February 7, 2002, on-line)—the experience sparked in him a passion for mountaineering.

When Greg was 15 the Mortensons returned to the U.S. and settled in St. Paul, Minnesota. In Ramsey High School, in Roseville, a St. Paul suburb, Greg felt like an outsider and was subjected to taunts and ridicule from his peers. He played football and was adept at languages, math, and science. Heeding the advice of his parents, he enlisted in the U.S. Army four days after his graduation, to help pay for college. (The army paid monthly education benefits to eligible veterans.) For two years beginning in 1975, Mortenson served as a field medic in Bamberg, Germany; in his leisure time he traveled to other cities in Europe. He earned the Army Commendation Medal for his prowess in evacuating soldiers in a live-fire exercise. In 1977 he enrolled at Concordia College, in Moorhead, Minnesota, on a football scholarship; during his two years there, his team won the National Association of Intercollegiate Athletics Division II football championship. He left Concordia to attend the University of South Dakota (USD) at Vermillion. Soon afterward his father was diagnosed with cancer. Every other weekend until his father's death, in mid-1981, Mortenson drove to his parents' home to help care for him; the round-trip commute took 12 hours. Mortenson earned a B.A. degree in chemistry and an associate's degree in nursing in 1983. He next worked as an emergency-room nurse in South Dakota hospitals, in places including the Pine Ridge Indian Reservation. He moved to Indianapolis, Indiana, in 1985, and the next year he entered a master's-degree program in medical neuroscience at the University of Indiana Medical School, with the goal of finding a cure for epilepsy; after realizing that he did not want to devote the years to that pursuit that it would probably entail, he left the school, without earning the degree. For much of 1988 he lived in Minnesota with his sister Christa, with whom he had always remained close. Then he moved to San Francisco, California, where he worked as a trauma nurse and spent his free time mountaineering.

## LIFE'S WORK

Christa's death, on the morning of her 23d birthday, devastated Mortenson. Seeking to honor her memory, he joined a 12-person expedition to climb K2, which lies within the Karakoram Mountains on the border of Pakistan and China; at 28,251 feet, K2 is less than 800 feet shorter than Earth's highest peak, Mount Everest. Mortenson hoped to leave Christa's amber necklace at the summit of K2, which is notorious for the fearsome hazards it presents to climbers; nearly one in four people have reportedly died in the attempt to conquer it. (Five members of Mortenson's expedition did not survive the climb.) Mortenson spent nearly four months on K2 and had come within 2,000 feet of the top when he lost his way and was forced to turn back. (That mishap occurred after he became separated from his climbing partner; Mortenson had helped another member of his party who had become incapacitated from altitude sickness.) By chance he wandered into Korphe, a tiny, impoverished Pakistani farming village 10,000 feet above sea level in the Karakorams. By that time Mortenson weighed 30 pounds less than he had before the climb, and he felt sick as well as overwhelmingly disheartened by his failure to achieve his goal; he was also bedraggled and filthy, having not showered for many weeks. Haji Ali, the chief of Korphe, and other peasants helped the physically and mentally exhausted Mortenson recuperate in their homes. Mortenson was amazed by their generosity and the strenuousness of the work that enabled them to live in such a difficult environment. He was also saddened by their extreme poverty: they suffered malnutrition, a high rate of infant mortality, chronic infections, and other problems linked to a poor diet and lack of access to modern methods of medicine and hygiene. During his three weeks in Korphe, Mortenson made use of

his nursing skills to set broken bones and stitch wounds, and he supplied aspirin and antibiotics to grateful villagers, who took to calling him "Dr. Greg."

Korphe was too poor to build a school or hire a full-time teacher, not least because corrupt local officials regularly pocketed government money allocated for education. Nevertheless, whenever possible, children gathered in the open air to study-even on days when frost covered the ground—with or without the help of a part-time instructor. When Mortenson saw children working on arithmetic by marking the earth with sticks or writing on slates with mud, he felt as if his "heart was being torn out," he told David Relin. "There was a fierceness in their desire to learn, despite how mightily everything was stacked against them, that reminded me of Christa. I knew I had to do something." Mortenson impulsively promised Haji Ali that he would come back and build a school in Korphe.

Back home in California in late 1993, Mortenson set about raising the $12,000 he and village leaders had estimated it would cost to build a five-room schoolhouse for 100 students up to the fifth-grade level. To save money he sold most of his possessions and gave up his apartment, living out of his car for a while. Using a rented typewriter, he painstakingly typed a few letters asking for contributions. Then, by chance, a Pakistani shopkeeper taught him how to use a computer, and he quickly printed 580 letters and sent them to people he knew and wealthy celebrities. Among his few responses was only one from a famous person: a check for $100 from the NBC broadcast journalist Tom Brokaw, a fellow USD graduate. Soon afterward, at the suggestion of his mother, he gave a talk about his project to pupils at the Westside Elementary School in River Falls, Wisconsin, where his mother was the principal. He later received $623.45 in pennies from the children. (Pennies for Peace, which he founded in 1995, grew out of that experience; it is now an arm of CAI.) Thanks to a doctor at the hospital where he was working, a story about him and his project was published in the newsletter of the American Himalayan Foundation in 1994. The article attracted the attention of the Swiss-born Silicon Valley inventor and entrepreneur Jean Hoerni, an avid mountaineer who had climbed in the Karakorams. Hoerni sent Mortenson a check for $12,000, along with a note reading, "Don't screw up."

In the fall of 1994, Mortenson returned to Pakistan to fulfill his promise, only to discover that before the school could be built, a bridge would have to be erected over the nearby Braldu River, so that the materials and equipment necessary for construction could be transported to the town. (The existing bridge, made of yak hair, was not strong enough for that purpose.) Mortenson flew back to California, secured funding for the bridge from Hoerni, and then returned to Korphe. Built with local labor, the 282-foot suspension bridge was completed in eight weeks. Meanwhile, realizing the importance of forming personal relationships and respecting local Pakistani mores, Mortenson had learned the language (a dialect of Urdu) spoken in Baltistan, that area of Pakistan. He worked to familiarize himself with the local culture and began to pray in the Islamic tradition.

During a trip back to the States in 1995, Mortenson attended a benefit dinner for the American Himalayan Foundation with Hoerni. There, he met Tara Bishop, the daughter of Barry Bishop, a National Geographic Society photographer who had climbed Mount Everest; Mortenson and Tara married six days later. Around that time Hoerni offered to donate $1 million to endow a nonprofit organization that would be set up to fund projects in Pakistan and Afghanistan. Mortenson became the director of that organization, the Central Asia Institute; his office was in the basement of the house he and Bishop had moved into. Hoerni saw a photo of the school, construction of which was completed in late 1996, shortly before his death, in January 1997. His will included provisions pertaining to CAI's endowment. The school admitted its first students in mid-1997; Mortenson, his wife, and their six-month-old daughter, Amira, attended the opening. In the next few years, with funding from the CAI, Mortenson and the residents of other impoverished villages were able to work more quickly to address the needs of youngsters and women in the region. By 1999 the CAI had undertaken the building of 11 schools, the installations of six potable-water systems, and the establishment of two women's vocational-training centers, and had launched a series of environmental-education workshops for teachers.

Though Mortenson's work was not politically motivated, it had significant political implications in the turbulent regions in which he was working. After the Soviet Union lost control of Afghanistan, in 1989, the Taliban began to recruit members from poor and uneducated mountain villagers in Afghanistan and near its border with Pakistan, attracting them with the promise of jobs. In 1996, when the Taliban in effect gained control of Afghanistan, females were banned from attending school and hundreds of radical Islamic religious schools, called madrassas, were opened. Mortenson came to see education as the key to providing children with the possibility of bettering their lives, improving societies as a whole, and preventing terrorism, "I've learned that Terror doesn't happen because some group of people somewhere like Pakistan or Afghanistan simply decide to hate us," Mortenson told members of Congress, as quoted by Richard A. Kauffman in the *Christian Century* [July 29, 2008). "It happens because children aren't being offered a bright enough future that they have a reason to choose life over death." Moreover, he concluded that educating girls is even more important than educating boys, in part because whereas young men often leave their villages and move to larger towns and cities once they finish school, women tend to stay in their communities and use their knowledge to improve the quality of life there. In addition, Mortenson has pointed out, the Koran stipulates that men must ask permission from their mothers before they can engage in jihad, whether militant or not. ("Jihad," which means "struggle" in Arabic, refers both to an individual's attempts to live according to the tenets of Islam and to an individual's or group's efforts to spread Islam to nonbelievers and increase the amount of territory ruled by Muslims. In the West "jihad" is usually interpreted to mean "holy war.") "When women have an education they're much less likely to condone their sons getting into violence," Mortenson told Sue Corbett for the *Miami (Florida) Herald* (January 24, 2009).

Earlier, in the midst of construction of the school in Korphe, Mortenson's activities had provoked suspicion among local Pakistani village leaders and mullahs (men educated in Islamic law and theology), who feared that he intended to incite youngsters to challenge Islamic traditions. In August 1996 Mortenson was kidnapped while traveling in Peshawar, a city in Pakistan's mountainous Waziristan region, on the Afghan border. During the eight days that he was held prisoner, he earned his kidnappers' trust by showing respect for Islamic culture: he requested a Koran and a translator, prayed, and told his captors that his wife was pregnant with his firstborn son. (Mortenson knew that to them, a firstborn son was considered more important than a daughter.) When he was released (he had been used as a bargaining chip in a tribal dispute), his kidnappers gave him a handful of coins to help fund his school-building efforts.

Mortenson has also been the target of two fatwas (rulings by Muslim scholars or clerics that hold the weight of official law) to prevent him from building schools; one came from Shiite and the other from Sunni scholars, and both were retracted after pressure by locals. The first was issued in 1997 by a local official who objected to Mortenson's efforts to educate Pakistani girls. In response to that fatwa, Mortenson contacted the Pakistani Shiite Islamic leader Said Abas Resvi and appealed to the Supreme Islamic Council, in Kholm, Iran. During the next year or so, the council dispatched "spies" to CAI's school sites to determine the extent of Western influence in the curriculum and to ask questions about Mortenson's intentions and behavior while he was working in Pakistan: Did he drink alcohol? Did he seduce Muslim women? The answers to those and other questions were no. In April 1998 the council sent word to Mortenson that they had ruled that his work "follows the highest principles of Islam" and granted him their permission to continue it. After earning that judgment the CAI received an increase in proposals from local village leaders to build schools for both boys and girls.

On September 11, 2001 Mortenson was in a village near the Pakistan-Afghanistan border, opening a new school. He learned about the attacks on the World Trade Center and Washington, D.C., about eight hours after they occurred, "Immediately , . . there was an outpouring of sympathy," he told Terry Gross. "I met with Islamic leaders in prayer sessions and they, without exception, told me that this was not in accordance with Islam and that these were terrorists. Village army commanders, village chiefs, children, women—they embraced me. . . . What I saw and felt over the next two months certainly didn't reflect what I saw in the press when I came back here to the States." When Mortenson returned to Montana, he received hate mail accusing him of "helping the enemy" and wishing for his "painful death." Speaking of those who made such accusations, Mortenson told Stephanie Yap for the *Singapore Strait Times* (January 27, 2008), "They are ignorant and they don't understand complex issues. Terrorism is based on fear, peace is based on hope. The real enemy, really, is ignorance."

An article about Mortenson in *Parade* magazine (April 6, 2003) by David Oliver Relin, a journalist who had traveled with him, brought a lot of attention to the CAI. Donations increased manyfold, and Mortenson, now seen as someone with a unique perspective on conditions in Afghanistan and Pakistan, was invited to testify before lawmakers on Capitol Hill and military

planners at the Pentagon. He presented his case for investing in education in the region rather than depending solely or mostly on military strategies. Mary Bono Clark, a Republican congresswoman from California, became one of his most vocal supporters. Mortenson has also argued in favor of forthrightly acknowledging the thousands of civilian casualties that have resulted from American military activities in Pakistan and Afghanistan and compensating the victims and their families. "By disavowing or denying the casualties," Mortenson told Gross, "what's happened has caused a schism and put up a wall instead of a bridge between us and the people there."

*Three Cups of Tea*, told from Relin's perspective, was subtitled (despite Mortenson's strong objections) *One Man's Mission to Fight Terrorism One School at a Time* when it was published in hardcover, in 2006. The title refers to traditions in Korphe and other parts of northeastern Pakistan that Haji Ali had described to Mortenson: "Here, we drink three cups of tea to do business," he said. "The first you are a stranger, the second you become a friend, and the third, you join our family, and for our family we are prepared to do anything— even die." The book sold sluggishly until the paperback edition arrived, the following year, with the subtitle Mortenson preferred: *One Man's Mission to Promote Peace One School at a Time*. The book appeared on the *New York Times* paperbacks best-seller list on February 17, 2007 and has remained there ever since. *Three Cups of Tea* was named *Time's* Asia Book of the Year in 2006 and the Pacific Northwest Booksellers Association Nonfiction Book of the Year in 2007, and it won the 2007 Kiriyama Prize for nonfiction, from the organization Pacific Rim Voices, among several other awards. A picture book based on *Three Cups of Tea*, called *Listen to the Wind*, and a young- readers' version of *Three Cups of Tea*, adapted by Sarah Thomson from the original book, were published in 2009. The latter contains a foreword by the celebrated primatologist, conservationist, and United Nations messenger for peace Jane Goodall and a section in which Mortenson's daughter, Amira, answered questions about herself and her experiences during trips with her father to Afghanistan and Pakistan. Amira and her father have occasionally given talks together about CAI and its offshoot, Pennies for Peace, which by 2008 had raised about $30,000 from children in 3,000 schools to support CAI's work. In March 2009 Mortenson received Pakistan's highest civil award, the Sitara-e- Pakistan (Star of Pakistan) Award, for his humanitarian efforts. A follow-up to *Three Cups of Tea*, entitled *Stones into Schools: Promoting Peace with Books, Not Bombs, in Afghanistan and Pakistan*, was scheduled for publication in December 2009. For that book, which will recount Mortenson's ongoing efforts in Afghanistan and Pakistan, he worked with ghostwriters. (His relationship with his previous co-author, David Oliver Relin, reportedly ended unamicably.)

## PERSONAL LIFE

Mortenson, whom Nicholas Kristof described as a "frumpy, genial man," is, "by his own admission, chronically disorganized and awkward in front of crowds," Simon Houpt wrote for the Toronto, Canada, *Globe and Mail* (March 21, 2009). Scrupulously careful and thrifty with CAI's funds, Mortenson hires CAI staff reluctantly. CATs board of directors is made up entirely of educators who have traveled or lived in Pakistan and/or Afghanistan. No volunteers work for CAI, mainly for security reasons but also because Mortenson is wary of the motives of would-be volunteers. (Many people, he has found, want only to experience something new for two or three months.) His permanent home and office are in Bozeman, Montana, where he lives with his wife, daughter, and son, Khyber (named after Pakistan's Khyber Pass], who was born in 2000.

## FURTHER READING

*Bozeman (Montana) Daily Chronicle (on-line) Apr. 13, 2009; Central Asia Institute Web site: Christian Century p35 July 29, 2008; Fresh Air (on-line) Feb. 7, 2002; Good Housekeeping p142+ June 2009; Miami Herald E p6 Jan. 24, 2009; (Toronto, Canada) Globe and Mail R p9 Mar. 21, 2009; Washington Post C p12 Feb. 11, 2009; Mortenson, Greg, and David Oliver Relin. Three Cups of Tea, 2006; Three Cups of Tea: One Man's Mission to Promote Peace One School at a Time (with David Oliver Relin), 2006; Stones into Schools: Promoting Peace with Books, Not Bombs, in Afghanistan and Pakistan, 2009*

---

# ROBERT P. MOSES

## Educator; Activist

**Born:** January 23, 1935; Harlem, New York
**Primary Field:** Civil Rights & Economic Equality
**Affiliation:** Algebra Project

## INTRODUCTION

*A hero of the American civil rights movement of the 1960s, Robert P. Moses is the creator of the Algebra Project, an unusual and highly effective program of school reform that aims to increase middle- school students' chances for academic success and, consequently, lifelong economic prosperity. In his book* Radical Equations: Math Literacy and Civil Rights *(2001), which he co-wrote with Charles E. Cobb Jr., Moses explained that the lessons he learned as a civil rights activist about empowerment, problem solving, and organizing underlie the philosophy and pedagogical tactics of the Algebra Project. In the early 1960s Moses, then commonly known as Bob, led the Mississippi voter-registration project organized by the Student Nonviolent Coordinating Committee (SNCC, pronounced "snick"). Despite considerable—-and sometimes violent—opposition from whites, he and his fellow activists refused* *to end SNCC's efforts to increase the number of blacks on Mississippi voting rolls, and he gained a reputation for fearlessness, strong leadership, and quiet strength. "Moses pioneered an alternative style of leadership from the princely church leader that King epitomized," the civil rights historian Taylor Branch told Julia Cass for* Mother Jones *(May/June 2002, on-line). "He was the thoughtful, self- effacing loner. He is really the father of grassroots organizing—not the Moses summoning his people on the mountaintop as King did, but, ironically, the anti-Moses, going door-to-door, listening to people, letting them lead." He later turned his attention to protesting the Vietnam War. After he was drafted into the military, he fled the U.S. He worked as a schoolteacher in Tanzania for half a dozen years before he returned to the States.*

*Moses, who had taught math in the U.S. in the late 1950s, founded the Algebra Project in 1982, with the goal of teaching algebra to poor, predominantly minority children by the time they reached eighth grade. In Moses's system, math problems are expressed in vernacular English and made applicable to the students' lives. Skeptics predicted that the program would not work, because, they implied, the youngsters he was target-*

*ing had little interest in learning, but Moses has proven them wrong. Since its inception the Algebra Project has helped thousands of students improve their academic performance. The program currently serves roughly 10,000 students annually in 28 cities across the country and involves more than 300 teachers. "Like sharecroppers demanding the right to vote 40 years ago, students will have to demand education from those in power," Moses told an interviewer for 4word (June 2001, online). "Math literacy is a civil right. Just as black people in Mississippi saw the vote as a tool to elevate them into the first class politically, math is the tool to elevate the young into the first class economically." He also said, "Change can't just come from the top, it must come from communities of people who organize to make demands, and in the process transform themselves." In a conversation with Alexis Jetter for the New York Times Magazine (February 21, 1993), Moses's longtime friend the Reverend James P. Breeden, who is also a civil rights activist and educator, said, "Bob combines Calvinist, absolute certainty with a deep commitment to democracy and poor folks. He can be the most charming, open guy you'll ever want to meet or a totally inside-himself,*

*enigmatic mystic. But one rarely runs into such an implacable being." Moses won a MacArthur Foundation "genius" grant in 1982.*

## EARLY LIFE

Robert Parris Moses was born on January 23, 1935 in Harlem, a section of New York City, and grew up in a public housing project there. His father had a low-paying job as a security guard at the historic 369th Regiment Armory, in Harlem. "He and my mother scrimped and saved to ensure that my brothers and I would get ahead," Moses is quoted as saying in William Heath's novelistic biography *The Children Bob Moses Led* (1995), which includes Moses's reminiscences and many factual references to his life and work. "The stress and strain took their toll: my mother once suffered a minor breakdown, and my father would sometimes slip into fantasies that his name was not Gregory Moses but Gary Cooper—a man brave enough, in spite of his cowardly town, to stand up for what was right." Thanks to his high score on a special entrance exam, Moses was admitted to Stuyvesant High School, a New York City public school known for its excellent mathematics and

---

### Affiliation: Algebra Project

A nonprofit corporation, the project currently operates with an annual budget of $2.5 million and employs 22 people full-time. The Algebra Project is built around the idea that youngsters will be more excited about math if it is applied to everyday life and taught in everyday language. In one exercise, the notion of negative and positive integers is conveyed by means of a field trip; from a designated starting point, the students walk in one direction, retrace their steps, and then walk in the opposite direction. Upon returning to the classroom, the youngsters are asked to assign negative and positive numbers to the places where they stopped on their outing. Another technique teaches ratios through African drumming. The results of such pedagogic methods have been striking.

According to Amelia Newcomb in the Christian Science Monitor (April 12, 2001, online), researchers at Lesley College, in Cambridge, Massachusetts, found that 92 percent of Algebra Project graduates in Cambridge had enrolled in upper-level math courses in ninth grade—a percentage twice as great as that in a control group of their local peers. Test scores among

students in the project have shot up, while the number of students being sent to detention and dropping out has fallen substantially.

Educators across the country have praised Moses and his program. Speaking with Newcomb, Freeman A. Hrabowski III, an African-American mathematician who is the president of the University of Maryland, Baltimore County, said, "The most important thing the Algebra Project shows is that kids from all backgrounds can succeed in math. It bridges the culture of the child and the world of math." "Each one, teach one," an Algebra Project motto, conveys Moses's conviction that, as 4word quoted him as saying, "there is a way that young people reach young people, are able to touch each other, that in my view is central to the future shape of the Algebra Project. It is not about simply transferring a body of knowledge to children, it is about using that knowledge as a tool to a much larger end. Young people in Mississippi changed the country. Now we are asking young people to step out into a different way of seeing themselves."

---

science programs. In his senior year he was elected president of his class.

After graduating from Stuyvesant, in 1952, Moses attended Hamilton College, in Clinton, New York, on a scholarship; he majored in philosophy and French. Thanks to one of his French professors, he began reading works by the humanist philosopher and writer Albert Camus; by his own account, Camus's ideas influenced him profoundly. In *The Children Bob Moses Led*, he was quoted as saying that during this period he "began asking hard political questions: 'Can revolution be humane?' 'Can the "victim" overthrow the "executioner" without assuming his office?'" For a time Moses belonged to a group of Pentecostal Christians at Hamilton; on weekends he would travel with them to New York City's Times Square to preach. When Moses told his father that he was thinking of becoming a preacher, as his grandfather had been, his father successfully dissuaded him, telling him, as Moses recalled for *The Children Bob Moses Led*, "That's not just any job. You've got to be called." As an undergraduate Moses traveled elsewhere as well; one summer, impressed by the Quakers' pacifist philosophy, he attended an American Friends Service Committee international work camp in France. The following year he went to Japan to help build wooden steps for juvenile residents of a mental hospital. By the time he earned a bachelor's degree at Hamilton, in 1956, Moses had become committed to the ideas of nonviolence and leadership through example.

## LIFE'S WORK

After completing college Moses began graduate study in philosophy at Harvard University, in Cambridge, Massachusetts. He earned an M.A. degree in 1957 and then started working toward his Ph.D. But the abstract aspects of that discipline increasingly troubled him. "I tired of thinking about thinking and the meaning of meaning," he explained, as quoted in *The Children Bob Moses Led*. "In that remote realm of tautologies, indexes, and surds, I was in danger of forgetting that the meaning of life was no abstract speculation but my immediate and concrete concern." In the spring of 1958, Moses's mother died of cancer, and his distraught father had to be hospitalized for months. Moses cut his studies short and returned to New York City, where he found work teaching junior-high-level math at the Horace Mann School, an elite private school in the Riverdale section of the Bronx. At around this time he became increasingly aware of the civil rights movement, reading

in the *New York Times* about the first sit-ins and student protests taking place in the South. Moses was especially affected by the photos of determined young protesters. "They weren't cowed," he recalled in *The Children Bob Moses Led*, "and they weren't apathetic—they meant to finish what they had begun. Here was something that could be done. I simply had to get involved."

Over spring break in 1960, Moses visited an uncle of his in Hampton, Virginia. During his stay he witnessed students picketing segregated stores in nearby Newport News, and he decided to join them. The experience left him feeling exhilarated, and he resolved to work in the movement. After he returned to New York, he volunteered with the Committee to Defend Martin Luther King, helping the group organize a rally to raise funds to defend the civil rights leader from legal prosecution. He soon realized that he did not feel comfortable working in an office while others were putting themselves in harm's way. At the suggestion of a friend, in the summer of 1960 he traveled to Atlanta, Georgia, to work for the Southern Christian Leadership Conference (SCLC). To his dismay, Moses again found himself assigned to office tasks. Moreover, as he was quoted as saying in *The Children Bob Moses Led*, SCLC struck him as "too hero-worshiping, media-centered, preacher-dominated, and authoritarian." He felt far more attracted to SNCC, which was attempting to build a grassroots civil rights movement. Although viewed with suspicion by some SNCC members because of his college degree and soft-spoken manner, Moses left SCLC and joined protests and picket lines organized by SNCC.

Later in the summer of 1960, Moses went to Mississippi, then the most racially segregated state in the nation, to view for himself the conditions of blacks and try to organize people to come to Atlanta in October for a SNCC conference. Upon arriving in Mississippi, he met Amzie Moore, a local official of the National Association for the Advancement of Colored People (NAACP), who made Moses aware of the plight of several poor black Mississippi families. In *The Children Bob Moses Led*, Moses recalled, "[Moore] showed me scenes that I'll never forget: children with swollen ankles, bloated bellies, and suppurating sores; children whose one meal a day was grits and gravy; children who didn't know the taste of milk, meat, fruits, or vegetables; children who drank contaminated water from a distant well, slept five in a bed, and didn't have the energy to brush the flies from their faces." Moore and Moses then planned a campaign to register African-Americans to vote—a huge and dangerous undertaking, the goal of which was to rid Mississippi of the racist politicians who controlled the state. At the time of the project's inception, less than 5 percent of black Mississippians had been registered to vote, although 40 percent of the state's population was black.

The next summer, after teaching one more year at Horace Mann, Moses returned to Mississippi, choosing the railroad town of McComb as his base. As he recalled in *The Children Bob Moses Led*, his purpose was "to break the Solid South by applying pressure at its strongest point. I sought out the worst part of the most intransigent stage, placed myself on the charity of the black community, located a few brave souls who would support civil rights workers, and set up a voter registration school. If enough people could find the courage to go down to the courthouse, confronting the system designed to oppress them, then blacks all over the South would take heart, the country would take notice, and maybe, one hundred years too late, the federal government would take action." The registration process was designed to make it almost impossible for the mostly poor and illiterate black population to gain the franchise; even blacks who could read were turned away, after failing tests that were nearly impossible to pass—tests on which whites were given passing grades, no matter how poorly they had performed. Moreover, armed white bigots harassed and even injured blacks who attempted to register. As a result, African- American Mississippians were fearful of taking any empowering action.

Moses and his SNCC colleagues began organizing classes in what they dubbed "freedom schools," to help local residents understand the voter-registration process. As their activity continued, racist whites targeted Moses and his fellow SNCC members for attacks and beatings. Pickup trucks filled with shotgun-toting whites would follow SNCC members. "You were always looking in your rearview mirror for headlights," Moses told Bruce Watson for *Smithsonian* (February 1996). One day in February 1963, a car filled with angry whites followed Moses and a colleague of his as they were traveling by car. The two men managed to shake that car, only to be attacked by people in a second car, who opened fire after pulling up alongside them. A bullet just missed Moses but hit the driver in the neck. Moses grabbed the wheel, pulled the car over to the side of the road, and drove his colleague to the hospital. In this instance and many others, law-enforcement officers did not help the civil rights workers; rather, they ignored and even encouraged the violence against them. In addition, they repeatedly placed many SNCC members, including Moses, under arrest. Despite such actions, the federal government refused to become involved on SNCC's behalf.

The violence and formidable odds did not faze Moses, and before long he had become known for his bravery. Once, he was found napping in a SNCC office that had been attacked by an angry white mob only hours before. Another time, he was beaten while accompanying two blacks to a registrar. Bleeding heavily from his wounds, Moses continued to lead the two to the registration site. Afterward, he pressed charges against his attacker, an action virtually unheard-of for a black man in Mississippi at that time.

In 1963 Moses co-founded and became the director of the Council of Federated Organizations (COFO), an association that aimed to coordinate the activities of all civil rights groups in Mississippi. As a way of publicizing blacks' unhappiness about their disenfranchisement, he organized the so-called Freedom Vote, a mock election in which 80,000 blacks participated. Encouraged by the turnout, in 1964 SNCC initiated Freedom Summer, a massive registration drive for blacks. After a lengthy debate SNCC members decided to recruit white students from the North to help in the effort. After a weeklong orientation, more than 1,000 students traveled to Mississippi to canvass cities and small towns to encourage blacks to register. Although the number of people who did so was small, the drive made more African-Americans aware of the civil rights movement, and it brought national attention to both SNCC and the civil rights struggle in Mississippi. Concurrently, attacks on SNCC members and volunteers increased. That summer at least 80 people were beaten, some 70 churches, homes, and businesses were destroyed by racists, and, most notoriously, three civil rights workers—James Chaney, who was black, and Andrew Goodman and Michael Schwerner, who were white—were murdered by members of the Ku Klux Klan. The publicity provoked by their deaths aroused resentment among African-American volunteers, who recognized that the murders were generating far more attention than had earlier killings in which all the victims were black. Many African-American volunteers also bristled at the behavior of white civil rights workers who acted as if they thought they were better equipped than their black counterparts to assume leadership roles in Freedom Summer activities. For those and other reasons, relations between white and black SNCC workers began to deteriorate. "That summer, people who were talking to each other stopped," Moses told Alexis Jetter. "People who had been working together left. The whole spectrum of race relations compressed, broke down and washed us away."

Another disappointment for Moses and SNCC was connected with their efforts at the 1964 Democratic National Convention, held in Atlantic City, New Jersey. Joining with other civil rights organizations, SNCC formed the Mississippi Freedom Democratic Party (MFDP), to protest the all-white composition of the official Mississippi delegation to the convention. Although the MFDP received nationwide publicity and a member of the protest delegation was given the opportunity to address the convention, the delegates were not allowed to participate in convention activities. As the summer wore on, Moses became increasingly disturbed by the slow progress of voter registration and the deaths of SNCC workers, for which he felt partially responsible. He was also angered by the federal government's lack of involvement in the registration effort. As United States military activities in Vietnam increased, Moses began to focus more on the antiwar movement. (A fictionalized version of Moses's experiences with SNCC was presented in the 2000 TNT made-for-television film *Freedom Song*, starring Danny Glover.)

In 1966 Moses was drafted into the army. To avoid having to serve in the Vietnam War, he fled to Canada with his second wife, Janet Jemmott, a former SNCC activist. He lived there under the name Bob Parris for two years. The couple then moved to the African nation of Tanzania, where Moses taught math. In Tanzania, as Moses told Julia Cass, he "lived a life as just another person. That helped me get grounded again and helped our family be just a family. " He and his wife returned to the United States with their four children in 1976. (President Jimmy Carter issued a blanket pardon of draft dodgers in January 1977.) With his family, Moses settled in Cambridge, Massachusetts, where he resumed working toward his Ph.D. in the philosophy of mathematics at Harvard University. In 1982 he became sidetracked from his studies once again, after finding out, to his surprise and dismay, that the school attended by his eldest child—his daughter Maisha—did not offer instruction in algebra. (According to the Harvard Archives, Moses has not yet earned a doctorate.) He asked the girl's teacher if Maisha could sit by herself in her math class and work on more advanced material.

The teacher responded by inviting Moses to teach Maisha and other students at her level of math proficiency. That invitation led Moses to design the Algebra Project, with the aim of teaching poor children algebra by eighth grade and the ultimate goal of stemming the number of school dropouts and the resulting high unemployment rate among minority teenagers. Since math is crucial in today's industrial and technological world, Moses hopes that impoverished communities can be uplifted with the help of the Algebra Project. Those who can learn algebra by eighth grade, Moses has theorized, will have a greater chance of getting into academically superior high schools, enrolling at college, and building successful careers. In his book *Radical Equations: Math Literacy and Civil Rights* (2001), he described how his experiences during the civil rights movement led to his creation of the Algebra Project.

## PERSONAL LIFE

Moses, whose home is in Cambridge, Massachusetts, is a devotee of the yogi Paramhasana Yogananda and is a vegetarian. Each morning he wakes before dawn to swim 1,000 yards at a gym, an activity he repeats at the end of the day. His wife, Janet (Jemmott) Moses, earned an M.D. degree in 1987; currently, she teaches at the Harvard-MIT Division of Health Sciences and Technology and is on the pediatric staffs at two Boston hospitals. The couple's four children— Maisha, Omowale, Tabasuri, and Malaika—have all worked to increase math literacy among school-children. Omowale and Tabasuri co-founded, and Omowale directs, an arm of the Algebra Project known as the Young People's Project, which, according to the Algebra Project Web site, "recruits, trains and deploys high school and college-age youth to work with their younger peers in a variety of math learning opportunities." In 2002 Moses and the Algebra Project were awarded the prestigious James Bryant Conant Award by the Education Commission of the States. Earlier that year he received the 2001 Margaret Chase Smith American Democracy Award, given by the National Association of Secretaries of States.

## FURTHER READING

*4word (on-line) pl+ June 2001, with photos; Algebra Project Web site; Christian Science Monitor (on-line) Apr. 12, 2001; Educational Leadership p6+ Oct. 2001, with photo; New York Times p30+ Jan. 7, 2001, with photos; New York Times Magazine p28+ Feb. 21, 1993, with photos; Smithsonian pll4+ Feb. 1996, with photos;*

Burner, Eric R. And Gently He Shall Lead Them: Robert Parris Moses and Civil Rights in Mississippi, 1994; Heath, William. The Children Bob Moses Led, 1995;

Moses, Robert P., and Charles E. Cobb Jr. Radical Equations: Math Literacy and Civil Rights, 2001

---

# JANET MURGUIA

## President and CEO of the National Council of La Raza

**Born:** September 6, 1960; Kansas City, Kansas
**Primary Field:** Latin Civil Rights
**Affiliation:** National Council of La Raza (NCLR)

### INTRODUCTION

*Janet Murguia is the president and chief executive officer of the National Council of La Raza (NCLR), which identifies itself as the largest nonprofit, nonpartisan Latino civil rights and advocacy organization in the U.S. "Demographics show that Hispan- ics are now the largest minority community" in the country, Murguia told Jerry LaMartina for the* Kansas City Business Journal *(November 26, 2004), when the U.S. Census Bureau estimated the number of people of Hispanic descent living in the U.S. to be about 40.5 million, or slightly under 14 percent of the total population. Murguia added, "Those numbers won't mean anything if we don't leverage those numbers into increased economic empowerment, political empowerment, and social advancement for the Hispanic community." In 2007—the most recent year for which the U.S. Census Bureau has provided data—descendants of Hispanics living in the U.S. numbered about 45.5 million, or about 15 percent of the total population. Currently, in terms of income, educational level, home and business ownership, medical coverage, and other measures of achievement and well-being, Hispanics lag behind all other ethnic groups except African-Americans. The goal of the NCLR, according to its Web site, is to "improve opportunities for Hispanic Americans," by means of "applied research, policy analysis, and advocacy" that aim to "provid[e] a Latino perspective in five key areas—assets/investments, civil rights/immigration, education, employment and economic status, and health." Other areas in which the NCLR is active include the availability of affordable housing and bilingual programs. The NCLR does not provide help directly to people; rather, it offers training and funding to its affiliates, which currently number close to 300 and are located in 41 states, Puerto Rico, and Washington, D.C. "We need to have institutions like NCLR so that our Latino community can have a voice in Washington and across the country—wherever decisions and policies that affect us are made," Murguia told Frank DiMaria for the Hispanic Outlook in* Higher Education *(February 27, 2006). Murguia has spent much of her time as the leader of NCLR responding to false and malicious statements about the organization and about Hispanics in the U.S. "When I took this job, I thought I would be talking more about taking advantage of our opportunities rather than defending our civil rights," she told Michael Humphrey for the* National Catholic Reporter *(February 22, 2008, on-line). "We should be talking about housing and personal advancement, building community. Instead we are fighting hate speech and distortions."*

*Murguia, whose parents' education ended with elementary school, has two bachelor's degrees and a law degree. She began her professional life in Washington, D.C., in 1987, as an aide to a Democratic congressman, Jim Slattery of Kansas. From 1994 to 2000 she held a series of jobs at the White House, during the presidency of Bill Clinton. In 2000 she served as the deputy campaign manager and director of constituency outreach for the ultimately unsuccessful candidates on that year's Democratic presidential ticket, Vice President Al Gore and his running mate, U.S. senator Joseph Lieberman of Connecticut. For three years beginning in 2001, she held the post of executive vice chancellor for university relations at the University of Kansas, her alma mater. She became the chief operating officer of the NCLR in 2004 and was promoted to its top leadership position in 2005. "I've seen the American dream be a reality, and I want to make sure we can make it a reality for others as well," she told Teresa Watanabe for the* Los Angeles Times *(July 20, 2006).*

### EARLY LIFE

The youngest, along with her twin sister, Mary, of the three sons and four daughters of a Mexican-American couple, Janet Murguia was born in Kansas City, Kansas, on September 6, 1960. She grew up in a Mexican-American community in the section of Kansas City known as Argentine. Her father, Alfredo Olivarez Murguia, was born in Oklahoma; during his childhood he returned to Mexico, then moved to Kansas after his marriage. He worked in a Kansas City steel plant; when he retired, in about 1990, after 37 years on the job, his salary was $18,000 a year (the equivalent of less than $30,000 in 2008). Murguia's mother, Amalia, operated an informal day-care facility in her home to supplement her husband's income. Amalia was a widow with a young daughter, Martha Hernandez, when she and Alfredo married. The children they had together, in addition to Janet and Mary, are Alfred Jr., Rosemary, Carlos, and Ramon. Janet Murguia told Janet Perez for *Hispanic Business* (April 2005) that her parents "set a terrific example" for her and her siblings. "The values that they imparted . . . reflect the positive aspects of our culture, the strong sense of faith, the strong sense of family, a strong sense of community that helps and supports one another." Her parents "scrimped" and "sacrificed" for their children, she wrote in a remembrance for *Newsweek* (October 15, 2007), and though neither had attended school beyond the sixth grade, they encouraged their children to excel academically. Murguia told Teresa Watanabe, "They always knew the importance of education. They knew . . . it was the key to the future for their kids." Six of the seven Murguia siblings' have earned college degrees, and four have earned law degrees. Mary Murguia and Carlos Murguia are the first brother and sister in U.S. history to serve as federal judges; Ramon Murguia practices law privately in Kansas City. Alfred is a hotel caterer, and Martha works in a restaurant. Alfredo Murguia died in 2002; Rosemary quit her job at around that time to serve as her mother's caregiver and as the caretaker of the family house.

Janet Murguia attended Harmon High School, in Kansas City. During her years there she participated in Girls State, a citizenship-training program sponsored by the women's auxiliary of the American Legion. She was one of the two female students from Kansas chosen in 1977 to attend Girls Nation, another American Legion activity, in which participants visit Washington, D.C., for a week to learn firsthand about the workings of government.

According to Watanabe, Murguia and her twin sister earned "near-perfect" grades in high school. Both attended the University of Kansas (K.U.) and lived in the same dorm room. A worker in the school's financial-aid office, Murguia told Watanabe, helped her enormously in her successful search for the scholarships, loans, and grants necessary to cover her tuition and expenses. She received two bachelor's degrees from the university: a B.S. in journalism and a B.A. in Spanish, both in 1982. Three years later she completed a J.D. degree at K.U.'s School of Law. From 1987 to 1994 she worked in Washington, D.C., as an assistant to Jim Slattery, a Democrat who represented Kansas's Second Congressional District in the House from 1983 to 1995. (That district encompasses the state capital, Topeka, and much of eastern Kansas, excluding the Kansas City metropolitan area.) Slattery became a mentor to Murguia and steadily increased her responsibilities; as a result she gained experience in a wide range of areas. Murguia, Slattery told Janet Perez, "was deeply committed to trying to make the country a better place for all people. When you meet Janet you can't help but be impressed by the warmth of her personality, her enthusiasm, and her genuine concern and compassion for others."

## LIFE'S WORK

Slattery opted not to seek reelection in 1994, deciding instead to run for governor of Kansas. At the recommendation of Bill Richardson, then a New Mexico congressman, Murguia was hired as a member of the White House Legislative Affairs Office under President Bill Clinton. Her titles during the next six years included deputy assistant to Clinton, deputy director of legislative affairs, and senior White House liaison to Congress. Murguia worked with First Lady Hillary Clinton's Task Force on National Health Care Reform. The extremely complex plan proposed by the task force never gained sufficient support among legislators and was abandoned in September 1994. Reflecting in 2007 on its failure, Murguia told Richard S. Dunham and Keith Epstein for *BusinessWeek* (July 3, 2007, on-line), "One of the big mistakes of the Clinton experience was to think that they could do this without business and industry. It was arrogance." (The Patient Protection and Affordable Care Act and the Health Care and Education Reconciliation Act were signed into law by President Barack Obama in March 2010.)

In 2000 Murguia served as a deputy manager of the presidential and vice presidential campaigns of the Democratic nominees, Vice President A1 Gore and U.S. senator Joseph Lieberman of Connecticut, respectively; she was also the director of constituency outreach during their campaigns. In 2001, after the Republican George W. Bush assumed the presidency, she returned to Kansas to take on the post of executive vice chancellor for university relations at K.U. She was in charge of public and government relations and trademark licensing and managed the K.U. Visitor Center, KANU-FM (the campus radio station), and the Audio-Reader Network, a university-managed reading service for blind students. Her duties also included attending meetings of the Kansas state legislature in Topeka and raising funds through the K.U. Endowment Association. In addition, she toured the state to promote K.U. and spread the word about the importance of education and of "making it accessible and affordable," she told Michelle Adam for the *Hispanic Outlook in Higher Education* (February 24, 2003). "I saw those dismal statistics in Washington, D.C., not only about the lack of Latinos in higher education, but the fact that we have poor rates in terms of high school. We need to create higher expectations for our community. We have to keep the bar high. I feel that maybe I can help do my part in that regard." In a 2002 issue of *Hispanic Business*, Murguia was listed as one of the "100 Most Influential Hispanics."

Working with NCLR's affiliates is one of Murgula's most important duties. She also strives to strengthen the NCLR's ties to other civil rights advocacy groups— the National Association for the Advancement of Colored People (NAACP) and the National Urban League, for example. Another priority is the registration of new Hispanic American voters; in the months preceding the 2008 presidential election, about 200,000 Latinos registered for the first time with the NCLR's help. "One of the clearer roads that we have to move forward on as a community ... is around civic engagement," Murguia told a reporter for the *Denver Post* (September 2, 2007). "I don't think this is a policy debate anymore. I think we have to work on changing the political landscape for the community. . . . That means making sure that all folks who are eligible to be citizens are being naturalized . . . making sure that people go out and vote once they are registered."

Under Murguia, NCLR has been active in advocating for immigration reform, which has become one of the most polarizing political issues in recent years. In an interview broadcast on *NBC News* (March 28, 2006), Murguia said, "If we're going to deal with this problem sensibly, orderly, fairly and humanely, we need a solution that is comprehensive. It can't just be enforcement only. . . . That alone won't work. We need to offer guest

worker options, and ultimately deal with those 11 to 12 million workers . . . [who do] back-breaking work that nobody else wants to do in this country. We need to recognize that they are contributing to the economic vitality of this country, and understand that they're already part of this country." According to the organization's Web site, "NCLR's immigration policy agenda supports a workable and humane immigration system that restores the rule of law and protects workers and families, measures that protect civil rights and due process and keep the nation safe, and integration strategies that help immigrants become fully participating and contributing Americans." The NCLR supported a bill proposed in 2007 by then-President George W. Bush that would have established a means for roughly 12 million undocumented immigrants to gain citizenship. It would also have toughened border security and established a guest-worker program. Critics of the bill complained that it offered illegal immigrants "amnesty," and it died in the Senate. NCLR has expressed frustration with the failure of the administration of President Barack Obama to act on immigration reform. In a July 10, 2009 NCLR news release, Murguia complained, "It's time to stop the missteps, half-steps, and back- steps on immigration, The country wants immigration reform, the Latino community is waiting for it, our families are suffering, and we need to see some serious progress." She added, "NCLR urges the administration and Congress to demonstrate leadership by avoiding piecemeal attempts to address the country's broken immigration system and instead advance an effective, comprehensive solution."

The NCLR has been among the civil rights organizations strenuously fighting an Arizona law, signed by Governor Jan Brewer in April 2010, that requires immigrants to carry at all times documents regarding their status. Provisions of the law, which went into effect on July 29, 2010, made failure to provide such documents on request by law- enforcement officers a criminal offense and gave those officers the power to detain immigrants suspected of being in the U.S. illegally. On July 28, 2010, a federal judge blocked those provisions—the most controversial parts of the bill. The state of Arizona appealed the decision, and a hearing on the judge's injunction was scheduled for November 2010. The NCLR has argued that those provisions would open the door to legalized discrimination against Hispanics, regardless of their legal status, since they would permit police officers to demand to see anyone's documents in the course of questioning concerning possible infringement of other laws, and since the officers would be far more likely to demand documents if those stopped appeared to be Hispanic. The NCLR maintains the Web site boycottintolerance.org, which provides information about ongoing protests against the law and— as many other civil rights organizations have done—urges that people avoid vacationing or holding conferences in Arizona. The NCLR has also asked Major League Baseball officials to abandon plans to hold the 2011 All-Star Game in Phoenix, Arizona's largest city.

The NCLR's stance on immigration, along with many of its other stands, as well as its activities, mission, and even its name have been heavily criticized by conservative politicians and media figures. In an "open letter to the public" (October 26, 2006, on-line), Murguia wrote, "As an advocacy organization engaged in the public arena, we know that some will disagree with our views. As Americans committed to basic civil rights, we respect anyone's right to do so. But it is also clear that some critics are willfully distorting the facts and deliberately mischaracterizing our organization and our work." Murguia wrote the letter in response to remarks by Republican congressman Charlie Norwood of

Georgia, who in a press release (September 20, 2006) had described the NCLR as "a pro-illegal immigration lobbying organization that supports racist groups calling for the secession of the western United States as a Hispanic-only homeland"; he had also charged that the NCLR had "mounted an all-out campaign to prevent state and local police from voluntarily aiding critically undermanned federal authorities" engaged in border patrols. "If Americans don't wake up now, they'll wake up one day soon to find their nation has been stolen by La Raza and pals," Norwood declared.

The conservative syndicated columnist Michelle Malkin has also demonized La Raza. Referring to the 2008 Democratic and Republican presidential candidates (and ultimate nominees), Malkin wrote (July 12, 2008, on-line), as posted on her Web site's archives, "Both Barack Obama and John McCain were scheduled to speak this week in San Diego at the annual conference of the National Council of La Raza, the Latino organization whose name is Spanish for, yes, The Race.' Can you imagine Obama and McCain paying homage to a group of white people who called themselves that? No matter. The unvarnished truth is that the group is

## Affiliation: National Council of La Raza (NCLR)

In 2004 Murguia left K.U. to become the chief operating officer of NCLR. The organization was called the Southwest Council of La Raza when it was set up, in 1968, in Phoenix, Arizona, by Julian Samora, Ernesto Galarza, and Herman Gallegos, the last of whom was its first executive director. The group began helping Hispanic community organizations with voter registration, leadership development, and other activities, in the process linking up formally with groups including the Mexican American Unity Council (MAUC) and Chicanos Por La Causa Inc. (CPLC).

In 1972, having drawn affiliates from all over the country, the organization changed its name to National Council of La Raza. In 1974 the NCLR board selected Raul Yzaguirre as NCLR's new executive director. Yzaguirre, who headed NCLR until the end of 2004, reorganized the group, obtained federal grants, and increased its involvement in public policy-making. Murguia became the head of the NCLR on January 1, 2005.

As of 2010, NCLR had a staff of 120, a 21-member board, eight regional offices, and a budget of $1.3 bil-

lion. It receives funding from corporate partners, dues from affiliates, donations from individuals (who are considered members), and the federal government. Its corporate partners include Johnson & Johnson, Bank of America, PepsiCo, Wal-Mart, and State Farm Insurance. A few representative organizations among its approximately 300 affiliates are Academia Avance, in Los Angeles, California (one of the 115 charter schools that receive NCLR support); the East Boston Ecumenical Community Council, in Massachusetts; the Hispanic Economic Development Corp., in Kansas City, Missouri; the Hispanic Women's Organization of Arkansas; the Michigan Commission on Spanish Speaking Affairs; the Mississippi Immigrants Rights Alliance; the Multicultural Career Intern Program, in Washington, D.C.; the Washington State Migrant Council; Valley Community Clinic, in North Hollywood, California (which, along with other NCLR-supported health centers, provided treatment to about 200,000 people in 2008); and Youth Development Inc., in Albuquerque, New Mexico.

a radical ethnic nationalist outfit that abuses your tax dollars and milks p.c. [politically correct] politics to undermine our sovereignty." She also wrote that NCLR "vehemently opposes cooperative immigration enforcement," "has consistently opposed post-9/11 national security measures," and "sponsors militant ethnic nationalist charter schools subsidized by your public tax dollars."

During an interview with Rick Sanchez for CNN (May 28, 2008) two days after President Obama nominated federal judge Sonia Sotomayor for a seat on the U.S. Supreme Court, a third outspoken critic of the NCLR, the Republican former congressman Tom Tancredo of Colorado, characterized the organization as "a Latino K.K.K. without the hoods and the nooses." (He was referring to the Ku Klux Klan, a white-supremacist organization whose modus operandi has included violence and intimidation.) "If you belong to something like that, you've got to explain it in a way that's going to convince me and a lot of other people it's got nothing to do with race, even though the logo is 'All for the race, nothing for the rest,'" Tancredo declared, according to Ernest Luning, writing for the *Colorado Independent* (May 28, 2008, on-line).

The La Raza Web site rejects Norwood's, Malkin's, and Tancredo's claims as distortions or outright lies. For example, it declares that the NCLR "unequivocally rejects" the precept "All for the race, nothing for the rest" (in Spanish, "Por La Raza todo, Fuera de La Raza nada"), which "is not and has never been the motto of any Latino organization." Moreover, "race" is only one meaning of "la raza"; according to the NCLR, "La Raza" "has its origins in early 20th century Latin American literature and translates into English most closely as 'the people' or, according to some scholars, as 'the Hispanic people of the New World.' The term was coined by the Mexican scholar Jose Vasconcelos to reflect the fact that the people of Latin America are a mixture of many of the world's races, cultures, and religions. Mistranslating 'La Raza' to mean 'the race' implies that it is a term meant to exclude others. In fact, the full term coined by Vasconcelos, (*La Raza Cosmica*,' meaning the 'cosmic people,' was developed to reflect not purity but the mixture inherent in the Hispanic people. This is an inclusive concept, meaning that Hispanics share with all other peoples of the world a common heritage and destiny." Hispanics, Murguia has often said, "are an ethnic group, not a race."

In addition, the NCLR does not support separatist organizations or the idea that any part of U.S. territory should be returned to Mexico. It does not encourage illegal immigration; rather, it "has repeatedly recognized the right of the United States, as a sovereign nation, to control its borders. Moreover, NCLR has supported numerous specific measures to strengthen border enforcement, provided that such enforcement is conducted fairly, humanely, and in a nondiscriminatory fashion." Mur- gufa herself was a member of the Independent Task Force on Immigration and America's Future, an independent, bipartisan committee chaired by former congressman Lee Hamilton, an Indiana Democrat, and former U.S. senator Spencer Abraham, a Michigan Republican, and she endorsed its recommendations for immigration reform, released in September 2006.

As summarized on the Web site of the Migration Policy Institute, the recommendations included the creation of "an independent body in the Executive Branch that would introduce flexibility into the system by making regular recommendations to Congress and the President for adjusting immigration levels . . . based on ongoing analysis of labor market needs and changing economic and demographic trends." The committee also recommended the provision of "a path to legal status for unauthorized immigrants who can demonstrate steady employment, knowledge of English, payment of taxes, and passage of a background security check, among other requirements."

The NCLR also maintains on its Web site, "It is in the best interests of the United States and of immigrants themselves to ensure that all immigration to the U.S. takes place legally."

Murguia has also responded to criticisms of NCLR, and discussed Latino affairs in general, on many television talk shows and news programs. As the head of the NCLR, she has testified before numerous congressional committees and subcommittees on matters directly affecting Hispanics. Mur- guia is a board member of the Independent Sector, a coalition of nonprofit groups and corporations; an executive-committee member of the Leadership Conference on Civil Rights; and a board member of both the Hispanic Association on Corporate Responsibility and the National Hispanic Leadership Agenda.

Since 2003 several magazines, among them *Hispanic Business*, the *Washingtonian, Hispanic, NonProfit Times*, and *Newsweek,* have included her on their lists of the most influential or powerful women or Hispanics in the U.S. She received the Kansas University Law Alumni Association Distinguished Alumnus Award in 2005 and the Community Service Award of the Mexican American Legal Defense and Educational Fund in 2008.

**FURTHER READING**
*Hispanic p32 June 2004; Hispanic Business p34+ Apr. 2005; Hispanic Outlook in Higher Education pi7 Feb. 27, 2006; Kansas City (Kansas) Star pll Feb. 8, 2004; Los Angeles Times p2 July 20, 2006; nclr.org; Topeka (Kansas) Capital-Journal A pi Nov. 4, 2002*

# N

## RALPH NADER

### Consumer Advocate; Lawyer; Author

**Born:** February 27, 1934; Winsted, Connecticut
**Primary Field:** Environmentalism
**Affiliation:** Independent

#### INTRODUCTION

*In the two decades since a young, unknown attorney took on the Detroit automobile industry with his hard-hitting tract, Unsafe at Any Speed: The Designed-in Dangers of the American Automobile, Ralph Nader has become known as the founder of the consumer rights movement in America. His name is synonymous with the seat belt in cars and with public safety issues generally. Even his critics acknowledge that Nader's achievements are "as immutable as FDR's" and that "No living American is responsible for more concrete improvements in the society we actually do inhabit" than Citizen Nader,* The New Republic *editorialized in 1985.*

*In the era of the "Reagan Revolution," when federal constraints on business and industry are being loosened, Nader's personal popularity has diminished somewhat and the causes he promotes are out of fashion. But Nader is a modern "man for all seasons," and his unremitting advocacy of the consumer's cause is institutionalized in the form of the network of organizations, called Public Citizen, Inc., that he founded in the early 1970s. "The most important question that can be asked about any society" Nader once said, in a statement that comes close to summing up his credo, "is how much effort do citizens spend exercising their civic responsibility. We can't possibly have a democracy with 200 million Americans and only a handful of citizens."*

*Ralph Nader.*

Don LaVange

#### EARLY LIFE

Ralph Nader was born on February 27, 1934 in Winsted, Connecticut, to Nadra and Rose (Bouziane) Nader, Lebanese immigrants who operated a restaurant and bakery in the small town of Winsted. He was the youngest of their two sons and two daughters. In an interview with Ken Auletta for *Esquire* (December 1983), Nader recalled that he had "read all the muckraker books before [he] was fourteen—*America's 60 Families, The Jungle.*"

Nader's dream of becoming a "people's lawyer" was instilled in him in adolescence by his parents, who in noisy free-for-alls conducted family seminars in the duties of citizenship in an industrial democracy. Mark Green, a former Nader associate, told Ken Auletta that "when [the Naders] sat around the table growing up it was like the Kennedys. Except that the subject was not power but justice." And in the *Esquire* article, Michael Pertschuk, a former "Nader's Raider" who chaired the Federal Trade Commission during the presidency of Jimmy Carter, compared Nader's father to "an Old Testament prophet—righteous."

Following his graduation in 1951 from Winsted's Gilbert School, Nader entered the Woodrow Wilson School of Public and International Affairs at Princeton University. There he demonstrated his nonconformity by refusing to wear white bucks, the style of loafers preferred by the Princeton elite in those years, and by attempting, unsuccessfully, to prevent the campus trees from being sprayed with DDT.

## LIFE'S WORK

Graduating *magna cum laude* in 1955, with a major in government and economics, Nader enrolled in the Harvard Law School. He became an editor of the *Harvard Law Record*, a staid academic journal that Nader tried to turn into a rostrum for the discussion of social reformist ideas. After earning the LL.B. degree with distinction in 1958, Nader served for six months in the U.S. Army as a cook at Fort Dix, New Jersey. At sub-bargain prices at the base PX, he purchased the twelve pairs of shoes and four dozen cotton socks that, in the mid-1980s, Nader has not yet worn out.

In 1959, when many of his law school classmates were settling into careers with high-powered New York firms or with the government in Washington, Nader set up a small legal practice in Hartford, Connecticut. In the early 1960s he traveled widely, in the Soviet Union, Africa, and South America as a freelance journalist for the *Atlantic Monthly* and the *Christian Science Monitor*, and in Scandinavia. Distressed by what he saw as indifference on the part of American corporations to the global consequences of their actions, Nader early in his career spoke out against the arrogance of corporate power. Though timely, his message was veiled in generalities, and failed to attract an audience.

By 1964, Nader had grown restless in Hartford. "I had watched years go by and nothing happened," he said of the decision to carry his fight to Washington, D.C. "Before that, decades had gone by. I decided it took total commitment." Moreover, he had found an issue whose time had come—one that both dramatized corporate negligence and aroused the concern of American consumers—auto safety.

Nader had become interested in highway safety as a college student, when hitchhiking was his primary means of transportation and the auto accidents he had seen alarmed and appalled him. As early as 1958 Nader had written his first article on unsafe vehicle design, "American Cars: Designed for Death," which was published in the *Harvard Law Record*. Sharing Nader's concern with the liability of automobile manufacturers for the mounting carnage on the nation's highways was Daniel Patrick Moynihan, then the Assistant Secretary of Labor for policy planning, who hired the young attorney for the position of staff consultant on highway safety. From the spring of 1964 until May 1965, Nader devoted his time to producing a legislative background document, "A Report on the Context, Condition and Recommended Direction of Federal Activity in Highway Safety," and to developing an extensive network of contacts among members of the Washington Press Corps and on Capitol Hill.

But, unsatisfied with a dusty tome on a government shelf, Nader turned his impeccable, exhaustively documented study into one of the century's most influential muckraking books. Published in November 1965, *Unsafe at any Speed* (Grossman) indicted the whole Detroit automobile industry for its emphasis on styling over safety, but Nader trained his fire on the General Motors Corporation and its sporty Chevrolet Corvair, which he called "one of the nastiest-handling cars ever built." As Jonathan Rowe observed in the *Washington Monthly* [March 1985], Detroit "had always preferred to keep safety discussions focused on the driver and the road," but Nader changed "the premise of the debate, directing attention to the car and the company that made it."

Support for highway safety legislation was building in Congress and in the administration of President Lyndon B. Johnson, but when Nader accused General Motors of having hired private detectives to investigate and discredit him, swift passage of the Traffic and Motor Vehicle Safety Act of 1966 was ensured. In a nationally televised hearing of Connecticut Senator Abraham

Ribicoff's subcommittee on executive reorganization on March 22, 1966, General Motors President James M. Roche admitted that there had been "some harassment" of Nader and publicly apologized to him.

Overnight, Nader became an American folk hero, the David who had slain an industrial Goliath, proof that "one man could still make a difference," as Rowe put it in the *Washington Monthly*. And when it became known that Nader lived alone in a cheap, one-room efficiency apartment in downtown Washington, owned no car, put in one-hundred-twelve-hour work weeks, and required only $5,000 a year for personal expenses, he acquired the aura of a "Jimmy Stewart hero in a Frank Capra movie," to quote *Newsweek* (January 22, 1968).

Ralph Nader now began to fight for the public interest on many fronts, and his efforts culminated in legislation that improved safety standards in the construction of natural gas pipelines and in underground coal mining. He was also instrumental in the passage of the Wholesome Meat Act of 1967, which established federal inspection standards for slaughterhouses and processing plants to protect against the contamination of poultry and meat. Dubbed a "zealous consumer crusader" by the news media, Nader began to spend one-quarter of his time crisscrossing the country, giving lectures in which he enlisted the support of ordinary citizens for the burgeoning consumer rights movement, More important, to quote Jonathan Rorve, Nader "tapped a vein of social concern among scores of young people then in college or law school."

To realize his goal of creating what Ken Auletta called "a Fifth Estate to represent the public against . . . an unholy alliance between corporations and the government," in 1969 Nader formed the Washington, D.C.-based Center for Study of Responsive Law. Staffed by what Harrison Well- ford, an early executive director of the Center, told the *Washington Post* (Sept. 13, 1981) were the "best and brightest [young] lawyers in the country," the organization became, in Auletta's words, "the guerrilla base of operations for. Nader's Raiders." Early Center projects included investigations of the Federal Trade Commission^ the Interstate Commerce Commission, and the Food and Drug Administration. The Nader group's close scrutiny demonstrated that, time and again, those government regulatory agencies were susceptible to influence exerted by the very industries they were designed to monitor and that, as Thomas Whiteside wrote in a lengthy profile of Nader in the *New Yorker* (October 8, 1973), "the agencies,

theoretically operating in the public interest, Were . . . providing a bureaucratic shield behind which special interests exerted control,"

In August 1970, in an out-of-court settlement of Nader's $16,000,000 lawsuit against General Motors for invasion of privacy, the consumer advocate received $425,000. Much of the $284,000 Nader retained after paying his legal fees was used as seed money for his Corporate Accountability Research Group. Among other activities, the Corporate Accountability Research Group has campaigned for the federal, rather than the state, chartering of corporations so that concentrations of economic power might be more easily monitored by shareholders and watchdog groups. In 1970 Nader also started the Public Interest Research Group (PIRG), which fights for consumer and political reform on the community and college campus level in twenty-six states.

In 1971 Nader founded Public Citizen, Inc., a consumer lobbying group, as a counter force to powerful corporate lobbies. Public Citizen in turn became the parent organization for the Tax Reform Research Group, the Retired Professionals Action Group, and Congress Watch, which publishes *Who Runs Congress*, an invaluable guide to the inner workings of Capitol Hill.

Because of their systematic exposes of industrial hazards, unsafe products, and governmental ineptitude in enforcing. consumer safety laws, Nader and his so-called Raiders have been compared to the renowned muckrakes of the late nineteenth and early twentieth centuries. But reformers like Upton Sinclair, Ida Tarbell, and Lincoln Steffens were writers, who inflamed with one issue, then moved on to another. But Nader and his associates, most of them lawyers, always built legal and judicial means of remedial action into the structure of their organizations. Nevertheless in the early 1970s he continued to score major legislative victories. He was credited with a key role in the establishment of the Environmental Protection Agency in 197Q and in securing passage of the far-reaching Freedom of Information Act of 1974.

By 1971 a Harris poll recorded that Nader was the sixth, most popular public figure in the United States. The following year presidential nominee George McGovern sounded out Nader on the possibility of running for the vice presidency on the Democratic party ticket. According to Jonathan Rowe, Nader had political clout because he had media clout. The news media were infatuated with Nader because he furnished them with accurate information as well as headlines, and politicians feared the bad publicity he could bring them.

By the middle of the decade Nader was. condemning the economic power of large corporations in terms of being responsible for a violence so pervasive that the American public had not yet begun to recognize, its subtly insidious extent. Not surprisingly, Nader had by now earned his share of powerful detractors.

In August 1971, just months before he joined the U.S., Supreme Court bench, Lewis F. Powell Jr. wrote a legal memorandum entitled "Attack on American Free Enterprise System." In developing his argument Powell called Nader "perhaps the single most effective antagonist of American business." He then quoted from a magazine article that said, "The passion that rules in [Nader]—and he is a passionate man—is aimed at smashing utterly the target of his hatred, which is corporate power." Powell further advised that there "should be no hesitation to attack the Naders" who decry corporate enterprise."

By the end of the 1970s Nader's influence was visibly on the wane. He had been instrumental in the creation of the Occupational Safety and Health Administration (OSHA) in 1976, but suffered a major setback two years later, when Congress fell just a few votes short of creating the Consumer Protection Agency, which had been Nader's dream. His efforts to compel Detroit to equip motor vehicles with inflatable air bags also met with failure, for by 1980 automobile manufacturers were the object of national concern, not outrage. .

Moreover, Nader himself was being described in the press as one "too busy for fiction, just as he's too busy to own a car, too busy to have a family, too busy to care about clothes, or anything but reforming the nation for consumers." However, a more substantive criticism of Nader appeared, in the *Chicago Tribune* (January 4, 1985). Thomas Ferraro reported that when Congress rejected the Consumer Protection Agency, "Some blamed Nader's refusal to compromise and his combative nature," Ferraro also observed that, on Capitol Hill, those who see him as "an effective lobbyist" often complain that "they might vote with Nader a hundred times and then be called 'a tool of industry' for a single vote he considers anti-consumer."

In the early 1980s it is conservative doctrine that "Naderism" results in the overregulation of industry. And for its part, the American public now takes Nader's accomplishments for granted, from seat belts and shatterproof windshields to smoking and nonsmoking

sections in public facilities. "I'm no longer seen as the Lone Ranger," Nader told the *Chicago Tribune*. "I consider myself a public citizen. I enjoy achieving justice in society."

In 1985 Nader headed just two of the almost two dozen National Consumer organizations he has formed. He continues to fund the Corporate Accountability Research Group largely from the fees he receives as a lecturer and from the many articles and books that he publishes. Most of the Public Citizen groups are funded by grants from small foundations and by voluntary contributions.

Since Ronald Reagan acceded to the Presidency in 1981, Nader's consumer groups have launched investigations into the nuclear power industry, the Educational Testing Service, the postal service, and the insurance industry. Nader himself still refuses to accept an economic situation in which "the manufacturer is the lord and the market place the manor" to quote Whiteside's *New Yorker* piece. Nader has targeted as the "enemy of the '80s" the vast power of the giant corporations. He has also blasted the Reagan administration for providing a "government of General Motors, by Exxon, for Du Pont."

In October 1980 Nader resigned as President of Public Citizen, Inc., so that he might devote more time to projects that organize citizens at the community level. Two such recently formed groups are Citizen Utility Boards, which monitor public utilities, and Buyers Up, which brings homeowners and small businesses together to negotiate lower prices for their home heating fuel.

In 1986 Nader and coauthor William Taylor published *The Big Boys* (Pantheon Books), a profile of nine corporate-power-wielding chief executive officers. In *Newsweek* (June 2, 1986) Rich Thomas praised Nader and Taylor for the evenhandedness of their view of business leadership, though he complained that the 571-page book was "rambling and badly organized." Although the authors hardly refrained from upbraiding their subjects, Thomas noted that *The Big Boys* had set "off in search of corporate pestilence but [found] excellence instead.... Nader views *The Big Ones* as genuine achievers, men whom he would gladly enlist as lieutenants in the utopian consumer autocracy he envisions— under himself, of course, as Chief Scold."

Nader is a five-time candidate for President of the United States, having run as a write-in candidate in the 1992 New Hampshire Democratic primary, as the Green

Party nominee in 1996 and 2000, and as an independent candidate in 2004 and 2008.

## PERSONAL LIFE

Ralph Nader is relaxed and witty in the presence of friends, who tend to be professional associates, but is too busy to socialize very much. As a baseball fan whose love of the game was instilled by his childhood heroes, the New York Yankees, Nader believes that professional sports teams should be owned by their fans.

Nader's sister, Laura Nader Milleron, an anthropology professor at Berkeley, told the *Christian Science Monitor* (April 29, 1980) that "He was the last child, the most relaxed, the most regular." Her brother is capable of working nonstop, she said, because "he's at peace with himself, and happier than ninety percent of the people who are running around, taking desperate vacations in Bermuda and Hawaii, spending money ..."

Ralph Nader is lean of build and stands six feet four inches tall. He is sallow-complexioned and has short, curly black hair that is now beginning to turn gray at the temples. He still favors the plain, narrow-lapeled suits and skinny ties that he has worn since he left the army in 1959.

## FURTHER READING

*Chicago Tribune II pl+ Ja 4 '85 pors; Christian Sci Mon B pl+ Ap 29 '80 pors; Esquire 100:480-/- D '83 pors; New Republic p4 D 9 '85; New Yorker p50-h O 8 '73, p46+ O 15 '73; Newsday p8+ Mr 9 '86 pors; Washington Post F pl+ S 13 '81; Who's Who in America 1984-85; Buckhorn, Robert F. Nader: The People's Lawyer (1972); Contemporary Authors vols.77-80 (1979); Corey, Hays. Nader and the Power of Everyman (1975); McCarry, Charles. Citizen Nader (1972)*

---

# KUMI NAIDOO

## Director of Greenpeace International; Activist

**Born:** 1965; South Africa
**Primary Field:** Environmentalism
**Affiliation:** Greenpeace International

## INTRODUCTION

*In November 2009 Kumi Naidoo became the director of Greenpeace International, a nearly four-decade-old organization committed to nonviolent activism to preserve the environment. A native of South Africa, a veteran of the antiapartheid struggle there, and a human-rights activist since his early teens, Naidoo has learned through sometimes bitter experience that meaningful change often takes time. Still, in his post, in which he seeks to combat and raise awareness of global warming, he has emphasized that time is short. "We are talking about being in an extremely inconvenient moment of world history where the future is at stake and the present is already proving to be hugely painful," he said in an interview with David Smith for the London* Guardian *(November 18, 2009, on-line). The task of persuading world leaders to implement the changes required to reverse global warming is not easy; Naidoo, however, has made a career of going against the odds for causes he*

*believes in. He said to Smith, "I think we will not make apologies for speaking truth to power and inconveniencing some political leaders." What will ultimately make the difference in our planet's future, Naidoo has said, is the involvement of ordinary citizens. "I strongly believe in the decency of ordinary men and women in rich and poor countries who all care about their children, and their grandchildren," he told Smith. "I think when they put the pictures of those kids in front of them and think [about] what kind of planet we [are] going to give them, I hope people will rise above whatever short-term economic and other interests they might have."*

## EARLY LIFE

Kumi Naidoo, who is of Indian ancestry, was born in 1965 in South Africa. He was raised in a lower-middle-class family in the township of Durban. At that time apartheid, or officially sanctioned racial segregation was brutally enforced in South Africa, where the white minority government relegated blacks and other nonwhites to second-class citizenship. Naidoo told Stephen Moss for the *Guardian* (November 30, 2009, on-line) that when he was 14, "the lights went on," and he saw the need to fight apartheid. As a 15-year-old student at a Durban secondary school that had no electricity or books, he marched as part of the national student uprisings of the 1980s. As a result, he was expelled. "We were shouting these ridiculous slogans, like 'You pay our teachers peanuts, no wonder we get a monkey education system,'" Naidoo told Annie Kelly for the *Guardian* (July 22, 2009, on-line). "It was like a big party, but three weeks later there were people being beaten all around me, people being hauled off into prison, being killed. It was then that I understood that we were up against something that was bigger than injustice in the education system. It was systematic. After that, there was no going back." Two weeks before those student demonstrations, Naidoo's mother had committed suicide. "She was 38 and had issues with my dad," Naidoo said to Stephen Moss. "She just reached a moment where it felt too much. During that apartheid period there were very high levels of suicide: there was no support for people. It was a surprise to us. She left a note, took an overdose, and was gone within hours. It feels like yesterday." Naidoo has said that he often wonders how his mother would have handled the repercussions of his activism, had she lived to see how tumultuous his life became as a result of it. "If you got involved in the struggle, the assumption was you'd end up dead, or in detention or exile," he told Kelly. "I spent much of my Early Life feeling like I was living on borrowed time, and it's a feeling I've carried around ever since." Following his expulsion, Naidoo studied at home and passed an entrance exam for the University of Durban-Westville, whose students were mainly South African Indians; he received a B.A. degree in law and political science, cum laude, in 1985.

For much of the 1980s, Naidoo was active in student and residents' associations, programs to foster youth leadership, and antiapartheid struggles. In 1986 he was arrested and charged with violating his country's state-of-emergency rules. Facing 15 years in prison, Naidoo spent one year underground before going into exile in Britain. (Afterward his younger brother was held in prison for a year without a trial.) Naidoo remained committed to the fight against apartheid, however, particularly after his good friend Lenny Naidu was murdered by South African special forces, in 1988. Naidoo recalled to Moss the last conversation he had with Naidu: "Before we fled in different directions into exile, he was very philosophical and asked me what was the best contribution you could make to the cause of humanity and justice. I said, 'That's very easy, it's giving your life.' He said, 'You mean participating in demonstrations and getting shot and killed.' I said, '1 guess so,'

and he said, 'No, that's the wrong answer. It's not giving your life, but giving the rest of your life.'" Naidoo, then 22 years old, did not fully grasp at the time what his friend meant. "I still think deep and hard over what he was trying to say," Naidoo said to Nell Greenberg for the *Earth Island Journal* (Summer 2010). "What he was saying is that the struggle for justice—the struggle, whether it is gender justice, environmental justice—is a marathon, not a sprint. And the biggest contribution that any one of us can make is maintaining a lifetime of involvement until we win on those struggles."

## LIFE'S WORK

While in exile in Britain, Naidoo was a Rhodes Scholar and earned a doctorate in political science from Magdalen College, at Oxford University. He remained in Britain until 1989. After the longtime antiapartheid activist Nelson Mandela was released from prison, on February 11, 1990, following decades spent behind bars, Naidoo returned to South Africa to work toward the legalization of the African National Congress (ANC). Mandela's release came as a shock to Naidoo and many of those involved in the antiapartheid movement. "Suddenly we had to think about a future, a career path, pensions, things that hadn't previously been in our vocabulary. It was quite an adjustment to have to make," Naidoo recalled to Moss. It was an exciting time, but also a difficult one. Not long after he returned to his newly liberated homeland, Naidoo lost another close friend, the social activist Joan Wright, in a car crash. Of that tragedy, Naidoo told Moss, "My story is an African story. We have to endure loss of loved ones on a much more regular basis [than in the West]. I've had more than my fair share of loss, but sadly it's not peculiar in the African context."

In 1993 Naidoo became the executive director of the National Literacy Cooperation of South Africa. That same year Walter Sisulu, a senior ANC member and one of Naidoo's heroes, had offered him a job as head of the ANC's media-production division. He chose to work instead in the area of literacy after a conversation with a mentor, Mary Mkwanazi, who told him, as Naidoo recalled to Moss, "If you want to be on TV and be famous then go and do the ANC job. If you really want to make a difference, go and do the adult literary job." Naidoo concluded that when it comes to achieving goals, activists have an advantage over politicians. "The constraints of election cycles and the compromises forced on you by the realpolitik of governing mean that often you can't speak truth to power. I think politicians are overrated, and the role they play in society is disproportionately more valued than the role faith leaders, trade union leaders, NGO [nongovernmental-organization] leaders and media people play," he said to Moss. Naidoo headed the National Literacy Co-operation of South Africa until 1997.

During the 1994 democratic elections in South Africa, Naidoo served as the official spokesperson of the Independent Electoral Commission and was responsible for overseeing the training of all electoral staff in the country. The election, in which Mandela won South Africa's presidency, marked the beginning of universal adult suffrage in the country and the end of apartheid. "What I learned from that time, which is helpful now," Naidoo told David Smith for the *Guardian* (November 18, 2009, on-line), "is not to believe that things cannot change and not to underestimate the power of the voices and actions of ordinary people. We never thought change would come as fast as it came. In the mid-80s it just seemed that it was going to be another 20 years."

From 1996 to 1998 Naidoo was the executive director of the South African National NGO Coalition (SANGOCO). SANGOCO is an umbrella group created to incorporate the work of provincial and sectoral NGOs in governmental policy and ensure that the traditions of civil society continue to have a place in South Africa. In 1998 Naidoo became secretary-general and CEO of the Civicus World Alliance for Citizen Participation, whose mission, according to the official Civicus Web site, is to "empower citizens to participate in the processes of public decision-making that affect their lives." Civicus is made up of several programs, among them Civil Society Watch (CSW), whose actions include analyzing the effects of laws and policies on civil society, issuing press statements, and coordinating such civic actions as protest marches. In 2008 Naidoo was named honorary president of Civicus, a position he still holds. In April and July 2009, Naidoo was a visiting fellow at the Carnegie UK Trust—an organization that, according to its Web site, "investigates areas of public concern to influence policy and practice"—and an international adviser for the trust's inquiry into the future of civil society.

In February 2009 Naidoo embarked on a hunger strike in solidarity with the people of Zimbabwe. In Zimbabwe, agriculture, the backbone of the country's economy, has been crippled by the combined effects of drought, HIV/AIDS, and government land reforms. Unemployment is rampant, and inflation has made basic necessities unaffordable for many of Zimbabwe's citizens, who have fled to neighboring countries by the millions. The shared-government agreement between Zimbabwe's longtime president, Robert Mugabe, and Morgan Tsvangirai of the Movement for Democratic Change, negotiated in 2008 with South Africa as mediator, has reportedly been undermined by impropriety and foot-dragging, preventing the changes required to address the humanitarian crisis. The international community has accused South Africa of standing by passively instead of taking steps to ensure that the power-sharing agreement actually works.

Naidoo was on the 19th day of the 21-day hunger strike when he was contacted by a recruitment company on behalf of Greenpeace International. The recruiters wanted to know if he was interested in applying to become the organization's head. "I was OK, I was still compos mentis, but I was a little weak and had already lost 14kg [about 30 pounds]," he explained to Moss. "I said, 'Guys, this is not the best time to be thinking about jobs.'" That might have been the end of the matter, had Naidoo not happened to mention the call to his 17-year-old daughter, the product of his relationship with a young woman while he was a student at Oxford. (The couple never married but remain friends; Naidoo's daughter lives in Glasgow, Scotland.) Naidoo told Moss, "She said, 'Dad, I will not speak to you if you don't at least think about it because Greenpeace is one of the best NGOs in the world, and when I grow up I would love to work for them.' It has a kind of magic for young people." When the recruiting company called again a week later, Naidoo showed more interest. In November 2009, when Greenpeace's leader, Gerd Leipold, resigned after nearly nine years in the position, Naidoo stepped in to take his place. While some criticized Greenpeace's choice, arguing that Naidoo's success as a human-rights activist did not guarantee his competence as an environmentalist, Naidoo expressed the view that all aspects of activism are interconnected. "I can understand that people might see it as somewhat of a disconnect," he said to Robin Powell for the *Sydney (Australia) Morning- Herald* (February 22, 2010). "I'm not your traditional environmentalist. But I see it as a logical development, not an abrupt move. I've come to a revelation: I think the environmental crisis is, in a sense, at the centre and connected to all other crises." Naidoo has pointed out, for example, that while the genocide in Darfur is a "crisis of violence" and an ethnic conflict, the lack of water and arable land there have played a huge role in it.

Greenpeace International was founded in 1971, when a group of activists leased a small fishing vessel called the *Phyllis Cormack* and set sail from Vancouver, Canada, to Alaska to protest nuclear testing. Today, Greenpeace's efforts are focused on banning commercial whaling, with activists taking to the water to physically thwart whaling ships; putting an end to nuclear testing; and combating the threats of global warming and toxins in the environment. Responsible for 1,500 staff members in 28 offices worldwide and a budget of 200 million euros (currently equivalent to about $260 million), Naidoo took his post at a critical time for Greenpeace—the eve of the 2009 conference on climate change, held in Copenhagen, Denmark. The conference was organized by the United Nations in cooperation with the Danish government; in attendance were representatives of the member countries of the United Nations Framework Convention on Climate Change. Naidoo's first act as director was to gather the whole staff (about 150 people) at the Greenpeace headquarters, in Amsterdam, the Netherlands, for a meeting. "I told them I thought the moment we are living in right now can best be described as a perfect storm," he told Moss. "First, we had the fuel price crisis three years ago, that led to a food price crisis. We have an ongoing poverty crisis where 50,000 men, women, and children die every day from preventable causes. We've known about the climate crisis for some time now; and then the financial crisis was the final boot in the solar plexus. When you have such a convergence of crises, you have two options: you can get out a couple of Band-Aids, try to do a temporary fix and keep it as business as usual; or you can take a leaf out of Chinese culture, where the symbol for crisis is the same symbol for opportunity. I feel that we have to turn this moment into a point where humanity sobers up."

In the days leading up to the Copenhagen conference, Naidoo stressed its significance and. attempted to convey to world leaders that their attendance was crucial. "The Copenhagen Summit offers the single greatest opportunity for leaders to come together and create a legally binding agreement to avert climate chaos," he told reporters at a press conference in Johannesburg, South Africa, as quoted on the Web site *7thSpace Interactive* (November 16, 2009). "Our leaders need to find the courage to do what is right instead of what is comfortable. They need to become the leaders we elected

them to be by acting to save the climate. They must avert the threat of mass migration, mass starvation, and mass extinction, all of which will be inevitable if climate change goes unchecked." Naidoo pointed out that while global warming may seem to be a "slow-burning" issue for much of the developed world, other places are already experiencing serious consequences of the problem. "Developing countries are least responsible for the climate chaos we find ourselves in and also the ones paying the most brutal price. They should therefore receive significant financing to help them adapt to the impact of climate change, recognizing the historical responsibility," he said in an interview with Caroline Hartnell for *Alliance Magazine* (January 18, 2010, on-line).

When the summit came to an end, in December 2009, no international, legally binding agreement had been forged. Although deeply disappointed, Naidoo saw the need to move forward. "Part of what is critically needed right now is for us to actually build, if you want, the broadest possible awareness and understanding of citizens who are voters, in the hope that there can be a bottom up kind of pressure. With the Copenhagen summit, some might justifiably say that we put too much of our eggs into the COP15 [the 15th Conference of the Parties] basket. ... So in the post- Copenhagen reflection we are saying we also need to continue to build other leverages of campaigning and resisting and popular mobilization," Naidoo said in his interview with Nell Greenberg. He told Hartnell, "History has shown us—the US slavery, anti-apartheid and so on—it's only when decent men and women are willing to stand up, put their lives on the line and take strong, vibrant action that the agenda can move forward. Citizens and civil society must recognize that governments will not act with the urgency that is needed unless they are pushed into it."

In July 2010 Greenpeace made headlines when it shut down between 30 and 50 British Petroleum (BP) gas stations in London, England, by disabling their pumps. That action was taken to protest BP's plans to continue deepwater drilling in the wake of the disastrous oil spill in the Gulf of Mexico, which was caused by the explosion of an offshore BP drilling rig the previous April. After BP announced that Robert Dudley would replace the firm's longtime chief executive officer, Tony Hayward, Naidoo declared, as quoted by *Press TV* (July 27, 2010, on-line), "Dudley should overturn current plans to extract oil from risky deepwater wells off Libya and in the Arctic, where a spill could have consequences even more devastating than in the gulf. A change in leadership is a key opportunity for BP to cut its losses in more ways than one, by turning away from high-cost and environmentally reckless sources of oil. . . towards an energy revolution based on clean energy sources."

In September 2010 Naidoo made public a letter he sent to Mark Zuckerberg, the chief executive officer of Facebook. The letter concerned Facebook's decision to buy electricity for its first data center, in Prineville, Oregon, from Pacific Power, which produces energy mainly by burning coal. In the letter Naidoo called upon Zuckerberg to turn to other, cleaner sources of energy and to use Facebook's enormous influence to spur other companies to do the same. "Greenpeace regularly uses Facebook to engage its supporters and their friends to hold corporations accountable for their environmental impact," Naidoo wrote, according to *Targeted News Service* (September 1, 2010, on-line). "Facebook is uniquely positioned to be a truly visible and influential leader to drive the deployment of clean energy." The news service reported that at least half a million Facebook users "have joined with Greenpeace to call on Zuckerberg and Facebook" to stop using coal-based energy.

## PERSONAL LIFE

Naidoo is currently based in Amsterdam. His longtime romantic partner remains in South Africa. Although the two have considered living together in Amsterdam, Naidoo travels so often that it would make little difference in terms of the time the couple spend together. Naidoo has acknowledged that life as an activist is difficult; change takes time, and sometimes even modest progress requires a seemingly disproportionate amount of work. He has learned to live with disappointment. Still, he has

said that he would not trade his career path for anything. "If I were to turn the clock back, I wouldn't choose to do anything differently . . . ," he told Greenberg. "When I reflect on my life now ... I think that activism actually gave my life much more meaning than anything else could have given it. . , . My best friendships, you know, my best relationships with people. I mean, there are people who I worked with when I was in my teens, I don't see them for 20 years, and I bump into them and it's like a long lost relative. The depth, the closeness of that relationship is very different when you combine with people working for justice." When asked by Greenberg what advice he would give to young people who are considering activism but feel hopeless in the face of seemingly insurmountable problems, Naidoo responded, "To young people I would say, 'Activism can be fun, it can be sexy, it can be ethical, it can enhance your place in the world, it can help you with your education, it can help you with the quality of your relationships with family, friends, and community, and it's a path of life very well worth taking. And it's not a grind. When I think about my life as an activist, I've laughed a lot. Even though I have had to bury many, many people I still think that I got a lot of meaning, laughter, friendship, love out of activism.'"

## FURTHER READING
*Alliance (on-line) Jan. 18, 2010; BBC News (on-line) Mar. 14, 2010; Earth Island Journal (on-line) Summer 2010; (London) Guardian (on-line) July 22, 2009, Nov. 18, 2009, Nov. 30, 2009*

# GROVER NORQUIST

## Conservative Activist; Founder and President of Americans for Tax Reform

**Born:** October 19, 1956; Sharon, Pennsylvania
**Primary Field:** Tax Reform
**Affiliation:** Americans for Tax Reform

### INTRODUCTION

*Grover Norquist "just may be the most influential Washingtonian most people have never heard of," Susan Page wrote for* USA Today *(June 1, 2001). In 1985, while Norquist was working as a speech-writer for the U.S. Chamber of Commerce during the administration of the Republican Ronald Reagan, the president asked him to form an ad-hoc committee to generate support for what became the Tax Reform Act of 1986. The committee, Americans for Tax Reform (ATR), with Norquist as president, went on to become a permanent fixture in the nation's capital and played a vital role in the passage of sweeping tax cuts under President George W. Bush. Another prominent Washington entity begun by Norquist is the Wednesday Meeting, a weekly gathering of politicians, strategists, businesspeople, and lobbyists dedicated to advancing a national conservative agenda. (Similar meetings are being held in 40 states.) Speaking with John Aloysius Farrell for an article in the* Boston Globe *(April 17, 2002), the combative Norquist described his followers as the "leave-us-alone coalition" and explained their desires. "Taxpayers: Don't raise my taxes. Property owners: Don't mess with my property. Home-schoolers: I just want to educate my kids. Gun owners: Don't take my guns away. Traditional-values conservatives—Orthodox Jews, Roman Catholics, Muslims, Evangelicals: I just want to raise my kids in my faith. Each of the groups is there on the issue that brings them to politics, which is that they want to be left alone." In keeping with his belief in a very limited federal government—he has often been quoted as saying that he wants to reduce government "to the size where we can drown it in the bathtub"—Norquist told Michael Scherer for* Mother Jones *(January 1, 2004), "My ideal citizen is the self-employed, homeschooling, IRA-owning guy with a concealed-carry [gun] permit. Because that person doesn't need the . . . government for anything."*

### EARLY LIFE

Of Swedish descent, Grover Glenn Norquist was born on October 19, 1956, the first of the four children of Warren Elliott and Carol (Lutz) Norquist, He grew up in Weston, Massachusetts, one of the wealthiest suburbs in the Boston area. His father was a vice president at Polaroid and a former engineer; his mother was a former schoolteacher who later became the town's tax assessor. From the time that he was very young, Norquist's parents taught him to live according to three principles: order, self-reliance, and individual responsibility. They also made their political views known to him: often, after church on Sunday, Norquist's father treated him and his three younger siblings to ice cream cones; he would then take bites out of the cones, playfully blaming each bite on a different tax levied by the government. Norquist's own political leanings began to show as early as the sixth grade, when he argued with classmates over the Vietnam War, which he apparently supported; he has recalled debating with a fellow student who tried to convince him that the Republican Richard Nixon was a fascist and that Alger Hiss—a former State Department official whom Nixon, as a U.S. congressman, had played a major role in getting convicted on perjury charges related to alleged Communist activity—was innocent. At 11, at a sale at the public library in Weston, he picked up anticommunist literature including *Masters of Deceit*, by the longtime FBI director J. Edgar Hoover, and *Witness*, by Hiss's accuser, Whittaker Chambers. Norquist's conservative ideology has its roots in the anti-Communist stance he adopted before his views on domestic policy were formed. When Norquist was 12 he volunteered for Nixon's successful 1968 presidential campaign. A short time later his ideas on tax reform began to take shape, when he formulated a "no new taxes" ideal for the Republican Party.

During his teenage years in Weston, in the early 1970s, Norquist wore his hair long, listened to rock music, played soccer, and learned how to shoot firearms at the target range in the family basement. He attended the prestigious Weston High School, where he focused more on academics and on studying politics than on dating. A standout student, he was listed in his senior-class yearbook as being "most intelligent," "most likely to succeed," "most studious," "most responsible," and "most ambitious." While other students quoted figures ranging from the philosopher Socrates to the singer

Joni Mitchell under their yearbook photos, Norquist, as noted in Nina J. Easton's book *Gang of Five*, wrote his own text: "A dictatorship is like a machine with a warranty—it works well for a while. A democracy has no guarantees and as such needs to be constantly maintained, nurtured, even pampered, lest the people allow her to rust and begin to cast covetous glances at her more expedient rival."

## LIFE'S WORK

In 1974 Norquist enrolled at Harvard University, in Cambridge, Massachusetts. One of few vocal conservative students on campus, he has said that he flourished in that atmosphere according to what he calls the "Boy Named Sue" theory—a reference to the Johnny Cash song in which the protagonist is given a girl's name by his departing father in order to force him to fight and learn to survive. Norquist recalled to John Aloysius Farrell for the *Boston Globe* (April 17, 2002) that the experience of being a conservative among liberal students (whom he called "Bolsheviks") "toughened you up. It made you think. It also convinced me that it all mattered: Those guys at Harvard were going to go out and run the country. We were cooked if some of us didn't get active . . . too." He attracted attention at the school as the co-publisher of a libertarian paper called the *Harvard Chronicle* and also wrote for the business section of the *Harvard Crimson*. He graduated in 1978 with a B.A. degree in economics.

The mid-1970s had seen, in some circles, an antitax movement spurred by high inflation, rising unemployment, and "bracket creep," or the placement of wages and salaries into higher income-tax brackets even as inflation caused workers' buying power to decrease. The movement culminated in the June 6, 1978 passage of California's Proposition 13, which slashed property taxes by an average of 57 percent, limited property-tax rates to one percent of market value, and outlawed any future tax increases that were not approved by a two-thirds majority in the state legislature. Proposition 13 created a domino effect, with other states passing similar measures in what has often been referred to collectively as a "modern Boston tea party." Norquist joined the movement, working briefly for the National Taxpayers Union (NTU) in Washington, D.G., and then—after earning an M.B.A. degree from Harvard—returning to Washington to become executive director of both the NTU and the organization National College Republicans. Those positions helped him to make vital contacts with rising stars of a new generation of right-wing conservative activists. He held both jobs until 1983, when he started working as an economist and as the chief speechwriter for the U.S. Chamber of Commerce. Then, in 1985, at the request of President Ronald Reagan, Norquist established an ad hoc group called Americans for Tax Reform, to help build grassroots support for Reagan's Tax Reform Act of 1986. The legislation simplified the income-tax code, broadened the tax base, and eliminated many tax shelters; it also marked the first time in history that the top tax rate was lowered and the bottom rate was increased simultaneously. Despite approving of the tax cuts, many conservatives were initially skeptical of the legislation, fearing that a double cross lay among the elimination of tax credits, breaks, and shelters. "They said, 'We're going to get rid of these credits and deductions, we're going to broaden the base and then they're going to come back and raise the [tax] rates again, and we won't even have the deductions and credits anymore,'" Norquist recalled to Nicholas Confessore for the *New York Times* (January 16, 2005). "At which point, I said, 'Well, what if we made it difficult for them to raise rates?'" Acting on the same "no new taxes" philosophy he had formed as a teenager, in 1985 Norquist circulated among members of the U.S. Congress a document that became known as the Taxpayer Protection Pledge (or simply the Pledge)—a promise never to vote to raise tax rates—which was signed by more than 100 members of Congress. (In 1988 the Republican presidential candidate George H. W. Bush used the very words "no new taxes" in making a campaign pledge, one he broke while in office.) Not long after the Tax Reform Act became law, Norquist took ATR private and began serving as its president.

During the latter half of the 1980s, Norquist took a hiatus from tax reform to work as an overseas liaison for the government in support of anti-Soviet guerrilla armies, deemed "freedom fighters." He visited the war zones of Pakistan, Afghanistan, and Angola and worked as a lobbyist alongside supporters of the Nicaraguan Contra rebels and other Reagan-backed insurgent groups. He rallied support for such anti-Communist groups as Mozambique's RENAMO and Jonas Savimbi's UNITA in Angola, both of which were backed by South Africa's apartheid regime. From 1985 to 1988 he also served as Savimbi's economic adviser; he was registered with the United States Department of Justice during that time as a foreign agent of Angola.

In the early 1990s Norquist began working closely with the Republican congressman Newt Gingrich of Georgia to make Americans for Tax Reform into a major force in the antitax movement. With the election of the Democratic president Bill Clinton in 1992, Norquist set out to instill an antitax mindset in politicians around the country, reemphasizing opposition to taxes as one of the central tenets of American conservatism; in the process he became a leader of conservatism's center-right. In 1993, in response to President Clinton's proposal for a government-run health-care system, Norquist launched the now-famous Wednesday Meeting, an invitation-only, weekly gathering of conservatives in his Washington office for the purpose of coordinating activities and strategy. Beginning with a dozen or so attendees, the Wednesday Meeting had grown to an average of about 45 a year later, with participants including representatives of the National Rifle Association, the Christian Coalition, and the Heritage Foundation. An early sign of the meetings' importance—and Norquist's power—emerged in 1994: Republicans, led by Gingrich, the new Speaker of the House, gained the majority of seats in the House of Representatives and the Senate for the first time in 40 years, in a victory attributed largely to Gingrich's "Contract with America." Co-authored by Norquist and other conservatives, the so-called contract detailed legislation that Republicans would introduce if their party gained control of Congress, including bills aimed at reforming the welfare system, requiring a three-fifths majority in both houses of Congress to raise taxes, passing a balanced-budget amendment, and setting congressional term limits.

Norquist used the Republicans' newfound power to expand Americans for Tax Reform through networking, direct-mail fund-raising, and pursuit of corporate backing; currently, the organization boasts an annual budget of approximately $7 million. He also helmed each Wednesday Meeting with a "big-tent" approach, deemphasizing such social issues as gay rights and abortion— which tend to divide conservatives—and placing a strong emphasis on tax cuts, tort reform, and the rollback of federal business regulations. That strategy helped to draw the support of major corporations including Microsoft, Pfizer, AOL Time Warner, UPS, and Philip Morris. While some conservatives maintained that catering to corporate interests would result in too many compromises of core conservative principles, Norquist insisted that his organization's alliance with corporations would benefit the Republican Party. For example, the promise of tort reform attracted millions of campaign dollars from corporations and undermined the clout of trial lawyers, who constituted an important segment of the Democratic support base; also, the anticipation of tax cuts for rich investors led them to give more money for Republican campaigns. In addition, the privatization of Social Security, a goal of conservatives, would greatly benefit Wall Street brokers, who were strong Republican allies and generous campaign contributors.

Norquist broadened his "leave-us-alone" coalition through alliances with a number of religious groups, among them evangelical Protestants, Mormons, conservative Catholics, and Orthodox Jews. In the mid-1990s he drew criticism when he cast his eyes on the American Muslim community, whose support he saw as necessary for the conservative movement. Many on the right condemned Norquist's efforts to make allies of such groups as the Council of American-Islamic Relations (CAIR), citing its members' failure to oppose the terrorist activities of Hamas and Hezbollah. Norquist viewed his pursuit of Muslim support as part of a larger purpose: defeating the Democrats. He told a gathering of *National Journal* reporters and editors, as quoted by Paul Starobin in that publication (November 19,2005), "The point of being an American is that you are for individual liberty and freedom and the Constitution. It doesn't matter, frankly, what language Mom speaks, or what religion you are."

In 1997 Norquist and the lawyer David Safavian founded a lobbying firm, the Merritt Group, which was later renamed Janus-Merritt Strategies. (The firm was sold in 2002 to the Virginia-based Williams Mullen Strategies.) Emphasizing free markets and seeking to reduce the size of the federal government, Merritt represented businesses including BP America (the U.S. division of British Petroleum), Seagram, Universal Studios, and a wide range of Mexican industrial groups. In the area of gaming interests, the firm, together with the lobbyist Jack Abramoff, advocated for Native American tribes such as the Saginaw Chippewa and the Viejas Band of Kumeyaay Indians. The firm became known for its controversial clients, such as Pascal Lissouba, the corrupt former president of the Republic of the Congo, and Abdurahman Alamoudi, the founder of the American Muslim Council, who was an outspoken supporter of Hamas and Hezbollah. In 1998 Norquist cofounded the Islamic Free Market Institute with the Washington lobbyist and libertarian Khaled Saffuri, who had numerous contacts in the U.S. Muslim community. The institute sought to inspire and facilitate the development of economically conservative grassroots Muslim movements. Alamoudi devoted tens of thousand of dollars to the group before being convicted, in July 2004, of tax and immigration violations and illegal dealings with Libya; he was sentenced to 23 years in prison, having confessed to a role in an assassination plot targeting Saudi Arabia's crown prince. Right-wing critics attacked Norquist's alliance with the Muslim community as being a hindrance to the conservative movement and a threat to the safety of the American public. In a December 2003 article for *Front- PageMag.com*, Frank J. Gaffney Jr., a Norquist nemesis and a former assistant secretary of defense in the Reagan administration, wrote, "Grover Norquist's efforts to legitimate and open important doors for pro-Islamist organizations in this country must be brought to an immediate halt." Norquist has refused to talk about Alamoudi for the record, and his partner, Saffuri, has claimed that he was deceived by Alamoudi and had no prior knowledge of his criminal activities.

Meanwhile, Norquist had been a major force in George W. Bush's first presidential campaign. In November 1998 he met with Bush and his top political aide, Karl Rove (later his deputy chief of staff at the White House), in Austin, Texas. Impressed with Bush's stances on tax cuts, school choice, tort reform, pension reform, and other subjects, Norquist decided that Bush was the best hope for the Republican Party in the 2000 presidential election. He started rallying support for Bush in Washington, helping to bring the majority of conservatives there into Bush's camp. He was also responsible for organizing the conservative counterattack against Bush's main Republican competitor, U.S. senator John McCain of Arizona. In early 2000, after McCain defeated Bush in the New Hampshire primary, Norquist led a crusade against the senator and his policies. He helped develop TV spots that assailed McCain's campaign-finance proposals as being in opposition to First Amendment rights and that showed an image of McCain's face being morphed into Clinton's. Bush went on to win the next 11 of 16 primaries and clinched the Republican nomination easily. Robert Dreyfuss wrote for the *Nation* (May 14, 2001, on-line), "To a significant degree, George W. Bush owes his election to Norquist." After Bush was elected, in November 2000, Norquist became the "field marshal," as some called him, of Bush's $1.3 trillion tax-cut package, known as the Economic Growth and Tax Relief Reconciliation

Act of 2001. To win bipartisan support for the legislation, he put pressure on congressional Democrats by coordinating a campaign to get state legislatures to pass resolutions of support; he also organized 17 conservative groups under the umbrella of the American Conservative Union to champion Bush's plan. When passed, in June 2001, the bill became the third-largest tax cut since World War II.

Norquist supervised Bush's second tax cut, the Jobs and Growth Tax Relief Reconciliation Act of 2003, which accelerated the tax-rate cuts that were enacted in 2001 and temporarily reduced the tax rate on capital gains and dividends to 15 percent. The cuts were controversial, with some calling them bad economic policy and noting that they favored the wealthy and other special-interest groups. Bush's supporters asserted that the cuts fostered job growth and increased the pace of economic recovery from the recession caused by the terrorist attacks of September 11, 2001. The Congressional Budget Office estimated that the tax cuts would increase budget deficits by $60 billion in 2003 and by $340 billion by 2008. Detractors have noted that increased deficits will leave the U.S. more indebted to other nations in the years to come, reduce the resources necessary to invest in the future of the country, and pass on debt to future generations.

In October 2003 Norquist found himself in the midst of more controversy when, during an interview with Terry Gross for National Public Radio, he compared the estate tax to the Holocaust. (He later apologized for the comparison.) Meanwhile, he was active in Bush's 2004 reelection campaign. After Bush's victory, Norquist's candor was on full display. He told the *Washington Post*, quoted in its November 4, 2004 edition, "Once the [Democratic] minority of [the] House and Senate are comfortable in their minority status, they will have no problem socializing with the Republicans. Any farmer will tell you that certain animals run around and are unpleasant, but when they've been fixed, then they are happy and sedate." In 2005 and 2006 Norquist's Americans for Tax Reform helped pass two more Bush tax bills, which extended through 2010 the rates on capital gains and dividends that had been enacted in 2003, raised the exemption levels for the Alternative Minimum Tax, and enacted new tax incentives designed to persuade individuals to save more money for retirement.

In 2006 Norquist's ties to the lobbyist Jack Abramoff, who had been sentenced to more than five years in prison after being convicted of fraud, conspiracy, and tax evasion, became a focus of media attention—as did the indictment of Norquist's former partner at Janus-Merritt Strategies, David Safavian, on charges of making false statements and obstructing investigations into his dealings with Abramoff. In June of that year, an investigative report on Abramoff's lobbying was released by the Senate Indian Affairs Committee, chaired by Norquist's longtime adversary John McCain. The report implicated Americans for Tax Reform in a money-laundering scheme. ATR was labeled a cash "conduit" for financing Abramoff s clients in other grassroots lobbying campaigns; Abramoff, it was determined, had been instructing his gambling clients, many of them Native Americans whom he had misled, to write checks to ATR, which passed them on to other conservative organizations, sometimes after keeping a percentage. As a result, Norquist faced possible indictment for violating the provisions of his organization's tax-exempt status. The potential charges against him included lobbying for companies without reporting that activity as a business expense and introducing Abramoff's clients to important Washington officials, among them Karl Rove, in exchange for donations to ATR. Norquist maintained his innocence, explaining to Rachel Van Dongen for *Congressional Quarterly Weekly* (November 3, 2006), "There are no tax implications at all." The Norquist-McCain feud turned public, as noted by Ryan Lizza for the *New Republic* (March 20-27, 2006), when Norquist called the Arizona senator a "nut job" and a "gungrabbing, tax-increasing Bolshevik." McCain's chief of staff countered Norquist by saying that "most Reagan revolutionaries came to Washington to do something more patriotic than rip off Indian tribes." While Norquist's reputation suffered, he was not indicted.

Norquist has expressed optimism about a Republican presidential and congressional win in 2008. In the meantime, he has urged his conservative peers not to work toward accomplishing anything in the 110th, Democratic-controlled Congress. At a March 2007 Conservative Political Action Conference, as quoted on a transcript posted on the Think Progress Web site (March 2, 2007), he said, "Get married, develop a hobby, learn to belly dance, learn to golf—you know, we got two years free, but we gotta spend time and effort playing defense here. Our job is to say 'no, no, no, no' for two years." Norquist has remained steadfast in his support for the war in Iraq but has acknowledged its detrimental effect on other national matters, explaining to Ronald Kessler

for the News Max Web site (July 26, 2007), "You have an unease among a lot of non-political people, but the real cost of Iraq is not even so much that unease as the drowning out of other issues. We can't run against the Democrats—calling them the party that wants to raise taxes—if the president can only talk about Iraq."

Norquist remains an influential figure in Washington circles as the head of ATR; his long-term goals include cutting the cost of government in half over the coming decades, converting Social Security and public-pension programs into systems of private investment accounts, and replacing affirmative action with "color-blind" policies. He explained to Susan Page, "As long as the Christians don't steal anyone's guns, the anti-tax activists don't violate anyone's property rights, the property owners don't interfere with the home-schoolers, the home-schoolers don't want to regulate the small businessmen and the gun owners agree not to throw condoms at the Christians' kids, then we can all work together."

## PERSONAL LIFE

Norquist "is often described as an eccentric," Laura Blumenfeld wrote for the *Washington Post* (January 12, 2004), before his marriage. "For a bedside table, Norquist uses a giant green canister for Kraft parmesan cheese. He displays what he hopes will be the world's largest collection of airsickness bags. At staff meetings, employees say, he holds court while variously sitting on a giant red plastic ball, eating tuna from a can, rubbing his feet against a massager and sniffing hand lotion as he kneads it into his fingers. He excuses himself to go to the 'ladies room.' His manner is charming, though bitterness creeps into his voice when he talks about classmates at Harvard." Norquist currently serves on the board of directors of the National Rifle Association and the American Conservative Union and is a contributing editor at the *American Spectator* magazine, for which he writes a monthly column. He is also a member of the Council on Foreign Relations and the chairman emeritus of the Islamic Institute. In 1995 he authored the book *Rock the House*, which gives an in-depth insider's account of the Republican takeover of Congress in 1994. Norquist exercises 40 minutes daily, enjoys reading murder mysteries, and occasionally listens to literary works on audiotape. He and his wife, Samah Alrayyes, whom he married in April 2005, reside in Washington, D.C. "From the moment [Norquist] gets up to the moment he gets to bed, he thinks, 'How am I going to hurt the other team?'" Stephen Moore, the president of the antitax group Club for Growth, explained to Scherer. "One time I was telling Grover about this woman I met. Most guys would say, 'Oh, is she really good-looking?' or something like that. Grover said, 'Is she good on guns?' He was being totally serious."

## FURTHER READING

*Boston Globe F pl+ Apr. 17, 2002; Mother Jones p42+ Jan. 1, 2004; Nation (on-line) May 14, 2001; National Journal (online) Nov. 19, 2005; New Republic p9+ Mar. 27, 2006; New York Times p35 Jan. 16, 2005; Slate (online) July 7, 2003; USA Today A pl3+ June 1, 2001; Washington Post A pl+ Jan. 12, 2004; Easton, Nina J. Gang of Five: Leaders at the Center of the Conservative Crusade, 2000; Rock the House, 1995*

---

# ELEANOR HOLMES NORTON

## Political Leader; Civil Rights Lawyer

**Born:** June 13, 1937; Washington, D.C.
**Primary Field:** Race & Gender Equality
**Affiliation:** American Civil Liberties Union

## INTRODUCTION

*Outspoken, able, and assertive, Eleanor Holmes Norton has been Washington, D.C.'s Congressional Delegate to the U.S. House of Representatives since 1991. Prior to that, she served as Chairperson of the Equal Employment Opportunity Commission from 1977 to 1981 and was Chairperson of the New York City Commission on Human Rights from 1970 to 1977. The first woman to head the Equal Employment Opportunity Commission and New York City's powerful anti-discrimination agency, Ms. Norton brought to her post five years experience as an A.C.L.U. lawyer specializing in First Amendment cases. As head of the Human Rights Commission, she became known for her ability to obtain federal grants to assist her in her all-out effort to end all forms of discrimination. "There are certain substantive principles that I believe in strongly," she once said. "One is racial equality. The other is free speech. As it turns out, if I want to implement the principle of equality, I do it through participation in the civil rights movement. To implement my belief in free speech, I represent anyone whose free speech has been infringed."*

*She continues the fight to get residents of the District Columbia full representation in Congress. Delegates to Congress are entitled to sit in the House of Representatives and vote in committees, but are not allowed to take part in legislative floor votes. The District of Columbia, technically a U.S. Territory, shares this limited form of representation with Puerto Rico, Guam,* *American Samoa, Northern Mariana Islands, and the U.S. Virgin Islands. Legislation strongly supported by Norton that would grant the District of Columbia a voting Representative in the House, the District of Columbia House Voting Rights Act of 2009, was passed by the United States Senate on February 26, 2009. However the legislation stalled in the House and failed to pass prior to the end of the 111th Congress.*

## EARLY LIFE

The eldest of three girls, Eleanor Holmes Norton was born Eleanor Holmes on June 13, 1937, in Washington, D.C. Her father, whom she once described as a "rabid New Dealer" was a Civil Servant in the Housing Department of the District of Columbia; her mother was a teacher. Both parents were college graduates and instilled in their children the importance of hard work and a good education. As if by example, her father returned to school to earn his law degree while Eleanor Holmes was still a child. "We were a close family and an egalitarian family" she said years later, as quoted in *Women Today* (1975). "My father always wanted a boy but never seemed fazed that he had all girls. He was terribly proud of us and just assumed that girls could do whatever boys did. My mother and grandmother felt the same way, and my sisters and I had a sense that a little girl can grow up to be somebody."

A diligent student in a segregated public school in Washington, D.C., Miss Holmes dreamed of becoming a missionary in Africa, or a teacher, "like all the nice little colored girls wanted to be," as she once put it. She remembered her childhood in an interview with Judy Michaelson for the *New York Post* (October 30, 1968): "I used to ask why I couldn't go to the bathroom in Hecht's Department Store or to the movies downtown.

The only thing that wasn't segregated was the buses. Middle-class Black parents went to great pains to indoctrinate their children, to mitigate the effects of all this. They attempted to give you a feeling of specialness."

Following her graduation from Dunbar High School, the only college preparatory secondary school in the nation's capital attended by Black children, she enrolled in Antioch College, in Yellow Springs, Ohio, in the autumn of 1955. Originally attracted to that small liberal arts college by its innovative work-study program, she switched her major from Science to History in her sophomore year. Encouraged by her professors, she went on to advanced studies at Yale University after taking her B.A. degree from Antioch in 1960. A "natural protester" and a "natural advocate" by her own estimation, Miss Holmes, having settled on a career in law, received her M.A. degree in American studies, in 1963, and her Doctor of Jurisprudence degree in 1964.

## LIFE'S WORK

In the course of her five-year career with the A.C.L.U., Ms. Norton represented alleged criminals, Vietnam War (formally known as the Vietnam Conflict) protesters, Civil Rights activists, Ku Klux Klansmen, politicians, and feminists. In one highly publicized case, she won promotions for 60 women employees who accused *Newsweek* magazine of job discrimination based on sex. "Society is organized so that it depends on discrimination against women," she observed to Prudence Brown in an interview for *Newsday* (January 23, 1971). "Blacks have felt it only in the last several hundred years, but for women it has been throughout history. The Newsweek management was not a malicious predator against women; it was a victim of society. And I don't think anything will work to change management's point of view short of coming down very hard on it."

Convinced that the First Amendment contributed to "almost every social change in the 20th century," Ms. Norton specialized in cases involving freedom of speech. For instance, she was a member of the team of lawyers that drew up a brief in defense of Julian Bond, a Georgia State Representative, when the Georgia House of Representatives voted overwhelmingly to deny the young Black legislator his seat for his outspoken opposition to the Vietnam War and military conscription. When New York City Mayor John V. Lindsay, fearing civil unrest, refused to grant Gov. George C. Wallace, the American Independent Party's candidate for the Presidency, a permit to hold a rally at Shea Stadium during the 1968

election campaign, Ms. Norton asked to represent him in his lawsuit against the city. "If people like George Wallace are denied free expression, then the same thing can happen to Black people," she explained to one interviewer. "Black people understand this. No Black person ever said to me, 'Sister, how come you're representing George Wallace?' They knew how come." (Wallace's A.C.L.U. lawyers won their case, but, when New York City appealed the decision, Wallace moved the rally to Madison Square Garden, to save the time and expense of another litigation.)

In October 1968, Ms. Norton argued and won her first case before the Supreme Court as the legal representative of the National States Rights party, a White supremacist group that had been denied permission for a rally in Maryland two years earlier, because worried local authorities thought that the group's vocal denunciations of Jews, Blacks, and others might provoke angry responses from nonparty members. "Some people think free expression leads to violence [and] there are some occasions when some speaker works people up," she conceded, as quoted in *Women Today*. "But that's very rare. Speech isn't what leads to violence. Free speech can avoid violence. If Civil Rights hadn't come by free expression, it would probably have come by revolution." In addition to practicing law, Ms. Norton was an Adjunct Professor at New York University Law School and taught Black History at the Pratt Institute in Brooklyn, N.Y.

In April 1970, Mayor John V. Lindsay appointed Eleanor Holmes Norton Chair of the New York City Commission on Human Rights. Hesitant at first, Ms. Norton decided to accept the appointment because the Human Rights Commission, by law, acts as the representative of and advocate for the complainants. At a press conference shortly after taking office, she told news reporters, "As commissioner, I will attempt to see that no man is judged by the irrational criteria of race, religion, or national origin. And I assure you I use the word 'man' in the generic sense, for I mean to see that the principle of nondiscrimination becomes a reality for women as well."

Because many working women are, in Ms. Norton's view, "classic [Uncle] Toms" who don't see themselves as objects of discrimination, women are more exploited by businesses than any other group. "Most people think Civil Rights today is about whether or not I'm turning down somebody at the door because he is Black or female," she explained to one interviewer. "It doesn't happen that way anymore. It is more subtle. It happens when women are asked at a job interview 'Do you intend to get pregnant within the next two years?' And it happens to women much more than it happens to Blacks, because Blacks have spent 300 years trying to educate the country about how perverse it all is." Taking the offense, Ms. Norton decided not to wait for specific complaints, and, instead targeted individual companies for investigation of possible discriminatory practices.

In response to individual complaints, she obtained maternity benefits, including maternity leave, for single women, from an airline, a major bank, and a blue-collar employer; convinced another company to allow a pregnant secretary to remain on the job past her seventh month of pregnancy; won for a woman sports reporter the right to sit in the press box at hockey games; forced the chic 21 Club to serve women on an equal basis with men; and ordered the Biltmore Hotel to change the name of its Men's Bar and to open that male bastion to women. Working closely with national and local women's groups, Ms. Norton promoted the revision of outdated federal and state laws regulating workmen's compensation and minimum wages, the liberalizing of abortion laws, and the establishment of adequate day care centers. "My whole position on working women is that women ought to have choices," she said. "The choices are not always available to women today. Without day care centers, without equal employment opportunities, the right to work is more mythical than real."

To provide a forum for the particular problems of Black women, who have had to contend with both racial and sexual discrimination, Ms. Norton helped found the National Black Feminist Organization, in August 1973. "The Black woman already has a rough equality [with men], which came into existence out of necessity, and, is now ingrained in the Black lifestyle," she explained to Charlayne Hunter in an interview for the *New York Times* (November 17, 1970). "Black women had to work with, or beside, their men, because work was necessary to survival. . . . That gave the Black family very much of a head start on egalitarian family life. Black men are the one group accustomed to women who are able and assertive because their mothers and sisters were that way," she continued. "I don't think they want their wives to be like the White suburban chocolate eaters who live in Larchmont."

To combat job discrimination against Blacks, Hispanics, Vietnam Veterans, ex-offenders, and older employees, the former Commissioner urged businesses to give these people access to "higher-level, skilled, and better-paid jobs in every industry." In a speech to the Association of Personnel Agencies of New York, at the Pierre Hotel, in New York City, on April 2, 1971, she contended that while most companies had made an effort to recruit minority group members for entry-level positions, few offered these employees any real chance for advancement. Without adequate employment opportunities for minorities, she warned, "the 1970s might well bring consequences none of us would like to envision."

One of the country's most outspoken advocates of tough anti-blockbusting legislation, Commissioner Norton helped to push through the New York State Legislature the nation's strictest law prohibiting discriminatory real estate practices. "People run from neighborhoods because they have no idea what Black people are like," she once explained. "They think Black people live in Harlem and are on welfare, and, 'Lord, some of them are going to move next to me, so I'm going to move to the suburbs.' The point is the Black who moves next door is most likely to be a policeman whose wife is a nurse, and together they make $25,000. It's a great financial sacrifice for them to move out of the ghetto and they're going to work hard to keep the new neighborhood from becoming another ghetto."

Horrified by the imbalance between minority students and minority teachers in New York City's schools, Ms. Norton convened public hearings on the Board of Education's employment practices, in January 1971, citing a 1969 Board of Education survey that showed that minority groups comprised 55 percent of the students, nine percent of the teachers, and four percent of the principals, she ordered Human Rights Commission investigators to look into recruitment, appointment, and promotion procedures, and, to outline constructive proposals for "immediate change and improvement in the way Blacks and Puerto Ricans are treated by the educational system."

"You can't just say there aren't enough Blacks and Puerto Ricans around who are eligible for the job," she argued, as quoted in the *New York Times* (November 2, 1970). "Private industry devised methods to improve minority employment. Other school systems have done it, and I think New York can do it, too."

Turning her attention to municipal government, she conducted a census of city employees to check for racial or sexual discrimination, set up Affirmative Action programs, and broadened maternity leave policies. In a

## Affiliation: American Civil Liberties Union

In late 1964, Eleanor Holmes moved to Philadelphia where she spent a year clerking for a federal judge. There she met Edward Norton, then a naval officer stationed in the city. They were married on October 9, 1965. "He liked the fact that I was a highly educated woman," she told Greta Walker in an interview for the latter's book, *Women Today*. "Nobody would have married me who didn't want a woman with a career. By the time my husband met me, a career was totally built into my being. I would never have attracted a man who wanted a wife to stay home." Later that year, the couple moved to New York City, where Ms. Norton took a job as the Assistant Legal director of the American Civil Liberties Union.

memorandum to Mayor Lindsay, made public on January 25, 1973, she complained that because only three of the 14 members of the Human Rights Commission were attorneys qualified to conduct hearings, vital work of the Commission was being unnecessarily delayed. She recommended that the Mayor hire two professional hearings officers to replace the 14 unpaid Commissioners and raise the Commission to the status of a full-fledged city department.

Impressed by her ability and her aggressiveness, Mayor Abraham D. Beame asked Ms. Norton, in 1974, to stay on for a second term. Her reappointment was supported by 100 Black Men, the NAACP, the National Urban League, feminists, leading city politicians, and both of New York City's Black newspapers. Among her few opponents were a handful of Black militants, who charged that she had neglected "the bread- and-butter issues that affect black people." Ms. Norton, who considers herself to be a Black militant, termed these accusations "ridiculous."

"I have a stake in the Black struggle and want my cohorts in the struggle to understand the role I'm playing," she has said, as quoted in *Ebony* (January 1969). "I believe that the peaceful approach to problems is the most viable way . . . , [but] when the brothers go into the streets, as in Newark and Detroit [in the late 1960s], I can number myself among the Black people who sit back and categorically condemn them. I have to ask myself, 'Was that violence totally unwarranted?'"

In 1977, Norton was appointed by then President Jimmy Carter as the first female Chairperson of the U.S. Equal Employment Opportunity Commission. She released the E.E.O.C.'s first set of regulations outlining what constituted sexual harassment, and, declaring that sexual harassment was indeed a form of sexual discrimination that violated Federal Civil Rights laws.

Before she became a Congressional Delegate, Norton served as a Senior Fellow of the National Urban Institute and a Professor at Georgetown University Law Center, in 1982. She was a vocal anti-apartheid activist and part of the Free South Africa Movement, and served on the Boards of several civic, Civil Rights, and public service organizations. In 1990, Norton and 16 other people formed African-American Women for Reproductive Freedom. She also contributed an essay to an anthology *Sisterhood Is Forever: The Women's Anthology for a New Millennium*, edited by Robin Morgan, entitled, "Notes of a Feminist Long Distance Runner."

When she was elected as a Congressional Delegate on the Democratic Party ticket, it was revealed that neither she nor her husband paid District of Columbia income tax returns between 1982 and 1989. She and her husband paid more than $80,000 in back taxes and fines. She is a member of the Congressional Progressive Caucus and the Congressional Black Caucus. Besides her fight to give residents of the District of Columbia better representation in Congress, Norton has repeatedly introduced a version of the Nuclear Disarmament and Economic Conversion Act, which would require the United States to disable and dismantle its nuclear weapons, when all other nations possessing nuclear weapons do likewise, since 1994. She serves on several House committees and subcommittees, including: Committee on Oversight and Government Reform; Subcommittee on Federal Workforce, Post Office, and the District of Columbia; Subcommittee on Information Policy, Census, and National Archives; Committee on Transportation and Infrastructure; Subcommittee on Aviation; Subcommittee on Economic Development, Public Buildings and Emergency Management; and, Subcommittee on Water Resources and Environment. She has sponsored and supported legislation and made several television appearances, such as appearing as a regular panelist on the PBS women's news program *To the Contrary*, interviews with Stephen Colbert, and *Democracy Now!*

On October 2, 2014, *ABC News* reported she co-sponsored a bill aimed at changing the National Football

League's tax-exempt status unless it supported changing the name of *The Washington Redskins* to a 'non-racist slur.'

## PERSONAL LIFE

Norton and her husband, Edward Norton, married in 1965. He passed away in 1993. They had two children, Katharine and John. She received a Foremother Award for her lifetime of accomplishments from the National Research Center for Women & Families in 2011.

## FURTHER READING

*Biog N p163 Ja/F 75 por; Ebony 24:37+ Ja 69 pors; N Y Post p55 O 30 68 por; p4 F 12 74 por; N Y Sunday News mag p2Q-f- Ja 12 75 por Newsday p40 Ja 23 71 pors; Bird, Caroline. Enterprising Women (1976) Walker, Greta. Women Today (1975)*

# O

## ALEXIS OHANIAN

### Internet Entrepreneur; Free Speech Activist

**Born:** April 24, 1983; Maryland
**Primary Field:** Freedom of Speech
**Affiliation:** Reddit

#### INTRODUCTION

*A year after graduating from college, Alexis Ohanian and his former college dorm mate, Steve Huffman, founded* Reddit, *the self-described "front page of the Internet." The social networking site and community board began to grow in popularity and, within a year, had become one of the fifty most popular websites. In 2006 Ohanian and his fellow cofounder sold the site to the publishing giant* Condé Nast. *Ohanian became a multimillionaire at the age of twenty-three. But he continued to be involved with the site for three years and would later, in the fall of 2014, return as chairman. He also wrote the best-selling book* Without Their Permission: How the 21st Century Will Be Made, Not Managed *(2013), went on to found and cofound various tech companies, and has passionately advocated for Internet freedom. He has twice appeared on the* Forbes *Thirty under Thirty list.*

#### EARLY LIFE

Alexis Ohanian was born on April 24, 1983. He was raised in Columbia, Maryland, by his mother, Anke, a night-shift pharmacy technician, and his father, Chris, a travel agent. When Ohanian was ten years old, his parents bought their first computer. The PC was primarily for their son, who became obsessed with it. Although on occasion he would break it, he would repair it himself as well. At that time, in 1993, the Internet was not ubiquitous, and at first the Ohanians did not have an Internet connection. When they did finally get one, much to their son's delight, it worked via a dial-up modem, which was slow but still provided a connection the rest of the world.

Ohanian was a big video-game enthusiast. He particularly loved *Quake II*, so he created a website, his first, which was a fan page for that video game. As he writes in *Without Their Permission*, he was thrilled by the "power" of being able to attract real people to see his fan site—his online creation. "I could build something from my suburban bedroom," he wrote, "and millions (okay, well, hundreds) of people all over the world could see just how much I loved a video game. That's how I got interested in making websites. There was no turning back." He also launched FreeAsABird.org, through which he designed custom websites for small nonprofit organizations, free of charge. Although he was only a teenager, nobody questioned Ohanian's age. He would e-mail the organization with a pitch to help, and no one had any idea how old he was.

Ohanian also held various paying part-time jobs during high school, including working for two-and-a-half years as a waiter at Pizza Hut. But it was his job for a company called Sidea that would go on to make the biggest impact. His job for Sidea involved doing software and hardware demonstrations at a booth at a CompUSA store. With the aid of a big computer monitor and a headset microphone, young Ohanian made presentations—every half hour, regardless of audience presence or attentiveness—about computer products current at the time. In *Without Their Permission*, Ohanian points out that that was genuinely a "fabulous way for me to start public speaking." Speaking to a room full of people, or a room with a few people, or an empty room day after day proved to be an invaluable lesson.

Ohanian was a big kid. The tallest boy in class, as a young teen he was also overweight, weighing around 260 pounds. In school he stood out, but he was not exactly popular with the "cool" kids or the opposite sex. But that did not seem to bother him much. He had his group of friends. "I cared too much about video games and computers," he writes in *Without Their Permission*, "to realize how not cool I was." In the world outside of school, however, he was presumed to be older just because of his size. He recounts an amusing story of one day, while working at CompUSA, being approached by a man shopping for a mouse for his computer. Although there were no significant differences between them, Ohanian suggested the color of one mouse as being a bonus "feature." Amused, the man gave him his business card and offered him a job in sales. "I didn't have the heart to tell the man I was only fourteen," Ohanian writes. After years of being overweight, Ohanian in his junior year decided to cut out junk food and soft drinks and to start exercising. He lost nearly sixty pounds as a result.

Another important lesson came from observing his father. For about three decades, his father had been a travel agent, but then his industry began to encounter turbulence—first a bit, then a lot. Because Ohanian was so fascinated by and good with computers and knew his way around the Internet, he understood all too well how people's ability to book their own plane tickets and hotel rooms dramatically affected his father's ability to make a living. His father, according to Ohanian's autobiography, adapted to the circumstances by switching his business model: his specialty became first-time and business travelers. Ohanian was privy to all these changes and developments because his father would openly discuss them during dinner. The lesson for Ohanian was simple and straightforward: "The Internet was a powerful tool, and I wanted to be sure I knew how to use it. The free market is ruthless. But it has to be. It's up to us to make the most of it." In other words, "disruptions" (to one's plans or business model) happen all the time, but to be ahead of the game it is best to be the one doing the disrupting.

## LIFE'S WORK

When, in the fall of 2001, Ohanian arrived at the Hancock House dorm on the University of Virginia campus, he had plans of becoming an immigration lawyer. He was also as enthusiastic about video games as he had ever been. That first day, across the hall from his dorm room, Ohanian noticed a fellow student playing the racing game *Gran Turismo*, and was instantly thrilled that someone at college was playing a video game. He and the other young man, Steve Huffman, instantly bonded over video games and would go on to be become best friends. Because these two young students would later create Reddit, one of the most popular websites on the Internet, this story would often be told and retold in many subsequent profiles and interviews.

Another part of this "origin story" is how Ohanian decided he did not want to become a lawyer after all. When he sat down to take the LSAT, the law school admissions exam, he chose not take the test, but instead walked out. Ohanian needed to think—and probably eat—so he went to a local Waffle House, which is where he decided he has no desire whatsoever to attend law school or be a lawyer. He would later call this moment an epiphany. He decided what he did want to do was start a company with his best friend, engineering student Steve Huffman.

During the summer between junior and senior year, Ohanian attended an international technopreneurship (technology entrepreneurship) conference in Singapore, an island country in Southeast Asia. He had been invited to attend the conference by Mark White, one of his favorite professors. By that point Ohanian and Huffman had already thought up a business idea, and in Singapore Ohanian shared the idea with his professor: MyMobileMenu, a service that allows users to order from restaurants on their phones. Professor White loved the idea and agreed to help. But this was in 2004, quite some time before from the proliferation of smartphones.

In the spring of 2005, Paul Graham gave a talk called "How to Start a Startup" before an audience in Cambridge, Massachusetts. In the crowd were college seniors Ohanian and Huffman, who had decided to attend over their spring break. Ohanian had no idea who Graham was, but Huffman surely did, the latter being the more tech-savvy of the two. After the talk Ohanian and Huffman approached Graham, asking to pitch him their business idea in exchange for a drink; Graham liked what he heard about MyMobileMenu and asked them to interview for Y Combinator, then a new company that trained and funded startups. The two could not have been more thrilled, but after the interview came some bad news: Graham told them Y Combinator would not support their idea but wanted to support them as entrepreneurs, so they needed to come up with a new plan. Upon their next meeting, Graham told them, as Ohanian recalled to Christine Lagario-Chafkin for *Inc.* magazine (June 2012), "You guys need to build the front page of the Internet." Ohanian and Huffman then went to work, with the help of the Y Combinator program. "We built Reddit in three weeks," Ohanian told Lagario-Chafkin. The site launched in 2005, and by the following year, due to its enormous potential and popularity, it was purchased by the publishing giant Condé Nast for an undisclosed sum (reportedly Ohanian received as much as $20 million). At twenty-three Ohanian was a multimillionaire.

The same year that they launched Reddit, Ohanian graduated from the University of Virginia with a bachelor's degree in history and commerce—with a concentration on management and international business—as well as a minor in German. Huffman graduated with an engineering degree.

After Condé Nast bought Reddit, Ohanian stayed on as a product manager but left that post in 2009 to pursue other projects and interests. That year he gave a popular TEDIndia talk about how the organization Greenpeace, in their campaign against the Japanese government allowing the practice of killing humpback whales, launched a campaign to name a whale to personalize the project and how Reddit users voted for Mister Splashy Pants—a name Greenpeace at first resisted and then embraced. In 2010 Ohanian volunteered for three months as a fellow in Yerevan, Armenia, for Kiva, a nonprofit organization that attempts to help people around the world through microloans. Upon returning to the United States, Ohanian resumed his entrepreneurial journey with Huffman, starting Breadpig, what he calls a "sidekick-for-hire," which publishes web comics as well as "other geeky novelties," according to his autobiography. Starting in 2010 Ohanian served as Y Combinator's ambassador to the East for three years. Also in 2010 he joined Hipmunk, a travel website Huffman founded, for which Ohanian primarily did prelaunch marketing and design. Ohanian is also an investor in dozens of startup companies.

Ohanian's book, *Without Their Permission: How the 21st Century Will Be Made, Not Managed* (2013), received publicity blurbs from the likes of statistician Nate Silver, Y Combinator partner Garry Tan, and Zappos.com CEO Tony Hsieh. A combination of memoir, guide on how to create a great startup, and manifesto on Internet freedom, it went on to become a *Wall Street Journal* business best seller.

In 2011 Ohanian used his influence and expertise to campaign against two congressional bills that had the potential to stifle Internet freedom: the Stop Online Piracy Act (SOPA) and Protect IP Act (PIPA). The opposition to these two pieces of proposed legislation came from both parties, as well as many average people and tech giants, including Wikipedia, Yahoo, Mozilla, and many others. As reported by Hayley Tsukayama for the *Washington Post* (5 Sept. 2012), Ohanian has pointed out how bipartisan the opponents of PIPA and SOPA were: "Republicans want to keep the open Internet safe from big government. Democrats want to keep it safe from big corporations. I say we agree to agree and move ahead. It was so successful because we literally had the Tea Party next to the MoveOn.org guys at these meetings. They don't often hang out together."

A couple years later Ohanian spoke out against paid prioritization of the Internet, the concept that Internet service providers (ISPs) should be allowed to charge higher rates for priority website access during times of peak web traffic. Ohanian and other advocates of net neutrality argue that the free, open Internet has facilitated innovation and startup growth and that government regulation of ISPs is needed to ensure that those conditions continue.

## PERSONAL LIFE

In June 2014 Ohanian became a partner at Y Combinator, and that November he returned to Reddit full-time as chairman after the company's CEO resigned. Ohanian lives in the New York City borough of Brooklyn. He has a cat named Karma.

## FURTHER READING

Koidin Jaffee, Michelle. "The Voice of His Generation: Reddit Co-Founder Alexis Ohanian Fights for a Free and Open Internet." *University of Virginia Magazine.* U. Va. Alumni Assn., Fall 2014. Web. 2 Dec. 2014; Lagorio-Chafkin, Christine. "How Alexis Ohanian Built a Front Page of the Internet." *Inc.* Mansueto Ventures, 30 May 2012. Web. 2 Dec. 2014; Ohanian, Alexis. *Without Their Permission.* New York: Grand Central, 2013. Print; Schulman, Michael. "Founder of Reddit and the Internet's Own Cheerleader." *New York Times.* New York Times, 22 Nov. 2013. Web. 5 Dec. 2014; Tsukayama, Hayley. "Alexis Ohanian, Reddit Co-Founder and Web Advocate." *Washington Post.* Washington Post, 5 Sept. 2012. Web. 2 Dec. 2014.

# Sean Patrick O'Malley

## Archbishop of Boston

**Born:** June 29, 1944; Lakewood, Ohio
**Primary Field:** Child Abuse Advocacy
**Affiliation:** Catholic Church

### Introduction

On September 7, 2003 Sean Patrick O'Malley, the archbishop of Boston, reached a landmark settlement with 550 people who claimed to have been sexually abused by priests. The settlement was a crucial step in helping the U.S. Catholic Church confront what many regard as the worst scandal in its history. The archdiocese of Boston had been rocked in 2002, when it was revealed that the city's archbishop, Cardinal Bernard Law, had covered up for priests accused of sexually abusing children by moving them to new parishes and failing to report the accusations to the proper authorities. Under intense criticism from both clergy and laity, Cardinal Law resigned in disgrace in December 2002. (He remained a cardinal, thus retaining the right to assume another church post as well as vote in a papal election.) O'Malley was appointed six months later to lead the country's fourth-largest diocese out of the crisis and begin the process of rebuilding the laity's confidence in the Church.

O'Malley began handling abuse cases during the 1990s, when he served as archbishop of the Fall River, Massachusetts, diocese, where, in the biggest abuse scandal of the decade, a priest was accused of molesting more than 100 children. While there he implemented a zero-tolerance policy toward priests accused of sexual abuse, established abuse-education classes, and reached settlements with most of the victims. O'Malley did the same with the Palm Beach, Florida, diocese, where he served as archbishop from 2002 until his appointment in Boston. Many saw his installation in Boston as a sign that the Vatican had finally begun to take the crisis seriously. "It's really a watershed moment for a diocese to receive a new bishop," Reverend James A. Field, the pastor of the Parish of the Incarnation of Our Lord and Savior Jesus Christ, in Melrose, Massachusetts, told Michael Paulson for the Boston Globe (July 30, 2003). "The installation is a way of symbolizing that a new day has begun and that we have a new shepherd." The Catholic Church in the U.S. is at a turning point in its history. In addition to the abuse crisis, the Church faces the closing of numerous schools and parishes due to declining numbers of students and parishioners, a shrinking pool of young priests, and low funds. Further, the ethnic makeup of the Church is changing in the U.S., as most new parishioners are immigrants who come from predominately Catholic countries. According to Monica Rhor in the Boston Globe (July 3, 2003), whites make up only half of all Catholic teenagers in America; within a few years, Latinos will make up the majority of Roman Catholics in the country. Many experts therefore believe that the future of the Catholic Church rests on the shoulders of immigrants. O'Malley, who holds a doctorate from the Catholic University of America, in Washington, D.C., and speaks six languages, has spent most of his career ministering to immigrant populations in the D.C. area, as well as in the U.S. Virgin Islands. Mario J. Paredes, one of O'Malley's coworkers at Centro Catolico Hispano, told Monica Rhor, "Rome made his appointment with all sorts of messages and meanings. He is being sent to a church that is no longer Irish, no longer the old boys. It is a church that is heavily Hispanic, heavily Portuguese, diverse, multicultural, and multilingual."

O'Malley's work with immigrants is part of his ministry as a Capuchin-Franciscan Friar. The Capuchin religious order is dedicated to following the teachings of the 13th-century Catholic mystic St. Francis of Assisi, an ascetic whose life was said to be characterized by humility, poverty, devotion, and joy. Members of the order live together in a community and take vows of poverty, chastity, and obedience; in addition to contemplation and prayer, they perform duties in accordance with the teachings of the New Testament. O'Malley was professed in the order at the age of 21 and ordained as a priest at 26. As a Capuchin, he wears sandals and a simple brown frock with a pointed hood, an outfit he wore even at his installation ceremony in Boston in 2003. He also insists on living in humble settings and refused to move into the archbishop's mansion, preferring instead a small apartment in an unfashionable section of the city. His views on Catholic life are orthodox; staunchly against abortion, he participates in the Church's annual rally in Washington, D.C. Above all else, O'Malley, who prefers to be called "Archbishop Sean," is known for his love of and commitment to the poor, his joyful demeanor, and his absolute devotion to others. As quoted by Linda Kulman, Jeff Glasser, Ange-

*la Marek, and Nancy L. Bentrup in* U.S. News & World Report *(July 14, 2003), Mary Ann Glendon, a member of the Pontifical Council for the Laity and a professor at the Harvard Law School, remarked after O'Malley's first press conference as archbishop, "[He] spoke words of great simplicity and power. This is really a case of what you see is what you get. The man radiates a certain kind of Franciscan personality that is going to be very, very good for wounded Boston."*

## EARLY LIFE

The younger of the two sons of Theodore and Mary Louise O'Malley, Sean Patrick O'Malley was born on June 29, 1944 in Lakewood, Ohio, and raised in Herman, Pennsylvania. His family was devoutly Catholic and often participated in religious retreats. It was after one such occasion that O'Malley had a formative encounter with a friar: returning home from a visit to a Franciscan retreat in Pennsylvania, the 10-year-old and his father met a mendicant dressed in a tattered robe and wearing a rosary around his neck. Afterward Theodore O'Malley commented to his son, "You know, that's the happiest man in the world," as Sean O'Malley recalled to Eric Convey for the *Boston Herald* (July 28, 2003). The encounter left a deep impression on O'Malley, who had already expressed a profound interest in matters of faith. He began to seriously consider entering the religious life and, two years later, enrolled at St. Fidelis Seminary, in Herman (other sources say Butler), Pennsylvania. A boarding school for teenagers wishing to enter the Capuchin order, St. Fidelis required its students to undergo rigorous training in the foreign languages: six years of Latin, four years of German, two of Spanish, two of Greek, and one of Hebrew. While other students spent much of their time playing sports, O'Malley preferred to participate in the school's theatrical productions and help out in the kitchen, where German nuns prepared meals for students and their teachers. "He's always been very unusual, really," Jack Healey, a human-rights worker and fellow student at St. Fidelis, told Convey. "Most of us were ballplayers hoping to be priests one day. Sean was a little priest the whole way through ... he was a little Franciscan the whole way through. He was the real thing from day one."

## LIFE'S WORK

O'Malley was professed in the Capuchin order in 1965 and ordained as a priest in 1970. After graduating from St. Fidelis, he continued his studies at Capuchin College, in Washington, D.C. At the Catholic University of America, O'Malley earned a master's degree in religious education and a doctorate in Spanish and Portuguese literature. Between 1969 and 1973 he taught at Catholic University and planned to eventually pursue missionary work oversees. That plan changed in 1973, when the archbishop of D.C. asked the Capuchins to help minister to the city's growing Latino population. O'Malley subsequently founded Centro Catolico Hispano, which provided immigrants and others with legal advice, employment referrals, English-as-a-Second-Language (ESL) and GED classes, and medical and dental services. He also confronted foreign ambassadors serving in D.C. about the way they treated domestic help, transported medical supplies to Central American countries, doled out food and medicine to those in need, opened a Spanish-language bookstore, and founded the first Spanish newspaper in the area. This work, coupled with O'Malley's Sunday Masses in English, Spanish, Portuguese, and French, cemented his connection to immigrant communities, a connection that would become the hallmark of his career.

O'Malley's commitment to immigrants was particularly manifest in his work at the Kenesaw, a dilapidated apartment building located in Adams Morgan, then one of the most impoverished neighborhoods in the nation's capital. For decades the building's owner, the Antioch Law School, had refused to provide tenants with even the most basic services, such as heat, hot water, and pest control. Nevertheless, the school continued to collect rent from tenants. In addition, drug dealers worked out of several of the apartments, and prostitutes routinely brought customers to unoccupied rooms there. In 1977 Antioch, which was in financial trouble and hoped to renovate and sell the building, served the tenants with eviction notices. When he heard about the plight of the tenants, O'Malley himself moved into the Kenesaw, taking two rooms—one in which he slept on the floor and one that he turned into a chapel. "It was a dangerous place to live, believe me," the lawyer and Kenesaw community activist Silverio Coy told Alan Cooperman and Pamela Ferdinand for the *Washington Post* (July 2, 3002). "He wanted to make a statement that not only was he going to help these people, he was going to share their needs and anxieties every single day." O'Malley helped the tenants renovate the building and fight the eviction. Refusing to pay rent to Antioch, the tenants repaired, cleaned, and painted the Kenesaw. They also took turns using a baseball bat to patrol the area for rats and drug dealers. Eventually, O'Malley helped the tenants organize themselves into a cooperative, which allowed them to secure enough funding from public agencies and banks to buy the building themselves. "A lot of good people lived there, but they didn't coordinate anything before Father O'Malley came," Coy said. "He transformed their lives."

O'Malley's work in the Washington, D.C., diocese prompted his installation as an Episcopal vicar for the Hispanic, Portuguese, and Haitian communities, and as executive director of the archdiocesan Office of Social Ministry in 1978. Six years later the Vatican granted his wish to serve in a foreign mission by appointing him coadjutor bishop of St. Thomas, U.S. Virgin Islands; a year later he was made full bishop. While there he built shelters for the homeless, established an AIDS hospice, and helped islanders rebuild after Hurricane Hugo, in 1989. One parishioner, Charlene Kehoe, said that attending a midnight Mass held by O'Malley inspired her to return to the Catholic Church after an absence of several decades. "I would never have come back to the church except for him," she told Thomas Farragher for the *Boston Globe* (July 27, 2003). "I thought I had found something better than the church. It wasn't until [the midnight Mass] that I saw that, aha, the church can be really spiritual— to really have truth within it. He has the ability to connect emotionally with people and to really hear them—to let them say their piece and to figure out what the next step would be with a deep spiritual understanding."

The U.S. Catholic Church was first confronted with a major sexual scandal in 1985, when a Louisiana priest, Gilbert Gauthe, was sentenced to 20 years in prison for molesting children. In 1992 Reverend James Porter of the Fall River diocese was accused of sexually abusing dozens of boys in five different states during the 1960s and 1970s. (He later pled guilty to 28 counts of abuse and was sentenced to 18 to 20 years in prison.) The Vatican subsequently sent O'Malley there to serve as bishop of the diocese and to help the largely Latino and Portuguese population heal. He helped settle 101 cases that had been brought against the diocese, instructing the church's lawyers that "it was the right thing to do." The bishop then initiated a zero- tolerance policy against sexual abuse (a policy that included running background checks on all clergy and church personnel) and provided sexual-abuse training to priests and lay volunteers alike. In addition, O'Malley set up the diocese's first Latino parish, Nuestro Senora de Guadalupe.

Ten years later, in 2002, the Vatican called on O'Malley to restore order to another diocese in crisis. This time he was sent to Palm Beach, Florida, where two consecutive bishops had left after sex- abuse scandals. Bishop J. Keith Symons had resigned in 1998, after admitting that he had molested five boys in three parishes; his replacement, Reverend Anthony J. O'Connell, resigned four years later, after admitting that he had repeatedly molested an underage student at a Missouri seminary where he had served as rector. As bishop, O'Malley promised to report all allegations of abuse to the proper authorities and to remove all guilty priests from service. He also issued a public apology to the victims and appointed a sheriff and a rabbi to an independent review board that had earlier been formed to handle sex-abuse accusations.

O'Malley's work in Palm Beach was stopped short, however, when the Vatican called on him to take over the archdiocese of Boston, the city that was at the center of the Church's sex-abuse crisis. After the Massachusetts priest John Geoghan was convicted, in January 2002, of molesting a 10-year- old boy, Cardinal Bernard Law, who was then archbishop of Boston, insisted that, while the case was an isolated incident, he would act decisively on all future charges of pedophilia brought against priests. Soon thereafter, documents were released showing that over the years Geoghan had been accused of molesting boys at several different parishes—yet instead of removing him from office, Cardinal Law had repeatedly reassigned him. Upon further investigation, a pattern of deception began to emerge: Law had regularly failed to report sex- abuse allegations to the proper authorities, had moved accused priests to new parishes (where many continued to molest children), and had either ignored or paid off victims. Amid calls for his resignation from both lay people and clergy, Cardinal Law stepped down as archbishop of Boston on December 13, 2002.

On July 1, 2003, Pope John Paul II appointed O'Malley to the position. The Capuchin priest was characteristically humble upon hearing the news, remarking, as quoted on CNN (July 2, 2003, online), "I feel acutely aware of my own deficiencies in the face of the task at hand, and I ask for everyone's prayers and collaboration as I embark on this ministry." During his installation ceremony, a sober affair devoid of the usual pomp and finery, O'Malley asked for forgiveness from those who had suffered sexual abuse at the hands of Catholic priests: "The whole Catholic community is ashamed and anguished because of the pain and damage inflicted on so many young people and because of our inability or unwillingness to deal with the crime of sexual abuse of minors," he said, as quoted on the CBS News Web site (July 31, 2003). "To those victims and to their families, we beg forgiveness and assure them that the Catholic church is working to create a safe environment for young people."

O'Malley's first act as archbishop was to replace the church's lead council working on the hundreds of civil lawsuits facing the Boston diocese, sending a signal to the city's Catholics that settling the cases was his top priority. O'Malley chose Thomas Hannigan, the attorney who had helped him settle abuse claims in Fall River, to replace Wilson Rogers Jr., who had been criticized for using hardball tactics against the plaintiffs. Within nine days of being installed, O'Malley offered a $55 million settlement to be divided among the victims, nearly twice the amount any diocese or archdiocese had paid at one time to settle claims of abuse. Although the settlement was rejected, both lawyers and victims were impressed by O'Malley's speedy offer, particularly considering that Cardinal Law and his lawyers had stalled negotiations for 18 months. "Any negotiation has to start in a certain place, and this is a good place," Roderick MacLeish Jr., a lawyer representing 260 victims, told Ralph Ranalli and Stephen Kurkjian for the *Boston Globe* (August 9, 2003, on-line). "We believe that there is a lot of good faith being shown by the archdiocese. There are still a lot of obstacles, but we are finally having a worthwhile and constructive dialogue." Negotiations continued, with O'Malley personally attending the bargaining sessions. He also met with many of the victims in private.

On September 7, 2003, barely a month after O'Malley became archbishop, the Boston archdiocese reached a settlement with 550 people who claimed to have been sexually abused by members of the church. The victims received an $85 million compensation package to be divided among them according to the severity and duration of the abuse, the largest amount ever in a clergy sexual-abuse case. The settlement also stipulated that victims would be included on all boards governing abuse, that the church would offer the victims mental-health counseling regardless of whether they accepted the settlement or not, and that the details of all such counseling would be kept confidential. Many credit O'Malley with persuading the victims to accept the offer. In addition to changing lawyers and participating

in the negotiating sessions, he won over many of the bitter victims through his attention, his patience, and his sensitivity. Many have said that they came to believe he truly cared about them. One example of O'Malley's personal attention to the victims was his response to the mental breakdown of a 25-year-old man who claimed he had been raped by a priest when he was five. After the breakdown, in September 2003, O'Malley immediately met with the man's parents and promised to do whatever was necessary to help their son, including paying for a residential treatment. A year earlier, Cardinal Law had sent a letter to the family in response to their lawsuit, suggesting that the parents' negligence had allowed the rape to occur. "It was a major change," the father told Kevin Cullen for the *Boston Globe* (September 10, 2003). "They reached out to my son at a time of need, no questions asked. This guy [O'Malley] has done everything he can since he got here to change the way things were done before, and he should get credit when he does the right thing." "Sean O'Malley has always struck people here as someone who puts people first, and there's no doubt in my mind that he will do so," Fall River's mayor, Edward M. Lambert, told Alan Cooper-man and Pamela Ferdinand. "I don't think it's the safe choice for the church. But I certainly think it's the right one."

In his position as archbishop, O'Malley has weighed in on some of the more controversial moral issues of the day, and he has been critical of elected officials over such matters. For example, according to LifeSiteNews.com (January 23, 2004, on-line), O'Malley said regarding Catholic politicians, "These politicians should know that if they're not voting correctly on these life issues [such as abortion] that they shouldn't dare come to communion." As quoted by the *Catholic Online* (March 12, 2004), he addressed the issue of marriage and homosexuality. Referring to proposals brought before the Massachusetts State Legislature, which sought to link the definition of marriage as a union between one man and one woman with a law giving same-sex civil unions the same protection under the law as marriage, O'Malley said, "We support the Marriage Affirmation and Protection Amendment as it has been presented, without the Introduction of civil unions language. The amendment seeks to protect a social institution that is essential to our society. A debate about social benefits given to other individuals in our law is a separate issue. . . . The amendment reaffirming marriage as the union between one man and one woman must be approved on its own merits. . . . Linking the two [proposals] coerces people in a way that is unfair." As quoted in the *Washington Times* (October 4, 2004), while speaking at the annual Red Mass at the Cathedral of St. Matthew the Apostle, in Washington, D.C., O'Malley said, "Too often when politicians agree with the Church's position on a given issue, they say the Church is prophetic and should be listened to, but if the Church's position does not coincide with theirs, then they scream separation of church and state."

## FURTHER READING

*Boston Globe (on-line) July 27, 2003; Boston Herald pl+ July 28, 2003, with photos; Providence Journal-Bulletin A pl+ May 5, 2000, with photos; U.S. News & World Report p36+ July 14, 2003, with photos; Washington Post A p3+ July 2, 2003*

# P

## WAYNE PACELLE

### President and CEO of the Humane Society

**Born:** August 4, 1965; Connecticut
**Primary Field:** Animal Rights
**Affiliation:** Humane Society

### INTRODUCTION

*Wayne Pacelle is the president and chief executive officer (CEO) of the Humane Society of the United States (HSUS), the largest organization working in the U.S. to "create a humane and sustainable world for all animals," according to its on-line mission statement. Pacelle is a vegan: he does not eat meat, fish, or fowl or consume or use any products obtained from animals, including milk, eggs, leather, wool, and items stuffed with goose down. But neither he nor HSUS expects others to emulate him. "I'm . . . conscious of the cultural complexities of this issue," he told Karen MacPherson for the Pittsburgh (Pennsylvania)* Post-Gazette *(December 20, 2004). "People are raised to think of animals in a certain way, and to use animals in some ways. I try to see where people are and give them encouragement to get to a place where they view animals not as tools for research or game to be harvested, but as individual beings that have the same spark of life that all of us have." Before he joined the HSUS, in 1994, Pacelle worked for six years with the Fund for Animals, a group whose main goal was to end sport hunting. He served as the HSUS's senior vice president for communications and government affairs until 2004, when he rose to its top position. "The arrival of Wayne Pacelle as head of the Humane Society in 2004 both turbo-charged the farm animal welfare movement and gave it a sheen of respectability," Kim Severson wrote for the* New York Times *(July 25, 2007). She also wrote, "Pacelle has retooled a venerable organization seen as a mild-mannered protector of dogs and cats into an aggressive interest group flexing muscle in state legislatures and courtrooms." In 2008* Supermarket News *named Pacelle to its annual Power 50 list of influential people In food marketing, declaring, "There's no denying his growing influence on how animal agriculture is practiced in the United States."*

### EARLY LIFE

The youngest of the four children of Richard and Patricia Pacelle, Wayne Pacelle was born on August 4, 1965. He grew up in New Haven, Connecticut. His father, who is of Italian descent, was a high-school gym teacher and football coach; his mother, whose ancestors were Greek, worked as a secretary for an uncle's construction business. "Ever since I was a kid I've been focused on animals," Pacelle told Patricia R. Olsen for the *New York Times* (December 24, 2006). "I dog-eared the pages with the animal entries in our encyclopedia and memorized everything about them, from a polar bear to a pronghorn antelope." Every week he watched the TV show *Wild Kingdom* and dreamed of meeting its host, Marlin Perkins. The family had pet dogs during Pacelle's childhood; one of them, he learned later, was a product of a puppy mill—in effect, a factory for producing what were touted as pure-bred dogs, for sale to dealers or pet stores. Typically, females at such facilities are overbred; that is, they are impregnated every time they go into heat and are often killed when they no longer produce litters of sufficient size or stop producing altogether. Also common in puppy mills is in- breeding, which results in increased frequencies of genetic defects; many of those problems do not become evident

## Affiliation: Humane Society of the United States (HSUS)

The HSUS was founded in 1954; currently, it has 10 million members. It works in both the U.S. and—through a subsidiary, the Humane Society International (HSI), established in 1991—the world over "to forge a lasting and comprehensive change in human consciousness of and behavior toward all animals in order to prevent animal cruelty, exploitation, and neglect and to protect wild habitats and the entire community of life." Thanks in part to images that have appeared in its ads and on address labels that have often accompanied its mailed fund-raising appeals, the HSUS is widely associated with the well-being of dogs and cats, but the welfare of pets is only one of its many concerns. (Indeed, the HSUS does not own or maintain any animal shelters, including those operated by local humane societies. It acts as an advocate for animal shelters when necessary, however, and publishes Animal Sheltering, a magazine regarded as the most comprehensive resource for shelter professionals.) High on HSUS's agenda is the reversal or slowing of global warming, which, if it continues unabated, according to the Intergovernmental Panel on Climate Change, will likely cause the extinction of up to a third of Earth's plant and animal species by 2050 (and have disastrous consequences for humans as well). Significantly contributing to global warming are the ways in which the 11 billion farm animals in the U.S. and more than 70 billion overseas are raised, the ways products are derived from them, and the ways those products are distributed. The HSUS and HSI urge major changes in the farm-animal industries and in the consumption of animal products. Toward that goal they have adopted what they call the "three R's" approach: "the refinement of production methods, the reduction of consumption, and the replacement of animal products with non-animal alternatives," according to the HSUS "Statements of Policy" (July 2009, on-line).

The top priorities of the HSUS include putting an end to the cruel treatment of animals in factory farms, in many of which pigs or calves raised for veal, for example, spend their entire lives in pens too small for them to turn around, and the beaks of chickens and turkeys are chopped off to prevent them from injuring or cannibalizing one another in their severely overcrowded enclosures. Among the other concerns of the HSUS are the use and treatment of animals in biomedical research and testing, in high-school and college classes,

and in the entertainment industry, which encompasses film, television, greyhound races, horse races, rodeos, and circuses. Other matters of importance to the organization are the treatment and uses of companion animals—those trained to assist people with physical, visual, or hearing impairments; the handling of animals by pet stores and pounds; policies regarding pets during disasters, such as Hurricane Katrina, which struck the Gulf Coast of the U.S. in 2005; the operations of so-called puppy mills; the lawful (in some states) and illegal (in most states) operations of "blood" sports, including dog fighting and cock fighting; hunting practices that HSUS regards as inhumane, including the use of certain types of traps and hunting on enclosed properties or from airplanes; trapping and ranching animals for the fur industry; activities of the fishing industry that threaten the existence of some marine species and cause the inadvertent destruction of others; and conditions at zoos and aquariums. In terms of individuals, the HSUS, Pacelle told Bridget Kelly for the Hartford (Connecticut) Courant (August 30, 2004), is "simply asking people to expand their sensitivity and to exhibit greater mercy and kindness to the less powerful. If you're concerned about the well-being of animals, then you inevitably should think about your food choices, your clothing choices, your recreational pursuits."

Some critics of the animal-rights movement believe Pacelle is a radical who is determined to ban all forms of hunting and force the American public into a vegetarian lifestyle. By contrast, some within the movement think that Pacelle is not radical enough. Pacelle contends that he understands both sides of the animal-rights debate. Although HSUS is energetically engaged in animal-rights activism, Pacelle has rejected the use of illegal or in-your-face tactics to achieve the goals of the HSUS—the sorts of methods sometimes employed by representatives of People for the Ethical Treatment of Animals (PETA), for example, or the more radical Animal Liberation Front, which advocates, according to its Web site, "radical abolitionism: total liberation by any means necessary." Rather, HSUS devotes its efforts to awakening the public to its philosophy and lobbying for the passage of legislation that would help to achieve its goals. Nevertheless, in press releases from organizations of furriers, livestock or poultry farmers, and dog owners (in particular, those whose members own

## Affiliation: Humane Society of the United States (HSUS) (*Continued*)

breeds commonly involved in dog fighting, such as pit bulls), HSUS is commonly and incorrectly equated with PETA or more-extreme groups. Pacelle has been quick to point out how they differ. He told Guy Raz for the National Public Radio (NPR) program All Things Considered (June 2, 2000), "There's no question that [PETA has] had some very significant victories in terms of getting major corporations to stop testing on animals. At the same time, I think it's clear that they have helped to contribute to the image of animal activism as sometimes a little too quirky and sometimes a little too radical." Pacelle told Alison Stewart for the NPR program The Bryant Park Project (November 6, 2007), "Really, our focus [at HSUS] is about human responsibility and less about animal rights. I mean, we're less concerned about whether animals have an inherent right than we are about what human responsibilities are in terms of our relationship with animals. ... We have all the power in the relationship over animals, and we think . . . being a good person means being decent and responsible in our care of animals."Affiliation: Humane Society of the United States (HSUS)

until long after the retail sale of the dogs. In addition, the animals are often inadequately fed and are kept in cramped, overcrowded cages. Many weaken or die during transport to dealers or shops. "There are millions of healthy adoptable dogs in shelters that are fine dogs," Pacelle told Don Oldenburg for the *Washington Post* (August 9, 2004). "And shelters end up killing dogs because our society fails to provide homes to them and people fail to sterilize their animals properly."

Pacelle planned to become a lawyer when he enrolled at Yale University, in New Haven, Connecticut, in 1983. The summer following his sophomore year, he interned as a ranger at the Isle Royale National Park, an island park in the part of Lake Superior that lies within the Michigan border. He has said his devotion to the animal-rights cause was sparked late one night as he canoed on the lake. "You're in this pristine environment," he recalled to Carla Hall for the *Los Angeles Times* (July 19, 2008). "Inside this area, the animals could be protected. It just spoke to me. I could be part of the larger process of protecting animals and the environment."

### LIFE'S WORK

Pacelle became a vegan shortly after that experience. As a junior at Yale, he established the Student Animal Rights Coalition. The group spurred the Introduction of vegan meals in the school's dining halls and protested the Yale Medical School's use of animals in research. Pacelle made connections to other animal advocates, among them the writer Cleveland Amory, who founded the Fund for Animals in 1967. When Pacelle was home from school, he would lecture family members about the inhumane slaughter of food animals. "I was kind of strident," he told Hall. "But I've changed."

Pacelle graduated from Yale with a B.A. degree in history and environmental studies in 1987. He then got a job as a writer for the *Animals' Agenda*, a magazine published by the Fund for Animals. He became associate editor and, soon, was named president of the fund's board. At 23 he assumed the post of national director. Five years later, in 1994, he joined the Humane Society of the United States as its vice president for communications and government affairs, a position he held for the next decade. During that time Pacelle figured in the successful campaigns for the passage of 15 pieces of animal-friendly legislation in various states, including laws banning the use of bait and dogs in the hunting of bears, cougars, and bobcats in Oregon, Massachusetts, and Washington State; outlawing cockfighting in Arizona, Missouri, and Oklahoma; and forbidding the use in Arizona of crates that make movement impossible for veal calves. He also campaigned successfully for the defeat of several measures deemed to be injurious to animal protection, including Proposition 197 in California (1996), which would have repealed mountain lions' status as specially protected mammals under the California Wildlife Protection Act of 1990, and State Question 698 in Oklahoma (2002), which sought to increase the number of voters needed to propose an amendment to the state's laws dealing with permissible methods for hunting, fishing, and trapping.

In the past two decades, Pacelle has also been instrumental in the passage of federal statutes to protect animals. Among them are the Great Apes Conservation Act of 2000, which aims to protect apes (chimpanzees, gorillas, bonobos, orangutans, and gibbons) in their native habitats in Africa (the first three) and Asia (the last two); the Captive Wildlife Safety Act (2003), which bans commerce in such exotic animals as lions, tigers, leopards, cheetahs, jaguars, and cougars for purposes of private ownership; and the 2008 farm bill (officially, the Food, Conservation, and Energy Act of 2008), part of which banned the import of dogs from overseas puppy mills.

In the wake of Hurricane Katrina, which flooded large parts of New Orleans, Louisiana, in August 2005 and caused widespread damage elsewhere along the Gulf Cost, HSUS tried to rescue some of the tens of thousands of pets that were left stranded. The Federal Emergency Management Agency and the U.S. Coast Guard, however, declaring that only people would be rescued, prevented HSUS volunteers from entering New Orleans in the days after the storm. "Government policies forced people to make an awful choice—to be rescued and leave behind their pets or to stay in a stricken city and risk their lives," Pacelle told Marsha Ginsburg for the *San Francisco Chronicle* (September 16, 2005), "We want to see a rescue policy that recognizes the incredible bond between people and their pets." As reported in *Time* (June 6, 2007), 44 percent of the New Orleanians who refused to leave their homes did so because they would not part with their pets, according to a survey conducted by the San Francisco-based nonprofit Fritz Institute. Eventually the HSUS, which raised more than $34 million for relief efforts, coordinated the rescue of more than 10,000 animals in the Gulf Coast region and reunited some 2,500 of them with their owners. For the HSUS's role in the rescue and relocation of pets following Hurricane Katrina, Pacelle, along with the leaders of several other rescue organizations, was named Executive of the Year by the *NonProfit Times* (a magazine for executives of nonprofit organizations) in December 2005. The following year Pacelle and the HSUS campaigned for the passage of the federal Pets Evacuation and Transportation Standards (PETS) Act, which was signed into law by President George W. Bush on October 6, 2006. The law requires that in planning for disasters, all local, state, and federal agencies must include provisions for pets and service animals.

The Humane Society's clout within political circles increased in 2008, when its two-month investigation into unlawful activities at a slaughterhouse and meat-packing plant sparked the largest recall of beef in U.S. history. In October 2007 an HSUS investigator (without identifying himself as such) had secured a job at the Westland/Hallmark Meat Packing Co. in Chino, California. The undercover agent videotaped workers kicking sick cows, applying shocks to them, and using forklifts to force them to walk. The federal government has banned the use of sick, or "downer," cows as food because of an increased risk of infection in consumers caused by bacteria or prions, the latter of which cause bovine spongiform encephalopathy; known colloquially as mad cow disease, that infection causes deterioration of the brain and spinal cord and is often fatal. In February 2008, following further investigations by Chino police and agents of the U.S. Department of Agriculture (USDA), the USDA called for the recall of 143 million pounds of ground beef that had originated at the Westland/Hallmark slaughterhouse. Several of the workers caught on videotape were prosecuted, and the plant was shut down. Pacelle and the HSUS also appealed to the USDA for the closure of a loophole in the ban on downer cows as sources of food. A partial ban on the cows was implemented after the nation's first reported case of mad cow disease, in 2003, but a loophole allowed cows that had already passed federal inspection and later were unable to walk to enter the food supply after further examination. In March 2009 the USDA ruled that all nonambulatory cows, including those who had passed inspection, must be humanely euthanized and their deaths reported to proper officials.

In May 2009 Pacelle announced that the HSUS would work with the former Atlanta Falcons quarterback Michael Vick to campaign against dogfighting. Organized dogfighting is a felony in every U.S. state. Nevertheless, fights between two dogs, most commonly pit bulls, continue to be staged for purposes of entertainment and gambling. The dogs are often seriously injured, and some are killed. Often the owner of the losing dog will kill or abandon it if it is injured. In August 2007 Vick pled guilty to funding and operating a dogfighting ring at a home he owned in Virginia. Four months later he was sentenced to 23 months in a federal prison. (Vick was released from prison on May 20, 2009 and served the final two months of his sentence in his Virginia home.) Speaking to William C. Rhoden for the *New York Times* (May 22, 2009) about HSUS's collaboration with Vick, Pacelle said, "I understand that there are people who don't want to work with Michael Vick. I want to end dogfighting. And he may be a very important role player in that process. . . . If he's sincere, and if he's committed in the long run to this goal for whatever reasons, he can be an agent of change, he can steer young kids in urban communities' vile activity toward more productive interactions with dogs. Our goal is not endless punitive treatment of Michael Vick. Our goal is to eradicate dogfighting in America."

Pacelle has written for publications including *Human Dimensions of Wildlife* and the *George Wright Forum*, the latter of which is "devoted to interdisciplinary inquiry about parks, protected areas, and cultural sites," according to its Web site. His op-ed pieces have appeared in dozens of major newspapers, among them the *Washington Post*, the *Los Angeles Times*, the *New York Times*, and the *San Francisco Chronicle*. He also writes an occasional column for *Bark* magazine. He is a board member, co-founder, and former chairman of Humane USA, a nonpartisan organization, formed in 1999, whose goal is the election of animal-rights advocates to political office. In 2006 Pacelle cofounded the National Federation of Humane Societies (NFHS). He currently serves on its board.

## PERSONAL LIFE

Pacelle's marriage to Kirsten Rosenberg, the former managing editor of the now-defunct magazine *Animals' Agenda*, ended in divorce. He lives in Washington, D.C., with his girlfriend, Christine Gutleben, and her cat, Libby. Gutleben directs the HSUS's Animals and Religion program, which, according to the HSUS Web site, "seeks to engage people and institutions of faith with animal protection issues, on the premise that religious values call upon us all to act in a kind and merciful way toward animals."

## FURTHER READING

*Hartford (Connecticut) Courant B p1 Aug. 30, 2004; hsus.org; Los Angeles Times A p1 July 19, 2008; New York Times III p9 Dec. 24, 2006; New York Times Magazine p47 Oct. 26, 2008; Washington Post C p1 Aug. 9, 2004*

# ROSA PARKS

## Civil Rights Activist

**Born:** February 4, 1913; Tuskegee, Alabama
**Died:** October 24, 2005; Detroit, Michigan
**Primary Field:** Civil Rights
**Affiliation:** Civil Rights Movement

## INTRODUCTION

*The modern civil rights movement began with Rosa Parks' refusal to surrender her seat on a bus to a white man on December 1, 1955 in Montgomery, Alabama. Her arrest for violating the city's segregation laws was the catalyst for a mass boycott of the city's buses, whose ridership had been 70 percent black. That boycott brought Martin Luther King Jr. to national prominence as president of the Montgomery Improvement Association, a group of ministers dedicated to the spiritual and organizational leadership of the boycott. The Montgomery Improvement Association filed a federal suit challenging the constitutionality of the segregation law on February 1, 1956, and the boycott continued until December 20, 1956, when a Supreme Court order declaring Montgomery's segregated seating laws unconstitutional was served on city officials. The next day blacks returned to the integrated buses, but not without violent incidents.*

National Archives and Records Administration Records

*Rosa Parks.*

*Rosa Parks' continuing involvement in the American civil rights movement antedated the Montgomery, Alabama bus boycott by more than two decades. From 1943 to 1956 she was a secretary for the Montgomery branch of the National Association for the Advancement of Colored People (NAACP). In 1957 she moved to Detroit, Michigan, where she worked for nonviolent social change with Martin Luther King Jr.'s Southern Christian Leadership Conference (SCLC). Mrs. Parks earned her living primarily as a seamstress until 1965, when she went to work for Congressman John Conyers Jr., Democrat from Michigan, and she has been his receptionist, secretary, and administrative assistant for twenty-five years. In 1987 she founded an institute to provide leadership and career training to black youth. Continuing to speak out on civil rights issues, she makes about twenty-five public appearances each year. In an interview with Marney Rich published verbatim in the* Chicago Tribune *(April 3, 1988), Rosa Parks said that she wants to be remembered "as a person who wanted to be free and wanted others to be free."*

## EARLY LIFE

Rosa Parks was born Rosa Louise (or Lee) McCauley on February 4, 1913 in Tuskegee, Alabama to James McCauley, a carpenter, and Leona (Edwards) McCauley, a teacher. At the age of two she moved to her grandparents' farm in Pine Level, Alabama with her mother and her younger brother, Sylvester. At the age of eleven she enrolled in the Montgomery Industrial School for Girls, a private school founded by liberal-minded women from the northern United States. The school's philosophy of self-worth was consistent with Leona McCauley's advice to "take advantage of the opportunities, no matter how few they were."

Opportunities were few indeed. "Back then," Mrs. Parks recalled in the *Chicago Tribune* interview, "we didn't have any civil rights. It was just a matter of survival; of existing from one day to the next. I remember going to sleep as a girl hearing the [Ku Klux] Klan ride at night and hearing a lynching and being afraid the house would burn down." In the same interview, she cited her lifelong acquaintance with fear as the reason for her relative fearlessness in deciding to appeal her conviction during the bus boycott. "I didn't have any special fear," she said. "It was more of a relief to know that I wasn't alone. If I was going to be fearful, it would have been as far back as I can remember, not just that separate incident."

## LIFE'S WORK

Rosa Parks' sensitivity to the injustices committed against black Americans was evident in her selection of a husband and in her work. In 1932 she married Raymond Parks, a barber who was active in black voter registration and other civil rights causes. After attending Alabama State College (now Alabama State University) in Montgomery for a time, Mrs. Parks worked for the Montgomery Voters League, the NAACP Youth Council, and other civic and religious organizations. In 1943 she was elected secretary of the Montgomery branch of the NAACP. She recalled her work with that organization during an interview with Roxanne Brown for *Ebony* (February 14,1988): "In the early 1940s and 1950s I worked on numerous cases with the NAACP, but we did not get the publicity. There were cases of flogging, peonage, murder, and rape. We didn't seem to have too many successes. It was more a matter of trying to challenge the powers that be, and to let it be known that we did not wish to be continued as second-class citizens."

During the 1940s and 1950s, Mrs. Parks supported herself by taking in sewing at home, working as a housekeeper and as a seamstress, and, for a time, as a life insurance agent. To get to work she was forced to depend on Montgomery City Lines buses, whose patronage was 70 percent black in a city of 50,000 black citizens and 70,000 white citizens. By 1955 seating arrangements in some southern cities, as well as in the northern, eastern, and western United States, had been integrated, but a pernicious system of segregated seating arrangements persisted in Montgomery.

The first ten seats of every bus were reserved for white passengers, regardless of whether there were any white patrons on the bus, so that it was not uncommon for black women to stand over empty seats with their arms full of packages. Occasionally a black passenger would sit in the white section, either from sheer exhaustion or because the person was from out of town, and therefore ignorant of the law. When that happened, the passenger would be ordered, often in obscene language, to move. The orders would sometimes be backed by the threat of physical violence, which was carried out in some cases. If the white section was filled to capacity when white patrons boarded the bus, passengers in the black section were required to relinquish their seats to white passengers. The bus drivers, all of whom were white men, were empowered by law to enforce those practices and to use their own discretion in allocating bus seats according to race.

Thus it happened that on December 1, 1955 Rosa Parks and three other black passengers were asked to vacate an entire row of seats, the first row behind the white section (not in the white section, as is commonly believed) so that one white man could sit down. Mrs. Parks recognized the bus driver, James F. Blake, as the same one who, in 1943, had evicted her from his bus for boarding through the front door. Black passengers were often forced to pay their fares at the front of the bus, then get off and reenter through the rear door. Sometimes the driver would drive away before a passenger could board the bus from the rear after having paid up front.

On December 1, when Blake asked the row of black passengers to get up, none of them moved at first. As recounted by Mrs. Parks in the *Chicago Tribune* interview, Blake then said, "You all make it light on yourselves and let me have those seats." All of them stood up except Mrs. Parks, who was tired from the day's work at Montgomery Fair department store, where she was employed as a seamstress. Blake asked her if she was going to stand up. "No, I'm not," she replied. When Blake threatened to call the police, she said, "You may go on and do so." Two police officers boarded the bus to arrest Mrs. Parks, who was still seated. When one of them asked her why she did not stand up, she said, "I don't think I should have to. Why do you push us around so?" He answered, "I don't know, but the law is the law, and you are under arrest."

Rosa Parks was taken to jail, booked, fingerprinted, incarcerated, and fined fourteen dollars. That day, three people arrived at the jail to obtain her release on bond: Clifford Durr, a white liberal lawyer; his wife, Virginia Durr, a white civil rights activist who had employed Mrs. Parks as a seamstress; and E. D. Nixon, the former president of the NAACP's state and local branches, for whom Mrs. Parks worked as a secretary. E. D. Nixon was also a Pullman porter, the regional director of the Brotherhood of Sleeping Car Porters, and the president of the Progressive Democratic Association of Montgomery.

Nixon and the Durrs escorted Mrs. Parks to her home. Nixon asked her if she would be willing to appeal the case, but her. mother and her husband feared for her safety if she challenged the segregation law she had been charged with violating. Raymond Parks was quoted by Taylor Branch in his book *Parting the Waters: America in the King Years 1954-63* (1988) as having warned, "The white folks will kill you, Rosa."

But she had no fear above or beyond that with which she had always lived. According to Branch, she replied to Nixon's request with the words, "If you think it will mean something to Montgomery and do some good, I'll be happy to go along with it."

Fred Gray, one of Montgomery's two black lawyers, agreed to represent Mrs. Parks in her appeal to the state courts. On the night of her arrest, Gray informed Jo Ann Robinson, an English professor and the president of the Women's Political Council (WPG), of the incident. Among the city's sixty-eight black organizations, the WPC was the group most involved in planning the ensuing bus boycott. Just four days after the Supreme Court declared school segregation unconstitutional in *Brown v. Board of Education of Topeka* (May 17, 1954), the WPG had sent a letter to the mayor of Montgomery complaining about the seating practices and requesting alleviation. The letter warned the mayor to act swiftly, "for even now plans are being made to ride [the buses] less, or not at all."

Instead of improving, the conditions for black bus passengers worsened that year and the next. In 1955 two black teenage girls were arrested in separate incidents, the circumstances of which closely resembled those surrounding Rosa Parks's case. The cases of the two teenagers, Claudette Colvin and Mary Louise Smith, heightened dissatisfaction in the black community. The WPC planned a boycott of the buses and drafted instructions that were lacking only in the date the boycott would take place. Rosa Parks convened the NAACP Youth Council to plan a campaign. As it turned out, both teenagers' cases were found unsuitable for the role of catalyst in the mass action, for reasons such as lost momentum, the unwed and pregnant condition of one of the teenagers, and the futility of fighting a charge of disorderly conduct rather than one of violating the segregation laws.

When Jo Ann Robinson heard of Mrs. Parks' arrest from Fred Gray, she saw in her an ideal candidate on whose behalf to launch the boycott, for she was a highly respected member of the community. As described by Mrs. Robinson in her memoir, *The Montgomery Bus Boycott and the Women. Who Started It*, Mrs. Parks was "quiet, unassuming, and pleasant in manner and appearance; dignified and reserved; of high morals and strong character."

On Friday, December 2, Jo Ann Robinson and the WPG produced and distributed throughout Montgomery thousands of leaflets announcing that a one-day bus boycott would take place on Monday, December 5, the day of Rosa Parks' trial. Each leaflet read, in part: "Another Negro woman has been arrested and thrown in jail because she refused to get up out of her seat on the bus for a white person to sit down. If we do not do something to stop these arrests, they will continue. We are, therefore, asking every Negro to stay off the buses Monday in protest of the arrest and trial."

The leaflets blanketed the town, informing nearly every black congregation of the boycott, and on December 2 the congregations decided to support the boycott, even if their ministers failed to take the initiative. Becoming aware of the level of support among their congregations and deciding that their guidance would benefit the movement, the clergymen formed the Interdenominational Ministerial Alliance (IMA). The IMA met that evening at Dexter Avenue Baptist Church, where Martin Luther King Jr., then twenty-six, was pastor, and drafted their own condensed version of the WPG's leaflet. They added a call for a mass meeting on the evening of December 5 at Holt Street Baptist Church, where they planned to determine whether they should continue the boycott.

Only a few white passengers rode the buses on December 5, and virtually no black passengers were on board. Helmeted policemen on motorcycles trailed the buses, ostensibly to protect black passengers from what the police called "Negro 'goon squads.'" Historians have noted that the black citizens of Montgomery had nothing to fear from each other, there were no 'goon squads,' but much to fear from the presence of extra policemen (all of whom were white). Ironically, the police only served to scare away those blacks who might otherwise have ridden the buses that day.

The people gathered in and around the Holt Street Baptist Church that night resolved to continue the boycott until their demands for improved bus service were met. The IMA absorbed many of those present and became the Montgomery Improvement Association (MIA), which elected Martin Luther King Jr. as its president., In the following weeks of the boycott, the MIA and the WPC met repeatedly with the city commissioners (three white men) and the bus company's management to press for three objectives. In the words of Mrs. Robinson, the boycotters wanted "more courtesy from drivers, that Negroes sit from rear toward the front and whites from the front toward the rear until all seats were taken, [and] that Negro bus drivers be employed to operate the buses on predominantly black routes."

The city commissioners refused repeatedly to grant any of the boycotters' demands, despite the mounting monetary losses sustained by the bus company. In January 1956 the city commissioners joined the White Citizens Council, whose membership included rabid segregationists, and that month a "get-tough" policy was adopted in a fruitless attempt to coerce black citizens into abandoning their aims. Policemen harassed carpool drivers by detaining them for inordinate lengths of time on spurious charges and by issuing tickets for miniscule or imaginary traffic violations. Blacks who walked to work risked being beaten by whites, who also threw bricks, rotten food, and urine-filled balloons from passing cars. Their hostility served only to inspire the boycotters to persevere.

Many boycotters, including Rosa Parks, lost their jobs. On January 30 King's house was bombed while he was away, and on March 22 he was convicted and fined $1,000 for violating the state anti-boycott law. Enjoined from most of its activities by a court order, the Alabama NAACP was unable to function normally for the following eight years.

Nevertheless, the boycott continued. The MIA's demands did not include full-scale integration until February 1, 1956, when Fred Gray filed a federal suit challenging segregated seating per se; According to Mrs. Robinson, Rosa Parks was not one of the plaintiffs named in the suit, but it was filed on behalf of all those affected by substandard treatment on the buses, as well as on behalf of the plaintiffs. On June 5, 1956 three federal judges voted two to one to rule bus segregation unconstitutional. The city of Montgomery appealed to the United States Supreme Court, which upheld the lower court's decision, but the buses were not officially desegregated until the order was served on city officials by United States marshals on December 20, 1956.

The boycott had lasted 382 days. When, on December 21, Rosa Parks was photographed sitting on the integrated buses for the first time, one of the drivers with whom she was photographed was James Blake, the man who had arrested her. "He didn't react at all, and neither did I," she recalled in an interview for the *Montgomery Advertiser* (February 24, 1982). Referring to the desegregation of the buses, she said, "I don't recall that I felt anything great about it. It didn't feel like a victory, actually. There still had to be a great deal to do."

The desegregation of the buses was a costly victory for all concerned. The Parks family was harassed and threatened continually over the telephone, Mrs. Parks lost her job, and her husband was unable to work after suffering a nervous breakdown. In August 1957 Rosa and Raymond Parks, by now both unemployed, moved with Leona McCauley to Detroit, Michigan, where Sylvester McCauley had rented a two-family flat for them.

Mrs. Parks' first few years in Detroit were especially difficult, according to an article by Alex Poinsett for *Jet* (July 14,1960). She found a job supervising guest rooms at the Hampton Institute in Virginia in 1958 for $3,600 a year, but was forced to quit because she was unable to move her family from Detroit, and when she returned to Detroit with $1,300 in savings, they were quickly depleted. In July 1958 her husband was hospitalized with pneumonia, and in December 1959 she herself was hospitalized with stomach ulcers. Having lost her apartment, she moved her family into two small rooms in the meeting hall of the Progressive Civic League in Detroit, where she took in sewing while her husband worked as caretaker of the building. By 1961 she had earned enough money to move into an apartment. Meanwhile, she had been raising funds at rallies for the NAAGP around the country.

Since March 1965, Rosa Parks has been working in the office of Congressman John Conyers Jr., a Democratic member of the United States House of Representatives who, since his election for the first time in 1964, has acquired a reputation in Congress as a leader in civil rights, welfare, opposition to American military involvement in Vietnam, and black voter registration drives. Mrs. Parks runs his office in Detroit, greets Visitors, and sometimes gets involved in cases dealing with job guidance and cultural planning. She remained active in the NAACP, the SCLC, and the Women's Public Affairs Committee of 1000. She also served as deaconess of St. Matthew A.M.E. church in Detroit,

For over three decades, in speeches at conventions, churches, and official celebrations, Rosa Parks tried to make her fellow Americans, especially young people, aware of the history of civil rights in the United States. Her services were especially in demand during the anniversaries of civil rights actions that are celebrated in December, the observance of Martin Luther King Jr.'s birthday in January, and the events of Black History Month, in February. In 1987 she founded the Rosa and Raymond Parks Institute for Self-Development, established to offer guidance to black youth in preparation for leadership and choice of careers. In 1988 she gave speeches around the country in celebration of her seventy-fifth birthday, the 125th anniversary of the

Emancipation Proclamation, and the twenty-fifth anniversary of the March on Washington. On June 30,1 989 she attended a White House celebration of the twenty-fifth anniversary of the Civil Rights Act, at which former President George Bush, in speaking of her momentous refusal to give up her bus seat, mistakenly referred to the town in which the act took place as Birmingham, not Montgomery. After the ceremony, which took place in the wake of several recent Supreme Court decisions that were inimical to civil rights progress, Mrs, Parks told reporters, "We need stronger, better leadership. Instead of having better ceremonies we need better programs."

Among Rosa Parks' awards are the NAACP's Spingarn Medal (1979), the Martin Luther King Jr. Award (1980), *Ebony's* thirty-fifth Service Award (1980), the Martin Luther King Jr. Nonviolent Peace Prize (1980), and the Martin Luther King Jr. Leadership Award (1987). She holds an honorary degree from Shaw College, and she had a street named after her in Detroit in 1969. In recognition of her service, the SCLC has annually sponsored the Rosa Parks Freedom Award since 1963, and since 1979 the Virginia-based Women in Community Service has sponsored its own Rosa Parks Award.

During her interview for the *Chicago Tribune*, Rosa Parks articulated her creed: "I do the very best I can to look upon life with optimism and hope and looking forward to a better day, but I don't think there is anything such as complete happiness. It pains me that there is still a lot of Klan activity and racism. I think when you say you're happy, you have everything that you tried and everything that you want, and nothing more to wish for. I haven't reached that stage yet."

## PERSONAL LIFE

Rosa Parks' silver hair framed a pleasant face in her later years, and she was often recognized on the street or in her office in Detroit where observers were struck by her youthfulness. Although her husband died in 1977, and her brother and mother died within a few years after that, she was an aunt to thirteen nieces and nephews to keep her from feeling lonely. In March 1988 she had a pacemaker installed to regulate an irregular heartbeat, and in February 1989 she was briefly hospitalized for chest pains. Her most recent recognition was bestowed on her in 1989 by the Neville Brothers, who wrote a song called "Sister Rosa" for their album *Yellow Moon*. Its reggae chorus is "Thank you Miss Rosa/You are the spark/You started our freedom movement."

Parks lived in Detroit until her final years and her death on October 24, 2005 at the age of 92. Parks died of natural causes and her Life's Work was commemorated by her body lying in honor in the rotunda at the U.S. Capitol. Parks was only the thirty-first person, and first American of non-government accord to have this proceeding. Parks' body was returned to Detroit where she was buried in Woodlawn Cemetery.

## FURTHER READING

*Parting the Waters: America in the King Years 1954-63 (1988); Famous American Women; When and Where I Enter: The Impact of Black Women on Race and Sex in America; In Black and White; Negro Almanac; The Montgomery Bus Boycott and the Women Who Started It;*

---

# POPE PAUL VI

## Former Supreme Pontiff of the Roman Catholic Church

**Born:** September, 26, 1897; Concesio, near Brescia, Italy
**Died:** August 6, 1978; Castel Gandolfo, Italy
**Primary Field:** Peace & Justice Movement
**Affiliation:** Roman Catholic Church

### INTRODUCTION

*With the ease and assurance of centuries-old practice that can bring about a new administration without doing violence to continuity of tradition, on June 20, 1963, the Sacred College of Cardinals elected the Archbishop of Milan, Giovanni Battista Cardinal Montini, as the 262nd Supreme Pontiff of the Roman Catholic Church. Montini, who took the name of Pope Paul VI, had occasionally been referred to as the spiritual son of both Pope Pius XII and Pope John XXIII.*

*A scholar and a linguist, intensely interested in international politics, and, for many years trained in Vatican administration and diplomacy, Pope Paul VI was expected to assure a continuity of Pope John's recognition of the need of the Church to adjust to changing world conditions and to deal directly with problems, such as Communism, instead of ignoring them. Even before his coronation on June 30, he had set an early date, in September, for the resumption of the Second Vatican (Ecumenical) Council, which Pope John had convened, in 1962, to study proposals for reform and modernization of some Church practices. It reopened on September 29, 1963, with his declaration that its task was "to build a bridge toward the contemporary world." Pope Paul VI worked tirelessly to implement its findings, after its conclusion in 1965, and also worked hard to promote*

*world peace. Now beatified after his death, Blessed Pope Paul VI is on the road to sainthood.*

### EARLY LIFE

Like Pope John XXIII, Pope Paul VI was a Lombard, but his background as a member of a landholding, upper-middle-class family contrasted strikingly with the peasant origins of his predecessor. Montini was born in the hamlet of Concesio near Brescia in northern Italy on September 26, 1897. His parents, Giorgio and Giuditta (Alghisi) Montini, in keeping with the family's traditional devoutness named him Giovonni Battista (John the Baptist). He had an older brother, Lodovico, who was a Christian Democratic member of the Italian Senate, and a younger brother, Francesco, who was a physician.

During the five centuries that the Montinis have lived in the Po region, several members of the family have served the Church as prelates or priests. The Pope's father was a lawyer and the editor for 25 years of a crusading Catholic newspaper *Il Cittadino (the Citizen)* of Brescia. He championed the progressive political views of the Popular Party (a forerunner of the Christian Democratic Party) in his paper, and also as a Deputy for three terms in Italy's pre-Fascist legislature.

Boyhood friends recalled Giovanni Battista Montini as an expert tree climber, who attributed his fearlessness to keeping his eyes on heaven. His physical frailty, however, made it impossible for him to complete his schooling at the Jesuits' Arici Institute in Brescia, where he had founded a student paper *La Fionda (the Catapult)*. Largely through private tutoring and independent study at home, he qualified for a degree in 1916 from the Arnaldo Lyceum in Brescia. Rejected for military service, he then began to study for the priesthood and was ordained four years later, on May 29, 1920, at the Church of St. Mary of the Graces in Brescia.

After a summer's service as a Parish Curate, Montini went to Rome for graduate work at the Gregorian University. He also took courses in literature at the University of Rome. His intensity and brilliance as a scholar came to the notice of Monsignor Giuseppe Pizzardo, who four years later, as an influential conservative Cardinal, was to vote in the conclave that elected Montini to the Papacy. Pizzardo recruited Montini for the Pontifical Ecclesiastical Academy, a training school for Vatican diplomats and officials of the Secretariat of State.

## LIFE'S WORK

As an apprentice Foreign Service Officer of the Holy See, with degrees in Theology, Civil and Canon law, and Philosophy, Montini was sent to Poland, in May 1923, to fill the position of Secretary to the Apostolic Nunciature, in Warsaw. His health apparently suffered from the change in climate, and, at the end of about six months, he returned to Rome. He became a *minutante (document writer)* in the Secretariat of State at the Vatican and, at the same time, assumed the far less routine duties of spiritual adviser to the Italian Federation of Catholic University Students. During his ten-year association with that organization, he often saw his students engage in street fighting with Fascist youth groups, and he befriended a number of anti-Fascists, including Alcide de Gasperi and Aldo Moro, who later became leaders of the Christian Democrats.

Eventually, Mussolini's suppression of non-Fascist organizations, and, the pressure of his own increasing responsibilities at the Vatican, forced Montini to give up his work with the student group. As early as 1930, he had caught the attention of Eugenio Cardinal Pacelli, who was then the Secretary of State of Pope Pius XI. Pacelli singled out Montini for special grooming and, in 1937, appointed him Substitute Secretary of State for Ordinary (Internal) Affairs and entrusted him with the key to the Vatican's secret code.

When Pacelli became Pope Pius XII, in 1939, he relied heavily on Montini as a friend and as a dedicated, tireless steward of the Vatican. Especially after the death, in 1944, of Luigi Cardinal Maglione, his Secretary of State, the Pope turned to Montini for advice, because instead of appointing a successor to Maglione, Pius XII chose to cope personally with the duties of the office. Montini dealt with all Papal correspondence, handled many delicate diplomatic problems during World War II, and, in the postwar period, strengthened the stand of the Roman Catholic Church against Communist aggression by supporting Christian Democratic liberals.

In 1952, Pius XII appointed Monsignor Montini to the post of Pro-Secretary of State for Ordinary Affairs. Monsignor Domenico Tardini, as Pro-Secretary of State for Extraordinary Affairs, had the responsibility of handling concordats. Some observers of events at the Vatican have suggested that Montini, who had been sympathetic toward the worker-priest movement in France, and, who advocated a more active role for the Church in co-operating with organizations for world peace, found himself in conflict with the older, conservative Tardini. Both men declined elevation to a Cardinalate in 1953—a refusal that Pope Pius attributed to their modesty. A rumor, however, prevailed that Tardini had rejected the honor to prevent Montini from accepting. "A pasquinade," Xavier Rynne recalled in the *New Yorker* (July 20, 1963), "at once became current: When Tardini would not, Montini could not."

The Vatican hummed with similar speculation the following year, when Pope Pius chose Montini to succeed Ildefonso Cardinal Schuster as Archbishop of Milan. To some observers the appointment meant a banishment of Montini from the center of power of the Church, and, therefore, a triumph for the reactionary faction of the Holy See. Others believed that the Pope acted in accordance with a petition from the clergy of Milan that Montini be made Cardinal Schuster's successor. Furthermore, as Archbishop of Milan, traditionally the see of a Cardinal, Montini could freely accept the red hat at the next consistory for the election of Cardinals.

Giovanni Battista Montini was consecrated Archbishop of Milan, on December 12, 1954, at St. Peter's Cathedral in Rome. When he arrived in Milan, in a dramatic gesture of humility, he knelt and kissed the frozen ground. Milan, the largest archdiocese in Italy and a stronghold of Communism, challenged Montini to bring the teachings of the Roman Catholic Church to bear on the many social problems that had arisen from the area's enormous postwar industrial expansion. To replace the churches destroyed during World War II, he launched a construction program for the building or renovation of about 220 chapels and churches that he felt should be used, not only as houses of prayer, but as centers of community activity.

Some 90 cases of books had followed Archbishop Montini to Milan, but in becoming "the Archbishop of the workers," he found less time for the pleasures of his library. A contemplative, scrutinizing man, whom Pope John XXIII reportedly referred to affectionately as "our Hamlet in Milan," Montini as Archbishop expressed another side of his personality. With the zeal of a missionary, he sought a pastoral encounter with the Milanese, and he visited factories, mines, business offices, Communist districts, banks, and the Chamber Of Commerce headquarters. He also attended bicycle races. To "the unhappy ones who gather behind Marx," he preached a doctrine of Christian love in an effort to win souls to the Church, rather than further alienate them.

Although not yet a Cardinal, Montini was among the candidates for the Papacy whom the Sacred College of Cardinals considered in the conclave to chose a successor to Pope Pius XII, upon his death in October 1958. The election went instead to Angelo Giuseppe Cardinal Roncalli, who as Pope John XXIII called a consistory later in the year, on December 15, and placed Montini's name at the head of his list of 23 new cardinals. Restored to prominence in the diplomatic service of the Church, Montini left Milan from time to time to carry out missions for Pope John abroad. In June 1960, he visited the United States to receive an honorary degree from Notre Dame University, and also, according to speculations in the press, to explain to American bishops that an editorial in *La'Osservatore Romano* justifying the Church's right to influence political thinking did not apply to the United States, where Marxism was not a real threat and where a Catholic, John F. Kennedy, was a candidate for President. Montini, later in the year, visited South America, and, in August 1962, made a tour of Africa to report to Pope John on the Church's problems in the newly established African states.

The principal act of Pope John's reign was his calling of the Second Vatican (Ecumenical) Council to enable the Church to consider modifications in its procedures that would allow a more effective handling of present-day problems. Alone of the Princes of the Church, Montini was invited to be a house guest of Pope John at the Apostolic Palace during the first session of the council in late 1962. The Pope, reportedly, listened to the Archbishop in preparing his opening address to the council, and, in turn, Montini may have been following John XXIII's advice in taking a somewhat nonpartisan stand in council debates.

Pope John XXIII died on June 3, 1963. When the Sacred College of Cardinals met, on June 20, to elect a new Pope, Archbishop Montini was the popular favorite

and was generally believed to have been also the choice of Pope John, who had, however, avoided influencing the Cardinals. On the second day of a relatively brief conclave, in the fifth or sixth ballot (the Church prescribes secrecy on details of voting), Montini was elected to rule as the 262nd Supreme Pontiff of the Roman Catholic Church. (Pope Pius XII and Pope John XXIII had also been elected as the 262nd Pontiff, but their positions were changed during their reigns.) In choosing the name Pope Paul VI, Montini seemed to many Catholics to have announced a program of evangelism and Christian unity such as that undertaken by St. Paul. He was crowned on June 30 in a spectacular open-air ceremony in St. Peter's Square. In his coronation sermon, which he delivered in nine languages—Latin, Italian, French, English, German, Spanish, Portuguese, Polish, and Russian—he declared his intention to encourage "greater mutual comprehension, charity, and peace between peoples."

In a funeral oration, in Milan, just after the death of Pope John, Archbishop Montini had said, "Pope John has shown us some paths which it will be wise to follow. . . . Can we turn away from paths so masterfully traced? It seems to me we cannot." A few days after his election, Pope Paul showed his readiness to follow immediately at least one path of his predecessor, when he set September 29, 1963, as the date of the resumption of the Second Vatican Council. He vowed that the continuation of the council would be "the pre-eminent part" of his Pontificate.

During the first three months of his rule, he gave much attention to streamlining the procedures of the council and to working out plans for the second session, including the decision to permit a number of qualified Catholic laymen to attend. Early, in September 1963, in the first direct denunciation of Communism that he made as the Pope, he said that "the council should not be viewed as a subtle but harmful submission to the pragmatism" of the times. He explained that the effort to apply remedies to "a contagious and deadly illness"—errors condemned by the Church, such as Marxist atheism—did not signify a change in opinion: "Rather it means trying to fight it, not only in theory, but in practice."

While the Second Vatican Council met, the Pope relaxed secrecy requirements and set up a press committee to make the council's work continuously known to news media. An additional number of non-Catholic observers were invited and some laymen admitted as auditors; in 1964, just before the third session, some women were invited to attend. One of his chief concerns was to assure that the council fathers could work in an atmosphere of freedom, and many of the procedures instituted were designed with this in mind.

He agreed to establish the Synod of Bishops, a representative body of bishops selected from all over the world to advise and assist the pope in governing the Church.

After four sessions and the publication of 16 vital documents (four constitutions, nine decrees, and three declarations), the council came to its solemn close on December 8, 1965. In the months and years that followed, Pope Paul worked tirelessly to implement its pronouncements: The first Synod of Bishops, met in Rome from September 29 to October 29, 1967; the Curia was reform; the Code of Canon Law was revised; the sacred liturgy was renewal, with emphasis on the use of the vernacular together with the preservation of Latin; the rules governing mixed marriages were liberalized; the Council of the Laity to promote the lay apostolate was created; and, the Pontifical Commission for Justice and Peace was formed.

The Pope, however, cautioned that renewal must not sacrifice any of the Church's sacred deposit of faith. He issued admonitions against unfounded theological speculations, unauthorized experimentation in the liturgy, and any attempts to weaken the authority of the Roman pontiff and the hierarchy.

The Pope also improved ecumenism, and met with Patriarch Athenagoras I of Constantinople during his 1964 trip at the Holy Land, and at the solemn closing of the Second Vatican Council, the historic occasion occurred when he and the Patriarch removed and consigned "to oblivion" the mutual excommunications, which in 1054, had resulted in the Great Schism between the Eastern and Western Churches.

Pope Paul's relations with Protestantism also were cordial. He accepted the 1965 proposal of the World Council of Churches to set up a dialogue between it and the Roman Catholic Church, and he promptly sent Cardinal Bea to Geneva to accept the proposal. He invited to the Vatican the Most Reverend Arthur M. Ramsey, Archbishop of Canterbury, and discussed relations between Catholicism and the Anglican Church. In 1968, Pope Paul, sent greetings to the Tenth Lambeth Conference of Anglican Bishops and to the Fourth General Assembly of the World Council of Churches. Both of these meetings were attended by Catholic observers. He also opened dialogues with the Lutheran World Federation, and traveled, in 1969, to Geneva to the headquarters of the World Council of Churches, where he was warmly welcomed. However, he cautioned against any attempt to modify or gloss over essential Catholic teachings, and insisted that unity cannot be brought about at the expense of doctrine.

Pope Paul VI became the first "pilgrim Pope," and traveled extensively, including, but not limited, to: the Holy Land; India; the United Nations headquarters in New York City (where and said mass at Yankee Stadium); Portugal; Turkey; Colombia; Switzerland; and Uganda.

The Pope was especially known for his attempts at World Peace; his Pontificate took place in a time of ever-increasing international tension and dangers. He repeatedly addressed letters to the heads of the warring nations and met with such world figures as U.S. president Lyndon B. Johnson and UN secretary general U Thant to discuss means of ending the Vietnam War (officially known as the Vietnam Conflict). He also sought to bring peace to other parts of the world: In the Middle East; in the Dominican Republic; in the Congo; and, in Nigeria. He entered whenever possible into negotiations with Communist nations, meeting with both Soviet President Nikolai Podgorny and Foreign Minister Andrei Gromyko. Agreements were reached with Hungary, Czechoslovakia, and the former Yugoslavia that resulted in a lifting of some of the restrictions on religious activities in those countries. The Holy See was also permitted to name bishops to vacant dioceses.

His encyclicals, however, maintained the centuries-old traditions of the Church. There were five major encyclicals: *Ecclesiam suam* (August 6, 1964; On the Church) dealt with the awareness that the Church has of its nature and on the fact that this awareness must be constantly increased and deepened. This can be done only by constant internal renewal; *Mysterium fidei* (September 3, 1965; The Mystery of Faith) restated the Church's traditional teaching on the Eucharist, especially the doctrine of the Real Presence and of transubstantiation, or the change effected by the words of consecration in the Mass; *Populorum progressio* (March 6, 1967; On the Development of Peoples) was one of Pope Paul's most important encyclical, and extended and deepened, in the light of modern conditions, the social teachings of his predecessors; *Sacerdotalis caelibatus* (June 24, 1967; On Priestly Celibacy), a response to widespread urgings for some relaxation of the Church's traditional rule of celibacy for the priesthood and religious, upheld celibacy by appeals to Scripture and tradition and declined to modify the law in any way; *Humanae vitae* (July 25, 1968; On Human Life) upheld the Church's traditional teachings on artificial contraception. He also upheld the Church's teachings that homosexuality and other sexual practices were sins. *Humanae vitae* angered Roman Catholics in the U.S. and Western Europe.

Later, in 1976, a gay French writer, Roger Peyrefitte, "outted" the Pope as being gay in an article published in *Tempo* (which was seized by Italian police) to retaliate against the Pope for his January document, restating that all sex outside marriage, including homosexuality, was sinful. The Pope later spoke from the window of his study and asked listeners to give study the January document and give it "virtuous observance," as a to counter the licentious hedonism practiced in the modern world.

Other allegations were made about the Pope's alleged homosexuality, all unproven.

Pope Paul VI died of a heart attack on August 6, 1978. Some observers attributed his death (he had, however, a history of "frail health") to the kidnapping and murder by the Red Brigades of Aldo Moro, a Christian Democratic politician, who was a friend dating back to the Pope's days of being spiritual adviser to the Italian Federation of Catholic University Students. He is buried beneath the floor of Saint Peter's Basilica with other popes.

Because of the Pope's continual pleas for peace and justice in global affairs, the Roman Catholic Church began the long road to declaring him a Saint. The diocesan process for the beatification of Pope Paul VI began on May 11, 1993, and he was given the title "Servant of God." On December 20, 2012, Pope Benedict XVI proclaimed that Pope Paul VI had lived a life of heroic virtue, which means that he could be called "Venerable." In 2012, he was elevated to "Blessed" by Pope Francis I due to a miracle attributed to the intercession of Paul VI. According to an article published in the October 18, 2014 issue of *National Catholic Reporter*, "Pope Paul VI is almost a saint. Here are four of his biggest legacies" all he needs is one more miracle to be canonized as a saint. (See https://www.ncronline.org/news/people/pope-paul-vi-almost-saint-here-are-four-his-biggest-legacies.)

### PERSONAL LIFE

Pope Paul VI was five-feet-ten-inches tall, weighed 154 pounds, and had deep-set blue eyes. He loved Mozart, but he also was a fan of the French Jesuit guitarist, Father Aime Duval. He was well known among the clerics for his subtle wit.

### FURTHER READING

*N Y Post Mag p2 Je 23 63 por; N Y Times p2 Je 22 63 por; New Yorker 39:74+ Jl 20 63 Newsweek 62:42+ Jl 1 63 pors; Sat Eve Post 263:79+ Jl 27 63 pors; Time 81:40+ Je 28 63 por; Washington (D.C.) Post B p5 Je 22 63 por; Chi è? (1961) Clancy, John G. Apostle for Our Time; Pope Paul VI (1963); International Who's Who, 1962-63; Panorama Biografico degli Italiani doggi (1956); Who's Who in Italy, 1957-58*

---

# LINUS C. PAULING

## Physicist; Chemist; Educator

**Born:** February 28, 1901; Oswego, Oregon
**Died:** August 19, 1994; Big Sur, California
**Primary Field:** Chemistry and Peace Studies
**Affiliation:** Linus Pauling Institute of Science and
    Medicine

### INTRODUCTION

*"The reasonable man adapts himself to the world,"* George Bernard Shaw once observed. *"The unreasonable one persists in trying to adapt the world to himself. Therefore, all progress depends upon the unreasonable man." Linus Pauling, the only person to have received two unshared Nobel Prizes, in chemistry and peace, is arguably one such unreasonable man, according to the admirer who sent him a poster inscribed with Shaw's aphorism. Frequently ahead of his time and consequently regarded by some observers with skepticism, Pauling has often been accused of obstinacy and intellectual arrogance. But those very qualities, along with his intuitive powers, his unquenchable curiosity, and his breadth of knowledge, are responsible for his many groundbreaking scientific discoveries in such diverse areas as crystallography, quantum mechanics, and biochemistry. "My success as a scientist," Pauling told*

*John Horgan, who profiled him for* Scientific American *(March 1993), "has been largely the result of having broader knowledge than most scientists, in particular having a remarkably extensive knowledge of empirical chemistry, and also knowing mathematics and physics." The editors of the British magazine* New Scientist *have ranked Pauling among the twenty greatest scientists who have ever lived, a list that also includes Albert Einstein, Charles Darwin, and Isaac Newton.*

*Pauling gained public attention for the first time shortly after World War II, when he began to warn the governments of the emergent superpowers about the dangers of nuclear testing, and for the second time in the 1970s, when his research into the healing properties of vitamin C created a controversy that has not yet abated. The impact of his thought on all aspects of conventional chemistry was celebrated in a meeting of leading chemists in Pasadena in 1991, in honor of the scientist's ninetieth birthday. The proceedings were recorded in the book* The Chemical Bond: Structure and Dynamics *(1992), edited by Ahmed Zewail. The scientist's quarter-century crusade for the adoption by the general population of a nutritional regimen involving mega doses of vitamin C has been likened by some observers to Einstein's fruitless pursuit of the unified field theory, although others have contended it is still too soon to draw a conclusion. If Pauling's track record is a reliable guide, his belief that vitamin C not only protects humans against the common cold but also promotes longevity and counteracts the ravages of many diseases, cancer among them, may someday be vindicated.*

## EARLY LIFE

Of German and English descent, Linus Carl Pauling was born on February 28, 1901 in Oswego, Oregon, the only son of Herman Henry William Pauling, a salesman and pharmacist, and Lucy Isabelle (Darling) Pauling. In the middle of the decade, the family, which by then included Linus's younger sisters, Pauline and Frances Lucille, moved to Condon, Oregon, where Herman Pauling established a drugstore. After her husband's death, in 1910, Belle Pauling, as Linus's mother was known, supported her family by running a rooming house in Portland. Linus Pauling developed an interest in science, especially in collecting insects and minerals, as a boy, and in chemistry at the age of twelve. As a teenager, he conducted his own experiments with chemicals obtained from an abandoned iron and steel smelter, and he read voraciously about mineralogy, chemistry, and

physics. "I mulled over the properties of materials," he recalled in his interview with John Horgan. "Why are some substances colored and others not? Why are some minerals or inorganic compounds hard and others soft? I was building up this tremendous background of empirical knowledge and at the same time asking a great number of questions."

According to Anthony Serafini's biography *Linus Pauling: A Man and His Science* (1989), Pauling was discouraged from pursuing his hobbies and from continuing his education by his mother, who needed his help in supporting his sisters. While attending Washington High School in Portland, Pauling contributed to his family's income by delivering milk, operating film projectors, assisting a photographer, working in a machine shop, and performing other odd jobs. He left high school in 1917 without his diploma, which was denied him because, in an early instance of his legendary intellectual cockiness, he refused to take a required course in civics, reasoning that his own reading in that subject area was sufficient. Washington High School finally awarded Pauling his diploma in 1962, after he had won his second Nobel Prize. Enrolling at Oregon Agricultural College (now Oregon State University), in Corvallis, in September 1917, he studied chemical engineering. In further demonstration of Pauling's disdain for authority, he may have irreparably damaged his candidacy for the recently established Rhodes scholarship, according to Serafini, when he told his Rhodes interviewer that he had spent his preparation time reading *La Vie Parisienne*, an erotic magazine. He was not awarded the grant. To help make ends meet, Pauling assisted his professor in quantitative analysis in his junior year, and as a senior he taught a course in chemistry for home-economics majors, one of whom was Ava Helen Miller, whom he married the following year.

Upon his graduation from Oregon Agricultural College in 1922, Pauling received a B.S. degree in chemical engineering. In the autumn of that year, he entered the California Institute of Technology, in Pasadena, where he worked in Caltech's chemistry department as a graduate assistant and, later, as a teaching fellow. Studying under Arthur A. Noyes, Richard C. Tolman, and Roscoe G. Dickinson, he was awarded a Ph.D. in chemistry, summa cum laude, in 1925. He spent the following two years as a research associate and a fellow of the National Research Council at Caltech. During the academic year 1926-27, he lived abroad on the proceeds of a Guggenheim Fellowship, studying quantum mechanics with

Arnold Sommerfeld in Munich, Erwin Schrodinger in Zurich, and Niels Bohr in Copenhagen. In 1927 Pauling was appointed an assistant professor of chemistry at Caltech. Two years later he was promoted to associate professor, and in 1931 he advanced to full professor, a position that he held until 1963. Concurrently, from 1937 to 1958, he served as chairman of Caltech's department of chemistry and chemical engineering and as chairman of the Gates and Crellin Chemical Laboratories at Caltech.

## LIFE'S WORK

Pauling's exposure to the nascent field of quantum mechanics during the mid-1920s thrust him into the unique position of being "the only person in the world who had a good understanding of quantum mechanics and an extensive knowledge about chemistry" at that time, as he told John Horgan. Using the new technology of x-ray diffraction, he pioneered the field of crystallography, the analysis of the structures of such inorganic crystals as the micas, the silicates, and the sulfides. Among the first scientists to apply quantum mechanics to systems with more than one electron, Pauling rendered chemical configurations in three dimensions for the first time by measuring the distances and angles of the chemical bonds between atoms. His book *The Nature of the Chemical Bond and the Structure of Molecules and Crystals* (1939) is still considered to be a classic in its field. In 1928 Pauling published his hybridization, or resonance, theory of chemical bonding in benzene and other aromatic compounds, and in 1934 he began studying the biochemistry of proteins. In 1942 Pauling and his colleagues produced the first synthetic antibodies by altering the chemical structure of globulins; five years later he embarked on a five-year investigation of the destruction of nerve cells by polio viruses.

In 1951, following fourteen years of research, Pauling and R. B. Corey expanded the frontiers of biochemistry by describing the molecular structure of proteins in three-dimensional terms for the first time when they discovered, via x-ray crystallography, the twisted, helical shape of chains of amino acids in the proteins in such substances as hair, wool, muscle, and fingernails. In the following year he demonstrated that a genetic defect in the globin, or protein-containing portion of a hemoglobin molecule, was responsible for the sickling of red blood cells in patients with sickle-cell anemia. Meanwhile, he was examining the structure of deoxyribonucleic acid, the molecule that contains the genetic code.

In 1953 Pauling made a rare error when he described the DNA molecule as a triple helix. Francis Crick and James D. Watson correctly identified the double helix a few months later.

Awarded the Nobel Prize in chemistry in 1954 for his "research into the nature of the chemical bond and its application to the structure of complex substances," Pauling used his newly prominent position to speak out against the testing of nuclear weapons. Although he had opted out of the Manhattan Project, the top-secret program that led to the American development of the atomic bomb by Enrico Fermi, J. Robert Oppenheimer, and other physicists during World War II, Pauling did supervise the development of armor-piercing shells and a new class of explosives. As a staff member of the National Defense Research Commission, he worked on rocket propellants and on oxygen indicators for submarines and aircraft. He also helped develop a substitute human plasma, under the auspices of the Office for Scientific Research and Development. In 1948 President Harry S. Truman awarded Pauling the Presidential Medal for Merit for his service during the war, an honor that did little to protect the scientist from the rising tide of McCarthyism in the years to come.

In an era dominated by the Cold War mentality that marketed backyard bomb shelters and promoted "duck-and-cover" schoolroom drills, Pauling was suspected by the United States government of harboring pro-Soviet sentiments because of his anti-nuclear activism. For a year after the end of World War II, he lectured on the dangers of nuclear war as a member of the Research Board for National Security. In 1946 he joined Einstein's Emergency Committee of Atomic Scientists, a group that agitated for a ban on atmospheric testing of nuclear weapons. He argued against the superpowers' developing and testing the hydrogen bomb in the early 1950s, and in 1955 he and fifty-two other Nobel laureates signed the Mainau Declaration, entreating world leaders to stop the arms race. In 1958 Pauling published his book *No More War!* and presented to Dag Hammarskjold, the secretary-general of the United Nations, a petition that was signed by more than eleven thousand scientists from forty-nine countries whose opposition to nuclear weapons led to a surcease of atmospheric testing by both the United States and the Soviet Union later in the year.

Called to testify for a second time before the Internal Security Subcommittee of the United States Senate in 1960 (the first was in 1955), Pauling risked being prosecuted for contempt because he refused to reveal the names of those who had worked with him in collecting the eleven thousand signatures. In the early 1950s he had been denied a passport (until he had to travel to Sweden to pick up his first Nobel Prize), and he was continually subjected to insinuations that he was a Communist, charges that he always denied. In fact, until the death of Soviet dictator Joseph Stalin in 1953, Pauling's resonance theory was criticized by authorities in Moscow for being out of step with Marxist doctrine.

Dismayed to find that the nuclear testing carried out in 1961 alone had doubled the level of radioactivity in the atmosphere, Pauling drafted a proposal that later served as the basis for the 1963 nuclear- test-ban treaty signed by the United States, the Soviet Union, and Great Britain. Although his antinuclear efforts were widely applauded, his unstinting peace activism antagonized many of his scientific colleagues, among them Edward Teller and Willard F. Libby. As members of the United States Atomic Energy Commission, Teller and Libby portrayed Pauling as an alarmist, contending that it was safe to continue nuclear testing. When Pauling received the 1962 Nobel Peace Prize, on the very day in 1963 that the test ban treaty took effect, the news "was greeted in a most unpleasant manner in the United States," according to R. J. P. Williams, who reviewed Serafini's biography of Pauling in *Nature* (November 1989).

Resigning from Caltech in 1963, Pauling became a research professor at the Center for the Study of Democratic Institutions in Santa Barbara, California, where he studied international affairs as well as science. During his four years in Santa Barbara he found a simple explanation for asymmetric fission and other nuclear properties when he posited his close-packed-spheron theory of the cluster arrangement of protons and neutrons in the nucleus. He also taught chemistry at the University of California in San Diego from 1967 to 1969 and for the following four years at Stanford University, in Palo Alto, California. In 1973, also in Palo Alto, he founded the Linus Pauling Institute of Science and Medicine, an independent nonprofit research and educational organization devoted to the study of orthomolecular medicine, a term Pauling coined in 1968 to describe the treatment of disease or illness by supplementation of the diet with optimum doses of vitamins, minerals, and other natural substances already present in the body.

Foremost among Pauling's treatments of choice is the administration of vitamin C, whose properties he began researching in the late 1960s. With publication in 1970 of his book *Vitamin C and the Common Cold,* for which he won a Phi Beta Kappa Award for the year's best book on science, Pauling was thrust once more into the public spotlight. His contention that mega doses of vitamin C, or ascorbic acid, could help prevent or cure the common cold was highly controversial at the time, eliciting fervent support from some sectors of the population and drawing intense criticism from some of his scientific colleagues, who felt that the issue had not been sufficiently studied to warrant Pauling's claims. In a Stanford University news release (March 16,1973), K. C. Hayes, a doctor at the Harvard School of Public Health, noted that "Pauling's nutritional comments of recent times have disappointed us, not only because they make no sense in terms of modern medicine or nutrition, but also in the irresponsible way they arouse false hopes in those who have diseases which Pauling feels can be successfully treated by his vitamin therapy.'"

Undeterred by such reproaches, Pauling continued his investigation of the potential benefits of taking vitamin C, extending his research to cancer. His efforts to publicize the results of his studies were thwarted by the medical establishment as early as 1972, when the editorial board of the *Proceedings of the National Academy of Sciences* refused to publish a paper he had written on the connection between vitamin C and cancer "because of its therapeutic implications." The incident marked the first time the academy had prohibited one of its own members from publishing in the *Proceedings*. Finally, in collaboration with the Scottish physician Ewan Cameron, Pauling wrote *Cancer and Vitamin C* (1979), in which he reviewed the evidence to date, including a 1978 Mayo Clinic study that showed that high doses of vitamin C had no effect on patients with advanced cancer. But, as Pauling pointed out, that study failed to mention that the treated patients had undergone chemotherapy, which had decimated their immune systems. Vitamin C was therefore naturally useless, because it works only in conjunction with a functioning immune system, according to Pauling's theory. Throughout the 1980s inconclusive evidence continued to mount on both sides, with each faction finding flaws in the design of the other's studies.

In 1986 Pauling published *How to Live Longer and Feel Better,* which launched him on yet another round of the television talk-show circuit. This time he applied his theory of orthomolecular medicine to all aspects of optimum health and longevity, prescribing a lifelong nutritional regimen comprising mega doses (six to eighteen grams a day) of vitamin C and high doses of vitamins E, A, B-complex, and minerals and restrictions on the consumption of sugar. He also emphasized the importance of drinking adequate amounts of water, exercising, drinking alcoholic beverages only in moderation, not smoking, and avoiding stress. While most experts agreed with those prescriptions, many of them took issue with Pauling's assertion that "eggs and meat are good foods," given the high cholesterol content of such foods. Pauling's approach was unique in drawing a connection between longevity and vitamin C's ability to decrease the incidence and severity of the common cold. According to one of Pauling's theories, human beings become a little more worn out with each cold, illness, or other stressor, no matter how minor. Therefore, the fewer colds one suffers, the longer one's life expectancy, all other factors being equal (which is never the case, right down to the level of biochemical individuality, as Pauling himself has often been the first to point out in caveats).

In a 1994 review of the evidence gathered since 1971 for or against vitamin C's alleviation of the common cold, Harri Hemila of the University of Helsinki, in Finland, concluded that the twenty-one placebo controlled studies that have been conducted "have not found any consistent evidence that vitamin G supplementation reduces the incidence of the common cold in the general population. Nevertheless, in each of the twenty-one studies, vitamin C reduced the duration of episodes and the severity of the symptoms of the common cold by an average of 23 percent. However, there have been large variations in the benefits observed, and clinical significance cannot be clearly inferred from the results. Still, the consistency of the results indicates that the role of vitamin C in the treatment of the common cold should be reconsidered."

Among the many awards Pauling has received are the Langmuir Prize from the American Chemical Society (1931), the Davy Medal of the Royal Society of London (1947), the Pasteur Medal from the Biochemical Society of France (1952), the Addis Medal from the National Nephrosis Federation, the Phillips Memorial Award from the American College of Physicians (1956), the Avogadro Medal from the Italian Academy of Science (1955), the International Lenin Peace Prize (1971), the National Science Foundation's National Medal of Science (1975), the Lomonosov Gold Medal of the Soviet Academy of Sciences (1978), the Award in Chemical Sciences from the National Academy of Sciences (1979), the Vannevar Bush Award from the National Science Board (1979), the Arthur Sackler Foundation Chemistry Award (1984), and the Priestley Medal from the American Chemical Society (1984). The holder of honorary doctorates from fifty universities, among them Princeton, Yale, Oxford, and Cambridge, Pauling is a member of the National Academy of Sciences, the American Physicists Society, the American Philosophical Society, and the American Academy of Arts and Sciences, among other associations.

## PERSONAL LIFE

Until his death, on August 19, 1994, Linus Pauling divided his time between a residence in Palo Alto and a ranch house on 160 acres in Big Sur, California that overlooks the Pacific Ocean. Pauling credited his wife, Ava, who died in 1981, with being instrumental in his success. "By handling all the family problems that might disrupt me, she saw to it that I could carry on my work," he told Elizabeth Gleick in an interview for *People* (August 31, 1992). She performed not only the traditional duties expected of a wife and mother but also worked alongside Pauling in many of his antinuclear endeavors, goading her husband to become as well versed in the subject of war and peace as he was in chemistry and physics. As the director of research at the Linus Pauling Institute, Pauling published about ten to fifteen scientific papers a year, and at the time of his death, he was working on three books. His lifetime output to date exceeds one thousand published papers and books. Pauling is survived by three sons, one daughter, fifteen grandchildren, and eighteen great-grandchildren.

## FURTHER READING

*How to Live Longer and Feel Better; Linus Pauling: A Man and His Science; Linus Pauling: Scientist and Crusader*

# JOHN PAYTON

## Lawyer; Activist

**Born:** December 27, 1946; Los Angeles, California
**Died:** March 22, 2012; Baltimore, Maryland
**Primary Field:** Civil Rights
**Affiliation:** NAACP

## INTRODUCTION

*"Despite the progress we have seen since the Civil Rights Movement and the passage of the 1964 Civil Rights Act, the 1965 Voting Rights Act, and the 1968 Fair Housing Act, the 21st century still continues to present significant challenges. In many ways, the problems of race have grown more challenging." John Payton made those remarks during an interview with the* Civil Rights Monitor *(Winter 2008, online), several months after he was named the president and director counsel of the NAACP Legal Defense and Educational Fund (LDF). The LDF's name was the NAACP Legal Defense Fund when it was founded, in 1940, as an arm of the National Association for the Advancement of Colored People, with the aim of fighting racial discrimination in the nation's courts. In one of the greatest triumphs for civil rights in U.S. history, the NAACP-LDF filed the six lawsuits known collectively as Brown v. Board of Education of Topeka, Kansas, in which in 1954 the U.S. Supreme Court ruled as unconstitutional the state-sanctioned segregation of public schools. Payton himself argued civil rights cases before the Supreme Court in 1988 and 2003, during his years with the firm Wilmer, Cutler & Pickering. He practiced with the firm as a general litigator from 1978 to 1991 and then as a partner, from 1994 to 2008; in the interim he served as the corporation counsel for the District of Columbia. As the head of the LDF, he has appeared before the Supreme Court once, on February 22, 2010, in the case of Lewis Jr., et al. v. City of Chicago. Payton has been a board member and co-chair of both the National Lawyers' Committee for Civil Rights Under Law and its Washington, D.C., chapter, and he was the president of the bar association of Washington, D.C. in 2001 and 2002. He has taught at the law schools of Harvard, Georgetown, and Howard Universities.*

*The primary mission of the LDF, according to the organization's website, is "to see that African Americans become full, equal and thriving participants in our democracy." Operating independently of the NAACP since 1957, the LDF has worked to improve the qual-ity of education for children of all races in low-income areas where schools lack adequate funding and where huge numbers of young people never graduate from high school. It has also strived to end all forms of discrimination in employment, business, housing, public transportation, and health care; to remove barriers to voter registration; to ensure that at every polling station, citizens can be confident that they will enjoy the protections of state and federal voting laws; to overturn state laws that disenfranchise for life anyone ever convicted of a felony; and to end inequalities in the criminal-justice system, including inadequate legal representation for the poor, the persistence of far harsher sentencing for people of color than for whites, and the disproportionately high number of blacks and Hispanics on death row. The LDF seeks to end the death penalty altogether. The organization is also fighting to end "environmental" injustice, because of which low-income and minority populations have suffered far more harm than others from hazardous substances released into the environment by various industries. "The problems of race and inequality in our country have proven to be enduring and deep-seated in nature," Payton told the* Civil Rights Monitor *interviewer. "Long term solutions for these problems of justice and equality will require far-reaching change. LDF has a unique role to play and decades of experience in developing strategies that have had a profound impact on our society. But we must recognize that this is a marathon and not a race if we are to find solutions that will work. The challenge is figuring out how to best leverage the momentum of communities across the country in the broader fight for equality and human rights. In my view, our democracy has never needed LDF more than it needs it today to achieve promises and possibilities not yet realized."*

## EARLY LIFE

John A. Payton was born on December 27, 1946 to an insurance agent and his wife. With the exception of the two years his family lived on Guam, which he described to an interviewer for the *Washington Lawyer* magazine (June 2001) as "an island paradise," he grew up in Los Angeles, California. "I think everyone remembers childhood as rather idyllic," he told that interviewer. "That's certainly true for me." As a high school student, Payton considered a career in science. In 1965 he entered Pomona College, in Claremont, California, where he was one of very few African-American students in the five colleges in the Claremont Colleges system. As an undergraduate he became more interested in social activism than in science. "Everybody was worried about the draft and the Vietnam War. We were all worried about civil rights and issues of equality and justice. I was among the students who were very active," he recalled to the *Washington Lawyer*. Payton co-founded the Black Student Association at Pomona and organized various protests. As a senior he helped lead a successful student effort to persuade Claremont Colleges administrators to create an Intercollegiate Department of African-American Studies, as one way to increase enrollment of African-Americans. He told the interviewer, "During those years I became interested in pursuing something that would have the possibility of helping to create social change, and that was how I became interested in becoming a lawyer." Payton majored in literature and wrote his undergraduate thesis about the civil rights activist, historian, sociologist, and writer W. E. B. DuBois and his important role in the Harlem Renaissance of the 1920s and 1930s, when African-American writing, composing, and other cultural activities flourished. Because his limited funds prevented him from attending college full-time, Payton did not earn a B.A. degree until 1973, after eight years at Pomona.

That year Payton worked briefly at the Claremont Colleges in the African-American admissions office, which he had helped to create. He then traveled to West Africa to study the literature and other aspects of that region, financed by a Thomas J. Watson fellowship, which supports one year of independent scholarship abroad with the goal of enhancing the recipients' "capacity for resourcefulness, imagination, openness, and leadership and to foster their humane and effective participation in the world community," according to the Watson Foundation's website.

## LIFE'S WORK

After Payton returned to the U.S., he entered Harvard Law School, in Cambridge, Massachusetts. At that time Boston, across the Charles River from Cambridge, was embroiled in a controversy regarding the city's attempt to end racial imbalances in its public schools by busing many pupils to schools outside their own neighborhoods. The issue was extremely contentious among Boston residents, and violence erupted on several occasions. As a law student Payton took affidavits from African-American students who had been victims of the

violence. In his first year at Harvard, Payton was the comments editor for the *Harvard Civil Rights-Civil Liberties* Review, and he and other students wrote briefs for a civil rights lawyer. "My view was that the law didn't work well on its own," he told the *Washington Lawyer*. "Therefore, it was important for people who cared about these issues to get involved, to push, to put in time, and to make the law work right." Payton earned a J.D. degree from Harvard in 1977.

Payton then moved to San Francisco, California, to serve as a law clerk for U.S. District Court judge Cecil F. Poole, the first African-American to serve as a federal judge in Northern California. Next, in 1978, Payton joined the venerable, nationally known Washington, D.C., law firm of Wilmer, Cutler, and Pickering (from 2004, Wilmer, Cutler, Pickering, Hale, and Dorr, and known informally as Wilmer Hale). At that time the firm was representing the NAACP in its appeal of the Mississippi Supreme Court's verdict in *NAACP v. Claiborne Hardware Co.* The plaintiffs in that case were a group of white Claiborne County, Mississippi, merchants who had sued the NAACP in 1966 for damages resulting from an NAACP-organized boycott of their businesses, launched with the goal of ending various forms of discrimination against Claiborne County's black residents. The Mississippi Supreme Court had ruled against the NAACP, which was represented by Wilmer, Cutler lawyers. Payton, who during his job interview with the firm had expressed interest in the case, was hired as a general litigator. Payton and seven other Wilmer, Cutler lawyers assisted Lloyd N. Cutler in preparing the NAACP's appeal, and in 1982 the U.S. Supreme Court decided unanimously (without Justice Thurgood Marshall, who had recused himself) in the organization's favor. "I don't think there's any question about the fact that our legal system has been affected by race, and that Mississippi in the 1960s and 1970s was affected by its legacy of racism and discrimination," Payton told the *Washington Lawyer*. "But at the same time, I think there were other factors at play, too. States routinely try to protect their local business interests, their merchants, and the U.S. Supreme Court was not subject to those pressures. So race was a factor, but it wasn't the only factor."

Payton also assisted in litigation involving many other clients, among them such major corporations as Cigna Insurance and ABC; the Nigerian government; the American Legacy Foundation, an anti-smoking foundation created after a 1998 agreement between the tobacco industry and 46 states; the Federal National Mortgage

Association (Fannie Mae); and, without charge, injured parties in cases of racial discrimination. He appeared before the U.S. Supreme Court for the first time in 1988, arguing in defense of a Richmond, Virginia, law that required 30 percent of municipal-construction contracts to be awarded to minority-owned businesses. Six members of the court ruled in favor of the defendant, the J. A. Croson Co.; Justice Thurgood Marshall, who wrote the minority opinion, was joined by Justices Harry Blackmun and William J. Brennan, the last of whom wrote, "I join Justice Marshall's perceptive and incisive opinion revealing great sensitivity toward those who have suffered the pains of economic discrimination in the construction trades for so long. I never thought that I would live to see the day when the city of Richmond, Virginia, the cradle of the Old Confederacy, sought on its own, within a narrow confine, to lessen the stark impact of persistent discrimination. But Richmond, to its great credit, acted. Yet this Court, the supposed bastion of equality, strikes down Richmond's efforts as though discrimination had never existed or was not demonstrated in this particular litigation." According to Michael Abramowitz, writing for the *Washington Post* (January 21, 1991), Payton's demonstration of the discrimination and his skillful arguments received "high marks" from other lawyers.

In 1991 Payton was tapped by the administration of the newly elected mayor of Washington, D.C., Sharon Pratt Dixon, to serve as the corporation counsel for the District of Columbia (now called the office of the attorney general). Among his many duties in that post, which he held until early 1994, Payton handled all civil cases brought by or against the district; prosecuted juvenile criminal cases and adult misdemeanor cases; conducted or helped with criminal investigations involving government fraud; and supervised attorneys working for the district's dozens of agencies. At that time the nation's capital was experiencing a soaring number of crimes, increasing drug use among young people, and severe racial tensions as well as a budget crisis. "It was a daunting task, no doubt about that," Payton told the *Washington Lawyer*. "Once I was on the job, I realized I had completely underestimated the problems. So it was very, very challenging. And also very rewarding."

In 1993 leaders of Washington's civil rights groups urged (former) President Bill Clinton to nominate Payton to head the Civil Rights Division of the U.S. Department of Justice. Before Clinton did so, Payton met with members of the Congressional Black Caucus to discuss his possible appointment. During that meeting he angered many caucus members when he refused to assure them that the Voting Rights Act of 1965 allowed the intentional creation of black majority congressional districts. The members were further upset when they learned that during his 16 years as a district resident, he lived in the Mount Pleasant section, he had never voted. Having lost the caucus's support, Payton withdrew his name from consideration for the Justice Department job.

Earlier, in 1991, Payton had married Gay McDougall, a lawyer who starting in 1980 had directed the Southern Africa Project of the Lawyers' Committee for Civil Rights Under Law (a group organized at the request of President John F. Kennedy in 1963). In 1994 McDougall was appointed to the Independent Electoral Commission, set up in anticipation of the April 27, 1994 presidential election in South Africa. As a member of the lawyers' committee, Payton joined a team of international observers who monitored the voting, in which more than 18 million black South Africans voted for the first time and which resulted in the election of Nelson Mandela as South Africa's first black president.

Later in 1994 Payton returned to Washington and resumed his practice of law with Wilmer, Cutler, and Pickering. He remained with the firm for the next 14 years, serving from 1998 to 2000 as the head of its litigation department. In 2003 he appeared before the Supreme Court a second time, to argue for the defense in *Gratz et al v. Bollinger et al*. In that case, filed by the Center for Individual Rights, a politically conservative organization, Jennifer Gratz and Patrick Hamacher, white applicants to the University of Michigan, accused the school's then-president, Lee C. Bollinger, and other school administrators of racial discrimination in their use of a points system that favored less qualified African-American applicants. Payton, representing the university, argued that affirmative action was necessary to ensure that a "critical mass" of minority students attended the school, to create an atmosphere in which students of all races could become acquainted with one another as individuals and also broaden their knowledge of the world in a multicultural atmosphere. The court considered that case in conjunction with one brought by Barbara Grutter, a white applicant to the University of Michigan School of Law who had similarly accused the school of illegally discriminating against her. The court ruled against the university in the Gratz/Hamacher case but in its favor in the Grutter case, on the grounds that diversity in schools is a compelling state interest and that affirmative action is constitutional, that is, universities may legally take into account an individual's race in their admissions processes; the consideration of race by the law school, the court ruled, was legal, but the point system used by the undergraduate division was not. While the undergraduate division and Payton lost their case, civil rights leaders hailed the court's decision regarding the necessity and legality of affirmative action.

On December 6, 2007 the LDF announced that Payton had accepted its offer of the job of president and director-counsel. He succeeded Theodore M. Shaw, its fifth president (and the lead counsel for the defense in the Gratz case). The LDF's first president was Thurgood Marshall, its founder, who held the post for 21 years. In 1952 and 1953 Marshall argued for the plaintiffs before the Supreme Court in *Brown v. Board of Education*, and later, in 1967, he became the first African-American to be seated on the U.S. Supreme Court. "This is both a very exciting and a very humbling moment for me," Payton said, as quoted in an LDF press release (December 6, 2007, online). "Racial justice and equality are issues that I deeply care about, and being at LDF will allow me to be involved in that fight every day."

In 2009 Debo P. Adegbile, the LDF's director of litigation, argued for the defense in a case that challenged an important provision of the Voting Rights Act of 1965. The case, Northwest Austin Municipal Utility District No. 1 v. Eric H. Holder Jr., et al arose when an Austin, Texas, utility filed a lawsuit against the U.S. Justice Department (headed by Eric Holder) charging that a section of the Voting Rights Act of 1965 is unconstitutional. Section 5, the so-called pre-clearance provision, requires Justice Department approval of proposed changes in voting procedures or any other aspects of voting (including, for example, location of polling stations) in 16 specifically named states or localities that in 1965 were found to have a history of racial discrimination. The lawyers for the utility argued that conditions in the South had changed significantly since 1965, making Section 5 irrelevant; Adegbile maintained that continuing racial discrimination made it necessary, noting that Congress voted to renew the Voting Rights Act in 2006 after considering more than 16,000 pages of evidence of voting-related discrimination since 1965. The court ruled, 8-1, that "we are now a very different nation" compared with the U.S. in 1965, in Chief Justice John G. Roberts Jr.'s words, but that "whether conditions continue to justify such legislation [i.e., Section 5] is a difficult constitutional question we do not answer

today," as Adam Liptak reported for the June 23, 2009 edition of the *New York Times*. Justice Clarence Thomas cast the dissenting vote. Roberts also suggested that the Austin utility might be able to take advantage of the Voting Rights Act's "bailout" provision, which enables "political" entities to avoid seeking Justice Department approval for voting-related changes; the bailout provision, he wrote, deserved a "broader reading." "This is one of the most important civil rights cases decided this year," Payton said in an LDF press release (May 30, 2008, online). "The Voting Rights Act does not stand at the periphery of the nation's long march to greater equality, it lies at its core. That a small utility district would think that it could take us off the path to political fairness by rehashing previously discredited arguments is unfortunate, but the Court declined that invitation." A lawyer for the utility company, however, described the court's ruling as "a complete victory as far as we're concerned," according to Liptak.

In September 2008 LDF was successful in persuading the 11th Circuit Court of Appeals to overturn the death penalty imposed on Herbert Williams, who had been on death row for 20 years. Williams's attorneys, the LDF argued, had failed to provide an adequate level of defense in his trial, as guaranteed by the Constitution. The next year the LDF persuaded the U.S. District Court for the Southern District of Texas to grant a prisoner named Mariano Rosales a new trial, because prosecutors had unconstitutionally excluded African-Americans and Hispanics from serving as jurors in his original trial. After his conviction Rosales had spent 23 years on death row. In 2008 the LDF filed with the U.S. Supreme Court a "friend of the court" brief in support of Andrew Cuomo, the attorney general of New York State, who in 2005 had attempted to investigate apparently discriminatory lending practices of many national banks, whereby those banks issued "a significantly higher percentage of high-interest predatory loans to African-American and Hispanic borrowers than to white borrowers," according to an LDF press release (March 4, 2009, online). A district court and then the U.S. Court of Appeals for the Second Circuit agreed with the argument presented by the Clearing House Association, a consortium of national banks, that state fair-lending laws cannot be imposed on national banks. In *Cuomo v. The Clearing House Association* (June 2009), the Supreme Court ruled in favor of Cuomo 5-4 (with Justice Antonin Scalia joining the four members of the court usually identified as liberals—John Paul Stevens, David

Souter, Ruth Bader Ginsburg, and Stephen Breyer), noting, in Scalia's words, that states "have always enforced their general laws against national banks and have enforced their banking-related laws against national banks for at least 85 years."

In February 2010 Payton appeared before the Supreme Court in the case *Lewis Jr., et al. v. City of Chicago*. He was representing African-American firefighters who had won a Federal District Court case against the city of Chicago for discrimination in the use of a job-placement test. According to a press release on the NAACP-LDF website ( February 22, 2010), "The test was designed so that anyone who scored above a 65 was qualified for a firefighter job. But the City invented an arbitrary cutoff score of 89 and hired only applicants who scored above, even though, as the district court found, the cut-off score was statistically meaningless and bore no relationship to job performance as a firefighter. By hiring from the falsely named 'well qualified' pool, which was mostly white, African- American applicants were disparately and unjustifiably denied employment opportunities." On appeal, the U.S. Court of Appeals for the Seventh Circuit had reversed that ruling, on the grounds that the firefighters failed to file their complaint with the Equal Employment Opportunity Commission within the federally mandated 300-day limit. Thus, although the city of Chicago admitted to discriminatory hiring practices, the date of the plaintiffs' filing became the issue. The city argued that the 300-day window began when the results of the test scores were revealed; the plaintiffs claimed that a new act of discrimination occurred each time the test scores were used to hire, thus beginning the 300-day time period over again. On May 24, 2010 the Supreme Court ruled in favor of the firefighters. "Today, the Supreme Court affirmed that job seekers should not be denied justice based on a technicality," Payton said, as quoted on *The Defenders Online* (May 24, 2010). "This victory goes well beyond the immediate results in Chicago. It should ensure that no other fire department or employer uses a discriminatory test, and LDF will go the extra mile to make sure that they do not." That month Payton was awarded the Charles Hamilton Houston Medallion of Merit by the Washington Bar Association.

On another front, in December 2009 the LDF, in a joint effort with the NAACP, the National Urban League, and the National Coalition of Black Civic Participation, launched Count on Change 2010, a national public-awareness campaign whose goal is an accurate count of African-Americans and other members of minorities in the 2010 census. "The 2000 Census overlooked 1 million people of color, more than 600,000 of whom were African American," Payton said, as quoted in *The Defenders Online* (January 5, 2010). "The distribution of federal funds to state, county and municipal governments and the distribution of political power at every level of government depend on the Census. We cannot afford to be excluded from the count again in 2010."

Recent cases in which the NAACP-LDF has been involved include *Davis v. City of New York*, a class- action lawsuit against the allegedly unlawful trespass policies in New York City Housing Authority projects; and *Georgia v. Holder*, in which the state of Georgia is suing to alter its voting laws. According to the NAACP-LDF website, with Georgia's proposed change, "qualified voters would be ineligible to register if the information they provide on their voter registration applications does not exactly match information maintained by the Georgia Department of Driver Services or the Social Security Administration, Eligible voters who are not perfectly matched must successfully navigate a series of steps before they can cast a regular ballot on Election Day. If they cannot complete the process before Election Day, but still turn out to vote, they must appear at a hearing to make sure the ballot they cast on Election Day counts. If the court will not allow Georgia to implement this voting change, the state asks the court to invalidate the federal preclearance provision of the Voting Rights Act, known as Section 5," the same provision the NAACP-LDF successfully defended in *Northwest Austin Municipal Utility District No. 1 v. Eric H. Holder Jr. et al.*

## PERSONAL LIFE

Payton and his wife, Gay McDougall, lived in New York City and then Washington, D.C. Payton died on March 22, 2012 in Baltimore, Maryland. The couple had no children. McDougall was the executive director of Global Rights, a U.S. based international human rights advocacy group, from 1994 to 2006. In 2005 she was appointed as the first United Nations independent expert on minority issues.

## FURTHER READING

*Civil Rights Monitor (online) Winter 2008; District of Columbia Bar (online) June 2001; Journal of Blacks in Higher Education (July 31, 2002); naacpldf.org;*

# FREDERICA PERERA
## Molecular Epidemiologist

**Born:** December 19, 1941; Boston, Massachusetts
**Primary Field:** Public Health
**Affiliation:** Columbia Center for Children's Environmental Health

### INTRODUCTION
*While the phrase "security of the womb" has often been used as a metaphor for a place that is totally peaceful and safe, the womb, or uterus, does not protect a developing fetus from all dangers. Scientists have known since the early 1900s, for example, that the babies of mothers infected with syphilis may contract that disease while in the womb, and they discovered in the 1980s that babies of pregnant women infected with the AIDS virus may carry the same infection at birth. For the past three decades, the molecular epidemiologist Frederica Perera has been gathering mounting evidence that pregnant women who live in polluted environments pass along to their fetuses not only nutrients essential to life but also harmful substances in the air they breathe. Perera is a professor at the Columbia University Joseph L. Mailman School of Public Health (CSPH, also known as the Mailman School), in New York City. She has served since 1998 as the founding director and principal investigator of the Columbia Center for Children's Environmental Health (CCCEH) and since 2006 as the director of Columbia's Disease Investigation Through Specialized Clinically-Oriented Ventures in Environmental Research (DISCOVER) Center, an initiative sponsored by the National Institute of Environmental Health Sciences.*

*In the late 1970s and early '80s, Perera pioneered the field of molecular epidemiology, a novel interdisciplinary approach to understanding the causes of disease. In 1982 she and I. Bernard Weinstein wrote the seminal paper on molecular epidemiology; published in the Journal of Chronic Diseases, it offered a conceptual framework for incorporating biological markers, or biomarkers, into epidemiology studies (a proposal later adopted by the National Research Council). A biomarker, according to the National Institutes of Health, is in part "a characteristic that is objectively measured and evaluated as an indicator of normal biologic processes [or] pathogenic processes." In her research Perera relied on techniques invented by molecular biologists,*

*who search for biomarkers in tissues or body fluids from animals that have been exposed to unnatural or uncustomary chemicals. Perera initially focused on biomarkers known as carcinogen DNA adducts, which form when chemicals bind to biological molecules, such as cellular DNA or proteins. Some adducts result in genetic mutations. Such mutations increase the probability that cancer will develop. Ideally, if a biomarker linked to pathology is identified in an individual before symptoms of disease can be detected, physicians and policymakers can take steps to prevent the disease. Perera's doctoral thesis was entitled "Report of a Pilot Project in Molecular Epidemiology: A Preliminary Study of Carcinogen-DNA Adducts in Human Subjects"; a paper constituting the first report of carcinogen-DNA adducts in a human p op ulati on base don that research appeared in the journal Carcinogenesis in 1982 with Perera as the lead author.*

*Molecular epidemiology incorporates "molecular, cellular, and other biologic measurements into epidemiologic research," according to the Introduction to Molecular Epidemiology: Principles and Practices (1993), a groundbreaking work that Perera edited with the epidemiologist Paul A. Schulte; it is a discipline in which laboratory scientists, primarily molecular biologists, collaborate with epidemiologists, who study the incidence and distribution of diseases within groups of people. In particular, Perera studies the effects of environmental pollutants on chromosomes, genes, and other cell molecules in human populations.*

*At present there are tens of thousands of pollutants in Earth's air, soil, and water, produced by industry, agriculture, and other activities of humans; according to the World Health Organization, an arm of the United Nations, an estimated one- quarter of the diseases that strike people today can be traced to prolonged exposure to environmental pollution. Perera's long term studies of thousands of pregnant women and their babies in New York City, Poland, and China have produced evidence that babies born to mothers who breathe polluted air may be harmed physically and mentally. "Early-life exposures, even occurring in the womb, appear to be important determinants of that child's respiratory health and development later on," Perera told Melissa Lee Phillips for* Environmental Health Perspectives *(October 2005). "We have enormous opportunities to prevent these diseases and conditions." Perera has also studied the effects of polluted air on smokers and nonsmokers and has investigated the roles of particular genes in individuals exposed to carcinogens—substances that cause cancer. She has been recognized internationally not only for her scientific work but also for her efforts to reduce children's exposure to pollutants, notably in several low income New York City neighborhoods as well as at sites in China and Poland, and for her repeated attempts to awaken policy makers to the serious hazards of environmental pollution on children and adults. Perera's honors include the first Irving J. Selikoff Cancer Research Award from the Ramazzini Institute, in Bologna, Italy, in 1995; the first Children's Environmental Health Award from the Pew Center for Children's Health and the Environment, in 1999; an honorary doctoral degree from Jagiellonian University, in Cracow, Poland, in 2004; the Children's Environmental Health Excellence Award from the U.S. Environmental Protection Agency, in 2005; and the Measure of Children Award from the Healthy Schools Network, in 2008.*

## EARLY LIFE

The second of the four children of Davis Clapp Drinkwater and the former Frederica Plimpton, Perera was born Frederica Plimpton Drinkwater in Boston, Massachusetts, on December 19, 1941. Beginning at age 12, she grew up on her parents' farm, in Panton, Vermont, with two sisters, Susan and Polly, and a brother, Davis Drinkwater Jr., now a cardiothoracic surgeon in Nashville, Tennessee. Her father, a Harvard University graduate, served as a commander in the U.S. Navy during World War II before becoming a farmer. In Vermont her mother held an elected position in the town, helping people in need; she was also a longtime Planned Parenthood volunteer.

Perera graduated magna cum laude from Harvard University, in Cambridge, Massachusetts, with a B.A. degree in 1963. She married that year, and during the next decade she gave birth to three sons and a daughter. She earned a Master's degree and a Doctorate, with honors, in public health at Columbia University in 1976 and 1981, respectively. In the latter year Perera joined the faculty of the Mailman School as an assistant clinical professor; she was promoted to assistant professor in 1983, associate professor in 1988, and full professor in 1995. From 1989 until 2004 Perera was associate director of the Division of Epidemiology, Prevention and Control at the Columbia-Presbyterian Cancer Center (now part of New York-Presbyterian Hospital/Columbia

University Medical Center), and from 1990 to 1991 she served as acting head of the Division of Environmental Sciences at the Mailman School.

## LIFE'S WORK

In the late 1970s Perera began to investigate the suspected causal connections between chemicals in cigarette smoke and air pollution and the occurrence of cancer. Cigarette smoke inhaled by smokers and people nearby (those breathing so-called secondhand smoke) is among many thousands of environmental pollutants. The vast majority have been introduced into the world's air, water, and soil since the start of the Industrial Revolution, in the 19th century, and most of those since World War II. They include polycyclic aromatic hydrocarbons (PAHs) and other emissions from fossil fuel combustion in vehicles, factories, homes, and power plants; waste from industrial processes; chemical fertilizers and pesticides in soil runoff that enters water supplies; motor oil, paint, batteries, electronic devices, and other things discarded improperly on land or in water; particles produced by incineration of garbage; and microscopic particles and vapors released from synthetic items such as carpets or plastics.

When Perera began her studies, most researchers used rats and mice to determine the effects of toxic substances on humans. Using the results of such studies, for example, the percentages of the animals that developed diseases, tumors, or organ abnormalities, the researchers would hypothesize about the results of exposure to those toxic substances in human populations. They would then conduct epidemiological studies of human communities exposed to those substances to find out the rates at which similar diseases, tumors, or abnormalities occurred in those people. Perera, however, wanted to work with human tissue and human populations directly. "Humans have a very different molecular response to the environment than rodents. But tests treat us like rodents, in a very uniform way," she told Jordana Hart for the *Boston Globe* (September 24, 1989).

In her early research Perera collected samples of tissues and body fluids (blood and urine) from human volunteers exposed to cigarette smoke and air pollution. Cigarette smoke contains not only nicotine and tars but chemicals including formaldehyde, ammonia, carbon monoxide, hydrogen cyanide, and PAHs. Perera focused on PAHs, a group of compounds released by the burning of organic matter including fossil fuel, many of which are used in industry; PAHs do not break down easily into their component parts and thus tend to persist in the environment for a long time. At least 15 PAHs are undoubtedly carcinogenic, and others have been implicated in high rates of cancer in workers whose exposure to them is direct, heavy, and prolonged. Perera searched for biomarkers in her subjects' tissues, blood, and urine that indicated exposure to PAHs. In the course of her research, she discovered that after PAHs enter a person's lungs, they pass into the bloodstream and damage blood cells by binding to the cells' DNA. With the aim of comparing damaged blood cells to healthy ones, she examined blood cells from the umbilical cords of newborn infants, thinking that such cells must be "pure," that is, uncontaminated by environmental toxins. When she analyzed such blood, however, she found PAH molecules attached to some of the cells' DNA. "I was pretty shocked," she told Jerome Groopman for the *New Yorker* (May 31, 2010). "I realized that we did not know very much about what was happening during this early stage of development."

In the early 1990s, in collaboration with Kari Hemminki, Regina Santella, and other scientists and physicians from the U.S., Poland, and Scandinavia, Perera investigated cell damage in people living and working in Silesia, a highly industrialized part of Poland where there were high levels of air pollution, including the presence of PAHs from the combustion of coal. The researchers examined blood samples from adult volunteers from urban areas and, for comparison, from "a rural, less polluted area of Poland," according to the paper in *Nature* (November 19,1992) in which they described their findings. Analyses of the volunteers' PAH- DNA adducts revealed that the quantities of adducts in their blood cells were significantly higher in the urban industrial area and coincided with seasonal fluctuations in air pollution. Byproducts of coal combustion were greatest during winter months, when buildings were heated. In measurements of the presence of adducts, the researchers also found huge variations among individuals: the presence of adducts in some people's cells was 200 times greater than in those of others. That finding supported the hypothesis that genes play a role in the extent to which environmental pollutants affect cells.

Also in the early 1990s, in a study of 87 Hispanic and African-American mothers and their preschool children, aged two to five years, in New York City, Perera found that exposure to mothers' cigarette smoke greatly increased the presence of PAHs in the children's systems. In another study during that period, Perera

examined tissue samples taken from 15 women being treated for breast cancer at the Columbia-Presbyterian Medical Center and from four women who had undergone breast-reduction surgery. Of the 15 women with cancer, the tissues of five longtime smokers showed a pattern of adducts associated with exposure to tobacco smoke. None of the tissues from nonsmokers showed that pattern. Those findings suggested that the formation of adducts in the female breast is associated with exposure to environmental carcinogens. Perera described those findings and other results of her research up to that point in a 12,800 word article, entitled "Molecular Epidemiology: Insights into Cancer Susceptibility, Risk Assessment, and Prevention," published in *JNCI: Journal of the National Cancer Institute* (April 17,1996). Perera and her team then carried out a case-control study of breast cancer and in 2000 reported a significant relation between PAH-DNA adducts in breast tissue and cancer risk.

In 1998, with support from the National Institute of Environmental Health Sciences (an arm of the National Institutes of Health) and the U.S. Environmental Protection Agency, Perera established the Columbia Center for Children's Environmental Health. Her aim, she told Jenn Preissel for the *Columbia Daily Spectator* (March 25, 2005), was to try to decrease the incidence of "serious childhood diseases through the identification of environmental risk factors that by their nature are preventable." As the director of the CCCEH since its founding, Perera has guided one of the largest and longest-standing studies of mothers and children in the U.S. At any one time the subjects include more than 700 women, who enter the study during pregnancy, and their newborn children, who are followed until age eight. The women and their families all live in New York City, some in the Washington Heights or Harlem neighborhoods of Manhattan and others in the South Bronx, places whose air contains greater levels of toxic substances than the air in many other parts of the city. All but a tiny percentage of the residents of those neighborhoods are low income Hispanics or African-Americans, among whom the incidence of respiratory problems, notably asthma, and learning difficulties are significantly greater than in residents of neighborhoods with cleaner air. After concentrating on exposure to PAHs in the early years of her study, Perera expanded her research to include many more chemical compounds and other materials, such as insecticides and pest allergens. Toward the end of their pregnancies, the women in the study wear backpacks containing devices that monitor the air they breathe, and the women provide the researchers with urine samples. When their babies are delivered, a sample of umbilical cord blood is drawn and the cells examined. The newborns are weighed and their head circumferences measured. As the babies grow, the researchers assess the children's physical and cognitive development and health.

Perera and her co-workers have conducted similar studies, though with fewer subjects, in other places with high levels of air pollution: Cracow, Poland's second-largest city, and Tongliang, a city in the municipality of Chongqing, China, where a local power plant burned more than 20,300 tons of coal each year before it was shut, in 2004. In another project, Perera focused on 330 infants born in Lower Manhattan on September 11, 2001 or up to half a year after that date, when the U.S. was attacked at the World Trade Center. The resulting fires and the collapse of the center's twin towers produced enormous clouds of smoke and dust, a mixture of particles of thousands of compounds, that continued to pollute the air in Lower Manhattan for more than four months. Scientists who monitored PAHs in the area during the six months following 9/11 recorded levels of pollution up to 65 times higher than normal.

Among other findings, Perera's research has produced evidence that babies whose mothers were exposed to higher-than-usual levels of PAHs from tobacco smoke or other forms of air pollution have lower birth weights and smaller heads than unexposed babies. Typically, newborns whose weights at birth are significantly lower than average are more likely than other newborns to experience respiratory disorders and other health problems in infancy and later on, and babies born with smaller-than-normal heads are more likely to experience learning difficulties as they get older. Although animal studies had suggested that the placenta filters out many of the PAHs to protect the fetus, Perera and her team found that mothers and infants had similar levels of PAH-induced DNA damage; babies with mothers who had been exposed to greater levels of pollutants had about 50 percent more persistent genetic abnormalities than babies with mothers exposed to lower levels of pollutants. "What gets across [the placenta] is not detoxified and the damage to the DNA is not repaired in the fetus as it is in the mother," Perera told Anna Gosline for *New Scientist* (July 3, 2004). Furthermore, Perera found, the babies had similar or higher adduct levels than their mothers, indicating that fetuses and newborns

are especially susceptible to air pollutants, which can also lead to a greater risk of developing cancer later in life, many scientists believe. "We already knew that air pollutants significantly reduced fetal growth, but this is the first time we've seen evidence that they can change chromosomes in utero," Perera said, as quoted by Karen Matthews for the *Associated Press* (February 15, 2005). She added, "While we can't estimate the precise increase in cancer risk, these findings underscore the need for policymakers at the federal, state and local levels to take appropriate steps to protect children from these avoidable exposures."

To learn whether PAHs from the World Trade Center disaster may have affected pregnant mothers and their fetuses, Perera and her collaborators measured PAH-DNA adducts in cord blood among newborns of mothers living near the site of the attacks in the following months. Levels of cord blood adducts were higher the closer the mother lived to the site, and higher adducts in combination with in utero exposure to secondhand smoke were associated with a reduction in birth weight and head circumference. The study in Tongliang revealed that infants born before the power plant was shut down, those whose mothers were exposed to combustion related power plant pollution during their pregnancies, had higher levels of DNA adducts and had less favorable birth measurements than babies born after the plant was shut down. At two years of age, children who had had the most exposure to PAHs, as evidenced by PAH-DNA adducts, performed significantly worse than others on neurodevelopment tests. The CCCEH's studies in Poland during the past decade have produced similar results. In 2009 Perera and colleagues reported that elevated prenatal PAH exposure in New York City was significantly associated with lower IQ scores at age five, a finding that was confirmed in the Polish study population.

In 2006 the CCCEH launched the DISCOVER initiative, four studies funded by the National Institute of Environmental Health Sciences that seek to further elucidate the relationships between air pollutants and childhood asthma, abnormal neurocognitive development, and cancer. An integral component of the project is community involvement: Perera and her team work with both families and neighborhood organizations to reduce residents' exposure to harmful pollutants, by means of educational efforts such as workshops and newsletters and visits to people's homes to advise on the best methods of controlling infestations of household pests.

## Personal Life

Perera's first husband, Phillips Perera, served as a U.S. deputy assistant secretary of commerce, then as a vice president of American Express, before becoming the founder and president of Interfin, a New York financial services company for international food businesses. From that marriage, which ended with her husband's death, in 1992, Perera has four children, Frederica, Christopher, Alexander, and Phillips Perera Jr., who is the director of ultrasound at the University of Southern California Department of Emergency Medicine. In 1996 Frederica Perera married Frederick A. O. Schwarz Jr., the great-grandson of the founder of the famous Fifth Avenue toy emporium, F.A.O. Schwarz. Frederick Schwarz Jr., chief counsel at New York University Law School's Brennan Center for Justice, has a son and two daughters from his previous marriage. Perera lives in Manhattan with her husband.

## Further Reading

*Respirable Particles: Impact of Airborne Fine Particulates on Health and the Environment; Risk Quantitation and Regulatory Policy; Molecular Epidemiology: Principles and Practices*

---

# Adolfo Perez Esquivel

## Activist; Professor

**Born:** November 26, 1931; Buenos Aires, Argentina
**Primary Field:** Human Rights
**Affiliation:** Nobel Peace Prize

### Introduction

*The winner of the 1980 Nobel Peace Prize was Adolfo Perez Esquivel, the devout Roman Catholic Argentine human rights activist, who at the time was almost unknown even to the public in his own country. Nominated for the peace prize by its 1976 winners, Mairead Corrigan and Betty Williams of Ulster, Perez Esquivel was chosen from a record number of candidates. In honoring him, the Nobel committee cited him for having "stone a light in the darkness" of strife-torn Argentina, and for having "devoted his life to the struggle for human rights since 1974," the year in which he became general coordinator of the Service for Peace and Justice, a church-based network of organizations working for social justice in Latin America by nonviolent means.*

*Before dedicating himself to the battle for human rights in his native Argentina, Perez Esquivel was a sculptor and professor of architecture. Since the armed forces took power in Argentina in 1976, he concentrated his efforts on behalf of the tens of thousands of Argentines imprisoned and tortured by the military regime, especially the so-called desaparecidos or "disappeared ones," who vanished without a trace, with the result that he was himself jailed without trial and held for more than a year. On the day he learned that he had been awarded the Nobel Peace Prize he told Edward Schumacher of the* New York Times *(October 14, 1980): "I accept this prize in the name of Latin America and its workers, in the name of its campesinos, and its priests who are working diligently for the peace and rights of all." Because of Perez Esquivel's ingrown reticence and the scant amount of public attention he attracted before winning the Nobel Peace Prize, Edward Schumacher described him in his article as "a backrooms man, a committee organizer, not a charismatic public leader.: It is therefore not surprising that relatively little is known about his background.*

### Early Life

Perez Esquivel was born on November 26, 1931 in Buenos Aires, Argentina to a Spanish fisherman who had immigrated to Argentina and his wife, who died when Adolfo was very young. The boy spent very little time with his father, who became a commercial representative for coffee firms. Although the family was poor, Adolfo attended private schools, where he acquired the habit of voracious reading. Prowling through the second-hand bookstalls of Buenos Aires, he found himself especially attracted to religious subjects, even as a teenager. In an interview with Carla Hall of the *Washington Post* (November 20, 1980) he recalled: "I read Gandhi's autobiography, where he says nonviolence is not just for saints. I read Thomas Merton, a Catholic monk. I was very impressed by his spiritualness. I read

St. Augustine." He began to meet with other Argentines in small groups that combined prayer and reflection with social welfare concerns.

After graduating from his private secondary school, Perez Esquivel enrolled at the National School of Fine Arts of Buenos Aires and La Plata. For the next fifteen years following his graduation from that institution on October 11, 1956, he pursued a successful and politically detached career as a sculptor and professor of art at the Manuel Belgrano National School of Fine Arts in Buenos Aires and at other art schools in or near the capital. When his sculptures were widely exhibited in Argentina, he won several prizes, including the important Premio La Nacion de Escultura. His work is in the collections of the Buenos Aires Museum of Modern Art, the Museum of Fine Arts in Cordoba, and the fine Arts Museum of Rosario.

During the earlier years of his career as a sculptor, Perez Esquivel explored themes from Latin American art and history. His 1966 terra cotta work Templo del Sol (Temple of the Sun), for example, employs rough architectural forms and a primitive standing figure reminiscent of pre-Columbian clay figurines. In a pamphlet that was published by the Argentine Ecumenical Movement for Human Rights while Perez Esquivel was in prison, he is quoted as having said, "While all the contributions of different cultures and artistic movements combine in our epoch into a universal language that reflects today's problems, I feel the need to find in our American roots the means of expression in symbols and signs that can fuse with today's concerns. For that reason I'm interested in deeper knowledge of Pre-Columbian cultures." Another theme often found in Perez Esquivel's work is that of motherhood. His Monumento a la Madre (Monument to Mothers) stands in the Argentine city of Azul, and another with the same subject can be seen in Bernal. But by the late 1960's the social and religious ideas that were increasingly important to Perez Esquivel came to dominate his sculpture.

Those later years of Perez Esquivel's artistic career were difficult ones for his country, for Argentina had never recovered from the bitter class antagonisms exploited by Juan Domingo Peron, the populist dictator overthrown by the military in 1955. The urban industrial class, organized into strong unions, and the lower-middle classes remained passionately committed to Peronism, but the military was determined not to let the exiled dictator or his followers return to power. The result was a long and ultimately catastrophic political

stalemate. Repression by a succession of military governments led many young Peronists and leftists to go underground and to organize urban guerrilla armies. By the early 1970's they were carrying out acts of terrorism that invited even more severe response from the armed forces.

## LIFE'S WORK

The progressive unraveling of Argentina's political fabric, and the wretched conditions in which much of its population still lived, led Perez Esquivel to turn from the absorptions of his artistic and academic career to political activism. In 1968 he attended a conference in Montevideo, Uruguay, where representatives of church, labor, student, intellectual, and community groups discussed means of achieving "change and development through a process of nonviolent liberation," as Perez Esquivel later described it. That conference was only one manifestation of a trend then developing throughout Latin America: the growing involvement of clergymen and deeply committed lay activists in social issues in behalf of the poor. At the 1968 meeting in Montevideo the "basic structure" of the Service for Justice and Peace (its full name in Spanish is the Servicio de Paz y Justicia en America Latina, Orientacion No Violenta) was created. At a second conference, held in Costa Rica in 1971, the Servicio was formally founded. That same year Perez Esquivel joined an Argentine group dedicated to Gandhian principles of "militant nonviolence," and one of his first projects was to organize weaving, carpentry, and ironworking workshops in urban neighborhoods to achieve the Gandhian goal of self-support through craft industry. In 1972 he carried out a hunger strike to protest the violence perpetrated both by terrorists and by police forces in Argentina; in 1973 he founded a monthly magazine, Paz y Justicia (Peace and Justice) that was later adopted as the official publication of the Service; and in 1974, at a conference in Medellin, Colombia, he was named general coordinator of the service, whose headquarters were officially established in Buenos Aires during that year.

From its inception, the Service for Peace and Justice has been a loosely structured, ecumenical network of disparate organizations pledged to maintain close contact and support each other's efforts. Its basic outlook was best enunciated by Perez Esquivel in an interview with Larry Rohter of Newsweek (October 27, 1980). "Unjust structures must be changed," he said. "But only through nonviolence can those structures be transformed to build a more just and humane society." Such a commitment to pacifism, however, was not a common stance in Latin America, and for the first years of its existence the major task of the Service for Peace and Justice was simply to bring isolated groups in distant countries into touch with each other. To that end, Perez Esquivel resigned his teaching positions and traveled tirelessly throughout South and Central America. In 1974 he launched a campaign in behalf of Indians in Ecuador whose attempts to acquire land were being repressed, and in the following year he visited Paraguay to help organize protests against the government's attacks on the church organized Agrarian Leagues. During a trip to Brazil in 1975 he was briefly jailed, and he was arrested again in Ecuador in 1976, a year in which he also traveled to the United States and Europe.

Meanwhile, in Argentina matters were moving from bad to worse. Peron's return and his election to the presidency in 1973 had little calming effect, and after Peron's death in 1974, his widow and successor, Isabel Peron, proved incapable of halting the slide into chaos. Raging inflation, pervasive official corruption, terrorism in the cities and guerrilla warfare in the countryside finally led the armed forces to seize power on March 24, 1976 and install as president the army commander in chief, General Jorge Rafael Videla, who with the junta set out to crush the Argentine left with extraordinary brutality. In 1976 and 1977 tens of thousands of Argentines were jailed and tortured without charges or trial, and countless others fled into exile. Anyone suspected of the least sympathy or connection with leftist or Peronist activities was vulnerable. Many of the victims were kidnapped and murdered by right-wing paramilitary death squads apparently operating with the sanction of the government.

In the face of that wave of terror, and similar repression by neighboring military regimes in Chile, Bolivia, Paraguay, Brazil, and Uruguay, the Service for Peace and Justice concentrated its efforts on the defense of human rights. Perez Esquivel led a campaign to publicize and press for enforcement of the Universal Declaration on Human Rights of the United Nations. Within Argentina, he helped found the Ecumenical Movement for Human Rights and served as president of the Permanent Assembly for Human Rights. His public denunciations of government atrocities did not endear him to the authorities, and in 1976, while he was traveling abroad, his headquarters of the Service for Peace and Justice in Buenos Aires were occupied and ransacked by security

forces. On April 4, 1977, when Perez Esquivel went to a local police station on a routine matter, he was arrested without warning and jailed.

During the fifteen months of Perez Esquivel's imprisonment he was never formally charged, although the government let it be known that he was being held as a "subversive." He was severely tortured, an experience he refuses to discuss in detail, but constant prayer and the performance of yoga exercises whenever possible helped him resist the attempt to break his morale. Of the ordeal of torture, he said in a 1980 interview, "When you experience this extreme situation of being between life and death, you try to understand what Christ said on the cross: 'Father, forgive them, for they don't know what they are doing.' But I thought that, yes, these people did know what they were doing. This was very contradictory for me, and I tried to understand more deeply, what was it that Christ was trying to say to us in this supreme moment? What I discovered, little by little, was that what [the torturers] did not know was that they were persons, and that we were persons. They had lost their identities."

Almost from the moment of his arrest, an international campaign took shape to demand Perez Esquivel's release. While he was still in prison, important religious leaders called for his release, Mairead Corrigan and Betty Williams nominated him for the Nobel Peace Prize, Amnesty International adopted him as a prisoner of conscience, and the Carter Administration interceded with the Argentine government. The Argentine government finally released Perez Esquivel in June 1978, but for nine more months he was kept under house arrest. Resuming his work, in 1980 he made another tour through Europe, by which time repression in Argentina had eased somewhat, largely because the junta had won its "war" on the left. But Perez Esquivel insisted that Argentines be informed of the fate of the estimated 10,000 to 20,000 desaparecidos, and he began working closely with the women known as "Las Locas de Mayo" (the madwomen of May Square), who meet each week in a central plaza of Buenos Aires to protest and demand information about their missing relatives.

The award of the Nobel Peace Prize to Perez Esquivel on October 13, 1980, after the committee had considered a record number of fifty-seven individual and seventeen organizational candidates, was clearly intended to aid his efforts in behalf of Argentine political prisoners. The citation stated that "Perez Esquivel is among those Argentines who have shown a light in the darkness. He champions a solution of Argentina's grievous problems that dispenses with the use of violence, and is the spokesman of a revival of respect for human rights. The prizewinner is an Argentinian, but the views he represents carry a vital message to many other countries, not the least in Latin America, where social and political problems as yet unresolved have resulted in an escalation of the use of violence." Shocked and angered by the flurry of international publicity that accompanied the award, the Argentine government at first maintained a stony silence, while the tightly controlled media tried to play down the significance of the story. Some days later the government issued a statement that defended its jailing of Perez Esquivel on the grounds that he had "contributed to the cause of those who promote terrorism in the nation." Meanwhile, congratulations poured in from all over the world, from such personages as Willy Brandt, Edward M. Kennedy, and Joan Baez.

Shortly after winning the Nobel Peace Prize, Perez Esquivel traveled to the United States for a one week tour that took him to New York City, Philadelphia, Washington, and Phoenix, where he addressed the annual convention of the Associated Press Managing Editors Association. He met with then U.N. Secretary General Kurt Waldheim, with members of Congress, and with Rosalynn Carter and was awarded an honorary Doctorate of Humanities from St. Joseph's University in Philadelphia. Throughout his brief visit he stressed the theme that human rights issues are inextricably linked to economic ones. As he told Larry Rohter, "You cannot talk solely of human rights in terms of torture and imprisonment and killing. True, this is the gravest aspect. But we must also look at the case of the peasant who has no land and is dying of hunger." On December 10, 1980 he received the Nobel Prize in Oslo, Norway, where he attacked "the old, well-known, and dilapidated structure of injustice" in his acceptance speech. He added: "The rules of this play, which have been laid down by the big powers and have been inflicted upon the rest of the world, also permit the biggest crime of our time, the arms race." The Argentine ambassador was conspicuously absent from the ceremony.

## PERSONAL LIFE

Adolfo Perez Esquivel is a slim man with thinning dark hair, usually disheveled, and the intense, austere appearance that one associates with a religious activist. He is usually described as being modest, soft-spoken and patient. His shabby, almost bare office in the Buenos Aires headquarters of the Service for Peace and Justice has pictures of Pope John Pual II and of Gandhi tacked on the wall. Perez Esquivel married his wife, Amanda, in 1956; they have three sons, the oldest of whom, Leonardo, is a staff member of the Service for Peace and Justice and helped to run the organization while his father was in prison. The family lives in a modest house designed by Perez Esquivel himself in the upper-class Buenos Aires neighborhood of San Isidro. Besides the Nobel Prize, Perez Esquivel has been awarded the Pope John XXIII Prize in 1977 by the international Catholic organization Pax Christi. Certainly the greatest irony about his Nobel Peace Prize is that the Argentine government passed a law in 1977 providing that any Argentine who won a Nobel Prize would be awarded a lifetime stipend equal to the salary of a Supreme Court Justice. Perez Esquivel was granted the lifetime pension in September 1981, ending a five-month delay. His son Leonardo said that the funds will be used to further the work of the Service for Peace and Justice. He remains an outspoken political voice in the contemporary moment of peace and conflict.

## FURTHER READING

*http://adolfoperezesquivel.com.ar/;    http://www.encyclopedia.com/topic/Adolfo_Perez_Esquivel.aspx*

# CHELLIE PINGREE

## Politician

**Born:** April 2, 1955; Minneapolis, Minnesota
**Primary Field:** Consumer Advocacy
**Affiliation:** Democratic Party

### INTRODUCTION

*In February 2003 Chellie Pingree, whose former occupations include farmer, small-business owner, chairperson of a local school board, and Maine state senator, and who in 2002 ran unsuccessfully as a Democrat for one of Maine's seats in the U.S. Senate, was elected president and chief executive officer (CEO) of Common Cause. A nonpartisan, nonprofit citizens' watchdog organization based in Washington, D.C., Common Cause was founded in 1970 by John Gardner; earlier, while serving in the Cabinet of President Lyndon B. Johnson and then as the chairperson of the National Urban Coalition Action Council, Gardner had concluded that ordinary U.S. citizens lacked a collective voice in the nation's capital. "Everybody's organized but the people," Gardner once said, "everybody" referring to the thousands of industries and other special interest groups whose lobbyists influence federal legislation, regulations, and policies. According to its website, Common Cause is "a vehicle for citizens to make their voices heard in the political process and to hold their elected leaders accountable to the public interest." It is "committed to honest, open and accountable government" and to "encouraging citizen participation in democracy." Pingree began to gain an intimate familiarity with the political process and its strengths and weaknesses three decades ago, when she became involved in community affairs in the small Maine community in which she ran her farm and knitting goods business and raised her three children. Among the high points of her highly effective, eight-year career in the Maine state Senate, in which for four years she served as the majority leader, were the passage of unprecedented healthcare and prescription drug bills that benefitted thousands of Maine residents who had no medical coverage and/or had very low incomes. In 2001 the national nonprofit organization Families USA, which is dedicated to making high quality, affordable health care available to all Americans, named Pingree "consumer health advocate of the year." As the head of Common Cause, she is working to enhance the transparency of government at all levels; strengthen and extend*

*campaign finance reform and promote increased public financing of political campaigns; implement changes in states' systems of electoral districting, which currently allow rampant gerrymandering in favor of one party or another; and limit the increasing control that a small number of giant corporations exert over the media. One of her prime goals is to convince people everywhere in the U.S. that each person can make a difference in the political process, whether by discussing issues with friends and relatives, writing letters or email messages to or phoning legislators, attending public meetings, voting, or seeking election to public office in their communities, towns, cities, or states.*

### EARLY LIFE

Rochelle Marie Pingree, known universally as Chellie, was born in Minneapolis, Minnesota, on April 2, 1955. As a 17 year old new high school graduate, she moved to North Haven, an island 12 miles off the coast of Maine, in Penobscot Bay. Pingree attended the College of the Atlantic, in Bar Harbor, Maine, where she studied human ecology, a discipline concerned in part with the consequences of human actions on the natural and manmade environments. After she graduated, with a B.A. degree, in 1976, Pingree bought a two acre farm in North Haven. For a dozen years beginning that year, she raised sheep, chickens, cows, and vegetables on the farm, which eventually covered 90 acres. Concurrently, in 1981, she established North Island Yarn, a retail store that sold products hand-knitted by Pingree and her employees. Later, after renaming the business North Island Designs, she also marketed knitting kits and books of knitting patterns to some 1,200 retail outlets nationwide, along with the mail order houses L. L. Bean and Lands' End. She wrote or co-wrote, with Debby Anderson, four books of knitting patterns, among them *Maine Island Classics: Knitting on a Maine Island* (1988), and she joined the National Writers Union, which is affiliated with the United Automobile, Aerospace, and Agricultural Implement Workers of America (familiarly known as the UAW), one of the nation's largest and most diverse labor organizations. North Island Designs continued operating until 1993.

Meanwhile, in 1975, while still an undergraduate, Pingree had married. During the next decade she became the mother of two daughters (Cecily and Hannah) and a son (Asa) and became involved in North Haven affairs. In the February 5, 2002 installment of an occasional "diary" that appeared in the UAW's online publication *Solidarity*, she wrote that in North Haven, she "learned what it is to be part of a community. On an island of 350, almost everyone serves on a board or committee at some time, or is an active volunteer or just involved in the morning conversations over coffee down at the store." According to Chris Mooney in *American Prospect* (October 7, 2002), North Haven is still a place where "people leave their keys in their cars so neighbors can borrow them." Its year round population includes many lobstermen and other rugged individuals with whom Pingree "rub[bed] shoulders" regularly, in Mooney's words. In the *Solidarity* piece, Pingree described the first time she stood up and spoke at a North Haven town meeting as "one of the scarier public speaking moments of my life." She soon became braver and, as she recalled, "found that being involved in small town politics was very rewarding and quite an education." During the 1980s she served on the North Haven Planning Board, as a tax assessor, and on the local school board, the last of which she chaired for some time. School board chair, according to Pingree, is "the hardest job in politics." "One thing that distinguishes local politics and makes it such a model for the way I believe policy should be made at all levels of government is accountability," she wrote for Solidarity. In a town as small as North Haven, "almost every decision you make will be discussed on the ferry, at the store over coffee and at the next baked bean supper. And, because most issues affect everyone's lives, community members feel an obligation to do their part when it comes to making decisions."

## LIFE'S WORK
In 1992 Pingree won election to the Maine state Senate as a Democrat in District 21, a strongly Republican area that encompassed North Haven and other Penobscot Bay islands and more than a dozen municipalities in Knox County, on the mainland. She was reelected to three additional two year terms in the Senate; because of reapportionment in Maine, she represented what had become District 12 during those three terms. Pingree quickly distinguished herself among Senate lawmakers through her ability to find creative solutions to problems and to build bipartisan consensus around issues. A poll conducted in 1995 by the now defunct *Maine Times* newspaper named Pingree the state's favorite legislator. The following year she was elected majority leader

of the state Senate. She was only the second woman in Maine history to win that position, which she held until 2000. As a Maine lawmaker she sponsored legislation that created the Parents as Scholars program, a student aid service that helped low-income parents to pursue two or four year college degrees. During the mid-1990s she served as co-chair of both Maine's Committee on Housing and Economic Development and the Maine Economic Growth Council. In recognition of her efforts to expand opportunities for small-business owners, she was named the Economic Development Council's legislator of the year in 1994. According to Mooney, Pingree's experience in those legislative and advisory bodies was instrumental in her successful fight to establish a law that requires corporations that do business in Maine to report state-tax breaks and how they use subsidies given by the state. Pingree also served as chairperson of Maine Citizens Against Handgun Violence and the Maine Women's Vote Project, the latter of which works to increase voter turnouts for state elections. Her priorities also included advocating for increased public access to public land.

As a state senator Pingree was best known for her efforts regarding health care. As Senate majority leader she successfully led the fight to extend health care to 10,000 low-wage Maine families and reduce their prescription-drug costs. With one of the highest percentages of senior citizens of all 50 states and as a state bordering Canada, where drug prices are regulated and often considerably lower than in the U.S., Maine has long been on the frontline of the national debate regarding the high costs of prescription drugs and the pharmaceutical industry's role in keeping prices high. Pingree spearheaded the passage, in 2000, of Maine Rx, an unprecedented piece of legislation that requires pharmaceutical companies to negotiate the prices of drugs with the state government in order to keep drug costs low for state residents who do not have health insurance or whose salaries or wages are significantly lower than average. In drawing up the law, Pingree was aided by the Center for Policy Alternatives, the country's "leading nonpartisan progressive public policy organization serving state legislators," according to its website. More than 250,000 uninsured Maine residents became eligible to enroll for discounts on prescription drugs after Maine Rx went into effect. The program served as a model for prescription-drug programs instituted in Hawaii and Illinois, and Legislatures in other states are considering similar measures. "We shouldn't have to pass this bill in Maine, then in New Hampshire, then in Virginia," Pingree declared to Robin Toner for the New York Times (May 11, 2002). "[The federal government] ought to have a Medicare prescription drug benefit, and they ought to negotiate a really good price. If we could do this in Maine, we can do it in Washington," meaning that such reforms should be nationwide and not limited to individual states. The Pharmaceutical Research and Manufacturers of America unsuccessfully challenged Maine Rx before the U.S. Supreme Court as an unconstitutional regulation of interstate commerce.

Thanks to Pingree's achievements in the Maine state Senate, in 1997 she earned an Eisenhower International Exchange Program fellowship, which enabled her to travel in Hungary to observe that country's continuing transition from Communist rule to open democracy. While in Hungary Pingree also met with female business leaders and women involved in the country's politics. In 1998 Pingree was a member of a special White House delegation that oversaw the democratic elections in Bosnia and Herzegovina, which took place after years of ethnic and religious bloodshed there. In 1999 she interacted with female political leaders in Northern Ireland as a member of another U.S. delegation. Also during the 1990s Pingree traveled in India with a group organized by the Global Peace Initiative.

Because of term limits regulations, Pingree was not permitted to seek re-election in 2001. That same year she was named a senior fellow at the Center for Policy Alternatives, in Washington, D.C. In 2002, after ruling out a run for the state governorship, Pingree campaigned for a seat in the U.S. Senate against the popular incumbent Maine Republican Susan Collins. Maine's other senator, Olympia Snow, is also a woman and a Republican. During her campaign, Chris Mooney wrote, "In her political ads and rapid-fire stump speeches, Pingree hones in on pocketbook issues, especially prescription drugs and corporate accountability. But she often approaches them not so much as an outraged corporate watchdog but from the folksy perspective of a small businessperson trying to keep the island's only general store running." The race was watched unusually closely nationwide, because some political observers believed that a Pingree victory was essential for the Democrats to hold onto their party's majority in the Senate. Senate Majority Leader Tom Daschle appeared with Pingree at several events during her campaign, and *Time* (June 10, 2002) ran a photo of Daschle and Pingree together. In an August 2002 entry for her UAW *Solidarity* "diary,"

Pingree wrote that the Maine Senate race began attracting further national press attention when it became public that the White House had conducted an "electronic slide show" revealing that the administration of Republican president George W. Bush considered "Maine's Senate seat to be one of a few in which a Democrat could unseat a Republican incumbent." In part because Senator Collins and the Maine Republican Party also come out in favor of health-care reforms, diminishing the selling power of Pingree's proposals, Collins defeated Pingree on Election Day, November 5, 2002, by 16 percentage points.

Pingree's record as a highly effective advocate of corporate responsibility and measures that would aid average, working-class citizens led the national governing board of Common Cause (chaired by Derek Bok, president emeritus of Harvard University) to elect her president and CEO of the organization on February 11, 2003. In a "public letter" to potential members issued in 1970, when Common Cause was launched, John Gardner stated, "The first thing Common Cause will do is to assist you to speak and act in behalf of legislation designed to solve the nation's problems. We are going to build a true 'citizens' lobby, a lobby concerned not with the advancement of special interests but with the well-being of the nation. We will keep you up-to-date on crucial issues before Congress. We will suggest when and where to bring pressure to bear. We want public officials to have literally millions of American citizens looking over their shoulders at every move they make. We want phones to ring in Washington and state capitols and town halls. We want people watching and influencing every move that government makes." In addition to Gardner, Common Cause's previous presidents were Archibald Cox, a former solicitor general of the United States, who was most famous as a special prosecutor during the Watergate investigations, which led to the resignation of President Richard Nixon, and Pingree's immediate predecessor, Scott Harshbarger, a former Massachusetts attorney general. During its first 34 years, Common Cause was instrumental in the establishment of "sunshine" laws that promote transparency in regard to the activities of the U.S. Congress; a ban that prohibits members of Congress from accepting gifts from special-interest groups; the demise of the so-called grandfather clause that in the past allowed senior members of Congress to pocket their remaining campaign funds when they retired; the enactment of tough financial disclosure laws for members of Congress;

the blocking of the federal government's expansion of weapon systems such as "Star Wars" (the missile defense shield); and, in 2002, the passage of the Bipartisan Campaign Reform Act.

Currently, Common Cause has about 300,000 members and supporters (the latter of whom receive the organization's email messages). Some four dozen employees work at its Washington, D.C., headquarters, aided by about 100 volunteers. As president and CEO Pingree oversees Common Cause's finances, public communications, and programs; she is the public face of the organization's mission to mobilize citizens to take stands and speak out on issues regarding civil rights, corporate accountability, and ethical practices in government. On its Web site Common Cause urges citizens to "take action" by contacting their local U.S. senators and representatives about current issues; to visit Causenet, the organization's online issues and news-alert network; and to "become an activist" by talking with Common Cause volunteers to find out what sorts of actions Common Cause recommends in local communities. In October 2005, according to its Web site, the top goals of Common Cause were to "increase the diversity of voices and ownership in media; make media more responsive to the needs of citizens in a democracy and to protect the editorial independence of public broadcasting; advance campaign reforms that make people and ideas more important than money; make certain that government is open, ethical and accountable; remove barriers to voting and ensure that our voting systems are accurate and accessible; increase participation in the political process; [and] make certain that our government is held accountable for the costs, in lives and money, for the invasion of Iraq."

In 2008, Pingree was elected to the U.S. House of Representatives and was sworn into Congress on January 6, 2008. Pingree ran for re-election in 2010 and won, defeating Republican challenger Dean Scontras.

Pingree ran for re-election in 2012 and joined the Congressional Progressive Caucus shortly after and has served as the vice-chairwoman since.

## PERSONAL LIFE

"It's hard not to think about raising carrots when you're trying to solve tricky issues in Washington," Pingree told Bill McConnell for *Broadcasting & Cable* (November 1, 2004, online). Among her other honors, in 1996 Pingree earned the Center for Policy Alternatives' Flemming Fellow Leadership Award. In 2004 the Maine state Legislature honored her with a Distinguished Achievement Award. Pingree contributed to the book *Sustaining Island Communities: The Story of the Economy and Life of Maine's Year-Round Islands* (1998). Since she assumed her post at Common Cause, she has become a resident of Washington, D.C. Her marriage, to Charles F. Pingree, ended in divorce in about 1990. In an online announcement released by the organizers of the Future of Music Policy conference, held in 2004, which addressed the issue of the increasing control of the nation's media by a decreasing number of mega corporations, Pingree (who spoke at that meeting) was quoted as saying that her son is an aspiring actor, and one of her daughters (Cecily) is building a career as an independent documentary filmmaker. Her other daughter, Hannah, is currently serving in the Maine House of Representatives, for a district that includes North Haven; at 27, she is the youngest member of the state House. Earlier, Hannah Pingree developed iVillage's Election 2000 website.

## FURTHER READING

*Maine Island Classics: Knitting on a Maine Island; Sustaining Island Communities: The Story of the Economy and Life of Maine's Year-Round Islands*

# ELIZABETH PISANI

## Epidemiologist; Journalist

**Born:** August 7, 1964; Cincinnati, Ohio
**Primary Field:** Public Health; Sexual Health
**Affiliation:** Ternyata Ltd.; UNAIDS

### INTRODUCTION

*"When people ask me what I do for a living, I say, 'Sex and drugs.' I used to say I was an epidemiologist, which is also true, but most people looked blank. Saying I do sex and drugs saves me explaining that epidemiology is the study of how diseases spread in a population. And it is a good conversation starter."* Those words are *from the preface of Elizabeth Pisani's book,* The Wisdom of Whores: Bureaucrats, Brothels and the Business of AIDS *(2008).* The Wisdom of Whores *grew out of Pisani's more than 10 years of work as an epidemiologist for the nonprofit organization Family Health International in Indonesia and as a consultant in epidemiology for UNAIDS, the United Nations Joint Programme on HIV/AIDS, based in Geneva, Switzerland. The book is also a product of her years as a journalist for the news agency Reuters and the newspaper Asian Times and her experiences of "debate, passionate disagreement, moments of enlightenment, misery and laughter shared with people in many countries," as Pisani wrote in* The Wisdom of Whores.

*According to the latest figures from UNAIDS (2009), in the last three decades, an estimated 60 million people were infected with HIV (the virus that causes AIDS) and about 25 million died of AIDS. The amount of money wealthy countries have spent to combat the HIV/AIDS pandemic in developing nations has increased dramatically in recent years, from $300 million to $500 million annually in the late 1990s to over $13 billion in 2008. Yet in 2008 an estimated 33.4 million people worldwide were infected with HIV, among them 22.4 million in sub-Saharan Africa. That year an estimated two million people died of AIDS, and another 2.7 million were newly infected with HIV.*

### EARLY LIFE

Elizabeth Pisani was born on August 7, 1964 in Cincinnati, Ohio, to an American father, Roger Pisani, and a British mother, Julie Pisani, both corporate executives. "My parents met when my father was hitchhiking around the world and my mother was hitching around

Europe. Perhaps not surprising, then, that they bred into me curiosity, a love of travel and a tendency to talk to strangers in immigration queues." Pisani dedicated her book to her mother and father, and in its acknowledgments she mentioned the enormous help she received from her brother, Mark, in writing it. Her family is Roman Catholic. During her childhood the Pisani's moved often, mainly in Western Europe, and she became fluent in Spanish and French. When she was 15 she visited a school friend who lived in Hong Kong (then a British territory). "I absolutely loved it," she told Lucy Knight for the *New Statesman* (August 11, 2008, online). "Up until that point home had been wherever we were living but here was my first sense of foreignness. I was taken with the idea that there was a quarter of humanity in one country [China] and that I couldn't communicate with them." Also while in Hong Kong she "discovered that everyone has something interesting to say," she wrote in her book, and she became "hooked on Asia, hooked on nightclubs and girlie bars, hooked on chatting to anyone who would chat." For a time the Pisani's lived in England, where Elizabeth attended a sixth form college (analagous to an academically rigorous U.S. high school) for students ages 16-19 in Richmond, a London suburb.

For a year between high school and college, starting in about 1981, Pisani worked for a fashion advertising agency in New York City. It was then that the public began hearing about a never-before diagnosed disease, called GRID, or Gay Related Immune Deficiency. It was renamed AIDS in 1982 after scientists and lawmakers discovered that the disease was not exclusive to the gay community. "Within a year, GRIDS had worked its way into New York's consciousness," Pisani wrote. "Cafes grew hushed when yet another skeletal figure shuffled in. Drinks with friends in the city's gay bars were often interrupted by volunteers from the Gay Men's Health Crisis, handing out leaflets and condoms."

Pisani next enrolled at Oxford University, England, where she studied classical Chinese and became fluent in Mandarin Chinese. She earned an M.A. degree in 1986. Since then her proficiency in Mandarin has waned. "I can speak it when it comes to discussing the contraction of AIDS but then I'll have trouble remembering the word for spoon," she told Knight. After her graduation Pisani traveled in China and Tibet and settled in Hong Kong for a time. In 1987 she joined the news agency Reuters as a foreign correspondent. She was posted to Reuters bureaus in Hong Kong, New Delhi, India, and Jakarta, Indonesia, and was sent to cover stories not only in Asia but in Latin America as well. She also wrote regularly for the *Economist* and contributed articles to the *International Herald Tribune* and the *Financial Times*. The many topics and events she wrote about included the Indonesian stock market, Hong Kong nightclubs, and wars of liberation. She was among the few foreign journalists present in Tiananmen Square, in Beijing, China, in the early morning hours of June 4, 1989, when Chinese troops attacked pro-democracy protesters.

## LIFE'S WORK

While with Reuters Pisani became interested in the politics of population control, an important issue in India, China, and other Asian nations. In 1993 she quit her job and, having followed a boyfriend who had moved to London (David Fox, whom she married in 1998), enrolled at the London School of Hygiene and Tropical Medicine, known informally as the London School, it is a college of the University of London. She concentrated on medical demography, the study of population dynamics and their influence on public health problems, and became fascinated with epidemiology, the study of the many factors affecting the health of populations: everything from the spread of disease through contaminated water, air pollutants, or insect bites and malnutrition to dangerous working conditions and unsafe toys. "The more I thought about it, the more I liked epidemiology," Pisani wrote. "It's actually not unlike investigative journalism. You need to ask the right questions of the right people. You need to record the answers carefully, analyse them correctly and interpret them sensibly, and in context. And you have to communicate the results clearly to people who might do something about them." More specifically, she was drawn to the study of HIV/AIDS. "AIDS didn't make it to the London School of Hygiene's curriculum until I was there, in 1994," she wrote. "By then we knew that almost all HIV-infected adults got their infection when having anal or vaginal sex, or while injecting drugs with shared needles. Sex, drugs and plenty of squeamish politicians. AIDS was the disease for me."

Pisani earned an M.S. degree in medical demography in 1994. In 1995 she returned to journalism, to work for the newly launched newspaper *Asia Times*, based in Bangkok, Thailand. Pisani served as the bureau chief for Indochina, covering Vietnam, Cambodia, and Laos,

with an office in Hanoi, Vietnam. In 1996, while still with *Asia Times*, she was hired as a consultant writer by the United Nations Joint Programme on HIV/AIDS, UN AIDS, based in Geneva. UNAIDS was launched in January 1996 in an effort to accelerate, coordinate, and expand the global response to the HIV/AIDS pandemic. Its partners, or co-sponsors, are the World Health Organization (WHO), the International Labour Organization, the World Food Programme (all three are U.N. agencies), the U.N. Refugee Agency, the U.N. Children's Fund (UNICEF), the U.N. Development Programme, the U.N. Population Fund, the U.N. Office on Drugs and Crime, the U.N. Educational, Scientific and Cultural Organization (UNESCO), and the World Bank.

AIDS is caused by the human immunodeficiency virus (HIV), which attacks the immune system and leaves the body susceptible to infection. AIDS is the final stage of an HIV infection, when the immune system has been so badly damaged that it can no longer fight infections. Generally, people develop AIDS symptoms about 10 years after they are infected with HIV. The virus is transmitted through direct contact of a mucous membrane or the bloodstream with a bodily fluid containing HIV, including blood, semen, vaginal fluid, or breast milk; it can occur during unprotected anal, vaginal, or oral sex, while using a contaminated hypodermic needle, and through blood transfusion. Mothers can pass HIV to their babies during pregnancy, childbirth, or breastfeeding.

Pisani's work for UNAIDS involved preparing reports that emphasized the importance of addressing the spread of HIV/AIDS and acquiring funds from governments and nongovernmental sources for that purpose. Pisani wrote the first two editions of UNAIDS' biennial report on the AIDS pandemic. She admitted in her book that a common practice among UNAIDS consultants was "beating up" the story, or exaggerating the severity of the situation. "We weren't making anything up," she wrote. "But once we got the [statistics], we were certainly presenting them in their worst light. We did it consciously. I think all of us at that time thought the beat-ups were more than justified, they were necessary. We were pretty certain that neither donors nor governments would care about HIV unless we could show that it threatened the 'general population.'" The reports of Pisani and her colleagues tried to convince politicians that AIDS was endangering innocent civilians rather than "wicked" people as drug users and prostitutes were deemed. "All the evidence suggested that governments don't like spending money on sex workers, gay men or drug addicts. There are no votes in being nice to a drug addict," she wrote. In order to secure government support, "AIDS couldn't be about sex and drugs. So suddenly it had to be about development, and gender."

In *The Wisdom of Whores*, Pisani argued that a huge portion of the billions of dollars spent to stop or slow the spread of HIV/AIDS has been wasted, because of factors that are ubiquitous on what she calls Planet Politics: "hypocrisy, shame and prejudice," "ideology and religion and culture," and "the self-interest of bloated institutions." But on Planet Epidemiology, where, in her scenario, scientific findings and humanitarian impulses prevail, there are effective weapons to be used in the continuing fight against HIV/AIDS: "We have the knowledge, the tools and the money to beat the HIV and many other diseases besides. The armies on Planet Epidemiology and Planet Politics have been waging their battles in isolation from one another, the one fighting for things that are effective but unpopular such as clean needles [for drug users], the other fighting for things which are ineffective but popular such as abstinence [from sex]. But we are beginning to see signs that common sense and common humanity are gaining the upper hand. If politics and epidemiology got off their separate planets and stood shoulder to shoulder in the war against disease, we'd have a better Planet Earth." One such sign: in December 2009 the U.S. Congress repealed the 21-year-old ban on federal funding of needle-exchange programs, through which drug users receive clean needles in exchange for their used needles, so that a needle possibly contaminated with HIV-laden blood could never be used by another person.

*The Wisdom of Whores* received positive reviews. Rachel Holmes, writing for the *London Times* (May 24, 2008), described it as "an engaging, well-written and entertaining confessional. Weaving anecdotes drawn from a rich cast of drug addicts, hookers, dive bars and street corners, the book investigates how these human stories are, or are not, effectively translated into the flip charts, colourful graphs and budgetary funding models that should influence and define global health policies." Stephen Lewis, a co-director of the U.S. advocacy group AIDS Free World and a former United Nations envoy on AIDS in Africa, wrote in his review for the Toronto, Canada, *Globe and Mail* (July 19, 2008), "This is an utterly fascinating book. Elizabeth Pisani writes with enormous verve and acerbity, her prose alive with anecdote and metaphor." He concluded, "The sad, sad

truth about the Pisani book is that the rude language and controversial nostrums will allow it to be dismissed by policy makers at all levels. But it should be mandatory, not voluntary, reading." In January 2010 Pisani founded Ternyata Ltd., a London based public health consultancy firm. The names means "an unexpected finding" or "a surprising result" in Bahasa Indonesian. One of her hopes is that information about HIV/AIDS and other diseases that is compiled by government researchers, university scientists, and others will be openly shared, to aid in coming up with the best approaches to prevention of infection.

In 2001 Pisani took a job in HIV surveillance with Family Health International, which was working with the Indonesian government. She is fluent in Bahasa Indonesian, Indonesia's official language. Her assignment involved determining how many people were infected with HIV among Indonesia's most at-risk populations. Such work involved late-night visits to remote railway stations to talk to people who injected illicit drugs into their bloodstreams, "injecting drug users," as they are known, and trips to red-light districts to interview prostitutes, waria (males who dress and live like women and sell sex to men), soldiers, sailors, and civil servants about their sexual habits. Pisani also worked for the ministries of health in China, East Timor, and the Philippines and conducted HIV policy research for WHO and UNAIDS. She quit her job in 2005. "I was like, I didn't need to do this job anymore because everyone knows what I'm going to say. Even though nothing changes," she told Prodita Sabarini for the *Jakarta Post* (November 23, 2008, on-line). Pisani completed her Ph.D. in infectious-disease epidemiology at the London School in 2006; her dissertation was entitled "Back to Basics: Putting the Epidemiology Back into Planning and Monitoring HIV Prevention Programmes: Case Studies in Indonesia."

The next year Pisani became a consultant for the Wellcome Trust, a London based, global charitable organization that supports biomedical research and activities "with the ultimate aim of protecting and improving human and animal health," according to its Web site. Around that time Pisani decided to write a book that would detail her experiences in Asia, sum up her criticisms of the global response to HIV/AIDS, and channel for the good of others the frustration and despair she had felt in the field. Written in only three months, *The Wisdom of Whores* was published in 2008 by W.W. Norton. The title refers to Pisani's realization that many of the

Asian sex workers she met knew more about HIV/AIDS prevention and transmission than many bureaucrats and people with power.

According to Pisani, many of the billions of dollars that have been spent to combat HIV/AIDS have been wasted on misguided programs and policies. One of the most persistent myths about AIDS, she has repeatedly said, is that everyone is at risk of contracting HIV, but that is true only in Africa, particularly sub-Saharan Africa. Everywhere else, AIDS "is confined to sections of society where there are clearly defined risk factors," she told Rosita Bolad for the *Irish Times* (May 16, 2008). "But governments generally aren't that keen to be seen to be spending tax money on drug injectors and sex workers and gay guys, these aren't hugely politically popular. So it's much easier to peddle the myth that everybody is at risk and that way, you can spend money on pregnant women and school children and other more popular groups and feel like you are addressing the problem, when in fact you are not."

Pisani and many of her colleagues have advocated a simple and relatively cheap solution to slow or stop the spread of HIV: provide the most at-risk populations (injecting drug users, gay men, sex workers and their clients) with clean needles and condoms. Every major study of needle-exchange programs has shown that such programs cut transmission of HIV and other viruses and do not increase the prevalence of drug use. Moreover, many studies have shown that condoms are 80 to 90 percent effective in preventing HIV transmission; among couples in which one partner is HIV positive and the other is not infected, the correct and consistent use of latex condoms results in an infection rate below one percent per year. Nevertheless, in most countries those who urge the distribution of clean needles among drug users and condoms among prostitutes have been stymied because of religious beliefs, pervasive ideas regarding morality, and in democratic nations, politicians who would rather remain popular with their constituents than support controversial programs. "The science tells us, for example, that making clean needles universally available to drug injectors can more or less wipe out HIV transmission in this group," Pisani wrote in an opinion piece for CNN.com (April 6, 2010). "The ideology tells us that providing such services for injectors is tantamount to condoning an illegal behavior that wrecks lives and families and increases crime. If you were running for election, faced with the choice of paying for clean needles and health services for injectors or with putting more cops on the streets and cells in the jails, which do you think would play best with the voters?"

Pisani has also charged that many HIV/AIDS programs and organizations have focused too much on treatment of people infected with HIV and not enough on preventive measures. In recent years antiretroviral therapies have maintained the well-being of many HIV-infected people who in the past would have succumbed to AIDS. Antiretroviral drugs (ARVs) suppress the replication of HIV in the body and reduce the viral load—that is, the quantity of the virus in the infected person's blood—thus delaying or even preventing the onset of AIDS. Pisani told Vicky Allan for the Sunday Herald Magazine (May 4, 2008), a Scottish periodical, "There aren't all these people with these whole clusters of symptoms that are in your face. It used to be that someone would shuffle into a bar with black blotches all over their face and you'd think, 'Oh, there's another one.' There were 10 years where it was a very visible thing and it has ceased to be so in developed countries." In The Wisdom of Whores she wrote, "Treatment makes HIV much, much less scary, because it makes it less fatal. There are fewer cadaverous people around, fewer funerals to go to. With treatment, people who were at death's door leap up and march back to the office and the nightclub." For that reason the advent of ARVs has a downside, because while the drugs lower the risk of transmitting the virus, many people have forgotten or choose to ignore the fact that they do not remove that risk entirely.

The gay community in San Francisco, California, illustrates that problem. By 1985, with the AIDS crisis becoming more acute, condom use among gay men in San Francisco rose from virtually zero to 70 percent. Condom use remained at that level until 1994, around the time that ARVs were introduced. By 2001, researchers found, half of the HIV-positive men within the community no longer used condoms, and of those men, a third were not using condoms even if their partners were HIV negative or did not know if they were infected. In 1999 the rate of new HIV infections tripled. Similar patterns were recorded in London, England; Amsterdam, the Netherlands; and Vancouver, Canada. ARVs keep people "alive longer, and healthy enough to want to have sex," Pisani explained to Decca Aitkenhead for the *London Guardian* (May 13, 2008). "You only have to look at the experience of the UK or US gay communities where we've had more or less universal access to ARVs for at least eight or nine years, and the number of new infections are rising. More people are living longer with HIV, and there is what we call behavioural disinhibition: '[Forget] the condoms, I don't need them any more, because if he's positive he'll be on drugs, so he probably won't infect me. And if I do get infected, it would be annoying, but not the end of the world.'" Pisani added, "Yes, it's great that all this stuff on treatment is happening. But it becomes all the more urgent to have effective prevention. And that's not happening."

The situation on the African continent is very different, but social scientists often ignore that difference, according to Pisani, for fear that they will be labeled racist. "Essentially there are two epidemics in the world," she explained to Terry Gross for the National Public Radio program *Fresh Air* (June 10, 2008). "One is in east and southern Africa particularly. And one is in all of the rest of the world. In most of the world HIV is spread mostly in behaviors that are fairly well defined as high risk, and that is: among people who buy and sell sex, among gay men who have many partners, and among people who inject drugs. On the African continent, because of different patterns of sexual behavior, HIV spreads among men and women in the general population." Although people from various parts of the African continent and people outside the continent may have the same total number of sexual partners in their lifetimes, non-Africans generally have a series of monogamous relationships ("sex in strings," as Pisani puts it), while people from the African continent, both males and females, are more likely to have two or three partners at once ("sex in nets"). The crucial factor when it comes to transmission of the AIDS virus is that HIV is highly infectious, and most contagious, during the two or three months immediately following a new infection. After that period, thanks to the production of antibodies, the newly infected person is less likely to infect another person. "So the likelihood that you spread HIV essentially depends on how many partners you have in that first very infectious period," Pisani told Gross.

In the African nations that have openly addressed their citizens' penchant for extramarital sex and concurrent, multiple sexual partners, and have promoted the use of condoms and assisted in their distribution, the occurrence of new HIV infection has dropped dramatically. Authorities in Senegal, in West Africa, took such action when HIV prevalence was low, and in 2006 fewer than 2 percent of adults in that country were infected. Similarly, in Uganda, in east-central Africa, HIV prevalence peaked at around 15 percent in 1991 and was

down to 7 percent by 2006. Those nations are the exceptions. More commonly, according to Pisani, AIDS organizations working in Africa and many African leaders have tended to ignore patterns of sexual behavior and instead talk about the spread of HIV/AIDS as a problem stemming from poverty and insufficient economic development. But there is evidence that refutes such assertions. In 2008 the central African nation of Niger ranked 163d in per capita income among 168 nations, and India's neighbor Bangladesh ranked 144th, but in those countries, according to the World Bank, fewer than 1 percent of adults are infected with HIV. By contrast, in the southern African nation of Botswana, which ranked 51st, higher than any other African country, the rate of HIV infection is 24 percent.

The Republic of South Africa, which ranks second in per capita income behind Botswana among Africa's 52 nations but whose gross domestic product is the highest on that continent, is home to the world's largest population of people infected with HIV: 5.7 million in 2007. Thabo Mbeki, who served as president of South Africa from 1999 to 2008, and his health minister, Manto Tshabalala-Msimang, were notorious for openly casting doubt on the causes of AIDS; Tshabalala-Msimang advised people to avoid taking ARVs and to eat foods including garlic and beetroot to treat HIV infection. "You don't need to dream up complex economic formulae to explain why HIV prevention in Africa is failing," Pisani wrote in *The Wisdom of Whores*. "Look at the leadership."

In 2003 the administration of President George W. Bush initiated the President's Emergency Plan for AIDS Relief (PEPFAR), committing $15 billion from the U.S. over five years to fight the HIV/AIDS pandemic, with most of the funding allocated for treatment. PEPFAR has greatly increased the amount of ARVs available to HIV-infected Africans, but Pisani and others have criticized it for its moral agenda: one-third of the program's HIV- prevention money was specifically dedicated to programs that promoted abstinence until marriage, and all organizations and governments that received PEPFAR funding were banned from using any of the money for needle-exchange programs and were required to sign an "anti-prostitution pledge." Those who sign such pledges, Pisani explained to Terry Gross, agree not to "recognize commercial sex as an industry or a legitimate activity" or to "engage in anything that promotes commercial sex or recognizes it in any way." Thus, no PEPFAR funds may be used to distribute condoms in brothels or for any other purposes aimed at preventing HIV infection among those prostitutes and their clients. (Except for the anti-prostitution pledge, those requirements were lifted when PEPFAR was renewed in 2008.) "It fills me with rage that the same people who will not spend a couple of cents on clean needles are perfectly happy to spend thousands of dollars on expensive and toxic antiretroviral drugs," Pisani told Brian Hutchinson for the *Canadian National Post* (June 14, 2008).

## PERSONAL LIFE

Ternyata, the consulting firm Pisani founded in 2010, provides training in infectious-disease epidemiology, surveillance methods, data management and analysis, and other vital skills. Pisani serves as a senior adviser to Wellcome Trust on matters related to public-health research in developing countries. She is an honorary

senior lecturer at the London School. In 2010 she was a featured speaker at the TED Conference (named for the increasing convergence of technology, entertainment, and design), held in Long Beach, California. In June 2010, a video of her talk was posted on her website, wisdomofwhores.com. She has also lectured at institutions including Harvard University, the Massachusetts Institute of Technology, the University of Oxford, and the Royal Tropical Institute, in Amsterdam. "Behind all the sex and drugs talk, I'm just a giant data nerd," Pisani has said. Pisani, who is divorced, lives in London. In her free time she enjoys sea kayaking.

## FURTHER READING

*The Wisdom of Whores: Bureaucrats, Brothels and the Business of AIDS*

---

# LETTY COTTIN POGREBIN

## Writer; Activist

**Born:** June 9, 1939; Queens, New York
**Primary Field:** Gender Equality
**Affiliation:** Feminism

## INTRODUCTION

*In 1970, when she was 31 years old, Letty Cottin Pogrebin had a high-powered job in publishing and had just written a chatty and humorous book, the well-received* How to Make It in a Man's World. *Then she read some feminist writings about the then-nascent women's liberation movement, and what she read so inspired her that she changed her life. She quit her job, began attending women's political meetings, and, in 1971, helped found* Ms. *magazine, With which she has been associated ever since. Her second book on achieving success,* Getting Yours: How to Make the System Work for the Working Woman *(1975), offered much more pragmatic advice than her first. A mother of three, Pogrebin became very interested in sex-role theories, and especially how they relate to child rearing. She explored their relationship in* Growing Up Free: Raising Your Child in the '80s *(1980), and its companion volume,* Stories for Free Children *(1982). She followed up those books with a discussion of family relationships, in* Family Politics: Love and Power on an Intimate Frontier *(1983), and*

*then an examination of platonic attachments, in* Among Friends: Who We Like, Why We Like Them, and What We Do with Them *(1987).*

*While continuing to be influential and active in the women's movement, Pogrebin grew increasingly disturbed by the anti-Semitic remarks she heard from some participants at international conferences. Those public expressions of anti-Semitism prompted her to re-examine her attachment to Judaism, which she had all but abandoned as a teenager. She eventually decided to return to her faith, and she became an active supporter of Israel. She wrote about that turning point in her life in* Deborah, Golda and Me *(1991). That book was followed by an even more personal account,* Getting Over Getting Older: An Intimate Journey *(1996), Pogrebin's description of the anger, fear, and dread she felt upon turning 50, and of the ways that she has learned to find fulfillment as she ages.*

## EARLY LIFE

Pogrebin was born Letty Cottin on June 9,1939, in New York City, to Cyral (Halpern) Cottin and Jacob Cottin, a lawyer. She comes from a family of rebellious women, including a grandmother who jumped out the window of her bridal chamber to elope with the man she truly loved, and an aunt who pretended she was infertile rather than admit that she didn't want to have children.

In a column about her family's secrets for the *New York Times* (November 29, 1992), Pogrebin revealed that she learned the biggest secret of all when she was almost 12. "To my horror, in 1951, I inadvertently discovered that my parents had not really been married for 28 years as they claimed; their wedding date had been a flat-out fiction," she wrote. "Both had been previously divorced and had met each other only 14 years before. What's more, the 26 year old woman I knew as my 'big sister' was actually my half-sister, my mother's daughter from her first marriage. And somewhere on the planet I had another half-sister, my father's daughter from his first marriage, whom he had stopped seeing shortly after I was born. The most positive thing I can say about my family's secrets is that they set the stage for my later involvement in the women's movement. Feminism's challenge to sexual hypocrisy and sex-role coercion seemed to directly address my experience growing up with a mother, grandmother, and aunts who had to cloak themselves in deception before they could face the world."

After graduating from high school, Pogrebin enrolled at Brandeis University, in Waltham, Massachusetts, where she earned an A.B. degree, cum laude, in 1959, with special distinction in English and American literature. She then moved to New York City, and not long afterward was hired as the director of promotion, advertising, and subsidiary rights at Bernard Geis Associates. In 1963, she met her future husband, Bertrand Pogrebin, on Fire Island, New York, "It was love at first sight across the volleyball net," she once said. They married six months later. Upon the birth of her twin daughters, Abigail and Robin, Pogrebin quit her job, because she thought that that was what she, a middle-class woman, was supposed to do. But after five months, she grew restless at home and returned to work on a part-time basis.

## LIFE'S WORK

Pogrebin moved up the corporate ladder at Geis Associates, and in 1969, she was appointed a vice president of the company. She described her success in her first book, *How to Make It in a Man's World*, a humdrous and practical guide for women in the workplace, which earned good reviews when it was published in 1970. But in an interview conducted 14 years later that was quoted in Newsday (January 3,1984), Pogrebin said she no longer stood by the advice she had offered in the book, describing them as "very simplistic, smug guidelines for being successful the old way. How to save a

man's ego if you're taking him out to lunch, and these things that as a feminist make my flesh crawl. But that's the way it was then."

Before embarking on a publicity tour for *How to Make It in a Man's World*, Pogrebin read some feminist writings, in preparation for questions from advocates of the women's liberation movement. Instead of being put off by the material, as she had expected, she was captivated by it, especially by articles about the burdens women struggle with in the workplace. As she considered her own career, Pogrebin realized that she had been making a lot of uncomfortable, and unfair, compromises. "At all the meetings, I was the only woman, but I had to make the drinks and serve the coffee," she said in the *Newsday* article. "I had control over tremendous amounts of money and staff and authority, but I was expected to defer. I was not expected to be resentful. And I was, but I put it away. That's why the movement spoke to me so clearly."

Before the year was over, Pogrebin had quit her job at Geis Associates to start a freelance writing career, and she was soon writing columns for *Working Woman* and the *Ladies' Home Journal*. Committed to becoming an active participant in the women's movement, she attended the first National Women's Political Caucus meeting in 1971. Later that year, Pogrebin became one of the founding editors of Ms., along with Gloria Steinem, a pioneering leader of the feminist cause, and several other women. Pogrebin continued to work as an editor at the magazine through 1987, after which time she became one of its columnists, as well as an editor at large. Since 1990, her title has been contributing editor.

Meanwhile, Pogrebin has continued to write books. *In Getting Yours: How to Make the System Work for the Working Woman* (1975), she offered practical advice on everything from hiring household help to the pluses and minuses of doing secretarial work. In a departure from her first book, she urged women to see the world not as "belonging" to men, but as women's world, too, from which they ought to insist on getting everything they deserve.

During the early 1970s, Pogrebin worked with the actor Mario Thomas on the production of the Emmy Award-winning musical television special *Free to Be You and Me* (1973), which encouraged children to pursue their dreams in all fields and not to be deterred by sexual stereotypes. Fascinated by this issue, Pogrebin wrote *Growing Up Free: Raising Your Child in the '80s* (1980), a guide to nonsexist child rearing. The book "engaged every bit of my consciousness for eight years," she told Penny Kaganoff for *Publishers Weekly* (November 21,1986). "It was so hard to challenge the wisdom of child development people and turn things upside down. I'm very gratified by the number of child psychologists and educators who took this book to their bosoms." Some reviewers, particularly those from conservative publications, thought Pogrebin had gone way overboard in her "opposition" to "natural sexual predispositions," but others found her examination of the different ways parents and teachers interact with boys and girls to be refreshing and insightful. Several years later, she helped produce another television special, *Free to Be A Family* (1988), which focused on the friendships of a selected group of American and Russian children.

Pogrebin's book *Stories for Free Children* (1982) was "an outgrowth of the feature Pogrebin had edited for Ms. since its inception," Kaganoff reported, and was "an anthology of 'nonsexist, nonracist, multicultural and high quality' literature for children that reflects the diversity of family life and such problems as divorce and unemployment." Next came *Family Politics: Love and Power on an Intimate Frontier* (1983), in which Pogrebin criticized the traditional, father-oriented structure within many families, a controversial position that was denounced by conservative critics. Pogrebin also contended in the book that the political establishment in Washington, D.C., had failed to help and support families in meaningful ways.

Turning from the world of parents and children, Pogrebin examined adult friendships in her next book. She got the idea for the book, *Among Friends: Who We Like, Why We Like Them, and What We Do with Them* (1987), after a dinner party she had hosted for the actor and director Alan Alda, who had started a conversation about friendships as research for his movie *The Four Seasons* (1981). "The question and animated discussion of that night triggered something very sensitive in me, my own inadequacies," she told Kaganoff. "I decided to write about friends because I felt as though I wasn't a good friend myself." In the book, she analyzed friendship patterns in the United States, categorized seven types of relationships, and discussed the factors that weaken and enhance platonic ties.

## PERSONAL LIFE

While working as a writer and editor, Pogrebin has remained active in the women's movement. Part of her attraction to feminism is its "universality message," as

she explained to Nina Burleigh of the *Chicago Tribune* (November 24,1991). "It says, at least where gender is concerned, we have enough commonality that we can reach out and cross barriers of race and class and forge a vision that lets us unite for the good of all." That utopian view was severely challenged in 1975, when Pogrebin attended an international women's conference in Mexico and was stung by the virulent anti-Semitic statements that were spouted by some representatives of Arab and countries from the developing world. Later during the conference, a resolution was passed that equated Zionism with racism. Five years later, at the United Nations Women's Conference, in Denmark, the resolution was reconfirmed. These events precipitated a personal crisis for Pogrebin, who concluded that "feminism might be empowering some women who hate Jews," as she once put it.

From that point on, Pogrebin began to re-examine her relationship with Judaism. As a child, she had attended synagogue regularly, and had had a bat mitzvah, the coming-of-age ceremony for Jewish girls. Then, when she was 15, her faith was shattered, because of something that happened at her mother's funeral: Her father had refused to bend the rule of Orthodox Jewish tradition that permits only sons to say *Kaddish* (the prayer recited by mourners). "My father decided to bring in a stranger [to chant the service] instead of bending the rules to allow me to participate," she told Burleigh. Deeply uncomfortable with the status accorded women in Judaism, Pogrebin abandoned her faith. After the incidents in Mexico and Denmark, she embraced her religion, and she has practiced it ever since. Her decision to do so was a lot easier than it might have been, she has said, because of the changes that have occurred in recent years in organized Judaism, particularly in the Reform branch. Leaders of the Reform movement agreed in 1922 that women could be rabbis, but it is only since 1972 that women have been ordained as rabbis in the U.S. "There was a sense of having something to return to that didn't compromise my dignity as a woman," she told Burleigh. In *Deborah, Golda and Me: Being Female and Jewish in America* (1991), Pogrebin recorded her journey back to her faith, how she melded it with her feminism, and how she was inspired to practice both Judaism and feminism by the examples of Deborah, the Old Testament judge, and Golda Meir, the late Israeli prime minister.

By the time *Deborah, Golda and Me* was published, Pogrebin had passed her 50th birthday, a milestone she "hated," as she has put it. "I was young for so long that I wasn't prepared for this," she told Amy Boaz Nugent for *Library Journal* (February 16, 1996). "This" included wrinkles, varicose veins, bifocal glasses, puffy eyelids, and occasional memory lapses, among other things. To help herself come to terms with aging, Pogrebin wrote *Getting Over Getting Older: An Intimate Journey* (1996). In that book, she discussed how she and other women have dealt with turning 50, and how being more mindful of the opportunities that become available in late middle age can make life meaningful.

Besides writing books, Pogrebin contributes freelance articles to many publications, including the *New York Times, Washington Post, Tikkun*, and *TV Guide*. She lives in New York City with her husband, Bertrand, who is a labor lawyer. A very close and active couple, they take hiking trips and travel overseas together in their leisure time. Besides being the parents of twin daughters, both of whom are writers, the Pogrebins have a son, David, who is a chef and works in restaurant management.

## FURTHER READING

*How to Make It in a Man's World; Getting Yours: How to Make the System Work for the Working Woman; Growing Up Free: Raising Your Child in the '80s; Stories for Free Children; Family Politics: Love and Power on an Intimate Frontier; Among Friends: Who We Like, Why We Like Them, and What We Do with Them; Deborah, Golda and Me: Being Female and Jewish in America; Getting Over Getting Older: An Intimate Journey*

---

# AI-JEN POO

## Labor Organizer; Activist

**Born:** 1974; Pittsburgh, Pennsylvania
**Primary Field:** Labor Issues; Human Rights
**Affiliation:** National Domestic Workers Alliance; Caring Across Generations

### INTRODUCTION

*In 2014, when Ai-jen Poo, director of the National Domestic Workers Alliance, was awarded a John D. and Catherine T. MacArthur Foundation fellowship, the organization cited her "compelling vision of the value of home-based care work [which] is transforming the landscape of working conditions and labor standards for domestic or private-household workers" and praised her for creating "a vibrant, worker-led movement." The editors of Time magazine had recognized her work in 2012, naming her one of the most influential people in the world. In the April 18, 2012, issue of the magazine, Gloria Steinman was effusive in her praise: "Once in a while, there comes along a gifted organizer, think of the radical empathy of Jane Addams or the populist tactics of Cesar Chavez, who knows how to create social change from the bottom up," Steinman wrote. Lauding the fact that Poo had helped spearhead the passage of the nation's first Domestic Workers' Bill of Rights, which entitles domestic workers in New York State to overtime pay, one day off per week, and three days of paid leave per year, Steinman continued, "Ai-jen Poo has done this by showing the humanity of a long devalued kind of work. This goes beyond organizing to transforming." Despite such accolades, Poo is widely recognized as a humble person who prefers the spotlight to be on the National Domestic Workers Alliance, rather than on herself. "[Awards are] really recognition of both the importance of domestic work in society today and the significance of domestic workers organizing, advocacy and leadership in the social change arena," she told Nathalie Alonso for Columbia College Today (Fall 2012). "I feel proud to be a part of a movement that inspires so many people."*

### EARLY LIFE

Ai-jen Poo was born in Pittsburgh, Pennsylvania. Some reputable sources describe her, however, as a native of New Haven, Connecticut. Her parents had emigrated from Taiwan as graduate students; her father, Mu-ming Poo, is a molecular neurobiologist, and her mother, an oncologist. She has one sister, Ting Poo, a film editor. In his native country, then led by Chiang Kai-shek, Mu-ming had been a pro-democracy activist, and Poo was deeply influenced by his activities. He now teaches and conducts research at the University of California, Berkeley. She was even more deeply influenced by her mother, who ran the household with no domestic help whatsoever, despite studying for a PhD in chemistry, working initially as a lab technician, and learning English. "I don't remember ever seeing her sit down and take a break or watch a movie or do anything for herself," Poo told Barbara Ehrenreich for *T Magazine* (1 May 2011). "She was always exhausted."

Poo attended the academically rigorous Phillips Academy in Andover, Massachusetts. Her propensity for activism was evident early on, and she once skipped an address by former President George H. W. Bush (himself a Phillips alum) in order to take part in a pro-choice rally. Upon graduating from the school in 1992, Poo, who was considering becoming a professional potter, entered Washington University in St. Louis, Missouri. After a year there, she transferred to Columbia University in New York City, excited to be in one of the cultural capitals of the world.

She soon switched her focus from pottery and art to women's studies. "When I got to Columbia, the women's studies department offered the opportunity to explore the intellectual work that had been done around women's rights and how gender has shaped our world and our history," she explained to Alonso. Columbia, on the Upper West Side of Manhattan, had long been known for its tradition of student activism and volunteerism, and Poo fit right into that environment. She was arrested in 1995 for blocking one of the city's major bridges during a protest against police brutality, and the following year she took part in campus-wide protests demanding more culturally diverse classes.

While in college Poo also began volunteering at the New York Asian Women's Center, which ran a shelter for victims of domestic abuse, and she was involved with the Committee Against Anti-Asian Violence (CAAAV), which hired her as a paid staff member upon her graduation from Columbia in 1996.

## LIFE'S WORK
While working at the CAAAV, Poo spearheaded a project to organize Asian immigrant women working in low-paying service jobs. It was an era in which several of New York City's garment factories were closing their doors and firing the predominantly female laborers; many of those whose immigration paperwork was in order became home health-care aides, while the undocumented among them flocked to restaurant kitchens, beauty parlors, and casual maid services. None of those situations was enviable: the women typically worked at least twelve hours per day and still remained below the poverty line.

Although the project began with Asian women, mainly Filipina workers, Poo quickly saw the need to branch out into a citywide, multiethnic effort. She was particularly moved by one Jamaican woman who approached her after hearing of her work. The woman had been lured to the United States as a teen, believing she could work as a live-in nanny and maid while attending school. Instead, her employers kept her busy from sunrise until late into the night, with no time to attend high school. Even worse, she never saw a dime of her promised wages: the couple employing her claimed they were sending the checks straight to her parents, but because they restricted her access to mail, she could never be certain that they were actually doing so. After almost two decades, she finally escaped with the help of one of the couple's children. "'I don't want to live in a society where people can treat others like that,'" Poo recalled to Ehrenreich. "And I certainly don't want to raise my own children in a society that doesn't value everyone's humanity.'"

In 2000, with the help of coworkers from CAAAV, Poo created and was lead organizer of Domestic Workers United, which in 2007 became an affiliate of a larger umbrella group, the National Domestic Workers Alliance (NDWA). Soon after its formation, Poo became the director of the NDWA. Poo and her staffers made dozens of trips to Albany to lobby New York State lawmakers to enact legislation protecting the rights of low-wage domestic workers. They were generally accompanied by large groups of the workers, who donned matching shirts and gathered on the steps of the New York State Capitol building to make their voices heard. After Assemblyman Keith Wright (D-Manhattan) and Senator Diane Savino (D-Brooklyn/Staten Island) introduced such a bill into the state legislature in 2004, some of the workers were invited to share their life stories. Among the most moving, Poo has recalled, was that of an elderly Colombian woman who worked for more than one hundred hours per week, cooking, cleaning, and providing child care for a family of six. For that, she was paid about three dollars per hour, money she used in part to buy insulin for her own child. Living in a sewage-filled basement, she was fired suddenly with no severance pay and no other job lined up. Other workers told harrowing stories of withheld pay, sexual harassment, and similar such indignities.

"The work that nannies, home health-care aides, and housekeepers do represents the 'wild west,'" she explained to Joann Weiner for the *Washington Post*

(September18, 2014). "You never quite know what you'll get. Maybe you'll get an employer who will give you time off when you're sick, provide a couple of weeks of paid vacation, pay you overtime when you work well over 40 hours a week and pay for your health insurance. Or, maybe you'll get an employer who forces you to work for up to 100 hours a week, docks your pay when you're sick and gives you no days off during the year." She continued, "Even worse, a bad employer might be one who engages in human trafficking or commits sexual assault."

On November 29, 2010, the state's Domestic Workers' Bill of Rights took effect, three months after Governor David Paterson signed it. The law, which was the first of its kind in the nation, entitles domestic workers in New York State to overtime pay, one day off per week, three paid days off a year after one year with the same employer, and inclusion in the state's Human Rights Law, which protects against sexual harassment and discrimination. The law applies even to undocumented workers. "It was a breakthrough moment," Poo told Alonso. "We forced the state of New York to recognize domestic work as real work that deserves inclusion and protection, and reversed a legacy of exclusion and discrimination." Since passage of the New York law, Hawaii, California, and Massachusetts have followed suit, and other states have organized taskforces or taken other steps toward enacting similar legislation.

In recent years Poo has turned her attention to the issues surrounding elder care and the estimated three million home-care providers in the United States. "They help our loved ones eat and bathe while providing emotional support and human connection," she wrote for the *Guardian* (29 Sept. 2014), pointing out that such workers earn an average of less than ten dollars per hour. Citing the fact that by 2035 there will be 11.5 million Americans over the age of eight-five, she wrote, "We've now entered a new era, where our collective failure to account for family care work has become untenable." Poo elaborated to Weiner, "Our society should support keeping people in their homes or providing for community-based care, rather than putting the elderly into nursing homes, which provide the most expensive form of care. I'd like to see another 2 million quality jobs in home care, where domestic workers are earning a living wage and have some economic security." To that end, in 2011 Poo spearheaded a new organization called Caring Across Generations, for which she is a codirector. The organization is devoted to encouraging a cultural shift in the way Americans feel about aging, multigenerational relationships, and caregiving; advocating for effective government policies; and building a platform for multigenerational civic engagement. She has also written a book on the topic, *The Age of Dignity: Preparing for the Elder Boom in a Changing America* (2015).

In 2014 Poo was awarded a fellowship by the John D. and Catherine T. MacArthur Foundation, which came with a stipend of $625,000 to be used to further her cause. She has been named to Time magazine's list of the world's 100 most influential people in the world and Newsweek's 150 Fearless Women list, both in 2012. In 2013 she was selected to be a World Economic Forum Young Global Leader. Her many other honors and awards include an Alston Bannerman Fellowship for Organizers of Color (2009) and an American Express NGen Leadership Award (2011).

## PERSONAL LIFE

Poo, who has also mounted initiatives to fight human trafficking and lobby for immigration reform, has on her upper right arm a tattooed image of a tiger, her Chinese zodiac sign. "Fear often gets in the way of our taking risks necessary to make real change in the world," she told Alonso. "The tattoo is a reminder to draw upon my inner tiger and to be courageous in the face of uncertainty in the service of a vision for a better world." Poo moved to Chicago in June 2014. She commutes to work in Manhattan.

## FURTHER READING

*The Age of Dignity: Preparing for the Elder Boom in a Changing America*

# JOHN PRENDERGAST

## Activist; Writer

**Born:** March 21, 1963; Indianapolis, Indiana
**Primary Field:** Human Rights
**Affiliation:** Humanitarian Aid

## INTRODUCTION

*"I felt very early on an affinity with those who would stand up against things that are wrong," the human-rights activist John Prendergast said on the Diane Behm Show (May 18, 2011), which airs on National Public Radio. "I felt injustice acutely, at a cellular level for many complicated reasons. When given an opportunity to fight against human rights abuses in Africa, I feel utterly compelled to do all I can." Prendergast has been working to end such abuses across the African continent for more than twenty-five years. He has done so under the auspices of Human Rights Watch, UNICEF, and other humanitarian aid and human rights organizations and think tanks; as a special adviser to Susan Rice, the assistant secretary of state for African affairs during President Bill Clinton's second term; as the director of African affairs at the National Security Council, an arm of the US executive branch; as special adviser on African issues for the International Crisis Group; and as the co-founder, in 2007, and co-chair of the Enough Project, whose stated goal is "to end genocide and crimes against humanity." Prendergast has focused mostly on atrocities that have occurred in Uganda, the Congo, and Sudan in the course of civil wars, which have often been abetted by outside governments that aid one side or another directly or indirectly. Those atrocities, which have affected many hundreds of millions of people, include killings and maimings, sometimes tantamount to genocide; sex slavery and the rapes of females of all ages; the starvation, malnutrition, and disease suffered by many refugees; and the conscription of child soldiers.*

*To stop and prevent such brutality and cruelty, Prendergast has traveled dozens of times to areas of conflict in Africa, on "fact-finding missions, peace-making initiatives, and awareness-raising trips," as he wrote for a widely quoted blurb about himself. He has held talks with politicians, military and rebel officers, and heads of various warring factions in different nations (at times finding himself in life-threatening situations) as well as with officials in the United States. To gain publicity for his missions and spur those in positions of power to act, he has teamed up with Hollywood stars including George Clooney, Javier Bardem, Ryan Gosling, Angelina Jolie, Brad Pitt, Mia Farrow, and Don Cheadle, all of whom have traveled with him in troubled spots and accompanied him to congressional hearings and offices of American policy makers. He and Cheadle have co-written two books:* Not on Our Watch: The Mission to End Genocide in Darfur and Beyond *(2007) and* The Enough Moment: Fighting to End Africa's Worst Human Rights Crimes *(2010). The Democrat Barack Obama and the Republican Sam Brownback, both US senators at the time, co-wrote the Introduction to Not on Our Watch. Prendergast has also written or co-written hundreds of commissioned reports and articles for professional journals, national and regional newspapers, and popular magazines as well as eight other books. Those books include the dual memoir* Unlikely Brothers *(2011), written with Michael Mattocks; in it, in addition to his professional life, Prendergast discussed his experiences as an unofficial "big brother" to Mattocks, one of seven children raised by a single mother in Washington, DC.*

## EARLY LIFE

The first of the two sons of John Prendergast (called Jack) and Claire Prendergast, John Prendergast was born on March 21, 1963, in Indianapolis, Indiana. His brother, Luke, is a high school teacher. The brothers were raised in a devoutly Roman Catholic family. Before their parents married their father considered doing good works by becoming a Catholic priest, and their mother by becoming a nun. Prendergast's mother, a trained social worker, volunteered with local Head Start classes and Catholic run programs during her years as a homemaker. His father, a Korean War veteran, worked as a traveling salesman for a frozen foods company and was often home only on weekends. In *Unlikely Brothers* Prendergast described his father as a brilliant storyteller who was ever ready to help others and extraordinarily skilled at connecting with people of all ages.

During Prendergast's elementary school years, he was a good student and excelled at sports, and he never engaged in serious mischief. Nevertheless, when he was about eight, his father began to subject him to "a new and growing impatience and anger that I couldn't figure out." "Again and again, it seemed, Dad would single me out for a harsh, relentless, and unexpected scolding, often when I felt I was doing nothing wrong. The forcefulness of the anger was shocking and profoundly destabilizing to me." His father's rages continued through Prendergast's high school years, "making me feel like a worthless loser," even though Prendergast got good grades, participated in school sports, never drank, smoked, or tried drugs, and held after school jobs. By his own account, as a child Prendergast also suffered because the family moved repeatedly, mostly within the Midwest, and in each new neighborhood and school, he would feel like an outsider. His unhappiness grew when, during puberty, he developed cystic acne, the most disfiguring form of acne, on his face and back; he feared that he looked like a monstrous lizard in the eyes of others. In his freshman year at college, the acne abated, thanks to medication. A series of injuries and other physical problems that ended his dream of becoming a professional basketball player compounded his misery when he was a teen.

After Prendergast completed eighth grade, his family moved to Berwyn, a suburb of Philadelphia, Pennsylvania. He attended a strict Catholic prep school for a year, then transferred, at his own insistence, to Archbishop Carroll High School, in Radnor, another Philadelphia suburb. At the school in Radnor, a more liberal Catholic institution that had a strong basketball program, three of his teachers influenced him greatly. One was Garrett Wiznicki, an English teacher who sparked his passion for the writings of authors including Jack Kerouac, James Joyce, Jean-Paul Sartre, Søren Kierkegaard, and Samuel Beckett and who expressed genuine interest in Prendergast's ideas and opinions. The second was Joseph Stoutzenberger, a teacher of religion who was "very Buddhist in his outlook" and talked about "the centrality of compassion" in the major religions; Stoutzenberger's requirement that his students serve the community led Prendergast to volunteer in a homeless shelter. From the third teacher, Joan Kane, who taught Spanish, he learned about the organizations Amnesty International and Bread for the World.

After high school Prendergast enrolled at Georgetown University, in Washington, DC. As a volunteer tutor of reading in children's homes in Washington, he witnessed firsthand the poverty related problems that prevailed in the city's low income housing projects. At the end of his freshman year, eager for "world knowledge and experience," he dropped out of college, equipped himself with a tent, sleeping bag, and

backpack, and began to hitchhike across the country on what Steve Hendrix, writing for the *Washington Post* (May 16, 2011), termed his "personal save-the-world tour." Money from his parents and earnings from odd jobs supported him. In several cities he helped in political campaigns; in Texas and Mexico he became acquainted with issues affecting manual and farm laborers. During his travels he met three social justice activists who "eliminated any doubts I might have had about whether one person can make a difference": Patrick Goggins, who worked toward peace among Northern Ireland Protestants and Catholics; Paul Comiskey, a Jesuit priest fighting against the death penalty and for improved prison conditions in California; and John Maher, the cofounder of the Delancey Street Foundation, which provides shelter and rehabilitation services for former convicts, substance abusers, and others in need.

## LIFE'S WORK
During the summer of 1983, Prendergast returned to Washington, DC, where he took courses at George Washington University and served as an intern at the Robert Kennedy Memorial Youth Policy Institute and as a volunteer coach for a boys' basketball team. That summer he met the Mattockses, a homeless African-American family headed by a single mother, who lived in a shelter supervised by a Georgetown friend of Prendergast's. He immediately became an informal "big brother" to Michael, the eldest boy, and James, who were seven and six years old then. On weekends the boys would stay with his parents in Berwyn while he worked for a landscaping firm. In the fall Prendergast moved to Philadelphia and was hired by the Democratic congressman William IT. Gray, an African-American Baptist preacher who was serving his second term in the House of Representatives.

Prendergast's job entailed helping constituents, mostly with problems involving bureaucracies or landlords. Also, through the organization Big Brothers Big Sisters, he became involved with Khayree and Nazir Lane, brothers living in Philadephia: on weekends he continued to visit Michael and James Mattocks or would have his parents take care of them. Later, Luke Prendergast took over as Khayree and Nazir's Big Brother. While nursing a sprained ankle at home one day, Prendergast saw a television news story about the famine then gripping Ethiopia, which had been triggered by civil war and other human actions and exacerbated by drought. "Somehow for the first 21 years of my life,

I'd missed the fact that such a level of human suffering could exist," he told Daniel Bergner for the *New York Times* (December 5, 2010). He immediately decided that he should go to Ethiopia to aid victims of the famine. Denied a visa both to Ethiopia and to its neighbor Sudan, Prendergast, who knew next to nothing about African politics or geography, secured a visa to Mali, which is nearly three thousand miles west of Ethiopia. He bought a plane ticket to Bamako, Mali's capital, giving little thought to how his absence might affect Michael, James, Khayree, and Nazir. "I was a do-gooder in the universal sense," he admitted to Gwen Ifill, who interviewed him for the weeknight TV show *PBS NewsHour* (June 17, 2011), "but not necessarily in the interpersonal sense."

On the flight to Mali, Prendergast met a specialist in Mali's Agriculture Ministry who had studied at Georgetown and recognized him. Prendergast accepted the man's invitation to board at his compound in Bamako and accompany him on his travels around Mali, during which the man talked about the ways in which developed countries and the World Bank kept the prices of agricultural exports from Africa artificially low. "Millions of small-scale farmers in developing countries in Africa and elsewhere are impoverished, and their families are needlessly hungry and poor so that Americans and Europeans can pay a penny less for a cup of coffee or a dime less for a t-shirt," Prendergast learned. "Now that I knew all this, what was I going to do about it?"

After three months Prendergast returned to his job in Congressman Gray's office, but he realized that he would rather help Africans than people in the United States. "I hungered to figure out the bureaucracy of foreign aid the way I'd once yearned to understand the way services were delivered to poor folks in America." He offered his services to the organization Operation Crossroads Africa and "signed on without even asking where they'd send me or what I'd have to do when I was there. All I knew was, it was a way to get back." The organization assigned him to a team that helped to build a school in Zanzibar, a semi-autonomous territory associated with Tanzania. Although he stayed to complete the project, he questioned the wisdom of spending so much money to send Americans to do a job that, given the necessary materials, the people who lived there could have accomplished.

While still in Zanzibar, Prendergast learned that the United Nations High Commissioner for Refugees and others had set up a camp in Hargeysa, in northwest Somalia, for refugees who had fled the famine in Ethiopia. He immediately traveled to Hargeysa, where he spent the next several months helping out in the camp. He soon learned that a substantial portion of the food and other supplies sent from overseas to aid the refugees wound up in the hands of the military and others loyal to the longtime dictator of Somalia, Siad (or Siyaad) Barre. Despite the well known brutality of the Barre regime, during the Cold War the United States government considered him a reliable ally; hundreds of millions of dollars in U.S. aid to Somalia helped Barre to remain in power. Prendergast realized that "it wasn't going to be enough to visit every conflict-torn corner on the African continent and understand each famine and war firsthand. I was going to have to become equally expert in the politics of foreign policy in Washington, D.C."

In 1986, back in the United States, Prendergast earned a BA degree in geography and urban studies from Temple University, in Philadelphia. By his own account, after he left Georgetown he had taken courses at three other colleges as well. He spent one term in graduate school at the University of Pennsylvania before transferring to the School of International Service of American University, in Washington, D.C., where he received an MA degree in international relations in 1990. Meanwhile, he had become a consultant for the organization Bread for the World, which according to its website is "a collective Christian voice urging our nation's decision makers to end hunger at home and abroad." As one of those voices, Prendergast would talk to congressional aides about food shortages overseas. He also served as a live-in supervisor to seven mentally challenged adult residents of a group home.

By then Prendergast was spending about two-thirds of the year outside the United States, in the Horn of Africa (Kenya, Somalia, Ethiopia, Eritrea, and Djibouti) and Central African countries including Angola, Congo, Liberia, Sierra Leone, and Rwanda. He worked at one time or another for many nongovernmental organizations, writing reports and popular articles about what he had observed. A turning point for him came in 1994, when, in Rwanda, over the course of three months, as many as 800,000 members of the minority Tutsi tribe perished at the hands of extremist members of the Hutu majority. The US government ignored what was happening, a White House official told him, because the American public expressed no interest in taking action. The failure of the United States to respond to the atrocities prompted Prendergast to expand his efforts to include ordinary Americans. Determined to build what he called "a popular constituency for peace in Africa," he began giving talks at colleges and conferences. "I had some pretty compelling material. I'd seen, with my own eyes, the starvation in Ethiopia, the anarchic mayhem in Somalia, the child soldiers in Uganda, the slave raiding in Sudan, and the genocide in Rwanda."

In 1996 Prendergast won a fellowship from the US Institute for Peace and a job as an adviser to Susan Rice, who, as a State Department assistant secretary of state, advised President Bill Clinton on African affairs. The fellowship paid his salary at the White House for six months, Prendergast had met Rice earlier, at a conference at Princeton University at which Prendergast had condemned the United States for making no effort to end the violence in Rwanda. At the end of the six months, Rice created a permanent position for Prendergast, as the National Security Council's director for African affairs. "I was right in the thick of things," he recalled. He regularly conferred face to face with Rice and Joseph C. Wilson, who had served as an ambassador in Africa before being appointed the National Security Council's senior director for African affairs, and sometimes with President Clinton himself. Prendergast sensed that Clinton felt haunted by what had happened in Rwanda; the president 'exuded a palpable hunger to do right by Africa," Prendergast wrote. Prendergast was with Clinton when, in Rwanda in 1998, the president publicly acknowledged, "We in the United States and the world community did not do as much as we could have and should have done to try to limit what occurred in Rwanda in 1994." During that period Prendergast was in Africa most of the time." I was traveling from one conflict zone to the next as an advisor to President Clinton's high-level peace envoys. We were negotiating with presidents, rebel leaders, militia commanders, and warlords, and we were trying to find peaceful solutions to some of the deadliest wars in the world since World War II." One successful effort in which he played a large role was the ending, in 2000, of armed conflict between Ethiopia and Eritrea.

In 2001, after Clinton left the White House, Prendergast became the co-director of the Africa program of the International Crisis Group (ICG). Based in Brussels, Belgium, the ICG is described on its website as "an independent, non-profit, non-governmental organisation committed to preventing and resolving deadly conflict"; toward that end the group advises governments, the United Nations, the European Union, and other such bodies. In that position Prendergast urged that economic sanctions be imposed against Zimbabwe, whose inhabitants had suffered decades of human-rights abuses and drastic economic deprivation under the rule of the nation's longtime ruler, Robert Mugabe, the European Union and the United States imposed such sanctions in 2002 and 2003, respectively; the sanctions remained in place as of late 2011. The United States provides humanitarian aid to Zimbabwe. Prendergast remained with the ICG until 2006. In the preceding years, in addition to Zimbabwe, he had investigated and reported on conditions in Somalia, Northern Uganda, and Sudan.

In 2007 Prendergast cofounded the Enough Project with Gayle Smith, with whom he had worked in the Clinton White House. The project was set up with funds from the foundation Humanity United and with the support of the Center for American Progress,, with which Enough is closely affiliated. The goal of the project, according to its website, is to help "build a permanent constituency to prevent genocide and crimes against humanity." "Too often," the post continued, "the United States and the larger international community have taken a wait and see approach to crimes against humanity. This is unconscionable. Genocide and war crimes are not inevitable, and we at Enough want to create noise and action both to stop ongoing atrocities and to prevent their recurrence. Our mission is to help people from every walk of life understand the practical actions they can take to make a difference." "Enough's strategy papers and briefings provide sharp field analysis and targeted policy recommendations," the website states. "Enough is also working to develop the policies, tools, and investments that can best be applied to prevent crimes against humanity and genocide now and in the future." The Enough Project currently concentrates on the complex continuing conflicts, and attendant massive human suffering, in Sudan and South Sudan, the Congo, Uganda, and Somalia.

## PERSONAL LIFE

With Tracy Me Grady and other basketball stars, Prendergast cofounded the Darfur Dream Team Sister Schools Program, which links American schools to a dozen schools maintained for children from Darfur, a region in Sudan, who are living in refugee camps in Chad. He is a board member of an adviser to the organization Not on Our Watch cofounded by George Clooney and four other Hollywood figures, which develops 'advocacy campaigns that bring global attention to international crises and give voice to their victims/' according to its website. "It's easy to see why celebrities are drawn to Prendergast," Christine Spines wrote for *Entertainment Weekly* (May 30, 2008). "With his shaggy hippie-chic haircut and rugged road map of a face, he's exactly the sort of righteous, world-saving warrior that actors love playing on screen. But Prendergast has earned his action-hero credentials."

In addition to the volumes he wrote with Cheadle and Maddocks, Prendergast's books include *Without Troops and Tanks: The Emergency Relief Desk and the Cross Border Operation into Eritrea and Tigray* (1994, written with Mark Duffield); *Civilian Devastation: Abuses by All Parties in the War of Southern Sudan* (1994, with Jemera Rone and Karen Sorenson); *Frontline Diplomacy: Humanitarian Aid and Conflict in Africa* (1996); *Crisis and Hope in Africa* (1996); and

*Crisis Response: Humanitarian Band-Aids in Sudan and Somalia* (1997). Prendergast's marriage to Jean, a nutritionist, in 1991 ended in divorce. In 2011 he married Sia Sanneh, a lawyer for the Equal Justice Initiative and a Yale Law School lecturer.

**FURTHER READING**
*Unlikely Brothers; Without Troops and Tanks: The Emergency Relief Desk and the Cross Border Operation into Eritrea and Tigray; Civilian Devastation: Abuses by All Parties in the War of Southern Sudan; Frontline Diplomacy: Humanitarian Aid and Conflict in Africa; Crisis and Hope in Africa; and Crisis Response: Humanitarian Band-Aids in Sudan and Somalia; Not on Our Watch: The Mission to End Genocide in Darfur and Beyond; The Enough Moment: Fighting to End Africa's Worst Human Rights Crimes*

# DAVID PROTESS

## Journalist; Activist

**Born:** April 7, 1946; Brooklyn, New York
**Primary Field:** Human Rights
**Affiliation:** Northwestern University

### INTRODUCTION

*David Protess, a former professor of journalism at Northwestern University, in Evanston, Illinois, believes that it is not enough for a reporter to reveal injustices in society. "The higher calling of journalism," he told Pam Belluck for the* New York Times *(March 6, 1999), "is that after you find the truth, you can in fact right the wrong." Protess' self-appointed mission is to right wrongs in the criminal justice system in particular, to overturn the convictions of people who have been sentenced to death for crimes that they did not commit. So far, he has been credited with securing freedom for eight innocent people, among them two men who had spent 18 years on death row and one who had remained there for 16 years and had come within two days of being executed. In unearthing evidence of forced confessions, false eyewitness accounts, failure of the police to act on promising leads or make available crucial evidence, systematic racism, and other phenomena that have resulted in gross miscarriages of justice, Protess has in-*

*creased his effectiveness by working in collaboration with his students at Northwestern; the students, in turn, get hands-on experience in investigative journalism in real, and sometimes life and death, situations. "We need someone to conduct these full-blown investigations because indigent clients aren't getting them through the legal system," Protess told Kari Lydersen for the* New Abolitionist *(February 1998), an anti death penalty publication. "I'm astonished to see how little preparation and legwork is done [by defendants' lawyers] for most Death Row defenses. And federal funding is gone at the same time that we're increasingly filling prisons. The problem's getting worse."*

*Protess strongly opposes the death penalty, without exception. In the* New York Times *(August 22, 1999), Caitlin Lovinger reported that "since the United States Supreme Court reinstated capital punishment in 1976, 566 people have been executed. In that same period, 82 convicts awaiting execution have been exonerated, a ratio of one freed for every seven put to death." "Capital punishment discriminates against minorities and protects the lives of white people as more valuable," Protess noted to Lydersen. "The death penalty makes politicians appear tough on crime," he added. "Instead of dealing with the causes, it deals with individual symptoms. It's a medieval system of dealing with social problems."*

## EARLY LIFE

David Protess was born on April 7, 1946 to Sidney Protess, a businessman, and Beverly (Gordon) Protess, a full time homemaker, in the New York City borough of Brooklyn. He grew up in Sheepshead Bay, a middle-class section of the borough. In his evolution as a seeker of justice, he has identified two historic events as especially significant. The first was the execution of Julius Rosenberg and his wife, Ethel, both of whom, in a highly publicized and bitterly controversial espionage case, had been found guilty of conspiring to transmit to the Soviet Union top secret information on the nuclear weapons being developed by the United States during World War II. On June 19, 1953 the Rosenbergs, who were the parents of two young boys, were put to death by means of the electric chair. The day after the execution, Protess, who was then seven years old, the same age as the Rosenbergs' younger son, saw a brutal headline on a local tabloid: "Rosenbergs Fried." "It seemed so unjust, and I'm not just taking a position about whether they were guilty or not," Protess told Pam Belluck. "What was unjust was that the state orphaned two young boys."

The second event that, by his own account, was crucial in his choice of career occurred two decades later, after Protess had earned a B.A. degree from Roosevelt University, in Chicago, in 1968, and a master's degree from the University of Chicago, in 1970. This was the Watergate scandal, which followed the break-in at the Democratic National Committee headquarters by Republican operatives in 1972 and led to the resignation of President Richard Nixon two years later. The scandal came to light through the efforts of the *Washington Post* reporters Bob Woodward and Carl Bernstein. Their accounts of the Watergate affair, which involved skullduggery, abuses of the office of president, and an illegal cover up, dominated the front pages during the period in which Protess was striving to complete his doctorate in public policy at the School of Social Service Administration at the University of Chicago. The coverage of Watergate by Woodward and Bernstein and other members of the media impressed Protess deeply. "I saw journalism as having a higher calling," he recalled to Ericka Mellon for the *Daily Northwestern* (February 8, 1999, online), the student newspaper at Northwestern

University. "I wanted to practice journalism that made a difference."

## LIFE'S WORK

After earning his PhD degree, in 1974, Protess taught political science for two years as an assistant professor at Loyola University, in Chicago. From 1976 until 1981 he served as research director of the Better Government Association (BGA), also in Chicago. Founded in 1923, the BGA is a watchdog group whose aim is to foster high standards of public service. According to an official BGA blurb, the organization "uses official documents, on the record interviews, undercover operations, and sophisticated techniques of investigative reporting to uncover corruption" in the government and "works closely with national and local media to expose waste, inefficiency, and corruption and to educate the public on the inner workings of the government."

In 1982 Protess joined the faculty of the Medill School of Journalism at Northwestern University as a professor of journalism and urban affairs. He was also named a faculty fellow in journalism at the university's Institute for Policy Research, which supports studies on issues connected with poverty, social welfare, race, employment, education, crime, and community development. Concurrently, from 1984 to 1989, he served as a contributing editor and staff writer at Chicago Lawyer, an independent investigative monthly that, in the words of Rob Warden, its editor and publisher, "was founded [in 1978] for the purpose of exposing corruption and other problems in the criminal justice system in Cook County, Illinois, and neighboring jurisdictions." In the course of pursuing a story for that magazine, Ericka Mellon reported, Protess helped to obtain a not guilty verdict for Sandra Fabiano, a Chicago resident who had been brought to trial on charges of child molestation. During later investigations for *Chicago Lawyer*, he enlisted the help of his students, counting their case-related activities as part of their course work.

As a professor, John Tang reported in the *Daily Northwestern* (February 3, 1998, online), Protess views his primary mission as teaching his students the techniques of investigative journalism. These include ways to conduct difficult interviews, such as those with prisoners who have not discussed their cases with anyone outside .the prison walls for years, or meetings with reluctant witnesses. Before attempting such encounters, the students practice by engaging in role play. They also get tips from private investigators. When carrying out assignments in the field that are potentially dangerous, the students are accompanied by Protess or a private investigator. "The best way of learning is by doing," Protess has observed, as quoted in the *Northwestern Observer* (February 11, 1999, online), the university's faculty and staff newspaper. Protess' outstanding contributions as a teacher of journalism were recognized in 1986 by the Poynter Institute, a school for "journalists, future journalists, and teachers of journalism" in St. Petersburg, Florida, which presented him with the National Teaching Award for Excellence in the Teaching of Journalism Ethics. In 1994 the Searle Center for Teaching Excellence, at Northwestern University, named him the Charles Deering McCormick Professor of Teaching Excellence, an honor associated with an endowed chair. In an online release, the Searle Center described Protess as a teacher "who brings his own research and investigative journalism into the classroom so as to create uniquely relevant, real world, thought-provoking learning experiences for his students. The excitement he arouses in his many students as he engages them in the subtle confluence of investigative journalism, the law, and ethics, is legendary in the University and in the broader educational and professional communities beyond this campus."

The first case in which Protess' students served as collaborators involved David and Cynthia Dowaliby, of Midlothian, Illinois, a town near Chicago, who in 1988 were prosecuted for the murder of their seven year old daughter, Jaclyn. The defense argued that the child had been murdered by an intruder who had broken into a basement window of the Dowaliby house and abducted her. Toward the end of the trial, the judge dismissed the charges against Cynthia, but not David, for lack of sufficient evidence. The jury decided that David was guilty, and he was sentenced to 45 years in prison, Dowaliby spent nearly two years behind bars before his conviction was overturned on appeal. In *Gone in the Night: The Dowaliby Family's Encounter with Murder and the Law* (1993), Protess and his co-author, Rob Warden, tried to demonstrate the Dowaliby s' innocence while lambasting what they regarded as the prosecution's many excesses. They also took to task the defense lawyers, members of the press who were unsympathetic to the defense, and Richard M. Daley, who was then the Cook County state's attorney and thus the county's chief prosecutor. Political considerations, Protess and Warden contended, had led Daley to approve the way the prosecution handled the case despite its lack of evidence.

In April 1989 Daley, who compiled a strong law-and-order record as state's attorney, was elected mayor of Chicago, which makes up a large part of Cook County. In their book, Protess and Warden also attempted to illuminate the ways in which journalists, government officials, and law enforcement agents influence decision-making in trial and appellate courts. In a review of *Gone in the Night* for *Library Journal* (May 1,1993), Gregor A. Preston wrote, "This is a tragic story, superbly narrated, of how a normal family was victimized by the criminal justice system," and he called the book "gripping" and "moving." "Despite their obvious bias," Sue-Ellen Beauregard wrote for *Booklist* (April 15, 1993), Protess and Warden "offer an illuminating look at a curious, tragic case that remains unsolved." *Gone in the Night* was named the best book of 1993 by Investigative Reporters and Editors, an organization "dedicated to improving the quality of investigative reporting within the field of journalism."

Another case in which Protess became deeply involved was that of Girvies Davis, who was sentenced to death for the murder of an elderly man in 1978. At his trial, the prosecution entered into evidence Davis's written confession of guilt in the murder. Protess later discovered that at the time that Davis had supposedly penned his confession, he could neither read nor write; furthermore, as a result of brain damage stemming from a childhood accident, his IQ placed him just above the level of a mentally disabled person. In addition to expressing serious doubts about the credibility of Davis's confession and questions about the conduct of the police (who had also charged him with complicity in several additional murders), Protess and his students raised issues of race and class in the handling of his case. Despite their efforts and those of other groups, in 1995 the state of Illinois executed Davis, by means of lethal injection. To help his students cope with the despair they felt when they heard of Davis's death, Protess brought a grief counselor to the class.

Before his death, Ericka Mellon reported, Davis urged Protess to take up the case of one of his fellow inmates, Dennis Williams. Davis already knew something about Williams's plight: In 1978 Williams and three other young African-American men, Verneal Jimerson, Kenneth Adams, and William Rainge, all of whom lived in Ford Heights, a poverty-stricken Chicago neighborhood, had been convicted of abducting a young man and his fiancé from a gas station where the man worked and then, after bringing them to an abandoned building in

Ford Heights, repeatedly raping the woman and shooting both her and her fiancé to death. Despite having alibis, the four had been arrested, on the basis of several accounts by ostensible eyewitnesses. Brought to trial and represented by court-appointed attorneys whom Protess later described as shockingly incompetent, all had been found guilty; Adams had gotten a prison term of 75 years, Rainge, a life sentence, and Williams and Jimerson, the death sentence.

Protess began working with several lawyers who had been making intermittent, unsuccessful attempts, without pay, to help the Ford Heights Four, as the men became known. He also assigned the case to three senior journalism majors, Stacey Delo, Stephanie Goldstein, and Laura Sullivan, in his investigative reporting class. He and the three students reviewed the transcripts of the trials and then, with the help of a private investigator, Rene Brown, who had looked into the case sporadically for years at the behest of a defense lawyer, began six months of legwork. Tracking down a witness who had placed the four men at the crime scene, they learned that the police had coerced her into making a false statement; other eyewitness reports also proved to be bogus. They also dug up, in a police file, papers that identified other potential suspects, most notably a group of men, among them the brothers Ira and Dennis Johnson, who had been spotted near the gas station shortly before the killings. Although those men had been seen the day after the murders selling distinctive items stolen from the station, the police had never questioned them. Protess has speculated that they failed to do so because, as Kari Lydersen put it, "in a tough-on-crime push, politicians were putting pressure on police to put someone behind bars for the murder," and the police, who had already locked up the Ford Heights Four, felt that having any poor young black men in custody was "good enough regardless of the defendants' guilt or innocence." "There's a police attitude toward young black men that if they didn't do this they probably did something else," Protess observed to Lydersen.

With the help of Brown, the students found Ira Johnson, in prison, serving a long sentence for a 1990 murder. When asked about the 1978 killings, Johnson admitted his guilt and implicated several others. Moreover, DNA testing, which had not been available in 1978, showed that the semen found in the body of the murdered woman could not have come from any of the Ford Heights Four. After 18 years in prison, including, for Williams, years spent in a cell only about 30 feet

from the electric chair, Williams, Rainge, Jimerson, and Adams were freed. Protess and Rob Warden described the four men's long ordeal in their book *A Promise of Justice: The Eighteen-Year Fight to Save Four Innocent Men* (1998). For his efforts to prove them innocent, Protess earned the 1996 Champion of Justice Award from the National Association of Criminal Defense Lawyers.

In 1999, in another case of criminal justice gone awry, Protess and five of his students, Shawn Armbrust, Erica LeBorgne, Tom McCann, Syandene Rhodes-Pitts, and Cara Rubinsky, along with Paul Ciolino, a private investigator with whom Protess has often worked, established the innocence of Anthony Porter, who had been sentenced to death in 1983 for the 1982 murder of a young couple during a nighttime robbery in a Chicago park. According to the transcripts from the trial and other court records, the gunman had used his left hand to fire the fatal shots; Porter, however, was right-handed. Moreover, the state's key witness, William Taylor, had sworn under oath that he had seen Porter shoot, but when the students went to the park to re-create the circumstances of the crime, they determined that from where Taylor testified he had been standing, about 500 feet from Porter, they could barely see the place where the couple had been slain, even in daylight. When the Northwestern sleuths talked to Taylor, he declared that the police had coerced him into making a false statement. The estranged wife of Alstory Simon, a man whom the police had identified as a witness in 1982, told the students that Simon was the killer, and a nephew of his told them that Simon had admitted his guilt to him. When Protess, Ciolino, and the students confronted Simon, he confessed. On February 5, 1999, on orders from a judge, Porter gained his freedom after 16 years of imprisonment. He was the 10th death-row inmate exonerated in Illinois since the state's reinstatement of the death penalty, in 1977. In May 1999 Illinois Attorneys for Criminal Justice (IACJJ, a group composed of public defenders and private defense attorneys, presented Protess and the five students with the organization's Advocates Award, in honor of what an IACJ official described as their "extraordinary efforts" in "uncovering] crucial evidence resulting in the freeing of Anthony Porter from custody and death row."

For a decade beginning in about 1980, Protess directed a study in which he and six of his colleagues at the Institute for Policy Research examined the impact of investigative reporting and media exposes on public opinion, government officials, and policy makers. The results of their research appear in *The Journalism of Outrage: Investigative Reporting and Agenda Building in America* (1991), by Protess, Fay Cook, Jack Dippelt, and James Ettema. With Maxwell McCombs, Protess edited the book *Agenda Setting: Readings on Media, Public Opinion, and Policymaking* (1991). He has also conducted studies of press coverage of hate crimes and other race-related matters in Chicago and media portrayal of the violence that erupted in Los Angeles and other cities in 1992, after a jury acquitted four white Los Angeles police officers charged with beating Rodney King in 1991. An onlooker had videotaped the police attacking King after pulling over his car, allegedly for speeding. In 2011, Northwestern University school officials put Protess on leave after they found he had deliberately falsified evidence. The scandal resulted in Protess not returning to Northwestern and the suing of Cook County by Simon. Simon's conviction was overturned in October 2014, and it remains unknown who committed the murders in the case.

## PERSONAL LIFE

In recent years Protess has received thousands of letters from prisoners seeking his help. "I pay attention to every case and personally answer each letter," he told John Tang. Prisoners even call him at home. "My home number is scribbled on every death row in the country," Protess said in an interview with Martha Brant for *Newsweek* (May 31, 1999). Protess lives with his second wife, Joan Perry, and their son, Benjamin; his first marriage, to Marianne Kreitman, which ended in divorce, also produced one son, Daniel. His honors include the Peter Lisagor Award for Exemplary Journalism, in 1989; the Amoco Foundation Faculty Award, from Northwestern, in 1993; and the Human Rights Award, from the National Alliance Against Racist and Political Repression, in 1996. Also in 1996, ABC Network News named him person of the week.

## FURTHER READING

*The Journalism of Outrage: Investigative Reporting and Agenda Building in America; Agenda Setting: Readings on Media, Public Opinion and Policy Making; Gone in the Night: The Dowaliby Family's Encounter with Murder and the Law; A Promise of Justice: The Eighteen-Year Fight to Save Four Innocent Men*

# R

## STEFAN RAHMSTORF

### Climatologist; Oceanographer; Activist

**Born:** February 22, 1960; Karlsruhe, Germany
**Primary Field:** Climate Change
**Affiliation:** Potsdam Institute for Climate Impact
Research

### INTRODUCTION

*Along with the majority of his colleagues worldwide, the climatologist Stefan Rahmstorf is certain that Earth's climate is warming. The dangerous rates at which the temperatures of the oceans and the atmosphere are rising can be traced, most scientists believe, directly to the activities of humans since the start of the Industrial Revolution, in the 1700s, and primarily to the growing use of fossil fuels. A native of Germany, Rahmstorf is a physicist and an oceanographer as well as a climatologist in Potsdam, Germany, and he holds the title of professor of physics of the oceans at the University of Potsdam, and he heads the department devoted to the analysis of Earth systems at the Potsdam Institute for Climate Impact Research (known by the acronym PIK). In 1999 he received from the James S. McDonnell Foundation a $1 million Centennial Fellowship Award, one of the world's most prestigious science prizes, for his work on the role of the oceans in climate change, including the ways in which the movements and temperatures of ocean currents affect temperatures in Earth's atmosphere. His work entails the gathering and interpreting of vast quantities of data disseminated by other scientists, not only to determine forces at work on Earth's climate at present but also to shed light on climate changes over thousands of years in the past. He* has used such information to create computer simulations to predict changes in climate in the future.

### EARLY LIFE

Stefan Rahmstorf was born on February 22, 1960 in Karlsruhe, Germany, to Rolf Rahmstorf, a manager in the pharmaceutical industry, and his wife, Hildegard, a pharmacist. Six years later his family, which includes his brother and sister, moved to the Netherlands. Rahmstorf has said that by the age of 12 he knew that he wanted to become a scientist. "I always wanted to understand how the world works," he told *Current Biography*. "I was particularly interested in astronomy and physics. I started to learn about oceanography in 1982, midway in my physics studies. I'd always loved the oceans and knew right away that oceanography was going to be the right field for me."

### LIFE'S WORK

Rahmstorf attended the University of Ulm and then the University of Konstanz, both in Germany; at the latter he wrote a thesis on general relativity theory and earned a diploma in physics. During his undergraduate years he also studied physical oceanography at the University of Wales (now Bangor University) in Bangor. He next pursued a PhD degree in oceanography at Victoria University of Wellington, New Zealand. He conducted research while on several cruises in the South Pacific. After he earned his doctorate, in 1990, Rahmstorf worked briefly as a scientist at the New Zealand Oceanographic Institute in Wellington. In 1991 he joined the Institute of Marine Sciences at the University of Kiel, in Germany. He has been working at the Potsdam Institute for Climate Impact Research since 1996 and has taught at the University of Potsdam since 2000.

Most of Rahmstorf's research on the role of ocean currents in climate change concerns what is known as the thermohaline circulation (THC) of the ocean (the world's connected seas). As Rahmstorf explained in a fact sheet posted on the PIK website (2002), the THC is different from wind-driven currents and tides, which occur at or near the surface and are controlled by the forces of gravity exerted on the ocean by the moon and the sun. The THC is linked instead to differences in seawater temperature and density; denser, colder seawater sinks below seawater that is warmer and less dense. The density of seawater depends on its salinity, the concentration of salt in it. Salinity increases as seawater evaporates and sea-ice forms; it decreases with rainfall, snowfall, runoff (water from rivers and rain, snow, and irrigation that is not absorbed into land but flows into the ocean), and the addition of meltwater, from melting glaciers, ice sheets, and other ice. Thermohaline circulation, sometimes called the ocean conveyor belt or the global conveyor belt, involves the sinking of huge masses of water (in a process known as deep-water formation) in particular areas such as the Mediterranean Sea, the Greenland-Norwegian Sea, the Labrador Sea, the Weddell Sea, and the Ross Sea; the spreading and upwelling of deep water; and the movements of certain near-surface currents, including the North Atlantic Drift (or North Atlantic Current). The North Atlantic Drift and the Gulf Stream (the latter of which is mostly wind driven) bring warm water from the Gulf of Mexico up along the eastern coast of the U.S. and across the Atlantic Ocean. The warm water releases heat that has kept the climate of Western Europe temperate for the past 10,000 years—since the last ice age. As the water grows colder, it grows denser and sinks; that sinking drives the currents. By the time the deep, cold water has returned south, it has reached depths of one to two miles below the surface. "The crux of the matter is that the strength of the circulation depends on small density differences, which in turn depend on a subtle balance in the North Atlantic between cooling in high latitudes and input of rain, snowfall, and river runoff," Rahmstorf explained in an article for *UNESCO Sources* (December 1997). Continued global warming, he has maintained, will upset that subtle balance. With an abnormally large input of freshwater from melting ice, for example, seawater will become less salty and thus less dense, deep-water formation in the Atlantic will slow, and the movement

of the "conveyor belt" will slow and eventually stop entirely. "We can see that such breakdowns have happened before in climate history," Rahmstorf wrote for *UNESCO Sources*, although precisely what caused them is not yet known. "Pulses of freshwater entered the Atlantic, causing cold spells lasting for hundreds of years. The last cooling occurred about 11,000 years ago. So the possibility of a circulation breakdown is not just in the computer, it is real." The evidence comes from painstaking examinations of cores of ice extracted from Greenland and cores of sediments extracted from the floor of the ocean. The cores, from drillings to depths of thousands of feet, show the accumulations of yearly deposits, the contents of which can be analyzed to reveal climate conditions at the time that each deposit settled. Such analyses are analogous to those of tree rings, which are added annually and reveal periods of drought, for example.

The presence in Earth's atmosphere of carbon dioxide and other so-called greenhouse gases— methane, nitrous oxide, carbon monoxide, and for the past 250 years or so, others produced by various industrial operations, such as sulfur hexafluoride, is not inherently harmful. On the contrary: such gases are vital for life, because, in a process dubbed the greenhouse effect in the mid-1800s, they trap long wave radiation escaping from Earth into space, which normally balances the energy coming from the sun. In a self-regulating, natural system, the trapped radiation heats the atmosphere and keeps air temperatures at levels favorable to life as we know it. As humans began to burn fossil fuels (coal and liquid-petroleum products) to provide energy to run machinery in factories and, later, to run power plants, cars, and planes, unnatural amounts of $CO_2$ and other greenhouse gases were emitted into the atmosphere. Scientists' understanding of climate and the forces that control it is incomplete (as is their understanding of weather, climatic conditions in small locales minute by minute). However, they know without any doubt that the burning of fossil fuels (and, to a much lesser extent, deforestation) has led to the increased concentration of $CO_2$ in the atmosphere. It is also known that increases in $CO_2$ concentrations lead to an increase in trapped long-wave radiation, a rise in atmospheric temperatures near Earth's surface, and higher temperatures in the surface waters of the ocean. By the early 1990s, according to Rahmstorf, global temperatures on average were 0.5 degrees Centigrade higher than they were before the

Industrial Revolution, and since then they have risen another 0.3°C.

Some of the effects of global warming are already apparent. Among the most dramatic is the loss of summer sea ice in the Arctic Ocean. "Ice extent in 2007 and 2008. was only about half of what it [was] in the 1960s," Rahmstorf wrote in his article "Climate Change—State of the Science," posted on the PIK website in 2009; "ice thickness has decreased by 20-25% just since 2001, and in 2008 the North-East Passage and North-West Passage were both open for the first time in living memory." One consequence of that melting of sea ice is that, in the past four decades, "sea levels have increased about 50 percent more than the climate models predicted," Rahmstorf told an *Agence France Presse* (December 14,2006) reporter. Rahmstorf provided evidence for that conclusion in a paper, co-written with six others, that was published in the May 4, 2007 issue of *Science*. If sea levels were to continue to rise, land at or slightly above sea level would disappear under water, leaving homeless many of the millions of people who live on low-lying islands or in coastal areas. Another result of global warming is that the acidity of the oceans is increasing along with higher levels of CO2. Such acidity threatens the well-being and even survival of marine ecosystems and fish and crustacean populations in many parts of the world.

For some years Rahmstorf was a member of the Abrupt Climate Change Panel of the National Oceanic and Atmospheric Administration (NOAA), a U.S. agency, and he currently sits on the German Advisory Council on Global Change. He was a principal author in 2007 of the Fourth Assessment Report of the Intergovernmental Panel on Climate Change (IPCC, established in 1988 by the World Meteorological Organization and the United Nations Environment Programme). The report concluded that global warming was "unequivocal" and has almost certainly resulted from human induced emissions of so-called greenhouse gases, particularly carbon dioxide (CO2 which consists of one atom of carbon, whose chemical symbol is "C," and two atoms of oxygen, "O"). Rahmstorf has written or co-written some 60 scientific papers, including 14 published in *Nature or Science*; 20 book chapters, in such reference works as *Encyclopedia of Ocean Sciences* (2001); and more than two dozen articles for *New Scientist* and other publications for laypeople. He has also co-authored three books: *Der Klimawandel* ("*Climate Change*," 2006), *Our Threatened Oceans* (2008), and *The Climate Crisis:*

*An Introductory Guide to Climate Change* (2009). He is a co-founder and regular contributor to Real Climate, a blog written by climate scientists for both experts and laypeople that has had over two million visits in the past five years. In 2005 the blog won a Science and Technology Web Award from *Scientific American*. In an October 3, 2005 online post, the magazine's editors described *Real Climate* as "a refreshing antidote to the political and economic slants that commonly color and distort news coverage of topics like the greenhouse effect, air quality, natural disasters and global warming" and "a focused, objective blog written by scientists for a brainy community that likes its climate commentary served hot."

In recent years Rahmstorf has become prominent among scientists who are vigorously challenging the views of so-called climate-change deniers, contrarians, and skeptics. He has strived to convince the public that a vast and growing body of evidence proves beyond doubt that the activities of humans have caused significant rises in oceanic and atmospheric temperatures; that failure to reverse that trend in the next few years will be catastrophic for hundreds of millions of humans and many other species of animals and plants; and that as many as a third of those species may well die out. "I wish [the skeptics and deniers] were right," he told *Current Biography*. "But unfortunately the recent data show that we have not exaggerated but underestimated the problem thus far. Arctic sea ice is vanishing much faster and sea levels are rising more rapidly than we expected just a few years ago." "I believe we will stop global warming," he said. "The question is just: how fast and at what level? I am less optimistic that we have enough political will and courage to curb emissions fast enough to limit warming to below 2 degrees Celsius, as is the goal that has now become a global consensus. I won't give up hope, but I worry that we will do too little, too late."

The reality of anthropogenic (human-caused) global warming has been accepted as fact by the IPCC, the NOAA, the U.N. Environment Programme, the World Meteorological Organization, the National Academy of Sciences of the U.S., the American Geophysical Union (the world's largest association of Earth scientists), the National Aeronautic and Space Administration of the U.S., and dozens of other scientific government agencies as well as climatologists from around the world and the leaders of many nations. Despite that consensus, Rahmstorf complained in his paper "The Climate

Sceptics" (2005, online), published in conjunction with a conference sponsored by the organization Munich Re, the media continue to convey to the public the false idea that the main conclusions of the scientific community regarding global warming "are still disputed or regularly called into question by new studies." In light of the voluminous evidence produced by thousands of studies, he wrote, "it is almost inconceivable" that those conclusions "could be overturned by a few new results." The media's persistent propagation of false ideas, in his view, "is mainly due to the untiring PR [public relations] activities of a small, but vocal mixed bag of climate sceptics who vehemently deny the need for climate-protection measures." Prominent among that "vocal mixed bag" are representatives of, lobbyists for, or politicians who have benefited from the contributions of corporations that sell petroleum products or other commodities whose manufacture and/or use leads to the emission of greenhouse gases. In "The Climate Sceptics" and elsewhere, Rahmstorf has shown that there is no scientific evidence to support any of their arguments but that there is a huge body of evidence to refute them. He has pointed out the fallacies in arguments that global temperatures are not rising; that natural processes account for nearly all the increase in CCh; that C02 plays little or no role in global warming; that greater solar activity has caused increased temperatures on Earth; that the potential effects of global warming are negligible; and that the costs of measures proposed for stopping or reversing global warming by limiting C02 emissions would be prohibitively high.

The last-mentioned argument was presented in an article for Newsweek (August 29, 2009, online) by Bjorn Lomborg of Denmark, whose academic training is in political science and who teaches at the Copenhagen Business School. According to Lomborg, "Even if all industrialized nations succeeded in meeting the most drastic emissions goals, it would likely come at a huge sacrifice to prosperity." Referring to figures offered by the economist Richard Tol of the Economic and Social Research Institute in Ireland, he wrote, "Using carbon cuts to limit the increase in global temperature to 2 degrees Celsius would cost 12.9 percent of [the world's gross domestic product, or GDP] by the end of the century. That's $40 trillion a year. Yet, such measures would avoid only $1.1 trillion in damage due to higher temperatures. The cure would be more painful than the illness." Lomborg suggested as far more cost-effective the use of "climate engineering": "For instance, automated

boats could spray seawater into the air to make clouds whiter, and thus more reflective, augmenting a natural process. Bouncing just 1 or 2 percent of the total sunlight that strikes the Earth back into space could cancel out as much warming as that caused by doubling pre-industrial levels of greenhouse gases. Spending about $9 billion researching and developing this technology could head off $20 trillion of climate damage." Rahmstorf has rejected such approaches. "First of all they do nothing to stop ocean acidification, which by itself would be enough reason to cut down our CO2 emissions, unless we want to destroy our ocean ecosystems," he told Current Biography. "Secondly they would make the climate system inherently unstable and requiring [of] human control, which would have to be maintained for thousands of years because of the long lifetime of the CO2 that is building up in the atmosphere. If you let those cooling measures slip for just a few years, the full force of CO2 warming would hit us immediately. I just don't trust humans can reliably manage such a complex system for millennia—I'd much rather keep it the relatively stable self-regulating system it is now." Rahmstorf has endorsed the work of the British economist Nicholas Stern, who, after a review of other economists' studies, has estimated that the cost of cutting emissions would total 2 percent of global wealth (as measured by the gross domestic product of all nations), while the damage resulting from inaction would cost anywhere from 5 to 20 percent of global wealth, and possibly far more. In an interview posted on the Allianz Knowledge website (June 9, 2009), Rahmstorf suggested that people could "build an energy system over the next decades based primarily on renewable resources"—biofuels, solar power, and wind power—and thus avoid the use of fossil fuels, at least to a significant extent.

On November 18, 2008, in taped remarks that Rahmstorf has sometimes quoted, President-elect Barack Obama addressed the Bi-partisan Governors Global Climate Summit, held in Los Angeles, California. Obama told some 30 U.S. governors and representatives of many nations, "Few challenges facing America, and the world, are more urgent than combating climate change. The science is beyond dispute and the facts are clear. Now is the time to confront this challenge once and for all. Delay is no longer an option. The stakes are too high. The consequences, too serious." The U.S., which in recent years has been responsible for at least 21 percent of greenhouse gas emissions, did not join the 185 countries that ratified the Kyoto Protocol, drawn up by 37 industrialized nations and the European Union during the U.N. Framework Convention on Climate Change held in Japan in 1997. A legally binding treaty that went into effect in 2005, the protocol aimed to reduce greenhouse gas emissions from 1990 levels by an average of 5 percent between 2008 and 2012. In December 2009, when the U.N. held its 15th conference on climate change, in Copenhagen, CO2 levels were continuing to increase, in part because of China's rapidly rising use of fossil fuels and the failures of nearly every other nation to cut emissions. Government heads and other delegates from 192 countries (among them Obama and Rahmstorf) attended that gathering. The agreement that resulted, known as the Copenhagen Accord, "fell short of even the modest expectations for the summit," according to the *New York Times* (December 18, 2009, online). "The accord drops what had been the expected goal of concluding a binding international treaty by the end of 2010, which leaves the implementation of its provisions uncertain. It is likely to undergo many months, perhaps years, of additional negotiation before it emerges in any internationally enforceable form." The *Times* also reported, "The maneuvering that characterized the final week of the talks was a sign of [global leaders'] seriousness; never before have [they] come so close to a significant agreement to reduce the greenhouse gases linked to warming the planet." The leaders agreed that global warming must never exceed 2°C above preindustrial levels and that by the end of January 2010, wealthy nations must register the emissions cuts they will implement by 2020. Those nations also pledged to fund efforts by poorer nations to reduce greenhouse-gas emissions and adapt to consequences of climate change.

## PERSONAL LIFE
In his free time Rahmstorf enjoys photography, yoga, and dancing. His first marriage, in 1991, to the New Zealand born actress Dulcie Smart, ended in divorce. He lives with his second wife, Stefanie, and their two children in Potsdam, where his wife owns a jewelry-design shop. The couple sell sterling-silver jewelry of their own design; each piece reads "OCO" or in some other way refers to CO2. The Rahmstorfs use the money from each sale to buy one of the limited number of CO2 emission credits issued by the European Union. They stamp each piece of jewelry with the serial number of the credit, to serve as evidence that with that purchase, the buyer has prevented the emission of one ton of CO2 into the atmosphere.

## FURTHER READING
*Der Klimawandel; Our Threatened Oceans; The Climate Crisis: An Introductory Guide to Climate Change*

# IGNACIO RAMONET

## Journalist; Activist; Educator

**Born:** May 5, 1943; Redondela, Galicia, Spain
**Primary Field:** Journalism; Public Intellectual
**Affiliation:** Alter-Globalization Movement

## INTRODUCTION
*"Globalization" refers to the merging of national economies into an international market. The Spanish-born journalist, author, and activist Ignacio Ramonet is best known for his prominent role in the "alter-globalization" movement, a grassroots struggle against what he and his compatriots see as the imposition of unrestrained capitalism and a global political and economic system that disproportionately benefits wealthy countries and classes. Most recently, Ramonet gained attention for his 100 hours of interviews with Fidel Castro, which cul-minated in the publication of* Fidel Castro: My Life—A Spoken Autobiography, *the most comprehensive volume on the life of the Cuban leader to date. As the editor in chief of the widely respected, Paris, France-based, leftist international-affairs journal* Le Monde Diplomatique *from 1991 to 2008, Ramonet wrote fiery editorials that resulted in the establishment of several important organizations, including ATTAC International, which proposes concrete solutions for what its officials see as the injustices of globalization; the World Social Forum (the alter-globalization movement's answer to the World Economic Forum), of which Ramonet is one of the main organizers and which has met annually since 2001; and the nongovernmental watchdog group Media Watch Global, which he co-founded in order to counter the corporatization of the media. Through his work at Le Monde Diplomatique in the 1990s, Ramonet helped cre-*

*ate the slogans "Another world is possible," the motto of the World Social Forum and an answer to the British prime minister Margaret Thatcher's famous statement "There is no alternative" to global free market capitalism; and "la pensee unique" ("single thought"), one of the terms now commonly used in examining globalization and its perceived inevitability. A professor of media studies and communication theory at Denis Diderot University, in Paris, and an adviser to the United Nations specializing in geopolitics, Ramonet is also a frequent contributor to the Spanish daily El Pais and an adviser to the pan Latin American television network Telesur.*

## EARLY LIFE

Ignacio Ramonet was born in Redondela, in Galicia, the northwest region of Spain, on May 5, 1943 to Antonio Ramonet, a tailor, and Antonia Miguez. To escape the fascist regime of the country's ruler, Francisco Franco, his family relocated to Tangier, Morocco, in 1946. "I do not belong to the generation whose real battle was fascism-antifascism. That was my parents' generation: my father participated in the Spanish Civil War [on the side that opposed Franco's forces] and my mother was a union militant," he told Rosa Miriam Elizalde for cubanismo.net (October 8, 2006). "The central battle of my generation, during its adolescence and early adulthood, was colonialism/anti-colonialism. Specially the liberation of colonized countries." Ramonet's childhood coincided with Morocco's gaining independence from France, in 1956, and with neighboring Algeria's war for independence from the same country, begun two years earlier; his schoolmates included Algerian refugees whose families had fled oppression in their own country. At a barbershop in Tangier, when he was 12 or 13, Ramonet learned about Cuban revolutionaries' struggle against the military dictatorship in that country, He recalled to Elizalde, "The barber was a man who had been to Cuba many times; he was a Spaniard very fond of the Island. The magazine he set out for his clients was *Bohemia*. With curiosity I began to read *Bohemia* in its salmon-colored pages, the red chronicles relating repressions of the dictatorship. One thing led to another: I discovered the personality of Fidel Castro," the revolutionary leader who went on to seize power in Cuba in 1959 and hold it for the next five decades. Reading about the oppression of Cuba's people by its own leaders, and about the Cuban revolutionaries' literacy campaigns and agrarian reforms, Ramonet came

to believe that "a country isn't sovereign just because it reaches independence but when its people are sovereign and not subjected to any kind of feudality," as he told Omar Gonzalez in an interview for cuba-now.net (February 2005).

Ramonet studied at the University of Rabat, in Morocco, and continued his education in France, at the University of Bordeaux III, where he earned an M.A. degree. He went on to teach at several schools in Morocco, including the College du Palais Royal a Rabat, where he was on the faculty from 1969 to 1972. Meanwhile, he had launched a network of film societies and embarked upon a career in journalism, both radio and print. He left in 1972 for Paris, where he began teaching at the University of Paris VII and earned a PhD in semiology and in cultural history from the Ecole des Hautes Etudes en Sciences Sociales; he was a pupil of the eminent philosopher Roland Barthes and the film theorist Christian Metz, among others. At that time he also began contributing film criticism to the French philosopher Jean-Paul Sartre's newly created leftist paper, *Liberation*, as well as writing for the influential film journal *Cahiers du Cinema*.

## LIFE'S WORK

In January 1973, concurrent with his lecturing, he began his long career with *Le Monde Diplomatique*. He started as a contributor to the paper, which had begun in the 1950s as a foreign affairs supplement to the French daily *Le Monde*. By the time Ramonet began his tenure there, the scholarly and opinionated paper, nicknamed "*Le Diplo*," had become known as a leftist journal that offered comprehensive foreign policy and geopolitical analyses. The paper is largely independent of *Le Monde*, as 49 percent of "Le Diplo" is owned by its readers and staff, Which "is extremely rare in the press, not only in France but in the world, and guarantees complete independence from all the powers that be, political, media or financial," as Ramonet wrote in its pages (January 1, 2007). Ramonet was elected editorial director and president of the board in 1990 and was reelected to the positions every six years until he resigned, in early 2008. He continues to write for the paper.

In an oft quoted January 1995 editorial for the paper, Ramonet introduced the idea of "pensee unique," or single thought. "We began to mobilize a group of intellectuals, thinkers, journalists and professors too, around *Le Monde Diplomatique* to try to identify the features of what we today call globalization," he told Gonzales.

"In that stage in which we were trying to identify the adversary's traits, I had proposed that this be called 'single thought.' In truth, single thought is what we call today globalization. This idea that there is only one good way of thinking, one useful way of thinking, one practical way of thinking, one modern way of thinking and that [it] consists in accepting the catalogue of ideas of globalization in economy, in work and in everyday life." Observers trace the development of modern-day globalization to the 1980s, during the conservative governments of Thatcher and U.S. president Ronald Reagan. Its proponents argue that free-market capitalism on an international scale enriches all involved through a trickle-down effect, providing for the democratization of technology and education, which over generations allows communities and nations to develop. Ramonet has characterized globalization as being based on an ideology in which economic considerations trump all others, leading to social Darwinism and ever increasing discrepancies in wealth between industrialized and Third World nations. "The aim of single thought," Ramonet told Gonzales, "is that people finally accept their own slavery. That's the project: how to make a person voluntarily consent and take part in his own exploitation and in addition, to think he's happy." In a now famous debate, printed in the journal *Foreign Policy* (September 22, 1999) between Ramonet and Thomas L. Friedman, a *New York Times* columnist and globalization advocate, Ramonet wrote, "Dazzled by the glimmer of fast profits, the champions of globalization are incapable of taking stock of the future, anticipating the needs of humanity and the environment, planning for the expansion of cities, or slowly reducing inequalities and healing social fractures. The most basic principle [of globalization] is so strong that even a Marxist, caught off guard, would agree: The economic prevails over the political. In this new social order, individuals are divided into 'solvent' or 'non-solvent,' i.e., apt to integrate into the market or not. The market offers protection to the solvents only. In this new order, where human solidarity is no longer an imperative, the rest are misfits and outcasts."

To Thatcher's famous line "There is no alternative," the alter-globalization movement responded, "Another world is possible." The movement identified globalization as progressing on several fronts: the economic front, in which nations' markets were forced open by more powerful countries as the price of debt relief, and their national resources were forced to be privatized; the ideological/media front, in which globalization was equated with modernization and progress and made to seem inevitable; and, particularly after the September 11, 2001 terrorist attacks on the U.S., the military front, in which the cause of globalization could be advanced by force, as was attempted in Iraq. Ramonet has argued that political sentiments matching those of the alter-globalization movement have been evident in grassroots campaigns throughout Latin America, particularly the Zapatista movement in Mexico led by Subcomandante Marcos and in measures adopted by Venezuelan president Hugo Chavez. "What happened in Latin America at the end of the 1980s? Globally, the military dictatorships that had marked the preceding 20 years in the continent started to disappear and Latin American societies welcomed with relief, the same as the whole world, the disappearance of those terrible regimes," Ramonet told Gonzales. "But, as soon as those democratic governments started to rule, they accepted globalization's 'solutions' with open arms; they started to privatize massively, to apply the recipes of the International Monetary Fund; and, with time, what we are now seeing took place: deep dissatisfaction in societies which consider that democracy doesn't fulfill its promises. Democracy isn't just the possibility of picking between one party or the other, to take part in civilian liberties; supposedly, it is also the will to create a fairer society, to distribute wealth better, without polarizing and, therefore, allowing greater economic democracy, social democracy, cultural democracy."

Out of those ideas grew three organizations: ATTAC, the World Social Forum, and Media Watch Global. In December 1997, following the collapse of Asian markets, Ramonet wrote in a *Monde Diplomatique* editorial, "Financial globalisation is a law unto itself and it has established a separate supranational state with its own administrative apparatus, its own spheres of influence, its own means of action. That is to say the International Monetary Fund (IMF), the World Bank, the Organization for Economic Cooperation and Development [OECD] and the World Trade Organization (WTO). This artificial world state is a power with no base in society. It is answerable instead to the financial markets and the mammoth business undertakings that are its masters. Absolute freedom of movement for capital undermines democracy and we need to introduce machinery to counter its effects." Warning that "the task of disarming this financial power must be given top priority if the law of the jungle is not to take over completely in the next century," he proposed three solutions, closing down tax havens, increasing taxes on unearned income, and instituting a tax on financial transactions, the last of which, he argued, could be achieved with the adoption of a reform tax, the Tobin tax, named after the Nobel Prize-winning economist James Tobin, who in 1972 advocated it to stabilize markets and generate revenue for the international community. "At 0.1%, the Tobin tax would bring in some $166 billion a year, twice the annual amount needed to abolish the worst poverty by the end of the [20th] century. Many experts have said there would be no particular technical difficulty about introducing this tax. It would spell the end of the . . . dogma subscribed to by all those people who love to tell us that there is no alternative to the present system," Ramonet wrote. He suggested the creation of a global pressure group that would lobby governments to introduce the measure. He wrote, "Why not set up a new worldwide non-governmental organisation, Action for a Tobin Tax to Assist the Citizen (ATTAC)?"

In the summer of 1998, ATTAC, with the acronym standing instead for Association for the Taxation of Financial Transactions for the Aid of Citizens, was formed in France. ATTAC, whose motto is "The world is not for sale," soon became active around the world, addressing many of the concerns of the alter-globalization movement, by calling for democratic control of financial markets; "fair" instead of "free" trade, that is, democratization of global financial organizations including the IMF, World Bank, WTO, and OECD; debt relief rather than austerity measures for poorer countries; defense of public goods and services against privatization; and sustainable development. "At a time when many pundits were writing off the left as dead, ATTAC gave new life and novel forms to traditional left ideals," David Moberg wrote for *In These Times* (May 14, 2001).

One of ATTAC's main projects was the organizing of the World Social Forum. In a *Monde Diplomatique* editorial (January 2006), Ramonet described the World Social Forum (WSF), which was first convened in Porto Alegre, Brazil, in January 2001, as "an international day of reflection" focusing "on rebuilding the internationalism of peoples and an anti-imperialist front." The forum began as a grassroots organizing and strategizing tool against globalization and free trade, operating under the theme "Another World Is Possible"; it aimed to coordinate the efforts of the various alter-globalization forces that were emerging at the time. The WSF was also intended as an alternative to the annual World Economic Forum, which Ramonet described in a 2001 editorial

as "the meeting place for the world's new masters, in particular the policy-makers who set the agenda for globalisation." Participants in the WSF have included such well-known thinkers, writers, activists, and statesmen as Arundhati Roy, Naomi Klein, Noam Chomsky, Immanuel Wallerstein, Joseph Stiglitz, Kofi Annan, Gilberto Gil, President Luiz Inacio da Silva of Brazil, and Hugo Chavez. While the WSF has been credited with bringing new ideas to the global conversation, it has also been criticized for being too vague in intent, for lacking follow-through, and, perhaps most significantly in recent years, for allowing well-funded, typically Western-based nongovernmental organizations to dominate the agenda, overshadowing grassroots movements. Another problem has been a lack of the sort of media coverage enjoyed by the World Economic Forum.

Ramonet's criticisms of the news media are central to his positions on globalization and the alter-globalization movement. In an editorial entitled "Set the Media Free" (October 2003), he described the news media as being, ideally, "the voice of those who have no voice," a "fourth estate" that is a key element in any healthy democracy. "Over the past 15 years, with the acceleration of globalisation, this fourth estate has been stripped of its potential, and has gradually ceased to function as a counter-power," he wrote. "Real power is now in the hands of a few global economic groupings and conglomerates that appear to wield more power in world politics than most governments. Globalisation now also means the globalisation of the mass media and the communications information companies. These big companies are preoccupied with growth, which means that they have to develop relations with the other estates in society, so they no longer claim to act as a fourth estate with a civic objective and a commitment to denouncing human rights abuses." In response to those developments, Ramonet wrote, "we have to create a new estate, a fifth estate, that will let us pit a civic force against this new coalition of rulers." He added, "Freedom of enterprise cannot be permitted to override people's right to rigorously researched and verified news, nor can it serve as an alibi for the deliberate diffusion of false news and defamation." Ramonet argued that while the choice to cover a story based on one's ability to sell it, particularly to advertisers, or based on one's commercial ties and interests, may be protected by the right to free speech, "these freedoms can only be exercised by media enterprises if they do not infringe other rights that are equally sacred, such as the right of each citizen to have access to uncontaminated news." Ramonet's call for a watchdog group emerged from discussions at the second World Social Forum, in 2002. Media Watch Global, of which he is founder and president, would, as Ramonet wrote in his editorial, "at last give people a peaceful civic weapon against the emerging superpower of the big mass media."

## PERSONAL LIFE

In 2001 Ramonet published a book of his interviews with Subcomandante Marcos, titled *Marcos: La Dignidad Rebelde.* He received far more attention after his 100 hours of interviews with Fidel Castro were published as the book Fidel Castro: *My Life—A Spoken Autobiography* (2008). Ramonet approached Castro with the idea for the project during the 2002 Havana International Book Fair, where Ramonet presented his book *Silent Propaganda.* The two met several times over the next three years; Castro added detailed footnotes and recollections to the resulting manuscript, making for an apparently exhaustive personal account. After the book appeared, Ramonet was relieved of his weekly column at the Spanish paper *La Voz de Galicia*, merely, by his account, for having published interviews with the controversial Cuban leader. In response to criticism that he had lacked the proper skepticism in his interviews with Castro, Ramonet told Elizalde, "Interrogations are for the police. A journalist does not interrogate. A journalist asks questions and the responsibilities for the answers are of the interviewee. I wanted to have a conversation. I have said it often: he never set any condition. Fidel Castro is the most [censored] person in the mass media, they mention him but his words are not heard. That is not right."

Ramonet is the author of a number of other books, among them *Le Chewing-Gum des Yeux, La Golosina Visual, The Tyranny of Communication, The Geopolitics of Chaos, La Post-Television, A World without Direction, Iraq: History of a Disaster*, and *Wars of the 21st Century: New Threats, New Fears.* He teaches media studies and communication theory at Denis Diderot University in Paris and has taught at the Sorbonne and been a visiting scholar at universities in Spain and Latin America. He has received several honorary doctorates and won many prizes for his work, including the Spanish Liber Press Award for best journalist of the year, the Rodolfo Walsh Award in journalism from the University of La Plata in Argentina, and the Spanish Turia Award for contributions to mass media.

Ramonet lives in Paris and is married to Laurence Villaume, a translator. The couple have four children.

## FURTHER READING

*The Tyranny of Communication; Wars of the 21st Century: New Threats, New Fears; Iraq: History of a Disaster; Fidel Castro: My Life—A Spoken Autobiography*

---

# MAMPHELA RAMPHELE

## University Administrator; Businesswoman

**Born:** December 28, 1947; Bochum, Transvaal, South
   Africa
**Primary Field:** Higher Education; Politics
**Affiliation:** University of Cape Town

## INTRODUCTION

*In an article she wrote for* Africa Today *(Winter 1990), the South African businesswoman and politician Mamphela Ramphele argued that the willingness of individuals to take risks is an essential prerequisite to political change. In her own life, Ramphele has not hesitated to challenge boundaries set by a racist and patriarchal society. Growing up under apartheid, she confronted a system that told her that as a black girl, she could aspire to*
*no higher vocation than teaching or nursing. Ramphele overcame the disadvantage of the inferior educational system set up for blacks, and in 1972, she earned a medical degree. That act of defiance set the tone for what followed in Ramphele's accomplished life. In the 1970s, she was an active member of the Black Consciousness Movement (BCM), a radical organization that, like the Black Power movement in the United States, promoted the idea that blacks had to rely on themselves for liberation. Her involvement with the BCM came at no small cost: in 1977, the government banished her for six years. Unbroken by that ordeal, Ramphele re-emerged in the middle of the 1980s as an activist turned academic who was willing to work within white institutions to effect change, despite criticisms from other activists that such a course was politically ineffective.*

*Since the dismantling of apartheid in the 1990s, Ramphele has gained recognition as one of the nation's most capable administrators. In 1996, she was named vice chancellor of the University of Cape Town (a position equivalent to president in American universities), and thus became the first black woman to head a South African university. Determined "to balance equity with excellence," in her words, she attempted to negotiate that university's difficult transformation into a truly inclusive institution.*

## EARLY LIFE

The third of seven children of two schoolteachers, Mamphela Aletta Ramphele was born on December 28, 1947, in a hospital in the Bochum district of the northern Transvaal, in South Africa. Having two professional parents meant that Ramphele's life was relatively privileged compared with that of her neighbors in Kranspoort, the village in the Soutpansberg district of the northern Transvaal where she grew up. She was taught in the lower grades by her father, Pitsi Eliphaz Ramphele, who set higher standards for her than for his other students. "Any mistake would unleash severe punishment. I had to be perfect," she wrote in her autobiography, *Across Boundaries* (1995).

Ramphele was a smart and confident child, and, like her mother, Rangoato Rahab (Mahlaela) Ramphele, she displayed an independent spirit and a willingness to challenge tradition. "[My mother] established boundaries beyond which she would not allow anyone to go," Ramphele wrote in her autobiography. "She tackled her brothers-in-law on many levels to let them know that she was not at their beck and call, but should be treated with respect if they expected respect from her. They were quick to blame her attitude on her professional status." The realities of South African apartheid became evident to Ramphele early on. The Bantu Education Act, which was passed in 1953, one year before she started school, decreed that education for blacks be only as advanced as necessary for semiskilled jobs. Educated black girls like Ramphele were expected at the most to become either teachers or nurses. At age 14, Ramphele entered Bethesda Normal College, a teacher training boarding school about 30 miles from Pietersburg. She was the top student in her class, and she quickly grew frustrated by the unchallenging curriculum (no math higher than arithmetic was taught, for example). Moreover, she and other students had to endure the humiliation of the "huiswerk" system, in which black students were forced to perform menial chores for their white teachers, to remind the black students of their supposedly inferior status.

Undeterred by the knowledge that extremely few black men and even fewer black women in South Africa received medical degrees, Ramphele decided to become a doctor. "It was not the desire to serve which influenced my career choice, but the passion for freedom to be my own mistress in a society in which being black and woman defined the boundaries within which one could legitimately operate," she wrote in her autobiography. Eventually, after struggling to overcome the inferior education she received at Bethesda, she gained admission to the University of Natal, the only school in South Africa where black Africans could study medicine without special approval from the government. There she had to deal with white professors who actively tried to prevent black students from graduating. One infamous professor who taught introductory chemistry "would breeze into the classroom, his cold blue eyes not making contact with anyone, but emitting sparks of hatred," she wrote in her autobiography. "He made learning almost impossible. He lectured from old scraps of notes which were visibly yellowing from age. He wrote some of the difficult formulae on the board, with a duster [eraser! in one hand, and as soon as he got to the end of a long formula, he would begin to erase what he had written, relishing the anxiety he read in our faces." Ramphele was one of the few who passed the course, with a D.

## LIFE'S WORK

While at the University of Natal, Ramphele met Stephen Biko, the charismatic leader of the Black Consciousness Movement, and she embraced his idea that blacks should seize control of the antiapartheid movement. White liberal organizations like the National Union of South African Students (NUSAS) had been prominent opponents of apartheid during the 1960s, but BCM advocates felt that their critiques were ineffectual and often paternalistic. BCM philosophy stressed that blacks should not depend on white liberals. Only through solidarity and self-reliance, BCM leaders argued, could blacks regain their self-esteem and psychologically emancipate themselves.

Ramphele's acceptance of the BCM's tenets was accompanied by changes in her appearance. She stopped wearing wigs to cover up her short, boyish hair and began wearing revealing attire, especially hot pants. She also started smoking. "As a woman, an African woman at that, one had to be outrageous to be heard, let alone be taken seriously," she wrote in her autobiography. She was soon befriended by Biko and accepted into BCM's inner circle. At the university, she led the local branch of the South African Student Organization, a group formed in accordance with BCM principles and presented as an alternative to NUSAS. After graduating, in 1972, Ramphele continued her work with the BCM by combining her medical skills with community organizing. In 1975, she helped set up and manage the activist run Zanempilo Community Health Center, in the Eastern Cape. In 1976, she became the branch manager of the Black Community Programs, also in the Eastern Cape.

Working closely together, Ramphele and Biko developed what became an intimate relationship. "We shared not only a passionate love affair but also a commitment to the liberation of the oppressed in South Africa," she wrote in *Across Boundaries*. "Ours was a complete relationship in which we mutually nurtured our shared values." Before she realized that she was in love with Biko, Ramphele had been romantically involved with a schoolmate, Dick Mmabane, and in around 1970, she and Mmabane married. Less than two years later, they separated, and in 1972, they divorced. By that time, Ramphele and Biko, who had married sometime before, had admitted their love for each other and had begun seeing each other in secret. In 1974, Ramphele gave birth to their daughter, Lerato. The baby died of pneumonia at two months of age.

Ramphele has been quite candid about her relationship with Biko, in order to set the record straight about her relationship with him and her role in the Black Consciousness Movement. The 1987 film *Cry Freedom*, which is based on the South African journalist Donald Woods's biography of Biko, is particularly inaccurate, she has claimed. "The peripheral role in which I was cast belied the centrality of my relationship, both personal and political, with Steve," she wrote in her autobiography. On the other hand, some reporters have tended to treat her relationship with Biko, who was murdered in 1977, as if it is the only notable thing she achieved in the 1970s. "I can only infer that my public persona is an uncomfortable one for patriarchal society to deal with, and has to be given 'respectability' by summoning Steve from the grave to accompany me, and clothe my nakedness," she wrote in *Across Boundaries*.

A turning point in the burgeoning antiapartheid movement came in 1976, when violence erupted between South African security forces and students in the black township of Soweto marching in protest of a government policy to have classes taught in Afrikaans (the language of the Afrikaners, who immigrated to South Africa from the Netherlands in the 17th century). The event triggered widespread protest and violence that continued throughout the country for the next two years. The South African police responded by killing, jailing, or banishing prominent black activists. In 1977, Ramphele was banished to Lenyenye, in northeastern Transvaal. Later that year, the government banned all BCM activities.

During one brief reunion with Biko during her banishment, "passion took its course," as Ramphele wrote in *Across Boundaries,* and she became pregnant again. While hospitalized because of complications in the pregnancy, she learned of Biko's death, on September 12, 1977, from head injuries that he had sustained while in detention. The police initially denied inflicting the fatal blows, and they continued to do so until 1996, when five South African policemen admitted their guilt. Describing how she felt after Biko's death, Ramphele told Wendy Woods for the *Guardian* (September 15, 1991) that "everything went dead. I literally wondered if I could survive physically." Her second child, a boy, was born in January 1978, and she named him Hlumelo, which in the Xhosa language means "shoot of a dead tree."

Citing Viktor E. Frankl, a survivor of the Holocaust and a world-renowned psychiatrist, Ramphele has said that "the most important survival strategy is to turn personal tragedy into triumph." During her banishment, Ramphele continued serving the community as a physician. "I was so angry that the government had taken me away from what I had been doing and away from my support networks that I thought, I'm going to show you,'" she told Wendy Woods. With borrowed money, she established several programs for local people, including a day-care center, an adult literacy program, and the Ithuseng Community Health Center. She also continued her education, and she received diplomas in tropical hygiene, in 1981, and in public health, in 1982, from the University of the Witswatersrand. She also earned a bachelor of commerce degree, in 1983, from the University of South Africa. Earlier, in 1982, she married Sipo Magele; their son, Malusi, was born in March 1983.

In the early 1980s, because of persistent black insurgency, international isolation, and an economic slump, South Africa's governing National Party, then led by

P. W. Botha, instituted its "Total Strategy," which involved, among other things, repealing "petty" apartheid laws in an attempt to alleviate international criticism. Thanks to that strategy, Ramphele's banning order was lifted, in 1983. After staying one more year in Lenyenye to ensure that her programs would continue to operate after her departure, Ramphele and her family left, much to the community's disappointment. She worked briefly in Port Elizabeth as a medical officer, before realizing that her marriage was destined to fail because her husband expected her to be a traditional wife. The couple separated in 1984, when she moved with her two sons to Cape Town.

The move to Cape Town, which resulted from an offer by her friend Francis Wilson, a professor at the University of Cape Town (UCT), to work with him on the Second Carnegie Inquiry into Poverty and Development in South Africa marks the beginning of Ramphele's career as an academic. She started studying anthropology at UCT, and in 1986, she became a research fellow there. From 1988 to 1989, she studied at the Bunting Institute, at Harvard University, in Cambridge, Massachusetts. "I had joined the ranks of armchair intellectuals who occupied the ivory tower of academic life, the very people we activists used to view with scorn," she wrote in her autobiography.

Ramphele's book *Children on the Frontline: A Report for Unicef on the Status of Children in South Africa*, which she wrote with Francis Wilson, was published in 1987. In it, she and Wilson dared to criticize black organizations that used black children in the fight against apartheid; in response, some people accused her of "blaming the victim." In 1988, she and Wilson published a second book, *Uprooting Poverty: The South African Challenge*, which presented lengthy statistics on black poverty in South Africa and discredited the notion that blacks were somehow better off under apartheid. She completed her PhD degree in social anthropology in 1991 at UCT, and was one of only nine black women to earn a doctorate there in a year when 400 white men did so. Her PhD dissertation, on migrant hostel workers, was published in 1993 as *A Bed Called Home*.

Since the dismantling of legal apartheid which began in 1990 with the freeing of the African National Congress leader Nelson Mandela after 27 years of imprisonment, and culminated in Mandela's inauguration as president of South Africa after the first election in which black South Africans voted, Ramphele has taken many high-level positions in formerly white institutions. In 1991, she became deputy vice chancellor of UCT, with responsibility for implementing the university's equal opportunity programs, and in 1996, she was named the school's vice chancellor.

Maintaining that a tradeoff between equity and merit is not inevitable, Ramphele has advocated a policy aimed at increasing the enrollment of blacks and women at UCT without sacrificing standards. "Contrary to popular myth, poor people did not struggle in order to have equal access to mediocrity," she told Suzanne Daley for the *New York Times Magazine* (April 13, 1997). Prominent on her agenda has been adding to the criteria for admission a measure of each prospective student's potential to succeed, so that admissions officers will consider more than merely the student's existing academic record. "We're not going to simply affirm people because they happen to be black," she told Charlayne Hunter-Gault on the *NewsHour with Jim Lehrer* (April 27, 1997). "The difficulty is how one helps young people coming from this divided past to see themselves as South Africans."

Ramphele has also stressed that the institutional culture of UCT must change to reflect black African traditions. She dramatically illustrated the sorts of changes she has in mind on the day she was installed as vice chancellor. At the installation ceremony, her mother performed "praise-song" for her, something perhaps never before seen on the UCT campus. Ramphele explained to Charlayne Hunter-Gault, "A praise singer in African culture is someone who weaves together the story of the extended family and celebrates the heroes, ridicules those who have gone astray, and admonishes those who think that they can go on without attention to the extended family."

Ramphele is the first black woman, and only the second woman, to head a South African university. Already there are signs that she has helped to ease UCTs difficult transition toward greater inclusiveness. Many newspapers have noted that while other South African universities have been the scenes of violence and protest, UCT has been relatively peaceful, perhaps because of Ramphele's attempts to create a climate of trust by, for example, having students participate in the drafting of the university's mission statement.

In 1992, Ramphele became the first woman and second black board member of the Anglo American Corporation, a mining conglomerate. She is also a board member of the Independent Development Trust, an organization that raises funds for educational projects.

Some activists have viewed her association with these white institutions with suspicion. In her own defense, Ramphele has insisted that "if one wants to make a difference to the structure of social relations, you've got to identify the major institutions you can influence," as she told Mary Ann French for the *Washington Post* (April 24, 1994). She has said that she has turned down many lucrative job offers in order to pursue her commitment to "human capital development," a commitment that has been consistent since her days as a BCM activist.

In 2013 Ramphele attempted to return to politics in South Africa and announced the launch of a new political party called Agang South Africa in February 2013. Agang is Northern Sotho for "build," and was intended to challenge the incumbent ruling party, the African National Congress (ANC). Agang South Africa did poorly in the general elections and gained 2 seats in the National Assembly of South Africa. Ramphele was criticized in the public eye during her short stint in the political arena when she apparently accepted an invitation from the opposition Democratic Alliance to stand as their presidential candidate in the 2014 election. Ramphele announced her withdrawal from politics in July 2014.

## PERSONAL LIFE

Ramphele remains a single parent, juggling her administrative duties with raising her two sons, Hlumelo Biko and Malusi Magele. "I don't imagine there are many black men who would like to interact with a woman like me," she told Wendy Woods. "I'm not going to cook supper or pick up underpants." In an interview for the *Chronicle of Higher Education* (November 3, 1995), she said that people who get to know her "find that I am not the witch or unreasonable militant that I am made out to be."

## FURTHER READING

*A Passion for Freedom: My Life; Children on the Frontline: A Report for Unicef on the Status of Children in South Africa; Uprooting Poverty: The South African Challenge; A Bed Called Home; Across Boundaries: The Journey of a South African Woman Leader*

---

# BERNICE JOHNSON REAGON

## Historian; Singer/Songwriter; Activist

**Born:** October 4, 1942; Doherty County, Georgia
**Primary Field:** Arts and Culture; Civil Rights Movement
**Affiliation:** Smithsonian Institute; Sweet Honey in the Rock

## INTRODUCTION

*"When I got out of jail in '61," Bernice Johnson Reagon, founder of the internationally acclaimed a cappella singing group Sweet Honey in the Rock, casually remarked to Michael Kernan for* Smithsonian *(February 1999), "I went to a mass meeting and I was hoarse because I sang all the time in jail. I opened my mouth to sing. I never heard that voice before. It was very similar to the way people describe religious conversion. For the first time I really understood what was in that singing that I had heard all my life." Jailed for her participation in a freedom march and expelled from college for her active support of the civil rights movement, Reagon embarked on a less than traditional educational journey. She traveled the country with the Student Nonvio-lent Coordinating Committee (SNCC) Freedom Singers, raising money and awareness for the fight for civil rights; organized folk festivals and collected old songs and oral traditions; and married and had two children.*

*Eventually recognizing that she needed academic legitimacy to further her goals, Reagon returned to college. She earned a PhD in history, studying oral culture and the musical traditions of the civil rights movement. Now a curator emerita at the Smithsonian Institution, a distinguished professor of history at American University, and a performer in Sweet Honey in the Rock, which specializes in politically charged songs as well as traditional African-American music, Reagon blends her backgrounds in history, music, and social activism to share her knowledge and experiences in a variety of formats. As Roger G. Kennedy, the director of the Museum of American History at the Smithsonian, told Barbara Gamarekian for the* New York Times *(June 17,1988), "Bernice is a real scholar, a hell of a performer, and a potent force here in a lot of ways. We listen to her, she discovers new truths for us all. Her special strength is the way she ties music to the social, historical, and political context of American cultural traditions." In fact, Reagon herself feels that she is on a mission. "I don't accept the world the way it works," she explained to Mary H. J. Farrell and Rochelle Jones for* People *(December 12, 1994). "I take on the world. I want to make the world the way it should be." As her daughter, Toshi, observed to Richard Harrington for the* Washington Post *(June 25, 1987), "She sometimes gets tired during her mission, but I don't think she ever gets tired of her mission."*

## EARLY LIFE

Reagon learned early on in life about hard work. Her parents each undertook more than one job while Reagon, who was born Bernice Johnson in Georgia on October 4, 1942, was growing up. Her mother, Beatrice, worked as a housekeeper and toiled in the cotton fields on her days off; her father, Jessie Johnson, was a carpenter and a Baptist minister. Her parents fostered her interests in activism and song. Her father was involved in voter registration drives as early as 1945, and her mother, although not involved in an organized effort, instilled the true meaning of activism in Bernice. "She could always see that we could operate in a different world with more opportunities," Bernice Reagon told Harrington. "She mortgaged her life to make sure we had a chance to do that. More than anybody, I take my sense of what a black woman is from her."

As a preacher's daughter, Reagon was introduced to music in church. "For the first 11 years, our church had no piano," she told Audreen Buffalo for *Ms.* (March/April 1993), "and I'm still an a cappella singer. I grew up singing in the 19th century congregational tradition, a style that can be traced to Africa. I learned three major repertoires in this style: spirituals, hymns, and children's secular play songs." She had to rely on her siblings to educate her about other styles of music. "My parents called the blues 'reals,'" she explained to Jon Pareles for the *New York Times* (April 18, 1986). "You weren't supposed to sing reals. But my brother would take the radio out of my parents' room and listen to the blues station, and since the boys' room was next to the girls' room, I'd hear them in my sleep. When I got old enough to buy records, the first one was by Howlin' Wolf, he's my favorite singer in the universe."

## LIFE'S WORK

In 1959 Reagon entered Albany State College, in her hometown of Albany, Georgia, to study Italian arias and German lieder as a contralto soloist, but her extracurricular activities put her at odds with the university administration. Fearing an onslaught of campus protests, in December 1961 school officials expelled those students, including Reagon, who were taking part in the growing civil rights movement. "On my first march in Albany, from the college, it was all students," Reagon recalled for Michael Kernan. "By the third march, when I was arrested, there were as many adults as students. The action became broader, and the songs, too. We would do our swinging freedom songs, but we'd also do old 19th century lined hymns. When the SNCC people came to town they found that the Albany sound was different. They'd heard, students sing, but they had never heard black people of all ages sing at that power level." In 1962 Reagon joined with three other SNCC members, Cordell Hull Reagon (to whom she was briefly married), Charles Nebbett, and Rutha Mae Harris, to form the SNCC Freedom Singers. Traveling the country to raise awareness and money, the group was "the movement's singing newspaper," as Audreen Buffalo described it, "reporting and defining the actions and issues from the civil rights war zones where they were frequently arrested." Only halfway through her junior year at the time of her expulsion, Reagon had transferred to Spelman College, in Atlanta, in 1962, to continue her course of classical music studies, but she completed only one semester before she dropped out to participate in the movement full-time.

The original members of the Freedom Singers disbanded in 1963, but Reagon kept herself busy organizing folk festivals and collecting and performing material drawn from African-American culture. At around the same time that Reagon divorced her husband, in the late 1960s, she grew disenchanted with the interracial folk-music circles. "I was trying to put my music in a sociopolitical context," she told Hollie I. West of the *Washington Post* (June 8, 1975). "But many white singers didn't want to address with any level of consistency the racism in this country. They focused on their own problems, like coal mining. Some of them would stop their music with the coal mining strikes of the '40s. I'd get so mad and say to them, 'Can't you get any closer to the '60s than that?'" As an alternative outlet for her singing, she organized the Harambee Singers, an all-female quartet with a social activist agenda. "[The Harambee Singers] were afraid of tape recorders," Reagon told Hollie I. West, "We saw ourselves as political activists. Everything had to be political. If somebody talked about love to us we'd think our politics was slipping." At around the time that the Harambee Singers were formed, Reagon tried to interest the Atlanta school board in a social-studies program for teaching oral traditions, but she was turned down. "I realized I could sing, I could produce festivals, I could work real well with audiences," she told Harrington, "but the minute I met the establishment structure, I would be turned around. So I went back to school, because I felt that wherever black people are, this material [oral history] should be, and that the oral process should be allowed right along with the written process." Returning to Spelman College, this time to the history department, Reagon earned her bachelor's degree in 1970. Starting in June 1970 and continuing into the following year, with the aid of a grant provided by the Southern Education Foundation, she developed a model to test the usefulness of oral traditions in public school social studies curricula.

Reagon moved to Washington, D.C., in the early 1970s to begin studies for her doctoral degree in history at Howard University. Because the school did not have a program in oral history, she completed a number of interdisciplinary independent studies while simultaneously pursuing passions outside academia. Since the late 1960s Reagon had been working as a field researcher for the Smithsonian Institution on a consultant basis. In 1972 she agreed to head what she christened the African Diaspora program, a research group formed to showcase African-American culture at the Smithsonian Institution Bicentennial Festival of American Folklife, which focused on various aspects of American culture. "Old Ways in the New World," one of the central themes of that festival, allowed Reagon to send scholars of black culture to Africa, the Caribbean, and South America and then to present to the public the antecedent cultural practices, such as cooking and music, of the Old World alongside the descendant practices of the New World. The program was the first in the Smithsonian's history to attempt to present African-American culture, and it met a lot of resistance and criticism from those who felt it couldn't be done or shouldn't be done in the way in which Reagon had envisioned it. "One of the most wonderful things that happened to me as a scholar," Reagon told Marvette Perez for the *Radical History Review* (Spring 1997, online), "was that one of the folklorists who had said about our festival program for the bicentennial, 'you can't do this concept and apply it to African Americans,' came to the program and said, 'I opposed this, but I was wrong, this absolutely worked.' That was really, really great. But others would

bring people there to look at what we were doing to actually say it was bad so that they could justify eliminating it." Reagon, who had hired only African-American scholars, was herself accused of being racist. Although at the time she didn't respond to that charge, she later admitted to Marvette Perez that the accusations were true: "Blacks who were coming up in university departments of folklore and ethnomusicology were not getting any of the grants to do field research. Therefore their CVs never looked right. And there were whites who were doing their field research and their dissertation research in Africa, all over the Caribbean, but Blacks in those same departments had difficulty securing support to do research outside of the United States. So as a result of our program several African American scholars were hired to conduct field research in these regions."

As if her work with the Smithsonian were not enough to keep her busy, Reagon assumed two more posts in 1972, spending the summer as a visiting lecturer in Black American music at Ithaca College, in Ithaca, New York, and serving as vocal director at the D.C. Black Repertory Theater Company. In the latter position she held a singing workshop that brought together four men and four women, but the group dissolved after a couple of months. At the urging of one woman, Reagon agreed to organize another workshop. Only four women showed up. "I was disappointed," she admitted to Richard Harrington, "but I was fairly dictatorial, so I started singing and it just fell in place and it was tight And we got through the first song and we looked at each other and went 'Yeah!' We went song after song after song and everything was right" The first song they sang was "Sweet Honey in the Rock," a song from Reagon's youth. "When I asked my father about its meaning," she told Audreen Buffalo, "he said it was a parable that referred to a land where, when rocks were cracked, honey would flow from them." Feeling that the image was an appropriate symbol of African-American womanhood, Reagon dubbed the new ensemble Sweet Honey in the Rock.

Over its more than 25 year history, Sweet Honey has comprised 22 members, though never more than five singers at a time; in 1980 a sign-language artist, Shirley Childress Johnson, was added. The group's sound is built on complex five-part harmony; the styles of doo-wop, gospel, soul, jazz, blues, folk, rap, and traditional African and Caribbean music are coupled with socially relevant subject matter. From the beginning Sweet Honey in the Rock proved very popular with audiences, even though its members, who hold down other jobs during the workweek, perform only on weekends. "The group saved my life and it made it possible for me to work at the Smithsonian," Reagon explained to Marvette Perez. "People would say to the women in Sweet Honey: 'Why aren't you singers full-time?' And we would say, 'Why should we be? Why should we choose between areas of work that we love to do, that combined makes us whole.'"

From February 1973 to May of the following year, Reagon was a teaching fellow in the School of Music at Howard University. In 1974 she also officially joined the staff of the Smithsonian fulltime, as the director of the African Diaspora Program in the Division of Performing Arts. That year, and again the next year, she traveled to Africa to do field research for the program. In 1975, after completing her dissertation entitled "Songs of the Civil Rights Movement, 1955-1965: A Study in Culture History," she received her PhD and began working as a lecturer in the History department at the University of the District of Columbia. At a folk festival hosted by the University of Chicago that year, *Sweet Honey in the Rock* was offered a recording deal with Flying Fish Records after a representative of the company heard them perform. Their first album, Sweet Honey in the Rock, was released in 1976, the same year that Reagon became the director of the Program in African American Culture (PAAC), a permanent program that grew out of the African Diaspora project. She also worked that summer as a visiting scholar in black culture and history at the American Studies Summer Institute at Skidmore College. In 1977 Reagon finished her stints as the vocal director at the D.C. Black Repertory Theater Company and lecturer at the University of the District of Columbia. That spring, she was a visiting fellow in black American culture at the University of California at Santa Cruz, and in the summer of 1980, she was a visiting fellow in the women's studies program at Portland State University.

In 1982 the PAAC was moved to the Public Programs division of the National Museum of American History, after the Smithsonian's Division of the Performing Arts was dismantled. Reagon designed the infrastructure of the PAAC and did not immediately notice the difference between her program and others in Public Programs. Instead of acting as a producer hiring writers and singers to present material, she and her staff conducted the research and found a way to present it to the public themselves. Part of her responsibilities

included fighting to ensure that her program received every penny of the $50,000 budget allotted by Congress. "And that was the beginning of my moving in the museum in a way in which nobody was supposed to move," she told Marvette Perez.

In 1988 Sweet Honey in the Rock won the Grammy Award for best traditional folk recording for its version of Leadbelly's "Grey Goose." Reagon decided to make a transition in her museum career that same year, leaving behind the directorship of the PAAC to become a curator in the Division of Community Life, a position that allowed her more time for research. Even though she had been studying black culture and oral traditions at the Smithsonian for almost 15 years by that point, she still met with constraints. "When I first came into the Division of Community Life as a curator," she told Marvette Perez, "I remember the collections manager saying to me: 'Here, we are interested in collecting three-dimensional objects,' and I thought, oh, here I go again. Why can't I just go someplace and just do what everybody else is doing? I remember when I asked for a promotion. They have a peer review committee, and I talked to the chairman of the committee, and he said, This is interesting, I wonder how people are going to look at this.' And the whole issue was that my work did not look like anything they were used to evaluating: it did not fit the usual curatorial categories." In 1989 she received a grant from the MacArthur Foundation, commonly called the "genius" grant, which she used in part to further her research for the museum.

In 1991 Reagon was profiled in a documentary entitled *The Songs Are Free: Bernice Johnson Reagon with Bill Moyers*. She also received a Candace Award for outstanding achievement from the National Coalition of 100 Black Women, a nonprofit organization that encourages leadership, development, and employment opportunities for black women. In 1993 Reagon was appointed distinguished professor of history at American University, and in January 1994 she became a curator emerita at the Smithsonian. In the same month, portions of the project she had worked on at the Smithsonian for the previous 10 years, *Wade in the Water: African American Sacred Music Traditions*, began airing on the radio. Consisting of 26 one-hour segments and supplemental educational materials, *Wade in the Water* traces the development of sacred music and its reciprocal impact on black history and culture. The program, produced conjointly by the Smithsonian and National Public Radio and funded in part by a portion of Reagon's MacArthur grant, won a Peabody Award for significant and meritorious achievement in broadcasting.

The awards continued to come Reagon's way. In 1995 the National Endowment for the Humanities awarded her the Charles Frankel Prize for outstanding contribution to public understanding of the humanities, for which she was honored at the White House. In 1996 she won the Isadora Duncan Award for her score to Rock, a ballet directed by Alonzo King for the LINES Contemporary Ballet Company. In that same year she also completed the traveling exhibition for *Wade in the Water*, which was set to tour in 16 U.S. cities over a period of four years.

In addition to her work in theater, film, and video, Reagon has written articles for numerous journals and anthologies and has made solo recordings. During her 1997 interview with Marvette Perez, she said, "I've had young people ask me how was I able to do so much. And I suggest that I'm not a good model, it really was over-extension. It's not a normal life to do what I did. But people who are oppressed cannot live a 'normal' life. Baby, you try to live a normal life if you're oppressed, you will never be free. I think you have to over-extend yourself."

On May 30, 1996, recognizing that she could not keep up the frenetic pace required for all her activities, Reagon resigned as the sole artistic director of Sweet Honey. She agreed, however, to become one of the six members of the new artistic directorship. Two years later, in 1998, Sweet Honey celebrated its 25th anniversary with the release of its album, *twenty-five*. On the same day Reagon also released *Africans in America*, a soundtrack that she had produced, compiled, and composed for a public-television documentary of the same name. She collaborated with Souleymane Koly on an opera that premiered in Abidjan, Ivory Coast, in 2001.

## PERSONAL LIFE

Although Reagon has not slowed her pace in recent years, she has learned to prioritize better. "As I've gotten older," she told Geoffrey Himes for the *Washington Post* (November 20, 1998), "I've felt it was important to reduce the amount of work I'm doing. I've had a very productive and intense life, but as I've gotten older, I had to find ways to keep doing this work and still keep myself going. And I've done it. I've found ways to do the work I love to do, whether it's singing or composing or doing research or teaching or working on radio and TV series, without carrying so much of the weight of the infrastructure." Reagon's son, Kwan, is a cook; her daughter, Toshi, is a musician.

## FURTHER READING

*Compositions One: The Original Compositions and Arrangements of Bernice Johnson Reagon; We'll Understand It Better By and By: African American Pioneering Gospel Composers; We Who Believe in Freedom: Sweet Honey In The Rock . . . Still on the Journey*

# CONSTANCE L. RICE

## Lawyer; Activist

**Born:** April 5, 1956; Washington, D.C.
**Primary Field:** Civil Rights
**Affiliation:** The Advancement Project

### INTRODUCTION

*The civil rights lawyer and activist Constance "Connie" Rice does not hesitate to tell people that in her job, she walks a tightrope. As the co-founder of the public advocacy and legal action group Advancement Project, the former litigator serves as a mediator between some of the poorest communities in Los Angeles, California, and the city's power structure, and between violent gangs and police officers who have sometimes been too willing to use force against them. "It may blow up in my face," she said about her work to Diane Lefer for the Chapel Hill, North Carolina based publication the* Sun *(April 2008), "but I'm trying to clear a place where new ideas can be vetted and tested. We have to create some safe zones for innovative people in both camps." She said to Lefer, "I always begin with the question, 'Who has the power to change this?' Sometimes it's the voters. When it comes to police reform, it's the police. I need to ally myself with the people who can solve the problem." Rice works tirelessly to end street violence, which she calls a "disease," through strategies that counter the forceful tactics used by police. She told Lefer, "My strategy is to figure out what people need in order to create change themselves." The last 20 years have seen "an epidemic of youth gang homicide," Rice told students at the University of California at Los Angeles in 2010, "which means that our kids are killing each other at such a high rate that epidemiologists are classifying it as an epidemic. We can't arrest our way out of this problem." Instead, Rice called for a "24/7 effort to build up the community so that they are inoculated against the virus that is violence." Most recently, Rice was enlisted by the U.S. Department of Defense to share innovative strategies for dealing with insurgencies in Iraq and Afghanistan, which have similarities to gang activity in the U.S.*

### EARLY LIFE

A second cousin of former U.S. secretary of state Condoleezza Rice (their fathers were first cousins), Constance LaMay Rice was born on April 5, 1956 in Washington, D.C. She has two younger brothers. Her mother, Anna L. (Barnes) Rice, was a science teacher, and her father, Phillip Leon Rice, was a colonel in the U.S. Air Force. Because of her father's career, the family moved often, and most of Rice's childhood was spent on military bases around the U.S. and abroad. Writing for the *Daily Beast* (October 18, 2010, online), Christine Pelisek described Rice as a "precocious and strong-willed" child. "At the age of 5," Pelisek wrote, "Connie was a budding champion of underdogs who, at the Cleveland Zoo, tried to coerce her brother into helping her free a lion." Education was very important to the Rice family. Genethia Hayes, a close friend of Rice's, told Pelisek that Rice's parents impressed upon their daughter the "obligation to do something credible and courageous and meaningful with your life." Rice attended Town and Country School in London, England, and graduated from Universal City High School, in Texas, in 1974. At 18, during her senior year, Rice offered to do all of the family ironing so that she could stay home from school and watch television coverage of the U.S. Senate hearings on the Watergate scandal. The scandal involved the break-in at Democratic National Committee headquarters at the Watergate complex, in Washington, D.C., by Republican operatives and the subsequent cover up by members of President Richard M. Nixon's administration. In July, when the House Judiciary Committee considered articles of impeachment against Nixon, Rice became entranced by the committee member and Democratic representative Barbara Jordan of Texas, who called for the impeachment of the president. Nixon resigned and was pardoned by his successor, Gerald R. Ford. Jordan was the first African-American congresswoman to be elected from the Deep South; her participation in the hearings made her a national figure. Inspired by Jordan, Rice decided to study law.

Rice attended Harvard University, in Cambridge, Massachusetts, where she received a B.A. degree in government in 1978. Her time there, shortly after the school became co-ed and during a particularly nasty desegregation battle was difficult. "When I was at Harvard, I never felt blacker in my life," Rice told Scott Shibuya Brown for the *Los Angeles Times* (November 27, 1994). "It was never an issue until I went there. It was a hostile environment in which to learn. Everything about you was under siege." During her first year, she

---

## Affiliation: The Advancement Project

In 1998 Rice left the Legal Defense Fund when she, Stephen R. English, and Molly Munger founded the nonprofit group Advancement Project, of which Rice is a co-director. The firm of English, Munger, & Rice handles the legal aspects of the Advancement Project's work, while the organization focuses on alternatives to litigation in its efforts to "dismantle structural barriers to inclusion, secure racial equity, and expand opportunity for all," as its website states. According to the site, the group's mission is "to develop, encourage, and widely disseminate innovative ideas, and pioneer models that inspire and mobilize a broad national racial justice movement to achieve universal opportunity and a just democracy." The group was instrumental in raising $25 billion for new school facilities throughout the state of California, including $5 billion to relieve overcrowding in urban schools.

---

was badly beaten by a classmate she had refused to date. Resolving to never again find herself defenseless, she studied the Korean martial art Tae Kwon Do, and by the time she graduated from Harvard, she was a national champion in the sport. In 1980 Rice was awarded both a first degree black belt and the Root Tilden Public Interest Scholarship to attend the New York University School of Law. She earned her J.D. degree in 1984.

## LIFE'S WORK

During law school Rice served as a clerk for the State of New York Department of Law in 1982 and was mentored by Lani Guinier, then with the NAACP Legal Defense Fund, in 1983. After graduation she clerked for Judge Damon J. Keith of the U.S. Court of Appeals for the Sixth Circuit in Detroit, Michigan, from 1984 to 1986. As a clerk, Rice, who told Lefer that she views capital punishment as an "obscenity," filed petitions on behalf of death row prisoners, among them a white supremacist. While her efforts failed in his case, the prisoner sent Rice a thank you note before his execution. Also during those years Rice became involved with the case of a deathrow inmate, Billy Moore, a young black man accused of killing a friend's uncle after a drunken altercation. Thanks to her work on his behalf, Moore was released in 1989. During her time as a law clerk, some of her male colleagues tried to limit her work to menial tasks and exclude her from important discussions, going so far as to make decisions in the men's room; when Rice and another female clerk discovered that practice, they began following the men inside.

Rice worked as an associate for the firm of Morrison and Foster, in San Francisco, California, from 1986 to 1987. In the latter year she served as special assistant to the associate vice chancellor of the University of California, Los Angeles, and in 1990 she joined the NAACP Legal Defense and Educational Fund in Los Angeles as western regional counsel; she eventually became co-director of the office. She also became president of the Los Angeles Department of Water and Power, a post she held from 1990 to 1995.

In 1992 the acquittal in the first Rodney King trial, in which four white police officers were tried for beating King, a black man, in an event captured on videotape, spawned riots in Los Angeles. In the wake of the violence, Rice was credited with fostering the truce between the city's infamous Bloods and Crips gangs. The gang leaders had decided that retribution killings, often for trivial offenses, had to stop. They modeled their truce on the Camp David Peace Accords between the Israelis and the Egyptians, with Rice supplying the gangs with copies of documents relating to the accords. She joked to Lefer, "I was like their research assistant." The truce, though no longer in effect, led to a significant drop in street violence. For Rice the truce proved that change could be enacted from within the community.

In 1993 gang leaders called upon Rice, whom they had come to see as a neutral, trustworthy figure, a second time. The occasion was Easter weekend (a time of many outdoor festivities), just before the verdict was to be announced in the civil trial of the officers accused of beating King; the city was on edge, with police, expecting the worst, preparing to don riot gear. As Rice recalled to Lefer, a gang member called her and said, "You need to call the police chief and tell him there are going to be some dead cops." Rice telephoned a police captain, Bruce Haggerty, and urged him to have officers in his division set aside their riot gear and enlist gang-intervention workers instead. The plan worked, and the weekend proceeded peacefully (perhaps aided by the verdict: two officers were convicted of violating King's civil rights). Those events marked the beginning of Rice's consistent role as mediator between the gangs and the LAPD.

Rice had brought many abuse-of-force lawsuits against the LAPD. "We won all of them," she told Lefer, "but we hadn't made a dent in the problem." Rice admitted, "I had fun suing them. They were so awful to our clients, and so racist and sexist and brutal." A canine unit case in 1992 changed Rice's approach to her work. The case involved the high number of incidents in which police dogs, handled by brutal officers, bit suspects, usually gang members or juvenile delinquents. Rice presented the statistics to the judge: the dogs had an 80 percent bite rate, and victims had a 47 percent hospitalization rate. When the judge suggested that the LAPD settle the case, the department asked the city for money to fix the problem themselves. "I recognized their sincerity," Rice told Lefer, "so we told the city to give them the money." Within six months the bite rate was 5 percent; the canine unit had fired some officers and hired replacements. That case led Rice to think of other ways to end what she called the "mentality of brutality" among officers. "Of course, one of the first lessons I learned was that they don't call it 'brutality.' They call it 'good policing,'" she told Lefer. "My language shut down the debate. I wasn't communicating. I was still fighting them."

From 1997 to 2001 the LAPD was embroiled in the Rampart corruption scandal, so named for the area of Los Angeles in which many police officers were accused of illegal activities that included stealing drugs from evidence rooms and killing or beating suspects and then framing them to hide the officers' abuses. In one such case Javier Ovando, an unarmed gang member, was shot and left paralyzed by Officer Rafael Perez and his partner. The officers then framed Ovando and testified against him in court. As the scandal and the subsequent trials ensued, the LAPD was accused of minimizing the scandal and failing to address the depth of corruption within the department. The city was the target of more than 200 lawsuits, resulting in the overturning of 156 felony convictions (including Ovando's), the prosecution of nine officers and the firing or suspension of 23, and the awarding of $70 million in legal settlements. In 2003 Rice was asked to author a report on whether the city had adequately addressed the causes of the police misconduct and, if not, what needed to be done.

Rice spent two years talking to various groups of officers in the LAPD. She asked about the practice of shielding corrupt officers and, as Melanie Mack wrote for the *Los Angeles Sentinel* (July 13, 2006), looked for ways to alleviate "the rampant mistrust and open hostility between poor underclass communities" and the police. She found that the LAPD was woefully understaffed and, as a result, had taken to overreaction and use of excessive force in many situations. "When you have too few officers," Rice told Lefer, "they puff themselves up like porcupines to look more fierce than they are." She encouraged the police to reward officers for improving communities rather than simply making arrests, because, she told Lefer, "if no one gets promoted for making sure a kid doesn't get arrested, why should anyone do it?" Of her research, she told Lefer, "I brought together police, gang intervention workers, sociologists, educators, demographers, and epidemiologists who study violence as a disease, a real dream team of experts on gangs. And that team told the city and the county what they had to do to end a youth gang homicide epidemic that their policies had helped create." Rice summed up her findings and recommendations in the landmark 2007 report "A Call to Action: The Case for Comprehensive Solutions to Los Angeles' Gang Epidemic." The report, which has been called "the Marshall Plan for gangs," called for programs balancing law enforcement with crime prevention. Rice currently co-chairs a commission to reform the LAPD's training and incentive programs.

Rice's report found that despite a decline in crime in the nation as a whole, crime in Los Angeles was surging; she also found that factions of larger gangs were spreading to other cities. Rice has been an outspoken critic of the methods employed by the LAPD in addressing gang violence, especially a policy called "containment suppression," which, Rice told Lefer, "actually guarantees high levels of violence in poor areas" by making sure it does not spread to other areas in the city. The LAPD, she argued, is "not there to provide public safety" but "to make sure the violence doesn't spread." The result, Rice reported, is bleak. "I started looking at some of the conditions in the communities where the violence was," Rice told Lefer. "The levels of post-traumatic stress disorder among children in hot spots for gang activity are the same as in [the war-torn Iraqi cities of] Mosul and Baghdad." The most recent official statistic, according to Landesman, is 47 percent. Those alarming levels of violence have not escaped the attention of the federal government; the U.S. military, according to Landesman, sends medics to train in local Los Angeles trauma units because the conditions there so closely resemble those of warfare.

At the height of the gang violence, in 2007, the number of gangs in Los Angeles County was estimated at more than 714, with upwards of 80,000 members, according to Peter Landesman, writing for *LA Weekly* (December 13, 2007). Many of the gangs formed in the 1960s from communities of African-Americans, Hispanics, Asians, and other racial and ethnic groups. Crimes committed by those gangs were comparatively minor, including petty theft and fistfights between rivals. In the 1980s drug trafficking was introduced into the gang culture, giving members a stronger reason to protect their home turf as they competed for customers. Drugs alone, however, do not account for the current state of affairs in Los Angeles, the country's epicenter of gang violence, with 70 percent of all homicides in the city attributed to street gangs. Landesman interviewed Father Gregory Boyle, a Jesuit priest and founder of Homeboy Industries, which helps reform gang members in the mostly Hispanic East L.A. neighborhood; Landesman wrote, "[Boyle] tells me that gang behavior is changing, and the change is chilling. Everywhere he sees signs of the erosion of known and protected codes of conduct, such as methods of assassination that used to protect the innocent, and territorial respect, which he says reflect an accelerating sense of desolation among poor urban youth. Gangs today are less about neighborhoods and rivalries. They've become repositories for hopelessness." Rice's experiences have mirrored those of Father Boyle. She talked to one gang member, she told Lefer, asking him where he saw himself in 10 years; "I don't," he replied.

The *Los Angeles Times* has called Rice one of "the most experienced, civic-minded, and thoughtful people on the subject of Los Angeles," and the publication California Law Business placed her on a list of the 10 most influential lawyers in the state. Rice has expressed an unwavering faith in the voices of individuals and the power of community and grassroots activism, because, as she told Lefer, "power concedes nothing without a demand." In her work during the 1990s for the Legal Defense Fund of the National Association for the Advancement of Colored People (NAACP), the nation's oldest and largest civil rights group, she is credited with winning $1.6 billion in awards in civil rights and class- action lawsuits; those include a landmark 1996 civil rights case against the Metropolitan Transit Authority (MTA) of Los Angeles, in which she won a decision in favor of the Bus Riders Union that allocated substantial funding to improve bus service in poorer neighborhoods. In

2000 she won a lawsuit that brought $750 million from the city for construction of new schools.

Despite her victories, Rice began to question the value of litigation as a means to effect change. "I always thought of litigation as the battering ram," she explained to Lefer. "You use it to break open the front door and make room for people to enter. Law is easy if you're in it only to win cases. But if I win a case against the police department and then send my clients back to a neighborhood where they dodge bullets and their kids aren't getting educated and their medical benefits have been cut off because they lost their second job, how much of a victory is that? Litigation," she concluded, "can't do the delicate work of creating the political will to solve problems." Rice has dedicated the past 12 years to such "delicate work," devoting her time and energy to engage with gangs in Los Angeles and staunch their proliferation.

Rice's supporters and enemies alike call her fearless; she has sued the Los Angeles Police Department (LAPD), the Los Angeles Housing Authority, and the Department of Water and Power (of which she was briefly president). "Many of my friends are in office. I've been suing my friends for 20 years," Rice told Lefer. "Even when you know the people in power, you still have to be a burr under their saddle and demand change."

In the summer of 2008, Rice teamed up with the city of Los Angeles to implement a program called "Summer Night Lights," which for the past three years has offered recreational activities, mentoring and counseling programs, meals, and other services at parks and housing complexes four days a week until midnight, safe activities during the times when most violent crimes occur. By 2010 the program was operating at 24 sites, feeding an average of 10,929 people free meals each night. In places where people were once afraid to turn on their lights at night for fear of drive-by shootings, the results were striking: "Overall, serious gang related crime has fallen 40.4% in the Summer Night Lights neighborhoods when compared with the summer of 2007," Scott Gold reported for the *Los Angeles Times* (October 31, 2010). "These neighborhoods are capable of transforming themselves away from violence," Deputy Mayor Guillermo Cespedes, who runs City Hall's Office of Gang Reduction and Youth Development, told Gold. "They will choose this over body bags. The city cannot afford to not do this program. It doesn't solve all of the problems we need to solve. But it is a wise strategy."

## PERSONAL LIFE

When contacted by the Defense Department to help quell insurgencies in Iraq and Afghanistan, Rice at first thought the department had confused her as others have, with her famous second cousin, Condoleezza Rice. The two met as adults, and while they do not share political views, they have formed a close friendship. After it was established that it was Constance Rice the Defense Department sought, Rice began applying the experience and expertise she has gained in her work with Los Angeles gangs to anti-insurgency strategies in the two war-torn countries.

Among dozens of other awards, Rice received an honorary doctorate from Occidental College in 2003, and in 2004 she was given the Women Lawyers of Los Angeles Ernestine Stahlhut Award. She is an occasional commentator for both National Public Radio and the *Huffington Post* and has appeared on *Nightline,* the *Oprah Winfrey Show*, and other TV programs. She published her first book *Power Concedes Nothing: One Woman's Quest for Social Justice in America*, from the *Courtroom to the Kill Zones* in 2012 to critical acclaim. Rice lives in Los Angeles.

## FURTHER READING

*Power Concedes Nothing: One Woman's Quest for Social Justice in America, from the Courtroom to the Kill Zones; advancementproject.org*

---

# CECILE RICHARDS

## Feminist; Activist

**Born:** July 15, 1957; Waco, Texas
**Primary Field:** Gender Equality; Family Planning/ Health
**Affiliation:** Planned Parenthood Federation of America

## INTRODUCTION

*In a climate in which the issue of health care has grown increasingly politicized, the traditionally nonpartisan organization Planned Parenthood Federation of America (PPFA) is becoming more politicized as well. The organization's decision in February 2006 to turn for leadership to Cecile Richards, the first PPFA president since its founding, in 1916, whose background is not in health care but in politics, is the foremost indicator of that shift. A daughter of the late Ann Richards, a governor of Texas and two-term state treasurer, she has been involved in politics and organizing for much of her life. As a college student and for years afterward, she coordinated grassroots efforts ranging from helping to unionize janitors in Los Angeles, California, to mobilizing hotel workers in New Orleans, Louisiana. After she returned to her native Texas, she formed the Texas Freedom Network, a group dedicated to monitoring and combating the expanding influence of conservative Christians on Texas school boards. After pro-choice work with the Turner Foundation and a stint as*

*deputy chief of staff for Democratic U.S. congresswoman Nancy Pelosi of California (currently the Speaker of the House), Richards became president of America Votes, a coalition of Democratic interest groups. During her time with America Votes, she was often praised for her persistence and diplomacy in bringing together disparate groups. Her supporters have noted that such characteristics and skills will serve her well as she tries to reenergize the pro-choice movement, which has lost much of its urgency in the decades since the U.S. Supreme Court's decision in* Roe v. Wade *(1973), which ruled as unconstitutional most state and federal laws that outlawed or restricted abortions. "For today's increasingly anti-choice, burned-out climate, Richards is just what Planned Parenthood's legendary founder, Margaret Sanger, might have ordered: quietly confident, friendly, and genuine," Jennifer Baumgardner wrote for the* Nation *(November 13, 2006). "Cecile has 'it' the way some people just have it," Jatrice Martel Gaiter, the head of Planned Parenthood Metropolitan Washington, told Baumgardner. "'It' being charm, class, beauty, brains, and being tough as nails." In light of her political pedigree and extensive experience, Richards has often been asked to run for elective office, but she has turned down all entreaties, preferring to remain in the more hands-on role of an organizer. "I love organizing," she told Dave McNeely for the* Austin (Texas) American-Statesman *(July 15,1998). "I love building something where there was nothing, giving people an opportunity to do something for themselves, particularly women." Richards told Robin Finn for the* New York Times *(March 11, 2006) that her job at Planned Parenthood is perfect for her at this stage of her career. "I've had the luxury all my life of having jobs where I got to feel like I was making an enormous difference in the lives of working people, and coming to Planned Parenthood is like coming full circle. I'm serving the women who grew up in the same families I was organizing. It feels totally right."*

## EARLY LIFE

The first of the two daughters and two sons of David Richards and Ann Richards (the former Dorothy Ann Willis), Cecile Richards was born on July 15, 1957 in Waco, Texas. Her father was a labor and civil rights attorney; at the time of her birth and for more than a dozen years afterward, her mother was a homemaker. During Richards's early years, in Dallas, both of her parents were active in Democratic politics in Texas. "I grew up in a very political family," she told S. C. Gwynne for *Texas Monthly* (August 2004). "Other families did bowling. We did politics." "Our four kids grew up in an atmosphere where you could not eat on the dining room table because it was always full of political mailings," Ann Richards, who died in 2006, told Gwynne. "When they were really small, they could fold letters and stuff them into envelopes and seal them. As they progressed in their abilities, they learned how to put a stamp on them and sort them out by precinct." The first dance Richards attended, when she was nine, was the kickoff for a protest march on the state capitol, in Austin, by Chicano farmworkers. When Richards was 10 she started a recycling campaign in her household. One day when she was 12, she wore a black armband to school to protest the Vietnam War and was sent home. In 1969 the Richards family moved to Austin. Two years later Cecile became the first female page in the Texas State Senate. In 1972, while attending Saint Stephen's Episcopal School, a private Austin high school, she worked on the successful campaign for a seat in the state House of Representatives of Sarah Weddington, one of the attorneys who, in 1971 and 1972, represented "Jane Roe" (the pro-choice side) in arguments before the U.S. Supreme Court in the case of *Roe v. Wade*. (Ann Richards managed Weddington's campaign and became her administrative assistant.)

After Richards graduated from high school, in 1975, she enrolled at Brown University, in Providence, Rhode Island, where she majored in history. As an undergraduate she actively supported a janitors' movement for better working conditions on campus. She earned a bachelor's degree from Brown in 1980. Richards told Diane Jennings for the *Dallas Morning News* (March 12, 2006) that her sense of duty contributed to her choice of career. "I had lived a very privileged life. I had an education that very few, very few people are so fortunate to get, and what was I going to give back?" After her graduation Richards became involved in various movements across the country; she organized garment workers in the Rio Grande Valley, nursing home employees in East Texas (an area encompassing all or parts of 49 counties), janitors in Los Angeles, and hotel workers in New Orleans, Louisiana. In New Orleans she met her future husband, Kirk Adams, who was also a labor organizer. The couple married in 1982.

## LIFE'S WORK

In 1990, Richards and Adams moved with their first child, a daughter, to Austin to help with Ann Richards's campaign for Texas governor. By that point Ann's political career was moving at full steam. The elder Richards endured a brutal campaign, which included frequent references to her former (and admitted) problems with alcoholism and unfounded allegations of drug problems. She narrowly won the race, becoming the first female governor of Texas to be elected in her own right. The previous female governor, Miriam A. "Ma" Ferguson, had run for office and served as a proxy for her husband, James E. "Pa" Ferguson, who had been impeached and removed from the governorship. In 1994 Richards helped with her mother's reelection campaign, this time against the Republican George W. Bush. Ann suffered a surprising defeat, losing to Bush by 7 percentage points. Although the loss was a blow for the Richards family, in some ways it helped Cecile. "I think my mom's loss was a liberating thing," Richards told Nancy Kruh for the *Dallas Morning News* (July 5, 1996). "I was no longer the governor's daughter." Nevertheless, Richards was deeply disturbed and angered by the smear campaigns against her mother, which included suggestions that her mother promoted homosexuality and was possibly a lesbian herself. "The whole tone and feeling about politics had changed, just in four years," she recalled to Kruh. "I was really alarmed by the whole dynamic of politics. I was really concerned that people were feeling very hateful. They were on a mission to eradicate these 'godless, anti-family officials' they thought were ruining the country."

Rather than blaming Republicans for the poisoning of the political atmosphere, Richards took a nonpartisan stance, focusing her energy on the increasing power of conservative Christian groups in Texas. In 1995 she founded the Texas Freedom Network, a nonprofit, nonpartisan group that, according to its Web site, "advances a mainstream agenda of religious freedom and individual liberties to counter the religious right"; currently, its membership includes more than 26,000 members of the clergy and community leaders. Richards formed the alliance in response to what she and many others saw as a movement by conservative Christian groups to win seats on local Texas school boards, where they could push for changes in school curriculums to mirror their personal beliefs, particularly in connection with school prayer and the controversial topics of evolution and creationism. "Regardless of party or background, people are not comfortable with extremists taking over, whether in the schools or in their political party or in running government," Richards told Sue Anne Pressley for the *Washington* Post (November 7, 1995). "They [the Christian right] definitely have a right to be involved and I applaud their efforts. Our concern is when folks with a fairly extreme ideology want to run everything and there's no room for people who look at things differently." In deciding to establish the organization, Richards was inspired by the example of her mother; as she told Kruh, "One thing my mom would always say to us is, 'What's the worst that could possibly happen?' I decided the worst thing is I could wake up when I was 70 and say, 'I wish I'd done that.' And that would be worse than any failure." In the early days of the network, Richards could afford to pay only herself and one full-time assistant, because she depended entirely on donations for funding; the rest of the work was handled by a band of devoted volunteers. The response of many sectors of the public to news of the group's formation was "amazing," as she recalled to Pressley. "The interesting thing to me is the diversity of folks. I was thinking this would only appeal to people who are very political. But what I'm finding are PTA [Parent Teacher Association] moms, people who have served on school boards, people who have been run out of their own churches. When you get right down to it, the question is, is the mainstream finally going to organize?" Members of the religious right, not surprisingly, reacted

negatively to the alliance's activities. "I think, by and large, they simply follow us around," Wyatt Roberts, the executive director of the Texas chapter of the conservative Christian group the American Family Association, told Sue Anne Pressley. "From what I can tell, they have no agenda other than to oppose conservative Christians. I think it goes deeper, though. I think there's a sincere dislike for Christians. I think it's religious bigotry."

To counter such claims, and to promote a more mainstream version of Christianity throughout the state by involving religious leaders in speaking out against aspects of conservative Christian movements, in 1996 Richards formed the Texas Faith Network, as an arm of the Texas Freedom Network (which already had religious leaders among its members). Richards, who was raised a Unitarian and had embraced Methodism as an adult, has said that her difficulties with politically and socially conservative Christians helped her to clarify her own religious beliefs. "I've said to people on the right, I have to thank them for getting me back to my religious faith," she told Kruh. "The Methodist church, besides my family, has been the single most important support this year." Jim Rigby, a Presbyterian minister and an early member of the Texas Freedom Network, praised Richards for her balanced approach to their work. "Her genes should be donkey-like, but she doesn't want to be a talking head for the Democrats," he told Kruh. "The issues are much deeper than that. The principles that animate her activities belong to both parties." Richards told Kruh, "I've made the best friends and best enemies in the past year." She also said, "I don't seek controversy, but we all have an obligation to stand up for what we believe in, no matter the consequences. That sounds so heroic, but that's the way I was brought up."

In 1998 Bill White, the chairman of the Texas state Democratic Party, announced that he Would not run for another term. Richards, who by then had three children, was the party favorite for the position, but she decided not to run. "For the first time, we really faced what being a full-time party chair would require and the sacrifices it would mean for us as a family," she told Ken Herman for the *Austin American-Statesman* (April 29, 1998). That year Richards's husband accepted the position of chief organizer of the AFL-CIO (the American Federation of Labor and Congress of Industrial Organizations), an association of national and international labor unions, and the family moved to Washington, D.C. There, Richards became involved in a variety of causes. She served as an AFL-CIO organizing director before working with the Turner Foundation (which makes grants in the areas of environmental conservation and population control), designing and directing a pro-choice project. She also created and served as president of Pro-Choice Vote, the largest 527 political committee active in the 2000 election season. Such organizations, named for the section of the federal tax code that regulates them, are permitted to raise unlimited amounts of money as long as they do not use the funds to actively support or oppose specific candidates. In 2002 Richards became deputy chief of staff for Congresswoman Nancy Pelosi, shortly after Pelosi's colleagues elected her the minority whip of the House. During the first year of her 18-month stint as Pelosi's aide, Pelosi won election as House minority leader.

Federal campaign finance reform measures in 2002 led to Richards's next job: president of America Votes, a Washington-based coalition of unions and liberal interest groups, founded in mid-2003, which was allowed to receive unlimited donations as long as it did not communicate directly with, or run advertisements for or against, specific candidates; it could, however, run ads about specific issues, which would imply which candidates the organization supported or opposed. Conservatives vehemently criticized America Votes, and some, among them Richard Poe, a senior fellow at the Center for the Study of Population Culture, a conservative think tank, questioned the coalition's legality. "The organization she ran was nothing more than a way to circumvent the campaign finance laws against groups that illegally coordinate with a political party," Poe told Michael Anft for the *Chronicle of Philanthropy* (March 23,2006). America Votes raised more than $350 million in 2003-04, most of which was spent to register voters in localities where the majority of residents were believed to be sympathetic to the Democratic Party platform. The party has historically been plagued by factionalism, which has caused many people to regard it as little more than a collection of strident special-interest groups; America Votes was an effort to coordinate Democrats' efforts in pursuit of the greater goal of electing a Democratic president. Although the 2004 Democratic presidential candidate, Senator John Kerry of Massachusetts, lost his bid for the White House, Richards considered America Votes to be a success. "I think it really grew into a much stronger coalition just because folks realized the benefit of people joining hands and working together from the labor movement, the environmental movement, women's movement, civil rights

movement," she told Robert Siegel for National Public Radio's Election Day news special (November 2, 2004), "And what we saw today was just an unbelievable coming together of this coalition across the country from Pennsylvania to Florida."

On February 15, 2006 Richards succeeded the interim president of PPFA, Karen Pearl, who had replaced Gloria Feldt, Planned Parenthood's head from 1996 to 2005. PPFA is the nation's largest provider of sexual and reproductive health care; it operates 860 clinics, with at least one health center or affiliate health center in each state. Beyond their common mission, the clinics have little holding them together. "We are a federation of separate and distinct entities trying to knit ourselves into a movement," PPFA's chief executive officer, Sarah Stoesz, told Baumgardner. "Before Cecile, we didn't have a chance. Now we do." Richards's background in political organizing rather than health care has been regarded, both positively and negatively, as evidence of the increasing politicization of PPFA. In 2004, while Feldt was still its president, PPFA endorsed a presidential candidate (John Kerry) for the first time in its history. "We have the potential to swing the vote in 2006, 2008, and 2010, and that's a lot of power," Richards told Baumgardner. "The question is, What are we going to do with it? And the answer is, We're going to use it. Planned Parenthood is going to become more political so that healthcare can become less politicized."

Weeks after Richards assumed the presidency of PPFA, South Dakota's governor signed into law a bill banning abortion under all circumstances except cases in which the life of a pregnant woman was endangered, making it the most far-reaching ban on abortion to be signed into law since *Roe v, Wade* legalized abortion in 1973. "Who knew it would actually happen?" Richards told Robin Finn. "I guess it's what I bargained for in general when I took this job. They're kind of going for broke to see if they can undo Roe." South Dakota voters rejected the new law, but it was a narrow victory for the pro-choice camp, and one that rested largely on the failure of the law to make exemptions for victims of rape or incest. The court also backed the rights of anti-abortion demonstrators to protest at abortion clinics, overturning a previous injunction by the Seventh U.S. Circuit Court of Appeals. Richards believes that the challenge presented in South Dakota is in some ways a necessary catalyst for a generation of women who grew up taking for granted the *Roe v. Wade* ruling and their right to undergo abortions. "I think it's going to be extremely hard for the average American to realize now that these people are talking about criminalizing abortion," she said to Finn. "Maybe it will be a bit of a wake-up call to everybody else in this country, is this a right that women have, or is this a right that politicians can take away?"

Meanwhile, the U.S. Supreme Court heard a case, called *Gonzales v. Carhart*, about the consitutionality of a federal ban on late-term abortion, the Partial Birth Abortion Act of 2003, which was struck down by judges in California, Nebraska, and New York. On April 18,2007, in a five-to-four decision, the Supreme Court upheld the consitutionality of the ban, marking the first time the justices banned a specific abortion procedure and the first time since *Roe v. Wade* that they approved a restriction on abortion that did not include an exception for the health of a woman. The majority decision was written by Justice Anthony Kennedy, who was joined by Justices Antonin Scalia and Clarence Thomas, as well as Bush's appointees, Chief Justice John G. Roberts and Justice Samuel A. Alito, In a blog that appeared in the *Huffington Post* (April 18, 2007, online) under the headline "A Dark Day for Women's Health and Safety," Richards called the decision "devastating." "The court told women that, with their health at risk during a pregnancy, deciding what to do is no longer up to them and their doctors," she wrote. "The Bush Supreme Court has let politicians come barging into that most personal of decisions." Richards also noted that Justice Ruth Bader Ginsberg, one of the four justices who opposed the majority's decision and the court's only woman, wrote in her dissenting opinion, "For the first time since Roe, the Court blesses a prohibition with no exception protecting a woman's health." Many joined Richards in interpreting the decision as representative of an ideological shift within the Supreme Court on the subject of abortion, especially since, in 2000, in *Stenberg v. Carhart*, the Court had rejected a Nebraska law banning late-term abortion for the very reason that it lacked an exception to preserve the woman's health.

Richards has been quick to point out that PPFA's primary focus is not abortion; more than 90 percent of the organization's services are not abortion-related. With an annual budget of $800 million, PPFA puts much of its resources into providing birth-control information and materials, giving Pap tests and pregnancy tests, and testing for sexually transmitted infections. According to PPFA, more than 600,000 unwanted pregnancies were prevented each year by the organization's clinics through birth-control services. "No one does more to reduce the need for abortions in this country than Planned Parenthood," Richards told Finn. "I would welcome legislators, including those from South Dakota, to work with us on family planning instead of focusing on making doctors and women criminals." Still, with two new appointees on the U.S. Supreme Court who are expected to be more sympathetic to pro-life arguments, and with pro-life advocates becoming increasingly vocal and increasingly critical of Planned Parenthood, Richards is ready for a struggle.

## PERSONAL LIFE

"I've never taken an easy job, I don't think. I can't remember one," she told Diane Jennings. She continued, "When [Planned Parenthood] turn[s] 100 in ten years, I want women and families to be able to access safe, affordable community-based health care in every state in this country. If I can do that I will feel like we, as my mom would say, we carried a bear over a mountain."

Richards lives in New York City with her husband, Kirk Adams, who is now chief of staff of the Service Employees International Union, the largest union in the U.S., and their three children.

## FURTHER READING

*https://www.plannedparenthood.org/; Sisterhood Is Forever: The Women's Anthology for a New Millenium*

# FAITH RINGGOLD

## Artist; Writer; Educator; Activist

**Born:** October 8, 1930; Harlem, New York City, New
    York
**Primary Field:** Arts and Culture
**Affiliation:** Narrative Quilts; Painting

## INTRODUCTION

*Driven by a fierce desire to communicate her ideas,
opinions, memories, and feelings as a woman, black
American, daughter, wife, mother, grandmother, politically aware citizen, resident of Harlem, and artist, Faith
Ringgold has produced a body of work of extraordinary
variety, power, and originality. Ringgold is perhaps best
known for her so-called story quilts, an art form of her
own invention, in which she mixed handwritten narra-
tives and paintings with traditionally pieced fabrics.
Continually looking for "alternative routes to get where
[she] want[s] to be," as she put it in her autobiography,* We Flew Over the Bridge *(1995), and ignoring
the "customs and biases of the art world mainstream,"
as her daughter Michele Wallace wrote in the catalog
for Ringgold's 20-year retrospective at the Studio Museum in Harlem, in New York City, she has also made
stretched canvas and fabric framed paintings, posters, murals, masks, costumed and masked figures, soft
sculptures, and dolls; created and acted in performance
pieces; and written the award winning* Tar Beach *and
other books for children. Insightful, provocative, and
spirited views not only of her own life but also of slavery and the civil rights, black nationalist, antiwar, and
feminist movements, her work reflects her commitment
to humanistic ideals and her determination to try to end
racism and sexism.*

*During an interview with Leigh Fenly for the* San
Diego Union *(February 16, 1991), Ringgold said that
gaining recognition as an artist proved to be far harder
than she had anticipated. "It's difficult for all artists to
succeed [in the United States], because art is not what
this society considers necessary," she explained. "And
then when the artist is outside the American mainstream, a woman and a woman of color, that makes it
even more difficult. The motto is: Knock on every door,
and when one closes, move to another one, but don't go
away. It will be hard, and it seems impossible. But it is
not impossible unless you stop." Ringgold's work has
been exhibited throughout the world, and her art is in*
*many prominent public and private collections, includ-
ing, in New York City, the Metropolitan Museum of Art,
the Museum of Modern Art, and the Solomon R. Guggenheim Museum. A New York City schoolteacher from
1955 to 1972, Ringgold has also held the rank of full
professor at the University of California at San Diego.*

## EARLY LIFE

Faith Ringgold was born Faith Willie Jones on October 8,1930 in New York City to Andrew Louis Jones Sr.
and Willie Edell Posey Jones. She had an older brother,
Andrew, and an older sister, Barbara; another brother
died shortly before her birth. Her maternal ancestors
include a line of talented seamstresses, among them a
great-great-grandmother who made quilts as a slave in
antebellum Florida. Ringgold's mother was a full-time
homemaker until the 1940s, when she got a job sewing clothing in factories. In around 1950 she launched
a successful business as a fashion designer and dress-
maker under the name Madame Willi Posey. Ringgold
often modeled clothes and emceed at her mother's fashion shows. "I openly adored her," she wrote in her autobiography. "Not only did she raise me carefully and
lovingly, but she was also my best friend. She left me
with a rich endowment of ideas and memories."

According to Eleanor Flomenhaft, who interviewed
her for *Faith Ringgold: A 25-Year Survey* (1990), the
catalog for the artist's retrospective exhibit at the Fine
Arts Museum of Long Island (which traveled to a dozen
other museums), Ringgold has "total recall of her personal odyssey through life." Often confined to bed as a
small child because of asthma, she would keep occupied
by drawing, reading, and sewing. When she felt better
but could not yet return to school, her mother would take
her to museums or to performances at Harlem's famed
Apollo Theatre. Her father, too, would take her on out-
ings on his days off from his job as a city sanitation
department truck driver. "My father always made me
feel special," Ringgold wrote in the dedication to her
memoir. She received as gifts from him her first paint
set and easel. "Art was the one thing I always loved to
do," she has said.

For years after Ringgold's parents separated, in
the early 1930s (they divorced in 1942), her father often socialized with his friends in the family's Harlem
apartment, entertaining them with stories that fascinated
young Faith. Her mother, too, was a skilled raconteur,

and Ringgold loved to eavesdrop as she and her women friends gossiped, reminisced, and shared their worries and dreams. "My childhood [years] were the best years of my life, I guess," she told Margaret Mazurkiewicz, who interviewed her for *Something about the Author* (1993). "I mean for good stories and wonderful connections with people and inspirations and positive affirmation."

According to Ringgold, the virtually all-white staffs at the racially mixed New York City public schools that she attended included many teachers "who thought nothing of [the students'] feelings and stereotyped all blacks as shiftless, lazy, and happy-go-lucky," as she recalled in her autobiography. "We were taught the most degrading things about our history: slavery was presented as if it were our fault, a kind of deserved penalty for being born black. Yet racist as [the teachers] were, they did teach us. Nothing was watered down or made easier to compensate for our so-called racial disadvantages; in fact, just the opposite was true. Knowing this, our parents raised us to understand that we had to be twice as good to go half as far."

Thanks to her parents, Ringgold also grew up assuming that she would go to college. In 1948, after graduating from Morris High School, she enrolled at the School of Education of the City College of New York, where she majored in art and minored in education. Her instructors focused on Western art to the virtual exclusion of all other art. "We copied Greek busts; we copied Cezanne and Degas; we copied the European masters," Ringgold told Eleanor Flomenhaft. "It was generally thought that we weren't experienced enough to be original; and if we were original, we were sometimes up for ridicule." Some of her professors, including one who gave her a grade of D in a drawing course, tried to dissuade Ringgold from pursuing a career in art. Nevertheless, having resolved, by the time she entered college, to become an artist, by her own account she "never for one moment doubted [her] ability to reach that goal."

In 1950 Ringgold married Robert Earl Wallace, a classical and jazz pianist. Their apartment served as a meeting ground where struggling jazz musicians and others among their acquaintances discussed racial prejudice and its effects on the lives of black people. The births of the couple's daughters Michele, in January 1952, and Barbara, in December of the same year, forced Ringgold to drop out of college temporarily. In 1954 she separated from her husband, moved with her children to her mother's apartment, and returned to City College. She earned a B.S. degree in fine art in 1955 and an M.A. degree in art, also from City College, in 1959. In 1962, six years after she and Wallace were divorced, she married Burdette ("Birdie") Ringgold, who has helped her with various facets of her career.

## LIFE'S WORK

Earlier, in 1955, Ringgold had begun working as an art teacher in the first of a series of a half-dozen public elementary, junior high, and high schools in New York City. "I really attribute a lot of my painting skills to my young students," Ringgold has said. "Because I had to go through this massive relearning process to go from Picasso and all the great artists I had to copy in college to me, via African art. I wanted to find a way of creating American art out of my experiences as an African-American. So the children really helped me to do that, they showed me what it is to be free, to be able to express yourself directly." In one example of their effect on her, in the early 1970s Ringgold started making African-style masks after seeing her students create them in class projects. Between 1970 and 1980 she also taught art at the Bank Street College of Education and, for periods during that decade, two other New York City colleges. In 1984 she became a visiting associate professor of art at the University of California at San Diego, and the next year she was promoted to the rank of full professor. "I'm very positive with my students," Ringgold told Eleanor Flomenhaft. "I would never tell students, no matter how much I might feel it is true, that they lack talent or ability, because I feel that the talent and ability is second to that person's drive and determination to be an artist. If they have that determination, and they are ready to do the work, everything else will fall into place. I know that from my own experience."

For a half dozen years beginning in the late 1950s, Ringgold painted landscapes and seascapes in the manner of the French Impressionists. In 1961, troubled by the suspicion that she "wasn't sure that [she] understood what being an artist was" and driven by the desire to "understand some of the aura of creating a work of art that could last 400 years," in her words, she toured museums in France and Italy. "I came back feeling that I would be an artist, that I could be, and that I should be an artist," she told Marguerite Mazurkiewicz. Sometime later, eager to acquire an audience for her work, she showed some of her paintings to the owner of a New York City art gallery. "You cannot do this," the owner told her, referring to the impressionistic style Ringgold had adopted, a judgment that, Ringgold has acknowledged, "helped [her] as an artist."

While vacationing on Martha's Vineyard, in Massachusetts, in 1963, Ringgold began a series of paintings, later named the *American People Series*, that marked what she has described as "the beginning of [her] mature work." "The idea was to make a statement in my art about the civil rights movement and what was happening to black people in America at that time," she explained in her autobiography. "I wanted to give my woman's point of view to this period." The writings of James Baldwin also served as a strong stimulus for her: "Baldwin understood, I felt, the disparity between black and white people as well as anyone; but I had something to add, the visual depiction of the way we are and look."

Highly stylized and rendered with flat colors, such *American People Series* paintings as *Between Friends* (1963) and *The Cocktail Party* (1964) depict "shocked-looking people in mostly unwilling interaction," as Terrie S. Rouse described them in *Faith Ringgold: Twenty Years of Painting, Sculpture and Performance* (1963-1983) (1984), the catalog for her retrospective at the Studio Museum in Harlem. The last, mural-sized paintings in the series, *Die, The Flag Is Bleeding*, and U.S. Postage Stamp Commemorating the Advent of Black Power (all 1967) reflect her reactions to the emergence of the black power movement. The latter two pictures are offshoots of the flag paintings of Jasper Johns, which, in Ringgold's view, "presented a beautiful, but incomplete, idea." "To complete it," she has explained, "I wanted to show some of the hell that had broken out in the States, and what better place to do that than in the stars and stripes?"

Earlier, in 1964, Ringgold had sent photos of some of her paintings to Romare Bearden, with the hope that he would invite her to join Spiral, the black artists' group that he had helped to establish. Bearden responded by critiquing her work and suggesting that she study the paintings of Max Beckmann and other European artists. "I was crushed," Ringgold recalled in her memoir. "Oh, 'Mr.' Bearden, I thought I was trying to forget all those theories about composition and asymmetrical balance, subtle harmony and subdued colors. It didn't apply to what I was doing." Two years later Bearden included a painting by Ringgold in *Art of the American Negro*, a group show that he curated. Sponsored by the Harlem Cultural Council, it was the first exhibition of work by black artists to be shown in Harlem since the 1930s.

In 1966, in response to an invitation from its members, Ringgold joined Spectrum, a cooperative New York City art gallery. She had her first solo exhibition a year later, when Spectrum mounted a display of the *American People Series*. "Although self-consciously ambitious, these paintings show exceptional talent," John Fischer wrote in *Arts Magazine* (February 1968), in one of several favorable reviews of the show. "The artist has a penetrating sense of irony which she graphically translates into pictorial emotion effectively." For her second, and, as it turned out, last solo show at the Spectrum Gallery, in 1968, Ringgold created her *Black Light Series*, as "a way of expressing on canvas the new 'black is beautiful' sense of ourselves," in her words, as well as her own "new interest in African rhythm, pattern, and repetition." Such paintings as *Soul Sister* (1967) and *The American Spectrum* (1969) illustrate the results of her experiments in creating black skin tones and in using a palette of darker colors. In what Ringgold has called her "first formidable sale," the Chase Manhattan Bank corporation bought *The American Spectrum* for $3,000. Chase representatives were about to buy a second painting, *Flag for the Moon: Die Nigger* (1969), a "black-light" image of an American flag, when they realized that the word "die" appeared among the stars and the word "nigger" formed the stripes. Ringgold has described that painting as her "way of saying that too many American people go to bed hungry, while the government spent billions to place their flag on the moon."

In the 1970s Ringgold created several political posters, among them one to raise money to help cover the legal expenses of the Black Panthers. She made *The United States of Attica* (1971), her most widely distributed poster, after 37 inmates and workers were killed in the course of an uprising through which inmates hoped to effect reforms at Attica State Correctional Facility, in New York. Ringgold's active involvement in racial, feminist, and other social and political issues includes her participation, in 1968, in a public demonstration that was organized at her suggestion to protest the omission of works by black artists from the exhibition *The 1930s: Painting and Sculpture in America* at the Whitney Museum of American Art, in New York City. "I was proud of myself," Ringgold wrote in her memoir, in recalling that she thus became "the originator of the first black demonstration against a major museum in New York City." Between 1968 and 1970, as a member of the Art Workers' Coalition, Ringgold devoted hundreds of hours to activities that succeeded in ending the exclusion of black artists from the exhibition schedule of the Museum of Modern Art, in New York City. In 1970, with her daughter Michele, she cofounded the advocacy group Women Students and Artists for Black Art Liberation. Her many efforts to increase opportunities for women artists also include her work with Where We At, an organization of black women artists that she cofounded; the Women's Caucus for Art; and Coast to Coast, the "Women of Color National Artists Book Project."

In 1972, inspired by Chinese landscape paintings, Ringgold created *Political Landscapes*, a series of 57 watercolors with handwritten messages, most of them in her own words, about war, violence, racism, and sexism. Already a sought-after speaker at feminist art conferences, she arranged to give talks about the series later that year at several college campuses. Meanwhile, in the summer of 1972, during a visit that she made to the Rijksmuseum, in Amsterdam, she saw a display of centuries-old Tibetan tankas, paintings bordered with fabric, and she realized that it would be much easier to transport cloth-framed paintings, which she could simply roll up, than her glass covered watercolors or stretched canvas oil paintings. With that in mind, she eventually assembled trunksful of what she called "traveling art," portable exhibitions that she would send for display at colleges, "thus widening her audience and bypassing the usual dependency on a dealer and gallery," as Moira Roth pointed out in the catalog for Ringgold's retrospective at the Studio Museum in Harlem. With the help of the speaker's bureau with which she had become affiliated, she also developed a package of lectures suitable for college audiences. At the end of the fall 1972 academic term, thinking that, with the lectures and traveling exhibits, she had found a relatively steady alternative source of income, she resigned her position as a schoolteacher to devote herself full-time to her career as an artist.

For nearly a decade beginning in 1972, Ringgold produced her artworks in collaboration with her mother. Willi Posey's asymmetrical pieced-fabric borders, which Ringgold has described as "an amazing and original blend, Tibetan and African inspired, and yet also [drawing] heavily from the African-American women's pieced quilting tradition," frame Ringgold's *Slave Rape Series* (1972), 16 paintings that form a narrative about female victims of the West African slave trade. The faces of the women in the series' "lavish, haunting scenes," as Terrie S. Rouse described them, resemble those of the

artist and her daughters. In 1973 Willi Posey produced the clothing for the 32 figures in Ringgold's *Family of Woman Mask Series*, which feature faces rendered in the style of the Dan masks of Liberia. "Powerful women who never had had a chance to be all they could be," in Ringgold's words, the figures portray people whom both the artist and her mother knew.

The many hanging or free-standing soft sculptures on which Ringgold and her mother collaborated include *Wilt, Willa, and Wiltina* (1974), the first work in Ringgold's *Dude Series*. Created in reaction to remarks by the black basketball star Wilt Chamberlain that were widely viewed as insulting to black women, the highly attenuated figures caricature Chamberlain and his imaginary family: a white wife and a racially mixed daughter. The masterfully fashioned faces of Ringgold's *Portrait Masks* (1975), which she made with spray-painted foam rubber, include representations of such real- life subjects as Adam Clayton Powell Jr., the militant black leader and congressman who was also the long-time minister of the Abyssinian Baptist Church, in Harlem, which Ringgold and her family attended for many years. Adopting a traditional West African style, she designed the portrait masks to be worn atop a wearer's head; eyeholes in the apparel that her mother sewed for each figure enable the wearer to see. In 1979, "determined to find a stable market for [her] art," as she has recalled, she and her mother launched Sew Real Soft Sculpture, an enterprise in which they made one-of-a- kind dolls. Sold for about $200 apiece, the dolls proved too labor intensive to be profitable and too expensive for many interested buyers.

For an exhibition called *The Artist and the Quilt,* Willi Posey fashioned a quilt using 30 of Ringgold's painted portraits of black men and women. Called Echoes of Harlem (1980) and later purchased for the Philip Morris corporate collection, it was among their last joint projects. For a few years after her mother's death, in 1981, the grief- stricken Ringgold "paint[ed] the inside of [her] head," as she put it. The results were the *Emanon, Baby Faith and Willi, Dah, and California Dah* series of abstract acrylic paintings. In 1984, driven by a compulsion to counter black people's negative image of the character Aunt Jemima, she wrote a story about Aunt Jemima. Encouraged by the enthusiastic response the story elicited from Moira Roth, then the chairman of the visual arts department at the University of California at San Diego, Ringgold created the quilt *Who's Afraid of Aunt Jemima?* (1984). Composed of pieced fabrics and painted portraits joined to rectangles of off-white fabric that bore her handwritten texts, it became her first story quilt. In Ringgold's version of the Aunt Jemima story, Jemima is someone who "could do anything she set her mind to"; when her employer makes Jemima his heir, she becomes rich and eventually opens two restaurants.

With the help of a series of assistants, Ringgold has since made about 85 quilts, some three dozen of them story quilts. Among the best known of the quilts without texts are *Sonny's Quilt* (1986), which shows the saxophonist Sonny Rollins playing his instrument as he floats above a multicolored version of the Brooklyn Bridge, and the *Woman on a Bridge Series* (1988), in which each quilt shows one or more black women exuberantly engaged in such activities as running or dancing on a New York City or San Francisco bridge. Ringgold's celebrated story quilts include *Tar Beach* (1988) and *Tar Beach 2* (1990), which are owned by the Guggenheim Museum and the Philadelphia Museum, respectively. Both *Tar Beach* quilts (which, according to some sources, are part of Ringgold's *Woman on a Bridge* Series) present a story narrated from the point of view of a young girl and show the girl and other residents of a Harlem apartment house relaxing on the tar papered roof of their building on a hot summer night, just as Ringgold often did with her family during her childhood.

Ringgold has also gained renown for her two *French Collection* story-quilt series (Part I, 1991; Part II, 1991-94), which tell the life story of her self described imaginary alter ego Willia Maria Simone, an African-American who becomes a successful artist in Paris. In 1992 *The French Collection Part I* appeared in one of the three solo shows of her work that were mounted at the Bernice Steinbaum Gallery, which represented Ringgold from 1986 to 1992. "Famous French masters and masterpieces put in appearances in these witty, immensely pleasurable images, as do Willia Marie's family and friends," Roberta Smith wrote in an enthusiastic review of the exhibit for the *New York Times* (February 14,1992). "Issues of race and sex abound, insinuated in complex and subtle ways, but never superseding the artist's sense of beauty."

*Change: Faith Ringgold's Over 100 Pound Weight Loss Performance Story Quilt* (1986), a work in the artist's *Change Series*, used photos etched on silk and cotton and a long text to chronicle Ringgold's history of weight gain and loss. The name of the quilt is also

the title of a solo performance piece in which Ringgold appeared 25 times between 1988 and 1991. Earlier, in 1980, frustrated because she could not find a publisher for the autobiography that she had written a few years before, Ringgold began describing her development as a woman and artist in *Being My Own Woman*, an hour long performance piece that she presented at colleges, the form of Being My Own Woman, she has said, was inspired by "the African tradition of combining storytelling, dance, music, costumes, and masks into a single production." Ringgold directed but did not appear in her first performance piece, *The Wake and Resurrection of the Bicentennial Negro* (1976), which she developed as an artist in residence at Wilson College, in Pennsylvania, and has described as "a visual narrative of the dynamics of racism, including the self imposed oppression of drug addiction." Ringgold's first husband was a drug addict who died of an overdose, in 1966, as did her brother Andrew, in 1961.

In 1988, at the suggestion of the book editor Andrea Cascardi, Ringgold began recreating for a children's book the story she had told in her quilt *Tar Beach.* Her book *Tar Beach* was published in 1991. "Combining the traditional association between flying and the escape of slaves to freedom with her own fantasies as a child who delighted in the sense of liberation and empowerment she felt on a rooftop from which she saw stars twinkling among the lights of nearby George Washington Bridge, Ringgold has fashioned a poignant fictional story about eight year old Gassie, who dreams that she can claim the bridge (and freedom and wealth) by soaring above the city," *Kirkus Reviews* (December 15, 1990) reported. "The triumphant soaring of imagination over reality is beautifully expressed in Ringgold's bold, vibrant paintings." The *Kirkus* reviewer concluded that the book was "marvelously evocative" and "beautiful, innovative, and full of the joy of one unconquerable soul." *Tar Beach* won some 20 awards, including the Coretta Scott King Award. It was named a Caldecott Honor Book and appeared on the *New York Times Book Review*'s list of the best illustrated children's books of 1991. Ringgold's other books for children are *Aunt Harriet's Underground Railroad in the Sky* (1992), *Dinner at Aunt Connie's House* (1993), *My Dream of Martin Luther King* (1995), and *Bonjour, Lonnie* (1996).

A large mural based on the life of the 19th century Latin American political and educational reformer Eugenio Maria de Hostos that Ringgold made for Hostos Community College, in New York City, was installed in 1994. "Flying Home: Harlem Heroes and Heroines," two 30 foot long, five panel murals that Ringgold created under the auspices of MTA Arts for Transit, a program of the New York City Metropolitan Transit Authority, were installed in a subway station at 125th Street and Lenox Avenue, in Harlem, in 1996. Bearing the name of a joyful composition by the jazz musician Lionel Hampton, "Flying Home" celebrates 32 African-American heroes of Harlem, each of whom is depicted floating above a New York City site associated with his or her celebrity, for example, the Cotton Club, Yankee Stadium, the Studio Museum in Harlem. The mural on the downtown side of the subway platform shows sports figures, artists, and performers, among them the prize fighter Sugar Ray Robinson, the painter Jacob Lawrence, and the singer Dinah Washington. Images of such writers as Nora Zeale Hurston, such civil rights activists as Malcolm X, and such political leaders as Adam Clayton Powell Jr. appear on the uptown side. Framed with colorful Moorish style borders, the panels are mosaics; they were formed from thousands of pieces of Italian glass by artisans from Miotto Mosaics, who replicated the many hued paintings and colorful Moorish borders that Ringgold created for the project.

## PERSONAL LIFE

In 1992 Ringgold and her husband, who worked at a General Motors plant until his retirement earlier that year, moved from Harlem, their lifelong neighborhood until then, to a house in Englewood, New Jersey. During the half of each year that the artist taught at the University of California, she lived in La Jolla, a suburb of San Diego. Her daughter Michele Wallace, who teaches at the City College of New York, has written several

books, among them *Black Macho and the Myth of the Superwoman* (1979); her daughter Barbara Wallace, an elementary school teacher, is the mother of Ringgold's three granddaughters, the oldest of whom, Faith, coined the name for Ringgold's *Dah Series* when she was a baby. By her own account, in her *Couples Series* (early 1970s) and other soft sculptures that focus on families, Ringgold tried "to make up for some of the closeness [she] missed in [her] relationship with [her] daughters." She has characterized her performance piece and story quilt series *The Bitter Nest* (1985 and 1987) as "a fictitious response" to the feuds she and her daughters have had.

Ringgold is the subject of Robyn Montana Turner's children's book *Faith Ringgold* (1993) and is one of the four artists profiled by Leslie Sills in *Inspirations: Stories of Women Artists for Children* (1989). She has received many honorary doctoral degrees, including one from City College, and many other honors and prizes, among them the Wonder Woman Foundation Award (1983), National Endowment for the Arts Awards (for sculpture, in 1978, and for painting, in 1989), and a Guggenheim Foundation Award (1987). "I don't want the story of my life to be about racism, though it has played a major role," she said in the concluding chapter of her memoir. "I want my story to be about attainment, love of family, art, helping others, courage, values, dreams coming true." She lives in Englewood, New Jersey and maintains her studio space.

## FURTHER READING

*Faith Ringgold: A 25-Year Survey; Faith Ringgold: Twenty Years of Painting, Sculpture, and Performance (1963-1983); We Flew Over the Bridge*

# BRUCE RITTER

## Priest; Activist

**Born:** February 25, 1927; Trenton, New Jersey
**Died:** October 7, 1999; Decatur, New York
**Primary Field:** Human Rights
**Affiliation:** Covenant House

## INTRODUCTION

*Bruce Ritter was a Franciscan priest stationed in New York City and active internationally, and dedicated his life "to the care of abandoned children for the love of God." Father Ritter began taking in homeless teenagers informally when he was living in a housing project on Manhattan's Lower East Side in the late 1960's. In 1972 he founded Covenant House, an international child-care agency that operates short-term "crisis centers," called Under 21, for street children in big cities, where their commonest means of survival is subservience to pimps, pornographers, and pedophiles. The Under 21 centers admit young runaways and castaways on a round-the-clock, no questions asked basis, offering food, shelter, and social, health, legal, educational, and vocational services. The oldest of the centers, Under 21/New York, in operation since 1977, annually serves some 20,000 desperate waifs, a large proportion of them victims of the billion dollar sex industry, which is protected by organized crime. Under 21/Toronto, which opened its doors in 1982, serves approximately 3,000, and an additional 10,000 are expected to seek sanctuary in the centers opening in Houston, in June 1983, and Boston, in October 1983. In addition to the short term Under 21 centers, Covenant House operates Casa Alianza, a long-term residential program for orphans and other homeless boys in Antigua, Guatemala. Ninety percent of the more than $15,000,000 needed to run Covenant House annually comes privately, from individuals, corporations, and foundations.*

## EARLY LIFE

One of five children, Bruce Ritter was born in Trenton, New Jersey on February 25, 1927. "I was baptized John," he explained to the interviewer for *Current Biography*. "Bruce is my religious name, taken when I made my vows as a Franciscan, My passport reads 'J. Bruce Ritter.'" His father, Louis Charles Ritter, who was the general supervisor of Trenton Potteries, died when Ritter was four. "We were very comfortable until my father died," he recounted to the interviewer. "We lost everything in the Crash. We moved out of a very fine home into a very poor one. My mother raised five kids by herself during the Depression. She lived on a $45 per month widow's pension, and she was a very accomplished seamstress." Mrs. Ritter, the former Julia Agnes Morrissey also played the organ in her younger years,

Ritter attended public schools, the Kuser School in Trenton and Hamilton High School in Hamilton Township, just outside the Trenton city limits, where the Ritter family lived. After graduating from high school, he worked briefly as a freight-car loader before joining the United States Navy, "It was in the Navy that my interest in spiritual matters developed," he related in the *Current Biography* interview, "I began to pray and read a lot, [including] a couple of books about Saint Francis from the base library."

## LIFE'S WORK

Discharged from the Navy in July 1946, Ritter went back to his old job loading freight cars for a year, During that time he "thought through the call to the priesthood [which] became persistent and finally undeniable," In 1947 he applied for admission to the Order of Friars Minor Conventual, one of the three distinct and independent branches of the Order of Friars Minor, popularly known as the Franciscans, founded by St, Francis of Assisi in 1209. The other branches are the Order of Friars Minor Capuchin, popularly known as the Capuchins, and the Order of Friars Minor, sans adjective, Members of the Order of Friars Minor Coventual are distinguished by the letters "O.F.M, Conv." following their names.

Ritter began his training for the priesthood at St, Francis Seminary on Staten Island in New York City. His studies there were interrupted by what he describes as "a foray into the monastic life" at the Trappist Abbey in Gethsemane, Kentucky. After a few months at Gethsemane he realized that his venture into Cistercian monasticism was "a mistake" and returned to the Franciscans on Staten Island.

In 1950 Ritter advanced to the study of philosophy at Assumption College in Chester, Pennsylvania, where he took his B.A. degree two years later. He began his study of theology at St. Anthony-on-Hudson Seminary in Rensselaer, New York and completed it in Rome, Italy. The Franciscan Pontifical Faculty of Theology in

Rome awarded him his doctorate in 1958, five years after his arrival in the Eternal City and two years after his ordination. His dissertation was on the history of medieval dogma.

After returning to the United States, Father Ritter taught at St. Anthony-on-Hudson for two years, at St. Hyacinth's Seminary in Granby, Massachusetts for one year, and at Canevin High School in Pittsburgh for two years. In 1963 he was assigned to Manhattan College in the Bronx, New York as campus chaplain and professor of theology.

It was at Manhattan College in 1968 that his students gave him, in his words, the "huge push" into the work that now consumes him. He recalled the details for *Current Biography*: "I was preaching at Mass one Sunday. My sermon was on zeal and commitment and the need for my students to be more involved in the life of the church. I had finished my sermon and was on my way back to the altar to finish Mass when one of the students stood up in church. He was president of the student body and captain of the track team. He said, 'Bruce, we think you're a pretty good teacher, but we don't like your sermons. We think you should practice what you preach and show us a little of that zeal and commitment you just talked about.' A pretty heavy shot. I thought about it and realized the students were correct. The next Sunday I apologized to the student body for not edifying them, and I asked for a new assignment, to live and work among the poor." Ritter got the assignment, a "non-specific" one, "simply to be useful to the poor."

He began the assignment by moving to the blighted eastern edge of New York City's East Village, at Seventh Street and Avenue D, on the East River, a neighborhood teeming with drug addicts and nomadic hippie "flower children." "I moved into this junkie's apartment near the river," he recounted to the *Current Biography* interviewer, "and became involved in all the problems you would expect to find, the poverty, the violence, the unemployment, the drug scene, and, without wanting or intending to, the problem of the hundreds of homeless kids there from all over the country."

According to Father Ritter, Covenant House began informally one winter night during a blizzard. "About two o'clock in the morning six kids knocked on my door, four boys and two girls, all under sixteen, runaways. They asked if they could sleep on the floor of my apartment. The next morning it was still snowing and very cold. The kids didn't want to leave. One boy went out and brought back four more kids and said, 'This is the rest of our family. They were afraid to come last night. They wanted us to check you out first. I told them you didn't come on to us last night, so that it was probably OK.'"

"That's how Covenant House got started. The kids had no place to go, I couldn't find a single child-care agency to take them in, I called over twenty-four of them, I didn't have the guts to throw them out, so I kept them." As word of his hospitality spread, the number of children knocking on Father Ritter's door swelled, To provide space for them he took over other apartments, and he enlisted a staff of student volunteers from Manhattan College and other Catholic colleges in the New York City area. "We survived hand to mouth for four years. To get money I begged, drove a cab, did whatever I had to do."

By 1972 hundreds of children were living in or coming to the group homes set up by Father Ritter. He obtained a child-care agency license, entitling him to some public funds, and the operation was chartered as Covenant House, an allusion to the Biblical Covenant between God and his Chosen People. "Runaway and homeless youngsters are our 'chosen people,'" he has explained, "and we have adopted this powerful model of faithful love as the basis of our relationship to them. Through our covenant with them, we care for our kids, and respond to their needs, not because they are beautiful, or clean, or well-behaved (many of them are not), but simply because they need us. In return, we expect them to respond, to the extent they can, by respecting us and each other. We are guided by the same principle that good parents instinctively follow with their own kids, the principle of unconditional love."

In 1976 Ritter was asked to "do something for the kids" specifically on the streets in and around Times Square, where the predatory sex industry uses and abuses thousands of them annually. Taking over a six-story building on Eighth Avenue between 43rd and 44th Streets, amidst the sleaze of peep shows, massage parlors, live sex shows, and pornographic bookstores, he opened in April 1977 Under 21, a crisis center for children sucked into the sinkhole of Times Square. The initial funding for Under 21 came from the Roman Catholic Archdiocese of New York, the Franciscans, and the Charles E. Culpeper Foundation. Other money was begged by Father Ritter at eight or nine Masses every weekend at churches around the metropolitan area.

During its first year of operation 6,000 children took refuge in Under 21, a tenth of them fifteen years old or younger. Thirty thousand meals were served, and 8,000 nights of shelter were provided, Many of the children were fleeing brutal pimps, as Ritter pointed out to Bill Reel of the *New York Daily News* (June 7, 1978): "We have one staff person who does nothing but take kids to hospitals. Many of the kids are sick from being beaten, raped, tortured." He gave the example of a thirteen year old girl who fled to Under 21 after her pimp beat her up and threw her down a flight of stairs. "What angered the pimp was that she earned him $180 that night, instead of her usual $300. After she came to us, he sent another of his girls in here to try to persuade her to go back to him."

As the Eighth Avenue center became overcrowded, with children sleeping on the floors and even around the altar in the chapel, Ritter searched for more space. Responding to his appeal, Governor Hugh Carey of New York turned over to him in 1979 three large, state-owned buildings at 460 West 41st Street, at Tenth Avenue, three blocks west of Times Square. The buildings, comprising a former detention and rehabilitation center for drug abusers, were leased to Covenant House for five years, with a five-year renewal option, for the nominal sum of a dollar a year.

The building on Eighth Avenue was retained as a residence for the Covenant House staff while the complex at Tenth Avenue was converted into a new home for Under 21. The penal ambiance of the facility was obliterated as much as possible by the tearing down of bars and gates and the application of bright paint and new carpeting. The spacious new headquarters made possible private bedrooms for the young guests; a cafeteria for the serving of meals three times a day; a licensed clinic under the direction of a medical doctor, a registered nurse, and other health professionals; schoolrooms for PS 106M, Covenant House's own New York City public school, set up on the premises for remedial education and staffed by professionals; a nursery and other necessities for a mother/child program instituted because of the large number of pregnant girls and young mothers with infants or toddlers coming for help; and space for legal services and individual and family counseling.

During the summer of 1981 Father Ritter and the board of directors of Covenant House made some legal changes in the way the agency operated. Covenant House was retained as the title for the corporate and administrative aspects of the agency. The crisis center was separately incorporated as a subsidiary of Covenant House and re-designated Under 21/New York. In July 1981 Covenant House and Covenant International Foundation opened Casa Alianza in Antigua, Guatemala, a residence for homeless "shoeshine" boys five to twelve years old, most of whom have been orphaned by the war in Guatemala. There were seven boys in residence at Casa Alianza the first night, and a year later there were 110 benefiting from the structured residential program, including education, medical care, twenty four hour supervision, counseling, and recreation. Unlike Under 21/New York, Casa Alianza was designed to meet the longer term needs of homeless children suffering more from starvation on the streets than subjection to prostitution or pornography.

Meanwhile, Father Ritter was receiving many requests to open Under 21 crisis centers in various locations throughout the United States and Canada. In January 1982 he opened Under 21/Toronto, a crisis center just off Yonge Street, the pornography strip in Toronto, Ontario, Canada, which accommodates an average of 230 young people a month. Other crisis centers are being opened in Houston, Texas, a nexus of interstate traffic in boy prostitutes, and in Boston, Massachusetts, near the notorious "Combat Zone."

Well over half of the children sheltered at Covenant House have been sexually exploited, through prostitution or pornography. On behalf of those children, the Covenant House legal staff played a significant role in the case of *New York v. Ferber*. Paul Ira Ferber, a Manhattan pornography dealer convicted of selling two films showing children under twelve engaging in explicit sexual activity, appealed his case on the ground that his "freedom of speech" rights under the First Amendment had been violated. The New York Court of Appeals in 1981 ruled in Ferber's favor, declaring unconstitutional New York's 1977 law making it a felony to use children in sexual performances. Covenant House immediately urged Manhattan District Attorney Robert Morgenthau to appeal the decision to the United States Supreme Court, and it put all of the resources of its legal staff and research department at his disposal. As "friends of the court," the Covenant House lawyers asked the Supreme Court to uphold the New York law against the selling of child pornography whether or not the material in question can be deemed "legally obscene." On July 2, 1982 Justice Byron White announced the unanimous judgment of the Supreme Court upholding the 1977 New

York ban on child pornography and removing all such pornography from the protection of the First Amendment. The court ruled that the fine points of legal obscenity were irrelevant in the light of "a government objective of surpassing importance," the prevention of sexual exploitation and abuse of children.

"We know that we have saved dozens of lives, literally, physically saved them," Father Ritter told James Brady in an interview for *Our Sunday Visitor* (March 21, 1982), "because this program is here, because my staff will get fired if they turn a kid away. Just fired, no questions asked." A child who walks into Under 21, at any hour of the day or night, is asked only his or her name, age, and hometown. He or she is offered medical attention often for venereal disease or drug addiction, a meal, a bath, and a bed, and is urged to make a free telephone call home, without necessarily divulging his or her whereabouts. The more serious medical cases are taken to St. Vincent's Hospital for treatment. All "walk-ins" are given a self set deadline for returning home, for going into long-term residence programs, or for finding jobs. To help children make the transition from street life to productive employment, Under 21/New York has an on-site work experience, Dove Services, Inc., in which up to eight residents of the center at a time take part in all phases of running a messenger service.

A typical Introduction of a pubescent runaway to New York City is to be greeted by a pimp in a big hat or one of his "catchers" at Port Authority Bus Terminal, beyond the forty-eight-hour mark, it is estimated, one in ten teenagers will be a prostitute. "If a kid has lived in the streets for a month or so," Father Ritter has pointed out, "it becomes very hard to reach him. If it's been six months, we've almost lost him, and if it's a year, he's gone." Covenant House has a 33 percent success rate in persuading the runaways and "throwaways" that there is an alternative to their destructive lifestyles. Two-thirds return to the streets, some to their deaths. In 1982 alone twelve former residents of Under 21/New York were killed by stabbing, strangulation, shooting, or overdoses. "You lose most of them because the city has no programs to offer," according to Father Ritter. "All you can do is care about them, feed and clothe them, and then bury them when they die." Because of explicit threats from pimps whose "women" take refuge in Under 21 (not to mention implicit threats from sex merchants inimical to Father Ritter), Ritter hires what he describes as "some very big staff" to guard the place. Many of the security personnel are off duty police officers.

Covenant House has a full-time paid staff of 500 worldwide. In New York it has a corporate staff of 350, professionals and religious. In addition to the salaried staff, there are approximately 200 part-time volunteers and seventy full-time volunteers. The latter comprise the Covenant Prayer Community, the members of which pledge a year's service, take meals together, pray three hours a day (mostly together), and live with Father Ritter in the residence on Eighth Avenue. Some of the members of the community remain beyond the year and take vows as Franciscans.

## PERSONAL LIFE

In the *Current Biography* interview, as in numerous others, Father Ritter gently protested his "mythologizing" by the press as a "pious, holy Franciscan who loves everybody." He finds it difficult to "hate the sin and love the sinner," he confessed, when the sinner is one who preys on children. As bald as his photographs would suggest, but not as heavy-set, Father Bruce (as everyone in Covenant House calls him) is round-faced, pleasant when relaxed, and tough in his low-keyed way. You believe him when he tells you that he has no time for recreation. He logged 100,000 miles visiting Covenant House's branches in a year, consulting with people trying to set up teen crisis shelters like his, and begging for donations and volunteers at Sunday Masses in parishes around the country, on campuses, and in corporate boardrooms.

Father Ritter's office at Under 21 in New York was a large, spare room, decorated only along one short space of wall with pictures, to which he guided the visitor with boyish enthusiasm: a painting by his sister of the site of the original Covenant House on the Lower East Side, garbage cans included; an artist's conception of the buildings, tennis court, and other facilities of Under 21/Houston; and a photograph of his "gorgeous kids" in Guatemala. Commenting on the growth of his project from six kids sleeping on his floor in 1968 to the international institution it is today, he said that he does not mind the institutionalization of what was once his private vision, even though "the price is loss of part of the vision," because he wants Covenant House to continue after he is gone. He said there will be nomadic armies of youths in cities around the world "trying to survive when they ought to be trying just to grow up," and in our decadent society, which makes pedophilia "almost fashionable," such youths will routinely be sexually exploited. "Covenant House and Under 21 exist to serve these lost sheep of the Twentieth Century Gospel. To help them find a way out of the gutters and brothels and strip joints, where their young bodies are in demand as objects of pleasure for lustful adults." Ritter ended up leaving the Franciscan order but remained a pious and devout religious practitioner. He was forced to retire to the small town of Decatur, New York amidst mounting

child sex scandal allegations. In his last decade celebrated mass in the privacy of his home. He enjoyed attending retreats in his later years and died of cancer at the age of 72.

## FURTHER READING

*Covenant House: Journey of a Faith-Based Charity*

# PAUL ROBESON
## Singer; Actor; Civil Rights Activist; Lawyer; Athlete

**Born:** Apr. 9, 1898; Princeton, N.J.
**Died:** Jan. 23, 1976; Philadelphia, Pa.
**Primary Field:** Civil Rights
**Affiliations:** Member of the Harlem Renaissance; Council on African Affairs; Provincetown Playhouse

## INTRODUCTION

*At the peak of his celebrity, while starring in Othello on Broadway, the immensely popular Black actor, singer, and political activist Paul Robeson was the guest of honor of a birthday party given, in April 1944, by the New York theatre world and an organization called the Council on African Affairs. So well-liked was Robeson that the celebration had to be held at the 17th Regiment Armory on Park Avenue to accommodate the nearly 8,000 guests. The sponsors of the tribute included some of the most famous names in show business, as well as several prominent figures from the Black community and the American left. By the end of the 1940s, with the Cold War in full swing and McCarthyism flourishing, such a gathering would have been highly unlikely. As the American political climate changed, however, Robeson clung to his admiration of the Soviet Union and to his denunciation of racial injustice. His commitment to views then considered radical and even subversive, cost him his passport from 1950 to 1958 and, although he later made concert tours of Australia and Europe, cut short his career as one of America's most eloquent singers and actors.*

## EARLY LIFE

Paul Leroy Bustill Robeson was born on April 9, 1898, in Princeton, New Jersey, the youngest of eight children

of William Drew and Anna Louisa (Bustill) Robeson. After escaping from slavery at the age of 15, his father had changed his name from Roberson, the surname of his former owner, to Robeson. He joined the Union Army, in 1861, and later worked his way through Lincoln University to become a Protestant minister. Paul Robeson's mother was a schoolteacher of African, Indian, and English ancestry. When the boy was six years old, she died of burns in a household accident. Paul, the only child still at home, and his father, who had lost his Princeton ministry, moved to Westfield, New Jersey, and then to Somerville in the same state, where the Reverend Robeson became Pastor of the St. Thomas African Methodist Episcopal Zion Church.

Shortly before his graduation from high school in Somerville, in 1915, Paul Robeson scored highest in a competitive examination for a four-year scholarship to Rutgers College (later Rutgers University). The following fall he became the first of his family to enroll in a White college. At Rutgers, he was the only Black student, and only the third Black student in the school's history. Despite his racial isolation, he was very popular with his classmates. Standing six-feet-three-inches tall and weighing 240 pounds as a young man, Robeson was described as "massive, beautiful in physique, muscular, strong and handsome." His deep voice and physical presence, then and later, impressed all who met him. He won the freshman prize for oratory and the sophomore and junior prizes for extemporaneous speaking. He earned twelve varsity letters in four sports—football, baseball, basketball, and track—and was named an All-American end in 1917 and 1918, winning the admiration of White teammates who had originally threatened a boycott if he were allowed to play on the football team. He served on the student council, gave the commencement address, and was elected to Phi Beta Kappa in his junior year, and also to the Cap and Skull Honor

Society. During all that time, Paul, like the other Robeson children, helped to support his college education by working at menial jobs in the summer.

## LIFE'S WORK

When he left Rutgers with his B.A. degree in 1919, Robeson took an apartment in Harlem, where his reputation as an up-and-coming Black youth had preceded him. In 1920, he entered the Columbia University Law School for training that he financed by playing professional football weekends. While in his first year at Columbia, he agreed to perform in an amateur production of the play *Simon the Cyrenian* at the Harlem Y.M.C.A. He made his professional debut, in 1921, in a presentation of the same play at the Lafayette Theatre.

A few of his dramatic roles gave Robeson the opportunity to sing as well as act, such as the title character in *Black Boy*, which had a short run in New York in October 1926. As Joe in *Show Boat* he sang "Ol' Man River" at the Drury Lane in London, in 1928, and at the Casino, in New York, in 1930. For British audiences, he also portrayed Robert Smith (Yank) in *The Hairy Ape* (1931), Balu in *Basilik* (1935), the Workman and Lonnie in *Stevedore* (1936), and Toussaint in *Toussaint L'Overture* (1936). In New York, in early 1940, he created the title role in *John Henry*, a play with music, but little dramatic force.

The role for which Robeson won highest critical tribute was *Othello*, which he first played in London, in May 1930. When that same production of Shakespeare's play, staged by Margaret Webster, opened at

---

## Affiliations: Member of the Harlem Renaissance; Provincetown Playhouse

For guidance in launching a career as an actor Robeson was primarily indebted to Eslanda Cardozo Goode, a chemistry student at Columbia whom he married on August 17, 1921. Having helped to persuade him to appear in Simon, she encouraged him to take time off from his studies to perform the starring role of Jim in Taboo, which ran briefly on Broadway, in 1922. Later in the year, renamed Voodoo, it was presented in Blackpool, England, with Robeson playing opposite Mrs. Patrick Campbell. His trip to England, where he and his wife were able to travel without the hindrance of Jim Crow laws and racial prejudice, began a lifelong love affair with Great Britain and the Continent.

In 1923, Robeson graduated from Columbia with an LL.B. degree, was admitted to the New York Bar, and was taken into a law firm headed by a prominent Rutgers graduate. His lack of enthusiasm for the limited opportunities that were open to him in law, along with his feeling that White clerks resented a Black giant in the office, combined to shorten his career as a lawyer. Observers recall that he was the victim of racism when a White secretary refused to take his dictation. He was, moreover, tempted to return to the theater by several members of the Provincetown Player, an experimental Greenwich Village company with which Eugene O'Neill was associate, who had seen his portrayal of Simon the Cyrenian. During May 1924, Robeson starred at the Provincetown Playhouse in two O'Neill plays, in The Emperor Jones as Brutus Jones, the Black dictator of a West Indian island, and in All God's Chillun Got Wings, a bold drama about an interracial marriage. Among those impressed by Robeson's apparently intuitive grasp of acting was the theater critic George Jean Nathan, who commented in the American Mercury (July 1924) that he "does things beautifully, with his voice, his features, his hands, his whole somewhat ungainly body, yet I doubt that he knows how he does them." Brutus Jones was the role in which Robeson made his triumphal London debut in September 1925.

Earlier, in 1925, Robeson had worked up a concert act with his friend, the pianist and composer Lawrence Brown. Their sellout concert in New York in April was so successful that they were signed to a 1925 to 1926 concert tour, playing and singing Negro spirituals and folk songs in the United States, Great Britain, and Europe. Robeson's voice, a deep and stirring baritone, soon became familiar all over the world. He had always had an aptitude for languages, and now he studied them so that he could sing folk songs of several nations. He eventually mastered more than 20 languages, including Chinese, Gaelic, and several African tongues. During the next 15 years, he made over 300 recordings, sang on the radio, and gave concerts in the United States, England, Europe, and the Soviet Union, which he visited for the first time in 1934. Robeson alternated his concert tours with appearances on the stage and in films, and eventually accumulated a large income.

the Shubert Theatre in New York, on October 19, 1943, Robeson drew uniformly ecstatic notices for his illuminating interpretation of the passionate and tragic Moor. The play made theater history on two counts: It was the first Othello on Broadway with a Black hero and a White supporting cast (José Ferre and Uta Hagen); and, its run of 296 performances exceeded that of any previous Shakespearean drama on Broadway. A coast-to-coast tour followed its New York presentation. Robeson's performance in *Othello* at Stratford-on-Avon in 1959 was also hailed as magnificent.

Two of the 11 motion pictures in which Robeson had leading or featured roles were film versions of plays in which he had appeared on the stage: *The Emperor Jones* (United Artists, 1933) and *Show Boat* (Universal, 1936). He played Basambo, an African chief, in *Sanders of the River* (United Artists, 1935); Umbopas, chief of another African tribe, in *King Solomon's Mines* (Gaumont British, 1937); a Black American dock worker in *Song of Freedom* (Treo Productions, 1938); and a coal miner in *Wales in Proud Valley* (Supreme, 1941). Among his other films were *Dark Sands* (Record, 1938) and *Tales of Manhattan* (Fox, 1942). In *Native Land* (Frontier Films, 1942), a documentary based on a Senate investigation of discrimination in the South, he spoke the commentary and sang the musical score. Sidney Poitier once said of Robeson, "Before him, no Black man or woman had been portrayed in American movies as anything but a racist stereotype." But Robeson felt he had not attained his goal. "I thought I could do something for the Negro race in films," he explained when he decided to give up working in motion pictures. "...The industry is not prepared to permit me to portray the life or express the living interests, hopes, and aspirations of the struggling people from whom I come."

Over the years, Robeson had acquired many interests and many friends beyond the entertainment business, becoming identified—and identifying himself—with left-wing causes. On his trip to the Soviet Union in 1934, he had been greatly impressed by the social experimentation he saw there. Revisiting that country often, he learned the Russian language and became as well known in Moscow as he was in London and New York. He once declared that Russia was the country he loved more than any other, and he sent his only child, Paul, Jr., to school there briefly, hoping that the absence of racial and class discrimination that Robeson believed was characteristic of Russia's schools would be to the boy's benefit.

During the 1930s, Robeson spent much time in England, where he was asked to give benefit performances for Jewish and other refugees from Fascist countries. He readily agreed and gained entree into British left-wing circles. Here he made the acquaintance of the young men of the West African Political Union, among them Jomo Kenyatta and Kwame Nkrumah. In the midst of the Spanish Civil War, he went to Spain to entertain Republican troops.

By the time the Robeson family returned to the United States, in 1939, to make America their home again, the Roosevelt years had wrought a perceptible change in the country's racial climate, and Robeson found it a more congenial place than the land he had left in 1928. He recorded a patriotic song called "Ballad for Americans," which became an instant hit and seemed to articulate the people's renewed faith in the vigor of the country and its democratic ideals.

Both Robesons considered themselves dedicated participants in what Paul Robeson once called "the struggle against anti-Semitism and against injustices to all minority groups." He joined organizations such as the Joint Anti-Fascist Refugee Committee, the Committee to Aid China, and the National Maritime Union, which made him an honorary member. His reputation as an entertainer was now fused with a new identification as a spokesman for the oppressed. That was no problem during World War II, when the "popular front against Fascism" was official United States policy. But in the late 1940s, as the Cold War intensified, Robeson began to suffer the same disrepute as thousands of other Americans with similar convictions.

Called before a committee of the California State Legislature in 1946, Robeson testified that he had never been a member of the Communist Party, but after that experience he refused to answer such questions, on principle. The House Committee on Un-American Activities routinely cited him in those days as a "Communist" or "Communist sympathizer," and people began to pay attention. Demands were made at Rutgers University that Robeson's name be removed from the alumni rolls and athletic records, and, that an honorary degree given Robeson earlier be rescinded. His recordings were withdrawn from stores and he was often denounced in newspaper editorials.

As the government and the public began to turn against him, Paul Robeson reaffirmed his views on the Soviet Union with increased vigor. In 1949, he made a controversial statement to the World Peace Congress in Paris: "It is unthinkable that American Negroes could go to war on behalf of those who have oppressed us for generations against a country [the Soviet Union] which, in one generation, has raised our people to the full dignity of mankind." Aside from feeling affection for the Russian people, who had warmly received him on so many occasions, Robeson had come to embrace "scientific socialism," as he wrote in his autobiographical *Here I Stand* (Dobson, 1958): "On many occasions I have expressed my belief in the principles of scientific socialism, my deep conviction that for all mankind a socialist society represents an advance to a higher stage of life."

The unpopularity of Robeson's views in a country grown increasingly fearful of Communism erupted in riots in the town of Peekskill, N.Y., in August 1949, when several liberal and radical groups held a music festival at which Paul Robeson was the featured attraction. Although Robeson finally managed to sing, more than100 concertgoers were injured. The experience angered and saddened him, and only confirmed his belief that America was becoming a reactionary nation.

In 1950, the State Department demanded that Robeson surrender his passport, and, refused to issue a new one, until he signed a non-Communist oath and promised not to give political speeches while abroad. In 1953, the C.A.A. was charged with subversion under the McCarran Act. Its principal leaders, including Robeson and Du Bois, were harassed. Robeson's unwillingness to comply led to a long and frustrating battle through the federal courts that did not end until 1958, when the Supreme Court in a similar case found the government's actions unconstitutional. During those years, Robeson was virtually prevented from earning a living, because the only concerts open to him in the United States were before small radical groups. In 1952, the Soviet Union awarded Robeson the Stalin Peace Prize, certainly a tribute that did nothing to alleviate his troubles at home.

By the time Robeson recovered his passport, the public's feelings about Communism had cooled somewhat, and in 1958 he gave a farewell concert at Carnegie Hall in New York City, his first appearance there in 11 years. He made a short tour of the West Coast, recorded

---

## Affiliation: Council on African Affairs

Although Paul Robeson was not a Communist Party U.S.A. Member, he served as The Council on African Affairs (CAA's) Chairman for most of its existence, while W. E. B. Du Bois served as Vice-Chair and head of the Africa Aid Committee. The CAA's most significant work took place in relation to South Africa. It supported striking Black miners and helped direct worldwide attention to the African National Congress's struggle against the Union of South Africa government and its policy of imposing racial apartheid.

The Council on African Affairs advocated an internationalization of domestic Civil Rights, support for African liberation groups, and a non-aligned stance on the part of developing nations toward the Cold War superpowers. Combined with many CAA leaders' past and current associations with the Communist Party U.S.A., this position became politically untenable by the early 1950s. The House Un-American Activities Committee (HUAC) put great pressure on Communist-affiliated organizations and activists.

---

an album, and then left the United States, remaining abroad until 1963. While in Russia in 1959, Robeson became ill and was hospitalized. From then until his return to America he was in and out of hospitals and nursing homes in Moscow, Eastern Europe, and London, suffering from exhaustion and from a circulatory ailment. According to his son, Robeson had become depressed and had tried to kill himself in Moscow. He underwent medication and electric shock therapy, but he never regained his health completely. In 1963, Robeson and his wife returned to the United States amid rumors, denied by Eslanda Robeson, that he had become disenchanted with Marxism. He would not speak to the press, however, except to announce his retirement from the stage and from all public affairs (he had not sung in public since 1961), and he went into a seclusion from which he had only occasionally emerged. After the death of Eslanda Robeson from cancer, in December 1965, Paul Robeson was able to keep his home only for a short time in New York City on Jumel Terrace, where his son and two grandchildren visited him. He eventually moved to Philadelphia to be with his sister, Mrs. Marion Forsythe.

The rich, powerful voice of Paul Robeson continued to be heard in recordings, such as the album *Songs of My People*, RCA Victor's 1972 selection of spirituals and other songs taken from old discs made by Robeson and Brown in the 1920s. Also available in the early 1970s were Vanguard's three albums, *Paul Robeson at*

*Carnegie Hall, Paul Robeson Recital*, and *Ballad for Americans*, as well as Columbia's album *Spirituals and Popular Favorites* and *Odyssey's Songs of Free Men*.

On April 15, 1973, a "75th Birthday Salute to Paul Robeson" was organized at Carnegie Hall by leaders in the entertainment world and the Civil Rights Movement, among them Harry Belafonte, Sidney Poitier, Zero Mostel, Coretta Scott King, and Angela Davis. Mrs. King paid tribute to Robeson for tapping "the same wells of latent militancy" among Blacks that her husband had inspired. Mayor Richard Hatcher of Gary, Ind., called Robeson "our own Black prince and prophet." Robeson was too ill to attend the celebration, but he sent a tape-recorded message, in which he said, "I want you to know that I am still the same Paul, dedicated as ever to the worldwide cause of humanity for freedom, peace and brotherhood."

Robeson's name reappeared in the news in 1975, following reports, originating with his son, that he would like to be inaugurated into the National Football Foundation Hall of Fame. The movement was headed by Rutgers President, Dr. Edward J. Bloustein, who appealed to the foundation on behalf of Robeson, calling him "a brilliant scholar-athlete and a brilliant artist in the finest tradition of collegiate higher education." He faced opposition, however, among directors of the foundation because of Robeson's political views and his long residence outside the country. (He was inducted into the hall of fame posthumously.) In addition to the Stalin Peace Prize, Paul Robeson received honorary degrees from Hamilton College and Rutgers University; the Spingarn Medal of the N.A.A.C.P; the Whitney Young, Jr., Memorial Award of the New York Urban League; and the Donaldson Award for the best acting performance of 1944 for his role as *Othello*.

In an era when Blacks were expected to step back, Robeson defied all expectations in the Jim Crow U.S. He unfailing continued to assert his Civil Rights, including the right to free speech, before there were any Civil Rights legislation to defend Blacks and other minorities.

On January 23, 1976, following complications of a stroke, Robeson died in Philadelphia at the age of 77. He lay in state in Harlem and his funeral was held at his brother Ben's former parsonage, Mother AME Zion Church, where Bishop J. Clinton Hoggard performed the eulogy. His pall bearers included Harry Belafonte. He was interred in the Ferncliff Cemetery in Hartsdale, N.Y.

## PERSONAL LIFE

Robeson married Eslanda Cardozo Goode, a Chemistry student who also was a Civil Rights Activist, in August 1921. Although the marriage started out strong, it was stormy because of Robeson's many infidelities. The couple almost divorced because of his affair with Peggy Ashcroft, a British actress who played Desdemona to his *Othello*. Robeson was persuaded by a friend to reconcile with his wife, because marriage to Ashcroft would have irreparably damaged his career. Eslanda died before Robeson in December 13, 1965. They had one child, Paul Robeson, Jr., who passed away in April 26, 2014.

## FURTHER READING

*Biog N 1:1317 N '75 por; N Y Times II p1+ Ag 6 '72 por; N Y Times Bk R p40+ O 21 '73 por; Biographical Encyclopaedia & Who's Who of the American Theatre (1966); Graham Shirley. Paul Robeson (1971); Hamilton, Virginia. Paul Robeson (1974); Hoyt, Edwin. Paul Robeson (1967); Robeson, Paul. Here I Stand (1958); Toppin, Edgar A. A Biographical History of Blacks in America (1971); Who's Who, 1974-75; Who's Who in America, 1974-75*

# RANDALL ROBINSON

## Lawyer; Author; Activist

**Born:** July 6, 1941; Richmond, Virginia
**Primary Field:** Human Rights; Immigrant Rights
**Affiliation:** U.S. Foreign Policy

### INTRODUCTION

*Why should African-Americans, or Americans of any race, for that matter, care about what is happening in Africa and the Caribbean? That is a question that Randall Robinson has been addressing for over 20 years. As the executive director of TransAfrica, a Washington, D.C. based lobbying group that he helped to found, he has sought to influence U.S. foreign policy in both Africa and the Caribbean. Since its establishment, in 1977, TransAfrica's annual budget has mushroomed from about $70,000 to $1 million, its staff has grown from two to about 16, and it boasts about 15,000 members. Under Robinson's leadership, TransAfrica has succeeded in shaping United States foreign policy regarding at least two issues. Back in the mid-1980s, Robinson emerged as a vocal opponent of the U.S. policy on South Africa, and after staging a protest against the South African government, he was arrested. This, in turn, helped spark a national movement aimed at forcing the U.S. to impose harsher sanctions on South Africa, and many observers believe that the movement was instrumental in bringing about an end to apartheid, in the early 1990s. In another case, Robinson went on a hunger strike in 1994 to protest the repatriation of Haitian refugees fleeing the military dictatorship of Raoul Cedras in Haiti. In response, the U.S. government reversed its policy and agreed to hold asylum hearings for the refugees. Within another half-year, the U.S. threatened to invade Haiti, and thereby succeeded in forcing Cedras to cede power.*

*Robinson readily admits that despite his organization's achievements, its impact on U.S. foreign policy has fallen short of what he has hoped it would be. "It has not changed the variously indifferent and hostile face of American foreign policy toward Africa and the Caribbean in general," he wrote in his memoir,* Defending the Spirit: A Black Life in America *(1998). U.S. foreign policy, he believes, has been racist in its neglect of African and Caribbean countries. He has questioned, for instance, why, since the end of the Cold War, the newly democratic countries in Eastern Europe have received more aid than the democracies in Africa or the*

*Caribbean. As Robinson wrote in his memoir, "Only from the study of America in its foreign relations can African-Americans hope to appreciate the full measure of America's insult to them."*

### EARLY LIFE

Randall Robinson was born on July 6, 1941 in Richmond, Virginia. He was the third of the four children of Doris Robinson, a former elementary school teacher who was active in the local Baptist church, and Maxie Robinson Sr., who taught history and coached several sports at Armstrong High School. The school's gym was named after him after he died, in 1973. When Robinson was growing up, segregation was still the norm in the South, and discrimination, both overt and subtle, was part of daily life. For Robinson, the statues of such Confederate heroes as Jefferson Davis, Stonewall Jackson, and Robert E. Lee along Monument Avenue in Richmond reflected the city's nostalgia for its racist past. "They never let you forget that Richmond was the capital of the Confederacy," Robinson told David Remnick for the *Washington Post* (February 5, 1985). "I remember going with my mother to a department store, and she'd have to put on a little cap before they'd let her try on ladies' hats. I recall sitting in the back of the bus with lots of empty seats up front. I remember delivering groceries to a white home, and when I came into the kitchen and they were discussing something very personal, they never stopped talking. It was as if I wasn't there. I was invisible." Robinson occasionally struck back. With his brother, he used to throw rocks at what had been the White House of the Confederacy.

Robinson and his family lived in a building where rats regularly gnawed holes in the walls. Early on, young Randall learned from his mother how to use wallpaper and paint to make their surroundings as livable as possible. His family put great stock in pride, as he found out when he asked his father whether he could get a job shining shoes. "He was appalled that I would even broach something like this to him, we were poor, but we were not that poor, and said no son of his would ever shine a white man's shoes," Robinson explained in an interview on the C-SPAN program *Booknotes*.

Robinson's two older siblings forged the way in academic and professional achievement: His sister

Jewell Robinson Shepperd was the first black student at Goucher College; she became a fundraiser for the Urban League and now has a career in theater. His brother, Max, the first black television anchor in the U.S., anchored ABC's *World News Tonight* for three years. Max Robinson died of AIDS, in 1988. Robinson's younger sister, Jean Yancey, became a public relations director at the Duke Ellington School of the Arts.

In contrast to his two older siblings, Robinson's performance in the all-black schools he attended was mediocre. "He was a cut-up. You would have thought he was going to be a comedian," Robinson's mother told the *Chicago Tribune Magazine* (October 16, 1985). "[His classmates] just can't imagine his doing what he's doing now." Athletic and tall (he now stands six feet, five inches), he played basketball in high school (with his father as coach) and, after graduating, in 1959, went to Norfolk State College, in Virginia, on a basketball scholarship. He dropped out of college after three years, and at the age of 22, was drafted into the army.

## LIFE'S WORK

Robinson hated the regimentation of army life, and he left after two years, just before his army division was sent to fight in Vietnam. He later learned that half of the men he had trained with were killed in one battle, in the la Drang Valley. With newfound discipline, he continued his undergraduate education at Virginia Union University, in Richmond, and earned a bachelor's degree in sociology, in 1967. Though he participated in civil rights protests at the time, he maintained a relatively low profile. In his memoir, he noted that though a disproportionate number of African-Americans were fighting and dying in the Vietnam War, "black students on black college campuses did not protest the war because those students believed, with reason, that they could not influence national foreign policy and therefore the war's outcome."

Robinson next attended Harvard Law School, in Cambridge, Massachusetts, where he sat in a classroom with whites for the first time. Also for the first time, he became aware that he was a greenhorn when it came to both the anticolonial struggles going on in Africa and the U.S.'s support for various dictatorships and colonialist regimes there. "I was incredulous," he wrote in his memoir. "Could I have been, for 26 years, that incurious? Could all these things actually be going on in the world (long have gone on, for that matter) without my

knowing a thing about them? Could there be a connection between my South and African's anguish?"

Following his graduation, in 1970, Robinson traveled to Tanzania on a Ford Fellowship. After returning to the U.S., he became an attorney for the Boston Legal Assistance Project, a federally funded program to provide legal aid to people who couldn't afford it. His legal career lasted only a year, because, he explained in his memoir, he was fired after continually demanding that the office, which served a predominantly black community, be headed by a black attorney. He next served as an administrative director of the Community Development Division of the Roxbury Multi-Service Center. During his tenure there, he organized protests against the Gulf Oil Co., which, he maintained, through its presence in Angola, Mozambique, and Guinea-Bissau, was in effect supporting Portugal's colonial administrations in those countries. Robinson also criticized Harvard for not divesting some $300 million invested in Gulf Oil. One wintry morning, students and faculty found Harvard Yard transformed into a symbolic graveyard of black crosses planted by Robinson and his fellow activists to protest the university's Gulf Oil holdings.

In 1975, Robinson became a foreign affairs aide to Congressman William L. Clay, a Democrat from Missouri. He also briefly served as a staff attorney for the Lawyer's Committee for Civil Rights Under Law before becoming, in 1976, an administrative assistant to Congressman Charles C. Diggs Jr., a Democrat from Michigan and, at the time, the most senior black member of Congress. As chairman of the House Africa Subcommittee, Diggs was one of the most prominent congressional voices speaking out on African issues. Diggs's career came to a disgraceful end after he was convicted, in October 1978, of falsifying congressional payrolls and diverting money to himself. Robinson resigned his position with Diggs that same year.

While working for Diggs, Robinson accompanied a congressional delegation to South Africa. Witnessing apartheid with his own eyes, he felt as if he were re-experiencing the discrimination and racism that prevailed in the segregated South of his youth. When Diggs demanded to know when black South Africans would be given the vote, Robinson overheard a white South African businessman answer, "To give a black the right to vote would be like giving a gun to a five-year-old!"

The Congressional Black Caucus met in 1977 to discuss creating a lobbying group for Africa and the Caribbean. The result was TransAfrica, which was incorporated on July 1, 1977, with Robinson as its executive director. "The idea for TransAfrica grew but of the broadly recognized need for an institutional mechanism through which African-Americans could be informed, galvanized, and moved to a focused, thoughtful participation in the formulation of U.S. foreign policy toward Africa and the Caribbean," Robinson wrote in his memoir. "Americans (unfortunately including African-Americans) knew little about Africa and the Caribbean. They knew even less about their nation's tradition of shameful attitudes and actions in these areas, a tradition often belied by the much ballyhooed image of America as a beneficent, compassionate, and freedom-loving superpower."

One of the first targets of TransAfrica's lobbying efforts was the U.S. government's reluctance to vigorously oppose apartheid in South Africa. President Ronald Reagan had endorsed a policy of "constructive engagement" with the South African government and the nation's business community, on the grounds that South Africa was staunchly anticommunist and was considered an ally of the U.S. in the Cold War. In testimony before members of Congress, Robinson presented reasons for his opposition to "constructive engagement," but his words made little impression. Reagan's landslide victory in November 1984 meant that the U.S.'s South Africa policy was unlikely to change for the next four years.

Refusing to accept the status quo, Robinson, along with the District of Columbia's representative in Congress, Walter Fauntroy, and U.S. Civil Rights Commissioner Dr. Mary Frances Berry, staged a sit-in at the South African Embassy on Thanksgiving Eve, 1984, in Washington, D.C. Both Robinson and Berry were arrested. The event generated much publicity and threw Robinson and TransAfrica into national prominence. He subsequently launched the Free South Africa Movement, of which he became national coordinator. Over the next 50 weeks, protesters in 26 cities demonstrated against the United States' policy toward South Africa. More than 4,000 people were arrested, including over 20 members of Congress. The protest eventually led Congress to pass the Comprehensive Anti-Apartheid Act of 1986, which established serious economic sanctions against South Africa for the first time. President Reagan vetoed the bill, but Congress overrode his veto. Many view the imposition of- sanctions as pivotal in the eventual release of Nelson Mandela and the establishment of non-racial democracy in South Africa.

TransAfrica has been active in connection with many other issues as well. In the late 1970s, Robinson worked to maintain U.S. sanctions against what was then white-governed Rhodesia (now Zimbabwe). He also criticized the U.S. for supporting Jonas Savimbi, the leader of the guerrilla force UNITA, which was fighting Angola's Cuban and Soviet backed government. Though his support of Communist leaders was anathema to his critics, Robinson does not consider himself a Communist. "I use a single standard for praise and condemnation," he told the *Washington Post* (March 13, 1990). "Wherever I see opposition to broad participation in the political system, I oppose it. I was arrested at [Marxist] Ethiopia's Embassy because of Ethiopia's deplorable human rights record. It is clear that Angola has to democratize its country; it must have national elections, though it's hard to do that in the middle of a civil war."

Robinson has also not hesitated to condemn countries governed by black Africans. He was critical of Sani Abacha's military dictatorship in Nigeria, which lasted from 1993 to June 1998, when Abacha unexpectedly died of a heart attack. The U.S. applied only limited sanctions (for example, cutting of economic aid and restricting visas) during Abacha's reign; in contrast, Robinson called for an oil embargo and the freezing of Nigeria's overseas assets. "It is a horrific situation only different from the old South Africa by the color of the oppressor," Robinson told the *Washington Post* (April 21, 1995).

A major foreign policy victory for Robinson occurred in 1994, when he went on a hunger strike to protest the treatment of Haitian refugees. Boats filled with Haitians fleeing the dictatorship of Raoul Cedras, who had seized power from the democratically elected leader Jean-Bertrand Aristide in 1991, were being turned back by U.S. ships on the high seas without giving the passengers on board an asylum hearing. Contrasting the plight of the Haitians to the treatment of Cuban refugees, Robinson pointed out that people in the latter group were often escorted to the U.S., where they would get an asylum hearing. "Race drives this policy as much as anti-Semitism in the State Department drove Roosevelt to turn around ships carrying Jews [during World War II]," Robinson proclaimed to the *Washington Post* (May 4, 1994). During the 1992 presidential campaign, Clinton had promised to reverse the Haitian policy, but after assuming the presidency, he did nothing, claiming that the Haitian boats were too rickety to make it to

U.S. shores and that turning the boats around was therefore necessary to save Haitian lives. Outraged, on April 12,1994, Robinson started a fast during which he ate nothing and drank only water and juice. Like his arrest at the South African Embassy, his hunger strike drew much media attention, particularly when he was hospitalized on May 4, because of his deteriorating condition.

On the 27th day of Robinson's fast, by which time he had lost around 13 pounds, one of Clinton's advisers informed him that the Haitian policy would be changed. Robinson ended his fast and began calling for military intervention to restore the democratically elected leader Aristide. This, as Robinson explained in his memoir, had been part of his strategy from the beginning. "The president had good reason to believe that he needed the electoral votes of Florida to be reelected [in 1996]. Overwhelmingly, Floridians were opposed to an influx of Haitians. Cubans were welcome, Haitians were not. I knew from the beginning that if I could persuade the President to screen the fleeing Haitians, the U.S. would soon run out of space for them at Guantanamo [and then the refugees would be resettled in Florida]. Then the president would have to choose between risking the loss of Florida and military intervention in Haiti [to stop the flow of refugees]. His decision was predictable." True to Robinson's prediction, Clinton did plan an invasion in September, the threat of which forced Cedras to abdicate power.

More recently, Robinson has protested the elimination of special European markets for bananas from such Caribbean countries as Dominica, Saint Lucia, Grenada, and Saint Vincent. Spurred by the multinational banana company Chiquita Brands, which wanted a greater share of the European market, the U.S. trade representative, Mickey Kantor, successfully represented Chiquita Brands' case to the World Trade Organization. Robinson opposed the action, because he believed that elimination of the protected European markets would devastate the economies of those Caribbean countries, all of which are democracies. In protest, on April 16, 1997, he and other activists dumped a ton of bananas in front of the U.S. trade representative's office building.

Robinson has also been lobbying for an increase in U.S. aid to Africa. "We are concerned that now, at the end of the Cold War, for the first time foreign policy toward Africa will not be driven by strategic concerns," he explained to *Black Enterprise* (August 1992). "The aid was never altruistic. Now it is being rethought. We have to fight to keep the United States engaged and supporting democracy in Africa just as we support Russia and the former Soviet republics."

While Robinson finds his work fulfilling, one aspect that he doesn't particularly like is the schmoozing that is de rigueur for lobbyists. "I'm not a good public person," he told the *Washington Post* (March 13,1990). "I don't think it shows when I'm in public, but it shows in my disinclination to be there. The substantive part of my work, the lectures, discussions with students across the country, I find rewarding. But there are things that you need to do that are essentially social for an operation that depends on funding. And I don't do them."

## PERSONAL LIFE

Robinson and his first wife divorced in 1982, after 18 years of marriage; they are the parents of two children, Anike and Jabari. In 1987, he married Hazel Ross-Robinson, a Trans Africa staff member who left the organization in 1985, after the two became romantically involved. Ross-Robinson served as a foreign policy adviser to U.S. Representative William Gray, a Democrat from Pennsylvania; she is now president of Ross-Robinson & Associates, which provides foreign policy related services. The couple have a daughter, Khalea.

Robinson, who once considered architecture as a career, enjoys spending his leisure time at home with his family and working on wood-carving projects. He has made many things, among them a staircase bannister carved with African-inspired symbols that spell out "I love you, Hazel." "This kind of thing is tremendously personal," he told the *New York Times* (August 22, 1991). "And I haven't any idea whether it would really appeal to others, and, frankly, I don't care. This is an extension of myself."

## FURTHER READING

*Defending the Spirit: A Black Life in America*

# ANITA RODDICK

## Social Activist; Businesswoman

**Born:** 1942; Littlehampton, Sussex
**Primary Field:** Environmentalism
**Affiliation:** The Body Shop

### INTRODUCTION

*"I hate the beauty business," the entrepreneur Anita Roddick declared in her autobiographical book* Body and Soul: Profits with Principles—The Amazing Success Story of Anita Roddick & the Body Shop *(1991). "It is a monster industry selling unattainable dreams. It lies. It cheats. It exploits women." Whereas most cosmetics companies profit from women's insecurities by promising that their expensive products will make women look and feel youthful, glamorous, and beautiful, the Body Shop has thrived on delivering affordable merchandise that sets out to do no more—and no less—than is possible for any cosmetic: "cleanse, polish, and protect the skin and hair," as Roddick has frequently intoned.*

*In keeping with Roddick's pared-down, no-nonsense approach to body care, the Body Shop uses mainly natural ingredients from renewable sources, offers to provide refills for its biodegradable, recyclable containers, does not use animals for testing, and actively supports environmental and human rights groups throughout the world. Flying in the face of conventional wisdom by refusing to advertise, Roddick has succeeded in an industry rooted in vanity and superficiality by making customers and employees feel good about purchasing and selling Body Shop products. In only sixteen years she has established an empire that encompasses more than seven hundred stores in forty-one countries, becoming one of the five wealthiest women in Great Britain in the process.*

### EARLY LIFE

Anita Lucia Perella was born in 1942 in the small English seaside town of Littlehampton, Sussex, the third of four children of Italian immigrant parents. Her mother, Gilda Perella, and her mother's husband, Donny Perella, owned and ran a cafe that served the local fishermen, and all the Perella children were expected to help in the cafe after school and on weekends. When Roddick was about eight years old, her mother divorced Donny Perella and married his cousin Henry, who died of tuberculosis

*Anita Roddick.*

eighteen months later. Roddick had always felt more attached to Henry than to Donny, and when she learned, at the age of eighteen, that Henry was, in fact, her father, she felt "as if an enormous weight of guilt had been lifted off [her] shoulders . . . ," as she recalled in *Body and Soul*. "[Knowing that Henry was my father] gave me a lot of confidence in gut feelings—taught me to trust my instincts above everything else, and stood me in very good stead when I came to open my first shop."

Roddick's life became arduous after her father's death, for she and her older sisters, Lydia and Velia (the daughters of Donny), and her younger brother, Bruno (the son of Henry), were required to work in the cafe as often as they were able. Perhaps because there was less leisure time available to Roddick for reading—she especially enjoyed books by authors whose work combined aesthetics with a social conscience, such as Walt Whitman, Bertolt Brecht, and Dostoevsky—she devoted her abundant energy and curiosity to her schoolwork, becoming enthralled with learning. After graduating from the Maude Allen Secondary Modern School for Girls, she applied to the Guildhall School of Music and Drama with the intention of becoming an actress. Although she was accepted, she declined to attend after her mother suggested that teaching would be a more "suitable" profession.

Confident that a classroom no less than a stage could serve as an outlet for her theatrical proclivities, Roddick attended the Newton Park College of Education at Bath for three years, studying English, history, and aesthetics. In 1962 she won a three- month scholarship to study the children of the kibbutzim in Israel. "I learned that it was a noble experience to be physically exhausted by honest labor, and I learned there was nothing more important to life than love and work," she wrote. Ejected from the kibbutz after she staged a practical joke for her young students by surreptitiously placing rocks just under the surface of a nearby lake and then having her bearded, long-haired colleague "walk" on the water, Roddick spent the remainder of her trip hitchhiking across Israel, learning valuable lessons in self-reliance along with the historical and cultural knowledge she picked up.

## LIFE'S WORK

After returning to England to complete her degree at Newton, Roddick spent a year in Paris working in the library of the *International Herald Tribune*. She then taught briefly in England, where she put her flair for the dramatic to good use in her classroom lessons by having her students act out historical events, write poetry as they listened to music, and generally have fun as they learned. "The only rule in my classroom was that no one should be bored," she wrote, "and at the end of a year the lethargic, dull-eyed kids that I had started with were unrecognizable. They were proud of themselves and proud of what they had achieved."

Restless once again, Roddick set off first for Greece and then for Switzerland. While in Geneva, Switzerland, she talked herself into a job with the women's rights department of the United Nations International Labor Organization. "Enthusiasm and energy either daunts people or it seduces them," she wrote, recalling how she was hired despite her lack of typing, shorthand, and other office skills. After a year in Geneva, she took her savings and set off on a self-directed tour of Tahiti, New Hebrides (now Vanuatu), New Caledonia, Australia (where she supplemented her dwindling financial resources by selling weatherboarding in Sydney), Reunion, Madagascar, Mauritius, and South Africa. "Everywhere I went I did my best to get to know the local people, to talk to them and eat with them and learn

about their lives," she revealed in *Body and Soul*. Her sojourn was cut short as a result of her disregard for the apartheid laws of South Africa; she was expelled from that country for attending a jazz club in Johannesburg on a night designated for blacks only.

By virtue of her itinerancy and her insatiable curiosity, Roddick became acquainted with the multifarious rituals and customs of many Third World peoples, including their forms of health and body care. "You change your values when you change your behavior . . .," Roddick told Cilia Duff Kent of the *Christian Science Monitor* (July 31, 1990). "When you've lived six months with a group that is rubbing their bodies with cocoa butter, and those bodies are magnificent; or you wash your hair with mud, and it works, you go on to break all sorts of conventions, from personal ethics to body care. Then, if you're me, you develop this stunning love for anthropology."

Back in England, Anita was introduced by her mother to Gordon Roddick, a kindred bohemian spirit who wrote poetry and traveled as freely as she did. The couple married in 1971, when Anita was pregnant with their second daughter, and shortly thereafter they opened a bed-and-breakfast hotel and, eventually, a restaurant. They learned much that would later prove valuable in establishing the Body Shop, including a division of labor that featured Anita out front, dealing with the public, and Gordon behind the scenes, organizing and managing. Finding themselves perpetually overworked and dissatisfied after three years of running both a restaurant and a hotel, with little time or money left over to attend to each other or to their children, the Roddicks sold the restaurant and began to consider alternatives to operating a hotel.

Around the same time, Gordon announced his intention to fulfill a long-standing personal goal: to ride a horse from Buenos Aires, Argentina to New York, which had been done only once, in the 1930s. Anita encouraged him to realize his childhood dream. "It blissed me out to have a partner who said, 'I've got to do this, I've got to be remarkable,'" she later told Suzie Mackenzie in an interview for the *Guardian* (September 11, 1991).

Faced with the urgency of earning a living for herself and her two children during her husband's projected two-year absence, Roddick decided to open a shop in order to ensure that she would have time for her children each day after closing. The idea of producing shampoos, lotions, and creams in a variety of sizes from natural ingredients arose from her experiences abroad and from her observation that no one was selling bath products in small or sample sizes. The concept of recycling and minimal packaging was generated by the need to keep start-up costs as low as possible, and her choice of a predominantly green interior decor began less as a symbol of her environmentally friendly practices than as a clever way to hide the damp spots on the walls. "I make no claim to prescience, to any intuition about the rise of the green movement," she stated forthrightly in *Body and Soul*. "At the forefront of my mind at that time there was really only one thought—survival. "

Using her hotel as collateral, Roddick obtained a $6,500 loan, contracted with an independent herbalist whom she found through the yellow pages, found a site in the upscale yet arty seaside resort of Brighton, some twenty miles from her home in Littlehampton, and opened the first Body Shop, next door to a funeral parlor, in the spring of 1976. Roddick's talent for garnering free publicity was evident from the beginning. When the morticians complained that her store's name would hurt their business, she anonymously leaked the story to the press. Before long, potential customers began arriving to see what all the hoopla was about. Since then, her only "advertisements" have been word- of-mouth recommendations from satisfied consumers and the high-profile stances the Body Shop takes on controversial social and environmental issues. "I think our genius came when we had the money but we didn't change things," she told Lisa Distelheim for *Life* (November 1988). "We just improved the business."

"There was a grace we had when we started— the grace that you didn't have to . . . tell lies," Roddick further explained to Bo Burlingham, who interviewed her for *Inc.* (June 1990). "We didn't know you could. We thought we had to be accountable. How do you establish accountability in the cosmetics business? We looked at the big companies. They put labels on the products. We thought what was printed on the label had to be truthful. I mean, we were really that naive." Thus, in a country that does not require the listing of ingredients, the Body Shop came across as sincere, honest, and up-front. There were also practical reasons for disclosing a product's contents. For example, reddish brown henna was prominently listed as the main ingredient in a shampoo that reportedly looked and smelled like horse manure. (The company now uses some synthetic fragrances, colors, and preservatives.)

Another of Roddick's innovations that derived from practical necessity was her decision to allow customers to choose from an array of perfume oils to scent their own purchases, which were otherwise fragrance-free. The process was much more cost-effective than adding expensive perfumes to each and every bottle of shampoo or lotion. "It all added to the wonderful smell in the shop and gave people the opportunity to experiment and create their own individual products," she explained in her book. "No one had ever done that before, and it was enormously popular: it was a combination of playtime, theatre, and a bit of fun."

Notwithstanding such blunders as labeling the bottles with ink that ran when exposed to steam, most of Roddick's instincts turned out to be right on target. She has attributed her initial success to her hard-driving need to survive, her ingenuity, proper timing, and her "zest for trading," a talent that, she believes, is "either in you or it's not." By September 1976 she had opened a second Body Shop, in Chichester, just west of Littlehampton. By the spring of 1977, when Gordon returned from his trip, having made it as far as Bolivia when one of his horses fell to its death in the Andes, the Body Shop had become so popular that the Roddicks were deluged with requests from customers who wanted to start a Body Shop branch of their own. Although the Roddicks had never heard of franchising, Gordon "invented" the practice, suggesting that others could open a Body Shop if they financed the operation themselves, in return for which they could use the Body Shop name and products. The first franchises began operating in 1978, including one in Brussels, Belgium; the following year shops were opened in Stockholm, Sweden and Athens, Greece.

All of the early franchisees were women, as most of them still are, which fits in with Roddick's passionate, caring, people-oriented ethic, as opposed to what she sees as the detached, traditional "male" focus on balance sheets, profit-and-loss calculations, and the bottom line. "The strength of women is the strength of instinct," she asserted in an interview with Libby Morse for the *Chicago Tribune* (October 20, 1991). "They don't want to make a science out of business. They only know that business is trading—and making that area where buyer and seller come together as magical and pleasant as possible."

By the fall of 1982 new Body Shops were opening at the rate of two a month, with the Roddicks charging a franchise fee and exercising strict control over the operation, image, and corporate identity of the stores. The day after the company went public in the spring of 1984, the share price increased by a whopping 50 percent. Just eight years later, the value of the Body Shop's gravity-defying stock had risen by more than 9,500 percent, and earnings for fiscal year 1990-91 had reached $41 million on sales of $231 million. The securities analyst John D. K. Richards told Rahul Jacob of *Fortune* (January 13, 1992) that he expected the company to sustain an annual growth rate of between 35 percent and 40 percent for the next five years.

When Roddick took the Body Shop public, she raised its name recognition as well as its earnings and realized that she could use her business as a potent vehicle for the expression of her social and environmental concerns. "From that moment, the Body Shop ceased to exist, at least in my eyes, as just another trading business," she wrote in *Body and Soul*. "It became a force for social change." She had been campaigning aggressively for years against the practice of animal testing in the cosmetics industry; with the success of the Body Shop, she had the clout to make her voice heard in other progressive movements of concern to her. The company's activism would serve three purposes concurrently: to effect change, to motivate her employees, and to substitute for advertising. While the latter goal is by no means her only motive, as some cynics have suggested, she has acknowledged its existence. "When you are [a] small [company]," she explained to Rahul Jacob, "you become the mouth of the product. Obviously we do use the press because we are run almost like a political campaign."

The first cause to which the Body Shop lent its window displays involved Greenpeace's lobbying efforts against the dumping of hazardous waste in the North Sea. The "Save the Whale" campaign followed shortly thereafter. Then, in cooperation with Friends of the Earth, the company highlighted the threat to the environment from acid rain and warned customers about the dangers to the ozone layer posed by the use of aerosol sprays. Soon Roddick was utilizing everything from bags to delivery trucks to convey a social message, and in 1986 she set up an Environmental Projects Department to coordinate campaigns and to monitor Body Shop products and practices for environmental safety.

Roddick's wide-ranging interests and projects have extended from renovating orphanages in Rumania to Amnesty International to starting an alternative London newspaper, called Big Issue, which is sold by homeless people. Her main focus, however, has been the empowerment of communities in the Third World. For example, her "Stop the Burn" campaign to save the Brazilian rain forests has been complemented by the development of a direct trading relationship with the Kayapo Indians that is intended to provide them with a livelihood while supplying the Body Shop with Brazil nut oil obtained from the rain forests. Her "Trade Not Aid" projects have involved American Indians and peoples in Somalia, Nepal, India, Burkina Faso, Malaysia, the Philippines, and Kenya. Unlike many multinational companies, the Body Shop does not exploit the Third World as a source of cheap labor; its overseas workers are paid wages comparable to those earned by British workers.

The dividends of Roddick's resourceful, creative approach to international business include a loyal clientele and a motivated work force. "You educate people by their passions, especially young people," she told Bo Burlingham. "You find ways to grab their imagination. You want them to feel that they're doing something important, that they're not a lone voice, that they are the most powerful, potent people on the planet." Her maverick attempts to humanize both the nature of business and the day-to-day work experience of her employees entail efforts to encourage each store's staffers to become involved, on company time, with at least one volunteer community project. In 1985 the Body Shop set up an in-house training school in London that focuses not on selling but on helping each individual employee realize his or her potential within the expanding Body Shop framework.

As the Body Shop and its projects have flourished, copycat imitations of the company's holistic concept and product line have proliferated. Two years after Roddick took her first plunge into the lucrative yet complex American market, with the opening of a store in New York City in July 1988, Estee Lauder launched Origins Natural Resources, a line of natural-ingredient cosmetics in recycled containers. In an even bolder attempt to capture the potential Body Shop customer, Leslie Wexler, the founder of the Limited Inc., began a chain of stores called Bath & Body Works, decorated in green and advertising itself as "dedicated to preserving the earth." (The Body Shop sued and reached an out-of-court settlement in July 1991.) And as of 1992, Kmart Corporation's Naturistics line was being sold in 1,800 stores. Undaunted by the competition, Roddick has been pursuing an aggressive expansion in the United States; by 1992 she had opened eighty-eight stores.

While she has acknowledged that the larger her company grows, the more challenging it will be to maintain its political and social activism, Roddick has averred that she intends to become "more radical, not less so." "We will compromise on almost anything," she wrote in the concluding pages of *Body and Soul*, "but not on our values, or our aesthetics, or our idealism, or our sense of curiosity. These are qualities drawn from the very core of our being and they are what keep us human in an alienating business environment."

Roddick's path-breaking innovations and phenomenal success have won her numerous awards and accolades, including Businesswoman of the Year in Britain, Communicator of the Year, Retailer of the Year, and the United Nations' "Global 500" environmental award. She was recently named an Officer of the Order of the British Empire. (She counts members of the British royal family among her devoted customers.) Having no intention of slowing down and resting on her laurels, Roddick has said, as quoted in *People* (October 10, 1988), "I wake up every morning thinking . . . this is my last day. And I jam everything into it. There's no time for mediocrity. This is no damned dress rehearsal."

## PERSONAL LIFE

As managing director of the Body Shop, with responsibility for marketing and product development (Gordon takes care of the administrative and financial operations as co-CEO), Roddick spends some five months of the year on the road, researching women's body-care rituals and delighting in the ancient occupation of trading with far-flung communities. "I think Gordon provides a sense of constancy and continuity while I bounce around breaking the rules, pushing back the boundaries of possibility and shooting off my mouth," Roddick wrote in *Body and Soul*. Her two grown daughters, Justine and Samantha, have become involved in some of the Body Shop humanitarian projects, although they have not yet committed themselves to the family business.

The Roddicks live in a spacious Georgian house, with four acres of land, on the Sussex Downs, fifty miles from London; they also own a seventeenth-century holiday home in Scotland.

## FURTHER READING

*Bsns W pU4+ Jl 15 '91 pors; Chicago Tribune VI p3 O 20 '91 pors; Christian Sci Mon p!4 Jl 31 '90 por; Guardian p37 S 11 '91 por; Inc 12:34+ Je '90 pors; Life 11:21+N '88 pors; Ms 17:50+ S '88 pors; People 30:97+ O 10 '88 pors; Roddick, Anita. Body and Soul: Profits with Principles—The Amazing Success Story of Anita Roddick & the Body Shop (1991)*

# ANTHONY ROMERO

### Executive Director of the American Civil Liberties Union

**Born:** 1965; Bronx, New York
**Primary Field:** Freedom & Equality
**Affiliation:** American Civil Liberties Union

## INTRODUCTION

*"I learned from my mom and dad the importance of believing in yourself and fighting for what you believe,"* Anthony Romero, the executive director of the American Civil Liberties Union, told Chris Bull for the Advocate *(June 19, 2001). "They taught me to treat others with respect but also to demand it in return." The ACLU, founded in 1920, is a nonpartisan organization devoted to defending the civil rights of people in the United States as those rights are delineated in the Constitution* and the Bill of Rights. Romero came to the organization in 2001, after a decade of defending human rights in the U.S. and around the world on behalf of the Rockefeller Foundation and then the Ford Foundation. The first Latino and first openly gay man to lead the organization, he arrived with an "overarching goal": "to promote a new generation of committed civil libertarians and civil rights activists," as he stated in an ACLU press release, as quoted in the Newsletter on Intellectual Freedom (July 2001). In a prescient statement not long before the September 11, 2001 terrorist attacks on the World Trade Center and the Pentagon, he told Lisa Balmesada for the Miami Herald (June 18, 2001), "Our own complacency is our greatest enemy. We give up a lot of our civil liberties because we choose not to fight. Americans have been lulled into a false sense of security." After the September 11 attacks, Romero and the ACLU worked as-*

*siduously to protect American freedoms, some of which the U.S. government sought to limit (through such procedures as wire tapping, racial profiling, and detention of immigrants) as a means of preventing further attacks or meting out immediate justice for terror victims. "We need to defend security and at the same time protect freedom," Romero explained to Arian Campo-Flores for* Newsweek *(December 31, 2001/January 7, 2002). "The two don't have to be on a collision course."*

## EARLY LIFE

The son of Demetrio and Coralie Romero, both of whom had immigrated from rural Puerto Rico, Anthony Romero was born in about 1965 in the New York City borough of the Bronx. He has one sister. His father held jobs as a janitor and maintenance worker at a big hotel. Impressed by her son's interest in reading, young Anthony's mother encouraged him to focus on school. He attended a Catholic elementary school in New York City until the family moved to Little Falls, New Jersey, when Demetrio Romero secured a job as a banquet waiter at the hotel. The move followed a long-fought racial discrimination battle that the elder Romero had won with the help of the hotel workers' union. Anthony Romero excelled in school, but because neither of his parents had completed high school, he never thought about attending college. His academic achievement, however—he graduated second in his high-school class—led college recruiters to seek him out. As a result, he enrolled at Princeton University, in Princeton, New Jersey.

At Princeton, Romero studied at the Woodrow Wilson School of Public and International Affairs. "I loved the focus on undergraduate teaching, and my interests were always in international affairs and human rights," he told Katherine Hobson for the *Princeton Alumni Weekly* (March 13, 2002, online). He spent his junior year at a college in Colombia. Fluent in Spanish, he wrote his senior thesis on a topic close to his heart: Latin Americans' immigration to the United States. After he graduated from Princeton, in 1987, he entered Stanford Law School (a division of Stanford University), in Stanford, California, where he again excelled. At both Princeton and Stanford, Romero was a beneficiary of affirmative action, a practice he staunchly supports. "I earned the grades, but affirmative action got me through the door," he told Lynda Richardson for the *New York Times* (January 8, 2002). "Very often, it's misunderstood as being about quotas or being unmeritorious. It's about leveling the playing field."

## LIFE'S WORK

After earning a law degree, in 1990, Romero felt a pull toward public-interest law. Focusing on charitable foundations, he returned to New York to work for the Rockefeller Foundation, where he oversaw the organization's civil rights endeavors. After two years he moved to the Ford Foundation, a global nonprofit organization that works to distribute grants and funding for various projects. In his first position there, he served as the foundation's program officer for civil rights and racial justice; after five years he was promoted to director of human rights and international cooperation. Through his work at the Ford Foundation, Romero traveled to far-flung locales, including China and Kenya. He also learned to manage funds and grants, a key qualification for working for the ACLU. In May 2001 he was named the ACLU's sixth director, succeeding Ira Glasser, who had headed the organization for 23 years. In a rare display of complete harmony, the 83-member ACLU board voted unanimously for Romero's appointment. "What I have achieved is an enormous testament to this country, so I am incredibly patriotic," he told Arian Campo-Flores. Defending civil liberties and human rights, he added, is "the ultimate act of patriotism."

As the director of the ACLU, Romero became responsible for overseeing a huge spectrum of activities. "Most civil rights and civil liberties organizations focus on a specific issue or a particular constituency," he explained in an ACLU press release (May 1, 2001). "The ACLU, in contrast, is the only organization that defends the civil liberties and civil rights of all Americans." As he explained to Rose Gutfeld for the *Ford Foundation Report* (Winter 2002), he believes there are four issues of particular importance to the ACLU: "The first has to do with free speech and new technologies. . . . The next generation of advocacy will require us to ensure that speech on the Internet is not just uncensored but free—in the sense of being open and available to all, and free from the restrictions on content and opinion that take place in the print and broadcast media, where powerful individuals and a handful of media companies exercise control." The second area of concern to the ACLU, Romero stated, is the U.S. criminal-justice system and the country's huge prison population—nearly two million men and women, the large majority of whom are members of ethnic minorities and are poorly educated or uneducated and were underemployed or unemployed before their incarceration. The ACLU opposes the death penalty and mandatory sentencing and advocates prison reform and a halt to racial profiling. "We may be headed for a situation where prison building is pursued with the same type of civic pride and support enjoyed by the national highway-building program of the 1950s," Romero told Gutfeld. The third priority of the ACLU is affirmative action— particularly with regard to redistricting, to equalize minority representation, and voting reform, to ensure that no registered voters are denied the opportunity to cast their ballots and that all votes are counted. As for the fourth issue, the ACLU has continued to pursue its goal of maintaining privacy for American citizens and visitors to the country. "Solutions to the privacy issues will not be easy because these involve highly technical matters and ethically complex choices," Romero told Gutfeld. Using the mapping of the human genome as an example, he added, "It is an awesome development, but it could be wrongly used. ... That information can be used to map your propensity for illness and disease, life expectancy and behavioral disposition. Such personal information can now be compiled in private databases, bought by the highest bidder and transacted cross-country with the stroke of a key."

One week after Romero took office, the United States was attacked by terrorists. In the weeks and months that followed, Romero and many other ACLU staffers worked overtime in an attempt to maintain the line between personal safety and violations of civil rights. "Civil libertarians are just like anyone else," he told Rose Gutfeld. "We understand the importance of increasing our safety and increasing our security. ... At the same time, we believe that we should not lose the basic freedoms and basic liberties that are the hallmarks of our democracy because of this fear and uncertainty. The terrorist attacks were meant not only to destroy; they were also meant to intimidate us as a people and to force us to take actions that are not in our best interests." Romero realized that the terrorist attacks marked a pivotal time for civil liberties. "We've been sounding the note that the U.S. must stay safe and free," he told Katherine Hobson. "Right now, young people will grow up in a new climate of civil liberties and civil rights that are being defined at this moment." Following the attacks, the ACLU protested the harassment of Arab-Americans as well as new federal policies allowing for the detainment of more than 1,200 immigrants whose names the Department of Justice refused to reveal. "By all accounts, the overwhelming majority of [the] detainees are Muslims or Arabs, come from Middle

Eastern countries, and are noncitizens," according to testimony presented before the Senate Judiciary Committee on December 4, 2001 by the ACLU's president, Nadine Strossen. "Most of these folks have nothing to do with the terrorist attacks, but we are treating them a certain way because of their national origin," Romero said to Gutfeld. "That's not right, and it cuts against our core principles of fairness and equality under the law." The ACLU filed lawsuits in protest, claiming that these immigrants had been denied due process. "Very little information is coming from our government on this key issue," Romero said during a San Francisco press conference, as reported by Alexis Chiu for the San Jose *Mercury News* (January 30, 2002). "That impedes the public's ability to know whether due process of law is alive and well."

Further, the ACLU sent letters to consulates, such as Pakistan's and Egypt's, offering legal advice and assistance for their detained citizens. "Our main concern is that there is a growing momentum focusing on a specific community, regarding them as suspicious merely because of where they are from. The government should focus on what they have done, not where they were born," Romero told Jennifer Barrett for *Newsweek* (January 18, 2002, online). The ACLU has also urged the U.S. government to honor guaranteed rights to privacy when crafting new legislation on issues ranging from airport security to the possibility of standardizing the licensing of drivers throughout the U.S., which would result in de facto national IDs for all drivers. "I worry about another attack and the loss of human life," Romero admitted to Lynda Richardson, "then the repercussions that would follow with a second attack, with a further curtailment of civil liberties and civil rights."

Romero's office, close to where the World Trade Center once stood, overlooks New York Harbor and the Statue of Liberty. "My job," he told Richardson, "is to make sure no one extinguishes her flame. So far, so good."

## PERSONAL LIFE
Romero, who enjoys cooking in his spare time, lives in Manhattan with his partner.

## FURTHER READING
*Miami Herald (on-line) June 18, 2001; New York Times A p20 Jan. 8, 2002, with photo; Newsweek p78 Dec. 31, 2001/Jan. 7, 2002, with photo; Wall Street Journal B pi Nov. 18, 2001*

# JOSEPH ROTBLAT

## British Physicist; Activist

**Born:** November 4, 1908; Warsaw, Poland
**Died:** August 31, 2005; London, England
**Primary Field:** Nuclear Disarmament / Peace
**Affiliation:** Nobel Peace Prize

## INTRODUCTION

*During World War II, the Polish-born British physicist Joseph Rotblat went to Los Alamos, New Mexico, to work on the Manhattan Project, the mission of which was to produce the world's first atom bomb. Of the scientists who left Los Alamos before that goal was reached, "he was the only one . . . who quit the Manhattan Project who cited moral reasons," William J. Broad reported in the* New York Times *(May 21, 1996). More than 50 years later, at the age of 86, Rotblat won the Nobel Peace Prize, for his subsequent efforts to stop the manufacture, testing, stockpiling, and spread of nuclear weapons.*

*After learning that he had won the prize, Rotblat said, "I see this honor not for me personally, but rather for the small group of scientists who have been working for 40 years to try and save the world, often against the world's wishes." Prominent among those scientists are people who have participated in the Pugwash Conferences on Science and World Affairs, an international organization that Rotblat helped to found, in 1957, and that was the co-winner of the 1995 Nobel Peace Prize. The purpose of the Pugwash Conferences is "to bring together, from around the world, influential scholars and public figures concerned with reducing the danger of armed conflict and seeking cooperative solutions for global problems." Pugwash participants meet as individuals, not as representatives of governments or institutions.*

*Rotblat believed that while all people must take responsibility for their actions, since World War II it has become especially important for scientists to do so. That is because for the first time in history, scientists have the ability to inflict disaster "on the whole of mankind," in his words, because of their crucial roles not only in the development of weapons of mass destruction but also in the development of technologies that can cause global environmental havoc. At a news conference held in 1995, Rotblat acknowledged that he did not expect the world to become safer simply because he and Pugwash*

*had won the peace prize. "But my hope is that more scientists will be encouraged to think seriously about the social impact of their work," he said.*

## EARLY LIFE

The fifth of seven children (two of whom, died in infancy), Joseph Rotblat was born into a Jewish family in Warsaw, Poland, On November 4, 1908. His father, Zygmunt Rotblat, prospered as a shipper of paper until World War I, when his business failed and the family plunged into poverty. "It came to the stage of literally hunger, starvation , . . ," Joseph Rotblat recalled to Susan Landau for the *Bulletin of the Atomic Scientists* (January/February 1996). "One had to fight for one's survival." To get by, the family sold vodka that they distilled illegally at home.

Zygmunt Rotblat's business never recovered, and after the war, Joseph Rotblat became an electrician. He worked outside, laying cable in Warsaw streets—a painfully difficult task in freezing weather. Determined to make a better life for himself, he enrolled at the University of Warsaw as a night student, and in 1932 he earned a master's degree in physics. While studying for his Ph.D., he began working at the Radiation Laboratory of Warsaw under the physicist Ludwik Wertenstein. In reminiscing about Rotblat to Susan Landau, a co-worker of his at the laboratory said, "There is hardly a man I know more devoted to science. Highly honest, a very good friend. He had high solidarity with all of his colleagues."

## LIFE'S WORK

Rotblat received his doctoral degree in 1938. In early 1939, he got an offer to work in Paris with the Nobel Prize-winning physicist Frederic Joliot-Curie and also an invitation to work at the University of Liverpool, in England, with the Nobel Prizewinning physicist James Chadwick, who discovered the neutron in 1932. Rotblat accepted the latter. "In Liverpool, they were building a cyclotron," he explained to Landau. "It was my intention to build a cyclotron when I came back to Warsaw so that we could start a proper school of nuclear physics."

Rotblat was preparing to leave for England when he learned about experiments in which bombardments of neutrons caused uranium atom nuclei to split, with a resulting burst of energy—a process dubbed nuclear fission. He also learned of a hypothesis, offered by the

Danish physicist Niels Bohr, proposing that when the nucleus was split, one or more neutrons might be released, and that neutron or neutrons might strike and divide other nuclei, thus beginning a chain reaction. Along with many other physicists, Rotblat began doing experiments to test Bohr's hypothesis. According to Landau, "He found that several surplus neutrons were released by the fissioning nuclei." Rotblat wrote up his results in Polish; then, before Ludwik Wertenstein had completed a translation into English for publication, a paper by Joliot-Gurie reporting precisely the same findings appeared in a professional journal.

Although Rotblat believed that his duty was "to do research and not think about how it was to be applied," as he put it, he grew concerned about the ramifications of the discovery—namely, the possibility that a chain reaction could proceed so rapidly that it could produce a massive explosion, and thus that it could serve as the mechanism of an atom bomb—-a bomb far more powerful than any in existence. What made that prospect especially frightening to him was that Germany was clearly preparing to attack Poland, and he thought that "if the Germans had such a new device, it would be quite terrible for our side."

Rotblat arrived at James Chadwick's laboratory in March 1939. Six months later, on September 1, the German army invaded Poland, and World War II erupted. Rotblat's wife, Tola Gryn, whom he had married in the early 1930s, had not accompanied him to England, because his stipend had been too small to support both of them, and she became trapped in Poland. His strenuous attempts to get her out of the country did not succeed, and after the spring of 1940, he lost contact with her. By that time he had concluded, in his words, that "the only way to stop the Germans from using [an atom bomb] against us would be if we, too, had the bomb and threatened to retaliate." Through experiments that he conducted with the help of the physicist Otto Robert Frisch, who was one of the original fission experimenters, he established by 1941 that the atom bomb was, in his words, "theoretically possible."

In June 1942, the British prime minister, Winston Churchill, and the American president, Franklin D. Roosevelt, agreed to combine the atom bomb projects of Great Britain and the United States. The bomb research and development, code- named the Manhattan Project, would be conducted in Los Alamos, out of range of attack by German bombers. For reasons of security, U.S. officials asked that the British government send only researchers who were British subjects. Since many of the people working on the bomb in Great Britain were 6migrds from other European countries, they had to become British subjects, literally overnight. Rotblat declined to take British citizenship, because he was concerned about his wife and other missing family members and he intended to return to Poland after the war. Thus he was not among the first group of scientists that came to New Mexico, in late 1943. Intervening on his behalf, Chadwick—the leading scientist in the British delegation—persuaded Leslie R. Groves, the American general who headed the Manhattan Project, to waive the citizenship requirement in Rotblat's case. (Rotblat became a British citizen at the end of the 1940s or the beginning of the 1950s, to enable his surviving family members to immigrate to England after Poland turned Communist. Earlier, he had learned that, along with six million other Jews and millions of other Europeans, his wife had been killed during the war.)

In Los Alamos, where he arrived at the beginning of 1944, Rotblat boarded with the Chadwicks. One evening in March 1944, General Groves came to their place for dinner. "It was at this time that [Groves] mentioned that the real purpose in making the bomb was to subdue the Soviets," Rotblat recalled to Landau. "I was terribly shocked. My unhappiness about the weapon had started even before this, but this certainly was wrenching. ... I felt that what I was doing was for no purpose." In the summer of 1944, word came from Europe that, as Rotblat had already begun to suspect, the Germans had made little progress toward building an atom bomb. Moreover, the defeat of Germany by the Allied forces seemed increasingly likely. So, soon afterward, Rotblat asked for permission to quit the Manhattan Project. Thinking that he might be a spy for the Soviet Union, the project authorities gave him a hard time about leaving, but, unable to substantiate their suspicions, they eventually complied with his request and merely asked him not to speak to anyone about the bomb effort.

After Rotblat returned to Great Britain, he became the acting director of Chadwick's laboratory in Liverpool. He remained silent about the bomb until 1945, when the United States dropped atom bombs on Hiroshima and Nagasaki. The bombing of those Japanese cities, which immediately killed or grievously injured an estimated 200,000 civilians, horrified him. "I did not think [the bomb] would be used as soon as it was made, without warning, and on a civilian population," he was quoted as saying in the *Chicago Tribune* (October 14,

1995). In an attempt to convince other physicists of the dangers of nuclear weapons, he began giving lectures throughout England. With the German-born physicist Albert Einstein and the British philosopher and mathematician Bertrand Russell, he founded the Atomic Scientists Association, a British group, as a vehicle for educating the public and influencing governmental policy with regard to nuclear weapons.

Meanwhile, after the war Rotblat grew fascinated with the medical applications of nuclear physics. In 1949 he joined the staff of St. Bartholomew's Hospital at the medical college of the University of London, where, with the physiologist Patricia Lindop, he did research on the effects of radiation on living organisms. "I became somewhat of ail authority on the hazards resulting from exposure to radiation," he recalled to Landau.

In early 1954, fallout from the detonation of a hydrogen bomb being tested by the United States on the Pacific island of Bikini rained down on a Japanese fishing boat. Exposure to a heavy dose of radiation from the bomb made the fishermen on the boat dreadfully ill. Soon after that incident, Rotblat appeared on Panorama, a British television program, where he said that the only difference between the atom and hydrogen bombs was the size of the blast. The hydrogen bomb, he said, was more powerful but did not produce any more radiation. But that statement turned out to be wrong, as he realized later that year; the hydrogen bomb, which is a thousand times more powerful than the atom bomb, actually produces a thousand times more radiation.

Rotblat wrote an article about the Bikini test, but he hesitated to submit it for publication because he didn't know exactly how much radiation had been released. Then, in 1955, in response to growing fears among Americans about the possibly harmful effects of the radioactive fallout produced by nuclear tests, the United States Atomic Energy Commission issued a statement suggesting that the dose of radiation that people in the United States received from nuclear tests was no more than what they would get from chest X rays. The statement stunned Rotblat. "If everybody in the United States—and also probably in other parts of the world—had received as much radiation from those few tests as you get from one X ray, then the radioactivity comes down very rapidly, before it has time to decay . . . ," he explained to Landau. "I thought this was terribly dangerous." Rotblat proceeded to publish his article. "As it turned out, the statement by the Atomic Energy Commission was wrong, and the amount of radiation was

much less than you get from a chest X ray . . . ," he told Landau. "But I didn't know at the time about this. I was as confused as the Atomic Energy Commission itself. The main thing was that people discovered it was a dirty bomb."

In 1955, prompted by Bertrand Russell, 11 distinguished scientists (including nine Nobel Prize winners)—among them Einstein, Joliot-Curie, the American chemist Linus Pauling, the Japanese physicist Hideki Yukawa, the German physicist Max Born, and Rotblat—joined Russell to draft what became known as the Russell-Einstein Manifesto, in which they urged scientists to gather to "appraise the perils that have arisen as a result of the development of weapons of mass destruction" and to discuss "what steps can be taken to prevent a military contest of which the [result] must be disastrous to all parties." The manifesto, which was widely publicized, ended with the following resolution: "In view of the fact that in any future war, nuclear weapons will certainly be employed, and that such weapons threaten the continued existence of mankind, we urge the governments of the world to realize, and to acknowledge publicly, that their purpose cannot be furthered by a world war, and we urge them, consequently, to find peaceful means for the settlement of all matters of dispute between them."

The manifesto provided the impetus for what became the Pugwash Conferences—annual meetings of scientists and public figures whose goals matched those of the signers of the manifesto. Twenty-two people attended the first meeting, which was held in Pugwash, Nova Scotia, in 1957. Because of "the climate of mistrust and fear that existed at that time" as a result of the Cold War, "it required a great deal of civic courage to come" to the meeting, Rotblat has recalled. "Anyone in the West who came to a meeting, who talked peace with the Russians, was condemned as a Communist dupe."

When Pugwash began, it provided the only channel of communication between the Eastern, Communist bloc of nations and the Western democracies on issues relating to global security and the threat of nuclear annihilation. Pugwash— sometimes called the Pugwash project or movement—helped to lay the groundwork for the Partial Test Ban Treaty of 1963, the Non-Proliferation Treaty of 1968, the Anti-Ballistic Missile Treaty of 1972, the Biological Weapons Convention of 1972, and the Chemical Weapons Convention of 1993. In a description of the organization that appeared in May 1997 on the Pugwash Web site, Vittore Mazzei of the

Rome Pugwash office wrote that with the warming of East-West relations since 1989 and "the emergence of a much wider array of unofficial channels of communication," the visibility of Pugwash has been "somewhat reduced," but "Pugwash meetings have continued . . . to play an important role in bringing together key analysts and policy advisers for sustained, in-depth discussions of the crucial arms-control issues of the day: European nuclear forces, chemical and biological weaponry, space weapons, conventional force reductions and restructuring, and crisis control in the Third World, among others. Pugwash has, moreover, for many years extended its [scope] to include problems of development and the environment." From 1957 to 1973, while teaching physics and doing research at the University of London, Rotblat held the post of secretary-general of the Pugwash Conferences. He became the president of the organization in 1988.

In naming Rotblat and Pugwash the winners of the 1995 Nobel Peace Prize, the Nobel Committee made it clear that in addition to honoring the recipients, its intention was to protest the refusal of France and Communist China to end their nuclear weapons tests—tests that Rotblat, too, has denounced.

## PERSONAL LIFE

When William J. Broad of the *New York Times* interviewed him in 1995, Rotblat appeared to the reporter to be "a study in perennial elan." "Courtly and full of old-world charm . . . , Rotblat at 87 acts like a man half his age," Broad wrote. Rotblat worked in London and shares a dwelling there with one of his sisters-in-law.

He wrote, co-wrote, or edited nearly two dozen books, and from 1960 to 1972, he edited the journal *Physics in Medicine and Biology*. He received many awards in addition to the Nobel Peace Prize, among them the 1983 Bertrand Russell Society Award and the 1992 Albert Einstein Peace Prize.

## FURTHER READING
*Radioactivity and Radioactive Substances (with James Chadwick), 1953; Atomic Energy: A Survey, 1954; Atoms and the Universe (with G. O. Jones and G. J. Whitrow), 1956; Science and World Affairs: History of the Pugwash Conferences, 1962; Pugwash: The First Ten Years, 1967; Scientists in the Quest for Peace, 1972; Nuclear Radiation in Warfare, 1981; as editor or co-editor: Aspects of Medical Physics, 1966; Nuclear Reactors: To Breed or Not to Breed?, 1977; Scientists, the Arms Race, and Disarmament, 1982; The Arms Race at a Time of Decision, 1984; Nuclear Strategy and World Security, 1985; Annals of Pugwash, 1986; World Peace and the Developing Countries, 1986; Strategic Defense and the Future of the Arms Race, 1987; Coexistence, Cooperation and Common Security, 1988; Global Patterns and Common Security, 1989; Verification of Arms Reductions, 1989; Nuclear Non-Proliferation and the Non-Proliferation Treaty, 1990; Building Global Security Through Cooperation, 1990; A Nuclear-Weapon-Free World: Desirable? Feasible?, 1993; Bulletin of the Atomic Scientists p46+ Jan./Feb. 1996, with photos, p26+ Mar./Apr. 1996; New York Times C pl+ May 21, 1996, with photos; Time p84 Oct. 23, 1995, with photo; Nobel Prize Winners Supplement 1992-1996, 1997*

---

# PAUL RUSESABAGINA

## Rwandan Humanitarian

**Born:** June 15, 1954; Rwanda
**Primary Field:** Human Rights
**Affiliation:** *Hotel Rwanda*

## INTRODUCTION
A hero, Paul Rusesabagina told Bob Nesti for the Boston-Bay State Banner *(January 13, 2005, online)*, *"is not someone who performs his duties and obligations. I didn't save people, I helped people; and that's the crucial difference. I did not save. I helped people to go*

*through. Being a hero is something different than helping people." Regardless of those sentiments, there are almost certainly at least 1,268 people who consider Rusesabagina a hero: the individuals he sheltered during the 1994 Rwandan genocide, when he was the manager of a luxury hotel in Kigali, the capital of Rwanda. The filmmaker Terry George dramatized the genocide and Rusesabagina's humanitarian response to it in a critically acclaimed motion picture, Hotel Rwanda, released in 2004. Largely due to the success of Hotel Rwanda, people around the world are now comparing Rusesabagina to Oskar Schindler, the German businessman who* saved more than 1,000 Jews during the Nazi Holocaust and whose actions were immortalized in Schindler's List (1993), a film by Steven Spielberg. In December 2004 the organization Amnesty International, which is helping to promote Hotel Rwanda in order to educate the public about ongoing atrocities in such regions as the Sudan and the Congo, presented Rusesabagina with its Enduring Spirit Award, one of a host of human-rights honors he has received over the last decade.

In the early 1990s the population of Rwanda, a nation in Central Africa south of Uganda, west of Tanzania, and north of Burundi, consisted mostly of ethnic Hutus; more than four out of five Rwandans were Hutus, who have traditionally been farmers. The Tutsi ethnic group, traditionally cattle herders, comprised 15 percent of the population, and about 1 percent of Rwandans were members of the Twa, a subgroup of African Pygmies. Despite their common culture and language, the Hutus and the Tutsis had long been at odds. Belgian colonists, who had arrived in the region in 1916, considered the taller, thinner, fairer Tutsis superior to the shorter, stockier, darker Hutus and issued identification cards to differentiate between the groups. The colonists' favoritism toward Tutsis on matters of power and influence bred resentment in many Hutus. In 1959, three years before Rwanda gained independence from Belgium, the Hutus rebelled, killing the Tutsi king and assuming control of the state. Over the ensuing years, thousands of Tutsis were killed or driven into exile. In 1990 a civil war began among the Hutus and a rebel Tutsi group called the Rwandan Patriotic Front (RPF). The conflict escalated after the airplane carrying the Rwandan president, Juvenal Habyarimana, a Hutu, was shot down above the Kigali airport, on April 6, 1994. The crash also killed the president of Burundi, Cyprian Ntayamira, who, with Habyarimana, had just attended a meeting of African leaders to discuss ways to allay the ethnic tensions in the region. Many observers have theorized that the plane was shot down by Hutu extremists unhappy with Habyarimana's moderate politics. Some Hutu politicians, along with people controlling a prominent local radio station, however, promptly blamed the deaths on Tutsi rebels; within hours, the Hutu militia—called the Interahamwe, or "those who work together"—began slaying Tutsis at a breakneck pace. They first killed Tutsis of prominence in business or politics, then turned on ordinary citizens. The militia instructed civilian Hutus to kill their Tutsi neighbors, friends, and relatives; the killers included some of Ruse-

sabagina's best friends, among them some who resisted the Hutus' orders until they realized that many of those who refused to kill others were put to death themselves. The slaughter lasted 100 days, during which more than 800,000 Rwandans— roughly 10 percent of the nation's population— were murdered.

## EARLY LIFE

Not all Hutus and Tutsis had regarded one another as enemies. Indeed, many families included members of both ethnic groups. Paul Rusesabagina's was among them. Rusesabagina was born into a farming family on June 15,1954 at Murama- Gitarama, in the south of Rwanda. He was one of nine children of a Hutu father and a Tutsi mother, and thus, according to the patrilineal system in place, was classified as a Hutu. In 1962 Rusesabagina entered the Seventh Day Adventist College of Gitwe, a primary and secondary school run by missionaries. From 1975 to 1978 he attended the Faculty of Theology, in Cameroon. In 1979 the Sabena hotel chain hired him as the manager of a newly opened hotel in the Akagera National Park. Realizing he had a talent in that field, from 1980 to 1984 he studied hotel management at Kenya Utalii College, in Nairobi. (A portion of his course work was done in Switzerland.) He then moved to Kigali, where he became the assistant manager of the elegant Hotel des Milles Collines, another Sabena facility. He remained there until 1993, when he was promoted to the top spot at the nearby Hotel Diplomats. Meanwhile, he had married a Tutsi woman named Tatiana and had four children with her.

One day in April 1994, Rusesabagina, Tatiana, their children, and many of their neighbors, most of them Tutsis, were rounded up by armed militants. The militants forced them out of their houses and onto a bus, where one of the militiamen handed Rusesabagina a gun. "Their leader told me to kill all the cockroaches [Tutsis]," Rusesabagina told Kyle Smith, Dietland Lerner, and Michael Fleeman for People (January 24, 2005). Horrified at the thought of murdering his friends and family, Rusesabagina thought quickly. "I showed [the leader] an old man and said, 'Do you really believe this old man is the enemy you are fighting against? Are you sure your enemy is that baby? Take me to the hotel, and I will give you some money. But I am the only one with a key, and if you kill me, you will not have the money." The bribe succeeded, and, after paying off the gunmen with money from the safe at the Hotel Diplomats, Rusesabagina promptly drove the group to the

Hotel des Mille Collines, a five-story building that had also been left in his care by its fleeing Belgium owners.

## LIFE'S WORK

Once Rusesabagina established the Hotel des Mille Collines as a refuge, its reputation spread quickly, attracting frightened Tutsis from across Rwanda. Though the hotel was designed to house 200 occupants, it was soon crowded with more than 1,200 people, who slept in rooms, corridors, and even the snack bar. "People came to the hotel raped, injured, bleeding," Rusesabagina told Anne-Marie O'Connor for the *Los Angeles Times* (December 28, 2004). Relief agencies dropped off orphans, some Hutu military officers brought their Tutsi wives, and a local priest, Father Wenceslas, deposited his Tutsi mother at the hotel, knowing that she would be safer there than in his own church. (Later, Rusesabagina watched helplessly from the roof of the hotel as machete-wielding Hutus attacked people hiding in the church.) Rusesabagina and his wife made a pact with each other: rather than be butchered, she would jump off the roof of the hotel with their children if the militia invaded.

Soon the militia cut off the hotel's electricity, water, and switchboard lines; Rusesabagina doled out water twice daily from the hotel pool and made use of one remaining phone line that the militia had missed. Via that one line, he made calls "like a madman," as he told O'Connor, dialing everyone he could think of who might be able to help, including employees of the French government and the White House. Few of Rusesabagina's frantic calls were fruitful. The United Nations withdrew forces after some of its peacekeepers were killed, and no one in the international community sent troops. (Both Bill Clinton, during his second term as U.S. president, and U.N. secretary-general Kofi Annan have publicly apologized for their inaction.) The militia regularly attempted to infiltrate the hotel and remove its temporary inhabitants; Rusesabagina managed to stall them repeatedly by bribing them with Scotch, cigars, and money—and by using all the connections he had made as a hotelier to call in favors from high-ranking officials. Once, his wife and children hid in a bathtub while he arranged to have the militia ordered out of the hotel. In the midst of widespread slaughter, Rusesabagina managed to protect everyone within the hotel.

Only when the approach of Tutsi guerrillas was imminent did the Hutu militia retreat, thus making it possible for Rusesabagina and the others to drive to a refugee camp near the Tanzanian border. Rusesabagina described the terrible journey to O'Connor: "There were no human beings; just dogs eating dead bodies," he recalled. "The whole country reeked. I never realized that all these people had been butchered. I felt like someone in a dream." At the refugee camp the Rusesabaginas found two nieces whose parents had been killed (along with most of Tatiana's family and some of Paul's relatives); Paul and Tatiana later adopted the girls.

After he left the camp, Rusesabagina returned to Kigali to resume his work as a hotel manager, but he found that the new Tutsi authorities viewed Hutu survivors with distrust, so he and his family moved to Belgium. He now lives in Brussels with Tatiana; their children, Lys, Diane, Roger, and Treasure (some sources spell the name "Tresor"); and their adopted nieces, Carine and Anaise (sometimes spelled "Karine" and "Anais"). He spends much of his time in Zambia (a nation southwest of Tanzania), where he runs a transport company. Rusesabagina told Anne-Marie O'Connor, "I never imagined so many people would join the killing mobs. That's why I don't trust people anymore. I know there are good people. But I'm always suspicious. I have completely changed."

In the aftermath of the genocide, many journalists, authors, documentarians, and filmmakers interviewed Rusesabagina in the vain hope of telling his story. After the director Terry George approached him, Rusesabagina watched films that George had either written or directed, including *In the Name of the Father* (1993), about a man accused of a terrorist bombing in England, and *Some Mother's Son* (1996), about a hunger strike among members of the Irish Republican Army in a British prison. Rusesabagina liked George's sensitivity and handling of politically charged issues and agreed to collaborate on the project. In early 2002 Rusesabagina spent several days with George and the writer Kier Pearson, recounting stories for them as they mapped out the script for *Hotel Rwanda*. George wanted the actor Don Cheadle to play Rusesabagina but feared that, in order to secure funding for the film, he might be forced to recruit an actor with proven box-office appeal, such as Will Smith or Denzel Washington. Then the producer Alex Kitman Ho joined the project and independently raised the needed funds, thus giving the filmmakers the freedom to hire Cheadle. Some critics have suggested that the reason why arranging both funding and studio distribution was difficult was that few in Hollywood cared about what had happened in Africa. "Ask anybody what was happening in '94, they probably remember [the former football star] O.J. Simpson [and his murder trial]," Ho told Justin Chang for *Variety* (January 3-9, 2005). "That was the big headline in this country."

Cheadle spent a week with Rusesabagina while preparing for the role, and Rusesabagina traveled to Johannesburg, South Africa, where the picture was being made, to lend support and supervise, when needed, during the filming. "When I met [Rusesabagina] I was struck that he wasn't 10 feet tall, he didn't swagger. He didn't cut an amazing path when he walked," Cheadle told Anne-Marie O'Connor. "He was just a man who did an extraordinary thing in an extraordinary circumstance. . . . The script really did a great job of not making him this huge heroic figure, but making him this common man who applied everything he knew as a hotel manager to survive." Cheadle continued, "He had to know how to talk to people, how to persuade, how to cajole, when to be forceful and when to back off. He applied that to save those lives, thinking every day was going to be his last day on Earth."

Ho told Justin Chang that the filmmakers "made a conscious effort to keep the slaughter [depicted on-screen] minimal." George explained further, "This has to be one of the most savage wars in a hundred years—just the enormity of the physical violence . . . people macheted to death. There's no way [to convey that] unless you use horror film tactics and prosthetics and all that stuff, and I didn't want to." Because of its relative lack of on-screen carnage, the movie secured a PG-13 rating. *Hotel Rwanda* premiered at the 2004 Toronto Film Festival. Although Rusesabagina has expressed his satisfaction at the depiction of his experiences, he found the film difficult to watch, as he still has nightmares about the genocide. Tatiana cried the first time she watched the picture, and some of their children have yet to see it. After the release of *Hotel Rwanda,* Rusesabagina and his wife decided that it was time to tell their nieces that they were adopted. (The girls were too young at the time of the genocide to comprehend or remember what had occurred.) "We did not want our children to learn their history from other people," he told O'Connor.

*Hotel Rwanda* was nominated for several Golden Globe Awards, and Cheadle was nominated for an Academy Award as best actor. Such acclaim is important to Rusesabagina only to the extent that it has brought the film and its message to the public. "The message of our movie is to say—look, this happened in Rwanda 10 years ago," he told a writer for collegenews. org (February 10, 2005). "The people of the world were not informed. Now today you are informed and again it is happening—are you not going to take action? Please do take action because it is happening in Sudan. It has been happening in the Congo for the last eight years—about [three and a half] million people have been killed. The world does not start and end in America and Europe. It goes beyond." He added, "The politicians keep saying, 'Never again, never again.' Those two words are the most abused words in the world."

## PERSONAL LIFE

Rusesabagina has won, among other honors, the Peace Abbey Courage of Conscience Award (shared with his wife) and the Immortal Chaplains Foundation Prize for Humanity. He launched the Rusesabagina Foundation to aid survivors of the Rwandan genocide. He has spoken at the White House and continues to give talks frequently in many other places around the world.

## FURTHER READING

*Amnesty International Web site; Boston-Ray State Banner (on-line) Jan. 13, 2005; Los Angeles Times E pi Dec. 28, 2004; People pll3 Jan. 24, 2005; Variety pl2 Jan. 3-9, 2005*

# S

## NAFIS SADIK
### Physician; Social Activist

**Born:** August 18, 1929; Jaunpur, India
**Primary Field:** Public Health / Family Rights
**Affiliation:** United Nations

### INTRODUCTION

*Nafis Sadik, the executive director of the United Nations Population Fund, is a guiding force in the effort to slow the exponential growth in the world's human population, which will soon reach six billion and, at current rates of increase, will climb to between 10 billion and 11 billion by the year 2050. "If we are to be successful, three conditions must exist simultaneously, and globally, to help reduce population," Sadik said during an interview with Leila Conners for* New Perspectives Quarterly *(Fall 1994): "first, the education and empowerment of women—the ability of women to participate in the decisions about family size and in the decisions about the shape and nature of society; second, the availability of family-planning services and information; and third, the confidence by parents that their children will survive." In pressing for full equality between men and women as a necessary condition for the success of population programs, as well as for the elimination of poverty, preservation of the environment, and sustainable economic development, Sadik has strived to change widely held attitudes of men toward women, with the aim of achieving a balance in male-female roles and responsibilities within and outside the home. She has also tried to spur men with influence in countries around the world to become advocates for women. "I do not see the empowerment of women as a zero-sum game in which women's gains are men's losses," she has said. "Rather,*

*I see women's empowerment as the rising tide which will lift all ships."*

### EARLY LIFE

Nafis Sadik was born Nafis Iffat Shoaib on August 18, 1929 in Jaunpur, India. Her father, Mohammad Shoaib, served as Pakistan's finance minister and also as a vice-president of the International Bank for Reconstruction and Development (commonly known as the World Bank); her mother, Iffat Ara Shoaib, was a homemaker. Raised in both Pakistan and India, Sadik attended the secondary school of the Loreto Convent, in Calcutta, India. Whereas her girlhood friends were "preoccupied with marriage," as she wrote in an article for the German weekly *Die Zeit* (September 1,1995), she "wanted to change the world," and she considered becoming an engineer. After abandoning that idea because she thought "the world was not ready to accept women engineers," in her words, she decided to seek a career in medicine. Her mother and, even more enthusiastically, her father supported her goal; unlike many others on the Indian subcontinent (and, indeed, in many other parts of the world), they did not believe that every girl's destiny lies solely in marriage and motherhood. In a speech that she gave in Berlin in 1995 at the Conference on Women in Muslim Societies, Sadik attributed her father's philosophy to his strict interpretation of Muslim teachings. "My father was a visionary, and he believed in educating girls and boys," she told Marguerite Holloway, who profiled her for *Scientific American* (June 1993). "All the family members kept saying to him, 'Oh, you are going to send your daughter to work, how terrible. Why are you sending her to college?'"

After graduating from the Loreto convent school, in 1944, Sadik spent two years at Loreto College, also in Calcutta. In 1946 she entered the College of Medicine of the University of Calcutta. Sometime later she transferred to Dow Medical College, in Karachi, Pakistan, from which she earned an M.D. degree in 1951. In 1952 she entered the internship and residency program at the City Hospital in Baltimore, where, following in the footsteps of the Dow professor who had most inspired her, she specialized in gynecology and obstetrics. She completed her training there in 1955. Her professional studies also included a stint, in 1958, as a research fellow in physiology at Queens University in Kingston, Ontario, Canada.

After returning to Pakistan in 1954, Sadik married Azhar Sadik, a businessman who was then an officer in the Pakistani army and, as such, was periodically transferred to military installations in different rural areas. At least partly as a means of ensuring her own employment in the same places, she got a job as a civilian medical officer. In the hospitals where she WQS posted, she took charge of women's and children's wards and supervised staffs of as many as 50 other medical officers. Sadik served in addition as a gynecologist and obstetrician at the hospitals. She treated many women who had given birth for the first time while still in their teens and had endured a long series of additional, closely spaced pregnancies. Many of the women suffered from serious reproductive tract infections or other maladies of varying severity from which some of them died. "They were really burdened," Sadik recalled to Marguerite Holloway. "I mean this childbearing was just like they were machines for having children. Their life was like a continuing bondage." When she would advise a mother of a newborn infant to wait a sufficiently long time before becoming pregnant again, for her own wellbeing as well as that of her children, the woman would almost invariably demur, explaining that her husband or others in her family would not allow it. Sadik realized that no matter what talents or skills a woman might possess and no matter what she may have accomplished, her status derived solely from her role as a wife and mother, and her family, indeed, the whole society in which she lived, imposed tremendous pressure on her to produce children, "preferably male, and as many as possible." "It was clear that in addition to health care, these women needed family planning, but even if it were available, many women were powerless to use it," Sadik observed in her article for *Die Zeit*.

## LIFE'S WORK

Determined "to change the way things were," in her words, in 1964, as a first step, Sadik studied public health and family planning at Johns Hopkins University, in Baltimore. After returning to Pakistan later that year, she became the head of the health section of the Planning Commission on Health and Family Planning. In 1966 she was named the director of planning and training of the Pakistan Central Family Planning Council, where she helped to design and implement a five year family-planning program. She was promoted to deputy director general of the council in 1968 and to director general in 1970.

In 1971 Sadik joined the staff of the United Nations Population Fund. Her husband supported her in that career move, which required resettling their family in New York City. According to Marguerite Holloway, "despite the problems of relocation and of finding a job, her husband said it was his turn to follow her." "He was very liberal in his attitudes and had no hang-ups about my working and doing whatever I wanted," Sadik told Holloway. After serving for two years as a UNFPA technical adviser, she was promoted to chief of the program division, and then, in 1977, to assistant executive director. When, ten years later, she was named executive director, she attained the rank of undersecretary general in the UN hierarchy. "Nafis Sadik's appointment is far more than a symbolic gesture from the male-dominated bastion of international deliberations that is the United Nations," an article in *Popline*, the newsletter of the Population Institute, declared when her new title was announced, as quoted by Mary Morain in the *Humanist* (November/December 1987). "Dr. Sadik's wisdom, intelligence, energy, and her firm commitment to reproductive rights are legendary among her colleagues in the field."

Established in 1969, the UNFPA is a subsidiary organ of the UN General Assembly. Its operations are financed not by allocations from the regular UN budget but entirely by voluntary contributions from member countries. In 1995 its income, which came from about 90 donor states, most of them developing nations, amounted to about $300 million. According to a UNFPA fact sheet, the agency "directly manages one-fourth of the world's population assistance to developing countries," and, to date, it has provided a total of more than $3 billion to virtually all of them. Its mandate is to acquire and share knowledge related to family planning and population; to build awareness of population problems and propose possible ways of responding to them; to help countries, at their request, to deal with such problems by suggesting strategies "best suited to the individual countries' needs"; to coordinate UN-FPA supported projects; and "to assume a leading role in the United Nations system in promoting population programs."

When Sadik arrived at the UN over a quarter of a century ago, she discovered to her dismay that the organization's male employees tended to treat women as their intellectual inferiors. "I found that I had better respect in Pakistan," she has recalled. "In order to be heard at the UN, I had to repeat myself, sometimes loudly. An idea would be picked up if a man in a meeting presented it, even though I might have already said the same thing and it had been ignored." After she became the UNF-PA's executive director, her male colleagues responded differently to her ideas. As the only woman present at high-level meetings, she noticed that they "paid special attention to what [she] said," as she wrote for Die Zeit. "Eventually, other people began talking about women's and population issues and then they would look at me to see if I heard them." She has also observed that in the early 1970s, population-related issues were "not discussed so openly." UN staff members "were uncomfortable if you talked about women's health and family planning," she explained to Marguerite Holloway. "It has taken a while to get over that embarrassment. But I suppose they get comfortable with someone. I mean, they know I am going to talk about it, so they get used to hearing it."

In the years since 1971, Sadik has witnessed major changes regarding fertility control not only as a subject of discussion but as an object of national concern. Family planning programs existed in only a few countries 25 years ago, for example, whereas currently, virtually all countries have them, and many of them are being expanded into reproductive health programs. In addition, the number of countries with UNFPA-supported programs has increased from fewer than five to more than 135. Worldwide, about 350 million couples have access to reproductive health services, and more than half of all couples use contraception, up from 10 percent in the 1960s. Fertility rates have decreased substantially in many countries; in some East Asian nations, the average number of children per family has dropped from between six and seven to less than three.

In many other places, however, millions of women who want to limit the size of their families cannot do so because they have no access to contraceptives and instruction in their use. "Surveys show that the demand for family planning services is much greater than the services available," Sadik told Monte Leach in an interview for *Share International* (May 1995). "If we had just catered to the demand, we would be at a much better global population level than we are now." High infant mortality rates, widespread illiteracy, the absence of sex education for adolescents, among other phenomena, and gender inequities in the economic, social, and political realms that force women into lives rigidly bounded by marriage and motherhood, in addition to the sort of familial and societal pressures that Sadik observed as a medical officer in Pakistan, have all contributed to persistently high birth rates in many developing countries in Asia, Africa, and Latin America. An estimated one billion people in those countries live under conditions of appalling poverty.

Currently, the world's human population is increasing by some 250,000 people every day. That amounts to about 90 million, more people than the entire population of Mexico, every year and close to a billion, "a whole extra China," in Sadik's words, in the course of a decade. "These increasing numbers are eating away at the earth itself," Sadik wrote in the *Futurist* (March/April 1991). "The combination of fast population growth and poverty in developing countries has begun to make permanent changes to the environment. They include continued urban growth, degradation of land and water resources, massive deforestation, and buildup of greenhouse gases." Reversing those trends, she advised, will require "a shift to cleaner technologies, energy efficiency, and resource conservation, especially for the richer quarter of the world's population," "a direct and all-out attack on poverty," and a decrease in the population growth rate. "Reducing the rate of population growth will help extend the options for future generations," she pointed out. "It will be easier to provide higher quality and universal education, health care, shelter, and an adequate diet; to invest in employment and economic development; and to limit the overall level of environmental damage."

As a Pakistani national, Sadik began her professional life as a physician. For nearly ten years, as a civilian medical officer, she practiced obstetrics and gynecology in rural communities in Pakistan. Deeply troubled by the circumstances of her patients, most of whom had borne many children in quick succession, she embarked on a career in family planning and public health. In 1971, after working for a half-dozen years with national family planning groups in Pakistan, she became a technical adviser at the United Nations Population Fund, which is the world's largest provider of multilateral assistance to population-related programs in developing countries and territories. She next worked for four years as chief of the program division of the UNFPA (an acronym based on the population fund's original name) and then, for a decade, as the UNFPA's assistant executive director. When, in 1987, she was named executive director, she became the first woman to hold the top position in a major voluntarily funded UN agency. In her worldwide staff of 800 people, 44 percent of the professional employees, 28 percent of those holding senior-level positions, and 50 percent of the division chiefs are women, far higher percentages of women than is currently the norm at the UN or in most other public or private institutions.

Sadik served as the secretary general of the 1994 International Conference on Population and Development, which was held in Cairo and which spawned a path-breaking agreement known as the Program of Action. A blueprint for the next 20 years, the plan calls for the revolutionary new approach to population control that Sadik has long advocated. According to the UNFPA's publication *The State of World Population* 1995, it "explicitly places human beings, rather than human numbers, at the center of all population and development activities" and "encourages the international community to address global problems by meeting individual needs, while maintaining the responsibilities and sovereignty of governments." "The plan focuses on both population and development," Sadik has explained. "It broadens the scope of population policy from the narrow focus on family planning and fertility to issues of sustainable development and empowerment of the individual, particularly women, to make decisions. The keystone of the Cairo plan is gender equality, equity, and empowerment of women." Transforming the proposals in the Program of Action into "tangible and effective action," as she has put it, is one of the greatest challenges facing Sadik, who began her third four-year term as head of the UNFPA in 1995. She currently holds the position of Special Adviser to the Secretary General and has additional responsibilities as Special Envoy for HIV/AIDS in Asia.

In the many articles that she has written for professionals and laypeople and in many of the hundreds of speeches that she has given, she sometimes addresses audiences in six different countries in a single month, Sadik has often emphasized the crucial importance of educating girls as well as boys and wiping out illiteracy among women as well as men. As she explained in the *Futurist*, "Education encourages a sense of control over personal destiny and the possibility of choices beyond accepted tradition. For women, it offers a view of sources of status beyond childbearing. The importance of literacy programs for adult women goes far beyond reading and writing: It also allows access to practical information on such matters as preventive health care and family planning, which are often part of the programs themselves." Moreover, "women with seven or more years of education tend to marry an average of almost four years later than those who have had none," and mortality rates among children of educated women are significantly lower than among those whose mothers have had no schooling, just as they are in families that receive adequate health care. Freed from the fear that they will lose children through illness, parents in such families tend to have fewer children.

It is because of overwhelming evidence that education and proper child and maternal health care almost inevitably result in reduced birth rates that Sadik has rejected what she has called "a purely 'numbers' approach" in population programs, which entails setting targets for population growth and quotas on family size. "The successful population control programs have responded to needs, and they have provided information and education programs which have also created an understanding of why you should space your children, not have children at a young age, and so on," she explained to Monte Leach. "They have also provided family planning services in the best possible manner. That is a very major difference from the past, and a very strong recommendation to move away from a demographic approach." Sadik is also convinced that, as she has said, "the attainment of sustainable development is possible only if it is based on the fulfillment of the needs and security of each individual person."

At the International Conference on Population and Development that was held in Cairo in September 1994, 20,000 delegates from a total of 150 countries adopted a "people-centered" plan of action that echoed the approach that Sadik has advocated. "Perhaps the most outstanding achievement at the Cairo conference was the clear affirmation that 'the empowerment and autonomy of women and the improvement of their political, social, economic, and health status is a highly important end in itself,' as well as a necessary condition for achieving sustained economic growth and sustainable development," Sadik wrote in her article for *Die Zeit.* In a *New York Times* (September 14, 1994) article that summarized the measures adopted by conference participants, Alan Cowell reported that the Program of Action implied that "in countries where abortion is not against the law, health care embraces safe conditions for abortion." "The plan does not legalize or seek legalization of abortion," Sadik said during her interview for *New Perspectives Quarterly.* "Rather, it seeks to make abortion less necessary through the provision of family planning and to make medical services available to women who resort to abortion in order to prevent health consequences, including death. Reproductive health does not contain a hidden agenda to legalize abortion. Reproductive health means information and education about reproduction, pre and post natal care, assisted deliveries, family planning services, and HIV/AIDS and STD (sexually transmitted disease) control and prevention."

Nafis Sadik has edited several books, among them *Population: The UNFPA Experience* (1984), *Population Policies and Programs: Lessons Learned from Two Decades of Experiences* (1991), and *Making a Difference: Twenty-five Years of UNFPA Experience* (1994). She has received awards from President Suharto, of Indonesia, for her assistance in developing that country's family planning program, and from the government of Pakistan, for her contributions in the field of medicine. Her many other honors include the Hugh Moore Award (1976), the Women's Global Leadership Award (1994) from the Center for Development and Population Activities, the highest category of the Bruno H. Schubert Prize (1995), and honorary degrees from three American universities: Johns Hopkins, Duke, and Brown. She was the 1994 laureate of the International Union for the Scientific Study of Population. In 1995 President Hosni Mubarak of Egypt signed a decree that gave her the Egyptian Order of Merit in recognition of her efforts in the areas of population and development and for her outstanding leadership at the 1994 International Conference on Population and Development. For her leadership role at the conference, she also earned a 1996 Prince Mahidol Award (which is named in honor of Prince Mahidol of Songkla, Thailand, "the father of Thai medicine").

## PERSONAL LIFE
According to Marguerite Holloway, Sadik is "direct but diplomatic"; her speech, which "preserves the cadences of Urdu," her native tongue, is rapid and forceful, and "her occasional monotone suggests she could blunt the thorns off any prickly topic." She and her husband, who has retired, have five children, including two whom they adopted, and five grandchildren. In her leisure time, she enjoys reading, playing bridge, and attending theatrical and operatic performances.

## FURTHER READING
*Population: The UNFPA Experience; Population Policies and Programmes: Lessons Learned from Two Decades of Experience; Making a Difference: Twenty-five Years of UNFPA Experience*

---

# FELICE N. SCHWARTZ

## Writer; Advocate

**Born:** January 16, 1925; New York, New York
**Died:** February 8, 1996; New York, New York
**Primary Field:** Gender Equality
**Affiliation:** Catalyst, Inc.

## INTRODUCTION
*In 1989 Felice N. Schwartz, the founding president and chief executive officer of Catalyst, a not for profit organization that works with businesses to effect change for women, ignited a controversy that reverberated through-* *out the feminist community, corporate America, and the national media by stating, in the opening sentence of an article for the* Harvard Business Review *(January/February 1989), that "the cost of employing women in management is greater than the cost of employing men." Observing that more women than men leave the work force for extended periods in order to rear children and that most corporations do not have effective strategies in place for retaining those women, Schwartz added, "The greater cost of employing women is not a function of inescapable gender differences. Women are different from men, but what increases their cost to the*

*corporation is principally the clash of their perceptions, attitudes, and behavior with those of men, which is to say, with the policies and practices of male-led corporations." Therefore, as she told Beth Brophy for* U.S. News & World Report *(March 13, 1989), "changing the attitudes of employers can reduce additional costs dramatically," to the mutual advantage of corporations and women.*

*Schwartz set out to do just that by taking the necessary but painful first step of challenging two powerful, competing orthodoxies: that of business, which associated all women with child rearing and low levels of commitment to their careers, and that of feminism, which preferred to treat men and women as though they were the same as well as equal. In her article for the* Harvard Business Review, *Schwartz focused on two types of women in the corporate environment: the "career-primary" woman and the "career-and-family" woman, who represent opposite ends of a continuum along which there are as many variations as there are individuals. She proposed that corporations recognize that the two types of women have different agendas and that companies design flexible programs to accommodate those women who choose both career and family. In referring to her ideas, a reporter for the* New York Times *coined the phrase "mommy track," which became the focus of a long and often bitter debate in which Schwartz was alternately cast as a maverick bravely spotlighting issues that corporations were afraid to tackle and as a traitor to feminist principles.*

## EARLY LIFE

Felice Nierenberg Schwartz was born on January 16, 1925 in New York City, the only daughter of Albert Nierenberg, who owned Etched Products Corporation, a metal-engraving and etching plant in Long Island City that produced decorative trim for automobiles, refrigerators, and other industrial products, and Rose (Kaplan) Nierenberg, a homemaker. In accordance with her father's wish that she become a doctor, Schwartz was a premed major at Smith College in Northampton, Massachusetts. Despite her lack of interest in her science courses, she dutifully applied to medical school, but, although she was accepted, she declined to attend, for in the meantime she had come under the influence of Ralph Harlow, the chairman of Smith's religion department, whom she has described as a "social activist with a marvelous moral imperative to his life." Harlow strengthened Schwartz's determination to spend her life

trying to change things that affronted her sense of justice, such as the fact that black students made up only .25 percent of Smith's enrollment.

## LIFE'S WORK

After graduating from college in 1945, Schwartz accepted a job with the National Association for the Advancement of Colored People (NAACP). Frustrated by the slow, bureaucratic pace she encountered there, she left the NAACP after nine months to found her own organization, the National Scholarship Service and Fund for Negro Students (NSSFNS). Based in Harlem, the NSSFNS was devoted to opening the doors of higher education to black students. To that end, Schwartz wrote and published *A Guide for Negro College Students to Interracial Colleges,* the first directory of its kind. She catalogued over $14 million in available scholarships and established a fund to supplement existing scholarships. By 1947 she had placed 750 black students in schools that had previously accepted few or none. For her efforts, she was honored with a Mademoiselle Merit Award in education in 1950.

In 1951 the death of her father prompted Schwartz to give up her position as executive director of the NSS-FNS in order to rescue the family company, which employed 750 people, from failure; Schwartz's brother, who was in charge of sales, invited her to step in as vice-president of production. The experience was very gratifying for Schwartz, as she explained in her book *Breaking with Tradition: Women and Work, the New Facts of Life* (1992): "Unencumbered by too much knowledge, I was able to go from one area to another, from purchasing, to production control, to cost accounting, to negotiating a labor contract with seventeen male shop stewards." With an office on the factory floor, Schwartz established herself as a visible, active presence who was unfazed by the shop stewards' sexist remarks. "You can make a class action suit out of it, or you can laugh at it," she observed in an interview with Julie Lawlor for *USA Today* (March 23, 1992). After three and a half years, the company was sold for a modest profit.

At that time, Felice Schwartz had married Irving L. Schwartz at the age of twenty and moved to the suburbs, and was pregnant with the second of their three children. For the next eight years, she stayed at home as a full-time mother. She was not concerned or anxious about returning to the workplace. "I felt secure that when I wanted to go to work I'd know what to do and it would work out," she has said. But she noticed that such was not the case for many of her peers. "I saw a lot of frustration and a lot of anxiety," she told Ellen Hopkins in an interview for *Working Woman* (October 1990). "What were these women going to do when the kids went on to college? What would the second half of their lives be like? I became consumed with wanting to do something about this terrible waste of talent." Thus, the same observations that inspired Betty Friedan to write *The Feminine Mystique* (1963) induced Schwartz to found Catalyst in 1962. Her husband, a physician, had just been named to a post at a medical school in Cincinnati. Realizing that New York City was the most logical place to base her efforts, Schwartz returned there with her children, and her husband flew out to see them every weekend for two years. "A lot of people thought it very odd," Irving Schwartz told Julie Lawlor. "But it didn't occur to me to stop her or oppose her idea of an agency that could be a real service to people." Like many other working women at that time, Felice Schwartz suffered her share of guilt for choosing to go to work as soon as her youngest child entered nursery school, as she explained to *Current Biography*: "I did feel massively guilty. There was no other way to feel. It was thought that you were being irresponsible. You were not really a woman. There was something wrong."

Nonetheless, in 1962, at the age of thirty-seven, Schwartz embarked on a cross-country journey to meet with nine college presidents whom she had targeted as potential founding board members for Catalyst. Headquartered in her suburban home, Catalyst was created "to bring to our country's needs the unused abilities of intelligent women who want to combine family and work," according to Schwartz. From the beginning, Catalyst was "a facilitating rather than a confrontational organization," as Schwartz has said, adding that "much more can be accomplished by opening doors than by breaking them down." She established a nationwide network of 250 resource centers as well as a counseling library that served twelve million women per year, and she wrote and distributed forty pamphlets that tailored job hunting strategies to women's needs.

"What we were trying to do in the early days," Schwartz has said, "was to demonstrate the feasibility and advantage of part-time work, because that's what women then wanted." At that time, her efforts centered on the public sector, because its traditionally low-paying positions normally attracted only one or two applicants per job opening. When the Boston Department of Public Welfare agreed in 1963 to fill twenty-five full-time positions with fifty half-time caseworkers, it received responses from more than 1,600 women, enabling the department to hire only the most qualified individuals rather than settle for anyone who requested an application.

Not satisfied to limit her endeavors to the public sector, Schwartz turned to the world of private enterprise. "I always wanted to work in the corporation," she told *Current Biography*, "because that's the powerful arena. Change that's effected there ripples across society." But corporate executives, faced with an abundance of male workers, were not motivated to hire women, and women themselves often experienced conflict when contemplating the prospect of "deserting" their husbands and children to go off to work. Schwartz addressed some of those issues in her first book, *How to Go to Work When Your Husband Is Against It, Your Children Aren't Old Enough and There's Nothing You Can Do Anyhow* (1968).

The following decade was was a transitional period both for Catalyst and for women in the workplace. Women who chose to go to work were being joined in increasing numbers by women who were forced to go to work out of economic necessity due to the recession of 1973-74 and the stagflation, an unprecedented combination of inflation and unemployment, of the late 1970s. Having focused on the career-counseling needs of individual women in the 1960s, Catalyst began to move into the corporate community in the 1970s. It conducted numerous groundbreaking studies on the availability of and demand for child care, the feasibility and usefulness of parental leave, and the complications faced by two-career families, including relocation and implementation of benefits. Catalyst disseminated the conclusions of its research in the 1980s in order to help employers deal with work and family issues by educating them in the proactive cultivation of women's leadership skills and the removal of obstacles to their advancement. In the 1990s the $2.5 million organization began serving its corporate contributors primarily in an advisory capacity as a solution oriented problem solver rather than merely as a gatherer, synthesizer, and provider of information.

Over the course of her three decades at the helm of Catalyst, Schwartz had become a highly reliable and widely respected expert on work and family issues, had established credibility with the business executives who contributed to Catalyst, and had been honored by feminist groups for the unique nature of her organization's contribution to rendering the corporate climate more amenable to the needs of professional women. Ironically, Schwartz was attacked by feminists, as well as by some business executives, in the wake of the publication of her *Harvard Business Review* article for advocating the very conditions that she had spent a lifetime trying to eradicate, namely, the relegation of female professionals to lower-paying staff positions and middle management while their male peers rose through the ranks of revenue producing line positions to corporate leadership posts. According to John Leo, writing in *U.S. News & World Report* (April 3, 1989), much of the criticism directed at Schwartz derived from misunderstandings spawned by the disparaging shorthand phrase "mommy track," which had been coined by Tamar Lewin of the *New York Times* (March 8, 1989) to describe the stagnant career path onto which Schwartz's "career-and-family" women would be shunted once they had been identified. "This is not a plan to dump all mothers onto the slow track," Leo wrote. "It's a way of giving people options on how long and hard they want to work and on what level. What's wrong with that?"

Schwartz conceded, in an interview with Lewin, that perhaps "at first, employers are going to be shocked and they're going to say, 'Let's not employ women,' but then they're going to realize that's ridiculous, that they absolutely depend on women." Given the fertility rate in the United States, which, according to the National Center for Health Statistics at the Department of Health and Human Services, declined from 25.3 live births per 1,000 people in 1957 to 15.6 in 1972 and was holding at 15.9 as of 1988, Schwartz told Beth Brophy that "the result will be a tremendous shortage of able, talented, educated, competent individuals." Moreover, more women than men are earning bachelor's, master's, and accounting degrees, and a third of M.B.A. degrees and nearly half of law degrees are awarded to women. In an article for *Fortune* (June 8, 1987), Schwartz had already provided corporate culture with a bottom-line rationale for enabling women to rise above middle management by removing the barriers to their advancement: "so that the company can capture the best people for leadership positions. Skimming the cream from both the male and female barrels, rather than digging deeper into the male barrel, pays off in quality gains that far outweigh the larger investment the company must make in women."

While many in the business community applauded Schwartz's efforts to draw attention to the differences between men and women, other corporate leaders objected. In a letter to the *Harvard Business Review*, Deborah Biodolillo, a vice president of human resources for Apple Computer, wrote: "Schwartz's recommendation for early identification of an individual's career path becomes not only impossible but also undesirable. It establishes barriers instead of providing the options people need." In another letter, Michael Maccoby, the president of the Maccoby Group, maintained that "business should not prejudge or categorize a woman by her attitude toward mothering but rather by her ambition, talent, and ability to balance values." But perhaps the most stinging commentary came from within the feminist movement. Betty Friedan wrote, "It is dangerous and deplorable for the *Harvard Business Review* and Ms. Schwartz to say that women managers have to make a choice between career and family. At a time when 95 percent of male executives have children but the majority of female executives are childless, it is dangerous to affirm the policies and attitudes that created just that situation."

In an interview with Diana Kunde for the *Dallas Morning News* (May 7, 1991), Schwartz admitted, "I had a couple of difficult months of adjusting to being accused of things I not only didn't say, but don't believe." Defending her position in an article for the *New York Times* (March 22, 1989), Schwartz argued that her main purposes were "to urge employers to create policies that help mothers balance career and family responsibilities and to eliminate barriers to female productivity and advancement." Barbara Presley Noble quoted her in the *New York Times* (February 23, 1992) as saying, "I was one of the first victims of political correctness. I dared to violate the party line that women are not different from men." "There is a conspiracy of silence that prevents us from putting the issues of maternity leave, parenthood, and flexible working arrangements on the table," she told Lisa Anderson for the *Chicago Tribune* (May 3, 1992). "Unless we put them on the table we can't analyze them and we can't address them. We will just continue in the way we are, with a deepening sense of discouragement on the part of employers and of frustration and anger on the part of women." In *Breaking with Tradition*, which received a much more balanced hearing than had her article, Schwartz expanded on her ideas about the ways in which corporations can best address the taboo issues surrounding women in the workplace that (usually male) employers and women have been reluctant to confront for fear of litigation and discrimination, respectively. Perhaps the most controversial tip

Schwartz offers young women in her book is to tell prospective employers their family plans. Maintaining in her interview with Ellen Hopkins that she understands the vulnerability of a job applicant who chooses to reveal whether she intends to have children, Schwartz said, "What that young woman doesn't understand is that simply because of her age and her sex she's suspect. And unless she initiates the conversation, the person on the other side of the desk is free to imagine the worst. I know that because I talk to corporate leaders."

Some of Schwartz's opponents believed that her close ties to corporate higher-ups influence Catalyst's findings and conclusions on women's issues. Ellen Hopkins quoted a former Catalyst employee as saying that Schwartz failed to see that "most people aren't in a position, either professionally or economically, to take the risks that Felice wants them to take in order to effect societal change." One of Schwartz's associates told Hopkins, "She's never been an employee, she's always been the boss. That's a weakness in that she doesn't understand readily what it's like to be vulnerable to the whims of your employer. On the other hand, it's the reason CEOs listen to her, they have the sense that Catalyst is willing to balance the advancement of women with what works for the company."

## PERSONAL LIFE

The recipient of Honorary Doctor of Humane Letters degrees from Pace University (1980), Smith College (1981), and Chatham College (1990) and an Honorary Doctor of Laws degree from Marietta College (1989), Schwartz was voted the Human Resources Professional of the Year in 1983 by the International Association for Personnel Women, and in 1987 she received the Excellence in Leadership Boehm Soaring Eagle Award from the National Women's Economic Alliance Foundation. In March 1990 she was one of 126 world leaders, thinkers, and trendsetters featured in *Fortune* magazine's sixtieth anniversary issue. In November 1992 she was admitted as a fellow at the National Academy of Human Resources. Schwartz serves on the advisory boards of the National Women's Political Caucus, the National Network of Hispanic Women, the Foundation for Student Communications, the General Motors Institute, and the Business Council of New York State, among other organizations, and she chairs the Nominating Committee of the Board of Planned Parenthood of America.

Schwartz retired as president and CEO of Catalyst in May 1993 and remained on the organization's board of directors. She continued to write and lecture. Her goal, she told Lisa Anderson, was "to make gender no longer an issue in the workplace." She has donated the proceeds from her book *Breaking with Tradition* to the Felice N. Schwartz Fund for the Advancement of Women in Business and the Professions, which is intended to ensure the continuation of key research projects already in progress at Catalyst. "Although I've loved every year better than every other year, and I think I've been privileged to have seen the whole thing, I'm ready to take this load off my back," she said in her interview with *Current Biography*. "My life will continue to be one that's addressed to social change, at a more modest intensity level, and with more time for my grandchildren and my children."

Schwartz lived in New York City until her death in 1996. Her husband, Irving, is Emeritus Dean of the Graduate Faculty and Lamport Distinguished Professor at the Mount Sinai School of Medicine of the City University of New York. They had three children, Cornelia Ann, Tony, and James Oliver, and many grandchildren.

## FURTHER READING

*How to Go to Work When Your Husband Is Against It, Your Children Aren't Old Enough, and There's Nothing You Can Do Anyhow; Breaking with Tradition: Women and Work, The New Facts of Life; The Armchair Activist: Simple Yet Powerful Ways to Fight the Radical Right*

# ALBERT SCHWEITZER

## Medical Missionary; Musicologist; Theologian; Organist

**Born:** Jan. 14, 1875; Kaysersberg, Alsace-Lorraine, Germany (now Haut-Rhin, France)
**Died:** September 4, 1965; Lambaréné, Gabon
**Primary Field:** Peace & Justice Movement

### INTRODUCTION

*Hundreds of missionaries in the 20th century sacrificed profitable careers and the comforts of civilization to help alleviate human misery in remote and dangerous parts of the world, but none had so dramatic an impact on man's conscience as Dr. Albert Schweitzer. At the age of 30, undeterred by the promise of brilliant achievement as a Biblical scholar, educator, preacher, concert organist, and musicologist, he turned to the study of medicine so that he could establish a medical mission in French Equatorial Africa (now Gabon). His hospital at the edge of the jungle at Lambaréné, founded in 1913, and his concept of Reverence for Life made him a legend and myth, a near Christ-like figure, a Nobel Peace Prize winner (1952), and one of the world's most admired men. During the later years of his life, his fame had been increased by controversy arising from his refusal to keep pace with, or even to recognize, the radical changes taking place in Africa.*

*After his death in 1965, his legacy lives on, fuelled by the direction of the Albert Schweitzer Fellowship, which was founded during 1940 in the United States to support Dr. Schweitzer's medical work in Africa during World War II. The hospital he founded in 1913, now the Albert Schweitzer Hospital, now a leading medical research institution, continues to operate in Lambaréné.*

### EARLY LIFE

Albert Schweitzer was considered a musical prodigy. Religion and music predominate in Albert Schweitzer's Alsatian origins. He was born in Kaysersberg in Alsace, then a part of Germany, to Louis and Adele (Schillinger) Schweitzer, on January 14, 1875. Six months later, his father, a minister in the Evangelical (Lutheran) Church in Kaysersberg, was transferred to Günsbach in the Münster Valley, where Albert grew up with an older sister, two younger sisters, and a younger brother. His maternal grandfather was also a pastor, and both his grandfathers were accomplished organists.

The church at Günsbach fascinated Albert Schweitzer from early boyhood. Having begun to study the piano when he was five years old, and the organ when he was eight, he was permitted by the age of nine to substitute for the organist at church services. He attended elementary school in Günsbach until 1884, when he enrolled in the *Realschule* in Münster. At the end of the year, however, his parents sent him to the Gymnasium in Mulhouse. He lived there, under strict discipline, in the home of his great-uncle and was allowed almost no diversion from schoolwork except music. He studied the organ under Eugen Münch, finding particular enjoyment in improvising.

In June 1893, Schweitzer passed his final examination at the Gymnasium, and, the following autumn, he entered the University of Strasbourg, where he took up residence at the Theological College of St. Thomas. There he concentrated his research on the Synoptic Gospels, eventually gaining proficiency in Hebrew, although his preparation for study in that language had been slight. His year of compulsory military training, which began in April 1894, scarcely interfered with his education. In spare moments on maneuvers, he read the New Testament in Greek; his reflections led to insights into the life of Jesus and to eschatological interpretations that later developed into his major contributions in theology.

Before he took his licentiate in theology in 1900, however, Schweitzer had decided to work for his Doctorate in Philosophy, which he obtained in 1899, submitting a thesis on the religious philosophy of Kant. Both his degrees were awarded by the University of Strasbourg, but, he did much of his research on Kant in Paris, where he attended a few lectures at the Sorbonne. In Paris, he also took organ lessons from Charles Marie Widor and piano lessons from Marie Jael-Trautmann. At the suggestion of Widor, he wrote a biography of Johann Sebastian Bach, which was published in French, in 1905, and then completely rewritten for a German edition, published in 1908. With Widor, and others, he founded the Paris Bach Society, in 1906, the year in which he also published a book on the art of organ building and organ playing. Both his biography of Bach and his critical editing of Bach's organ works are considered authoritative.

Meanwhile, Schweitzer had settled down—or so it then appeared—in Strasbourg. He became a preacher, in

1899, at St. Nicholas Church and, later, filled the posts of deacon and curate. He also served as Acting Principal, in 1901, of the theological college at the university, as Principal in 1903, and as Privatdozent from 1902 to 1912. His early theological writings, in fulfillment of academic requirements, had been devoted primarily to the Messiahship and the suffering of Jesus, and had tried to reconcile belief and knowledge. Extending his research, he completed, in 1906, what some scholars regard as perhaps his most important book, *The Quest of the Historical Jesus: A Critical Study of its Progress from Reimarus to Wrede.* Among his departures from established Christian views was his contention, as he expressed it in one of his autobiographical volumes, that "Jesus had announced no kingdom that was to be founded and realized in the natural world by Himself and the believers, but one that was to be expected as coming with the almost immediate dawn of a supernatural age" (*Out of My Life and Thought,* Holt, 1933).

In Strasbourg, Schweitzer was also occupied with charitable work among the city's homeless people and released prisoners, but these humanitarian efforts did not satisfy him. He had earlier vowed that he would devote his first 30 years to art and science and the rest of his life, in gratitude, to the direct service of mankind. A turning point in his career came in the autumn of 1904, when he happened to read an article on the needs of the Congo mission in a magazine published by the Paris Missionary Society, and he decided at once what form his service to humanity would take.

## LIFE'S WORK

Schweitzer spent the next seven years, from 1905 to 1912, in the study of medicine and obtained M.D. degree in, 1913, after a year's internship in a Strasbourg hospital. For his medical thesis he wrote a psychiatric study of Jesus, refuting the theory that He was paranoiac. During his medical training, he remained on the faculty of the University of Strasbourg, and, he also gave organ concerts to earn money for his projected mission, which he also financed through royalties from his book on Bach. Although a theologian, Schweitzer had decided to go to the Congo as a medical missionary rather than as a preacher. As he explained in *Memoirs of Childhood and Youth* (1924): "This new form of activity I could not represent to myself as being talking about the religion of love, but only as an actual putting it into practice."

On Good Friday, of 1913, Schweitzer left Günsbach for the mission at Lambaréné, on the River Ogowe, in French Equatorial Africa (now Gabon). His only companion was Helene (Bresslau) Schweitzer, whom he had married on June 18, 1912. With his wife, who had trained as a nurse in order to help him, he founded a jungle hospital that immediately attracted the African Blacks because he gave his settlement the atmosphere of a native village, where patients could bring members their families to cook for them and help nurse them.

Sixteen months after Schweitzer's arrival in Africa, World War I broke out, and he and his wife, who were German citizens, were interned as enemy aliens. They were eventually allowed to work at the hospital, but, in the fall of 1917, they were sent to France as prisoners of war, and were held in internment camps until their release in July 1918. Schweitzer then spent some time in Strasbourg, as preacher at St. Nicholas Church and as a doctor at the municipal hospital, in addition to taking additional courses in medicine and dentistry. He also gave organ concerts, including one in Barcelona, and lectured in Sweden, England, and other countries.

Schweitzer's seven-year absence from Lambaréné gave him an opportunity for thinking and writing that would have been impossible at his jungle hospital. As he had in some of his lectures, he discussed his work in Africa in his book *On the Edge of the Primeval Forest,* published in Bern in 1921, and, in New York by the Macmillan Company in 1922.

He devoted most of his attention, however, to philosophy and religion, completing the first two volumes of his projected four-volume *The Philosophy of Civilization.* The two volumes, *The Decay and Restoration of Civilization* and *Civilization and Ethics,* were published in German in Munich in 1923, and an English translation was published by Macmillan in 1939.

In analyzing contemporary civilization, Schweitzer finds that "the abdication of thought has been the decisive factor in the collapse of civilization." In his second volume, he discusses his ideas on the reconstruction of civilization, including his "Reverence for Life," a phrase that came into his mind one day, in September 1915, when he was journeying up the River Ogowe on a mission of mercy. The words struck him as if by chance in answer to his struggle, as he wrote in *Out of my Life and Thought,* "to find the elementary and universal conception of the ethical which [he] had not discovered in any philosophy."

Also in Europe, after World War I, Schweitzer completed his study on comparative religion, *Christianity and the Religions of the World*, which appeared in German and British editions, in 1923, and, was published in the United States by Henry Holt and Company, in 1939. His later important publications, except for several autobiographical volumes, also resulted from studies carried out over a period of time that included the World War I years: *The Mysticism of Paul the Apostle* (Holt, 1931) and *Goethe* (Beacon Press, 1949).

When Schweitzer returned to Lambaréné, in 1924, he found his hospital in ruins. The rebuilding and expansion of his settlement had progressed almost continuously since then until his death in 1965, despite setbacks during World War II. His task had been eased by his fame, which was spread by his autobiographical and other writings and by eyewitness reports of his accomplishment by visitors to Lambaréné. His own example of dedication brought many men and women, often medically trained, to his hospital for varying periods of service. International honors—such as many doctorates from universities throughout the world, the Goethe Memorial Prize of Frankfurt (1928), and the Nobel Peace Prize (1952)—also made his hospital a global point of interest that attracted monetary contributions both directly from individual donors and through the Albert Schweitzer Fellowships of America, established in the late 1930s. His visit to the United States in 1949, when he made guest addresses at the Goethe Festival in Aspen, Colorado, heightened his popularity among Americans in a tide of admiration that engulfed him in hero worship.

The $33,000 Nobel award enabled Schweitzer to begin construction of a leper hospital, about a quarter of a mile from his settlement, which had the capacity for treating some 200 lepers. It is said that nobody counts the population at Schweitzer's hospital, but estimates made during the 1960s indicate that it cared for more than 500 patients at any one time, with a staff of about three dozen White doctors, nurses, and aides, and many native workers. The figures did not include the many outpatients. In addition to tropical diseases, the Africans treated at the hospital suffered mainly from hernia, heart diseases, and pneumonia. The settlement also provided a refuge for a sizable number of animals.

Advanced age ended Dr. Schweitzer's practice as a surgeon, but he continued to visit patients and to supervise medical treatment, including the Introduction of new drugs and new equipment. He directed the construction of all buildings, which numbered about 70 in 1965, and, when he was still able, he did part of the work with his own hands. He also regularly conducted simple religious services at the hospital. Several of his critics had charged that he exercised a dictatorial, or paternalistic, control over all hospital activities, not only treating the natives like children, but, refusing to delegate authority to White members of his staff. He had been described as an enigma: A "throwback" to 19th century European thoughts and mores, authoritarian and paternalistic, but also a humble, self-sacrificing human being.

Even some of the "pilgrims" to Lambaréné found themselves appalled by the primitive sanitary conditions of what Schweitzer called "an African hospital built for Africans" and by the fact that he used electricity only in the operating rooms. Schweitzer's answer was that his hospital suited the needs of the jungle people and that thousands upon thousands of Africans came to him for help because he met them on their own terms. Those who felt that Schweitzer had buried his head in the sand pointed to his opposition to the atom bomb as another count against him. (Schweitzer, along with Albert Einstein and George Bernard Shaw, endless campaigned against the atom bomb and other weapons of mass destruction.)

A man of vibrant and dynamic personality, unpretentious but enormously complex, the white-haired, six-foot Grand Docteur continued to impress his visitors to Lambaréné even after it had become fashionable to disparage him. "For me," the photographer Erica Anderson had said, "the meeting with Dr. Schweitzer was a turning point, as it has been for countless others." His wit and perceptiveness seemed scarcely diminished by age. He was well into his 80's when he gave his last public organ concert, having been able to keep in practice by playing his piano at the hospital. Thousands of magazine articles and perhaps as many as 400 books have told throughout the world the story of Schweitzer's work at Lambaréné. His film biography, made by Erica Anderson, won an Oscar as the best documentary of 1958. Among the many medical missionaries whom Dr. Schweitzer had inspired are William Larimer Mellon, Jr., who founded the Hospital Albert Schweitzer, in Haiti, and Theodor Binder, who founded the Hospital Amazónico Albert Schweitzer in Peru. Missions such as these and similar humanitarian undertakings had largely succeeded because of Schweitzer's personal encouragement, his willingness to answer vast numbers of letters and to welcome hosts of visitors. He believed that every man can, in some measure, have his own Lambaréné, even though he may not be so fortunate as to be able to make the relief of suffering his entire lifework.

Schweitzer passed away at the age of 90 on September 4, 1965, of "circulatory disease brought on by old age," and was buried with his wife at Lambaréné. After their daughter, Rhena (Schweitzer) Eckert Miller, took over as Director of the hospital in Lambaréné, it was modernized. Gabanese physicians and other medical staff were brought on board, and more control of the hospital was given to the Gabanese. Its Medical Research Unit is one of the leading scientific institutions in Africa working to end the scourge of malaria, and it also serves as a highly regarded training site for African physicians and scientists. The hospital is supported by the Albert Schweitzer Fellowship.

## PERSONAL LIFE
Schweitzer married Helene (Bresslau) Schweitzer, on June 18, 1912. She died in 1957. They had one daughter,

Rhena (Schweitzer) Eckert Miller (died February 2009), who was born on his birthday in 1919. Mrs. Miller took over as director in 1965, after her father died, and ran the hospital until 1970.

## FURTHER READING
*Christian Cent 82:38 Ja 13 65; 82:11164- S 15 65; Life 58:834- F 19 65 por; N Y Times II pll Ja 17 65 por Sat R 48:194- S 25 65; Anderson, Erica. Albert Schweitzers Gift of Friendship (1964); Berrill, Jacquelyn. Albert Schweitzer: Man of Mercy (1965); Canning, John, ed. 100 Great Modern Lives (1965); Cousins, Norman. Dr. Schweitzer of Lambaréné (1960); McKnight, Gerald. Verdict on Schweitzer (1964); Picht, Werner. The Life and Thought of Albert Schweitzer (1964); Schweitzer, Albert. On the Edge of the Primeval Forest (1922); Memoirs of Childhood and Youth (1924); Out of my Life and Thought (1933); More from the Primeval Forest (1931); Who's Who, 1965;' Who's Who in America, 1964-65*

---

# AL SHARPTON, JR.

## Minister; Activist; Politician

**Born:** October 3, 1954; Brooklyn, New York
**Primary Field:** Civil Rights
**Affiliation:** Democratic Party

## INTRODUCTION
*"Al Sharpton is an insurgent, an insurgent who will bring to the public's attention those conditions that ordinary poor black people have to live under," Andrew Cooper, the editor of the City Sun, a Brooklyn-based weekly newspaper, told Malcolm Gladwell of the* Washington Post *(June 2, 1994). "That's why people look to him and have no problem following his lead. He is the symbol of our attempt to get through the maze with the truth." Operating primarily in New York City, the Reverend Al Sharpton Jr. has promulgated his "No Justice, No Peace" stance by staging well-orchestrated protest marches to draw attention to what he considers racially motivated murders or other crimes against black people who otherwise might have died or suffered anonymously. From the mid-1980s through the early 1990s, he has been involved with one notorious case after another, in-*

*cluding the alleged rape and abduction by white men of Tawana Brawley, a black teenager, whose claims were found by a grand jury to have constituted an elaborate hoax; killings in Howard Beach, Queens and Bensonhurst, Brooklyn; and riots in Crown Heights, Brooklyn. Sharpton has been agitating for justice for African-Americans for as long as he can remember. "I yelled when I was hungry," he has said in speeches, describing his earliest protests in infancy. "I yelled when I was wet. I yelled when all those little black bourgeois babies stayed dignified and quiet. I learned before I got out of the maternity ward that you've got to holler like hell sometimes to get what you want."*

## EARLY LIFE
Alfred Charles Sharpton Jr. was born on October 3,1954 in the Crown Heights section of the New York City borough of Brooklyn, the son of Al Sharpton Sr., a successful carpenter/contractor, and Ada Sharpton, a seamstress who had a son and a daughter from a previous marriage. A few years after Sharpton's birth, the family, which included his older sister, Cheryl, moved into a

two-family home in the middle-class neighborhood of Hollis, in the borough of Queens.

From his earliest years, Sharpton's life was centered upon religion, particularly through the Washington Temple Church of God in Christ in Brooklyn, a Pentecostal church whose pastor, Bishop Frederick Douglas Washington, fascinated him. Baptized at the age of three, Sharpton preached his first sermon, titled "Let Not Your Heart Be Troubled," a year later, before he had learned to read or write. At the age of ten he was fully ordained as a Pentecostal minister. In the same year, his father deserted the family and withdrew all financial support, thrusting them into poverty. Ada Sharpton supported her children by working first as a domestic and later as a machinist. After living in a housing project for a year, they moved into what Sharpton has described as a "five-room ghetto apartment" in Brooklyn's Brownsville section.

The reduction in his standard of living did not escape the notice of the young minister, who acquired a keen awareness of social contrasts and inequalities. "I knew that the world was better than this," he told Catherine S. Manegold in an interview for the *New York Times Magazine* (January 24, 1993). "In the projects, I thought: 'No, I don't have to accept this. I know there's a better life. I know there's good schools. I know that the garbage man picks up garbage in some neighborhoods, because I lived in them.' So that really gave me indignation." Sharpton became politically active at an early age. At various times throughout his educational career, he served as class orator, associate editor of the school newspaper, student council president, and leader of several student committees devoted to peace and civil rights. He also served as a student intern to Jule Sugarman, then New York City's human resources administrator.

As a teenager, Sharpton was influenced by several other prominent African-Americans in addition to Bishop Washington, among them Congressman Adam Clayton Powell Jr., who was also a minister at the Abyssinian Baptist Church in Harlem, and Jesse Jackson, an up-and-coming leader in the national civil rights movement who had been an aide to the Reverend Martin Luther King Jr. In 1968 Sharpton served as the youth coordinator of the unsuccessful congressional campaign of James Farmer of the Bedford-Stuyvesant section of Brooklyn. In the following year Jackson chose Sharpton to be the youth director of the Greater New York chapter of Operation Breadbasket, a food-distribution program

under the auspices of King's Southern Christian Leadership Conference.

When he was sixteen Sharpton founded his own political group, the National Youth Movement, whose aims included the eradication of drugs in black neighborhoods, the establishment of internships for teenagers with black entrepreneurs, and training programs for black health-care workers. In 1972, the year he graduated from Tilden High School in Brooklyn, Sharpton was chosen to be the youth director of Congresswoman Shirley Chisholm's presidential campaign. In the same year, Adam Clayton Powell died, but not before he had exhorted Sharpton to carry on for him, as Sharpton recalled in an interview with Peter Noel of the *Village Voice* (August 4,1992): "Just before Adam died he told me, 'I want to tell you something. These yellow Uncle Toms are taking over the blacks in New York. Don't you stop fighting. If you wanna do something for Adam, get rid of these Uncle Toms.' I think what I am fighting is Adam's fight."

As he entered adulthood, Sharpton was temporarily sidetracked from the political activism of his youth. In 1973 he became closely associated with the soul singer James Brown, whose son, Teddy, had recently been killed in an auto accident. "James sort of adopted me as the son he lost," Sharpton told Joy Duckett Cain of *Essence* (August 1994), "and he became like the father I never had." During much of the 1970s, Sharpton arranged Brown's schedule, promoted his tours, and hired his musicians. He even adopted the singer's hairstyle, reportedly promising not to change it until after Brown's death. Brown introduced Sharpton to Don King, the flamboyant and influential boxing promoter, whose ability to successfully market million-dollar boxing matches was equaled by his affinity for self-promotion. "I did a lot of on the job training with people who are masters," Sharpton told Manegold. "To grow up under people like James Brown, Jesse Jackson, and a promoter like Don King, I would have to be totally incompetent not to learn something." The apex of Sharpton's career as a music promoter came in 1984, when he served as a community relations adviser for the Jacksons' *Victory* tour.

## LIFE'S WORK

Beginning in the mid-1980s, a series of racial incidents in New York City catapulted Sharpton into the limelight, and his role as an activist and protester increasingly became that of a recognized, albeit controversial, spokesperson for the African-American community. The first of those events was the death, on December 20, 1986, of Michael Griffith, a twenty-three year old black construction worker, who was fatally struck by a car after being chased onto a highway by white youths in the Howard Beach area of Queens, New York. His stepfather, Cedric Sandiford, was badly beaten in the attack. A third black man, Timothy Grimes, escaped unharmed. A day after the first anniversary of Griffith's death, Sharpton staged well attended protests that snarled rush-hour traffic in Brooklyn and Manhattan for hours before the verdict in the first trial of the young white defendants was announced. Some of the protesters became enraged on hearing that no one was convicted of murder; three of the defendants were instead found guilty of manslaughter.

The case that garnered national attention for Sharpton was that of Tawana Brawley, an African-American teenager from Wappingers Falls in Duchess County, New York, who in November 1987 was found nude in a plastic garbage bag, her body covered with excrement and scrawled racial slurs. Brawley, who had been missing for four days, claimed that during that time she had been raped repeatedly by six white men, one of whom she thought was a police officer. After rejecting legal representation by the local chapter of the NAACP, Brawley's family chose Sharpton as their spokesperson and Alton H. Maddox Jr., who had represented Sandiford in the Howard Beach case, and C. Vernon Mason as their lawyers. On January 26, 1988 Governor Mario Cuomo of New York named as special prosecutor Attorney General Robert Abrams, who on February 29 empaneled a grand jury to investigate the case. In the same month, the actor and comedian Bill Cosby and Essence magazine publisher Edward Lewis put up a twenty-five thousand dollar reward for information leading to the arrest and prosecution of Brawley's alleged assailants, and the heavyweight boxing champion Mike Tyson contributed fifty thousand dollars to a foundation for young victims of violence; an equal amount was donated by Don King.

The story immediately became a media sensation, fed largely by unsubstantiated allegations originating from Sharpton organized news conferences about the identities of Brawley's attackers, the "corrupt" American criminal system, a "massive cover-up" by the police, and even a connection to the Irish Republican Army. Sharpton, who advised the Brawleys not to cooperate with the grand jury investigation on the

grounds that they could not expect justice from a racist system, a tactic that had produced results in the Howard Beach case, never provided any evidence to support his claims. The American public, which had at first seemed outraged by what allegedly happened to Brawley, soon became skeptical of the story, especially as it began to seem that Sharpton was using his influence to gain name recognition for himself. As his credibility began to suffer, so, too, did that of the silent Brawley, whose "statements" were made exclusively through Sharpton.

In the early months of the Brawley case, a reporter for *New York Newsday* (January 20, 1988) disclosed that Sharpton had been an FBI informant in investigations of organized crime syndicates and of black civic leaders in the mid-1980s. Sharpton has acknowledged that he helped the FBI, but only in its drug investigations, to gain protection from threats by a certain unnamed mobster in the music industry. Seven months after Brawley's alleged abduction, Sharpton's image was further damaged when Perry McKinnon, a private investigator and former aide to Sharpton, denounced Brawley's trio of advisers, saying that they were fabricating accusations to gain political power for themselves. Having found no evidence of rape (hospital tests in the aftermath of the alleged attack turned up only a minor bruise on Brawley's scalp), the grand jury concluded in October 1988 that the whole affair had been a hoax. Abrams filed judicial complaints against Maddox (whose license was later suspended) and Mason for obstructing the investigation and making false statements about the case, and in 1989 Abrams convened a grand jury that investigated Sharpton on sixty-seven counts of tax evasion, larceny, and fraud. The felony counts were dropped after Sharpton pleaded guilty to the misdemeanor of failing to file a New York State personal income tax return for 1986.

The Brawley case generated a lot of publicity for Sharpton, but much of it was negative. A poll conducted in the spring of 1988 by the New York Times and a local television station found that although black respondents ranked Sharpton as the best known African-American political figure in the city, they also gave him a rating that was more unfavorable than that given any other black leader. Writing in the *New Republic* (July 11,1988), Stanley Crouch observed that the three self-appointed Brawley counselors had "successfully utilized an ethnic version of McCarthyism," in which the enemies are white racists and "rent-a-Toms" who collaborate with their oppressors. Sharpton's self promotion also received a lot of negative press, but some observers of the Brawley case have credited him with possessing more than just media savvy. "Al Sharpton has gained prominence because he understands that there is in the inner city a constituency for a politics based on resentment, anger, and race hatred," according to Arch Puddington, writing in *Commentary* (January 1991).

In the early 1990s Sharpton, who, along with Maddox and Mason, was overseeing an organization called the United African Movement, again captured national attention by placing himself at the center of another violent crime with racial overtones. In the spring of 1990, a young, white Wall Street professional who was jogging in Central Park was attacked by a group of black and Hispanic teenagers, who raped and beat her nearly to death. Several of the defendants in the case made videotaped confessions to the police about their roles in the attack. As in the Brawley case, Sharpton leveled wild accusations, though this time not at the alleged attackers, but at the victim, charging variously, during protests outside the Manhattan Court House, that her boyfriend had committed the crime or that there had been no crime at all. "During the trial the testimony centered on constitutional rights and forensic evidence," Erika Munk reported in the *Nation* (October 8, 1990). "Meanwhile, the rhetoric outside the courthouse, though violently misogynous, was shouted as if it were a cry for racial justice. Sharpton's demonstrators insisted they were talking race, not gender." Sharpton also helped to raise money for the defendants.

In August 1991 another racially charged crisis erupted in Crown Heights, Brooklyn, when a car driven by a Hasidic man jumped a curb, killing Gavin Cato, a seven year old black West Indian boy, and severely injuring his cousin, Angela Cato. Riots immediately broke out throughout Crown Heights, where underlying tensions between blacks, on the one hand, and Hasidim, on the other, had long been smoldering. Sharpton, then the leader of an organization called the National Action Network, tried to organize some of the rioters to protest the failure of the New York Police Department to charge the driver with murder. In the course of three days of rioting, during which a visiting rabbinical student was killed and 67 civilians and 158 police officers were injured, Sharpton's role became that of negotiator. He met frequently with Mayor David N. Dinkins and other black leaders in order to bring the situation under control and to ensure that the black community's grievances received attention.

Sharpton has been widely criticized, and also admired, for using his extensive knowledge of the media to promote his own agenda while ostensibly acting altruistically. "Most public relations people wish they were as good as he is," Dominick Carter, a reporter for the New York radio station WLIB, told Martin Gottlieb and Dean Baquet of the *New York Times* (December 19, 1991). "He knows how to manipulate the press. I mean that as a compliment." Sharpton does not pretend otherwise, acknowledging as much to Gottlieb and Baquet. Referring to his long, wavy hair, his trademark running suits, and his portly frame, he said, "I created Al Sharpton. I wore my hair like this. I dressed like this. I talked like this. I weighed this much. That was my persona. The media just covered it." By the late 1980s he had become so recognizable that he inspired a character in Tom Wolfe's novel of racial and class tensions in New York City, *The Bonfire of the Vanities* (1987).

By 1992, when Sharpton first ran in a Democratic primary for the United States Senate, his image had been overhauled to increase his appeal to mainstream voters. Although he lost that primary election, coming in third in a field of four, his showing was respectable enough to convince him to try again in 1994. His second attempt was also a failure, in that he lost to the Democratic incumbent, but he captured a larger percentage of the vote than he had two years earlier. The philosophy he had espoused in an interview with Mike Sager for Esquire (January 1991) perhaps explains why his electoral defeats have not discouraged him from running in future elections. "To a white mind, it's tangible wins and losses that count in the world," he told Sager, "so you can look at it like this: I got money in black banks, a seat on the MTA board, Howard Beach, Bensonhurst. Those, you could say, are wins. Brawley and them others might be losses. That's to a white mind. But to a black mind, I'm successful 'cause I'm still here."

By the time he decided to enter the 1992 Democratic primary for the United States Senate seat held by the Republican Alfonse M. D'Amato, Sharpton had apparently realized that his image was sorely in need of renovation. A 1990 poll by the *New York Daily News* had found that 90 percent of whites and 73 percent of blacks in the city felt Sharpton was worsening, not improving, race relations. During the campaign he stopped making inflammatory remarks and accusations and began wearing business suits. He also broadened the range of issues he discussed and gathered endorsements from such prominent citizens as filmmaker Spike Lee and Betty

Shabazz, Malcolm X's widow. It was not the first time Sharpton had tried to run for political office. In 1978 he had declared his candidacy for the New York State Senate from the Seventeenth District, which included the Ocean Hill-Brownsville area, but his name was removed from the ballot because he had used two different addresses when registering to vote.

Sharpton's luck was much better in 1992. Not only did he get his name on the Democratic ballot automatically, without having to submit nominating petitions, but he also won 15 percent of the vote in the primary election on September 15, including 21 percent of the vote in New York City and 67 percent of the black vote statewide, a surprisingly strong finish in the opinion of most observers. In that election Sharpton came in third in a field of four, trailing both Attorney General Robert Abrams, the victor, and former vice-presidential candidate Geraldine Ferraro, a member of Congress from Queens, and besting New York City comptroller Elizabeth Holtzman. Abrams was defeated by D'Amato in the general election in November by one percentage point, prompting Jim Sleeper to observe in the *New Republic* (September 19-26, 1994) that Sharpton's candidacy may have hurt the Democrats: "Black voters who had turned out heavily for Sharpton that year in his primary against Abrams sat on their hands in November."

Soon after the 1992 congressional elections, Sharpton once more found himself embroiled in controversy. In February 1993 the New York State Court of Appeals refused to hear his appeal of a 1990 criminal trespass and disorderly conduct conviction stemming from the marches he had organized to protest the murder of Michael Griffith. Sentenced to forty-five days in the Brooklyn House of Detention, Sharpton served twenty-five days before being released on March 30. During his imprisonment he fasted, preached to fellow inmates, and read about Martin Luther King Jr.

Meanwhile, Sharpton had never really stopped running for the United States Senate, having kept his campaign offices open as voter registration centers following his defeat in the 1992 primary. In the 1994 primary, he ran against Democratic incumbent Daniel Patrick Moynihan, garnering 26 percent of the vote to Moynihan's 74 percent. Moynihan went on to triumph over the Republican candidate, Bernadette Castro, in the general election in November, capturing 55 percent of the vote. In 1995 Sharpton returned to his role as an organizer. His most recent activities have included leading a march from New York City to Albany, the state capital, to protest proposed budget cuts by Republican governor George E. Pataki; traveling to Fairfax, Virginia, the home of Supreme Court Justice Clarence Thomas, to lead a protest against his conservative voting record; and speaking in Washington, D.C., to a huge crowd (estimates raged from four hundred thousand to a million and a half) of black men at the Million Man March rally, organized by Louis Farrakhan, the leader of the Nation of Islam, on October 16, 1995.

## PERSONAL LIFE

Al Sharpton, who in February 1994 was re-baptized into the Baptist faith, has returned in recent years to preaching, giving sermons to the congregations of three different churches in the Brooklyn area. He has recently trimmed nearly seventy pounds off his formerly three hundred-pound frame. Since 1980 he has been married to the former Kathy Lee Jordan, whom he met in 1977 while she was a backup singer for James Brown and who has served in the United States Army reserves since the 1970s. The Sharptons and their two young daughters, Dominique and Ashley, live in Englewood, New Jersey; Sharpton also maintains an apartment and an office in Brooklyn.

In 1993 Sharpton received the National Action Network's Dr. Martin Luther King Jr./Adam Clayton Powell Jr. Memorial Award for his "untiring efforts to keep the legacy of King and Powell alive." In his free time Sharpton enjoys reading history and biography and playing word games with his daughters. His decision to enter mainstream politics has been attributed to his brush with death in January 1991, when he was stabbed in the chest by one Michael Riccardi while leading one of thirty marches that he organized in the Bensonhurst section of Brooklyn to protest the verdicts in the racially motivated August 1989 slaying of Yusuf K. Hawkins, an African-American.

## FURTHER READING

*Go and Tell Pharaoh; Al on America; The Rejected Stone: Al Sharpton and the Path to American Leadership*

# ANATOLY SHCHARANSKY

## Jewish Activist; Dissident

**Born:** January 20, 1948; Donetsk, Soviet Union
**Primary Field:** Political Dissident
**Group Affiliation:** Jewish Dissident Movement

### INTRODUCTION

*On February 11, 1986, the internationally renowned Soviet-Jewish dissident Anatoly Shcharansky walked across a bridge to West Berlin and freedom, following years of imprisonment. A founding member of the Moscow Helsinki Watch, a group devoted to monitoring Soviet violations of human rights, Shcharansky was jailed by Soviet authorities in 1977 for his outspoken criticisms of his country's repressive policies on Jewish emigration and political dissent. Combining liberal political convictions with a strong Jewish identity, Shcharansky provided a link between the two previously separate strands of dissent in the Soviet Union—the Jewish emigration movement and the broader human rights movement.*

*Thanks to the tireless efforts of his wife, Avital, and his brother Leonid, Shcharansky's fate became an international cause célèbre. Finally, in February 1986, apparently as part of an effort to improve relations with the United States, the regime of Mikhail Gorbachev released Shcharansky in an East-West prisoner exchange, and he was allowed to join his wife in Israel. Since gaining his freedom, he has visited the United States to press the cause of Soviet Jews and political prisoners. For many, Shcharansky's great courage and strong convictions have made him a "hero of our time."*

### EARLY LIFE

Anatoly Shcharansky was born on January 20, 1948, in Donetsk, a Ukrainian coal mining town near the Black Sea. He was the second of two sons born to Boris Shcharansky, a filmwriter and journalist, and his wife, Ida Milgrom, an economist. Anatoly received a gold medal for scholarship when he graduated from high school and, having played chess since he was eight, became his city's chess champion when he was just fourteen. Growing up in an assimilated Jewish family, he learned little about Judaism and, because of his parents' protectiveness, remained unaware of the widespread anti-Semitism of post-Stalinist Russia.

Shcharansky's awareness of his Jewish identity began to grow during his student years in Moscow, where he went in 1966 to attend a special mathematics school. His first brush with anti-Semitism came on a hiking trip with his best friend, who during an argument called him a "Yid." He later told an American reporter, "I think it was then that I decided [the Soviet Union] was no place for me."

### LIFE'S WORK

But it was the dramatic Six-Day War of 1967, in which tiny Israel defeated a strong coalition of Arab enemies, that brought Shcharansky, along with many Soviet Jews, to a new consciousness of his Jewish heritage. In the late 1960s and early 1970s, the "Jews of Silence," as Elie Wiesel once termed them, began to find their voice: to organize classes in Hebrew language and Jewish culture, to memorialize the victims of the Holocaust, and above all, to dream of going to Israel.

In April 1973, a year after graduating from the prestigious Moscow Physical-Technical Institute with a specialty in cybernetics and taking a job as a computer specialist with the Moscow Research Institute for Oil and Gas, Shcharansky applied for an exit visa to go to Israel. His request was rejected, on the grounds that his work had given him "access to classified materials," though none of the work he had done at the Moscow Physical-Technical Institute had been of a military nature. His thesis was on programming computers to play chess, and the institute where he worked was classified as an "open" institution, not involved in secret work.

But Shcharansky's visa never came. That second refusal, coupled with separation from his wife, redoubled his commitment to the dissident movement. He became part of a team, closely watched by the KGB, that traveled to outlying towns and provinces during October and November 1974, collecting information on the experiences of the "refuseniks" and was one of nine signatories to a letter to President Gerald Ford that detailed many cases of abuse and harassment that they had discovered on their journeys. The letter was dated November 18, 1974, five days before Ford flew to Vladivostok to meet with Soviet leader Leonid I. Brezhnev. As a result of a compromise negotiated by Henry A. Kissinger during those talks, the United States Senate in 1974 passed the Jackson Amendment to the Trade Reform Act of 1972, linking East-West trade to the easing of Soviet emigration restrictions. A further amendment to the act, introduced by Senator Adlai Stevenson 3d, set a $300 million limit on United States banking credits to the Soviet Union, making Soviet-Jewish emigration one of the conditions for any increase in those credits. The amended Trade Reform Act was signed by President Ford on January 3, 1975, but Soviet authorities, irate over the amendment, canceled the agreement seven days later. With others who had pinned their hopes on the Jackson Amendment, Shcharansky now took part in new letter-writing campaigns and protest demonstrations, including a rally on the steps of Moscow's Lenin Library on February 24, 1975. Two of the organizers were arrested, tried, and sentenced to five years of exile in Siberia.

In August 1975, even as reprisals against the "refuseniks" increased, the Soviet government signed the Helsinki accords, which recognized Soviet hegemony over Eastern Europe in exchange for a guarantee of human rights, including the right of emigration. Shcharansky later observed in an interview in the *Washington Post* (May 4, 1986) that the agreement was meaningless: "The moment they signed it, they started to take steps to discourage people from using it." Nevertheless, the Helsinki accords gave Soviet dissidents a new platform around which to organize. In May 1976, led by the physicist Yuri Orlov, a small group of activists, among them Anatoly Shcharansky, founded the Moscow Helsinki Watch to monitor Soviet compliance with its human rights provisions. In the following months, the group collected information on a wide range of abuses and published regular reports that were distributed to the embassies of the nations that had signed the Helsinki accords, as well as to the press.

Because of his central role in the Helsinki group, Shcharansky lost his job and was subjected to constant surveillance and threats. Then he was accused in *Izvestia* of spying for the CIA, and on March 15, 1977, he was arrested and charged under the Soviet penal code with "treasonable espionage" and with anti-Soviet agitation and propaganda.

Despite the fact that his former roommate, Sanya Lipavsky, named him as a CIA agent, Shcharansky insisted that he was not a spy. Even President Jimmy Carter came to his defense by issuing a statement that the Jewish activist had no links with the United States intelligence agency. Western observers agreed that the spy charge was a trumped-up cover for Shcharansky's real "crime," his prominent role in the dissident movement.

The authorities intended to make an example of him, to frighten other dissidents.

Shcharansky's trial began on July 10, 1978, two days before the start of United States-Soviet Strategic Arms Limitation Talks (SALT) in Geneva. Western observers and supporters of Shcharansky were barred from the courtroom, but his brother Leonid was allowed to attend (except for a secret session on July 11 and 12, which met to consider classified material that Shcharansky was alleged to have passed to foreign agents) and he conveyed information about the proceedings to about 150 supporters and journalists outside the courtroom. The prosecution charged Shcharansky with passing classified documents to agents posing as journalists, in particular to Robert Toth, a reporter for the *Los Angeles Times*, who was accused by Soviet authorities of working for the CIA. Conducting his own defense, Shcharansky rejected the charges as "absurd." Denied permission to call witnesses for his defense and restricted by the judge in his questioning of prosecution witnesses, Shcharansky was convicted on July 14 and sentenced to three years in prison, to be followed by ten years in a labor camp.

Then began almost a decade of nightmarish imprisonment. Shcharansky spent the first three years at Chistopol prison in solitary confinement. To keep his sanity, he did mental exercises: playing imaginary chess games with himself (which he always won, as he once jokingly told a reporter), outlining a book that he wanted to write, and singing Hebrew songs as loudly as he could, "I was sure that my people and my friends hadn't forgotten me," Shcharansky recalled, as quoted in the *Washington Post* (May 4, 1986), and that gave him the strength to resist the KGB's continued efforts to break his will.

Indeed, his family and friends had not forgotten him, and after the immediate protests over his imprisonment died down, they worked ceaselessly to keep his memory alive. His mother and his brother Leonid kept petitioning the Soviet authorities in his behalf and met regularly with Western journalists in Moscow. Those activities cost Leonid his job. Because he was considered a security risk; he was fired in 1982 from his position as a computer programmer for a Moscow industrial firm. Meanwhile, in Jerusalem, Avital founded the Association for the Release of Anatoly Shcharansky. With the support of international Jewish organizations, she took his case to Western heads of state, embarrassing the Kremlin with her outspoken condemnation of her husband's treatment.

Shcharansky remained optimistic and good-humored in his imprisonment. Moved to Perm 35, a labor camp for political prisoners, where he was assigned to work as a welder, he had more access to the outside world. His reading was heavily censored, but occasionally the camp authorities slipped up; an anti-Zionist magazine that they once gave him to read included a facsimile of a letter from Ronald Reagan to his wife, Avital. Shcharansky's spirit of resistance remained strong. Since he refused to work unless he was allowed to keep prayer books and candles, he was often sent to the "punishment cells." Accused of being a "bad influence" on other prisoners, he was sent back in January 1981 to Chistopol prison to serve a three- year sentence. In February 1982 he began a four-month hunger strike to protest the confiscation of his mail, during which he was forcibly fed.

Although his emotional stamina was exceptional, Shcharansky's physical health was poor. As a result of his severely restricted diet, his weight dropped at one point to less than 110 pounds. He suffered from chronic heart and blood pressure problems, and lack of medical attention for his eyes left him nearly blind. Fearing for her husband's life, Avital became increasingly outspoken in her public appeals in his behalf. Ignoring hints from the Soviet leader Yuri Andropov that Shcharansky might be released if she stopped her "noisy campaign," she went to the United States in 1984 for a White House ceremony on human rights and unexpectedly asked for a private interview with President Ronald Reagan. His administration later used every opportunity to tell Soviet authorities that the United States would regard the release of Shcharansky and his fellow "prisoner of conscience," Andrei Sakharov, as an important sign of their willingness to work for better East-West relations.

With Mikhail Gorbachev's accession to power, the Soviet Union became more receptive to the idea of freeing Shcharansky as a way to help thaw Soviet-American negotiations. Although the precise details were never revealed, Reagan and Gorbachev evidently reached an agreement on his release at the Geneva summit conference in November 1985. After some unexplained delays on the Soviet side, final plans were made to include the activist in an East-West exchange of captured intelligence operatives. To underline their insistence that Shcharansky had never been a spy, the United States authorities insisted that he be released before the other prisoners. As hundreds of journalists watched, along with the United States ambassador to Bonn and West German officials, Anatoly Shcharansky walked across the Glienicke Bridge from Potsdam into West Berlin on February 11, 1986, and at long last became a free man. Shcharansky immediately flew to Frankfurt, where he met Avital and, demonstrating his usual wit, greeted her with the words, "I'm sorry I'm late." That same day, nine years after their wedding, husband and wife finally realized their dream to go to Israel together. At Jerusalem airport, where they were met by Prime Minister Shimon Peres and a joyful crowd, Shcharansky said that it was the "happiest day of our life" and added, "I am not going to forget those whom I left in the camps, in prisons, who are still in exile or who still continue their struggle for the right to emigrate and for their human rights."

---

## Affiliation: Jewish Dissident Movement

Now branded as a "refusenik"—a Jew denied an exit visa—Shcharansky was subject to special harassment by the authorities. Angered by that state of affairs, he joined the Jewish dissident movement which, starting in the late 1960s, had begun to challenge the government's restrictive emigration policy. Those who protested too openly or tried to escape were given harsh prison sentences. As the numbers of the imprisoned grew, other Jews, among them the twenty-five-year-old Shcharansky, began to organize public protests in their behalf.

It was at one such public protest in October 1973, that the young activist met Natalia Shtiglits (or Stieglitz), an ardent Zionist, whose "refusenik" brother was serving a brief prison term for his political activities. The young couple began to live together soon after and, having decided to marry the following spring, both applied for exit visas to go to Israel. In June 1974, while Shcharansky was serving his first prison term as part of the "suspicious and subversive element" that was hidden from view during President Richard Nixon's second visit to the Soviet Union, Natalia learned that her visa had been granted. Believing that Anatoly's visa would soon follow, they were married the day he was released from prison, on July 4, 1974, and on the following day Natalia, now using her Hebrew name, Avital, left for Israel.

Physically and emotionally exhausted, Shcharansky went into seclusion for a few months to prepare for a trip to the United States, which he planned and financed himself, to thank his American supporters. He arrived in New York City on May 7, 1986, to a hero's welcome. Four days later he was the guest of honor at the annual Solidarity Parade in behalf of Soviet Jews, which culminated in a rally at Dag Hammarskjöld Plaza that drew an estimated 300,000 people. The following day, in the office of Random House publisher Robert Bernstein, who is chairman of the United States Helsinki Watch Committee, Shcharansky met for the first time in a decade with Yelena Bonner, another founder of the Moscow Helsinki Watch, who had been sentenced, along with her husband, the Nobel Prize-winning Soviet physicist Andrei D. Sakharov, to internal exile in Gorky for "anti-Soviet slander," but was in the United States on medical leave. Shcharansky then flew to Washington, D.C., where on May 13 he received the key to the city from the mayor and was awarded the Congressional Gold Medal, at a reception in the Capitol Rotunda. On the same day, he met with President Reagan, Vice-President George Bush, Secretary of State George P. Shultz, national security affairs adviser John M. Poindexter, and White House chief of staff Donald T. Regan, in a closed forty-minute conference in the Oval office, but the details of that conference were not released because of the administration's emphasis on "quiet diplomacy." During the next two days he met individually with leaders of the Senate and the House of Representatives and testified at hearings before the congressional committee that monitors compliance with the Helsinki accords.

During his visit, Shcharansky repeated the same message at every opportunity. While acknowledging that "quiet diplomacy" had helped to gain his release, he urged the United States to continue putting public pressure on the Soviet Union to release the estimated 400,000 Jews still awaiting exit visas and to moderate its policies on human rights in general. He told reporters that the United States "must leave no doubt with the Soviet authorities that the human rights problem is not a propaganda issue but a question of principle on which all the structure of the relationships between East and West can be built." Describing his release as a "cosmetic" gesture, Shcharansky expressed the view that the Soviet regime would not change markedly under Gorbachev unless it was subject to relentless pressure, including economic sanctions. "Just the fact that Gorbachev understands things better than his predecessors

gives some reason for optimism," Shcharansky told Francis X. Clines in an interview for the New York Times (February 8, 1987). He added, however: "The West must not be deceived by his campaign of gestures and must be firm. ..."

Shcharansky, who now uses his Hebrew given name "Natan" and has changed the spelling of his surname to Sharansky, continued to face some difficult challenges in his new homeland. Although he tried to steer clear of Israel's bitter factional politics, he has on occasion become embroiled in controversy. In the late summer of 1986 he came under fire for insisting that arms controls talks with the Soviet Union be tied to human rights issues and for opposing a meeting between Israeli and Soviet negotiators to reopen diplomatic relations between their two countries. Asked how he felt about the criticism, Shcharansky replied, "That's the beauty of democracy."

But in November 1986 the activist became embroiled in a more embarrassing controversy by meeting with two Palestinians, who asked him to investigate alleged human rights violations by Israeli authorities on the West Bank—in particular, the expulsion of a Palestinian newspaper editor. Rightist spokesmen maintained that the two men had connections with the Palestine Liberation Organization and bitterly attacked Shcharansky for listening to them. He issued an apology, explaining that he had been ignorant of their PLO ties and affirming that Israeli efforts to suppress the PLO "birds of prey" could never be considered a violation of human rights.

## PERSONAL LIFE

In the midst of his turbulent new life, Shcharansky's family has been a special source of joy. Honoring a commitment made at the time of his release, the Soviet Union allowed his brother Leonid, along with his wife and their two sons, and his mother, to immigrate to Israel in August 1986. Then, in November, Shcharansky's wife presented him with their first child, a girl. Asked how he and his wife were getting along after their long separation, Shcharansky replied that he had always felt spiritually close to her in their years apart. "But I was surprised," he admitted, "how we started understanding one another from the very first moment" after his release, and added that he was very proud of the political prominence she had acquired in his absence. Avital Shcharansky, a convert to Orthodox Judaism, is religiously more observant than her husband and has been identified with the religious right.

Described by Richard Grenier in *Insight* (March 17, 1986) as an "awesomely cheerful little man" who is "amiable, intelligent, even amusing," Anatoly Shcharansky is five feet two inches tall, stocky, and bald. After reading his moving letters from prison, which are quoted at length in Martin Gilbert's biography *Shcharansky: Hero of Our Time* (Viking, 1986), reviewers were eagerly awaiting his memoirs, scheduled to be published by Random House. On November 1, 1981 a flight of steps opposite the United Nations building in New York City was named the "Shcharansky Steps" at a ceremony sponsored by the Greater New York Conference on Soviet Jewry, the Student Struggle for Soviet Jewry, and Mayor Edward Koch of New York City. An honorary degree, conferred by Yeshiva University, was accepted for him by his wife in 1984.

## FURTHER READING
*Insight 2:32+ F 2 '86 por; N Y Rev of Bks 33:13+ S 25 '86 por; Newsday II 4+ My 19 '86 por; Washington Post C pl+ My 17 '86 por; Gilbert, Martin. Shcharansky: Hero of Our Time (1986). International Who's Who, 1986-87*

---

# CINDY SHEEHAN

## Political Activist; Writer

**Born:** July 10, 1957; Inglewood, California
**Primary Field:** Anti-War Movement
**Affiliation:** Peace and Freedom Party

## INTRODUCTION
*Cindy Sheehan is a political activist and writer whom some credit with reviving protest against the Iraq war. Her most highly publicized activity took place in 2005, when she camped out near President George W. Bush's Crawford, Texas, home, demanding to speak with him about the loss of her son, U.S. Army specialist Casey Sheehan, who was killed in Iraq in 2004. Her son's death contributed to Sheehan's transformation from a politically inactive mother and office worker into one of the antiwar movement's most visible exponents. Sheehan has accused President Bush of deceiving the American public during the buildup to the U.S.-led war in Iraq, which was launched in March 2003, 18 months after the terrorist attacks on the U.S, ostensibly to rid Iraq of so-called weapons of mass destruction. No such weapons were found there, and many, including Sheehan, have charged that the Bush administration knowingly rushed to war on the basis of faulty intelligence and that it implied connections between Iraq and the 2001 attacks in order to justify the war. "Before Casey was killed, I thought that one person couldn't make a difference," Sheehan explained to Deanne Stillman for* Rolling Stone *(December 15, 2005, online). "Millions protested against the invasion [of Iraq] in 2003, but it didn't do any good. Then, after Casey was killed, my daughter Carly read me a poem she wrote. It moved me to action. I thought, if one person can't make a difference, at least I'm gonna go to my grave trying.'" Through her actions and often-incendiary words, she has labeled Bush a terrorist and demanded his impeachment, likened the Iraq war to genocide, and publicly clashed with the parents of other soldiers who have died in the Iraq war, parents who continue to support the war and the president, Sheehan has become a lightning rod for controversy, reflected in the wide variety of ways she is portrayed in the media and particularly in the sphere of Web logs. To some, Sheehan is an inspiring figure with the courage to stand up to the president of the United States. To others, she is at best a tool of wealthy radicals who exploit her sympathetic story for their own political ends or, at worst, an anti-American, publicity seeking narcissist, an abettor of terrorism, or an anti-Semite, the last charge stemming from her comments on the Israeli-Palestinian conflict.*

## EARLY LIFE
Sheehan was born Cindy Lee Miller on July 10, 1957. She grew up in Bellflower, California, a small suburb of Los Angeles. She has said that as a child she was shy and introverted and had few friends. Her family life, by her account, was dysfunctional; her father was an alcoholic and her mother was physically abusive to Cindy and her sister, Dede. Sheehan, the only member of her family who belonged to the local church, found solace there and enjoyed both the stability of the church community and the feeling of independence that came with attending services.

Cindy's future husband, Patrick Sheehan, attended high school in nearby Norwalk, California. The two met and started dating when Cindy was 16 and were married on April 30, 1977; they moved into a small home in Norwalk. Patrick worked as a hardware-store sales representative in California and Nevada, while Cindy had a job as a loan adjuster for the Security Pacific National Bank. She left that position in 1979, prior to the birth of her first child, Casey Austin, in order to raise her family. The couple had three other children in the next six years: Carly, Andy, and Jane. When Casey was 14 the family moved to Vacaville, a town in northern California, and Sheehan, who had converted to Catholicism after her marriage, served in Vacaville as a youth minister at St. Mary's Church. (Sheehan has since left the church because of the historical role organized religion has had in global conflicts and what she sees as the inaction of religious leaders with regard to the antiwar movement in the United States.) Sheehan later took a position with Napa Valley Health and Human Services.

## LIFE'S WORK

Casey Sheehan joined the U.S. Army with an eye toward earning money for college while serving as a chaplain. Instead, he was assigned as a Humvee mechanic, and in early 2004 he was deployed to Iraq. On April 4, after less than a month there, Casey was killed in an ambush near Sadr City while attempting to rescue wounded soldiers. On June 17, 2004 the Sheehans, along with 17 other families who had lost children in the Iraq war, were invited to meet with President Bush at a military base near Seattle, Washington. Although Cindy Sheehan and her family were upset by the war and questioned its purpose, (Carly had begun to write poetry about the conflict), they decided to approach the meeting as Casey would have wanted them to and refrained from venting their frustration at President Bush. The president initially seemed to make a positive impression on the family, who praised him for coming to the meeting without political motivation. Sheehan told David Henson for the *Vacaville Reporter* (June 24, 2004, online) that she was affected by President Bush's apparent sympathy for their loss and his being a "man of faith."

The most comforting and satisfying part of the experience for the Sheehans was the chance to meet with other families of soldiers who had been killed, to share their grief with those families and engage in mutual support. Referring to that, Sheehan told Henson, "That was

the gift the president gave us, the gift of happiness, of being together." In an interview a year later with Wolf Blitzer for CNN (August 7, 2005), however, Sheehan accused the president of having been callous during the interview. "We wanted to use the time for him to know that he killed an indispensable part of our family and humanity," she said. "And we wanted him to look at the pictures of Casey. He wouldn't look at the pictures of Casey. He didn't even know Casey's name. He came in the room and the very first thing he said is, 'So who are we honoring here?' Every time we tried to talk about Casey and how much we missed him, he would change the subject. And he acted like it was a party." According to Greg Szymanski, writing for the LewisNews (July 5, 2005, online), Sheehan recalled her meeting with Bush as "one of the most disgusting experiences I ever had."

Sheehan held herself partially responsible for his son's death, feeling that she had not done enough to dissuade him from joining the army. Partly for that reason she suffered from depression and stress, which caused her to miss work. In July 2004 she was fired from her job. That year Sheehan, who had until then been a nominal Democrat and would not have described herself as politically active, began speaking out against the war in Iraq. In October 2004 she appeared on nationally broadcast television spots sponsored by the political action committee Real Voices. In one, according to Michelle Goldberg, writing for *Salon* (October 1, 2004, online), Sheehan was filmed addressing the president with the words, "I imagined it would hurt if one of my kids was killed, but I never thought it would hurt this bad, especially someone so honest and brave as Casey, my son. When you haven't been honest with us, when you and your advisors rushed us into this war. How do you think we felt when we heard the Senate report that said there was no link between Iraq and 9/11?" Sheehan told Goldberg that by speaking out against President Bush, she was able to assuage some of the sense of helplessness she felt about her son's death. "I need to speak out for what I think is right, and I have this chance right now because people want to listen to me," she said. "If I didn't do that, I wouldn't be able to get up in the morning or face a new day." She went on to refer to the 2000 presidential election, which was so close that votes were recounted in Florida, until the U.S. Supreme Court halted that process, effectively declaring Bush the winner. "My biggest regret in my entire life is that when Bush was selected as president by the Supreme Court that I didn't go out and say, 'No, this is b.s., we can't stop this election until we count every single vote.' I just regret it so much. I don't know if I did something more maybe my son would still be alive." Reportedly, Sheehan, along with a number of others who had lost family members during the Iraq war, was approached by the Democrat John Kerry's presidential campaign staff about appearing in additional television broadcasts against the war. As Sheehan became more involved in the antiwar cause, she alienated nearly all of her friends, who for the most part supported Bush in the 2004 election, as well as her husband's family, who were mostly conservative Republicans. Her television spots spawned hate mail and angry telephone calls, and some derided her as a traitor to the United States. Referring to those who wanted to silence her, Sheehan told Goldberg, "I think those people are traitors, because my son and millions of brave Americans before him have died for my right to speak out against the government." Using the insurance money that she received after her son's death, Sheehan spent the rest of 2004 traveling around the United States to speak out against the war.

During the January 2005 presidential inauguration of George W. Bush, Sheehan protested in Washington, D.C. She spoke at the opening of "Eyes Wide Open: the Human Cost of War", a traveling exhibition, sponsored by the American Friends Service Committee, that featured the combat boots of slain military personnel and otherwise honored U.S. soldiers and Iraqi civilians who had been hurt or killed in wartime. Sheehan later became one of the nine founders of a group called Gold Star Families for Peace. Inspired by the name of the organization American Gold Star Mothers, and by the U.S. military tradition of presenting gold stars to the mothers of soldiers killed in combat, Sheehan and others sought to extend similar recognition to all family members of deceased soldiers and to work toward the prevention of warfare. Through her appearances in television broadcasts and her attendance at numerous antiwar protests after her son's death, Sheehan became the group's spokesperson and most visible member.

Sheehan appeared at many more antiwar functions in 2005. One appearance of hers that drew particular criticism was at a San Francisco State University forum in support of the civil rights lawyer Lynne Stewart, who in February of that year was found guilty of giving support to terrorists. In a widely quoted speech, Sheehan took aim at the American public-school system for what she saw as its incorrect and politically motivated interpretation of U.S. history; attacked President Bush; and

otherwise engaged in what her detractors would later describe as anti-Americanism. In one of the most controversial and widely quoted parts of her speech, Sheehan, while discussing the deaths of soldiers in the Iraq war, stated: "This country (the U.S.) is not worth dying for."

Sheehan's continued political activism strained her Personal Life considerably. While her sister, Dede, and daughter Carly publicly supported her, few others of her acquaintances did. Her husband's family wrote opinion pieces denouncing Sheehan's views, and Patrick Sheehan himself disapproved of his wife's activities; the couple separated in June 2005 and divorced in August of that year. Cindy Sheehan has said that her conflict with her husband grew from the difference between their ways of handling grief. While Cindy Sheehan found comfort in making public appearances and statements, her husband grieved privately. As for his feelings about his wife's activism, Patrick Sheehan told Jill Smolowe for *People* (August 29, 2005) that "Casey's life isn't being honored" by it. "I'd like you to know that Casey was proud to be a soldier." In the same interview, he said, "My kids and I feel like we've had two losses: Casey, and now our wife and mother. The kids are angry and lonely for her. I don't think she's done the best for the family. When we see Cindy talking about Casey, we all relive the loss."

Sheehan's most widely publicized action came in August 2005, when she camped roughly three miles from the home of President Bush, in Crawford, Texas, and announced that she would remain there until he spoke with her about the Iraq war. Sheehan called for the immediate removal of U.S. troops from Iraq and railed against Bush for misleading Americans during the buildup to the war. The president, who spent most of August in Crawford, refused to meet with her, on the grounds that he had already done so. He publicly stated his sympathy for Sheehan's loss but argued that removing troops from Iraq would be a mistake. Bush sent National Security Adviser Stephen Hadley, Deputy Chief of Staff Joe Hagan, and other top White House aides to meet with Sheehan, but she continued to demand to meet with the president himself. Sheehan explained during her interview with Wolf Blitzer that she had brought her protest to Crawford because she took offense at comments the president had been making in regard to the U.S. soldiers who had been killed. "He said that the families can rest assured that their children died for a noble cause. And he also said that we have to honor the sacrifices of the fallen soldiers by continuing the mission in Iraq," Sheehan told Blitzer. "And I have said this so many times: I do not want him to use my son's name to continue the killing. Why would I want one more mother, either Iraqi or American, to go through what I'm going through?"

Sheehan began her vigil, which ultimately lasted 26 days, in the company of four supporters. Later, Gold Star Families for Peace sponsored a TV spot featuring Sheehan, which was broadcast in the Texas towns of Waco and Crawford, and further publicized her demands to meet with the president. The group also conducted a march to a police station just outside the perimeter of Bush's ranch to deliver letters written by activists to First Lady Laura Bush; the letters appealed to her as a mother to support their antiwar cause. To many opponents of the Iraq war, Sheehan's personal tragedy granted her an unassailable moral authority, and she was quickly embraced as an icon of the antiwar movement. Hundreds soon joined her at her campsite, not only to protest the war but to speak out on issues ranging from women's rights to U.S. support of Israel. Sheehan's campground, which became known in the media as "Camp Casey," drew up to 1,000 visitors each day, including members of Congress and prominent actors and musicians. The activity there, one of the biggest news stories of the summer of 2005, attracted a huge media contingent that documented the daily goings-on, which in turn prompted as much controversy and counter-demonstration as support. A counter-protest organized by the Dallas, Texas based talk-show host Darrell Ankarlo took place at the Yellow Rose gift shop, a few hundred yards from Camp Casey, and at times drew as much local support as Sheehan's group.

Sheehan's critics included Robert L. Jamieson Jr., who wrote for the *Seattle Post-Intelligencer* (August 13, 2005), "That Sheehan would allow her private grief to be plied for a public stunt seems unfathomable even if her underlying message about unnecessary blood being shed by American soldiers hits the mark." Cathy Young, writing for the *Boston Globe* (August 22, 2005, online), compared Sheehan's political relevance to that of Terri Schiavo, the St. Petersburg, Florida, woman whose death, following years spent on life support, was preceded by a highly publicized and politicized legal battle between her husband, who sought to remove life support, and her parents, who opposed the move. "The Sheehan circus has a lot in common with the Schiavo circus, none of it good," Young wrote. "Both stories represent a triumph,

on different sides of the political divide, of emotion and sentiment driven politics. Schiavo's parents could go off on crazy, paranoid, vitriolic rants, and enjoy a certain immunity by virtue of their unthinkable tragedy. The same is true of Sheehan. Sheehan's grief entitles her to sympathy. But her loss does not give her, as *New York Times* columnist Maureen Dowd (August 10, 2005) has claimed, an 'absolute' moral authority—any more than it would if her reaction to her son's death was to demand a U.S. nuclear strike against the (Iraqi) insurgents." In the activist's defense, the columnist Frank Rich of the *New York Times* (August 21, 2005) argued that what he deemed the smearing of Sheehan was similar to previous attacks against opponents of Bush's policies, such as the former government official Richard Clarke. Many believed strongly in Sheehan's protest and in her right to be critical of the government and President Bush but felt that her message was being undermined, and her credibility compromised, by the various activists and groups who had aligned themselves with her.

Sheehan's protest ended in late August, when Hurricane Katrina caused flooding that devastated much of New Orleans, Louisiana, and its surrounding areas and prompted President Bush to leave Crawford. Sheehan left as well, but not before declaring her intention to return each time Bush went to Texas on vacation. "I look back on it, and I am very, very, very grateful he did not meet with me, because we have sparked and galvanized the peace movement. If he'd met with me, then I would have gone home, and it would have ended there," Sheehan told Angela K. Brown for the *Associated Press* (August 31, 2005).

Following her stay in Crawford, Sheehan wrote articles for various online sites, restating her antiwar position, denying what she termed inaccurate rumors about her, and attempting to maintain the momentum that her vigil had brought to the antiwar movement. In those articles Sheehan argued that President Bush had falsified information during the buildup to the Iraq war and that he continued to fabricate reasons for maintaining a U.S. military presence in Iraq. She contended that he had made the U.S. less safe by sending personnel and equipment to Iraq, thereby leaving vulnerable regions of the country ill-prepared to cope with disaster, and she called for the impeachment of the president. In September 2005 Gold Star Families for Peace teamed with Iraq Veterans Against the War, Military Families Speak Out, and Veterans for Peace, among other groups, to organize the Bring Them Home Now Tour, a traveling antiwar protest that began in Crawford and crossed the United States to raise awareness about the war in Iraq. Sheehan spoke at many rallies along the way, and the tour culminated in a September 24 protest in Washington, D.C. Sheehan returned to Crawford when Bush vacationed there during Thanksgiving.

Sheehan used her celebrity in an attempt to persuade government officials to seek an end to the Iraq war. In the fall of 2005, she met with U.S. senator John McCain of Arizona, and on a separate occasion she urged Arizona governor Janet Napolitano to withdraw Arizona National Guard troops from Iraq. In October 2005 Sheehan tried unsuccessfully to earn an audience with California governor Arnold Schwarzenegger; she wanted to ask him to limit the number of California National Guardsmen made available for duty in Iraq. At the time, 16,000 of the roughly 20,000 National Guardsmen of California were in Iraq. Sheehan argued that this reduced the manpower that would be available to Californians in the event of a natural disaster, such as an earthquake or flood.

In late 2005 Sheehan traveled to London, England where she addressed the International Peace Conference, sponsored by the Stop the War Coalition and held at the Royal Horticultural Hall. In London she attended the premiere of a play by the Nobel Prize winner Dario Fo, *Peace Mom*, which was inspired by her story. She also participated in a series of interviews with the *London Guardian* newspaper and BBC Radio. Traveling to Ireland, she met with that country's foreign affairs minister, Dermot Ahern, to discuss the policy of allowing U.S. warplanes to refuel at airbases in Ireland, In January 2006 Sheehan made headlines when she traveled to Venezuela, whose government, headed by Hugo Chavez, has had strained relations with the U.S. to attend the Caracas World Social Forum, which drew more than 10,000 anti-globalization activists. Her trip was financed by Venezuela's foreign ministry, a fact that, together with Sheehan's speech at the event, generated controversy in the United States. According to Jan James, writing for the Associated Press (January 24, 2006), Sheehan said, "We really need to stop the imperialist tendencies of countries like the United States and Great Britain." In May 2006 Sheehan spoke at a rally in Melbourne, Australia, to call for the release of David Hicks, an Australian citizen who had been detained without trial for over five years at Guantanamo Bay, in Cuba, as a terror suspect. Hicks was freed in April 2007, after pleading guilty to one relatively minor charge.

Sheehan maintained her activism in the United States as well. On January 31, 2006 she gained notice when she was arrested at the U.S. Capitol during President Bush's State of the Union address, for wearing a T-Shirt that read "2,245 Dead. How Many More?" a reference to the number of U.S. soldiers who had died in Iraq up to that point. The dress code for the State of the Union address prohibits the wearing of clothing containing type of any kind, and at least one other person, the wife of Republican representative Bill Young of Florida, was also told to leave the premises; her shirt read, "Support Our Troops." Sheehan was arrested again, in New York on March 7, 2006, for obstructing entry to the office of the U.S. Mission to the United Nations while participating in a protest with Iraqi-American women against the Iraq war. She participated in a wider antiwar protest in New York on April 9, 2006.

Sheehan has written numerous articles published on Web sites including *Common Dreams, Truth Out, Daily Kos*, and the *Huffington Post*, as well as on the Web sites of the filmmaker Michael Moore and the political commentator Lew Rockwell. She has also published three books: *Not One More Mother's Child* (2005), an account of her first year of activism; *Dear President Bush* (2005), a collection of writings and speeches; and the memoir *Peace Mom: A Mother's Journey through Heartache to Activism* (2006). In August 2007 Sheehan announced her candidacy for the seat in the House of Representatives currently held by the House Speaker, the Democrat Nancy Pelosi, who represents California's Eighth Congressional District. She has attributed her decision to oppose Pelosi to the failure of the Democrats in Congress to take steps to impeach President Bush or end the war in Iraq.

Sheehan also continued to contribute pieces to blogs and other Web sites, urging readers to get involved in the antiwar movement and defending herself and the movement against attacks from the political right. In an article published on the Web site Common Dreams (April 7, 2006), Sheehan wrote about her frustration over conservatives' predictions of the demise of the antiwar movement and over what she saw as a complacent, easily manipulated U.S. citizenry. She argued that although many people shared her belief that the Iraq war was a misbegotten and failed enterprise, few were willing to speak out against it, or make sacrifices, as she had done, to achieve the goal of ending the conflict. "Some, like Casey and almost 2400 other Americans and their families give all, while some, like the people of Iraq, have everything stolen from them by unlawful war; some, like myself, give a lot; some give some, by writing letters, attending an occasional vigil or march; but the majority of Americans give nothing except an occasional vote, which we all know counts practically for nothing with our electoral process being so corrupted and almost rendered meaningless," she wrote. "The challenge of the peace movement, now that we have identified the problem so well, and have the vast majority of Americans on our side, is to convince each and every last American that he/she has a very intimate and personal stake in what we are allowing our government to do in Iraq and the world,"

In July 2006 Sheehan invited further controversy by meeting again with Venezuelan president Chavez and suggesting that he was a better leader than President Bush. She also purchased five acres of land in Crawford, with some of the insurance money she received after her son was killed. She announced that she would return to Crawford in August, when President Bush went on vacation, and that this time she would go on a hunger strike until the U.S. troops returned home. Soon after that announcement, on July 6, 2006, Sheehan appeared on MSNBC's program Hardball, whose guest host, Norah O'Donnell, expressed her suspicion that Sheehan's planned hunger strike was "just more of a publicity stunt" and questioned whether her politics truly reflected the beliefs of the American people or were in fact "extremist." O'Donnell also referred to Sheehan's connection with the "socialist dictator Hugo Chavez." The MSNBC interview brought Sheehan a great deal of hate mail. She responded with an article published on the Web site TruthOut.org (July 18, 2006), in which she defended herself against charges of anti-Americanism while repeating her assertion that Chavez is a better leader than Bush. Pointing out that Chavez is a democratically elected president, having carried 60 percent of his country's vote in 2004, and referring to Bush's actions as a presidential candidate and president, Sheehan wrote: "From stealing two elections and saying and acting like you [Bush] have a mandate to destroy the world; to circumventing Congress at every turn with 'signing statements' and just not telling them things; to wiretapping Americans without proper warrants; to reading our emails and looking at bank records without warrants; to illegally detaining people and torturing them; to insisting on staying a course in Iraq that is killing nearly more innocent people per month than were killed in our country on 9/11; to authorizing the

leak of covert agents' names; to selling our democracy to the highest bidders, such as [federal lobbyist] Jack Abramoff; to appointing avowed [United Nations] hater John Bolton to the UN in a recess appointment because he [Bush] knew that a normal confirmation process would fail; to allowing the neo-cons to take over our foreign policy to the detriment of our nation; to etc., etc. I ask Norah O'Donnell and MSNBC, who is the dictator here? George or Hugo?" She added, "I didn't say that I would rather live in Venezuela. I am an American, and I love my country which I believe is on a distinctly disordered course right now."

In 2006 Melanie Morgan and Catherine Moy published the book *American Mourning: The Intimate Story of Two Families Joined by War, Torn by Beliefs*. That controversial work, which chronicles both Sheehan's story and that of the family of another soldier who was killed in Iraq, attacked Sheehan on a personal level, describing her as a philanderer and as having ties to the Ku Klux Klan in addition to Chavez. Alan Colmes of the television program *Hannity & Colmes* described the book as "disgusting" and the authors' attack on Sheehan as "despicable." In September of that year, Sheehan published her memoir, *Peace Mom: A Mother's Journey through Heartache to Activism*. The book polarized opinions, as had most of her public activity. *Peace Mom* recounts Sheehan's experience of losing a son, her struggle to recover from the loss, and her transformation into an antiwar activist. Included in the book is criticism not only of President Bush but of John Kerry, John McCain, and Democratic U.S. senator Hillary Rodham Clinton of New York, among others. In the book's foreword, Sheehan described writing the memoir as one of the hardest things she had ever done, as it forced her to relive Casey's death daily; she also found, however, that the process was cathartic in the end. The foreword includes this passage: "This book is a story of one mom's journey from being a 'normal' mom to one who went to the seat of power and challenged the king and triumphed and who meets and is lauded by heads of state and also vilified and hated by other heads of state and much of the American media. This book is a story of one mom's journey from believing that her son was a 'war hero' to believing that her son died as a victim of the war machine. This is a book of one mom's journey from ignorance of history (even though, ironically, she majored in history) to being an active participant in making history and having an effect on social change. This is a book of one mom's journey from trusting her leaders even when they so brazenly take our country to bogus war, to one of pacifism and nonviolence at all costs."

In December 2006 Sheehan participated in a forum on impeachment at Fordham University with Carolyn Ho, the mother of Ehren Watada, a commissioned army officer who refused to go to Iraq. The next month she traveled to Cuba, where she called for the closing of the U.S. military prison in Guantanamo Bay. On May 4, 2007 Sheehan spoke at Kent State University, at an event commemorating the anniversary of the shootings in 1970 of four Kent State students by members of the Ohio National Guard during a Vietnam War protest on the school's campus.

That month Sheehan announced that she was abandoning the antiwar movement, because she had become disillusioned with the stubborn resistance to change that, in her view, characterizes the American system of government. In July 2007, however, she again spoke out publicly, after President Bush commuted the prison sentence of Lewis "Scooter" Libby, a former aide to Vice President Richard B. "Dick" Cheney. Libby had been convicted of lying and obstructing justice in an investigation into the leak of a CIA officer's identity. Sheehan also stated publicly that if, by July 23, 2007, Congress did not take action toward impeaching President Bush, she would run as an Independent for the seat in the House held by Nancy Pelosi, the House Speaker, who represents California's Eighth Congressional District. Sheehan told a reporter for the *Associated Press* (July 8, 2007), "Democrats and Americans feel betrayed by the Democratic leadership. We hired them to bring an end to the war." On August 9, 2007, in light of Congress's inaction regarding the president's impeachment, Sheehan announced her candidacy for Pelosi's seat, offering a platform that focused on universal health care, affordable college tuition, and higher ethical standards in government. Although she had no campaign funds, she insisted that she would not accept contributions from corporations. On September 10, 2007 Sheehan, along with nine others, was arrested for shouting outside a Senate hearing room in which General David H. Petraeus, the commander of the multinational force in Iraq, and Ryan C. Crocker, the U.S. ambassador to Iraq, were to testify about the war.

## FURTHER READING
*Not One More Mother's Child; Dear President Bush; Peace Mom: A Mother's Journey through Heartache to Activism*

# EUNICE KENNEDY SHRIVER
## Social Activist; Social Worker; Organization Official

**Born:** July 21, 1921; Brookline, Massachusetts
**Died:** August 11, 2009; Hyannis, Massachusetts
**Primary Field:** Human Rights / Children's Rights
**Affiliation:** Democratic Party

## INTRODUCTION

*Since the mid-1950s, when she became the executive vice-president of the Joseph P. Kennedy Jr. Foundation, Eunice Kennedy Shriver has been a leader in the worldwide struggle to improve the lives of people with intellectual disabilities. Through her fierce determination and unrelenting efforts in their behalf, Shriver sparked nothing less than a revolution in research on the causes of mental disability, the care of the mentally disabled, and the acceptance of the mentally disabled by the community, an accomplishment for which she was honored with the prestigious Albert Lasker Public Service Award, in 1966, and the Presidential Medal of Freedom, in 1984, the nation's highest civilian award. During the administration of President John F. Kennedy, Shriver played a key role in gaining the involvement of the federal government in that revolution. In 1968 she founded Special Olympics, which, with more than 1 million athletes and half a million coaches and other volunteers participating, has become the largest year-round program of sports training and competition in the world for mentally retarded (sic) children and adults. An international endeavor that has been labeled "a precursor of the larger disability rights movement," Special Olympics has demonstrated the humanity and long-unsuspected abilities of mentally disabled people and thereby has helped to remove barriers that separated them from their neighbors and society as a whole. In an address that she made at the fifth International Summer Special Olympics Games, in 1979, Shriver told the athletes, "What you are winning by your courageous efforts is far greater than any game. You are winning life itself, and in doing so you give to others a most precious prize, faith in the unlimited possibilities of the human spirit." A sister of President Kennedy (whom she always called Jack); Senator Edward M. "Ted" Kennedy of Massachusetts; Robert F. Kennedy, a United States attorney general and senator who was assassinated in 1968; and Rosemary Kennedy, who is mentally disabled.*

*Eunice Kennedy Shriver.*

*Shriver began her career in public service in the mid-1940s, when she worked with female prisoners, juvenile delinquents, runaways, and abandoned children. She was honorary chairman of Special Olympics International, and also the president of Community of Caring, a program that she founded in 1981 to reduce the incidence of mental disability among the babies of teenage mothers and that has since been expanded to address such problems as substance abuse by teenagers.*

## EARLY LIFE

The fifth of the nine children of Joseph P. Kennedy Sr., a multimillionaire financier, and Rose (Fitzgerald) Kennedy, Eunice Kennedy Shriver was born Eunice Mary Kennedy on July 10, 1921 in Brookline, Massachusetts, a suburb of Boston. Shriver's grandfathers, both sons of Irish immigrants, were the prominent Massachusetts Democrats Patrick J. Kennedy, who served in both houses of the state legislature, and John F. "Honey Fitz" Fitzgerald, a mayor of Boston. Her father served as the chairman of the Securities and Exchange Commission

(1934-35) and as the director of the Maritime Commission (1937) during the presidency of Franklin D. Roosevelt. In addition to John, Robert, Edward, and Rosemary, Shriver's siblings are Patricia Kennedy Lawford; Jean Kennedy Smith, the United States ambassador to Ireland; Joseph Kennedy Jr., a navy pilot who was killed in World War II; and Kathleen Kennedy Cavendish, who died in a plane crash in 1948. Many observers have characterized relations among the Kennedy siblings as very close and marked by steadfast loyalty.

Shriver's mother, a devout Roman Catholic, tried to instill in her children a sense of religious obligation. That feeling became so highly developed in young Eunice that people predicted she would become a nun. In an interview with Nora Ephron for the *New York Post* (November 19, 1966), her brother Robert said that his sister "was always very compassionate and very interested in the unfortunate." "Eunice really loves the outcast," R. Sargent Shriver Jr., her husband, told Kristin McMurran for *People* (August 27, 1979). "In any room she'll seek out the loneliest person. She really loves the people who have the least." Since childhood Shriver has also been unusually active physically (hyperkinetic, according to some reporters), athletic, and competitive. Joseph Kennedy Sr. encouraged a spirit of competitiveness in his sons and daughters. "We don't want any losers around here," he has been quoted as telling them. "In this family we want winners. Don't come in second or third, that doesn't count. Win."

The Kennedys moved from Brookline to an exclusive section of the New York City borough of the Bronx in 1926 and to the nearby suburban town of Bronxville several years later and they vacationed in Palm Beach, Florida and Hyannis Port, Massachusetts. Shriver received her primary and secondary school education at Roman Catholic convent schools. During her father's tenure as United States ambassador to Great Britain (1938-41), she lived in England and, according to the *Guardian* (October 6, 1972), graduated from a British boarding school. She attended Manhattanville College, in Purchase, New York, until illness forced her to drop out. After recuperating, she transferred to Stanford University, in California, where she earned a B.S. degree in sociology in 1943. She later took classes at the University of Chicago's School of Social Work.

According to one source, after her college graduation Shriver worked briefly with residents of Harlem, in New York City, before moving to Washington, D.C., where she began sharing a townhouse with her

brother John. As an employee in the Special War Problems Division of the United States Department of State, from 1943 to 1945, she helped to reorient to civilian life Americans who had been prisoners of war. In 1946 John Kennedy announced his bid for a seat in the House of Representatives, and Shriver joined his campaign, canvassing what *Time* (August 21,1972) characterized as "dingy walkups" in the Boston wards. She stumped with equal enthusiasm during his later successful campaigns, for the United States Senate, in 1952, and the presidency, in 1960; in races that Robert and Ted Kennedy made for elective office; and during the 1972 presidential contest, in which her husband ran for vice-president on the unsuccessful Democratic ticket headed by Senator George S. McGovern of South Dakota. Most recently, in 1994, Shriver solicited votes door-to-door during her son Mark's successful run for a seat in the Maryland House of Delegates. "She loves to go into people's kitchens and talk to them about their children," her son Robert told Kristin McMurran.

From 1947 to 1948 Shriver worked for a salary of one dollar a year at the Department of Justice as executive secretary for the National Conference on Prevention and Control of Juvenile Delinquency. At age 21 she had reportedly gained control of a $1 million trust fund. In 1950 she served as a social worker at the Federal Penitentiary for Women, in Alderson, West Virginia. After moving to Chicago, in 1951, she did social work at a youth shelter and at the city's juvenile court. She left those jobs shortly before the birth of her first child, in early 1954.

## LIFE'S WORK

In 1956 Eunice Kennedy Shriver became the executive vice-president of the Joseph P. Kennedy Jr. Foundation, which her father had established in 1946. In its first decade the foundation had served largely as a source of operating funds for Catholic organizations and institutions for the mentally disabled. Among them was the St. Coletta School, in Wisconsin, where Rosemary Kennedy has lived for half a century. Mildly mentally disabled when she was born in 1918, Rosemary Kennedy grew up at home, where, more than anyone else, it was her sister Eunice who always made a special effort to include her in family activities. "Eunice was the one who ensured that Rosemary would have her fair share of successes," Ted Kennedy told Victoria Dawson, as quoted in the *Los Angeles Times* (November 20, 1987). In her early 20s Rosemary became, in

Shriver's words, "increasingly irritable and difficult," and her memory, powers of concentration, and judgment began to decline. In 1941, without the knowledge of other family members, their father arranged to have Rosemary undergo a prefrontal lobotomy, a controversial procedure in which brain tissue was destroyed in an attempt to induce permanent calmness. In his book *The Kennedy Women* (1994) and in the *Washingtonian* (August 1993) Laurence Learner reported that such radical surgery, a treatment of last resort for severely mentally ill people, had probably never before been performed on a person with mental disability. Rosemary emerged from the operation much more seriously disabled than before. Reflecting on her sister's move to St. Coletta's, Shriver wrote in the *Saturday Evening Post* (September 22, 1962), "It fills me with sadness to think this change might not have been necessary if we knew then what we know today."

With Shriver at the helm, the Joseph P. Kennedy Jr. Foundation changed its main objectives to the prevention of mental disability and the adoption by society of more humane, just, and beneficial ways of dealing with the mentally disabled. With the goal of distributing funds "in areas where a multiplier effect is possible," it has awarded millions of dollars in grants for research into the causes of mental and intellectual disability and has awarded scholarships to students of bioethics at the Kennedy Institute of Ethics at Georgetown University. Shriver was the driving force behind the creation of that institute and a similar one founded at Harvard University in 1971.

Strengthened by the authority that her foundation title carried, soon after John Kennedy's inauguration as president, in 1961, Shriver began to push him to take action on behalf of the mentally disabled. Within months he set up the 'President Kennedy Committee on Mental Retardation' (sic), for which she served as a consultant. Its recommendations led to the establishment, in 1962, of the National Institute for Child Health and Human Development, which has supported thousands of basic research, clinical, and large scale population studies in normal and abnormal growth and development. The recommendations also resulted in the passage of bills, signed into law by President Kennedy one month before his assassination, in 1963, that aimed at addressing mental disabilities. The legislation allocated funds for maternal and child health services, construction of research and university-affiliated clinical centers, teacher

training, and projects to increase public awareness of mental disability programs.

The public's understanding of the plight of the mentally disabled increased exponentially with the publication of Shriver's landmark article in the *Saturday Evening Post*. After revealing that her sister Rosemary was mentally disabled, Shriver reported that about 3 percent of Americans were similarly disabled. "Like diabetes, deafness, polio, or any other misfortune, mental retardation (sic) can happen in any family," she wrote. Addressing widespread prejudices, she explained that mental disability is not the same as mental illness, and that there is no foundation for the beliefs that the mentally disabled are "belligerent" or "unmanageable" and may "go berserk" at any moment. She compared the dreadful conditions in some of the state institutions she had visited, places "where several thousand adults and children were housed in bleak, overcrowded wards of 100 or more" and received minimal attention, to the environments of well run facilities, where children and adults led happy, productive lives. "The truth is that 75 to 85 percent of the retarded (sic) are capable of becoming useful citizens with the help of special education and rehabilitation," she wrote. "Another 10 to 20 percent can learn to make small contributions, not involving book learning, such as mowing a lawn or washing dishes."

Shriver went on to describe the day camp that she had set up at Timberlawn, the 20-acre Maryland farm that she and her husband rented year round. In the camp's first season, in 1962, three dozen mentally disabled youngsters had blossomed under the care of volunteer counselors, and Shriver herself, who, as Patricia Smith wrote in the *New York World Journal Tribune* (November 16, 1966), pitched in to help "with verve, patience, and affection." Many campers (in later summers their numbers grew to 100) showed that they were far more capable in sports and other activities than even many experts realized. Their achievements, and those of the girls in the gym class that Shriver taught weekly at a school for the mentally disabled, her memories of Rosemary Kennedy's prowess at swimming, and the Fitness Awards program that had been launched by President Kennedy inspired two other path-breaking Shriver initiatives. One was the Kennedy Foundation's establishment, in 1963, of fitness standards and tests for the mentally and intellectually disabled and its support of ongoing research to refine them. The other was the foundation's creation, in 1968, of Special Olympics.

A two-day event held in July of that year in Chicago's Soldier Field, the first International Special Olympics Games attracted 1,000 mentally disabled athletes from 26 states and Canada, who competed in track and field events, floor hockey, and aquatics. "The world will never be the same," Richard J. Daley, then Chicago's mayor, said to Shriver as they watched two of the athletes carrying an Olympic torch into the stadium at the opening ceremonies. "He was right!" Shriver told Dick Died for the *Journal of Rehabilitation* (April-June 1983). "Because the world saw, for the first time, what its most neglected, least appreciated, most scorned and hidden citizens could accomplish." In 1975, at the five-day fourth International Special Olympics Games, 3,200 athletes from 10 countries took part. The first International Winter Games, which offered contests for 500 skiers or ice-skaters, were held in 1977. In 1993 the World Winter Games were held outside North America for the first time, when 1,600 athletes from more than 50 countries competed in five sports in Austria. During the nine- day ninth Special Olympics World Games, in 1995, more than 7,000 athletes, including people in wheelchairs, from 143 countries competed in 21 sports. As in previous Games, some of the world's top athletes provided instruction at sports clinics, which were open to the public as well as to the athletes free of charge. Consummately skilled in public relations and well known in high society, through the years Shriver has had great success in securing the help of leading entertainers as well as sports celebrities and financial support from major corporations.

The more than 1 million athletes, ages eight and over, who are currently in the Special Olympics program work year-round with a total of 140,000 specially trained coaches. Close to 400,000 additional volunteers, affiliated with about 25,000 community Special Olympics programs, assist as organizers, Games officials, drivers, or in other capacities. "Faith is not enough to win the battle," Shriver pointed out to Dick Died. "The spirit of Special Olympics, skill, sharing, and joy, must be based on the substance of Special Olympics training, practice, and participation." More than 15,000 Special Olympics meets and tournaments in winter and summer sports are held worldwide each year, and in a selection process that resembles that of the regular Olympics, athletes may advance from chapter to national games and then to the World Games.

"From the very beginning of Special Olympics, we have followed one guiding star, the conviction that most mentally retarded (sic) individuals, with proper coaching and training, can exceed the limits that we set for them at any given time or place," Shriver told Dick Died. "Over and over again, we have proved that principle. We proved that retarded athletes (sic) could run a 300 yard race. Then a 400 meter race. Then a mile. And now even the marathon. We proved that mentally retarded (sic) athletes could play team sports. First, volleyball, then floor hockey, then basketball, and even soccer." In the *New York Times* (July 8,1995), William C. Rhoden observed, "The search for meaning through commercialized athletics has been increasingly difficult. Yet, virtues in sports remain: The joy of competition, an appreciation for bucking the odds. The hunger for winning, an appreciation for sometimes falling short. An unbroken dedication for being prepared. With Special Olympians, all of this comes with no promise of scholarships or lucrative contracts, just the prospect of thriving beyond obstacles. They give a fresher, deeper meaning to the idea of being all that you can be."

As Shriver has pointed out in the hundreds of speeches she has given throughout the world in the last quarter century about the program and issues concerning the mentally disabled, participation in Special Olympics leads not only to improved physical fitness and motor skills but also to great gains in the athletes' self confidence and in their formation of a much more positive self image. By ending the isolation that so often limits the lives not only of the retarded but also of their families, the program helps mentally disabled people grow intellectually and socially and enables them and their families to fit into their communities. At the same time, family members and people in the community gain a greater appreciation for all the abilities of the individuals affected, not only those related to sports. "Without Special Olympics my daughter wouldn't have known she was a person, and neither would we," one mother told Shriver. "It's the families that come here and expand the program," Shriver explained to an *Associated Press* reporter, as quoted in the *Norwich (Connecticut) Bulletin* (July 6, 1993). "They go home and they're the ones that keep demanding more training, more education, more rights to jobs. That's the important thing to remember."

When, in 1966, a reporter asked her what had attracted her to social work, Shriver said, "I think that really the only way you change people's attitudes or behavior is to work with them. Not write papers or serve on committees. Who's going to work with the child to change him, with the juvenile delinquent and the retarded (sic)? Who's going to teach him to swim? To catch a ball? You have to work with the person. It's quite simple, actually." "When the full judgment of the Kennedy legacy is made, including JFK's Peace Corps and Alliance for Progress, Robert Kennedy's passion for civil rights, and Ted Kennedy's efforts on health care, workplace reform, and refugees, the changes wrought by Eunice Shriver may well be seen as the most consequential," Harrison Rainie wrote in *US News & World Report* (November 15,1993). "With a lot of help from her very powerful brother Jack and inspiration from her powerless sister Rosemary, Eunice Shriver helped move the nation for good and for all."

In 1981 Eunice Kennedy Shriver founded Community of Caring, with the goal of preventing teenage pregnancy and thus reducing the incidence of mental disability. Teenage mothers give birth to a higher percentage of mentally disabled babies than do older mothers. A school-based program that involves teacher training, discussions about values, student forums, parent involvement, and community service, Community of Caring is now designed to address other self-destructive behaviors as well, among them drug and alcohol abuse and dropping out of school. The program, which focuses on the values of caring, respect, trust, responsibility, and family, has been adopted by some 200 elementary, middle, and high schools in 20 states and the District of Columbia, and it has been endorsed by the National Association of Secondary School Principals, the nation's largest principals' organization. Shriver, who is the president of Community of Caring, edited its publications *A Community of Caring* (1982, 1985) and *Growing Up Caring* (1990).

According to Victoria Dawson, Eunice Kennedy Shriver "operates with a kind of high-octane fervor." "Even when she sits, she's always moving," Dawson wrote. Shriver has been described as intellectual, witty, hard-driving, steel-willed, elusive, abrupt, irreverent yet spiritual, and both sensitive and insensitive. "People say the most contradictory things" about her, Dawson reported. "But on one thing they agree: she knows what she wants, and she is relentless in the pursuit of it." According to her son Timothy, Shriver is "always committed to the possible." "She has a way of making people exceed their reach," her brother Ted has said. In *Newsday* (April 22, 1963), Helen Thomas wrote that she bore a remarkable resemblance to President Kennedy, with "the same lankiness, the same mannerisms, the same

Boston twang and quickness of speech, and the same intensity when she gets wound up in her cause." "She has a great sense of priorities in her life," her friend Donald Dell, a sports attorney, told Victoria Dawson. "Whereas most people worry about 'What should I do with my life next year?' For Eunice all that stuff is stuff. With her, it's family, religion, and causes."

## PERSONAL LIFE

Eunice Kennedy Shriver was been married May 23,1953 to R. Sargent Shriver, who served as the president of Special Olympics International from 1986 until 1990, when he was named chairman of its board. He is a former director of the Office of Economic Opportunity and of the Peace Corps and a former United States ambassador to France. The Shrivers' children are the broadcast journalist Maria Shriver Schwarzenegger; Robert, a lawyer, who is chief of Special Olympics Productions; Timothy, a teacher; Mark, a social worker and Maryland legislator; and Anthony, an organizer for Best Buddies, a program for the mentally handicapped. Eunice Kennedy Shriver's many honors include the National Volunteer Service Award, the AAMD Humanitarian Award, the AFL-CIO's Phillip Murray-William Green Award (which she received jointly with her husband), the Legion of Honor, the Common Wealth Award for public service, the Order of the Smile of Polish Children, the Prix de la Couronne Frangaise, and nine honorary degrees. When, in 1995, the United States Mint issued a commemorative coin bearing a portrait of her, as founder of Special Olympics, she became the first living woman to be depicted on an American coin.

It is believed that Shriver suffered from Addison's disease and she broke her hip and had a stroke in the years 2005-2007 and was admitted to hospital. In August 2009 she was again admitted to Cape Cod Hospital in Hyannis and she passed away at the hospital on August 11, 2009. An invitation-only Requiem Mass was held at St. Francis Xavier Roman Catholic Church in Hyannis and she was buried at nearby St. Francis Xavier parish cemetery. Pope Benedict XVI sent his condolences. With the passing of Shriver and her brother Ted Kennedy two weeks later, their sister Jean Smith remains the only living child of Joseph and Rose Kennedy.

## FURTHER READING

*A Community of Caring; Growing Up Caring*

# ELEANOR (MARIE) CUTRI SMEAL

## Social Activist; Writer; Lecturer

**Born:** July 30, 1939; Ashtabula, Ohio
**Primary Field:** Gender Equality
**Affiliations:** President of the Board of the Feminine Majority (Founder) and the Feminine Majority Foundation; President of National Organization for Women

### INTRODUCTION

*Now the President of the Boards of the Feminine Major-ity and the Feminine Majority Foundation, in Arlington, Va., Eleanor Cutri Smeal entered the national spotlight when, in 1977, the homemaker from Pittsburgh, Pa., was elected to succeed Karen DeCrow, a Syracuse law-yer, as President of the National Organization for Wom-en (N.O.W.). Smeal was expected to enlarge the appeal of a group that some had criticized for elitism, because of its leadership by professional women, since its found-ing in 1966. Upon her re-election in 1979, Eleanor Smeal was able to state that, within two years, NOW had doubled in size. With a membership now exceeding 500,000, N.O.W. is the world's largest feminist organi-zation and was the most militant of the various groups within the Women's Movement in the fight for ratifica-tion of the Equal Rights Amendment in the United States (which was three states short of passing). Under Elea-nor Smeal's guidance, N.O.W. doubled its membership and addressed itself to family problems and expansion of its political and economic goals. She won a third term in 1985. After her tenure as President of N.O.W. ended, she became the primary founder of Feminine Majority.*

### EARLY LIFE

Born in Ashtabula, Ohio, on July 30, 1939, Eleanor Ma-rie Cutri Smeal is the fourth child and the first daughter of a Roman Catholic family. Her father, Peter Anthony Cutri, had moved to the United States from Calabria, Italy, and worked as an agent for the Metropolitan In-surance Company, briefly in Ohio, and then in Erie, Pa., where his children were brought up. Her mother, the former Josephine E. Agresti, came from an Italian immigrant family. "Everyone asks me why I'm so good at debating and public speak" Eleanor Smeal told Greg Walter during an interview for *People* (August 8, 1977). "I started at four or five, like in any good Italian family."

In another interview, with Susan Dworkin for Ms. (Feb-ruary 1978), Eleanor Smeal described father as a politi-cally concerned man, a Democrat, and a champion of the underdog. "Everything he knew, he had learned the hard way," she said. "He wasn't naive, he was a realist, and he believed in the American dream." Having herself experienced the restrictions of a Victorian upbringing, Mrs. Cutri insisted that her daughter was going to have the advantage of a solid education and "was going to do anything she could do." Although raised as Roman Catholics, the Cutri children attended public schools in Erie because their mother wanted them to know people of varied backgrounds.

A notably diligent student, Eleanor Cutri achieved excellent scholastic records both in high school and at Duke University, in Durham, N.C. While in college, where she served as President of her dormitory, she lost favor among some of her follow students by arguing and voting in the affirmative on the issue of racial integra-tion for Duke. After graduating, in 1961, with a Phi Beta Kappa key and a B.A. degree, she considered the pos-sibility of studying law. When, however, she was told that women lawyers seldom practiced in courtrooms, she settled for courses in Political Science and Public Administration at the University of Florida, earning her M.A. degree in 1963.

At the University of Florida, Eleanor Cutri met Charles R. Smeal, a student in metallurgical engineer-ing, whom she married on April 27, 1963. She intended to continue her graduate study, but illness forced her to stop work on her doctoral thesis, an investigation into the attitudes of women toward woman political candi-dates. Somewhat later in the early years of her marriage, she wanted to complete requirements for her Ph.D. degree, but found that there was no child-care center for her young son, Tod. In 1969, after the family had moved to the Pittsburgh area, where her husband was employed as a metallurgical researcher with the West-inghouse Corporation, a back ailment forced a year of complete bed rest on Mrs. Smeal. Day-care services the children—Tod, then four years old, and a daughter, Lori, ten months old—were unavailable.

### LIFE'S WORK

During that ordeal of constrained leisure, as she became increasingly aware of the need of disability insurance for wives and mothers, Ms. Smeal read everything her husband could bring home about the suffragists and the developing Women's Movement. Both she and her husband, who had taken on much of the responsibility of child care and housekeeping, came through that period as confirmed, radical feminists.

When Ms. Smeal, along with her husband, joined the National Organization for Women, in 1970, she was midway in a four-year term as a member of the Board of the Upper St. Clair (Pennsylvania) chapter of the League of Women Voters. Her civic activity also concerned the Allegheny County Council, of which she was to serve as secretary-treasurer, in 1971 to 1972. Of her readiness to become steadily more deeply involved in N.O.W, she once said, as quoted in the *Christian Science Monitor* (September 4, 1979), "I made up my mind that the fight for the equality of women was the most important historical thing I could participate in and would always be important to me."

Eleanor Smeal made her initial contribution to the Women's Movement as convener and first President, from 1971 to 1973, of a N.O.W. chapter in South Hills, a Pittsburgh suburb. With day care as one of their priorities, the Smeals organized a nursery school in that community. Elected president of Pennsylvania N.O.W., in 1972, to serve through 1975, Ms. Smeal made educational injustice a target, leading the fight for equal opportunity for girls in physical education and sports programs in the Pennsylvania schools. N.O.W. won a guarantee by basing its arguments on Pennsylvania's constitutional prohibition against sex discrimination, a state E.R.A., rather than on the Federal Title IX of the 1972 Education Amendments, which denies federal funds to school districts and colleges that practice discrimination. Discussing that early victory, Eleanor Smeal explained to Christine Terp of the *Christian Science Monitor* (September 4, 1979), "The current laws are simply not enough. Essentially, this country has hedged its bets on sex discrimination. They say it's against the law, but. . . . We want all the buts taken out. That's essentially what it's [the Federal E.R.A. is] all about."

In 1973, Eleanor Smeal was elected to the National Board of Directors of N.O.W., and, in 1975 she became its Chairperson. That same year she was seated on the Board of Directors of N.O.W.'s legal defense and education fund, which supports, among other programs, the monitoring of equal educational rights enforcement by the government under Title IX. Because she believed that N.O.W. had to be decentralized from the large cities

where most of the organization's chapters were located in the early 1970s, Eleanor Smeal had previously become head of a new chapters committee. Susan Dworkin quoted her in *Ms*: "I went to every village and town, organizing; if you have just one or two people you can get a chapter going. I organized housewives. Because that's where I was."

During a period of internal dissension for N.O.W., Eleanor Smeal fought for the concept of many local units rather than a few larger centralized chapters, arguing that the struggle for equality is a concern of every community and that grass-roots organization would strengthen the alliance of women. It was a voting delegation sent by local chapters that elected Eleanor Smeal President of N.O.W., on April 23, 1977, at the seventh national conference, in Detroit. For the first time in N.O.W.'s history, the post of President carried a salary —$17,500. The decision to pay a salary to the top elected officers was another victory for Ms. Smeal, who wanted the leadership of N.O.W. to be accessible to women from all walks of life, not only those with independent incomes or those well supported by their husbands. She took over an organization of about 55,000 members that, in July 1976, had had a deficit of $120,000. By the end of her first year, N.O.W. was running in the black.

Seeing her election as a symbol of house support for Women's Rights, Eleanor Smeal repeatedly asserted that the economic security of homemakers is vital and that passage of the Equal Rights Amendment is a most important step toward that goal. Ratification of the E.R.A. became N.O.W.'s priority. At her election in 1977, she was designated chief of a national strike force charged with developing a strategy to fight for ratification of the amendment.

As a first move in the E.R.A. campaign, N.O.W. urged organizations planning conventions to boycott the then 15 states that had not ratified the amendment. The idea for the boycott had originated with the California chapters of N.O.W. and the League of Women Voters, which advocated a boycott of Nevada when that state's legislature was considering the E.R.A. in February 1977. Suits brought by Nevada and Missouri charged N.O.W. with violation of the antitrust laws, but, on February 21, 1979, United States District Judge Elmo Hunter, in Kansas City, Mo., upheld N.O.W.'s right to engage in its boycott as a legitimate political action. According to N.O.W. estimates, Kansas City and St. Louis together lost more than $19,000,000 in convention business because of the boycott, and, by mid-1979, more than 350 organizations, ranging from academic societies to labor unions and even local governments, were participating in it. As reported in *U.S. News and World Report* (March 20, 1978), "There's no question that the boycott is being felt."

The E.R.A. became probably the key issue of the three-day National Women's Conference, held in Houston, beginning on November 18, 1977. Eleanor Smeal was one of its leaders, having been appointed by President Jimmy Carter to serve on the National Commission on the Observance of International Women's Year, which organized the meeting. At the conference, for which the United States Congress provided $5,000,000, some 2,000 delegates and more than 12,000 observers, the largest political gathering of American women ever held, met in the Houston Coliseum and considered, among other matters, "barriers that prevent women from participating fully and equally in all aspects of national life." Over 1,400 of the delegates had been chosen at fifty- six state and territorial meetings. They were ethnically as diverse as America and represented a wide variety of views.

In another part of Houston, meanwhile, "pro-family" leader Phyllis Schlafly and a coalition of right-wing groups drew a large crowd to a counter-conference. Gail Sheehy described in *Redbook* (April 1978) a tension-laden confrontation between Eleanor Smeal and the "formidable, duchesslike" Phyllis Schlafly on the *MacNeil/Lehrer Report* news analysis television show. Mrs. Schlafly had earlier declared that the National Women's Conference would sound "the death knell of the Women's Movement" and that its delegate selection had been rigged to favor the "women's lib" factions. A national Roper survey, unveiled on the show, demonstrated that 20 percent of the people polled identified themselves with the anti-E.R.A. movement. Eleanor Smeal quickly pointed out that Roper's figure was the same as the percent of anti-E.R.A. delegates elected to the Houston conference. In a *Meet the Press* interview telecast from Houston, on November 20, 1977, she spoke with confidence about the positive results of the National Women's Conference: "The people who are here represent large constituencies. I think they are going away from here committed to improving the status of women in the United States."

With the E.R.A. still bogged down three states short of the 38 needed for passage, and, with some opposing state legislators apparently stalling a showdown vote beyond the March 22, 1979, ratification deadline, Eleanor Smeal announced on February 10, 1978, an all-out effort to gain Congressional extension of the original seven-year time limit for ratification. Insisting that "there can be no time limits on equality," she planned a grass-roots campaign to pressure Congress, led a march of nearly 100,000 people down Washington's Pennsylvania Avenue, and testified before Congress on behalf of the extension resolution introduced by Representative Elizabeth Holtzman and 20 co-sponsors. Upon the Senate's passage of the measure on October 6, 1978, an extension of the E.R.A. ratification deadline until July 30, 1982, took effect. Although his approval was not required, President Carter signed the measure on October 20.

Some of the other N.O.W. goals on which Eleanor Smeal had expended her considerable energy involved issues that, in the past, have proved to be divisive ones for the organization, such as rights of homosexuals and reproductive freedom, including abortion as one of the options for women in birth control. On behalf of women she has testified before Congressional committees on discriminatory health care, the Susan B. Anthony dollar, job preferences for veterans, and other questions. She served on the Board of Directors of the Full Employment Action Council in 1977 to 1978, considered employment discrimination of primary concern for women, and repeatedly underscored the economic significance of the E.R.A.

Economic themes claimed increased attention at N.O.W.'s 12th national conference, in Los Angeles, where many delegates wore 59-cent buttons to show their awareness that women then earned 59 cents to every dollar that men earned. During the three-day conference, which opened on October 5, 1979, Eleanor Smeal was re-elected to a two-year term as President of an organization that then had more than 100,000 members and a 1980 budget of $3,500,000. She became, moreover, the $39,000-a-year executive of a group that some feminists saw as having grown too structured, with a membership too largely made up of White, middle-class women. The plan of action, however, on which Eleanor Smeal and other national officers based their administration, included the goal of "dramatic increase in minority participation and action in N.O.W. at all levels."

The platform of Eleanor Smeal's executive team also called for the "establishment of N.O.W . . . . as a major political force in the nation." In early December 1979, members of N.O.W.'s political action committee voted to oppose the nomination and re-election of President Carter, primarily because of what they reasoned was his failure to use the power of his office for the ratification of the E.R.A. In the wake of that resolution, later, in December, the White House rescinded its invitation to Eleanor Smeal to take part in a discussion on the E.R.A. between Carter and representatives of national women's groups, a meeting that she herself had originally requested.

President Carter had earlier recognized the authority of N.O.W.'s President by appointing Eleanor Smeal to the National Advisory Committee for Women, in 1978 (the successor to the National Commission on the Observance of International Women's Year), and to the National Advisory Committee to the White House Conference on Families, in July 1979. She was listed as one of the 25 most influential women in the United States by the 1978 World Almanac, and, as one of the 13 women among the persons chosen for "50 Faces for Americas Future" by *Time* in its cover story of August 6, 1979.

"The sense of boldness that remains the prime prerequisite for leadership in any era," is the characteristic that all persons on Times list shared. If boldness is one of the qualities of Eleanor Smeal's leadership, another is her intense dedication. Gail Sheehy quoted the explanation of one of her associates in the organization: "When you see Ellie working twenty hours a day, you can't bear the idea of letting her down." Most of her friends and members of her family call her "Ellie," and she often signs her name "Ellie Smeal" on letters to N.O.W. members. Congresswoman Barbara Mikulski once introduced her as "the sister of us all."

Despite the hard work of Smeal and N.O.W. to ratify the E.R.A., the amendment was never ratified. (It fell short of the three states needed.) The proposed amendment is as follows: "Equality of rights under the law shall not be denied or abridged by the United States or by any State on account of sex."

According to the West's Encyclopedia of American Law, there were many opponents of the amendment despite polls showing that a majority of people in the U.S were in favor of it. Opponents of the amendment held that certain inequalities between men and women are the result of biology and that some legislation and state policies must necessarily take this fact into account. Some also contended that the ERA would undermine the social institutions of marriage and family. Still others argued that women had adequate protection under existing laws, such as the Civil Rights Acts of 1964 and 1968, Title IX, and the U.S. Supreme Court decision, *Frontiero v. Richardson*, 411 U.S. 677, 93 S. Ct. 1764, 36 L. Ed. 2d 583 (1973), which struck down a federal law that gave preferential treatment to married males over married females in securing salary supplements while in the armed services.

Supporters of the E.R.A. reintroduced the amendment in Congress yet again on July 14, 1982. The House of Representatives voted down the proposal on November 15, 1983.

Smeal, after her last term in office as President of N.O.W., was barred from running again. In 1987, she was one of the founders of the Feminine Majority and the Feminine Majority Foundation, and continues to serve as President of both of the Boards of Directors of the organizations. According to the biography on the website: "Smeal has been at the forefront of almost every major Women's Rights victory – from the integration of Little League, newspaper help-wanted ads, and police departments to the passage of landmark legislation, such as the Pregnancy Discrimination Act, Equal Credit Act, Civil Rights Restoration Act, Violence Against Women Act, Freedom of Access to Clinic Entrances Act, and Civil Rights Act of 1991. She has pushed to make Social Security and pensions more equitable for women, and to realign federal priorities by developing a feminist budget. She has campaigned to close the wage gap and to achieve pay equity for women. Expanding feminist activism to a global level, Smeal in 1997 launched the international Campaign to Stop Gender Apartheid in Afghanistan to counter the Taliban's abuse of women."

Smeal and the Feminine Majority organizations have shifted their focus to reproductive rights of women. ". . . she led the first national abortion rights march in 1986, drawing more than 100,000 participants to Washington, D.C. She has been in the leadership of every major reproductive rights march ever since, including the 2004 March for Women's Lives, the largest march in our nation's history. Over 1.1 million people gathered on the National Mall to demand that women's health, access to contraception, and abortion receive adequate funding."(See http://feministmajority.org/eleanor-smeal/)

Smeal serves on several boards, including the National Council for Research on Women, the National Organization for Women, the Executive Committee of the National Council of Women's Organizations, and the Leadership Circle of the Alliance for Ratification of CEDAW. She received an honorary Doctor of Law from

Duke University, an honorary Doctor of Science from the University of Florida, and an honorary Doctor of Humane Letters from Rutgers, the State University of New Jersey.

Despite the failure of the E.R.A. amendment, Smeal has successfully chipped away at discrimination and laws against women that have kept them down.

## PERSONAL LIFE
Smeal married Charles Smeal, on April 27, 1963. They had a son and daughter, Tod and Lori.

## FURTHER READING
*Christian Sci Mon B pi4- S 4 79 por; Ms 6:64+ F 78 por; N Y Times A pl8 Ap 28 77 por, A p!2 S 2 77 por; Los Angeles Times I p22 O 6 79; People 8:66+ Ag 8 77 pors; Redbook 150:243+ Ap 78; Time 111:16+ Mr 27 78 por; Britannica Book of the Year, 1979*

---

# TAVIS SMILEY
## Radio Talk-Show Host; Writer, Commentator; Lecturer

**Born:** September 13, 1964; Gulfport, Mississippi
**Primary Field:** Black Rights Advocacy
**Affiliation:** Media & Entertainment Industry

## INTRODUCTION
*Tavis Smiley, the host of the daily, nationally broadcast Tavis Smiley Show since January 2002, is known as one of black America's favorite radio talk-show hosts and respected as one of the most prominent voices of black advocacy in the country. "What I tell black people every day on radio is to be advocates,"* Smiley told Bomani Jones in an interview for the Africana website, *"You've got to fight for these things you believe in to make a difference. When you are disrespected and disenfranchised, you've got to speak up and be heard about those things." Prior to hosting the one-hour Tavis Smiley Show, which airs on National Public Radio (NPR), Smiley was the executive producer and host of the award-winning current-affairs show* BET Tonight with Tavis Smiley *on Black Entertainment Television (BET) from 1996 to 2001; since 1996 he has contributed political and social commentary twice a week to the Tom Joyner Morning Show, the number-one nationally syndicated radio program in the United States, and occasionally to ABC's World News Tonight with Peter Jennings, among other major media outlets. He is the author of six books, including the best-selling* How to Make Black America Better: Leading African Americans Speak Out *(2001). From 2001 to 2002 Smiley served as a correspondent for CNN and as a special correspondent for ABC-TV's* Good Morning America *and* PrimeTime Thursday.

Time *magazine has named Smiley one of the 50 most promising young leaders in the country, and in 1999 Newsweek listed him as one of the nation's "captains of the airwaves" and one of 20 people changing the way Americans get their news. Through his lectures, writing, broadcasts, and the Tavis Smiley Foundation, he works to uplift, inform, and inspire people, in particular African-Americans. Speaking of Smiley, NPR's president and chief executive officer, Kevin Klose, told Lynn Elber for the Associated Press (June 25, 2002), "This man's presence, his charm, his humor about life and his thoughtfulness about the human condition, in a universal sense, are immediately affecting to listeners."*

## EARLY LIFE
One of 10 children of Emory G. and Joyce M. Smiley, Tavis Smiley was born in Gulfport, Mississippi, on September 13, 1964. His father was a noncommissioned officer in the United States Air Force, and his mother is an Apostolic Pentecostal minister. When Smiley was young, the family moved to Bunker Hill, Indiana. His family, numbering 13 people, including his grandmother, lived in poverty in a three-bedroom trailer. Smiley spent a good deal of time in church in Kokomo, Indiana, while growing up, and today listeners sometimes liken his verbal cadence and power to those of a preacher. When Smiley was 13 he worked for Douglas Jr., who ran the New Bethel Tabernacle Church Sunday school and served as a Kokomo city councilman. Speaking of that formative experience, Smiley told Dan Geringer for the *Philadelphia Daily News* (February 13, 2002), "I was always moved by how people were so appreciative of Hogan's efforts to empower them, to get their kid a summer job, to get their tree trimmed, to get a pothole

filled. I saw constituent service first hand. I saw people's lives touched." Smiley recalled to Geringer the time he sat between Hogan and U.S. senator Birch Bayh of Indiana during a campaign event. "That night, I gave up my dreams of being a first baseman in the major leagues. I was a standout player and a big Cincinnati Reds fan. But that night I decided I wanted to devote my life to public service."

At Maconaquah High School Smiley was elected president of both his junior and senior classes, served as captain of the debate team, and directed the junior and senior choirs at the New Bethel Tabernacle Church, where his mother serves as a minister. Smiley attended Indiana University, in Bloomington, where he was a member of the Kappa Alpha Psi fraternity, on a debate scholarship. "I enjoyed the intellectual rigor of going back and forth with professors. I just enjoyed being around people who were smarter than I was and learning and growing," Smiley recalled to Devona Dolliole for an article on the *Black Collegian* website. During his sophomore year at the school, an African-American friend of Smiley's was shot and killed by white Indiana police officers who claimed to have acted in self-defense. Believing that his friend had been killed wrongfully, Smiley helped to lead the ensuing protests. "When my friend was murdered by those cops, it was the first time in my life that I connected politics with social advocacy," he told Geringer. "I wanted the ability to use the political apparatus, not just to get potholes fixed and trees trimmed and get kids summer jobs, but also to right wrongs and force people to reexamine their assumptions."

Smiley was active in student government at Indiana University, working for both the school's chancellor and the school's vice president. During his junior year he steadfastly pursued, and finally received, an internship with Tom Bradley, who was making history as the first African-American mayor of Los Angeles, the country's second-largest city. Returning to Indiana University after the internship, Smiley received his bachelor's degree in law and public policy in 1986, then went back to Los Angeles and served as an aide to Mayor Bradley from 1988 to 1990. In 1991 Smiley left the mayor's office to run for a seat on the Los Angeles City Council; he lost the race, winning 9 percent of the vote in a crowded field.

## LIFE'S WORK

Finding himself without a job, Smiley next thought of becoming a radio commentator. He created *The Smiley Report*, each installment of which was one minute long, and found sponsors for it on KGFJ-AM in Los Angeles, a black-oriented station. Events in Los Angeles in the early and mid-1990s provided much fodder for public debate, and thus for Smiley's reports. During those years national attention focused on the beating of a black man, Rodney King, by four Los Angeles police officers; the riots that ensued after the officers were acquitted of assault charges; and the O. J. Simpson murder trial. Smiley's radio broadcasts attracted a large following. Devona Dolliole quoted Tom Bradley, who was mayor for part of that time, as saying of Smiley, "At last, those on the left have a fast talking champion with fresh ideas to counter the outrageous barbs of the conservatives." In 1994 and 1995 Smiley co-hosted a talk show on the Los Angeles station KMPC-AM. An outspoken and liberal African-American, Smiley became known to many as a kind of anti-Rush Limbaugh, a reference to the highly opinionated, conservative radio commentator who is, along with Howard Stern, one of the most listened-to radio personalities in the country. Esther Iverem, writing for the *Washington Post* (June 22, 1998), quoted *Time* magazine as having stated, in the same 1994 issue that named Smiley one of the top 50 leaders for the future: "In the wildly popular and largely conservative medium of talk radio, a young black man unafraid to take on the white establishment would not seem to have a promising future. But Tavis Smiley, self-styled 'practical progressive,' is making a name for himself, in part because he is equally willing to admonish fellow African Americans who too quickly blame racism for their problems."

In 1996 Smiley began hosting and executive producing Black Entertainment Television's talk show *BET Tonight with Tavis Smiley*. On the show Smiley interviewed major figures from all walks of life, including Cuban leader Fidel Castro and Pope John Paul II, and discussed everything from police brutality to the latest celebrity gossip. Smiley conducted then-President Bill Clinton's first interview following the disclosure of his extramarital relationship with the one-time White House intern Monica Lewinsky. Smiley has since interviewed Clinton on the air a number of times. He ended each show by exhorting the audience to "keep the faith." The January 18, 1999 issue of *Newsweek*, the same one in which Smiley was named one of 20 people changing the way Americans get their news, praised *Tonight with Tavis Smiley* as a "smart Larry King-style" program and Smiley as a "high- octane host" who used the forum to speak out on a range of issues. Among Smiley's detractors was the conservative African-American talk-show host Larry Elder, who opined to John L. Mitchell for the *Los Angeles Times* (August 21, 2001), "[Smiley's] agenda is all too much 'The white man done me wrong,' and that the government owes us. He's a walking refutation of the racism about which he speaks. He is like many who are constantly crying out against the establishment but have become fantastically wealthy." The critic and author Mark Anthony Neal, a professor of English and Africana studies at the State University of New York at Albany, was quoted by Mitchell as criticizing Tonight with Tavis Smiley for its "cronyism," citing as an example the program on which Smiley introduced high-profile guests Johnnie L. Cochran Jr. and Cornel West as his good friends, an act that, in Neal's opinion, "effectively undermined his value as a host." Those comments notwithstanding, *Tonight with Tavis Smiley* was widely regarded as the most intelligently produced program on BET. Smiley was honored with the National Association for the Advancement of Colored People's (NAACP) Image Award for best news, talk, or information series for three consecutive years (1997-99) for his work on *Tonight with Tavis Smiley.* He won two other Image Awards for a *Tonight with Tavis Smiley* special called "Black and Blue: A Town Hall Meeting in New York City."

Initially citing declining ratings as the reason for its decision, BET announced in March 2001 that the station was not going to renew Smiley's contract with *BET Tonight* after he completed that season's schedule in the fall. Following the announcement, Tom Joyner, on the *Tom Joyner Morning Show*, sought to rally his audience to protest BET's move, and Smiley aired his own disapproval of the way BET had handled his dismissal: according to most sources, including Smiley, BET and its parent company, Viacom, informed Smiley of the decision by faxing his agent a four sentence memo. BET founder Robert Johnson subsequently stated that Smiley had been fired because he had sold an exclusive interview to ABC News without first offering the story to BET, even though Smiley's contract with BET did not require him to do so. Johnson, who referred to the difficult relationship he had had with Smiley during the five years of the show's run, then made Smiley's dismissal effective immediately. Smiley claimed that he had offered the story, an interview with Sara Jane Olson, an alleged former member of the Symbionese Liberation Army, an infamous 1970s American terrorist group, to CBS, which is owned by Viacom. Smiley sold

the interview to ABC, he said, only after CBS passed on the offer. Referring to Johnson's having sold BET to Viacom, Smiley said to Gregg Braxton for the *Los Angeles Times*, as quoted in the journal of the *National Association of Black Journalists* (July 31, 2001), "They terminated my contract immediately because I sold one independent project to a mainstream white corporation, when Mr. Johnson sold an entire Black network to a major white corporation. Go figure."

Thousands of people sent faxes, E-mail messages, and letters to BET and Viacom to express their support for Smiley and to protest BET's decision. Some Smiley supporters even made public demonstrations in Los Angeles and Washington, D.C.; among the prominent demonstrators and organizers of those protests were the Reverend Al Sharpton and the Princeton University professor and author Cornel West. "I have been humbled by the outpouring of Black love that I have received over the last few months. I will never forget this outpouring and I will never take it for granted," Smiley told *Jet* magazine (August 27, 2001). "What this experience has done for me is to make me more committed to Black people. I am more committed now than I was even eight weeks ago. Anybody would be if you had been lifted by Black love in the way I have been lifted, sustained, embraced by Black love." Smiley told Bomani Jones, "My firing became the catalyst for a great deal of commentary in all kinds of papers, mainstream and black outlets, in print and in radio. My firing became the catalyst for a real conversation about the lack of quality programming for black people. It was clear to me when I started reading all those articles that it wasn't about me. I just happened to be the jumping off point." The real issue, he said, was "the quality of programming that black people deserve." Reflecting on his years at BET, Smiley told *Jet*, "I really do thank BET for the opportunity. I am eternally grateful for the chance I had over five years to host [*Tonight with Tavis Smiley*]. I am proud of the work we did."

Since 1996 Smiley has provided political and social commentary twice a week on the *Tom Joyner Morning Show*, which is the number one nationally syndicated black radio program in the country and is carried on more than 100 stations nationwide. According to Esther Iverem, Smiley was introduced to Tom Joyner by then-President Clinton during the summer of 1996 at a White House meeting designed to test campaign material on a black audience. The *Tom Joyner Morning Show*, which, according to most figures, has a national audience of seven million listeners, provides Smiley with a platform from which to send out his messages of empowerment and awareness to black Americans.

"Say what you want about [Smiley], but he's a man with a plan," Joyner told Miki Turner for the Fort Worth, Texas, *Star-Telegram* (November 21, 2001). "He really cares about his people and wants to make things better for them." Together, Joyner and Smiley have taken advantage of the show's reach to effect change. By urging listeners to make telephone calls and send E-mail messages and faxes of protest to companies putatively engaged in discriminatory practices, Smiley and Joyner succeeded in halting the planned sale of slave memorabilia by Christie's Auction House, in **New York**, in 1997; in bringing about the temporary reinstatement of *Living Single*, which had been the top rated television show among African-Americans, after Fox canceled it in 1998; in getting CompUSA, the largest U.S. computer retailer, which had been reaping large profits from African-American customers, to direct more advertising business to black-owned media; and in pressuring the Katz Radio Group, a New York City based advertising sales firm, to buy more advertising spots on black owned radio stations. Smiley and Joyner accomplished the last named feat after they and others got their hands on an internal Katz memo that urged clients not to buy spots on minority-owned stations because "advertisers should want prospects, not suspects." Smiley and Joyner were also the force behind national campaigns that brought about the awarding of a Congressional Gold Medal to the civil rights leader Rosa Parks in 1999; led to the reversal, in 2001, of a decision by Republican congressmen to assign matters connected with historically black colleges and universities to a new congressional committee rather than to the existing committee that dealt with all institutions of higher learning, a move that, according to Smiley, Joyner, and others, would have been disadvantageous for those traditionally black schools; and resulted in the registration of hundreds of thousands of voters.

Just weeks after his dismissal from BET, Smiley signed lucrative deals to serve as a correspondent and guest host for the Cable News Network (CNN), on shows such as *TalkBack Live* and *Inside Politics,* and as a correspondent for ABC-TV's *Good Morning America* and *PrimeTime Thursday*. Smiley also renewed his contract as a commentator on the ABC Radio Networks' *Tom Joyner Morning Show* and agreed to host his own syndicated daily commentary show, *The Smiley Report,*

also for ABC Radio Networks. *The Smiley Report*, which premiered in November 2002, airs as a 60-second commentary on matters relevant to African- Americans. In addition, Smiley signed a development deal with Buena Vista Television, which is owned by the Walt Disney Co., for a syndicated, one-hour, daytime television talk show. That show, which Smiley envisioned as a "Phil Donahue-type" program on which issues of substance would be discussed, was scheduled to premiere in 2002. As of March 2003 the show had not aired. Lastly, he signed a two-book deal with the publisher Random House and a distribution deal with Hay House Inc., a self-help book-publishing company based in Carlsbad, California, to organize seminars on personal success and create a series of products, including "mini-books" and audiotapes of his speeches. Smiley's first product, called the Empowerment card deck, appeared in stores in March 2003.

Regarding the abrupt changes of fortune that his career has seen since 2001, when he was dismissed from BET, Smiley told *Jet* (August 27, 2001), "I didn't know that it would be this sweet this soon. But I also know that life is not a spectator sport. You have to be in it to win it. And I am still in it. I am not any less talented today than I was the day before BET fired me. And I know I was just as talented the day after BET fired me."

Smiley began hosting the *Tavis Smiley Show* on National Public Radio in January 2002. As of March 2003 the one-hour daily program, which covers topics of interest to African-Americans while at the same time trying to appeal to a broader audience, is carried on close to 60 stations nationwide on the NPR network. The idea for the show came about in 2000, after leaders from several dozen black public-radio stations met with NPR representatives to discuss what they felt their audiences wanted, but were not always receiving, in the way of programming. The show, NPR's first to originate from Los Angeles, offers interviews, news, and commentary on everything from politics to pop culture. Among the high-profile special guests Smiley has interviewed on the show are former president Clinton, basketball legend and businessman Magic Johnson, and Microsoft mogul Bill Gates. Regular guests include the University of Pennsylvania religion and Afro-American studies professor Michael Eric Dyson; the well-known scholars Cornel West and Charles Ogletree; Omar Wasow, the technology pundit and executive director of *blackplanet.com*; and the civil rights advocate and lawyer Connie Rice. Smiley's reports for NPR have included stories on diversity in newsrooms and on how movies portray black- white "buddy" relationships. Recent shows have featured discussions on what it means to be white in America, dual citizenship, and the Democratic Party's preparations for the 2004 presidential election. Observers have said that Smiley's liberal stance on many issues, and the diversity of perspectives presented on the show, are what set it apart from similar programs. Praising the *Tavis Smiley Show*, Florida Democratic representative Alcee Hastings, who has been one of Smiley's guests, told Mike Janssen for *Current* (June 24, 2002), "The point is that it's not only race-based issues that get a different treatment [on the show] it's nearly all issues." "An enlightened white American could host this show every day," Smiley told Janssen, "so long as he or she opens up the airwaves to a diversity of voices. That just doesn't happen enough." The University of North Carolina professor and media critic Chuck Stone gave his assessment of Smiley to J. Shawn Durham for the Durham, North Carolina, *Herald-Sun* (February 17, 2002), saying, "I've listened to [the *Tavis Smiley Show* on NPR] and he is a really intense man. He comes at you with a lot of information. He is very well read and when he talks, you can't help but hear what he is saying about something. He obviously cares a lot about what he is talking about and that gets others interested in hearing what he has to say."

Smiley is the author of six books, including *Hard Left: Straight Talk About the Wrongs of the Right* (1996) and *On Air: The Best of Tavis Smiley on the Tom Joyner Morning Show* (1998). As quoted by Esther Iverem, Smiley, attempting to motivate progressive-minded people to speak out and become more active, wrote in *Hard Left*, "It's not that the country has gone conservative, it's that those of us who are left of center have allowed the right to take control of the dialogue." In a *Publishers Weekly* review posted on the Barnes and Noble Web site, a writer called Hard Left a "thoughtful political statement" and "a hard-hitting counterpunch that liberals will endorse." A *Kirkus* review on the same Web site was less laudatory, with the writer calling *Hard Left* a "liberal pulpit-pounding from a young master of the exploding what's wrong with America genre. [Smiley] is too obviously impressed by his own influence ('the real power in this country today is in the media,' he avers) to be entirely convincing. Some of his facts are questionable, too. But no matter: Smiley is on a roll throughout this book, and his enthusiasm for his cases bears his argument along even when pure logic doesn't."

Explaining his reasons for writing *Doing What's Right: How to Fight for What You Believe—and Make a Difference* (2000), Smiley told Natalie Hopkinson for the *Washington Post* (January 19, 2000), "We have textbooks, manuals and guides for everything in America, except how to make a difference when you find something about which you are passionate. We are the realization of [Martin Luther King Jr.'s] dream. We are the first generation not born of struggle. I think that makes a book about advocacy more important than ever." In *Doing What's Right*, while seeking to help readers identify the issues they care about, Smiley offered tips on how to organize a movement, deal with the media, set up an Internet site, and make telephone contacts. In the bestselling *How to Make Black America Better: Leading African Americans Speak Out* (2001), Smiley encouraged blacks to take control of their own destiny. In the first section of *How to Make Black America Better*, Smiley offered 10 challenges to the African-American community. The middle portion consists of essays by 28 prominent African-Americans, including the Reverend Jesse Jackson, basketball star Shaquille O'Neal, lawyer, author, and children's advocate Marian Wright Edelman, and the editorial director of *Essence* magazine, Susan L. Taylor, among others. The book ends with excerpts from "Advocacy in the Next Millennium: New Paradigms for Progress," a symposium Smiley organized in Los Angeles before the 2000 Democratic National Convention. As it appears on amazon.com, a review of How to Make Black America Better by *Essense* magazine stated, "Smiley and Co. offer deft advice that encourages us to take positive action to make things right." A *Publishers Weekly* review posted to the same Web site found that "while only the committed will buy and read this cover to cover, there are enough quotable bits to generate interest." Smiley's latest book is *Keeping the Faith: Stories of Love, Courage, Healing and Hope from Black America* (2002). *Just a Thought: The Smiley Report 1991-93*, a collection of his radio commentaries, was published in 1993.

Smiley publishes a bimonthly newsletter, the *Smiley Report*, which, according to the Web site *sisterfriends.com*, has several million readers, and he is a contributing editor for the publication *USA Weekend*. In addition, he has provided political analysis for the television shows *Politically Incorrect*, hosted by Bill Maher, *Today*, and *World News Tonight* with Peter Jennings. Smiley's advocacy work has been showcased on *60 Minutes*.

In 1999 Smiley established the Tavis Smiley Foundation, a nonprofit organization dedicated to empowering and enlightening black youth through scholarships, seminars, and mentorship programs. One of the foundation's principal efforts is the Youth to Leaders (Y2L) program, which consists of an annual series of free, one-day leadership building conferences that are held in cities across the country. The headquarters for Smiley's many media ventures is the Smiley-owned, 6,000 square foot Smiley Group Inc. office building, on Crenshaw Boulevard in Los Angeles. According to Smiley's Web site, *tavistalks.com*, the Smiley Group Inc. (TSG) is a communications corporation established by Smiley "in support of human rights and related empowerment issues," and is the holding company for his various enterprises. Completed in 2001, the multimillion-dollar facility, which was once a dilapidated, graffiti-marked building, includes the offices of the Tavis Smiley Foundation, a technology center for local youth, and a state of the art radio studio, from which Smiley produces all his radio shows. He has filled the building with African handicrafts and original artwork by renowned African-American artists.

Smiley travels the country regularly, conducting seminars centered on his message of black empowerment and speaking to college students and representatives of corporations and other organizations. In February 2002 Smiley delivered the keynote speech at the Massachusetts Institute of Technology's 28th annual presidential breakfast honoring Martin Luther King Jr. In 2001 he conducted a symposium entitled "State of the Black Union: It's About Us" in Washington, D.C., the first installment in what Smiley sees as a series of "black think-tanks" in which African-American leaders and the public can come together to discuss the state of black America. In February 2002 Smiley organized a second such panel discussion, in Philadelphia, Pennsylvania, titled "Where Do We Go from Here: Chaos or Community? Black America's Vision for Healing, Harmony, and Higher Ground." The event, which ran all day and was free to the public, was broadcast live on C-SPAN, a public affairs cable channel, and featured civil rights leaders Al Sharpton and Jesse Jackson, social critic Stanley Crouch, Harvard law professors Charles Ogletree and Lani Guinier, and United States representatives Chaka Fattah and Maxine Waters, among others. His most recent "State of the Black Union" symposium, "The Black Church," was held in Detroit, Michigan, in February 2003.

Smiley has been honored for his public activism with the Mickey Leland Humanitarian Award from the National Association of Minorities in Communications. *Vanity Fair* inducted Smiley into its hall of fame in 1996. Along with Tom Joyner, in 2000 Smiley won the Congressional Black Caucus Harold Washington Award. In 2001 he was honored with the NAACP President's Image Award and the Los Angeles Press Club Headliner Award. He founded and served as chairman of the operations committee of Los Angeles' Young Black Professionals from 1988 to 1990; was a member of the steering committee of the United Way of Greater Los Angeles in 1989 and 1990; and sat on the advisory boards of the Inner City Foundation for Excellence in Education (1989-91), Scouting USA (1991), and the Martin Luther King Jr. Center for Non-violent Social Change (1992-93).

## PERSONAL LIFE

Smiley lives in Los Angeles, California. He is a fan of the singer Al Jarreau and fond of playing basketball and the board game Scrabble. "One day when I was about 3 or 4, I was running my mouth at a family gathering," Smiley recalled for Lynn Elber. "My aunt said to me, 'Boy, do you ever shut up? Why do you talk so much?' I shot right back, 'Because I've got a lot to say.' All these years later, I've still got a lot to say."

## FURTHER READING

*Just a Thought: The Smiley Report; Hard Left: Straight Talk About the Wrongs of the Right; On Air: The Best of Tavis Smiley on the Tom Joyner Morning Show; Doing What's Right: How to Fight for What You Believe—and Make a Difference; How to Make Black America Better; Keeping the Faith: Stories of Love, Courage, Healing and Hope from Black America*

# HAZEL BRANNON SMITH

## Newspaper Publisher; Editor

**Born:** February 4, 1914; Alabama City, Ala.
**Died:** May 14, 1994; Cleveland, Tenn.
**Primary Field:** Civil Rights
**Affiliation:** Secretary of the Holmes Country Democratic Executive Committee

### INTRODUCTION

*The first woman to win the Pulitzer Prize for editorial writing, Hazel Brannon Smith, owner-editor of four weekly newspapers in rural Mississippi, had been exposing political and social injustice in her home state for more than a quarter of a century. The 1964 Pulitzer award, presented to her as racist boycotts threatened her newspapers with extinction, cited the "whole volume of her work..., including attacks on corruption." Mrs. Smith, who prefers to be known as a newspaperwoman who reports the facts honestly, has minimized her editorial influence, describing herself as "just a little editor in a little spot" and pointing out, "A lot of other little editors in a lot of other little spots is what helps make this country. It's either going to help protect that freedom that we have or else it's going to let that freedom slip away by default."*

### EARLY LIFE

Of antebellum Southern ancestry, Hazel Freeman Brannon Smith, the daughter of Dock Boad Brannon, an electrical contractor, and Georgia (Freeman) Brannon, was born in Gadsden, the seat of Etowah County, Ala. The Black nurse who raised her was, she recalled in an interview with Senior Editor T. George Harris of *Look* (November 11, 1965), "treated as a member of the family." An exceptionally bright child, she graduated from the local high school in 1930, when she was sixteen. Too young to enroll in college, she began writing personal items at five cents an inch for the *Etowah Observer*, a small-town weekly newspaper. The editor, impressed with her talent, quickly promoted her to front-page reporting. She also sold advertising space on a 10 percent commission, and she earned so much in commissions that the paper put her on a regular weekly salary as an economy measure.

While on the staff of the *Observer*, Miss Brannon, as she was known before her marriage, developed an overwhelming desire to "write" her own newspaper.

With that goal in mind, she enrolled at the University of Alabama majoring in journalism, in 1932. At the university, she was managing editor of the campus newspaper and beauty queen of her social sorority, Delta Zeta. Upon taking her B.A. degree, in 1935, Miss Brannon, with borrowed money, acquired the failing *Durant News*, a weekly serving Holmes County, Mississippi. The paper, called the "Durant Excuse" by disgruntled subscribers, had exhausted three editors in the 13 months prior to the purchase. Realizing that her small weekly could not begin to compete with the larger daily newspapers in the coverage of state and national news, Miss Brannon made the Durant News a truly local paper, printing news of particular interest to the citizens of Holmes County: Births, deaths, marriages, graduations, family reunions, arrests. As circulation more than doubled, to 1,400 readers, advertising revenues increased, and within four years the young editor completely paid for her paper.

In her editorial column, "Through Hazel Eyes," Miss Brannon attacked social injustices and promoted unpopular causes. At the request of local public health officials, for instance, she supported a proposed venereal disease treatment clinic, provoking considerable local criticism. Many of her shocked readers insisted venereal disease was not an appropriate subject for public discussion, particularly by a well-bred Southern lady. In other columns, she assailed slot machine operators, bootleggers, gamblers, small-time hoods, and corrupt local politicians.

### LIFE'S WORK

In 1953, Sheriff Richard Byrd of Holmes County shot a young Black man in the leg. After talking to several eyewitnesses, Mrs. Smith became convinced that the shooting had been unprovoked. Attempting to provide a balanced account, she sought comment from the sheriff but, was told by his office that he was "out of town." She printed a story based solely on the testimony of witnesses and, the following week, wrote a scathing front-page editorial condemning Sheriff Byrd: "The laws of America are for everyone—rich and poor, strong and weak, Black and White. The vast majority of Holmes County people are not rednecks who look with favor on the abuse of people because their skins are black. Byrd has violated every concept of justice, decency, and right. He is not fit to occupy office."

When Sheriff Byrd filed a $57,500 libel suit against Mrs. Smith and the *Advertiser*, an all-male, all-White jury convicted her of libel and ordered her to pay $10,000 in damages. The Mississippi Supreme Court, citing the Constitutional guarantee of press freedom, reversed the libel award in a decision stating that her criticism of the sheriff was justifiable and "substantially true." Speaking at a dinner in honor of Mrs. Smith several years later, Dr. Arenia C. Mallory, president of all-Black Saints Junior College, remembered her editorial courage: "This story reduced her from a woman of almost wealth to a woman who has had to struggle like the rest of us. She defended a little boy who couldn't defend himself."

Mrs. Smith's four papers, reasonably successful until she became an editorial partisan of the Civil Rights Movement, steadily lost money. Advertising fell off substantially as intimidated businessmen succumbed to pressure from White Citizens' Councils in Holmes County towns. "Ours is the only paper in the county," she told Mary Hornaday in an interview for the *Christian Science Monitor* (October 17, 1964), "and I just cannot permit Citizens' Councils to tell me how to run my newspaper." Public service announcements filled the empty advertising space in the *Lexington Advertiser.* An opposition paper was founded in 1959 to cut into Mrs. Smith's readership, but, by mortgaging her business and personal property, paring her staff from fifteen to five, and borrowing money, she continued to publish.

One hundred thousand dollars in debt, Mrs. Smith went on extended speaking tours, earning from $300 to $1,000 per speech. The prestigious *Columbia Journalism Review* established the Hazel Brannon Smith Fund to ensure the survival of the *Lexington Advertiser,* and Black subscribers to the newspaper presented Mrs. Smith with $2,852 collected in support of her editorial policies.

Despite constant public harassment, economic boycotts, threats, acts of vandalism, and even a cross-burning on the lawn of the Smith home in Lexington, Mrs.

---

## Affiliation: Secretary of the Holmes Country Democratic Executive Committee

In 1943, Miss Brannon purchased a second newspaper, the Lexington Advertiser, an independent weekly published in the Holmes County seat. Characteristically, she took a personal interest in the political, economic, and social development of Lexington. From 1940 to 1948, she served as Secretary of the Holmes County Democratic Executive Committee, and, in 1940 and 1944, she was a delegate to the Democratic National Convention. When a lingerie manufacturer expressed a willingness to locate a new mill in the Lexington area, Miss Brannon visited the company's headquarters in the North and questioned the executives. Convinced that the proposed plant would bring needed benefits to Holmes County, she persuaded her readers to support a bond issue for construction of the plant.

Her business sense and instinctive ability as a reporter rejuvenated the Advertiser, which paid for itself within three years. With her profits, she purchased two more Mississippi weeklies, the Banner County Outlook in Flora, in 1955, and the Northside Reporter, in Jackson, in 1956. In the meantime, she had found in Walter Dyer Smith not only a husband, but, a helper in the running of her little journalistic empire. The most influential enterprise in that empire remained the Advertiser, serving a rural population dominated numerically by poor Blacks, but socially, economically, and politically by White truck farmers, small businessmen, and an occasional cotton planter. "Without her and her paper," one Black resident confided to T. George Harris of Look, "a Negro's life in Holmes County wouldn't be worth a plugged nickel."

---

Smith refused to desert the zealous Civil Rights workers who poured into the South in the early 1960s. In her "Through Hazel Eyes" column she noted that "these young people wouldn't be here if we had not largely ignored our responsibilities to our Negro citizens." A week after the disappearance and suspected murder of three Civil Rights workers in Neshoba County, Mississippi, in the summer of 1964, she appeared with Civil Rights leaders of both races in a panel discussion before a national meeting of the American Newspaper Women's Club in Washington, D.C. On that occasion, describing the climate in which the three youths died, she said, "You don't have to have a sheet to belong to the Klan. It's as much a state of mind as anything else."

In retaliation, her editorial offices of the Jackson, Miss., paper she owned, *The Northside Reporter*, were firebombed while she was attending the Democratic National Convention in 1964 as a commentator for NBC-TV News. In spite of the damage to equipment and files,

Mrs. Smith believed the bombing was potentially beneficial to her community. Eventually, she felt, there would be a backlash against such violence. "The pendulum is beginning to swing...," she said. "One of these days, a Southerner...will realize the Negro is a man like himself with the same desires, the same tastes.... We have to live together; we must get along together. We must have respect for each other and each other's rights."

For her editorial courage and honesty in the face of racist attacks and harassment, Mrs. Smith in 1964 was named Mississippi Woman of the Year by newspaper, radio, and television executives in her home state and Woman of Conscience by the National Council of Women of the United States. In New York City to accept her award from the National Council of Women, she told a news conference at the Overseas Press Club, on October 14, 1964, that her opponents were "scared to call me an integrationist to my face; they say it to my advertisers." About herself she said, "Since I was a little girl, I have been very independent. I reserve the right to do my own thinking, to act as a human being.... I just can't keep quiet." Although she has never considered herself to be a "crusading editor," Mrs. Smith told George Moneyhun of the *Christian Science Monitor* (July 6, 1966), "You finally come to a point when you must decide whether you're for law and order or against it, and it's also been a matter of people being able to pressure the free press with its rights and responsibilities."

In the Democratic primary, on August 9, 1967, Mrs. Smith finished second in the race for nomination for the state Senate, but, two weeks later, she lost the run-off election to incumbent state Senator Ollie Mohamed. Her faith in the people of Mississippi was confirmed in the late 1960s, when advertisers began returning to her newspapers and the total circulation of the four weeklies surpassed that of the largest daily in the state. According to Mrs. Smith, the circulation of the *Advertiser* had never dropped significantly. "Oh, a handful of people cancelled their subscriptions during the Civil Rights years, but they sent their cooks down to buy the paper issue-by-issue," she told Henry Mitchell of the *Washington Post* (May 4, 1973). In the same interview, she estimated that the *Advertiser's* losses, in 1972, had been "but $17,000 or $18,000." The interview with Mitchell took place when Mrs. Smith was in Washington for the premiere of the 28 minute documentary film *An Independent Voice* at the Henry R. Luce Hall of News Reporting in the Smithsonian Institution's Museum of Science and Industry. That film is about outstanding small-time newspaper editors, including Mrs. Smith. Her life was dramatized in the ABC-TV movie *A Passion for Justice: The Hazel Brannon Smith Story* (1994), with Jane Seymour in the title role. The movie aired several weeks before Smith died. In 2001, a biography about her, written by John A. Whalen, was published: *Maverick Among the Magnolias: The Hazel Brannon Smith Story*.

The Mississippi Press Association, of which Mrs. Smith was past President, awarded her a special citation, in 1957. Her other honors include the highest editorial award of the National Federation of Press Women, in 1948, 1955, and 1956; the Elijah Parish Lovejoy Award of Southern Illinois University, in 1960; Theta Sigma Phi's National Headliner citation, in 1962; and the Golden Quill of the International Conference of Weekly Newspaper Editors, in 1963. She was a former director of the Mississippi chapter of the National Editorial Association and a member of the Mississippi Council on Human Relations, the Mississippi Advisory Committee to the United States Civil Rights Commission, and the Mississippi Delta Council. She was President of the International Society of Weekly Newspaper Editors in 1981 to 1982.

According to the *New York Times* May 16, 1994, obituary on Smith, Hazel Brannon Smith, 80, Editor Who Crusaded for Civil Rights, she eventually was forced to sell the *Lexington Advertiser* because the boycott and opposition paper bled her financially. Other observers stated she had to sell an additional paper and left the newspaper business in 1985. Widowed since 1983, she moved to Cleveland, Tenn., to be closer to relatives. She spent the last years of her life at Royal Care Nursing Home until her death on May 14, 1994. (See http://www.nytimes.com/1994/05/16/obituaries/hazel-brannon-smith-80-editor-who-crusaded-for-civil-rights.html)

Smith's 1945-1976 papers are available to researchers at the Special Collections department of the Mississippi State University Library.

## PERSONAL LIFE

She was described as a handsome, dark-haired, buxom woman. Her eyes, contrary to the title of her editorial column, were deep blue. Talkative and gregarious, she possessed a sense of hospitality which, according to Ann Geracimos of the *New York Herald Tribune* (May 10, 1964), "oozes fried chicken and biscuits." She and her Yankee husband, Walter, met as passenger and ship's purser, respectively, on a round-the-world cruise, in 1949, and married within the same year. After settling in Lexington with his wife, Mr. Smith became administrator of the county hospital, but he was fired from that post when his wife went to war against the Citizens' Councils. Besides helping in the publication of Mrs. Smith's newspapers, he had served as Executive Director of Mississippi Action for Progress, Inc., which launched the Head Start program. The Smiths had no children. With offspring to worry about, Mrs. Smith conceded, she could never have been so daringly outspoken in her Civil Rights editorializing.

"God has been with me," Mrs. Smith, a lifelong Baptist, had said. "If he hadn't, I'd be insane or dead."

In her spare time she edited *Baptist Observer,* the monthly newspaper of the largest Black Baptist association in Mississippi. She and her husband, who passed away in 1983, rarely attended social functions outside of those public events where they appeared in their capacities as newspaper people and social activists. "We work too hard for one thing," Mrs. Smith explained. "Anyway, we'd only get into terrible rows at any party we went to."

## FURTHER READING
*Look 29:121+ N 16 '65 pors; Washington Post B p3 My 4 '73; Foremost Women in Communications (1970); Who's Who of American Women, 1970-71*

---

# JOE SOLMONESE

## Gay Rights Activist

**Born:** November 27, 1964; Attleboro, Massachusetts
**Primary Field:** Gender Equality; Human Rights
**Affiliation:** Human Rights Campaign (HRC)

## INTRODUCTION
*In 2005 Joe Solmonese became president of the Human Rights Campaign (HRC), an organization representing the lesbian, gay, bisexual, and transgender (LGBT) communities. He has since built that Washington, D.C. based political action committee (PAG) into one of the largest and most successful lobbying groups in the U.S., one that has been at the forefront of the fight for legal recognition of same-sex marriage. "This is a long-term struggle," Solmonese told Don Aucoin for the* Boston Globe *(April 7, 2005). "It's going to take a lot of back and forth. We're going to take three steps forward and two steps back. A lot." HRC is the nation's largest LGBT rights organization, with roughly 750,000 members and a budget of over $30 million. Since its formation, in 1980, it has invested in the campaigns of numerous pro-LGBT rights politicians and spoken out against antigay discrimination in society and the workplace. Its efforts with regard to same-sex marriage have pitted the organization against religious groups and conservatives who believe that families with same-sex parents are damaging to children and an affront to the institution of marriage. According to the group's Web site, HRC "works to secure equal rights for LGBT individu-*

*als and families at the federal and state levels by lobbying elected officials, mobilizing grassroots supporters, educating Americans, investing strategically to elect fair-minded officials, and partnering with other LGBT organizations."*

*Mary Breslauer, a former board member of HRC, told Aucoin that Solmonese "has one of the greatest gifts you can have in politics, and that's understanding that it's all about relationships, that the conversation with the receptionist or the driver or the field director can be just as important as the conversation with the candidate. Because he really focuses on you, you really focus on him. It's a kind of contagious quality he has." Prior to his work with HRC, Solmonese was the chief executive officer of EMILY's List, a PAC dedicated to supporting the election of pro-choice female candidates to all levels of government. From 2006 to 2009 he hosted, with Breslauer, the XM Satellite Radio show* The Agenda with Joe Solmonese, *on which LGBT issues were discussed.*

## EARLY LIFE
One of three children, Joe Solmonese was born on November 27,1964 and grew up in the town of Attleboro, Massachusetts. His parents, both schoolteachers, inspired his interest in politics. In high school he served on the student council and became vice president of his class. He also ran track. Solmonese attended Boston University (BU), where he majored in communications. For several summers during his years there, he worked

as an intern in the scheduling office of then Massachusetts governor Michael Dukakis. Dukakis, the 1988 Democratic presidential nominee, lost to the Republican George H. W. Bush in that year's general election. After graduating with a B.S. degree, in 1987, Solmonese became a fulltime staff member in Dukakis's office. Before leaving his job there, he was invited to a lunch with the governor, who advised him to remain in public service. "He is one of the most honest, decent people I know," Solmonese told *Aucoin* about Dukakis. "There are legions of people in my generation who are still in politics because he didn't just inspire us to stay in public service, he directed us to stay in public service, that was all you were supposed to do."

### LIFE'S WORK

Solmonese came out as gay when he was in his early 20s. His decision to do so coincided with the height of the AIDS (Acquired Immune Deficiency Syndrome) epidemic. A sexually transmitted disease that severely weakens the body's immune system and leaves victims vulnerable to potentially fatal infections, AIDS proved devastating to the gay community. "There is that on your consciousness, and you're coming out," Solmonese told *Aucoin*. "It compounded everything that you experienced coming out." He told *Aucoin* that the AIDS epidemic brought the gay community closer together. In 1990 Solmonese joined the successful reelection campaign of U.S. representative Barney Frank of Massachusetts, one of the first openly gay members of Congress. In that capacity Solmonese learned the basics of campaigning, analyzing polls, building a donor base, finding supporters, and reaching out to voters.

Solmonese next worked as a strategist for a succession of political figures. In 1993 he served as a campaign worker for Dawn Clark Netsch, then a candidate for governor of Illinois. Solmonese was impressed by Netsch's well financed campaign and learned that she had received a substantial amount of funding from EMILY's List. At the time the organization's executive director was Mary Beth Cahill, a former member of the Dukakis campaign, who had persuaded Solmonese to work for Frank; when Cahill learned of Solmonese's interest in EMILY's List, she invited him to join the group as deputy political director. In 1998 he became the group's chief of staff, and in 2003 he was named chief executive officer. "EMILY" is an acronym for "Early Money Is Like Yeast," a reference to the fact that yeast makes bread rise; similarly, early funding of a political campaign raises a candidate's visibility and chances of victory. The organization was founded by 25 women in 1985, at a time when there were few Democratic women in the U.S. House and Senate. The founders, including the current president, Ellen R. Malcolm, set up EMILY's List as a donor network through which members send campaign money to pro-choice candidates selected by the organization. Today EMILY's List boasts more than 100,000 members. According to its website, the organization "is committed to a three-pronged strategy to elect pro-choice Democratic women: recruiting and funding viable women candidates; helping them build and run effective campaign organizations; and mobilizing women voters to help elect progressive candidates across the nation."

Initially, EMILY's List supported only candidates for the U.S. Congress. After Solmonese became chief of staff, the group shifted its approach. In 2000 the number of women serving in state legislatures declined for the first time in 30 years, and EMILY's List responded by launching its Political Opportunity Program (POP), which supports progressive female candidates on the state and local levels. Solmonese told Shaun Bugg for the Washington, D.C., *Metro Weekly* (May 12, 2005, online), "We realized that the work of electing a woman to the United States Senate has to begin long before the 24 month election cycle. So we went about electing women to the state senate or house, or the mayor's office, or the county commission. We strengthened them by building their political operation so that when a U.S. Senate seat opened up the powers that be in that state said ' She's the one who should go.' So when people asked, is that a policy shift? Are you helping women get elected to the state legislature instead of the U.S. Senate?' No. It's just another way of getting women elected to the U.S. Senate."

Solmonese received mixed responses to his work as the CEO of EMILY's List. During his tenure, in which he emphasized outreach to "heartland and mainstream voters," as *Aucoin* reported, membership tripled and fundraising records were broken. In 2003 EMILY's List had two noteworthy victories: Kamala Harris became the first African- American district attorney in California, and Annise Parker was the first openly gay candidate to win a city wide election in Houston, Texas, where she was elected controller. EMILY's List was criticized, however, for supporting the Democrat Inez Tenenbaum for a seat in Congress in 2004 (she lost to the Republican Jim DeMint). Although pro-choice, Tenenbaum was opposed to same-sex marriage, and when EMILY's List recommended her as a choice to its membership, several gay-rights groups objected. In defense of his organization's support of Tenenbaum, Solmonese told Chad Graham for the *advocate.com* (March 10, 2005), "It's Emily's List's mission to elect pro-choice Democratic women. And I had been charged by the 100,000 members of Emily's List to uphold that mission." In 2004 results were mixed for candidates supported by the organization; many lost state Senate races in Florida, South Carolina, and Missouri. Still, out of the 225 candidates the organization endorsed that year, 140 won seats. All of the incumbents backed by the organization won re-election, including the U.S. senators Barbara Boxer of California, Patty Murray of Washington, and Barbara Mikulski of Maryland. Delaware's governor, Ruth Ann Minner, was reelected, and Christine Gregoire was elected to her first term as governor of Washington.

In the spring of 2005, after 12 years with EMILY's List, Solmonese was named president of the Human Rights Campaign, replacing another Massachusetts native, Cheryl Jacques. He took over the group at a tumultuous time in the gay-rights movement, when, as David Crary put it for the *Associated Press* (March 17, 2005), the same-sex-marriage debate rivaled the controversy over abortion "for volatility and virulence." The same-sex marriage debate first came to widespread attention in the U.S. in 1993, with the case of *Baehr v. Lewin*, in which three homosexual couples challenged Hawaii's marriage law. The law had allowed only for heterosexual marriages, but the Supreme Court of Hawaii ruled that a compelling reason was needed to deny the extension of marriage rights to homosexual couples. The Hawaii state legislature soon overruled the court. In 1996 the U.S. Congress passed and President Bill Clinton signed the Defense of Marriage Act, which forbade the federal government from recognizing homosexual unions. In 1998 Clinton signed an executive order banning the federal government from discriminating in employment on the basis of sexual orientation. California passed a domestic partnership policy in 1999, allowing homosexual couples to obtain many of the same benefits as married couples. In 2000 Vermont became the first state to allow civil unions, which grant same-sex partners the full legal benefits of marriage. Three years later the U.S. Supreme Court struck down all remaining laws barring gay sex, which was illegal in 13 states at the time. Massachusetts became the first state to legalize gay marriage, in 2004. Although the California

Supreme Court legalized same-sex marriage in May 2008, the ruling was overturned in November of that year when a majority of California voters favored a ballot measure known as Proposition 8. In 2014, the U.S. Supreme Court struck down a key part of the Defense of Marriage Act and same-sex marriage was allowed to resume in California.

Solmonese assumed his role as president of HRC in April 2005, with a salary of $225,000 per year. He began his tenure by traveling the country to meet with various community and religious leaders, gay and straight, to gauge how people felt about the gay-rights movement and same-sex marriage. He also spoke with corporate leaders from companies including Ford, Sprint, Hallmark, and Coca-Cola. At a news conference in June, Solmonese said of his travels, as quoted by Political Transcript Wire (June 6, 2005), "From Ford in Detroit to Sprint in Kansas City, it was reinforced to me that the American workplace is really a microcosm of America generally, because like no other part of American life, it's in the American workplace where strangers get to know each other and realize that we're united by our shared hopes and dreams and not divided by stereotypes and stigma." He noted that since 2002, when HRC began rating companies based on their LGBT policies, "over 8,000 employers now offer domestic partner benefits. That's a 13 percent increase from [2004]. Eighty-two percent of Fortune 500 companies include sexual orientation in their nondiscrimination policies. That's a 4 percent increase over [2004]." Nonetheless, he conceded that there was still much work to do. A year later Solmonese observed still more progress in HRC's efforts to affect the way corporations treat LGBT employees. He told Bugg in another article for the *Metro Weekly* (March 16, 2006), "A year ago we had 66 companies with a score of 100 [on HRC's corporate index]. This year we gave 104 companies a score of 100. That means that 5.6 million people are now working in a place where [everyone is] treated with the same benefits, same respect, same access to opportunity."

In 2006 HRC and XM Satellite Radio partnered to produce the show *The Agenda with Joe Solmonese,* which featured discussions of politics and culture, interviews with politicians and other celebrity guests, and calls from listeners. "This is a unique opportunity to engage millions of Americans in a real conversation about what it means to be gay, lesbian, bisexual, and transgender today," Solmonese said in a press release published by *PR Newswire* (June 8, 2006). The show was co-hosted by Mary Breslauer, a former HRC board member. Noteworthy guests included Democratic U.S. senator Edward M. Kennedy; Gene Robinson, an openly gay Episcopal bishop; and journalists from the *New York Times* and the *Washington Post*. The show proved so popular that by 2008 it had moved from Channel 120 on XM to Channel 155, a lifestyle XM channel that also features popular shows including *Good Morning America Radio* and *Dr. Laura Schlessinger*. The final installment of *The Agenda* aired on January 22, 2009.

In 2007 Solmonese announced further progress in HRC's work with corporations. "This year, more major American businesses received a perfect rating for equality and fairness than in any other year," he said, as quoted in *Health & Medicine Week* (February 12, 2007). "At an ever increasing pace, corporate executives understand that supporting their gay, lesbian, bisexual, and transgender employees is not only the right thing to do but it is also good for business. The findings in this year's report sends a clear message that the American workplace is rapidly becoming more inclusive of diversity." That year HRC also appointed its first chief diversity officer, Cue Vu, whose mission is to establish relationships with LGBT communities of color; she reports directly to Solmonese. In August 2007 Solmonese served on a panel that questioned that year's Democratic presidential hopefuls on LGBT issues.

HRC suffered a blow in 2007 with regard to legislation targeting hate crimes against gay and transgender individuals, a proposed measure known informally as the Matthew Shepard Hate Crimes Prevention Act. HRC had been lobbying tirelessly for the measure, calling on organization members to encourage their congressional representatives to support it. Democrats in the Senate had hoped to pass the hate-crimes measure by attaching it to the National Defense Authorization Act (NDAA), which President George W. Bush was expected to sign. However, the hate-crimes component was abandoned when House Democrats threatened to vote against the bill because it lent support to Bush's policies regarding the war in Iraq. "Today's decision is deeply disappointing, especially given the historic passage of hate crimes legislation through both Houses of Congress this year," Solmonese said? as quoted by Lou Chibbaro Jr. for the *Washington Blade* (December 6, 2007, on-line). "However, we are not giving up on efforts to find another legislative vehicle, in the second half of this Congress, to move the Matthew Shepard Act." In 2008 President Barack Obama, Bush's successor, pledged to sign the

act if Congress approved it. Congress did so the following year, and on October 28, 2009, Obama signed into law the renamed Matthew Shepard and James Byrd, Jr. Hate Crimes Prevention Act. Named for two victims of separate hate crimes, the act was appended to a $680 billion defense spending bill (which was signed in a separate ceremony).

HRC has received criticism from the transgender community over its reluctance to support a provision for the protection of transgender individuals in the Employment Non-Discrimination Act (ENDA). Although HRC initially said that it would support the ENDA only if it included transgender protections, the organization continued to support the act after those protections were removed in 2007 by Democrats who were concerned that they would hamper ENDA's passage in the House. Solmonese told Cynthia Laird for the *Bay Area Reporter* (January 10, 2008) that HRC continued to support ENDA because abandoning it might have kept the measure from reaching a vote until 2011. "That's how I evaluated it," he said. "We are very much at the beginning of the ENDA process. In spite of all the criticism, we started a process. Now, we build on that in a more expeditious way than if we walked away." The bill has yet to pass the Senate, but if it does, Obama is expected to sign it. HRC has pledged to continue to fight for a bill protecting transgender individuals.

HRC endorsed Obama for president in 2008, citing his commitment to civil rights for the LGBT community. Solmonese said in a press release on the HRC website (June 6, 2008), "Senator Obama has consistently shown that he understands, as we do, that LGBT rights are civil rights, and human rights." Although he does not support same-sex marriage, Obama opposes a constitutional ban on it. He supports civil unions, hate-crimes legislation, the repeal of the military's controversial "Don't Ask, Don't Tell" policy, and expanded funding for HIV/AIDS research. In December 2008, the month after the election, HRC's support for the victorious Obama flagged, when the presidentelect's team announced the selection of Rick Warren, pastor of the Saddleback Church in Lake Forest, California, to give the invocation at the presidential inauguration in January 2009. Warren, a vocal opponent of same-sex marriage, was a supporter of Proposition 8. Although Obama's team also chose the LGBT-friendly Reverend Joseph E. Lowery to close the ceremony, many in the LGBT community were offended. In an opinion piece in the *Washington Post* (December 19, 2008, online),

Solmonese wrote, "It is difficult to comprehend how our president-elect, who has been so spot on in nearly every political move and gesture, could fail to grasp the symbolism of inviting an anti-gay theologian to deliver his inaugural invocation." On December 17 HRC sent a letter to Obama, signed by Solmonese and available on the HRC website, which read, "Our loss in California over the passage of Proposition 8, which stripped loving, committed same-sex couples of their given legal right to marry, is the greatest loss our community has faced in 40 years. And by inviting Rick Warren to your inauguration, you have tarnished the view that gay, lesbian, bisexual and transgender Americans have a place at your table."

Despite his criticism of Obama, Solmonese has continued to support the president and believes he will take the steps necessary to help the LGBT community achieve full equality. In an October 2009 message, Solmonese predicted to HRC supporters that on the last day of the president's term, the LGBT community would be proud of the accomplishments it had made under Obama. Some believed Solmonese meant that the LGBT should be content to wait for change; in response to that charge, Solmonese wrote, in an HRC weekly update on the social media site Facebook (October 18, 2009), "The fact is, we've got an agenda. It includes repealing Don't Ask, Don't Tell, passing an inclusive ENDA (Employment Non-Discrimination Act), repealing DOMA (Defense of Marriage Act), and getting real protections for families and people with HIV/AIDS. How do we make all this happen? We have to pass laws. When it comes to changing the lives of LGBT Americans, that's the name of the game. Whatever the president does or doesn't say, whatever I say and however anyone decides to read it, there is only one way to pass a law: secure a majority of votes in the House and a filibuster-proof 60 votes in the Senate." Solmonese added, correctly predicting that the Matthew Shepard and James Byrd, Jr. Hate Crimes Prevention Act would become law during the Obama administration, "This is a lot easier said than done, but one thing is certain: when an LGBT bill gets to the Oval Office, this president will sign it."

In 2005 Solmonese launched the Religion and Faith Program, which provides resources to religious LGBT individuals. He has overseen the Campaign College program, which selects 40 college age individuals to attend a campaign training seminar in Washington, D.C., and work with the HRC on a campaign. He is also credited with personally overseeing many efforts to support pro-gay congressional candidates, including the Democrat Bob Casey, who defeated the incumbent Republican senator Rick Santorum of Pennsylvania, a particularly outspoken opponent of gay rights, in 2006. HRC raised over $350,000 and committed over 200 volunteers to Casey's campaign.

## PERSONAL LIFE

Solmonese, who lives in Washington, D.C., told Graham about HRC, "You know, in everything that we do, we're working toward marriage. We're working toward equality and marriage. It is a thread that runs through everything that we do."

## FURTHER READING

*Associated Press Online Mar. 17, 2005; Boston Globe Apr. 7, 2005; hrc.org; (Washington, D.C.) Metro Weekly (online) May 12, 2005*

# GEORGE SOROS

## Philanthropist; Financier

**Born:** August 12, 1930; Budapest, Hungary
**Primary Field:** Philanthropy
**Affiliation:** Democratic Party

## INTRODUCTION

*George Soros is widely regarded as one of the most successful investment managers in history. The first American to earn more than $1 billion in one year, his hourly income that year easily surpassed what the average American makes annually, he has accumulated his fortune through management of the Quantum Fund, an offshore investment vehicle that has averaged returns of approximately 35 percent for more than 25 years. So potent is his reputation as a shrewd market analyst that the very disclosure of his investments can create changes in the market as others imitate his investment decisions.*

*If that were all Soros were known for, he would be justly famous, but he has also made a name for himself as a philanthropist and philosopher. A proponent of the philosopher Karl Popper's idea of the "open society," Soros has established, with close to $1.5 billion of his own money, foundations throughout the world to promote Popper's vision of a just society. Much of that money has been spent in the former Soviet bloc to advance democratic reforms. In October 1997, for example, he announced that between 1998 and 2000, he plans to donate up to $500 million to Russia, "to improve health care, expand educational opportunities, and help retrain the military for civilian jobs," as Judith Miller reported in the* New York Times *(October 20, 1997). Miller noted that with that gift, which is to be made through his foundation the Open Society Institute Russia, Soros's presence in Russia will exceed that of the United States, which last year gave that nation $95 million in foreign aid. "He's the only man in the U.S. who has his own foreign policy, and can implement it," Morton Abramowitz, a former American ambassador to Turkey, told Connie Brack for the* New Yorker *(January 23, 1995). More recently, Soros has turned his attention towards the U.S., where he has criticized aspects of capitalism and has supported such causes as prison reform, better care for the dying, and, most controversially, changes in America's drug policies, including the*

*legalization of medicinal marijuana use and the establishment of needle-exchange programs.*

## EARLY LIFE

George Soros was born on August 12, 1930, to Tivadar Soros and Elizabeth Szucs, upper middle class Jews living in Budapest, Hungary. Despite the fact that the family did not embrace their Jewish identity ("My mother was quite anti-Semitic and ashamed of being Jewish," Soros admitted to Connie Brack), they were deeply affected by the advent of World War II and the Holocaust. Hungary's Jewish community of 1 million was one of the last to be touched by the Nazis, who invaded the country in 1944. According to reports, approximately 400,000 Hungarian Jews had perished by the time the war ended, a year later. Soros's father, an attorney, was a pragmatist who had prepared for the arrival of the Germans. He had experienced turmoil before, having been a prisoner during World War I and having witnessed firsthand the Russian Revolution of 1917. Tivadar Soros secured false identity papers for the family, and the young Soros pretended to be "Janos Kis," the son of a Hungarian government official whose job it was to deliver deportation notices to Jews and take possession of their property. Living under the constant threat of being discovered and executed, Soros often accompanied that Hungarian official as he carried out his work.

Surprisingly, Soros has described that period of his life in positive terms. "In many ways it was the happiest year of my life," he told Michael Lewis for the *New Republic* (January 10 & 17, 1994). "It was dangerous and exciting. It made me a bit of a risk taker. And I got to see my father at his very best." Also surprising, perhaps, is the fact that Soros came away from that experience suspicious of Jewish identity. In an incident that he recounted to Michael Lewis, Soros remembered that at one point, the Jewish Council asked him and other children to hand out deportation notices. The notices turned out to be lists of people slated to be executed. The fact that many Jews willingly followed the Jewish Council's directive made Soros wary of the power of all ethnic and religious affiliations.

The family survived the Nazi occupation intact, and Soros said later that the survival skills he learned as a 14 year old helped him as an investor. In 1947, he left his home country, which was by that time under Soviet control, and moved to London. Lonely and poor, he later described this period as being much more difficult than his World War II experience. He enrolled at the London School of Economics (LSE) and supported himself by working a number of part-time jobs, one of which was as a waiter at Quaglino's, where he often ate the leftovers of the restaurant's rich patrons.

Soros thought he might become another John Maynard Keynes or Albert Einstein. According to Brack, he considered the prospect of becoming a mere financial operator beneath him. At the LSE, he was influenced by the theories of Karl Popper, who argued that both fascist and communist regimes were "closed societies" in which elites regarded themselves as the sole possessors of the truth. Popper contrasted such societies with "open societies" where people realized that human knowledge could be fallible and where institutions existed to encourage argument and debate.

## LIFE'S WORK

In 1952, Soros graduated from the LSE. His diploma had no immediate value, and he started working as a handbag and jewelry salesman in Blackpool, a British seaside resort. He eventually landed a job as a trainee at Singer and Friedlander, a British investment bank, where he gained in-depth exposure to the operation of the stock market for the first time. In 1956, he emigrated to the U.S., and over the next decade, he worked as an arbitrage trader for various firms, among them F. M. Mayer, Wertheim & Co., and Arnhold & S. Bleichroeder. Fluent in French and German, he specialized in foreign securities, a relatively new field at the time. During this period he continued his philosophical reflections by attempting to write an essay, "The Burden of Consciousness," dealing with open and closed societies. In 1961, he became a naturalized American citizen and married Annaliese Witschak.

In 1969, Soros and a partner, Jim Rogers, started a hedge fund with several million dollars raised from private investors, primarily wealthy European clients. The fund was called Quantum, a reference to the revolution in quantum mechanics sparked by Werner Heisenberg's indeterminacy principle. The fund was based in Curaqao, in the Netherlands Antilles, and thus was not subject to the stringent regulations that applied to United States based public investment companies. Hedge fund managers typically employ more risky financial techniques than do mutual and pension fund managers. One of these is leveraging, in which a large percentage of one's investment consists of borrowed money; another

is shorting, in which one sells securities or currencies one does not yet own, hoping that by the day the security or currency has to be delivered to the buyer, its purchase price will have dropped. Hedge funds are more likely to use options, futures, and other derivatives, as well as to employ a "macro" approach to investing, in which one bets not on individual companies but on currencies, interest rates, and other financial barometers.

It was through his hedge fund, and his prescient bets on the prices of everything from cosmetics to laser-guided missiles, that Soros made a name for himself. Quantum is generally recognized as the most successful hedge fund ever operated. Ten thousand dollars invested in 1969 would be worth $21 million in 1994. The fund is limited to wealthy investors who (with the sole exception of Soros) live outside the United States and who pay very high premiums. Since the investors' profits are not taxed until money is repatriated, the fund effectively serves as a tax shelter. Today, Quantum, along with several subsidiary funds, has over $11 billion in assets.

One of Soros's more spectacular financial coups occurred in September 1992, when he bet $10 billion against the value of the British pound. Under the European Exchange Rate Mechanism (ERM), several European currencies are supposed to have a relatively fixed value in relation to each other. One key to maintaining the fixed value and preventing currency speculation is keeping interest rates at the same level in each country. Soros reasoned that individual countries would not adjust their interest rates, and hurt their own economy, to preserve the ERM. After analyzing events in Germany and England and determining that the British pound was overvalued relative to the German deutschmark, Soros made a series of complex bets and investments based on his prediction that the pound would have to be devalued. His prediction turned out to be correct, and the Bank of England was forced to withdraw the pound from the ERM. According to various accounts, Soros made between $1 billion and $2 billion on "Black Wednesday," the day he "broke the Bank of England," as the London press put it. Seemingly unfazed, Soros maintained that his gamble, involving approximately $10 billion, was actually a low risk.

While that event made Soros's reputation, his losses have been just as colossal. For instance, he was the biggest individual loser in the stock market crash of 1987. Although he claimed to have predicted the crash, he thought it would hit Japan instead of the United States first. He converted his Japanese assets into American assets, and when the crash hit the U.S. first, he ended up losing $800 million. On February 14,1994,he suffered another staggering loss, $600 million, by betting the wrong way on the Japanese yen. Soros, quick to defend his notion of "fallibility," has claimed that he, like any other money manager, has imperfect knowledge and that losses like these are inevitable; what is more important is minimizing losses and maximizing gains.

In explaining his success, Soros has claimed that the theory of "reflexivity " has helped him analyze the market. According to the theory, which he wrote about in his book *The Alchemy of Finance* (1987), perceptions affect events and events in turn affect perceptions; there is no truly objective measure of how things "really" should be. As a result, markets do not tend toward equilibrium but are instead prone to wild fluctuation as misperceptions build upon misperceptions. Hence, investors can make lots of money on both overvalued and undervalued stocks and commodities. Soros is not the first to have realized this "boom/bust" cycle of the market, though, and many have commented that his theory still does not precisely explain how he has been so successful. Soros, perhaps understandably, has remained elusive. "I have often done the right thing for the wrong reason," he told Michael Lewis. In the same interview, he said one of his guiding maxims has been to "invest first and investigate later."

More helpful in explaining Soros's success may be his worldwide network of contacts, which, an unnamed observer told Bruck, once allowed Soros to pull out of the Japanese market right before the U.S. government enforced trade restrictions on the country. "George has transactional relationships," Byron Wein of Morgan Stanley told Bruck. "People get something from him, he from them." Another factor to take into consideration is whether or not he has engaged in illegal manipulation of the market. In 1977, he was charged with stock manipulation, following a public offering of shares from the Computer Sciences Corporation. He eventually signed a consent decree neither admitting nor denying guilt, and settled a $1 million suit with Fletcher Jones Foundation, which had sued him because of the stock's decline in value. In 1994, a U.S. congressional hearing determined that hedge funds like Soros lacked the ability to manipulate markets.

Soros's success in financial speculation has allowed him to display considerable generosity in many well publicized philanthropic projects. Initially, though, he had difficulty determining what causes to support,

as he did not feel he could claim an American, Jewish, or Hungarian identity. Soros decided that the one thing he did care about was Popper's "open society," a universalistic concept that transcends particular identities. In 1979, he set up the Open Society Fund, with the objective of using well-placed grant money to help "closed" societies become more "open." He gave some money to South Africa for educational scholarships, but pulled out after deciding that he wasn't having enough impact. He then created foundations in Hungary, in 1984; China, in 1986; the Soviet Union, in 1987; and Poland, in 1988. Critical of most philanthropic foundations, which, to him, seemed more intent on gratifying the giver than aiding the receiver, Soros declared that his foundations would be different: They would operate with minimal bureaucracy and oversight from Soros. Between 1984 and 1989, he gave approximately $30 million, most of which was spent on photocopying machines, travel grants, theaters, filmmaking, sociological research, newspapers, and magazines, seemingly innocuous things that might promote the spread of democratic ideas and institutions.

Soros's increased involvement in philanthropic activities may stem in part from a midlife crisis he experienced between 1979 and 1982, a period during which he questioned what he was going to do with all the money he had earned. "It was a very simple quandary: Am I the slave of my own success, or am I the master of my own destiny?" he told Christian Tyler for the *Financial Times* (January 23,1993). "It really was a struggle between me as a person and my fund as an organization. It was a struggle that I won and that my fund actually lost." The year 1981 was the worst for Quantum, when it suffered its only negative return ever. That same year, Jim Rogers left the company, and Soros underwent a divorce. In a self-destructive move, he openly questioned his abilities and encouraged investors to pull out of the Quantum fund; in response, investors actually withdrew one-third of Quantum's funds. Soros eventually rebounded, making Quantum profitable again, and in 1983 he married Susan Weber, an art historian 25 years his junior.

In 1989, Soros distanced himself even further from the daily activities of investing by assigning management of the Quantum Fund to Stanley Druckenmiller. Devoting most of his energy to his philanthropy, Soros continued to establish foundations all over the world. In December 1992, just three months after "Black Wednesday," he announced some of his most ambitious

charitable projects to that date. He made direct donations and promises of $50 million in humanitarian aid
to Bosnia. He contributed $250 million to the Central
European University, which he had established in Budapest and Prague in 1990 and which by 1993 had 400
students from over 22 countries. Soros donated another
$250 million to aid humanities education in Russia, and
another $100 million went to the International Science
Foundation, established in 1992 by Soros to help scientists in the former Soviet Union continue their research.

By the end of 1996, Soros had given away close to
$1.5 billion of his money, and had established founda-
tions in approximately 30 countries. He had also written three books, *Opening the Soviet System* (1990), *Underwriting Democracy* (1991), and his autobiography,
*Soros on Soros: Staying Ahead of the Curve* (1995), to
help explain the philosophy behind his philanthropy.
While many people are still skeptical of his ideas (he
was unable, for instance, to convince Western countries
to launch a new Marshall Plan for post-Communist
countries), his reputation as the "man who broke the
Bank of England" has made it easier for him to gain
access to world leaders and convince them of the merits
of his agenda. In Ukraine, for example, Soros proved instrumental in securing an International Monetary Fund
(IMF) loan of $4 billion for the country in exchange
for economic reforms. "If this isn't meddling in the
affairs of a foreign nation, I don't know what is!" he
proclaimed to Brack. "I look at Ukraine with the same
frame of mind as I look at REITs [real estate investment
trusts]. By my intervention, I make it happen!"

Not all commentators have viewed Soros's largesse
sympathetically. There has been some concern about
possible conflict of interest between his foundations
and investments made by the Quantum Fund. Before
1994, Soros had been able to allay such criticisms by
voluntarily recusing himself from making financial investments in any country where a foundation existed.
In 1994, he suddenly reversed his position, maintaining
that conflict of interest was no longer an issue, because
the foundations were autonomous organizations.
Conflict of interest is not the only reason that some
people have criticized Soros's philanthropy. In Albania,
Kyrgyzstan, Croatia, Serbia, and Belarus, his foundations have come under attack by government leaders
who accuse them of fomenting dissent; the foundation in
Belarus was actually forced to shut down in September
1997. Other commentators worry about whether Soros
is equipped to handle the delicate diplomatic situations

that arise through his foundation work. "Soros, unsur-
prisingly, is to a considerable degree a creature of his
experience in the markets: idiosyncratic, intuitive, prone
to quick judgments often based on scanty information,
aggressive, manipulative, so self-reliant that he trusts no
one's judgment but his own—a profile, in sum, hardly
suggestive of a diplomat," Connie Brack wrote, citing
the example of Macedonia, where Soros's support of the
Kiro Gligorov government may have strained relations
between that country and Greece. (Brack also noted that
in 1987 the U.S. government was able, through new legislation, to tax Soros's Quantum Fund profits. Soros's
increased tax burden may have prompted him to be
more generous in his philanthropy.)

Soros has recently turned critical attention toward
the West. "Although I have made a fortune in the financial markets, I now fear that the untrammeled intensifi-
cation of laissez-faire capitalism and the spread of market values into all areas of life is endangering our open
and democratic society," Soros wrote in the *Atlantic
Monthly* (February 1997), "I contend that an open society may also be threatened from the opposite direction,
from excessive individualism. Too much competition
and too little cooperation can cause intolerable inequities and instability." Soros noted that the idea that individuals pursuing their own interests leads to the most
just distribution of resources loses credibility because
individuals have imperfect knowledge (fallibility), and
since imperfect knowledge affects events and vice versa
(reflexivity).

Soros's philanthropic projects in the United States
include the Emma Lazarus Fund, which provides assistance to legal immigrants who were denied government assistance as a result of the 1996 welfare reform
act; the Project on Death in America, which works to
enhance the comfort, dignity, and care of the dying (a
project inspired in part by his own experiences dealing
with his father's death, in 1968, and his mother's death,
in 1994); the Center on Crime, Communities, and Culture, which seeks to promote alternatives to incarceration; and, perhaps most controversially, the Lindesmith
Center, a research institute that seeks to develop alternative drug policies. Soros, who believes that the current
"war on drugs" is misguided, gave $1 million in 1996
to promote successful ballot initiatives in California
and Arizona to legalize medicinal marijuana use. He
has also given $1 million to support needle-exchange
programs. While many people have been outraged at
what they perceive as his encouragement of drug use,

he denies that his activities amount to encouragement. Far from believing that all drug use should be legalized, Soros believes that treatment, rather than incarceration, should be the appropriate response regarding the use of certain drugs. In the case of needle-exchange programs, he cites studies that show that such programs decrease the transmission of the AIDS virus and do not encourage drug use.

Soros's dual career as an ultra-rich financier and philanthropist has provoked varied opinion. To his supporters, he is the personification of the American dream and living proof that the pursuit of profit and beneficent intentions can go together. "[He is] a national resource, indeed, a national treasure," Strobe Talbott, the deputy secretary of state, told Connie Brack. To his detractors, on the other hand, he is a greedy financial speculator who does not so much invest in businesses as take advantage of short-term market fluctuations, heedless of the havoc he may wreak on world financial markets. Soros's critics range from leaders in post-Communist countries who believe he encourages dissent, to intellectuals in the U.S. who believe his recent critiques of capitalism are muddled and naive. But perhaps the harshest critic of Soros is Soros himself, who has admitted to harboring delusions of grandeur. "If the truth be known," Soros wrote in his book *Underwriting Democracy* [ 1991), "I carried some rather potent messianic fantasies with me from childhood which I felt I had to control, otherwise they might get me into trouble."

## PERSONAL LIFE

When he is not making millions or dining with heads of state, Soros enjoys the company of people with whom he can debate philosophy or play chess. These include the Polish intellectual Adam Michnik; the Hungarian economist Marton Tardos; and the Harvard economist Jeffrey Sachs. Soros has homes in London, New York City, and Southampton, on New York's Long Island. His wife is the founder and director of the Bard Graduate Center for Studies in the Decorative Arts, which opened in 1993. Soros has three children from his first marriage and two from his second.

## FURTHER READING

*The Alchemy of Finance; Opening the Soviet System; Underwriting Democracy*

# GLORIA STEINEM

## Writer; Political Activist

**Born:** March 25, 1934; Toledo, Ohio
**Primary Field:** Feminism

### INTRODUCTION

*Once considered a cultural lightweight, or the "pinup girl of the intelligentsia," as she was called in the late 1960s, Gloria Steinem has become part of the American political landscape. A founding editor of the journalistic linchpin of the American feminist movement,* Ms. *magazine, Gloria Steinem has been a symbol of women's liberation for more than fifteen years, continuing to pursue her original career as a journalist and working tirelessly as a political organizer. Although some younger women might now view her as an anachronism, for Gloria Steinem "there is nothing outside of [the movement]." "I once thought I would do this for two or three years and then go home to my real life," she has recalled. "But that was a symptom of the movement's tone at the time, which was, 'Surely, if we just explain to everybody how unjust this is, they will want to fix it.'"*

### EARLY LIFE

The second of the two daughters of Ruth (Nunevillar) Steinem and Leo Steinem, Gloria Steinem was born on March 25, 1934 in Toledo, Ohio. Her father, who died in 1962, was Jewish, and her mother, who died shortly before she would have turned eighty-two, in 1980, was a Theosophist of French Huguenot descent. Gloria Steinem is a full decade younger than her sister, Susanne (Steinem) Patch. Ms. Steinem's paternal grandmother, Pauline (Mrs. Joseph) Steinem, was a proto-feminist who served as president of the Ohio Women's Suffrage Association from 1908 to 1911 and was one of the two United States delegates to the 1908 meeting of the International Council of Women.

As Gloria Steinem herself described him, her charming, free-spirited father was "a truly American character." A former antiques dealer and summer resort operator, he prided himself on never wearing a hat and never working for anyone, and he was chronically out of money, "He was always going to make a movie, or cut a record, or start a new hotel, or come up with a new orange drink," Ms. Steinem has recalled. In a *Washington Post* profile (October 12, 1983), Elisabeth Bumiller wrote that Gloria Steinem spent "a lot of her childhood

*Gloria Steinem.*

Ms. Foundation for Women

in a household finance office, waiting for her father and yet another loan." Nevertheless, she remembers Leo Steinem as "a sentimental, kind, childlike man." "He was wonderful," she told Elisabeth Bumiller, "because it was like having a friend your own age. We'd go to the movies. He wasn't like a father."

Gloria Steinem's early years were spent traveling around the country in a house trailer while her itinerant father tried to make a living. In about 1946 Leo and Ruth Steinem were divorced, and Gloria went to live with her mother in Toledo. There, they settled into a rat-infested basement apartment in an East Toledo slum neighborhood, and Gloria began to attend school on a regular basis for the first time. Although Ruth Steinem had been a capable woman, a graduate of Oberlin College who had given up a career in journalism when she got married, she suffered her first nervous breakdown before Gloria was born. Crippled by recurrent bouts of anxiety and depression, she was unable to work; Susanne was living in another city, leaving Gloria to become her mother's sole caretaker.

## LIFE'S WORK

Gloria Steinem has been chastised for criticizing certain aspects of the traditional role of motherhood when she herself has never expressed any regret about not having children. But as she explained to Elisabeth Bumiller, "It may be true that since I had taken care of my mother for so many years that I felt I had done that already. I had already fed and looked after and nurtured another human being." "She was just a fact of life when I was growing up," Ms. Steinem wrote in "Ruth's Song [Because She Could Not Sing It]," her moving article about her mother; "someone to be worried about and cared for; an invalid who lay in bed with eyes closed and lips moving in occasional response to voices only she could hear; a woman to whom I brought an endless stream of toast and coffee, bologna sandwiches and dime pies, in a child's version of what meals should be. She was a loving, intelligent, terrorized woman. . .

To escape the dreariness and pain of her life at home, Gloria fantasized that she had been adopted and that her real parents would come and take her away. Her imaginary mother and father were calm, cheerful, and "uripoor," or as she told an interviewer from the *Chicago Tribune* (October 2, 1983], "just your stock central casting parents." Dreaming of someday tap-dancing her way out of Toledo, the teenaged girl danced at the local Elks Club, entered amateur-night competitions, and even won a local TV talent contest. It was not until her senior year of high school, when she moved to Washington, D.C., to live with her sister, that she left Toledo behind. In 1952 she applied to Smith College. Her grades were not high, but she was admitted on the strength of her scores on the entrance examinations.

Free of distractions in her Personal Life, she excelled academically, winning scholarships, gaining election to Phi Beta Kappa, spending her junior year in Geneva, Switzerland, and graduating magna cum laude in 1956, with a major in government. "I loved Smith," she remarked in a *Publishers Weekly* interview (August 12, 1983). "I couldn't understand women who were not happy there. They gave you three meals a day to eat, and all the books you wanted to read—what more could you want?" Following graduation, she went to India on a Chester Bowles Asian fellowship to study at the universities of Delhi and Calcutta. Subjected to course work that she considered "pointless," she joined the "Radical Humanist" group and traveled throughout southern India during a period of convulsive social unrest. At that time she began to publish freelance articles in Indian newspapers and also wrote a guide book, *A Thousand Indias*, for the government in New Delhi.

Returning to the United States in 1958, Ms. Steinem looked unsuccessfully for a reporting job in New York City. She eventually settled in Cambridge, Massachusetts, where she became codirector of the Independent Research Service, an offshoot of the politically liberal National Student Association, which in the 1960s was revealed to have been substantially funded by the CIA. One of her responsibilities was to recruit American students to attend Communist youth festivals in Europe. In later years some of her political opponents on the left later tried to smear her for having been a "CIA agent," a charge that she vehemently denied.

Still determined to become a journalist, Gloria Steinem moved to New York City in 1960, where she landed a job with *Help!*, the cartoonist Harvey Kurtzman's magazine of political satire, as a writer of photo captions and as a liaison with the celebrities chosen to appear on its covers. As Kurtzman told a *Washington Post* interviewer (October 12, 1983), "She would just pick up the phone and talk to people, and charm them out of the trees.... I was probably in love with her back then, just like everyone else." She gained modest recognition for her first published article, a 1962 piece on the sexual revolution for *Esquire* magazine called "The Moral Disarmament of Betty Coed." One of her observations was especially prescient, since it anticipated a contradiction that the women's movement would later have to address. "The real danger of the contraceptive revolution," she wrote, "may be the acceleration of woman's role-change without any corresponding change of man's attitude toward her role."

In 1963 Ms. Steinem published "I was a Playboy Bunny," a dryly witty expose for the now defunct *Show* magazine about her experiences while working undercover as a bushy-tailed, scantily clad waitress at Hugh Hefner's Playboy Club in midtown Manhattan. Her byline began to appear frequently on feature articles for such magazines as *Vogue, Glamour, McCall's,* and *Cosmopolitan*. In the middle of the decade of radical chic, Gloria Steinem herself became a minor celebrity. She championed the "right" causes and was seen at all the "right" places with the "right" men* including such companions as Ted Sorenson, Mike Nichols, and John Kenneth Galbraith. It was with one of her trendy friends, the film director and screenwriter Robert Benton, who was then an art director for *Esquire*, that She collaborated td produce *The Beach Book* (Viking, 1963), a coffee-table picture book dedicated to the frivolous art of basking in the sun. During the television season of 1964-65, she worked as a scriptwriter for *That Was the Week That Was*, the highly regarded show of topical satire that was aired by the NBC TV network.

In 1968 Gloria Steinem made the transition from writing about glitzy celebrities and sun-drenched beaches to chronicling the grittier realities of the political scene when the publisher Clay S. Felker assigned her a weekly column, "The City Politic," in his recently launched venture, *New York* magazine. Combining advocacy journalism with political activism, she accompanied Cesar Chavez on his Poor People's March in California; Served as treasurer for the Committee for the Legal Defense of Angela Davis; supported Eugene McCarthy's insurgent campaign for the Democratic presidential nomination in 1968, though she later switched her allegiance to Robert F. Kennedy; and backed Norman Mailer in his quixotic run for the mayoralty of New York City.

Despite her involvement in those causes, the mainstream media still tended to regard Ms. Steinem as the Hildy Johnson of Manhattan political and journalistic circles—intriguing and smart but in the end frivolously marginal. For instance, in 1969 a *Time* magazine scribe patronizingly called her "one of the best dates to take to a New York party these days . . . , a trim, undeniably female, blonde-streaked brunette. . . . She does something for her soft suits and clinging dresses, has legs worthy of her miniskirts, and a brain that keeps conversation lively without getting tricky." According to Elisabeth Bumiller, Ms. Steinem "prefers to remember her prefeminist life as more schizophrenic than trendy."

Gloria Steinem was joked into feminism in November 1968, when she attended a meeting called by the Redstockings, a radical women's group. To protest an official state hearing on New York's abortion laws, the Redstockings had asked women to discuss the illegal abortions to which they had been forced to resort. "I had had an abortion when I was newly out of college and told no one," Ms. Steinem recalled in her talk with .Miriam Berkley for *Publishers Weekly*. "If one in three adult women shares this experience, why should each of us be made to feel criminal and alone?" And as she has written, "Suddenly, I was no longer learning intellectually what was wrong. I knew." Ms. Steinem's resulting article was "After Black Power, Women's Liberation," her first openly feminist essay. At that time she began to reconsider her "own capitulation to all the small humiliations" and to read "every piece of feminist writing [she] could lay [her] hands on."

With her ability to articulate the goals of the women's movement, her glamour, and her trenchant sense of humor, Gloria Steinem quickly became one of feminism's "superstars." She became popular on the lecture circuit and on TV talk shows, even though she suffered from what she termed "an almost pathological fear of speaking in public," which she has since overcome. More important, she did not appear to possess the feminist rage that discomfited unradicalized men and women. As Clay S. Felker observed, "Some women come into my office armed with their new philosophy and they radiate hostility. Gloria brings the good news that it's going to make your life better."

In matters of political organization, by July 1971 Gloria Steinem had joined with Betty Friedan, Bella Abzug, and Congresswoman Shirley Chisholm to found the National Women's Political Caucus (NWPC), which encouraged women to run for political office. She had also helped to establish the Women's Action Alliance, a tax-exempt organization geared for mobilizing nonwhite, non-middle- class women and men to combat social and economic forms of discrimination. It was also in 1971 that Ms. Steinem had begun to explore the possibility of creating anew kind of magazine for women, one that would reflect the emerging feminist consciousness and be fully owned, operated, and edited by women, With the initial financial and promotional help of Clay S. Felker, Ms. Steinem, as editor, and Pat Carbine, as editor in chief and publisher, produced Ms., a thirty-page sample magazine that appeared as an insert of the December 1971 issue of *New York*.

The first complete issue of *Ms.*, financed and promoted by *New Yor*k magazine, hit the newsstands in January of 1972 and was labeled the "Spring" edition because the staff did not know when or how the next issue would be published. However, that issue, which included a full-page petition for safe and legal abortions signed by over fifty prominent women who had had abortions, including Gloria Steinem, sold out its first 300,000 copies in eight days. Financed by a Warner Communications investment of $1 million, Ms. became a monthly magazine in the summer of 1972, Featuring early articles with titles like "Why Women Fear Success," "Down With Sexist Upbringing," and "Can Women Love Women?" Ms. had attracted a monthly following of some 500,000 readers by the mid-1970s.

When the Equal Rights Amendment passed Congress in 1972, Ms. Steinem, like most feminist leaders, took to the hustings and lobbied with state legislators throughout the country for its passage. The ERA was never ratified, but even before its defeat the women's movement had gone through a period of ideological strife and internecine warfare. As the former *New York Times* editor A. M. Rosenthal has noted, the feminist movement "is not played with bean bags." Some Marxist and lesbian sects on its left wing repudiated the whole idea of "equal rights" and middle-class feminist assimilation, vilifying Ms. Steinem and her magazine as mouthpieces for "backsliding bourgeois feminism." The Redstockings, in particular, singled out Ms. Steinem for attack, dredging up the pseudo-issue of her past involvement with an organization that had been funded covertly by the QIA. The campaign, to ostracize, Gloria Steinem from the women's movement because of her alleged former ties to the CIA reached a crescendo when a *Village Voice* columnist, writing in the May 21,1979 issue, darkly hinted that she might have prevailed upon Random House to delete a chapter entitled "Gloria Steinem and the CIA" from *The Feminist Revolution*, a collection of essays by writers affiliated with the Redstockings, Steinem's denials of complicity in CIA chicanery were eventually accepted as truthful, but the "Steinem controversy" prompted the seminal contemporary American feminist, Betty Friedan, to offer her faint praise, saying, "Gloria's contribution was welcome and good, although it's not part of the mainstream of the movement."

While continuing to edit Ms., Gloria Steinem was one of the commissioners appointed in 1977 by President Jimmy Garter to the National Committee on the Observance of International Women's Year (IWY), That same year she was also awarded a Woodrow Wilson Scholarship to study feminist theory at the Woodrow Wilson International Center for Scholars. Giving generously of her time to progressive political organizations, Ms. Steinem has quipped that if her fate was to become a dispossessed woman, she would survive—by "organizing the other bag ladies." Since the mid- 1970s, she has participated in the founding of such groups as the Coalition of Labor Union Women, Voters for Choice, Women Against Pornography, and Women USA.

In the 1980s the contemporary feminist movement entered its third decade, and as the "second stage" of the movement has put forward its agenda for reform, Ms. Steinem is still a role model for young women, a kind of "adventurous aunt who inspires others to follow her off the high diving board," as Newsweek (June 4, 1984) put it. Gloria Steinem agrees with the thinker Rollo May that there are three historical stages—the formation of a myth, its period of social authority, and its dissolution—and she believes that in the current era old myths about women and men are breaking down. The newly emerging values, she insists, will be more humanistic. "The goal now is to complete ourselves," she told *Esquire.* "Progress for women lies in becoming more assertive, more ambitious* more able to deal with conflict. . . . Progress for men will lie in becoming more empathetic, more compassionate, more comfortable working inside the home. . . . We're not trading places. We're just completing ourselves." According to Ms. Steinem, the groundwork for social change was laid in the past two decades, but in feminism's second stage, structural innovations will be emphasized. "We accept the idea of equal pay; we don't have the reality of equal pay," she said in the *Esquire* interview. "We accept the idea of equal parenthood; we don't have the possibility of equal parenthood as a real choice. We don't even have parental leave instead of just maternity leave, much less the chance of a shorter workday or week for both parents.

Gloria Steinem continues to believe fervently that when the goals of women's liberation are realized, men will at last "have the opportunity to become whole people." However, the movement has thus far failed to "establish the principle that men should do 'women's jobs,'" as Ms. Steinem has asserted. Consequently, until men begin to take equal responsibility for child rearing, she fears that social patterns of authority will go unchanged. "Until men raise infants and children as much as women do," she has explained, "we—men and women—will all grow up fearing the power of women as the overwhelming, visceral, and irrational experience associated with childhood. And thus we will all define growing up as growing away from women." Ms. Steinem has promised that the movement will now begin to emphasize reproductive rights—the right to have children, the right to have an abortion, and the right to engage in homoerotic partnerships. As she told *Esquire*, "No longer will sex be seen as only a way of having children, which is the stand taken by the Moral Majority." One of the recent myths that Gloria Steinem has been at pains to debunk is that of the overachieving superwoman, the idea, often promoted in women's magazines, that says, as Ms. Steinem paraphrased it in *People* magazine (June 23, 1980), "Yes, you can be a nuclear physicist or a plumber providing you have three charming children, are a gourmet cook and the perfect wife." She views that myth as "ridiculous" and beneficial only to conservative men, who do not want the basic order of things to be disturbed.

In 1983 Gloria Steinem published *Outrageous Acts and Everyday Rebellions* (Holt), a collection of essays, magazine articles, and diary jottings that she had written over two decades. The book included "I Was a Playboy Bunny" and the acclaimed "Ruth's Song" as well as articles on "sisters" as diverse as Marilyn Monroe, Patricia Nixon, Linda Lovelace, and Jacqueline Onassis. In the *New York Times Book Review* (September 4, 1983), Diane Johnson asserted that "one is struck by [the] intelligence, restraint and common sense [of her essays], as well as by the energetic and involved life they reflect." But in the *Washington Post Book World* (October 9, 1983), Angela Carter complained that "there is, throughout the essays, a curious blindness to history— to the economic forces that created the conditions for the emancipation of women in industrialized countries in the nineteenth century, and the way those same forces have determined the nature of the struggle since then."

Collaborating with the photographer George Barris, in 1986 Ms. Steinem published *Marilyn* (Holt), a biography of the late film star Marilyn Monroe. While writing it, she felt "empathy arid connected" to the motion picture sex goddess: "The things that happened to her were things the women's movement has tried to prevent." In the *New York Times Book Review* (December 21,1986), Diana Trilling called *Marilyn* "a quiet" and "well-researched" book, having "none of the sensationalism that has colored other purportedly serious books about the film star, Norman Mailer's in particular." Gloria Steinem is also the author of the Introduction to *The Decade of Women* (Putnam, 1980), a collection of photographs with news bulletins and text celebrating events in recent feminist history. Her "I Was a Playboy Bunny" article served as the basis for *A Bunny's Tale,* a made-for- TV movie broadcast in 1985 over the ABC network. Although she was offended by the smarmy pun of the show's title, she approved of the script and the casting of actress Kirstie Alley as the young Gloria Steinem.

In 1987, the fifteenth anniversary of Ms., the magazine was sold to John Fairfax, Ltd., a large Australian communications conglomerate, for an undisclosed price rumored to be in the neighborhood of $15 million. Since 1979, Ms. had been operated as a tax-exempt foundation,

and in recent years the monthly readership has tapered off to about 480,000, 10 percent of whom are men. Ms. has "suffered from operating losses and from a decline in advertising pages as a growing number of [women's] publications began to address the subjects on which it was a pioneer," according to a report in the *New York Times* (September 24,1987). Gloria Steinem and Patricia Carbine did not profit directly from the magazine's sale, but each will be paid about $200,000 to serve for five years as consultants to Ms., which will continue to espouse the philosophy of the feminist cause. However, in the aftermath of an internal takeover that left Fairfax Publications in the control of politically conservative owners, the conglomerate announced in 1988 that Ms. would be sold, leaving the magazine's future in doubt.

Although she celebrated her fiftieth birthday in 1984, Gloria Steinem is still chic, glamorous, and enviably svelte. She told *People* (November 21, 1983) that she has not "faced the inevitable problem of age yet." "I've never been in a hospital," Gloria Steinem remarked, "and I have more energy than over," She has admitted to being a "sugar junkie," but manages to stay in trim without strenuous dieting or following an exercise regimen, although she walks u lot and loves to go dancing. "If I look good," she told *People*, "it's probably genes, plus the gift of having work that I care about. Women who have mental stimulation every day actually age up to ten years Jess, physiologically, than more isolated women do. . . . Revolution may keep us young."

## PERSONAL LIFE

In a culture besotted with celebrities and celebrity-watchers, Gloria Steinem maintains a very high profile. Nonetheless, she is reluctant to disclose the intimate details of her Personal Life. "It's a tremendous feat . . . wrote Garrison Keillor in the *Washington Post Book World* (September 19, 1983), "a decade of chastity in the face of seductive attention, a refusal to chit-chat or to let us in on her life, her romances. ... Not only does she not say, she makes no great show of not saying. She simply speaks her piece in behalf of women, and moves on." Although always on the go, she seems to keep her day-to-day routine simple. "I never saved a penny until this year," she told *People* in 1983, "and I've never owned a car. My only property is a two- room apartment." It is unlikely that she will ever settle into marriage, for as Ms. Steinem has said, she cannot "mate in captivity." Ms. Steinem signed lucrative contracts with Random House, to write a book about women born into families of inherited wealth, and with Little, Brown, to write *The Bedside Book of Self-Esteem*. She has also been hired by Random House as a contributing editor, with responsibilities in the areas of book acquisition, editorial policy, and marketing.

## FURTHER READING

*Chicago Tribune XV pl+ 0 2 '83 pors; Christian Sci Mon p21+ Mr 16 '84 pors, p29+ fe 30 '87 por; N Y Newsday II p3 fa 13 '88 por; New York 19:50+ Ag 25 '86; People 13:30+ fe 23 '80 pors; Who's Who in America, 1988-89*

# SANDRA STEINGRABER

## Biologist; Writer; Environmental Activist

**Born:** August 27, 1959; Champaign, Illinois
**Primary Field:** Environmental Activism
**Affiliation:** Reproductive Health

## INTRODUCTION

*"You can drink filtered water, but taking a ten minute shower is the equivalent of drinking a halfgallon of tap water,"* Sandra Steingraber told Karen Lindsey for Ms. Magazine *(January/February 1998). "You can eat organic vegetables, but the dioxin that gets into the air from incinerators is going to fall on organic as well as conventionally grown foods. We're not going to shop our way out of this crisis."* The crisis Steingraber referred to is the huge number and volume of toxins polluting the environment, substances linked to manufacturing, the use of pesticides, dry cleaning, and other human activities; many scientific studies have linked these toxins, which humans absorb through the air, water, food, and other products, to birth defects and a growing incidence of cancer and other serious diseases. Steingraber, a biologist, nonfiction writer, and poet, became interested in the links between environmental degradation and illness when she was diagnosed with bladder cancer at the age of 20. For many years she has fought to prevent the release into the environment of chemicals that may cause cancer. She is the author of two influential books, *Living Downstream: An Ecologist Looks at Cancer and the Environment* and *Having Faith: An Ecologist's Journey to Motherhood,* in which she described her battle against cancer and her first pregnancy, respectively. In both books she also offered discussions of toxins that she believes contributed to her disease. Steingraber has often urged parents, particularly mothers, to get involved in the environmental movement in order to protect their children. *"I see no real distinctions between my responsibilities as a mother and my work as*

*an environmental scientist and activist: I'm trying to keep my son and daughter, and the sons and daughters that they someday might want to have, safe from harm,"* she told an interviewer for the Organic Trade Association's *O'Mama Report (2002, online). "Just as I need to know about car seat recalls, I need to know about reproductive toxicants in the food chain, in the drinking water, in the air I breathe. This knowledge forms a starting point for social change."*

Steingraber regards the environmental movement as being among the latest in a series of campaigns for major social change in the U.S., its forerunners being the struggles to abolish slavery, give women the right to vote, and ensure equal civil rights for African-Americans. *"I always look backwards in order to look forwards,"* she told Neil deMause for Here magazine *(October 2001, online). "I think seeing yourself in a long line of people trying to make the world a better place, at least for me, makes me feel less despairing. The long view seems to be showing us that more and more people are aware of the issue [of environmental pollution], more and more people are trying to do something about it, the science is on our side, the more data come in, the more clear it is that we're taking needless risks, especially to the health of our kids."*

## EARLY LIFE

Born on August 27,1959 in Champaign, Illinois, Sandra Kathryn Steingraber was adopted early in life by Wilbur Francis and Kathryn Marie (Maurer) Steingraber. She was raised just outside the city limits of Pekin, Illinois, a rural area not far from Peoria. Kathryn Steingraber was a biologist, and as a child Sandra loved both that subject and English; she began to write poetry at age seven. At 15, after her mother was diagnosed with breast cancer, she decided to study biology. "I could easily have gone into poetry or drama," she told Lindsey, but she chose biology "because my mother was ill and maybe dying, and I wanted to carry her banner on." Her mother survived. Steingraber did not resume writing until 1979, when, as a 20 year old sophomore at Illinois Wesleyan University, in Bloomington, she was diagnosed with cancer and began writing poetry about the experience. Despite the disease and her treatment, which was successful, she earned a B.A. degree in biology from the college two years later, and a master's degree in English from Illinois State University, in Normal, in 1982. She received a Ph.D. in biology from the University of Michigan in 1989.

Earlier, in 1986 and 1987, Steingraber had spent several months in the Sudan interviewing Ethiopians in refugee camps set up along the border and investigating the effects of the Ethiopian civil war on the Blue Nile River. She described some of her findings in the book *The Spoils of Famine: Ethiopian Famine Policy and Peasant Agriculture*, co-written by the World Wildlife Fund anthropologist Jason W. Clay and Peter Niggli and published in 1988 by the organization Cultural Survival, which promotes the rights of indigenous peoples. In Ethiopia she saw close links between human health and the environment. "I had a number of epiphanies while working in the camps and talking to the displaced farmers there," she told *Current Biography.* "One was how clearly people there saw how their health, indeed their very humanity, was dependent on the surrounding ecology." One refugee, a farmer, told her about a river in his homeland that had become filled with silt after the construction of roads by the army; all the fish in the river had died. "He asked me about the rivers in my homeland and how the fish tasted," Steingraber recalled to *Current Biography.* "I told him that I had never eaten fish from the Illinois River where I grew up because they were too poisoned. He then expressed bewilderment as to why I had come all the way to Ethiopia to worry about his river when my own river was under attack. He encouraged me to go home immediately and take up arms against those poisoning my river."

## LIFE'S WORK

Spurred by what she had learned in Ethiopia and the knowledge that bladder cancer has a closer link to environmental factors than most other forms of the disease, Steingraber began to investigate the possible causes of her illness. In addition to her adoptive mother, her aunt had had the disease, a fatal case of bladder cancer. Furthermore, Steingraber discovered significantly higher than average rates of non-Hodgkin's lymphoma and

ovarian cancer in people who shared her home zip code, which covered portions of Tazewell County.

After working as a part-time newspaper reporter and teacher, Steingraber turned to writing full-time in 1993, when she received a Bunting Fellowship from the Radcliffe Institute of Harvard College, in Cambridge, Massachusetts. Her first book as sole author, *Post-Diagnosis* (1995), is a collection of poems about her struggle with cancer. "I think I needed the poetry to serve as an encoded expression of the grief, despair, and fear I was feeling," she said in a lecture at the University of Michigan, as reported by David Bricker for the *Michigan Daily* (October 31, 1997, online).

Steingraber's next book, *Living Downstream: An Ecologist Looks at Cancer and the Environment* (1997), examines research indicating that environmental factors may be among the causes of cancer. "Cancer is a bigger issue than ever," she said in her University of Michigan lecture, according to Bricker. "Cancer rates are rising. As they cast a long shadow over all of us, people are really starting to ask why." Steingraber had thought that the contents of *Living Downstream* would be new to most readers, but she discovered during the book tour that followed its publication that many people were already aware of the health risks associated with environmental contaminants and wanted to know what could be done about the problem. "One of the interesting things is that the cancer community, which for so long had been focused around therapeutic issues, how to provide emotional support through a diagnosis, where to find a wig, how to talk to your kids about it, they got very politicized in the early '90s, particularly the breast cancer movement," she told Neil deMause. "They began to ask questions about prevention, and the environment, and why more and more younger women were getting the disease. And really took a lesson from AIDS activists about ten years before us, who in the middle '80s showed how you could lay bare the political root causes of a disease, and profoundly alter the way scientific questions were posed, how they were funded, and what role patients and patient advocates played in the process of science. They really brought science to its knees and forced it to be what it should be, which is a public servant."

Reviews of *Living Downstream* were largely positive. "Far more than one woman's personal saga, this is a book about the wide scale use of pesticides and other chemicals and the gradual increase of cancer rates across the United States," Gary Lee wrote for the *Washington*

*Post* (August 24, 1997). "Using federal and state statistics to document both trends, the author seeks to establish the link between the two in her own life and for the larger population. While she falls short of proving her case, she backs it up with suggestive figures. Current U.S. annual use of pesticides is estimated at 2.23 billion pounds, she says, while 40 percent of persons now living can expect to receive a cancer diagnosis. By skillfully weaving a strong personal drama with thorough scientific research, Steingraber tells a compelling story. For anyone curious about the possible effects of contamination on the environment or personal health, it is well worth reading." Karen Lindsey wrote, "A compelling indictment of the role of pollutants in rising cancer rates, *Living Downstream* is an intricate weaving of scientific data, personal stories, and an intensely lyrical writing style that has defied the unwritten rules both of 'scientific objectivity' and of staying within a strict genre."

Steingraber maintains that the widely held idea that most cancers stem from genetic flaws is incorrect, and that even if it were true, to focus on genetics in the battle against cancer is counterproductive. "You can't change your genes," she said, as quoted by Bricker. "What we can change is the environment. We put [a contaminant] in, we can take it out. Even those of us who have inherited so- called cancer genes might not get cancer at all." Steingraber has pointed to studies showing that mortality rates from cancer among adoptees correlate more closely with such rates in their adoptive families than in their biological relatives. "We forget that families share environments as well as chromosomes," she told Lindsey. "Our genes are less an inherited set of teacups enclosed in a cellular china cabinet than they are plates used in a busy diner. Cracks, chips, and scrapes accumulate."

Steingraber's next book was *Having Faith: An Ecologist's Journey to Motherhood* (2001), an examination of ecological issues relevant to pregnancy. Written when she was expecting her first child, it intertwines personal narrative with scientific analysis. "This book is both a response to the chaotic, unpredictable process of motherhood in the face of modern technology and an assessment of the ecological precariousness into which we are now birthing our children," Stephanie Guyer-Stevens wrote in a review of *Having Faith for Whole Earth* (Spring 2002). "It moves smoothly through hard facts. This is a personal journal of pregnancy through childbirth, brilliantly integrating a touchingly personal

story with the data about the polluted ecosystem faced by mothers and children the world over." *An Economist* (February 16, 2002) critic called *Having Faith* "an intelligent and detailed scientific elucidation" of pregnancy. "Thoughtful and beautifully written, Ms, Steingraber's book deserves to be called a classic." *The Library Journal* selected *Having Faith* as one of its best books of 2001, *Having Faith* presents much scientific evidence that the environmental pollutants in a pregnant woman's body may have a profound impact on her fetus. "The old idea of the pregnant body as a space capsule sealed against hostile elements, and the developing fetus as its miniature astronaut, really blinded us to the intercourse between the human body and the larger environmental world," she told the Organic Trade Association. "An ecological understanding of the pregnant body, I think, helps us see more clearly the environmental threats to fetal development." Pregnant women's exposure to many substances, various solvents and pesticides, polychlorinated biphenyls. PCBs, which were used as coolants and lubricants and, though now illegal in the U.S., still contaminate the environment, as well as the chemical elements lead and mercury, has been linked to miscarriages, birth defects, premature labor, fetal brain damage, and low birth weights. Steingraber has said that it is difficult to know if the rates of miscarriage and birth defects are rising, because some states do not keep track of such information, and the records of those that do are often incomplete.

Steingraber advises pregnant women to reduce the risks to their unborn babies by avoiding the use of pesticides in their homes or yards, using the services of dry cleaners as little as possible, and limiting their consumption of seafood. She has emphasized, however, that the burden should rest not on individual women but on society: the best way to decrease the risks of birth defects is by reducing the presence of toxins in the environment. According to researchers, for example, fetal mercury exposure results in the births of approximately 60,000 babies with neurological problems and learning disabilities every year in the U.S. There are currently no prohibitions against the release of mercury into the environment by coal-burning power plants. The mercury enters the water supply through rainfall; from there it enters the cells of fish and other freshwater or seawater animals or plants, the main sources of the mercury ingested by people. Steingraber advocates using alternative, renewable energy sources rather than burning coal. She has also expressed the hope that the agriculture industry will decrease and eventually end its dependence on what she terms "neurotoxic pesticides."

Steingraber has paid close attention to safety issues connected with breast feeding. "Speaking as a biologist," she told the Organic Trade Association, "I can say that breast milk is a far better food for babies than its inferior pretender, infant formula. Breast milk is literally alive: it swims with white blood cells that confer protection against disease. It contains special sugars and fats that help knit together neurons in the brain. It protects against diabetes, obesity, juvenile arthritis, and certain cancers. Human milk is un-substitutable. And yet, it has also become the most chemically contaminated human food on the planet." Researchers have found traces of pesticides, flame retardants, toilet deodorizers, termite poisons, dry cleaning fluids, PCBs, and dioxins among the many substances detected in breast milk. Indeed, per pound of body weight, breastfed infants ingest daily an average of 50 times more PCBs than their parents. "The very substance that is supposed to boost immunity now contains immunosuppressive chemicals," she told the Organic Trade Association. "The very substance that is designed to protect a child against cancer now contains carcinogens." Nevertheless, she believes that the benefits of breast feeding still outweigh the liabilities.

Steingraber has criticized the idea that people can avoid environmental pollutants easily, by eating only organic food or drinking only bottled water. While she supports the growing and buying of organic food, she warns that it too contains toxins. For example, she has noted that because DDT (an insecticide whose use the U.S. government banned in 1972) has a half-life of 15 to 40 years in soil, crops grown in DDT contaminated soil will contain DDT. Moreover, bottled water, in her view, is an inefficient use of resources, because it is sold primarily in unrecyclable, nonbiodegradable plastic containers and its shipment, usually via trucks, requires the burning of huge quantities of fuel. "It makes a whole lot more sense on a political level to drink tap water than bottled water," Steingraber told deMause. "And it probably makes equal sense for your health, too, since bottled water is completely unregulated, and you get most of your exposure [to chemicals in water] from bathing and showering anyway." Steingraber favors detoxifying the nation's water supplies, nearly all of which are chlorinated to kill bacteria, but has acknowledged that doing so presents a difficult challenge: on the one hand, chlorination has made epidemics of such potentially fatal diseases as cholera unknown in the U.S.; on the other

hand, chlorinated water, which contains chloroform and other toxic byproducts of the chlorination process, has been linked to bladder and colon cancer. Other water purification technologies, including ozonation and carbon filtering, are either significantly more expensive than chlorination or produce byproducts whose safety level is unknown. Steingraber believes that scientists will find solutions to such dilemmas. "I tend to be really optimistic about human ingenuity," she told deMause. "There have been a lot of things that are really hard to do that we've done. Going to the moon was hard, but it was considered a campaign that we had to do, and we did it."

Steingraber has suggested various ways of reducing the amount of hazardous material released into the environment. One is the replacement of the most prevalent form of dry cleaning, which uses perchloroethylene, a chemical linked to bladder cancer, with so-called wet cleaning, which uses biodegradable soap, water, and computerized machines to achieve results that, in monitored tests, have closely resembled those of dry cleaning. Another suggestion is the phased replacement of incinerators with recycling programs. "The whole idea of solving a waste problem by shoveling things in an oven and lighting it on fire seems profoundly primitive to me," Steingraber told deMause. "And you can't possibly control the way these incinerators become de facto chemical labs as these molecules rearrange themselves and form new molecules like dioxins and other awful things that go up the stacks."

Steingraber is also pushing for a ban on the use of polyvinyl chloride (PVC), a component of credit cards, water pipes, wire casings, and other products. Although PVC is not harmful to the average consumer, the health of workers in factories where PVC is made is at risk, because the manufacture of PVC requires the use of, and produces as byproducts, toxic chemicals; furthermore, PVC is not biodegradable, and its incineration leads to the release of toxins into the atmosphere.

In addition to a Bunting Institute Fellowship, Steingraber was awarded a fellowship in women's public health policy at the University of Illinois in 1996. She has taught biology at Columbia College in Chicago; held a visiting fellowship at Northeastern University; and conducted fieldwork in East Africa, Costa Rica, and northern Minnesota. She was appointed to the National Action Plan on Breast Cancer (overseen by the U.S. Department of Health and Human Services) by President Bill Clinton in 1997. In 1999 she joined the faculty of Cornell University's Center for the Environment, in Ithaca, New York, working in the Breast Cancer and Environmental Risk Factors program, which is affiliated with the university's Institute for Comparative and Environmental Toxicology. She left that post in July 2003 to take a two-year position as distinguished visiting scholar in the interdisciplinary studies program at Ithaca College.

In 1997 Steingraber was named one of *Ms. Magazine's* women of the year. The following year she received the first annual Altman Award from the Jennifer Altman Foundation, for "the inspiring and poetic use of science to elucidate the causes of cancer," and the Will Solimene Award from the New England chapter of the American Medical Association, for "excellence in medical communication." She has often been compared to the pioneering environmentalist and writer Rachel Carson (1907- 64), who warned about the dangers of pesticides in her landmark book *Silent Spring* (1962). Steingraber, who has named Carson's work among her inspirations, received the 2001 Rachel Carson Leadership Award from Carson's alma mater, Chatham College, in Pittsburgh, Pennsylvania. She has spoken at conferences on human health and the environment throughout the U.S. and Canada and has lectured at many universities, medical schools, and teaching hospitals. In 1999 in Geneva, Switzerland, she testified about breast milk contaminants before a United Nations group that was drawing up a treaty regulating persistent organic pollutants. Her autobiographical chapbook, *The Organic Manifesto of a Biologist Mother,* was published by Organic Valley in June 2003.

## PERSONAL LIFE

Steingraber was married to Brian Wayne Burt from 1982 to 1994. In 1996 she married Jeffrey de Castro, a sculptor. The couple live in Ithaca, New York, with their daughter, Faith, born in 1998, and son, Elijah, born in 2001. After her son's birth Steingraber began attending meetings of the Religious Society of Friends (Quakers). Quakerism, which advocates nonviolence and respect for the natural world, "has become a spiritual practice for me that helps guide my writing about human rights and the environment," she told *Current Biography.* "I see my work now, as biologist, author, and activist, as an attempt to enact the Quaker ideas of bearing witness in times of extremity and speaking truth to power."

## FURTHER READING

The Spoils of Famine: Ethiopian Famine Policy and Peasant Agriculture; Post-Diagnosis; Living Downstream:An Ecologist Looks at Cancer and the Environment; Having Faith: An Ecologist's Journey to Motherhood

---

# BRYAN STEVENSON

## Lawyer; Social Activist

**Born:** November 14, 1959; Milton, Delaware
**Primary Field:** Civil Rights
**Affiliation:** Equal Justice Initiative

## INTRODUCTION

*Bryan Stevenson is an attorney and human rights activist whose mission is to end the racial and class linked biases that have made the criminal justice system in the Deep South and elsewhere in the United States, in his words, "largely unjust, unfair, and unavailable to protect the rights" of members of racial minorities and the poor. Those biases are strikingly evident in the administration of the death penalty: virtually all the people on death row in American prisons are poor, and the majority are black. "I could go through the South's prisons and put together five death rows of men not condemned [to death] whose crimes were far more vicious," Stevenson told Walt Harrington, who profiled him for the* Washington Post Magazine *(January 6, 1991). An African-American convicted of killing a white person, he has often pointed out, is 22 times more likely to get the death penalty than a white person whose victim was black; indeed, no white person has been executed for the killing of a black man or woman since 1976, when the Supreme Court reinstated the death penalty by upholding the constitutionality of certain death penalty statutes. As the legal representative of death row inmates in Alabama, Stevenson has set as his immediate goal the reversal of each sentence of death. "I remain convinced that each of us, including my clients, is more than the worst thing we have ever done and that we must pursue strategies for redemption and rehabilitation and not revenge and retribution," he said recently. In several cases he has won the release from prison of people awaiting execution who, he demonstrated, were wrongfully convicted. His long, ultimately successful struggle to prove the innocence of Walter McMillian, who spent six years on death row in Alabama for a crime he did not commit, was featured on the television program 60 Minutes in 1992.*

*Stevenson has devoted almost all his waking hours to fighting inequities in the legal system since he graduated from Harvard Law School a decade ago, first as a staff attorney with the Southern Center for Human Rights (1985-90), then as the executive director of the Alabama Capital Representation Resource Center (1990-95), and currently as the director of the Equal Justice Initiative of Alabama (EJI), which he founded in late 1995. He is using the entire $230,000 award that he received from the John D. and Catherine T. MacArthur Foundation in 1995 to support the work of his organization. In addition to litigation on behalf of juvenile offenders and people who were wrongfully charged or convicted of crimes, among others, the work of EJI includes documenting such pervasive problems in Alabama as the inadequacy of most court appointed defense attorneys and widespread racial discrimination in jury selection.*

*Through such means as the many lectures that he gives, Stevenson is attempting to awaken policy makers, civic leaders, and others to those problems so as to stimulate action to correct them. Although, by choice, he has earned only a small fraction of what he might have earned if, like most of his Harvard classmates, he had joined a large corporate law firm, he maintains that he does not envy people who have acquired wealth at such jobs. "I feel really enriched by the kinds of experiences I've had working with people [in communities in the South] and feel very rewarded to have seen hope increase in communities where hopelessness had prevailed previously," he told Earnest Reese of the Atlanta Journal-Constitution (June 23,1995). "Right now, I would not stop doing what I'm doing for any amount of money."*

## EARLY LIFE

The middle child of Howard Stevenson Sr. and his wife, Alice (Golden) Stevenson, Bryan Allen Stevenson was born on November 14,1959 in Milton, a town of about 1,500 in southern Delaware. He is a year younger than his brother, Howard Stevenson Jr., who is a clinical psychologist, and a year older than his sister, Christy Stevenson Taylor, who is a music teacher. His father worked for the General Foods Corporation as a laboratory technician, and his mother did bookkeeping at Dover Air Force Base. In the *Washington Post Magazine*, Walt Harrington wrote that the family's home, a ranch house that Alice and Howard Stevenson had built on a three-acre plot, was "elegant by local black standards of the day." The Stevensons spent all day every Sunday at the Prospect AME (African Methodist Episcopal) Church. For years Bryan Stevenson usually took part in church activities two or three weeknights as well. A self-taught musician, starting in adolescence he played piano and organ at the church. In the 1970s he participated in the charismatic Christian movement.

"I had the happiest childhood," Stevenson told Walt Harrington. "My parents cared about me, and I wanted to make them care about me more." By all accounts, he was a remarkably well behaved, considerate boy. His mother has recalled that whenever she slipped into a bad mood, young Bryan "was always the first to notice"; "he'd say, 'You all right, Mom?'" The high standards that Alice Stevenson set for her children included their speech; she frowned on so-called black English and expected them to use proper grammar, diction, and pronunciation. "Appalled by the docility she perceived in southern Delaware's blacks," Walt Harrington reported, "she admonished her children never to show false deference to whites." She repeatedly told her sons and daughter, "I never want to hear that you can't do something because you're black. You can do anything you want." From his father, who was a strict disciplinarian, Bryan Stevenson absorbed the lesson that "most white people will treat you well if you treat them well." According to Harrington, "between the two of them, Howard and Alice Stevenson sent a singular message" to their children: "Whites were not to be feared."

Thanks to the determined efforts of his mother, who wanted her children to get a better education than what the all black neighborhood school could offer, Stevenson began his formal education at the all white local elementary school. When the school was integrated two years later, and he was placed with other black children in the third-grade class ranked lowest academically, his mother forced school officials to transfer him to the top class, where he obviously belonged. Until he entered junior high school, he was the only black pupil in his class, and he was one of only a few black students in the advanced classes at his high school.

From early on, Stevenson was keenly aware of the hardships suffered by the many poverty stricken members of his community and by the many migrant workers who found temporary employment in the Milton area. "You saw how poverty and race affected life's options," he told Earnest Reese during his interview for the *Atlanta Journal-Constitution*. "I understood that and was always vexed by it." At times he felt the pain of racism firsthand. On the school bus, for example, some of his elementary school classmates triggered fights with him by addressing him with racial epithets. In first grade, although he often raised his hand, his teacher never called on him. The next year a teacher's aide forbid him to use playground equipment while white children were using it. In high school, a series of guidance counselors urged him to take vocational classes, advising him that "everyone needs to know how to make bricks." Stevenson entered Cape Henlopen High School, in the town of Lewes, in 1973. During his sophomore year his maternal grandfather, Clarence L. Golden, died of multiple stab wounds inflicted during a burglary at his home in Philadelphia. In an interview with Meg Grant for *People* (November 27, 1995), Stevenson said that the murder "seemed particularly cruel" because of his grandfather's advanced age. Nevertheless, he approved of the sentence the killers received, life imprisonment, not the death penalty. To this day, despite the intense empathy he feels for the families of murder victims, arid even in the cases of the most brutal murders, he believes that putting people to death can never be justified. "When we execute someone, we're saying their life has no value or purpose," he told *Current Biography.* "I've met people on death row who are dangerous or disturbed, but none about whom I could say, 'This person's life has no value or purpose.'"

In high school Stevenson made the varsity soccer, track, and baseball teams, belonged to the drama society (he played the leading role in its production of *A Raisin in the Sun*), served as a musician at various school events and as president of the student council, and participated in speech contests. In his senior year he won the Delaware high school oratorical championship, and he earned the highest grade-point average in his class. In 1977, after graduating from Cape Henlopen High School, Stevenson enrolled at Eastern College, a small Baptist institution in St. Davids, PennSylvania. He attended as a Presidential Scholar and on a soccer scholarship, and in one or more of his four years at college, the National Association of Intercollegiate Athletics

selected him for its all-star soccer team. He also played varsity baseball, and in 1980-81 he served as president of the student government. As an undergraduate he won the Phi Alpha Theta Award for scholarship, the Junior Scholarship Award for highest academic average, the Community Service Award, and the 1981 Outstanding Performance in Music Award. During his summer breaks he worked as a pianist and singer.

In 1981, after graduating magna cum laude from Eastern College with a B.A. degree in history and political science, Stevenson entered Harvard University Law School, in Cambridge, Massachusetts, with a full scholarship. In the Roxbury section of Boston, where he attended church, he volunteered his time to help residents of low-income black communities tackle problems connected with welfare and housing, and he gave piano lessons free of charge to children. "Bryan radiated a sense of goodness and kindness, which sounds so mushy," one of his Harvard classmates recalled to Walt Harrington. "But he definitely radiated it. He has some kind of inner peace." Another classmate told Harrington, "Maybe Bryan is the clearest example of what true character is all about."

To fulfill the requirements of one of his courses, Stevenson spent some weeks in Atlanta at the Southern Center for Human Rights (then called the Southern Prisoners' Defense Committee), which represents inmates who have been sentenced to death. While assisting Stephen Bright, the founder and director of the center, and other lawyers on the staff, Stevenson was struck by their deep commitment to their work and their clear sense of purpose. He realized that death-penalty litigation represented "an opportunity to confront race and poverty issues for folks who desperately needed legal assistance," as he explained to Earnest Reese. "It was an area where there was a great deal of neglect. People on death row were literally dying for lawyers to help them." The prisoners whom the center had taken on as clients resembled people he had known in Milton, "guys I'd grown up with, who I played basketball with, who didn't get the breaks I did," he told Jan Hoffman, who interviewed him for the *New York Times* (May 10, 1992). "They were condemned long before they got to death row." Stevenson has expressed the conviction that, but for his "breaks," he might "easily have ended up as one of the men" he has defended. "I've had friends, cousins who fell into trouble," he told Walt Harrington. "It could have been me."

## LIFE'S WORK

When he graduated from Harvard Law School with a J.D. degree, in 1985, Stevenson was awarded the Harvard Fellowship in Public Interest Law. That same year he received a master's degree in public policy from Harvard's Kennedy School of Government, where he was awarded the Kennedy Fellowship in Criminal Justice. Immediately after leaving Harvard, he began working in Atlanta as a full-time staff attorney at the Southern Center for Human Rights. "He literally could have written his own ticket, could've gone to a big law firm in New York or Washington or anywhere," Stephen Bright commented to Earnest Reese. "Instead, he chose to take on the most difficult work in the legal profession." In 1989 Stevenson moved to Montgomery to became the executive director of the newly formed Alabama Capital Representation Resource Center (ACRRC). Although he was offered an annual salary of more than $50,000, he refused to accept more than $18,000. The difficulty he experienced in finding an affordable place to live in Montgomery was compounded by the racial prejudice he encountered. "None of my Harvard degrees, my suits, meant anything next to my little black face," he said to Walt Harrington, in recalling the rebuffs he received from white homeowners and landlords.

Like centers set up in 19 other states in which a substantial number of people were on death row, the ACRRC received financial support from the federal government. Out of $19.8 million in federal funds allotted to the centers in 1995, the Alabama center got about $400,000, an amount equal to more than half its budget that year. In the fall of 1995, in what was touted as a cost-saving measure in a comprehensive appropriations bill, Congress voted to end federal funding of the ACRRC and the other post-conviction defender organizations, as they are formally known, and thus, in effect, to eliminate them. Earlier, in an interview with Lis Wiehl for the *New York Times* (August 11,1995), Stevenson had said, "The idea that the government will save money on this is ludicrous"; the cost of hiring private lawyers to represent death-row inmates, he and many other people in his field predicted, would far exceed the cost of the centers. In the *New York Times* (August 11, 1995), the columnist Anthony Lewis suggested that the "real motivation" of many congressmen who voted for the bill was "to look tough on the death penalty." President Bill Clinton's veto of the bill meant an extension of support for the centers only until the spring of 1996.

In anticipation of the expected total cutoff of funds, in the fall of 1995 Bryan Stevenson established a new, private, nonprofit organization, the Equal Justice Initiative of Alabama, to take the place of the ACRRC. For as long as it lasts, the $230,000 fellowship that he received from the MacArthur Foundation in 1995 will provide his salary (currently $27,000 a year) and those of the rest of EJI's small staff, four attorneys, one paralegal, and one administrative assistant, and will cover additional costs. To ensure that future expenses will be met, Stevenson devotes a lot of time to applying for grants and soliciting contributions.

Stevenson believes that the deficiencies in legal services for poor people in the Deep South have reached crisis proportions. "Without resources to obtain adequate legal representation or a state public defender system, poor people in Alabama are being sentenced to long-term imprisonment and to death at record levels, an EJI pamphlet reported. "Alabama's prisons are overcrowded with black, indigent, and teenage inmates; its death row is disproportionately black and 10 percent poor; and it is still not uncommon for poor defendants to be wrongly convicted or for black people to be unfairly sentenced to death by all-white juries." Contributing significantly to those situations is not only what Stevenson has described as "race and poverty bias" in the administration of criminal justice but also, in his view, an increasing acceptance of such bias as well as "an increasing hostility to the plight of the poor and disadvantaged among us."

Alabama is one of just a few states that has not set up a network of public defenders, and people charged with criminal offenses who cannot afford to hire their own lawyers become the clients of court appointed private attorneys. Most of those attorneys have little or no experience in handling criminal cases, particularly ones involving capital offenses, that is, crimes that resulted in one or more deaths. Yet properly handling such cases requires especially high levels of skill and knowledge, in part because the laws pertaining to capital crimes are very complex and are constantly changing, as Stevenson and Ruth Friedman, an EJI senior attorney, pointed out in an article for the *Alabama Law Review* (Fall 1992). Doing the legal research, conducting essential investigations, interviewing witnesses, and performing all the other tasks associated with conscientiously preparing a defense requires an enormous amount of time.

In Alabama, there is little incentive for a court appointed attorney to expend the necessary time, because the state has limited compensation to $20 per hour, up to a maximum of $1,000, for the legal research and all the other work that must be done outside the courtroom to prepare a defense. Thus, whereas Stevenson's preparation for a capital defense case invariably consumes at least 800 hours, court appointed attorneys often devote just a few hours to their cases. Many of them do not even try to establish whether their clients are competent to stand trial (many death row inmates are mentally disabled and/or suffer from schizophrenia, Vietnam War related emotional disorders, or other mental illnesses). Sometimes attorneys do not prepare any defense at all and call no witnesses. Commonly, they do not bring attention to prosecutorial misconduct or object to obvious constitutional errors made by prosecutors. It is not unusual in Alabama for poor people to be convicted of murder and sentenced to death after trials lasting only two or three days. According to EJI, "death-row prisoners have been convicted even though their lawyers were cited for being drunk in court."

Many of the people whom Stevenson has represented have also been the objects of blatant racial bias in judicial proceedings. In "Deliberate Indifference: Judicial Tolerance of Racial Bias in Criminal Justice," an article published in the *Washington & Lee Law Review* in 1994, Stevenson and Ruth Friedman reported that they had seen "the pervasive presence of racial bias in painfully obvious ways in case after case." In some instances, the judge, the prosecuting attorney, or even the court appointed defense attorney voiced racist views. Stevenson has also handled appeals for many African-Americans who were tried before juries from which black people had been deliberately excluded. According to EJI, "even in 1995, it is not unusual to see a prosecutor use 90 or 100 percent of his jury challenges against black people." Among the reasons that prosecutors have given for preventing blacks from serving on juries are that the potential jurors "went to a black university" or "looked unintelligent" or "seemed hostile." "In the deep South, black people have marched, fought, and died for the right to vote, serve on juries, and participate in making moral judgments for their communities," Stevenson and Friedman wrote in their *Washington & Lee Law Review* article. "To be casually excluded from meaningful participation after enormous struggle is deeply discouraging and disheartening."

"Racial bias within the legal system is not just an issue affecting how guilty people are treated in courtrooms across America, but rather one that implicates the moral authority of the law and the promise of equal justice," Stevenson and Friedman declared in the same article. "There is a clear relationship between race and the administration of criminal justice and race relations in this country. The presence of racial bias in the justice system is central to the concerns of people of color precisely because our society defines itself by a commitment to law and fairness. To the extent that this commitment is compromised or even abandoned in the context of administering criminal law, African-Americans are given every reason to view themselves as excluded from the system that dispenses justice." Stevenson and Friedman also wrote, "It is significant that in the last quarter-century, America's most devastating domestic civil disturbances have been ignited by perceptions that the criminal justice system operates in a racially discriminatory manner. While a host of socioeconomic factors underlies recent race riots and civil disturbances, these events clearly reflect a profound absence of hope in systems of justice and a belief that the promise of equality and fairness for people of color is meaningless."

The arrest, conviction, and death sentence of Walter McMillian had what EJI described as a "devastating impact" on the black community of Monroeville, Alabama, the town in which he lived. After being charged with murdering a young white woman during a robbery in Monroeville in 1987, McMillian, a black man who did not have a criminal record, spent 13 months in a cell on death row before his case went to trial. The nearly all-white jury found him guilty at the end of a two day trial despite his assertion that, at the time that the crime was committed, he was 41 miles away from the site of the murder, at a gathering attended by a dozen other people, several of whom corroborated his alibi in court. The jury voted for a penalty of life imprisonment without chance of parole, but the judge overruled their decision (a prerogative available to judges in Alabama) and sentenced him to death. It was thus that his plight came to the attention of Bryan Stevenson, who, with the help of his staff, determined that McMillian had been accused of the murder largely because he had incurred the wrath of local white people by having an affair with a white woman, that key witnesses against him had lied, and that the prosecutors had withheld from McMillian's original lawyer crucial evidence that pointed to McMillian's innocence.

After three years of litigation, which involved five appeals, the Alabama Court of Criminal Appeals overturned his conviction and he was released from prison.

"The fortunate thing about Mr. McMillian's case is his innocence was demonstrable," Stevenson told Peter Applebome for the New York Times (March 3,1993). "It's clear he had nothing to do with this crime. There are other folks in prison who don't have the money or the resources or the good fortune to have folks come in and help them."

Stevenson has written two guides on death penalty litigation: *Alabama Capital Postconviction Manual* (1991) and *Alabama Capital Defense Trial Manual* (1992). He was a visiting professor of law at New York University School of Law and the University of Michigan School of Law in the spring and fall of 1995, respectively. His professional activities include service on the American Civil Liberties Union (ACLU) national board of directors from 1992 to 1995 and on the steering committee of the ACLU's National Prison Project from 1990 to the present. In addition to the MacArthur Foundation award, Stevenson's honors include the Reebok National Human Rights Award (1989); the ACLU's National Medal of Liberty Award (1991), for which he was nominated by United States Supreme Court Justice John Paul Stevens; the American Bar Association Wisdom Award for Public Service Litigation (1993); the M. L. King American Dream Award, from the Alabama Democratic Conference (1993); and the Thurgood Marshall Medal of Justice, from Georgetown Law School (1994). In 1990 *Barrister*, a magazine published by the American Bar Association Young Lawyers Division, named him one of the country's top 20 outstanding young attorneys.

## PERSONAL LIFE

Because he works seven days a week, from 8:30 in the morning until 11:30 at night on weekdays and nearly as much on weekends, Stevenson has little time to pursue his avocational interests, reading for pleasure, composing music, playing jazz and gospel music on his electronic piano, and playing basketball and soccer, or even to attend church. When he has time to be with them, he enjoys the company of his nieces, Victoria and Mia Taylor, and his nephew, Bryan Gabriel Stevenson. "I want to be a witness for hope and decency and commitment," he has said. "I want to show in myself the qualities I want to see in others." "[Some] people act like I'm a priest, making such [financial and other] sacrifices," he observed to Walt Harrington. "I'm not. It's easy for me to do what I do. What people don't understand when they say I could be making all this money is that I couldn't be making all this money. I could not do it. If the death penalty were abolished tomorrow, I couldn't be a corporate lawyer. I'd probably be a musician."

## FURTHER READING

*Just Mercy: A Story of Justice and Redemption; Cruel and Unusual: Sentencing 13 and 14 Year Old Children to Die in Prison; The Politics of Fear and Death: Successive Problems Capital Federal Habeas Corpus Cases; The Ultimate Authority on the Ultimate Punishment: The Requisite Role of the Jury in Capital Sentencing; Confronting Mass Imprisonment and Restoring Fairness to Collateral Review of Criminal Cases*

# T

## OLIVER TAMBO

### Political Activist; Lawyer

**Born:** October 27, 1917; Nkantolo, Bizana, South Africa
**Died:** April 24, 1993; Johannesburg, South Africa
**Primary Field:** Anti-Apartheid Politics
**Affiliation:** African National Congress

#### INTRODUCTION

*"The most peculiar thing about South Africa is that you have twenty-eight or twenty-nine million people living in the same country, and twenty-four or twenty-five million don't exist! They're virtually foreigners in South Africa, without any rights. This must end." That ultimatum came from Oliver Tambo, the president of South Africa's most influential liberation organization, the African National Congress, in a 1982 interview. The soft-spoken Tambo has for many years been targeted as the "public enemy number one" of his country's white minority government, having campaigned throughout the world to isolate that regime, both economically and politically, ever since he first established a foreign base for the outlawed ANC in Lusaka, Zambia, in 1964. His diplomatic successes since then include the securing of long-term financial backing for the ANC from Scandinavian and other Western countries; the garnering of weapons and other types of aid from the Soviet Union and the Eastern bloc, and the winning of acceptance as a de facto head of state in the nonaligned countries.*

*In January 1987, after decades during which the ANC had been ignored by the American government, Tambo achieved another significant diplomatic triumph when he met with United States Secretary of State George P. Shultz in Washington, D.C. That*

*Oliver Tambo.*

Nationaal Archief

*meeting, and its tacit acknowledgment that the ANC's prestige among South African blacks made it a powerful player in that country's politics, infuriated American conservatives and South African government officials because of what they perceived as the ANC's links to communism and terrorism. A significant amount of cross membership existed between the ANC and the pro-Moscow South African Communist party (SACP), and the organization resorted not only to mass demonstra-*

768

*tions and boycotts but also to hit-and-run violence in its attempts to dislodge the white South African regime and its policy of apartheid, or legalized racial discrimination. Tambo has dismissed complaints about SACP connections as attempts to foster "tribalism" and has echoed the American Declaration of Independence by declaring that "in the face of systematic tyranny it becomes a duty and a right to take up arms."*

## EARLY LIFE

Oliver Tambo, one of seven children, was born on October 27,1917, to peasant subsistence farmers of the Pondo tribe in the Transkei village of Bizana, near Johannesburg. During what he has described as a politically "sheltered" childhood, he attended Anglican and Methodist mission schools, took part in inter-village horse races, and was an outrider in the equestrian section of a tribal chief's entourage. After graduating from the Anglican St. Peter's School in Johannesburg with an impressive first-class pass in 1938, he received a scholarship to Fort Hare University (some sources call it University College at Fort Hare), where he studied science and education. When an assault on a black woman dining-room employee by a white male superior went unpunished, Tambo, previously known mainly as a brilliant student, found himself "playing quite the leading role" in a student protest. After obtaining his B.S. degree in 1941, he stayed on at Fort Hare to work towards a diploma in education. "I didn't really want to be a teacher," he has said, "but there was nothing else I could be. It was just the racial restriction on Africans." He was expelled from Fort Hare, and thoroughly politicized, in 1942 when he led a large student protest against arbitrary restrictions on the use of a tennis court.

Ignoring his expulsion, St, Peter's promptly hired Tambo as an instructor of science and mathematics, a post that he held until 1947. In addition to teaching at St. Peter's, Tambo composed music and conducted the school's choir on occasion. He also seriously considered entering the Anglican ministry, but began to find his true vocation in the black protest movement. In 1944 he became a founding member, with Nelson Mandela, his former schoolmate at Fort Hare, several of his fellow teachers at St. Peter's, and others, of the Youth League of the African National Congress.

## LIFE'S WORK

"We were never really young," Tambo has said of that period. "There were no dances, hardly a cinema, but meetings, discussions, every night, every weekend." The discussions covered topics that ranged from the ineffectiveness of the genteel ANC parent body to the overlapping membership, then hotly opposed by Tambo, of the ANC and the South African Communist party. The Youth League that emerged from those bull sessions declared its intention to "galvanize" the ANC by becoming "the brain-trust and power-station" of the struggling black liberation movement.

As the Youth League hammered out its policies, Tambo became increasingly interested in law and was apprenticed to a Johannesburg law firm through Walter Sisulu, another Youth League member, who had already performed a similar service for Nelson Mandela. The law books that Tambo pored over began to change in 1948, when the Afrikaaner Nationalist party, which came to power that year, began to codify and elaborate existing repressions under its new apartheid policy. Laws were passed limiting, among other things, the education, freedom of movement, and choice of dwelling place of blacks, who also continued to be denied the franchise.

In 1949 Oliver Tambo and Nelson Mandela were elected to the ANC executive body. It was at their insistence and that of their supporters, that the Youth League's carefully orchestrated "Programme of Action," calling for boycotts, strikes, civil disobedience, and general defiance of the laws of apartheid, was adopted by the ANC as a whole. The Programme of Action was launched in 1952 with a massive "defiance campaign" that for months brought tens of thousands of demonstrators into the streets of South Africa and pushed membership in the ANC from 7,000 to 100,000. In 1955, in Kliptown near Johannesburg, a multiracial "Congress of the People" convened and adopted the Freedom Charter, the seminal document of the South African liberation movement and the embodiment of the vision of Tambo and the rest of the new ANC leadership. It opened with the promulgation of the ANG's keynote concept: "South Africa belongs to all who live in it, black and white."

Tambo and Mandela simultaneously battled apartheid in the courts, beginning in 1952 when they opened the first black law firm, in Johannesburg in defiance of official orders to relocate to a township. Tambo still wistfully recalls the way his name and Nelson Mandela's appeared in "the gold lettering on the glass" of the law firm door. "To reach our desks each morning," he wrote in his Introduction to Mandela's *No Easy Walk to Freedom* (1965), "Nelson and I ran the gauntlet of patient queues of people overflowing from the chairs in the waiting room into the corridors." "South Africa," he added, "has the dubious reputation of boasting one of the highest prison populations in the world. To be unemployed is a crime. To be landless can be a crime, and weekly we interviewed the delegations of grizzled, weatherworn peasants from the countryside who came to tell us how many generations their families had worked a little piece of land from which they were now being ejected. Our buff office files carried thousands of these stories and if, when we started our law partnership, we had not been rebels against apartheid, our experience in our offices would have remedied the deficiency." He and Mandela, sometimes handling seven cases a day, "had risen to professional status in our community," Tambo continued, "but every case in court, every visit to the prison to interview clients, reminded us of the humiliation and suffering burning into our people."

In 1956 Tambo and Mandela were themselves arrested along with 154 others and charged with treason. Tambo had recently been accepted as a candidate for ordination in the Anglican church, but the treason charge forced him to abandon all thoughts of entering the clergy. When not in court for the long preparatory session for the treason trial, he and Mandela practiced law as best they could. The treason trial finally opened officially in August 1958. The prosecution set out to establish, under South Africa's sweeping anticommunist legislation, that the Youth League Programme of Action, the ANC's Freedom Charter, and other documents in effect declared the ANC's intention to found a communist state. Evidence was flimsy, and charges against Tambo were dropped almost immediately. All defendants were found not guilty in March 1960.

At that time Tambo still believed that the ANC would never "have to go for violence as opposed to nonviolence." In March 1960 in Sharpeville, a town forty miles from Johannesburg, police opened fire on unarmed persons in a demonstration sponsored by the Pan Africanist Congress, an ANC splinter group, killing sixty-nine people and wounding 181. "It is hard to overstate the impact that Sharpeville made on us," Tambo once said. "We were unarmed, we were peaceful, and they shot us down in the street." At that point Tambo "knew that nonviolence had become meaningless." "We couldn't take it any further," he added. Anticipating a crackdown by the government, the ANC executive decided that Tambo should prepare to flee the country and establish a foreign base.

Two days after the now historic Sharpeville massacre, the ANC was banned. Its members went underground, and after forty-eight years of nonviolence, began building an armed wing, Umkhonto we Sizwe (Spear of the Nation). A state of emergency was declared, and Tambo left South Africa for Botswana to begin the establishment of the foreign headquarters. According to Peter Godwin of the *London Sunday Times* (June 29, 1986), his "escape, however, was very nearly undone when masked South African agents tried to kidnap him by drugging him with chloroform, but locals spotted them and reported their presence. It was only the first of a string of threats against Tambo's life." Another reporter noted that Tambo's life after that became, of necessity, one of "secret itineraries and meetings in anonymous offices behind heavily padlocked doors." In June 1960 he traveled to the United States in search of funds and political support, but American officials, pressured by South Africa, hesitated to give him a visa. His request for aid "received no real response," he has said.

Meanwhile, Umkhonto we Sizwe carried out sabotage attacks against government buildings that it felt symbolized apartheid until 1962, when Mandela and his colleagues were betrayed by an informer and rounded up, tried, and given life sentences almost to a man. In 1963 Tambo traveled to the Soviet Union in quest of the funds and arms he had failed to obtain in the United States and succeeded in his mission. The Soviet Union later became the ANC's main supplier of arms and even provided some academic scholarships for ANC recruits.

While Mandela was serving his life sentence and taking on mythical proportions in the minds of the majority of South Africa's people, Tambo remained "incredibly self-effacing," in the view of Bishop Trevor Huddlestone of South Africa. He assumed the role of "the workaholic who [made] all the difficult decisions" that held the ANC together in exile and won new financial support for it, especially from the Scandinavian countries, during a number of years when its prominence in the South African black community was replaced by a more radical black consciousness movement. This movement grew in influence until 1976, when, in the township of Soweto, government security forces fired upon unarmed students demonstrating against a number of newly imposed restrictions on education for blacks. There followed a sixteen month explosion of unrest in the townships during which 700 people were killed by the authorities. The importance of Tambo's work in establishing the ANC outside South Africa now became obvious, as thousands of young blacks poured across the border to join the ANC and Umkhonto we Sizwe, which represented the only surviving organized resistance to the government.

The immediate problem that Tambo and the other ANC leaders faced with those new recruits was to convince them, as one ANC official explained, that "there is more to this than simply grabbing a gun and going back to kill the people who have been stepping on them." A more subtle and lingering problem, as Tambo discovered in subsequent years, was South African security's use of informers to infiltrate the steady stream of ANC recruits. Tambo told the American journalist Joseph Lelyveld, in an interview for Lelyveld's 1985 book, *Move Your Shadow*, that on one occasion "there was a group of ten [recruits], and only one was genuine." Despite careful screening, it became "awkward to have large groups because you can't be sure when they just come." The first waves of recruits after Soweto, however, enormously bolstered the strength and effectiveness of the ANC and those that followed eventually gave it an effective fighting force of 10,000 men. By using hit and run guerrilla tactics, they tried to gain political leverage against a regime backed by a vastly superior defense force of 400,000 men who were supported by a yearly budget of $3 billion and some of the world's most sophisticated weapons.

By 1981 the government's Terrorism Research Center was reporting an ANC military strike every 53.2 hours. Employing Soviet made explosives, Umkhonto we Sizwe struck against what it felt to be symbols of South African repression, including police stations, pass records offices, military headquarters, and such economic pillars of apartheid as the SASOL oil refinery and, in 1982, the Koeberg nuclear power plant.

The government in Pretoria viewed the ANC attacks and the presence on the thirty-member ANC executive body of members of the South African Communist party as evidence of an indirect but "total onslaught" against South Africa by the Soviet Union. It followed up its rhetoric by attacking the ANC directly, staging reprisal raids against suspected ANC headquarters in the neighboring "front-line" states. In 1981 a bombing raid against a suspected ANC base in Lesotho, a country surrounded by South African territory, resulted in the deaths of fifty-four civilians who were "asleep in their beds," according to Mark Uhlig, Another attack and two

parcel bombs accounted for the deaths of fifteen ANC members in other front-line states. Tambo declared that "our violence compared to the regime's violence, physically, is minimal. Sharpeville, Soweto, hangings, shootings by the police, the number of people they have killed!" He also noted that Angola, Mozambique, and Zimbabwe had all won independence by fighting "serious armed struggles, while we were looking for economic targets."

In its first attack that resulted in civilian deaths, the ANC exploded a car bomb in May 1983 outside the South African Air Force headquarters close to the center of Pretoria, killing eighteen people, including eight blacks, and wounding some 200. Pretoria cited the attack as new evidence of ANC links to "international terrorism," and it helped Pieter W. Botha, South Africa's prime minister since 1978, to perpetuate the ANC's pariah status in the United States and Great Britain. Within Africa, Pretoria exerted so much economic and military pressure on three long-time ANC supporters, Mozambique, Lesotho, and Swaziland, that those countries closed their borders to the ANC.

In February 1985, through the nightly broadcasts of the ANC's Lusaka, Zambia based "Radio Freedom" and through ANC agents within South Africa, Tambo exhorted blacks to make their townships "ungovernable." A new government policy that took effect in January 1985 and allowed Asians and coloreds, or mixed-race South Africans, token representation in Parliament but denied it to blacks, accomplished that goal for him by setting off demonstrations and riots on an unprecedented scale. The Botha government declared two states of emergency, one in July 1985 and the other in June 1986, during which 22,000 blacks, including small children, were imprisoned, many without charges. Some 2,300 blacks were killed between September 1984 and June 1986, the great majority struck down by South African security forces. Scores died as a result of power struggles, mob justice, and raw frustration within the black community itself. As the death toll rose, Tambo announced in 1985 that Umkhonto we Sizwe would attempt to force the violence into the insulated and oblivious white areas, still striking at inanimate military and government targets but now also attacking military personnel and abandoning special efforts to limit the casualties that might result among nearby civilians. As rioting in the townships and international pressure for the South African government to make reforms steadily intensified, in September 1985 a group of prominent

South African businessmen traveled to Lusaka to meet with Tambo and other senior ANC leaders. Tambo assured them of the ANC's non-racialism and insisted that black and white sit side by side, not face to face at the conference table, "because we are all South Africans."

The ANC economic program, calling for the nationalization of banks, mines, and monopoly industry to create a mixed economy and thus facilitate South Africa's incontrovertible need for a redistribution of wealth, has been compared to that of the British Labour party. Although it troubled some of the businessmen, others felt that a mutually acceptable solution was within the range of negotiation. Pretoria condemned the meeting, but subsequent "pilgrimages to Lusaka," as one journalist called them, were made by clergymen and by members of the South African Parliament's white opposition party.

In September 1986 Tambo traveled to London for exploratory talks with Sir Geoffrey Howe, the British foreign secretary, and, separately, with Chester H. Crocker, the American assistant secretary of state for African affairs. That grudging recognition of the ANC by both governments came in the wake of indisputable evidence of ANC influence within South Africa, including clenched-fist salutes to Tambo and Mandela and ANC banners flown at mass funerals for many of the blacks killed by the South African security forces; the adoption of the goals of the ANC Freedom Charter by the umbrella opposition group, the United Democratic Front; and polls showing strong support for the ANC among millions of blacks despite the presence of a growing number of young radicals who, seeming to disregard all authority, including the ANC, often set up their own tribunals, and meted out justice with the "necklace," a gasoline soaked tire in which a "collaborator" or an "informer" was burned to death.

Abroad and in South Africa, the ANC began increasingly to be seen as an indispensable factor in averting a bloodbath, and one former South African police spy complained that "the ANC's real weapon isn't the AK-47, it is the ability to popularize and politicize discontent." Realizing that fact, the South African government narrowed press freedoms to the vanishing point throughout its two emergencies, but what journalists managed to report was enough to inspire the United States Congress to impose limited economic sanctions on South Africa in October 1986, over the objections of the Reagan administration. In December 1986 the South African government prohibited journalists from photographing "visible signs" of unrest such as corpses, or even from being "at a place within sight of any unrest, restricted gathering, or security action."

In January 1987 Tambo traveled to the United States to meet with Secretary of State George Shultz not long after celebrating the ANC's seventy-fifth anniversary with a speech in which he invited South Africa's whites into a "massive democratic coalition" with blacks. In the same speech he exhorted blacks to spread the unrest of their townships to white areas. Tambo continued to walk that rhetorical tightrope in the United States, where conservatives expressed outrage at his meeting with Shultz in newspaper ads. The North Carolina Senator Jesse Helms, the former U.N. ambassador Jeane Kirkpatrick, and many others called on Shultz to cancel the meeting. The fifty minute meeting with Shultz took place behind closed doors on January 28, 1987, while conservatives staged a protest outside.

Tambo pressed, unsuccessfully, for a "total break," both economic and political, between Washington and Pretoria and for special aid to the front-line states that Pretoria tries to intimidate and destabilize. When Tambo was questioned by Shultz and by journalists on the issue of ANC terrorism, he responded that the South African regime practiced the worst terrorism in all of Africa, apartheid being in itself an act of violence. Throughout his visit, the issues that Tambo wished to discuss were pushed into the background by questions of the influence on ANC policy of its pro- Moscow Communist members and of the Soviet Union itself. "I dominate the ANC," Tambo assured one reporter. At a Washington, D.C., church he drew an analogy familiar to Americans. "We are like the Jews in Hitler's concentration camps," he said. "When they looked among themselves, who cared what the next person believed or did not believe? Who cared among the Allies whether the Soviet Union was a socialist state? The overriding issue was the destruction of the Nazi system. The issue today is destruction of a Nazi system."

## PERSONAL LIFE

Oliver Tambo was a small, professorial-looking man, and his owlish appearance was reinforced by his spectacles. His wife, Adelaide, was a nurse, and they were married in 1956. They had three children who spent much of their lives living abroad. Living with them, Peter Godwin reported, "would have signed [Tambo's] death warrant." His own address was kept secret. Tambo enjoyed listening to classical music on a pocket recorder before going to bed. He also wrote his own music, including what Godwin described as "the haunting melodies sung by the ANC choirs in beautiful harmony."

In 1993, just months before the first democratic general election of 1994 in which Nelson Mandela would be elected president of South Africa, Tambo suffered a stroke and died at the age of 75. Many figures of the liberation struggle attended his funeral and Tambo was buried in Benoni, Johannesburg.

## FURTHER READING

*Nelson Mandela: The Man and the Movement; Oliver Reginald Tambo: teacher, lawyer & freedom fighter; Oliver Tambo: Beyond the Engeli Mountains; Oliver Tambo Remembered; Oliver Tambo and the struggle against apartheid; Preparing for power: Oliver Tambo speaks; Oliver Tambo, apartheid and the international community: addresses to the United Nations committees and conferences; Oliver Tambo*

---

# JILL BOLTE TAYLOR

## Neuroanatomist

**Born:** May 4, 1959; Louisville, Kentucky
**Primary Field:** Mental Health Advocate
**Affiliation:** Neuroscience

## INTRODUCTION

*While all neuroanatomists study the structure of the brain and other parts of the nervous system, few can claim to have as deep and personal an understanding of the field as Jill Bolte Taylor. In 1996 Taylor, who had trained at Harvard Medical School's Department of Neuroscience, suffered a stroke that affected the left side of her brain, which largely controls logic, language, and calculation. Unlike other stroke victims, she has been able to give a detailed and vivid explanation of her experience. "I think that I had an advantage because the brain was my area of expertise," she told Terry Gross for the National Public Radio program* Fresh Air *(June 25, 2008). "I do believe that it is unusual for someone to be so consciously tuned in to every step along the way during the process of cognitive degeneration."*

*In 2006, after years of recuperation, Taylor wrote a memoir,* My Stroke of Insight: A Brain Scientist's Personal Journey, *which became a bestseller when it was published by Viking in 2008. In it, she described the transformation she underwent in the wake of her medical emergency. She wrote: "I remember that first day of the stroke with terrific bitter-sweetness. In the absence of the normal functioning of my left orientation association area, my perception of my physical boundaries were no longer limited to where my skin met air. I felt like a genie liberated from its bottle. It was obvious to me that I would never be able to squeeze the enormousness of my spirit back inside this tiny cellular matrix. "*

*Taylor began spreading the word about the importance of tapping into the right side of the brain. In February 2008 she gave a speech at the annual Technology, Education, Design (TED) conference in Monterey, California, in which she passionately asserted, "We are the life force power of the universe, with manual dexterity and two cognitive minds. And we have the power to choose, moment by moment, who and how we want to be in this world. Right here, right now, I can step into the consciousness of my right hemisphere, where we are, at one with all that is. Or I can choose to step into the consciousness of my left hemisphere, where I become a single individual separate from the flow, separate from you. I am Dr. Jill Bolte Taylor, intellectual, neuroanatomist." She concluded, "Which would you choose? Which do you choose? And when? I believe that the more time we spend choosing to run the deep inner peace circuitry of our right hemispheres, the more peace we will project into the world and the more peaceful our planet will be." The speech was posted on the TED Web site and quickly became an Internet sensation, with several million viewers to date.*

*Taylor, who was chosen as one of Time magazine's 100 most influential people in the world for 2008, acknowledges that she is lucky to have recuperated so fully, of the people who experience the same form of stroke, 10 percent die immediately, while half remain in a vegetative state. She does not, however, wish she had avoided the stroke. "It was one of the most fascinating experiences of my life," she told Rebecca Webber for* Psychology Today *(July/August 2008). "How many brain scientists have the opportunity to study their brains from the inside?"*

## EARLY LIFE

Jill Bolte Taylor was born in May 1959 to Hal and Gladys (Gillman) Taylor. Her father was an Episcopal minister, and her mother taught math at a local college. They later divorced. Taylor was raised in Terre Haute, Indiana, with her older brother, who was diagnosed with schizophrenia as an adult, "During our childhood, he was very different from me in the way he experienced reality and chose to behave," Taylor wrote in *My Stroke of Insight*. "As a result I became fascinated with the brain at an early age." After graduating from Terre Haute South Vigo High School, in 1977, Taylor studied at Indiana University (IU), on the Bloomington campus. The school did not have a formal neuroscience program at the time, so she majored in human biology and physiological psychology. Taylor graduated in 1982 with a B.A. degree and was hired as a lab technician and teaching assistant at the Terre Haute Center for Medical Education (THCME), located on the campus of Indiana State University (ISU). Forgoing a master's degree, in 1984 Taylor enrolled in the ISU Department of Life Science Ph.D. program and spent the following years studying neuroanatomy. She also worked as a teaching assistant and later a visiting lecturer in gross human anatomy at the THCME.

Upon receiving her doctoral degree, in 1991, Taylor was offered a postdoctoral fellowship in the department of neuroscience at Harvard Medical School, in Boston, Massachusetts. She spent two years there working to locate Area MT, the part of the brain's visual cortex that controls a person's perception of motion. The project interested Taylor because many schizophrenia patients exhibit abnormal eye behavior while watching moving objects. In 1993 she became affiliated with Harvard Medical School's Department of Psychiatry, and she began conducting research in the Laboratory for Structural Neuroscience at the Harvard affiliated McLean Hospital, in Belmont, Massachusetts, under the guidance of Francine M. Benes, an expert on postmortem investigation of the human brain as it relates to schizophrenia. During that time Taylor also taught human head-and-neck anatomy at the Harvard School of Dental Medicine.

McLean Hospital is home to the Harvard Brain Tissue Resource Center, known informally as the "Brain Bank." At the facility, donated postmortem brains are collected and distributed for the purpose of medical research. Taylor became a spokesperson for the center, lecturing all over the region and urging audience members to become brain donors upon their deaths and to inform their families accordingly.

## LIFE'S WORK

At the age of 35, Taylor became the youngest person ever elected to the board of directors of the National Alliance on Mental Illness (NAMI), the country's largest grassroots organization dedicated to improving the quality of life for people with mental illness and their families. From 1995 to 1996 she also served as a vice president of the organization. Taylor had learned in the course of her own research that there was a shortage of donated brain tissue from people diagnosed with psychiatric illnesses. She explained in her memoir, "I decided this was merely a public awareness issue." In a link to her work with the Brain Bank, Taylor's NAMI platform focused on the need for brain donations from mentally ill patients, and she began to take her donation lecture across the country. At the end of each presentation, she brought out her guitar and sang a jingle she had written to lighten the mood: "Oh, I am a brain banker / Yes, banking brains is what I do / Oh, I am a brain banker / Asking for a deposit from you." Taylor was soon being billed on the lecture circuit as the "Singing Scientist," and thanks in large part to her efforts, an average of 30 brains from deceased psychiatric patients are now donated each year. Taylor has stated that that figure is still inadequate.

On December 10, 1996 Taylor awoke with a sharp pain behind her left eye. Thinking that it was just a headache, she continued with her normal morning routine of exercising and showering. Soon, however, she realized she was having trouble keeping her balance and began to feel detached from her body. "In addition to having problems with coordination and equilibrium, my ability to process incoming sound (auditory information) was erratic," Taylor wrote in *My Stroke of Insight*. "I understood neuroanatomically that coordination, equilibrium, audition and the action of inspirational breathing were processed through the pons of my brainstem. For the first time, I considered the possibility that I was perhaps having a major neurological malfunction that was life threatening."

Taylor was, in fact, suffering a hemorrhagic stroke caused by a birth defect known as arteriovenous malformation (AVM). As she explained in an essay for the *London Daily Mail* (July 22, 2008, online), "Normally, the heart pumps blood through the arteries with high pressure, while blood is retrieved through the veins, which are low pressure. A capillary bed acts as a buffering system between the two. But with AVM, an artery is connected to a vein with no buffering capillary bed in between. Over time, the vein can no longer handle the pressure and the connection between the artery and vein breaks, spilling blood into the brain."

In the human brain, the right and left sides have separate functions. The right side is the center of creativity and processes emotions, while the left side is more analytical, focusing on details, facts, calculations, and words. Because Taylor's hemorrhage was located on the left side of her brain, above her language center, Taylor began to lose all concept of language and numbers. The chatter she generally heard within her mind was silenced, and memories of her ill brother and demanding career faded. Taylor said at that point she experienced Nirvana, or a state of perfect peace. "As the language centers in my left hemisphere grew increasingly silent and I became detached from the memories of my life, I was comforted by an expanding sense of grace," she wrote in her memoir. "In this void of higher cognition and details pertaining to my normal life, my consciousness soared into an all-knowingness, a 'being at one' with the universe, if you will."

The moment Taylor's right arm became paralyzed, however, her euphoria was marred by the certainty that she was having a stroke. She told Terry Gross, "At this point people say, 'Well why didn't she just call 911?' Well, the group of cells in my left hemisphere that understood numbers, the group of cells that understood what 911 was, were swimming in a pool of blood and no longer functional." She continued, "So, eventually I did decide that I was going to call work and I had to locate a business card that had my phone number at work on it. And by the time I finally found my business card I could not read. And eventually I had to match the shape of the squiggle of the number to the squiggle on the telephone pad in order to get that phone number dialed." Once she had dialed successfully, Taylor could no longer speak but was able, by grunting, to make her co-worker understand that she needed help.

On her way to the emergency room at Massachusetts General Hospital, Taylor accepted the idea of her own death and was surprised to wake up in the hospital hours later. "I was not necessarily happy to find myself in that condition," she told Gross. "I really had to grieve the death of the woman whom I had been because I had none of her memories. I had none of her recollection of her life. And I was essentially now an infant." Two and a

half weeks after she was admitted, Taylor had surgery to remove a golf ball-sized blood clot in her brain. When she was sent home, her mother moved in with her to help with her recovery.

Over the next eight years, Taylor was forced to relearn many everyday functions. "I had to learn to read again, wash dishes, do puzzles: I didn't know anything any more about edges, about how you use color as a clue when you're doing a puzzle. I had to start from scratch," she told Susan Schwartz for the Montreal, Quebec, *Gazette* (September 11, 1997). "Because I understood my brain so well, how it organizes information, it was probably easier for me: I believe in the ability of the brain to reroute itself." Aside from her regular visits to a speech therapist, Taylor did not follow conventional recovery methods, which dictate that a patient be roused from sleep early in the day, given amphetamines, and subjected to large doses of stimulation from television and radio. At first, Taylor slept most of the day, waking only to eat and use the bathroom. She never watched television and did not talk on the phone. Taylor used children's toys to master basic skills and also watched videotapes of herself giving lectures in order to imitate her own speech patterns. She ultimately regained the scientific knowledge she had lost and began giving lectures again, which she did at first by memorizing scripts and hoping no one would ask questions. "I had the advantage that I didn't lose my right hemisphere. After enough time for the swelling in [my] brain to go down and after brain surgery, I had enough awareness that I still understood, for example, the head of the pancreas and how the duodenum fits around the head of the pancreas," she told Terry Gross. "I had the picture in my mind, but I didn't have any language. So I had to go back and re-learn all the terminology." Although many neurologists think that within six months of a stroke, the brain will have achieved whatever level of recovery is possible, Taylor believes that her eight years of steady improvement refute that. "I am living proof that you can lose your mind and get it back," she told Gina Barton for the *Indianapolis Star* (October 18, 2001).

## PERSONAL LIFE

Since her stroke, Taylor has said, she has become a more compassionate person, and she now makes time for such artistic endeavors as writing and playing music. "When I lost my left hemisphere I lost all of the normal 'in the box' thinking," she told Sandra Kiume for *Inkling* magazine (May 24, 2007, on-line). "When I lost the ability to define, organize and categorize information, I gained the ability to be intuitive and creative." Taylor also crafts anatomically correct depictions of brains in colorful stained glass, a hobby she began as part of her therapeutic regime. Her creations are sold online and can be seen on display at the National Institute of Mental Health, in Bethesda, Maryland, and the Harvard Brain Tissue Resource Center.

Taylor now lectures frequently about her belief that, as she said at the TED conference, "if I have found nirvana and I'm still alive, then everyone who is alive can find nirvana." Although some have tried to explain her experience in religious terms, Taylor asserts that the enlightenment she felt was scientifically based. "Religion is a story that the left brain tells the right brain," she told Leslie Kaufman for the *New York Times* (May 25, 2008).

Taylor, who hopes to one day open her own rehabilitation facility, continues to be a national spokesperson for the Harvard Brain Tissue Resource Center and now serves as president of the Greater Bloomington (Indiana) Area Affiliate for NAMI. She currently teaches part-time at the IU School of Medicine and works as a consulting neuroanatomist for the Midwest Proton Radiotherapy Institute, a cancer-treatment facility. She is the recipient of Harvard's Mysell Award, for scientific presentation, as well as several honors bestowed by NAMI.

Taylor, who frequently cites her mother as her dearest friend, currently lives in Bloomington. She has a dog and two cats.

## FURTHER READING
*My Stroke of Insight: A Brain Scientist's Personal Journey*

---

# RANDALL A. TERRY

## Anti-Abortion activist

**Born:** April 25, 1959; New York, NY
**Primary Field:** Christian Evangelical
**Affiliation:** Operation Rescue

### INTRODUCTION
*The most visible figure on the "pro-life" side of the fiercely divisive abortion issue is Randall A. Terry, a Christian Evangelical lay missionary based in Binghamton, New York. In 1984 he founded Operation Rescue, a direct-action antiabortion group that is fueled by religious fervor (some would say zealotry or fanaticism) and that uses traditional nonviolent, civil-disobedience tactics in "rescue missions," the sit-down blockades of entrances to abortion clinics, aimed, in his words, at stopping "the slaughter of innocent lives." "This is a life and death struggle," Terry, who believes he has a Biblical mandate, has explained. "To the people on the other side, it's an issue, but to us it's a baby who's going to die." Counter demonstrators at the blockades have an answering slogan: "Operation Rescue, that's a lie. You don't care if women die." Operation Rescue is much larger, better organized, more rigorously disciplined, and more sophisticated in strategy and tactics than any of its scattered predecessors, which date back*

*to groups of ragtag Roman Catholic demonstrators, some of whom were veterans of the peace movement, in the early 1970s. "The pro-life activists had no succinct phrase to describe exactly what they were doing," Philip F. Lawler observed in his book* Operation Rescue: A Challenge to the Nation's Conscience *(1992). "The word that would eventually emerge to describe this movement, rescue, did not appear [until] Randall Terry had an inspiration that gave pro-life activism its rallying cry and crystallized the emerging nationwide movement into Operation Rescue." In Terry's long-term view, "child-killing is the flashpoint" in a broader "cultural civil war." The ultimate goal of the rescue movement, he has said, is rescuing our society "from the path of destruction it's on" and effecting a "reformation [that] will cause America to better reflect Judeo-Christian ethics in her laws and cultural norms, a reflection that she possessed as recently as the 1950s."*

*In the hundreds of "rescue missions" mounted by Operation Rescue and its local chapters since 1987, tens of thousands of American and Canadian citizens have risked arrest. Terry himself has served several jail sentences, and he owes the National Organization of Women a court judgment of $50,000. The legal sanctions against Operation Rescue took a quantum leap upward in November 1993, when Congress passed a* *bill making the blocking of access to abortion clinics a federal felony. The bill did not distinguish between non-violent blockaders and the occasional fringe mavericks who perpetrate violence against clinics and abortion-ists. While Terry has tried to distance himself from the violent extremists, the officials of the mainstream National Right to Life Committee in their turn have taken no public position on Operation Rescue.*

## EARLY LIFE

Randall A. Terry, the older son of Rochester, New York public school teachers, Michael Terry and Doreen (Di-Pasquale) Terry, was born on April 25, 1959. Before they embraced Randall's evangelical faith, in the late 1980s, his parents were apparently perfunctory Chris-tians at best. His mother seems to have been more re-luctant to endorse Randall's pro-life stand than his fa-ther was, but descriptions of her in published profiles of Terry suggest that she is now firm in that support.

"Terry's roots, at least on his mother's side of the family, have long been matriarchal, progressive, and iconoclastic," Susan Faludi observed in *Mother Jones* (November 1989). "One branch quit the Catho-lic Church for good in the early 1900s, because Terry's maternal great-grandmother refused to put up with a bossy parish priest. Terry's grandmother fought racism at every opportunity. And few can match the DiPasquale women, Terry's mother, Doreen, and her three younger sisters, Diane, Dawn, and Dale, for commitment to so-cial change."

Rejecting offers of more lucrative and less stress-ful jobs in suburban schools, Doreen Terry has dedi-cated herself professionally to teaching in inner-city schools in Rochester. Diane Hope is a professor of communications at the Rochester Institute of Technol-ogy. Dawn Marvin is a former communications direc-tor of the Rochester chapter of Planned Parenthood. Diane, Dawn, and Dale have worked for more than two decades in the causes of civil rights, peace, women's equality, and women's reproductive rights. "I think the Randy that goes around as leader of Operation Rescue is someone I have very little connection with as the Randy that I knew as a kid," Diane Hope told Susan Faludi. Her sister Dawn disagreed. "You cannot separate who he is as a fundamentalist Christian with who he was as a teenager," she said. "He didn't just come from a middle-of-the-road Protestant family where he learned about Jesus and the little lamb. He came from a family where at family gatherings he absorbed feminist arguments

from really strong-willed women. I don't think we have any choice but to explore his roots."

Terry grew up in a tract housing development in the Rochester suburb of Henrietta. Inheriting a talent for music from his father, he has been playing the piano and writing songs since childhood, and he originally aspired to become a rock musician. After interviewing Terry, Francis Wilkinson wrote in *Rolling Stone* (October 5, 1989), "He pointedly alludes to his teenage habits of smoking pot and playing rock music in a neighborhood garage band, almost as if to revel momentarily in the sin he has so fully expunged." Terry still plays rock music, of the Christian variety, and he wrote and performed the antiabortion songs on *When the Battle Raged*, a tape he distributes to people in the pro-life movement. Asked if he had ever engaged in premarital sex, Terry told Wilkinson, "Well, I was a product of my times. I was delivered from the whole rock and roll culture."

Although he was an accelerated honors student just four months short of graduation, Terry dropped out of high school at the age of sixteen, partly in temporary re-bellion against his parents. He later earned a high school equivalency certificate. Hitchhiking across the country for four months, he traveled as far as Galveston, Texas. During his journey he had some unsettling encounters, which made him realize, as he later remembered, that "if there was a dark side, then there had to be a God." On his way home he began studying a Gideon Bible he had taken from a motel room. Back in Henrietta, while working behind the counter in an ice cream parlor, he served a customer who turned out to be a lay minister from the Elim Bible Institute, an evangelical mission-ary training school in Lima, New York. The rapport between the two men was immediate, and Terry's reli-gious conversion was completed. By his own account, he became a Christian on September 6, 1976.

## LIFE'S WORK

Terry joined a charismatic Christian congregation, one that believes in the Pentecostal gifts, including speak-ing in tongues, faith healing, and other manifestations of the Holy Spirit. On the recommendation of his pas-tor, he was accepted as a student at Elim Bible Institute in 1978. As a student at Elim, he wrote, produced, and starred in *Turn Again*, a partly autobiographical rock-opera version of the Biblical story of the Prodigal Son. In a homiletics class at the institute, he was introduced to the works of Francis Schaeffer, who is regarded by many American Evangelicals as their equivalent of C.

S. Lewis, the British author of *The Screw tape Letters* and other books on Christianity, and by Terry as "the greatest modern Christian philosopher." A conservative and populist Presbyterian who rebelled against the hegemony of liberalism in theology and Biblical criticism that began in the 1920s, Schaeffer wrote books of apologetics, Christian intellectual history, and criticism of a Western culture steeped in secular humanism and situational ethics. Believing that the thinking of the Founding Fathers was grounded in Biblical principles, he looked for a catalyst issue on which to challenge what he considered to be the nation's contemporary waywardness. After considering the "godlessness" of the public schools, he settled on abortion as the springboard issue, and in 1981, three years before his death, he published the book *A Christian Manifesto*, which would become a charter document of Operation Rescue.

After graduating fourth in his class of thirty-nine at the Elim Bible Institute in 1981, Terry could have been ordained an Evangelical minister, but he chose instead to be a lay missionary. With his wife, Cindy, whom he married in the same year, he intended to do missionary work in Central America. He had learned Spanish for that purpose. "In the fall of 1983, God interrupted our plans to be missionaries and called us to the mission field of abortion clinics," he wrote in the preface to his book *Operation Rescue* (1988). In an interview with Susan Faludi for her *Mother Jones* article, he recounted how "the vision of Operation Rescue was birthed in [his] heart": "The first time I remember being cognizant of child killing was in 1977. I was driving my car home from work one day, and I saw a bumper sticker that said, 'Abortion, Pick on Someone Your Own Size,' and I thought, 'Yeah, that's right.'" The next defining moment in the chronology he related was the day in 1983 when a woman new to his prayer group at the Church at Pierce Creek, in the Binghamton area, suggested that they pray for an end to "the Holocaust in America" that had begun, in the view of pro-lifers, in state after state in the late 1960s with federal judicial decrees and nationally in 1973 with the Supreme Court's sanctioning of abortion in the *Roe v. Wade* decision. The scope of that decision was reduced by the court's *Webster v. Reproductive Health Services* decision in 1989. As the group prayed, Terry was struck for the first time with a full realization of the inconsistency of Christians like himself who "were saying that abortion was murder" but were protesting only by "writing a letter now and then."

In the early 1980s Terry earned a living by selling tires. Later he ran a used-car business, until 1989. In May 1984 he began spending much of his free time picketing a Binghamton abortion clinic and doing what pro-lifers call "sidewalk counseling," trying to persuade pregnant women entering the clinic to "choose life" for the offspring they were carrying. "Then my wife went out there full-time, forty hours a week for like four months," he recalled to Francis Wilkinson during the interview for *Rolling Stone*. "Finally, the people of our church rallied, made a whole bunch of pickets, and came down and started standing with us." In his book *Operation Rescue*, he wrote, "The extra strength in numbers had a tremendous effect. In a two-week period, five young women who were pregnant and planning to abort their children turned away and chose life for their babies, the first among hundreds in the years to come who would be rescued."

In developing his organization and refining its strategy and tactics, Terry was influenced by the nonviolent civil disobedience of civil rights activists as well as by the example of his seniors in direct action in the religious pro-life movement, most of them Roman Catholics with whom he became personally acquainted and sometimes collaborated. Today the membership of Operation Rescue, according to several estimates that vary only slightly, has a strong representation of Catholics, almost 40 percent, although the majority of its members, nearly 60 percent, are Evangelicals. Those Catholics included the highly dedicated pacifist and human rights crusader Joan Andrews, who was described by Garry Wills as "the one authentic hero of the pro-life movement," Joseph Seidler, who founded the Pro-Life Action League in Chicago, and John Ryan, who set up the Pro-Life Direct Action League in St. Louis. In 1984 Terry played a leadership role in at least one of the first national antiabortion actions, staged jointly by organizations including Seidler's and Ryan's groups.

In October 1984 Terry and his wife opened in Binghamton the Crisis Pregnancy Center, the prototype of many facilities that he would help open across the country. The center offered women free pregnancy tests, confidential counseling, baby clothes, formula, and other necessities for newborns as well as access to a range of supportive referral services, including some that help unwed mothers find lodging in private homes. When the Binghamton center and its referral services became overburdened, Terry began planning and raising funds for the House of Life, a residence for unwed mothers that opened in Binghamton in the fall of 1987. In addition to rescuing "babies and their mothers from the nightmare of abortion" and educating people "to the value of human life from the Bible-based Christian perspective," Terry's purpose was, in his words, "to call the church to repentance for [its] apathy, cowardice, [and] selfishness [in] having allowed child-killing to occur" for so long without protesting.

Before settling on the blockade as his standard tactic, Terry experimented with invading abortion clinics, a tactic patterned after Joseph Seidler's sit-ins. His first "rescue mission" took place one morning in January 1986, when he and six members of his group entered the abortion clinic in Binghamton just after it opened, before any patients had arrived, and locked themselves in one of the inner rooms. The seven were arrested for and found guilty of criminal trespass and resisting arrest. Terry refused to pay his fine of sixty dollars and spent ten days in jail in the spring of 1986. Following another rescue mission a few months later, he was again imprisoned. After twenty-two days in jail, he was released pending appeal just before his daughter was born. He eventually lost the appeal and served the remaining twenty-three days of his sentence in March and April 1987.

Terry unveiled his plan for a nationwide Operation Rescue at a meeting of antiabortion leaders in Pensacola, Florida in November 1986. The response was mixed. Focusing on those who approved of the idea, Terry began, in his words, to "spread the vision" by calling on pastors and church people across the country to join him. On November 28, 1987 he led nearly three hundred people, including many clergy, in a blockade of the Cherry Hill (New Jersey) Women's Clinic. After long planning, Operation Rescue activists from all over the United States and Canada converged on New York City and Long Island from May 2 through May 6, 1988. In a series of blockades of various abortion clinics, more than fifteen hundred demonstrators were arrested, among them a Roman Catholic bishop, two monsignors, fifteen priests, four nuns, a Greek Orthodox priest, two rabbis, and more than twenty ministers of various evangelical denominations. Counterdemonstrating pro-choice partisans, restrained behind police barricades during the incidents, chanted such slogans as "Racist, sexist, anti-gay, born-again bigots go away!"

The national publicity drawn by Operation Rescue escalated during the following months, when Terry and his cohorts descended on abortion clinics in Atlanta,

Georgia before, during, and after the Democratic National Convention there. Between June and October 1988, 1,235 people were arrested in twenty-four separate "rescues." The bookings were complicated by the fact that many of the arrestees had begun the practice of identifying themselves only as "Baby Doe," reflecting their view of themselves as surrogates. Convicted on charges of criminal trespass in Atlanta, Terry refused to pay the $550 fine. After several delays, he was incarcerated in the local county jail and served four months, until January 30, 1990, when an anonymous donor paid his fine.

The "siege of Atlanta" generated an increased flow of financial contributions to Operation Rescue, including a check for $10,000 from the Reverend Jerry Falwell's Moral Majority. In the months following the events in Atlanta, the organization's average monthly income, previously about $1,000, grew to several tens of thousands of dollars. As Operation Rescue leaders, seasoned in Atlanta, recruited new activists in numerous cities, the membership climbed, eventually reaching an estimated one hundred thousand. Terry himself traveled widely throughout the country teaching his principles and tactics to local groups. From the end of October 1988 to the middle of February 1989, there was at least one locally organized clinic blockade every weekend. Early in 1989 the national organization staged another large event in the New York City area, in which more than one thousand people were arrested. John Cardinal O'Connor, the Roman Catholic archbishop of New York, addressed the participants before that blockade. The New York "rescue" was followed by a series of Holy Week blockades in Los Angeles, by various "theme" blockades, including two in Washington, D.C. "Rachel's Rescue," organized and conducted exclusively by women, and "Veterans' Rescue", by a series of blockades at a clinic in Dobbs Ferry, New York, and by "national days of rescue" held in dozens of cities. Mary Suh and Lydia Denworth reported in *Ms.* (April 1989) that there had been a total of at least 130 blockades of abortion clinics in thirty-five states and some twelve thousand arrests of participants. In his book *Operation Rescue*, Philip F. Lawler reported that between May 1988 and August 1990 Operation Rescue had mounted blockades at 683 sites, resulting in the jailing of approximately forty-one thousand people.

At the same time, the counterattack of the pro-choice forces, chiefly the National Organization for Women, Planned Parenthood, and the National Abortion Rights

Action League, was gaining momentum, eventually forcing Operation Rescue into a retrenchment. In 1990 Terry closed his Binghamton headquarters, stopped soliciting donations, moved Operation Rescue's financial operations virtually underground, and formed the Christian Defense Coalition "to teach Christian communities to defend themselves against police brutality, judicial tyranny, and political harassment" and "to speak out against the abuse of fellow Christians." Those defensive moves were at least partly in reaction to the escalating sanctions against Operation Rescue. Among other things, the United States attorney's office in New York had seized the organization's bank accounts, and the courts had levied a $50,000 judgment against Terry and a $110,000 contempt fine against his organization (he has refused to pay either). Operation Rescue was also subjected to novel applications of the federal RICO act, which was intended to provide a mechanism for confiscating the assets of organized crime, and of a post-Civil War anti-Ku Klux Klan act.

In a surprising resurgence of vitality, Operation Rescue staged the project called the "Summer of Mercy," involving several thousand pro-lifers over a period of six weeks in July and August 1991 in Wichita, Kansas. For blockading abortion clinics, including that of Dr. George Tiller, a specialist in late-term abortions, at least 1,773 people were arrested, including, on one occasion alone, eighty-three priests and ministers. Eugene Gerber, the Roman Catholic bishop of Wichita, expressed his "solidarity" with the blockaders, and Joan Finney, the governor of Kansas, complimented them on their "orderly manner and dignity." A year later Terry and Joseph Slovenec were sentenced to jail terms of up to six months for violating a judge's order requiring them to stay at least one hundred feet away from abortion clinics in Houston, Texas during the Republican National Convention there. They began serving their sentences on August 27, 1992. The recent Freedom of Access to Clinic Entrances Act set a maximum fine of $100,000 for first-time violent offenders, who would also face up to a year in prison; nonviolent first offenders faced a maximum fine of $10,000 and up to six months in jail. Subsequent offenses would nearly triple the penalties.

Citing the 1993 murder of an abortionist outside a Florida clinic, President Bill Clinton said, at a White House signing ceremony on May 26, 1994, "We simply cannot, we must not, continue to allow the attacks, the incidents of arson, the campaigns of intimidation upon law-abiding citizen that have given rise to this law."

## PERSONAL LIFE

Lanky and gangly, Randall A. Terry stands six feet, one inch tall, weighs 175 pounds, and has a loping gait. His voice is slightly high-pitched, and his conversational style has been described as "Christian hip." "Terry has an almost Jacksonesque knack for pithy phrases turned with a sort of evangelical jive," Francis Wilkinson observed in *Rolling Stone*, referring to the Reverend Jesse Jackson. In his private relations with his associates, Terry is easygoing, informal, and playful to the point of indulging in such practical jokes as water gun squirts. But in the clinic blockades, he is very much the commander, using his bullhorn to direct maneuvers, such as the tactic of "going limp" after the arrival of police. He regards the antiabortion struggle as "the fiercest battle in a war of ideologies and allegiances" that must be waged on many fronts against those who are in the process of stamping out "virtually every vestige of Christianity from our laws, morals, institutions, and, ultimately, our families." "The pollution and degradation of this culture did not happen overnight," he told Richard Lacayo in an interview for *Time* (October 21, 1991), "and neither will our ability to reclaim it and reform it happen overnight." In addition to their daughter, Faith, Randall Terry and his wife, the former Cindy Dean, have three mixed-race foster children, born to a woman Terry became acquainted with outside the clinic where she had gone to have the third child aborted. The Terrys live outside Harpursville, New York, a thirty-minute drive from Binghamton. Terry enjoys hunting, fishing, volleyball, and reading, especially the thrillers of Tom Clancy.

## FURTHER READING

*Operation Rescue: A Challenge to the Nation's Conscience; Accessory to Murder; Operation Rescue*

# JACOBO TIMERMAN

## Journalist; Author; Social Activist

**Born:** January 6, 1923; Bar, Ukrainian SSR, Soviet
Union
**Died:** November 11, 1999; Buenos Aires, Argentina
**Primary Field:** Human Rights
**Affiliation:** Zionism

### INTRODUCTION

*One of Argentina's most distinguished journalists, Jaco-
bo Timerman became the focal point of an international
human rights issue after he was seized in April 1977
by Argentine security forces and held captive for thirty months. He described that harrowing ordeal in his
book* Prisoner Without a Name, Cell Without a Number *(Knopf, 1981). A Jew, a dedicated Zionist, and an
outspoken defender of social justice, Timerman, as publisher of the liberal Buenos Aires daily La Opinion from
1971 to 1977, provoked controversy with his attacks on
government corruption and repression, his allegations
of officially sanctioned anti-Semitism in Argentina, and
his efforts to get to the bottom of the unexplained dis-
appearances of an estimated 15,000 to 20,000 Argentines seized by official authorities or paramilitary death
squads. More recently, Timerman, who is now a journalist in Israel, has challenged the human rights policy
of the Administration of President Ronald Reagan and
its tendency to tolerate right-wing "authoritarian" regimes while condemning those of the "totalitarian" left.*

### EARLY LIFE

In the foreword to his book, Jacobo Timerman revealed
that his family, "by way of those strange, bi-forked
paths of Judaism, escaped the Spanish occupation of
the Netherlands, and the Inquisition, and wound up in
a small town of Vinnitsa Oblast in the Ukraine, called
Bar." He was born there on January 6, 1923, the older
of the two sons of Nathan and Eva (Berman) Timerman.
Although his parents were poor, according to "family
accounts" the Timermans "were prominent in the community and fought for Jewish rights." He was only five
when his family left Bar for Argentina to escape the po-
groms that were rampant in the Ukraine in the 1920's,
but he remembered attending the town's Great Synagogue with his father, his uncles, and his cousins, and
he bore away with him "a vague longing for those tall,
bearded, unsmiling men."

When Jacobo Timerman was twelve his father died,
leaving his mother with having to support him and his
brother, Yoselle, who is now known as Jose. "His closeness to this strong woman is one of the grand tones of
his character," Ted Solotaroff concluded in the *Nation*
(June 13, 1981). "Her dream of a Jewish homeland became his Zionism." The Timermans lived in the Once
(Eleventh) District of Buenos Aires, the heart of the
Jewish quarter, in a one room apartment they occupied
rent free in exchange for performing janitorial duties in
their tenement building. While his mother worked as
a street vendor selling clothes, Jacobo attended public
schools, working afternoons as messenger boy for a
jewelry store. A "neurotic obsessive" about the suffering of world Jewry, Timerman recalls, his mother constantly reminded her sons of it. After the rise of Hitler,
she would ask them during meals: "How can we be eating while the Jews in Germany are being mistreated?"

Timerman had his first contact with Zionism at
eight, when his mother enrolled him in the Jewish sports
club Macabi. At fourteen he joined Avuca, a student
group that organized discussions on Zionism and Jewish history. Later he learned the techniques of agriculture, hoping eventually to work on a kibbutz in Israel.
A major influence on his life was his encounter, through
Avuca, with two Jewish Boy Scouts who were Socialist Zionists. "When I heard them speak," he wrote, "I
became destined for that world I would never abandon
and never try to abandon a world that at times took the
form of Zionism, at times the struggle for human rights,
at times the fight for freedom of expression, and at other
times again the solidarity with dissidents against all
totalitarianisms."

### LIFE'S WORK

Thereafter Timerman concentrated his reading on works
by such socially committed writers as Jack London,
Upton Sinclair, John Dos Passos, Henri Barbusse, and
Erich Maria Remarque. He joined Socialist May Day
demonstrations and identified with returning Jewish
veterans of the Zionist organization Hashomer Hatzair
who had fought against Franco in the Spanish Civil War.
In 1944 he was arrested while attending a film festival
of the Argentine League for Human Rights, allegedly a
Communist affiliate, and was detained for twenty four
hours. He also became a member of the Youth League
for Freedom, which supported the Allied cause at a time

when the Argentine government backed the Germans and was eventually dissolved by police as a Communist front. On one occasion, Timerman was arrested and detained overnight after leading a group of young antifascists in an attack on the headquarters of a Nazi newspaper. Anxious to enlist as a volunteer in the struggle against the Axis, Timerman offered his services to the Free French Committee and the British and American embassies in Buenos Aires but was not accepted.

Although Timerman once told Richard Eder of the *New York Times* (December 15, 1979) that he did not "become a journalist" but "was born one," he originally started out on another course. For a year he went to the school of engineering in nearby La Plata. Among his teachers there was Ernesto Sabato, who eventually became one of Argentina's foremost novelists. Timerman began to make his mark in journalism in 1947, when he became a freelance writer for several literary magazines. In the late 1950's he joined the staff of *La Razon*, then one of Buenos Aires' leading newspapers. His resourcefulness as a reporter became widely known, according to his longtime friend Jacob Kovadloff, after the February 1958 election of Arturo Frondizi as President of Argentina on a nationalist, anti-imperialist platform. Before Frondizi assumed office in May of that year, Timerman traveled with him by air on a series of visits to heads of state of other countries in Latin America. His front page dispatches for *La Razon* gave the nation up to date news about Frondizi's plans for governing.

Timerman's restless, inventive journalism carried him into radio, television, and publishing. In the early 1960's, with a group of young fellow journalists, he launched *Prim era Plana*, a highly successful weekly news magazine patterned on the format of *Time* or *Newsweek* magazine. Timerman sold it and in 1969 founded *Confirmado*, another popular newsweekly. Having in turn sold it, he again joined other colleagues and founded the newspaper *La Opinion*, of which the first issue appeared on May 4, 1971.

Modeled on the liberal Parisian daily Le Monde, Timerman's newspaper was greeted, in Kovadloff's words, as a "breath of fresh air in Argentine life" by the intellectual, politically-minded readers to whom it catered. As its publisher and editor, Timerman announced that *La Opinion* would support Israel, that its stance would be left of center, and that it would give extensive coverage to the arts. *La Opinion* took no private advertising and, unlike other Argentine newspapers, it allowed its writers to sign their articles. When

La Opinion prospered, attaining a circulation of some 150,000, Timerman sold a 45 percent share to David Graiver, a young Jewish financier. In 1974, with Graiver's help, he built a modern printing plant that serviced his newspaper. He also founded a small but successful book-publishing firm, Timerman Editores, which under the direction of his son Hector published works on contemporary issues, many of them especially commissioned from their authors.

From 1971 to 1977, the years in which Timerman published *La Opinion*, Argentina experienced one of the most trying and violent periods of its history. Always outspoken and politically aware, moving within the nation's most influential circles, Timerman was constantly involved in national affairs. Although *La Opinion* remained left of center it became a force for moderation and opposed extremism of all political shades. As a result, Timerman became the target of harassment and violence from both left and right. In July 1972 Timerman's home was among twenty places time bombed by the Montoneros, an ultra-leftist faction of the Peronists, who remained a major political force in Argentina seventeen years after the forced exile of President Juan Peron. With the proliferation of terrorist groups, Timerman's life was in constant danger.

When in the spring of 1973 Argentina reverted to civilian government with the resignation of President General Alejandro Agustin Lanusse, Timerman supported the election of Hector Campora, whose undisguised function was to prepare the country for the return of Juan Peron. *La Opinion's* Peronist allegiance continued after Peron returned and was overwhelmingly reelected President in September 1973. It ceased, however, after Peron's third wife, Isabel Martinez de Peron, who assumed the Presidency upon her husband's death in July 1974, proved completely unable to govern effectively.

Meanwhile, Timerman continued to champion democratic institutions and human rights, irrespective of ideological boundaries. Taking positions that later confounded his prison interrogators, he condemned the Soviet Union's persecution of dissidents, right-wing tendencies in Israel's government, terrorist acts of the Palestine Liberation Organization, and Fidel Castro's treatment of political prisoners and exportation of terrorism. On the other hand, Timerman supported the Marxist government of Salvador Allende, who was elected President of neighboring Chile in 1970, and after Allende's overthrow in a bloody military coup in 1973, he was named "public enemy number one" by the

Chilean press because of *La Opinion's* denunciations of human rights violations by that country's new dictatorship. In February 1976 Timerman urged in *La Opinion* that Argentina's military move against Isabel Peron's government, following twenty months of economic chaos, political corruption, and inability to prevent terrorist acts by the left wing Montoneros and Trotskyite People's Revolutionary Army (ERP) and the far-right "death squads" of the Argentine Anticommunist Alliance. As a result, *La Opinion* was shut down for ten days.

When President Isabel Peron was overthrown in March 1976 by a three-man military junta headed by Lieutenant General Jorge Rafael Videla, who became President, Timerman's position was perilously ambiguous. On the one hand, he backed Videla's promises of national unity, economic reconstruction, and ultimate return to traditional constitutional processes. On the other, he deplored the government's free-market policies, the mounting violence, and the increasing numbers of *desaparecidos*, or missing persons, most of them abducted by extreme right-wing elements of the military. *La Opinion*, along with the English language *Buenos Aires Herald*, edited by Robert Cox, soon were almost alone among periodicals in insisting upon cessation of all terrorism and upon *habeas corpus* proceedings for those taken into custody, whose stories and names Timerman published regularly in his paper.

Ironically, while the Videla government mounted pressures on *La Opinion* to stop marshalling public opinion, it pointed to the continued existence of that opposition organ as proof of its own moderation. As means of exerting pressure on *La Opinion*, the authorities at times withheld official government advertising from its pages and compelled the paper to bear excessive production costs. As the danger increased, some reporters quit, and a few loyal ones eventually joined the scores of journalists who disappeared. Timerman received many death threats, from both left and right, and published responses to some of them on the front page of La Opinion. In his editorials he insisted that the newspaper would maintain its standards and expressed curiosity about who would eventually claim his corpse. In answer to advice from friends that he leave Argentina, Timerman asserted: "I am one who belongs to Masada, referring to a first-century Jewish community whose citizens chose to die rather than surrender to the Romans."

At 2:00 A.M. on April 15, 1977, twenty armed men in civilian clothes broke into Timerman's Buenos Aires home and, allegedly on orders from the Tenth Infantry Brigade, carried him off. His family did not learn of his whereabouts until six weeks later. In the months that followed, Timerman was moved about, to three clandestine places of confinement and two regular prisons. In *Prisoner Without a Name, Cell Without a Number* he recounted his experiences, a simulated execution, beatings, electric shock tortures, extended periods of solitary confinement under humiliating circumstances, and intense interrogations. Timerman concluded that although most of his fellow prisoners were not Jews, a Nazi-like element of the military looked towards a "final solution" for Argentina's more than 300,000 Jewish citizens and subjected Jewish prisoners to especially harsh treatment. When he openly admitted to his interrogators that *La Opinion* was a Zionist organ, his captors seemed determined to use him as showcase proof of an alleged worldwide Zionist plot to seize Patagonia in southern Argentina for a second Jewish state. Their futile plan, Timerman believes, may have saved his life.

Since no formal charges were filed, official motives for Timerman's imprisonment were never clear. The military at first spoke vaguely of "subversive acts" and "economic crimes." Eventually, however, Timerman was publicly linked with David Graiver, the part-owner of *La Opinion*, whose financial empire had grown to include banks in Brussels and New York. Following reports, not fully substantiated, of Graiver's mysterious death in August 1976 in a plane crash in Mexico, his empire collapsed. It was alleged that he had looted his own banks. Eight months later, shortly before Timerman's arrest, Argentine authorities alleged that Graiver was the financial agent through whom the Montoneros invested millions extorted through ransom. Timerman's connection with Graiver was presented as part of a Jewish-Marxist-Montonero conspiracy, and authorities tried to support that contention by reprinting leftist *La Opinion* articles in the press.

Timerman's release on September 25, 1979, following more than a year of imprisonment and seventeen months of house arrest, came after three judicial declarations of his innocence on all charges. In October 1977, after sixteen hours of questioning, he had been cleared by a military special war council of links with guerrilla forces. Then, in July 1978, Argentina's supreme court, acting on a writ of habeas corpus filed by Timerman's wife, decided that there was no legal basis for holding him. Nevertheless, Timerman remained under house arrest. The supreme court's unanimous second verdict of innocence on September 18, 1979 precipitated a face-off between military hard-liners and moderates, but after a few days of indecision Timerman was finally released, put on a plane with a visa to Israel, and stripped of his Argentine citizenship and his property.

During Timerman's incarceration, worldwide attention focused on his case. Cyrus Vance, Alexander Solzhenitsyn, and Henry Kissinger were among the many who spoke out for his release, as were Amnesty International, the Inter-American Press Association, and the human rights commission of the Organization of American States. In interviews and in his book, Timerman credited his life to those efforts, and particularly to those of the Vatican and the Administration of President Jimmy Carter, which withheld aid to Argentina because of human rights violations. Timerman singled out for special praise Patricia M. Derian, Carter's Assistant Secretary of State for Human Rights. On the other hand, he leveled increasingly harsh criticism at the lack of support he received from Argentine Jewish leaders. "I had not been humiliated by torture, by electric shocks on my genitals, but had been profoundly humiliated by [their] silent complicity," he wrote in his book. Their "panic," he continued, "constituted a nightmare within a tragedy."

When Timerman's eloquent story of his imprisonment, translated from the Spanish by Toby Talbot, appeared, in condensed form in the New Yorker (April 20, 1981), and as the book *Prisoner Without a Name, Cell Without a Number* (Knopf, 1981), the response was sympathetic. Many critics concurred with Barbara Amiel, who said in her *Maclean's* review (June 15, 1981) that the book was "both horrifying and hypnotic in its revelations," and that it reinforced an undeniable point: "no possible political system of the extreme left or right can offer human beings any degree of stability, prosperity and justice."

Soon, however, Timerman became once more a center of controversy. During a book promotion visit to the United States he repeatedly criticized Argentine Jewish leadership and the Reagan Administration's policies on human rights. Appearing on *Bill Moyers' Journal,* presented over WNET-TV on May 29, 1981, Timerman vigorously condemned the State Department's low-keyed response to human rights violations in "authoritarian" nations like Argentina, and he compared Argentine Jewish leaders to members of a Judenrat, or Jewish council, of the kind that cooperated with the Nazis during World War II. Timerman attended

confirmation hearings of the Senate Foreign Relations Committee in May 1981 on Ernest W. Lefever, President Reagan's nominee for Assistant Secretary of State for Human Rights. Although he did not testify against Lefever's policy of "quiet diplomacy" toward allies like Argentina that violated human rights, his presence at the hearings was regarded as a significant factor in mustering Congressional opposition that caused Lefever to withdraw from consideration.

Timerman's views were met by volleys of sometimes acerbic responses from such commentators as William F. Buckley Jr., Irving Kristol, and Norman Podhoretz. In the *Wall Street Journal* (May 29, 1981), Kristol suggested that the "Graiver Affair," rather than the fact that he was a Jew, was the cause of his imprisonment, while the former Israeli diplomat Benno Weiser Varon, in an article in *Midstream* (December 1980), refuted contentions that the Timerman case constituted another "Dreyfus affair." Disagreement with Timerman also came from Mario Gorenstein, president of the Jewish Associations of Argentina. On the other hand, Timerman had many supporters, including Argentine human rights leader Emilio Mingone, Rabbi Morton Rosenthal of the Anti-Defamation League of B'nai B'rith, and New York Times columnist Anthony Lewis. Ted Solotaroff observed in the *Nation* (June 13, 1981): "He is, quite simply, an extraordinary man: reflective, humane, righteous and withal extremely brave, resourceful and hard-headed."

As a resident of Tel Aviv, Timerman was a columnist for the daily Ma'ariv and also wrote for the newspaper *Davar*. In 1979 he was awarded the Hubert H. Humphrey Freedom Prize of the Anti-Defamation League of B'nai BYith and the David Ben-Gurion Award of the United Jewish Appeal, in 1980 he received the Golden Pen of Freedom from the International Federation of Newspaper Publishers, and in 1981 he was presented the Maria Moors Cabot Prize for contributions to inter-American understanding. He holds the Arthur Morse Award of the Aspen Institute and has been honored by Hadassah, the United Synagogue of America, and the American Jewish Committee.

## PERSONAL LIFE

Jacobo Timerman married Riche (or Risha), a former law student, whom he married on May 20, 1950. They had three sons: Daniel, who works on a kibbutz in Israel; Hector, an editor at Random House in New York; and Javier, a student at Hebrew University in Jerusalem.

Timerman was described as robust and stocky, with thinning gray hair and a wide-mouthed, rugged face. He wore tinted glasses owing to an eye injury in his youth. When he appeared on television with Bill Moyers he spoke in fluent but accented English. To those who knew him he was an admirable but difficult man with considerable ego, sometimes harsh in his judgments, and not inclined to mince words or shy from controversy in causes he has supported all his life.

Following his wife's death in 1992, Timerman suffered from severe depression and failing health. He died of a heart attack on November 11, 1999 in Buenos Aires.

## FURTHER READING
*Prisoner Without a Name, Cell Without a Number; Chile: Death in the South; The Longest War: Israel's Invasion of Lebanon*

---

# PETE TRIDISH

## Community Radio Activist

**Born:** November, 17, 1969; Brooklyn, New York
**Primary Field:** Micro-broadcasting movement
**Affiliation:** Prometheus Radio Project

### INTRODUCTION
*Pete Tridish is the co-founder and leader of the Prometheus Radio Project, a nonprofit organization whose motto is "freeing the airwaves from corporate control" and whose mission is to fight media consolidation by providing legal, technical, and organizational support to low-power, community-based FM radio stations. Tridish, whose real name is Dylan Wrynn, has been fighting against the monopolization of radio since 1996, the year he helped to establish and operate the pirate radio station Radio Mutiny in Philadelphia, Pennsylvania. The Federal Communications Commission (FCC) shut the station down in 1998, having banned such low-power stations 20 years earlier with the rationale that the signals of low-power community-based stations would interfere with the broadcasts of a national radio network and large commercial radio outlets. After agitating for the rights of noncommercial groups, such as nonprofit organizations, community collectives, and schools, to set up small radio stations, in the late 1990s Tridish worked with the FCC to establish rules that once again legalized the existence of and granted licenses to low-power FM radio stations. Since that time Tridish and his Prometheus Project colleagues have been successful in helping to establish several small, community radio stations in rural areas around the United States. Tridish told Laurie Kelliher for the* Columbia Journalism Review, *as posted on the publication's website, that a large part of community radio's mission is to "broad-*

*en and deepen the listening experiences of its audience. [People] want to hear Britney Spears because that's what they've heard. That doesn't mean they wouldn't appreciate music from Kenya. It's really a question of what people are exposed to and what their options are. It really is important for there to be a place on the dial that in some ways is less successful, that presents programs that are not going to be as popular, but is a place where you can go when your ear grows past the bubble pop of our culture. I think those are the sort of green spaces, the common public spaces, that we need to be thinking about as a culture. They have an effect that goes beyond the audience numbers." Along with a number of other concerned parties, in 2003 he and his Prometheus colleagues persuaded a federal court to temporarily block the FCC from easing restrictions designed to prevent large media companies from monopolizing the airwaves. The Prometheus Radio Project's work has been recognized and supported by the Open Society Institute and the Ford, List, and MacArthur Foundations.*

### EARLY LIFE
Pete Tridish was born Dylan Wrynn on November 17, 1969 in the New York City borough of Brooklyn. His father, Stephen Wrynn, sporadically held jobs as a maintenance worker, keeping in good repair the heating, ventilating, and air conditioning systems in various New York City office buildings. After his father's death, Tridish's mother, Phyllis Wrynn, a public-school teacher, married Mitch Friedlin, who worked as a roadie for blues musicians, then in a hardware store. Tridish has a half-brother and a stepsister, neither of whom was present while he was growing up. His mother and stepfather operated a small picture framing business out of their home.

For 10 years during the 1980s and 1990s, Tridish worked intermittently as a carpenter and, to a lesser extent, in various other trades, among them masonry, plumbing, and electrical wiring. Some of his jobs involved solar heating; he told *Current Biography* that his original goal after finishing his schooling was to become a solar-heating contractor or a housing rights organizer. He received a B.A. degree from Antioch College, in Yellow Springs, Ohio, in 1992; his self-designed major was called "appropriate technology."

## LIFE'S WORK

After college, social activism became the focus of Tridish's life. 'I was working with activists in various movements," Tridish recalled to Kelliher, "and we all thought that our voices had been marginalized in the campaigns we were working on. I had been involved ever since high school in campaigns, from the nuclear freeze to the antiapartheid movement, and had always found that the stumbling block to getting exposure for our issues had to do with corporate control of the media. We felt that to make a difference in the way people thought about these issues we'd have to try to change the way the airwaves are regulated." In 1996 Tridish co-founded Radio Mutiny, a pirate radio station (91.3 FM) that broadcast from secret locations in Philadelphia, Pennsylvania. It was referred to as a "pirate" station because it was operating without a license and so in violation of FCC regulations. "None of us had been on the radio and none of us knew much about radio," Tridish told Kelliher. "For about seven or eight months, we tried to build a transmitter and finally, after blowing it up a couple times, got it going early in 1997." As a way to hide his identity and avoid the heavy fines that operating a pirate radio station would incur, that same year he assumed the name that he goes by, which sounds like "petri dish," a small glass or plastic container for growing bacteria for research. Other members of Radio Mutiny became Millie Watt, from "milliwatt," Anna Tennah, as in "antenna," Noah Vale, as in "no avail," and Bertha Venus, as in "birth of Venus."

Radio Mutiny offered an eclectic mix of programming, which included reggae, poetry, dramas, plus a segment called the "Condom Lady," which offered safe sex tips, and "Incarceration Nation," a regular report on the U.S. penal system. After broadcasting for less than a year, Radio Mutiny received a knock on the door. "FCC, open up," the visitors said, according to Tridish as quoted in the Indianapolis Star (September

15, 2003, online). He continued, "The girl who went to the door said, 'Yeah, right,' because there were always people coming to the door and making jokes. But then she looked out, she saw some guy she didn't know and a couple of cops. She told them she wouldn't open the door unless they had a warrant, so they went away." Soon afterward Tridish and his Radio Mutiny partners demonstrated in front of the site where Benjamin Franklin's printing press once stood, in downtown Philadelphia, and challenged the FCC to arrest them. They held a large banner that read, "1763, Benjamin Franklin challenges the Stamp Act and refuses to pay taxes to King George. 1996, Radio Mutiny defies the FCC for Freedom of Speech." During a similar demonstration held at the building where the Liberty Bell is displayed, also in Philadelphia, Tridish and his Radio Mutiny colleagues again broadcast from their transmitter, which they had carried with them, in open defiance of the FCC rules prohibiting low-power community broadcasting. In 1998 the FCC returned to the group's broadcast location with a court order, broke down Radio Mutiny's door, and confiscated the transmitter, thus shutting down the station for good. Nevertheless, Radio Mutiny's members continued to agitate for freedom of the airwaves. In 1998 Tridish organized a 25 city Radio Mutiny tour, during which he was the principal speaker for the group, which spoke out against commercial monopolization of radio and FCC restrictions. He also served as an organizer for the initial micro-radio conferences, meetings of advocates of low- power FM radio stations on the East Coast; the first was held in Philadelphia in April 1998, and the second, during which fellow radio pirates broadcast directly into the FCC's main offices, was held in Washington, D.C., the following October.

After the demise of Radio Mutiny, in about 1998, Tridish helped to found the nonprofit Prometheus Radio Project (named for the character in Greek mythology who steals fire from the gods and gives it to man), setting up offices in the basement of Calvary United Methodist Church in Philadelphia. In addition to Tridish, members of the Prometheus Project include Anthony Mazza, Jaclyn Ford, Levi Roman, and Hannah Sassaman. The Prometheus Radio Project has been a leading advocate for community groups that want to establish low-power FM stations, mostly in rural areas underserved by commercial broadcasters. The push for the legalization of low-power community based radio stations is sometimes referred to as the micro-broadcasting movement. "Prometheus staff members started their voyages on the oceans of aether as pirates to protest media concentration and demand access to the airwaves," the group's Web site explains. "With the possibility of legal low-power radio stations on the horizons they turned in their hooks and patches to help foster the free radio movement." Tridish explained to Kelliher that his objective in forming the Prometheus Project was to "take the FCC at its word, that they really did care about community radio, and try to get them to pass a proposal that would actually be good for community broadcasters around the country." A typical commercial radio station has a 50,000-watt signal that can reach listeners within a radius of hundreds of miles; the signals of low-power stations, which by federal law may not exceed 100 watts, seldom extend beyond 10 miles.

In the late 1990s, spearheaded by the likes of Tridish and his colleagues, the micro-broadcasting movement expanded, "using exponential growth, mass media exposure, and stubborn noncompliance with FCC 'cease and desist broadcasting letters,'" as Kate Duncan wrote for *Z Magazine* (July/August 1998). "Pirates also adhere to the safety-in-numbers rule, helping establish and keep other stations on the air." The FCC expressed its willingness to discuss the possibility of legalizing low-power FM stations, though commission members often contended that interference from such stations would disrupt preexisting licensed programming. The commission began to reconsider its position on community radio and began discussing ideas with leaders of the micro-broadcasting movement, among them Tridish. As quoted by Duncan, then FCC chairman William Kennard stated that proponents of noncommercial low-power FM radio stations "have a legitimate issue in that there are, in some communities, no outlets for expression on the airwaves, and I believe that is a function, in part, of the massive consolidation that we are seeing in the broadcast industry."

In 1999 Tridish led the Prometheus Radio Project on a 20 city tour around the U.S. to bring attention to the group's crusade. He began working closely with the FCC on proposals for establishing the legality of community radio stations. "There was a long period of time when many of [my fellow radio pirates] called me a sell-out for working so closely with the FCC," Tridish recalled to Kelliher. He actively participated in the FCC rulemaking process that led, in 2000, to the adoption of regulations sanctioning low-power FM (LPFM) stations and offering radio licenses to select nonprofit groups,

community organizations, and schools, among other interested parties.

Despite the FCC's issuance of licenses to small community stations beginning that year, Tridish was not satisfied, "because low-power FM has done nothing for the big cities," as he told Kelliher. Indeed, returning to the familiar objection that low-power stations would create unwanted interference, large broadcasting entities (including the National Association of Broadcasters, a powerful trade association representing the interests of established radio and television broadcasters) persuaded Congress to pass a bill that overrode the FCC's changes and limited new licensing to low-power stations in, for the most part, small towns or rural areas. Low-power stations in urban areas were all but banned. Therefore, according to Eils Lotozo in the *Philadelphia Inquirer* (March 7, 2002), the FCC rejected nearly 80 percent of the thousands of license requests that had poured in after the new regulations were announced in 2000. "That was very unusual," Tridish told Lotozo. "We were kind of blindsided. Congress doesn't know a watt from a volt, and it has never overruled the FCC on a technical issue." He told Kelliher, "To this day Philadelphia, where I come from, doesn't have a low-power radio station. It's kind of ironic that I haven't been able to bring to Philadelphia the dreams and successes we had as pirates back in 1998. I think the FCC put together low-power FM as a patch to its rules so it could maintain authority over the airwaves because, frankly, it had badly misallocated the airwaves in the past."

In 2001, to examine the common claim that LPFM stations create detrimental interference, the FCC, at Congress's command, hired the Mitre Corp., a federally funded research and development center, to conduct independent LPFM field tests. The FCC's report to Congress on the findings of the Mitre study (dated February 19, 2004 and posted on the official FCC Web site) concluded that interference from LPFM stations was very minimal and that no significant interference from an LPFM station existed beyond a radius of a few hundred meters around the LPFM station's transmitter site, meaning that the FCC's relegation of LPFM stations to areas outside urban centers or locations with preexisting full-service FM stations is unnecessary. The FCC report, which counseled Congress to "re-address this issue and modify the statute" that relegates LPFM stations to areas outside major urban centers, signaled a victory for Tridish and his colleagues. Tridish told *Current Biography* that U.S. senator John McCain, an

Arizona Republican, for one, has expressed his desire to introduce legislation that would further empower the LPFM or microbroadcasting movement.

Despite having had to contend with financial and technical difficulties, the Prometheus Radio Project has helped to establish and construct a number of small, community-based, independent radio stations around the U.S., including, in 2002, KOGZ-FM in Opelousas, Louisiana, which plays zydeco music, offers local news, and is owned by a civil rights group; WRYR-FM in Arundel County, Maryland; and KRBS in Oroville, California. Prometheus members, and others of like mind, say that these start-up stations, while somewhat unpolished and limited, are much needed outposts standing against the rapid consolidation occurring in the radio industry, a trend that is making it increasingly difficult for people with viewpoints that differ from those of the mainstream media to have their voices heard.

In the summer of 2003, the Republican dominated FCC passed new regulations that, if implemented, would have allowed individual companies to own as many as three television stations and eight radio stations in the same market and to own television stations serving up to 45 percent of the nation's viewers. (The FCC regulations previously allowed up to 35 percent.) After the commission passed the new regulations, members of Congress received from constituents hundreds of thousands of letters, E-mail messages, and phone calls questioning or objecting to the new rules, as reported by Suzanne Charle in an article on the Ford Foundation website. In July this strong public response led the House of Representatives to stop funds required by the FCC to carry out the rule changes.

The administration of President George W. Bush has argued that new FCC regulations easing rules on media ownership are necessary to help broadcasters compete in a market altered by the dominance of television and the advent of the Internet. The FCC and representatives of major television networks assert that, in the face of rapidly advancing digital technology, the proposed FCC changes would actually promote competition and preserve diversity in the nation's media. Among other concerned groups and individuals who do not agree with those opinions, Prometheus members have argued that the FCC changes threaten diversity, competition, and the public nature of the airwaves. As an example of media consolidation, the company Clear Channel owns more than 1,200 radio stations around the United States. "[Big media companies] need to be curtailed in how far they can spread their arms over the countryside," Hannah Sassaman, a Prometheus staff member, told David B. Caruso, an Associated Press reporter quoted in the Indianapolis Star. "It will change the way broadcasting sounds in America if it is all centralized out of the big cities." Among those who do not agree with Prometheus's grievances is the National Association of Broadcasters' senior vice president, Dennis Wharton, who told Caruso, "We don't buy into their claim that radio has somehow lost its local flavor. The reality is that today most successful stations are highly committed to serving their local audiences."

In August 2003 Tridish and his associates filed a little-noticed suit against the FCC stating that the commission's changes furthered the monopolization of media and undermined the diverse and public nature of the airwaves. The Prometheus Project was the "lead plaintiff" or "plaintiff of record," as Tridish told Current Biography; later, other media-justice groups, as well as organizations pushing for consumer rights and other causes, joined the suit on Prometheus's side. In September a Third Circuit federal court in Philadelphia ruled in favor of the Prometheus Group's complaint, granting an emergency stay that temporarily barred the FCC from implementing the new rules. Soon afterward, the U.S. Senate, employing a rarely used legislative device called the Congressional Review Act (CRA), voted to repeal the new FCC regulations. Echoing the sentiments of Tridish and his colleagues, as quoted in an Associated Press article posted on the Virginia Press Association Web site, Democratic U.S. senator Patty Murray of Washington State said, "We have to ensure that the marketplace of ideas is not dominated by a few conglomerates at the expense of our citizens and our democracy." While pleased with those results, Tridish remains skeptical: "I'm always cautious about getting too excited about court victories," he told Caruso. "Eventually, the weight of the system always seems to wind up catching up with you."

Despite considerable bipartisan opposition, in January 2004 Congress passed, and President Bush signed into law, the Omnibus Appropriations Bill, which contains a provision setting at 39 percent the maximum allowable percentage of U.S. television households reached by outlets under the ownership of a single company. Critics deplored the decision to raise the cap from the previous 35 percent and said the easing of the restriction was a White House-tailored concession to the media companies Viacom (which owns CBS) and

News-Corp (which owns Fox), both of which already owned outlets that reached between 35 and 39 percent of all television households: thus, before the Omnibus Bill passage, both companies had actually been operating in violation of the law.

In early February 2004 Prometheus's case against the FCC was heard in the United States Third District Court of Appeals, in Philadelphia. Though the Omnibus Bill passed in January rendered moot Prometheus's fight against raising the broadcast-ownership cap, the judge who reviewed the case examined all other current FCC regulations concerning issues of media consolidation: for example, broadcast cross-ownership (a television station's current right to own a newspaper, for example); the diversity index (which deals with what percentage of a station or stations an individual party owns); and the definition of radio markets. On June 24, 2004 the court ruled that the FCC's recent attempts to loosen media-ownership regulations were unjustified. According to a press release on the Prometheus Web site, "The court determined that the FCC relied on 'irrational assumptions and inconsistencies' in determining the new cross-ownership caps, and ordered them to make a new decision that takes seriously their duty to regulate media to preserve the public interest." Although the ruling was a major triumph for Prometheus and other independent radio stations seeking media diversity, Tridish has emphasized the importance of sustaining activist efforts on behalf of LPFM radio in order to ensure that the verdict is upheld by the U.S. government. "Our next step," he told Katherine Stapp during an interview for the *Inter Press Service* (June 29, 2004), "will be a campaign to get the president to respect this decision, and persuade the administration not to appeal it."

The most recent victory for the LPFM movement occurred on July 22, 2004, when the U.S. Senate Commerce Committee voted to approve legislation authorizing low-powered radio stations to broadcast in areas previously deemed off-limits due to "potential interference" with major stations. The bill, which received bipartisan support from John McCain and Patrick Leahy, a Vermont Democrat, has the potential to increase substantially the number of low-power community radio stations broadcasting in the United States.

On the Prometheus Radio Project Web site, the group states that they are "looking for potential stations and potential volunteers." Prometheus is accepting proposals from groups "in cities throughout the northeast region [of the U.S.] to be subjected to our 'Special Treatment.' If selected, the lucky group (and lucky city!) will receive a special visit or two from Prometheus Radio People, complete with workshops, technical info, obnoxious advice, a good bit of never-do-welling, and perhaps a little bit of something that might help your group establish a community radio station." Prometheus offers a mentorship program that helps to link those aspiring to start community radio stations with already-established licensed stations in the same area. Two or three times a year, Prometheus members tour different sections of the country, visiting anywhere from five to 20 groups in each region. In addition to its work in the U.S., Prometheus has taken its message abroad, helping to establish community stations in Colombia and Nepal. In early March 2004 Tridish traveled to Guatemala to conduct for local groups a standard Prometheus Project workshop on how to set up a small noncommercial community radio, station.

## PERSONAL LIFE

Tridish has lectured widely around the U.S., everywhere from small coffee shops to the Cato Institute, and has been interviewed by *National Public Radio, CNN,* and the *Freedom Forum* as well as the *Philadelphia Inquirer*, the *Chicago Tribune*, the *Nation*, the *Los Angeles Times*, the *Washington Post*, and *Broadcasting and Cable*, among other publications. He told Bruce Schimmel for the *Philadelphia City Paper* (July 17-23, 2003, online) that his office, in the basement of the United Methodist Church in West Philadelphia, is filled with posters from radio stations, props from political demonstrations, bullhorns, bits of electrical wire, and hulks of half-built transmitters. "Yeah, I'm a geek, and I have a lot of geek pride." At the end of an email response to *Current Biography*, in the place where his name would have gone, Tridish wrote, "petri dish: a squat, cylindrical, transparent article of laboratory glassware, useful in observing resistant strains of culture in ethereal media."

## FURTHER READING

*http://www.prometheusradio.org/*

# TANYA TULL
## Social Activist

**Born:** March 22, 1943; San Francisco, California
**Primary Field:** Housing Rights
**Affiliation:** Poverty and Homelessness

## INTRODUCTION

*As Tanya Tull and Ruth Schwartz reported in an opinion column in the* Los Angeles Times *(March 6, 2004), on any given night in Los Angeles, California, alone, more than 8,000 children in homeless families struggle to find places to sleep. According to the National Coalition for the Homeless, as of mid, 2003 more than 14 million families in the United States had critical housing needs and were at risk of becoming homeless. In 2011, there was an estimated 46.2 million people living in poverty. Tull has dedicated her professional life to the eradication of those problems, and her innovative solutions for alleviating them in Los Angeles and elsewhere around the U.S. have won national and international attention. Tull is the president and chief executive officer (CEO) of Beyond Shelter, an award-winning, Los Angeles-based nonprofit organization that she founded in 1988. Much of Beyond Shelter's focus is on helping homeless families to find permanent housing and then providing social services for six months to one year, to help those families rebuild their lives; in Los Angeles more than 3,000 families have benefitted from those services. The organization's programs have served as blueprints for new ways of attacking the societal scourge of family homelessness and poverty on a national level. For example, beginning in 1999 the organization's methods were praised, documented, and disseminated by the Pew Partnership for Civic Change as part of the latter's national initiative known as* Wanted: Solutions for America. *In 2004 Beyond Shelter employed more than 60 people and operated on a budget of $3.4 million. Through Beyond Shelter Tull has developed six permanent, affordable, multi-unit housing projects for low-income persons or homeless families in Los Angeles County, with six additional new housing projects in development. Over the years she has raised millions of dollars in grants and donations to fund her humanitarian work. She has been an Ashoka Fellow and recipient of various awards and fellowships.*

## EARLY LIFE

The older of two children, Tanya Tull was born on March 22, 1943 in San Francisco, California. Her father, Sam Cherry, was a painting contractor who later owned and operated a bookstore and art gallery in San Bernardino, California; her mother, Clare Cherry, was a noted early childhood educator and the author of several books on teaching children. Tull's brother, who goes by the name of Neeli Cherkovski, is a poet and the author of biographies of the writers Lawrence Ferlinghetti and Charles Bukowski, among other books. Tull's parents were first-generation American Jews whose parents had fled persecution in the Ukraine and immigrated to the U.S. as teenagers. In San Francisco Sam and Clare Cherry "were involved in the Bohemian world of artists and writers for a few years," as Tull informed *Current Biography.* "My parents were extremely liberal, offbeat and non- judgmental, with friends from all walks of life and ethnicities." Her father's older brother, Herman Cherry, was a New York-based artist, a leading abstract expressionist closely associated with such figures as Jackson Pollock and Willem de Kooning. That artistic world "provided a background for my life, albeit from a distance," Tull told *Current Biography.* After Tull's birth, her family moved to Los Angeles. As a child she was an avid reader; she has also done abstract painting.

Tull graduated with a B.A. degree in arts and humanities from Scripps College, in Claremont, California, in 1964. She then spent a year working on a kibbutz in Israel. In 1967 she moved with her husband, a Moroccan-born Israeli artist, and their baby boy to Los Angeles. Tull and her husband were unable to find employment, and the young family was forced to rely on welfare for three months. Told by a social worker who had visited her family about a job opportunity at the Los Angeles County Department of Public Social Services, Tull applied and was hired for on-the-job training as a social worker. Within weeks, in 1967, she had begun her career in social work, handling the cases of 60 families in need in South Central Los Angeles. "Our [family's] nightmare was over," Tull said in a speech she gave upon accepting the National Citizen Activist Award from the Gleitsman Foundation, in 1996, as quoted in a Beyond Shelter press release. She added, however, that she has "never forgotten how I felt, the helplessness, bewilderment, and feelings of despair. If things could go so wrong for me, then how much more wrong can they go for those who did not have the opportunities and education that I had? My life work eventually was directed by those feelings."

## LIFE'S WORK

Dispirited by what she saw as government malfeasance and insensitivity, in 1970 Tull left her job at the Department of Public Social Services. The next year she earned a life-teaching credential from the School of Education at the University of California, Los Angeles (UCLA); she then taught elementary school for a short while, spending most of the rest of the decade raising her growing family. Her first marriage had ended in 1968; in 1971 she had remarried and had two more children. In 1980, as she recalled in her speech at the Gleitsman Foundation award ceremony, she was moved to action by an article in the *Los Angeles Times* describing the hundreds of poor children living among rats and garbage in the transient hotels of Los Angeles's Skid Row. "Within a week, a woman possessed, I was walking the streets of Skid Row," she said. Within two months, despite her lack of experience in the field, she had founded Para Los Ninos, Spanish for "For the Children." Armed with a letter of support from Mayor Tom Bradley, with whom she had met, she began seeking grants for the organization from foundations and corporations. Focused primarily on the immigrant community in downtown Los Angeles, Para Los Ninos runs child-care and family-support programs. Tull served first as executive director and then as president of the organization until 1996.

While maintaining that post, Tull also cofounded, in 1983, and served as co-director of L.A. Family Housing Corp., a nonprofit agency that operates emergency shelters and transitional housing and develops permanent housing for the homeless. From 1986 to 1988 she was executive director of the organization. In 1988 Tull founded two more nonprofit organizations, A Community of Friends and Beyond Shelter. The former develops permanent housing for the mentally ill throughout Los Angeles County. The latter organization, Beyond Shelter, has been the chief focus of Tull's work.

According to both the U.S. Department of Health and Human Services and the U.S. Interagency Council on Homelessness, an estimated two to three million people find themselves homeless at some point each year. A study conducted by the National Alliance to End Homelessness has found that families with children are the fastest-growing group among the homeless. Because of poor credit and histories of being evicted from housing, many homeless people have a very difficult time finding places to live. Further, those families who have recently been placed in housing are still at a high risk of becoming homeless again. In their *Los Angeles Times* article, Tull and Ruth Schwartz, executive director of the Shelter Partnership in Los Angeles, wrote that in Los Angeles the "majority of families that become homeless are headed by single mothers, surviving on incomes as low as $600 per month for a family of four if the parent is unemployed to about $900 per month if the parent is working." The authors wrote that homeless families are "generally 'invisible' to the public," but that "their numbers are growing."

Beyond Shelter's chief program is Housing First, through which Tull helps homeless families move from emergency shelters to permanent, affordable housing in residential neighborhoods throughout Los Angeles County. Much of the program's methodology arises from Tull's and Beyond Shelter's conviction that homeless families, once housed, can begin to regain self-confidence and control over their lives, and, furthermore, are much more likely to benefit from the other social services provided by groups such as Beyond Shelter and mainstream programs. Therefore, placing homeless families in housing as quickly as possible is Beyond Shelter's primary goal. The program's methods are described on the organization's Web site: homeless families are referred to Housing First by more than three dozen agencies throughout Los Angeles County. After being enrolled in the Housing First program, a family is assigned a case manager, who, working through Beyond Shelter's Housing Resources Department, moves the family into affordable rental housing in a neighborhood of the family's choice. Next, the case manager helps to introduce the family members to their neighborhood, educating them as to the shops, local transportation, and community services available in the area, and helps to enroll the family's children in schools. The Beyond Shelter Web site states that even six months to a year after a family has been moved into new housing, the case manager "provides individualized, supportive social services to help each family move toward improved social and economic well-being." The success of Housing First has attracted both national and international attention. The program, funded through donations and grants, was chosen by the U.S. Department of Housing and Urban Development to represent the United States as one of "25 U.S. Best Practices" at the United Nations

Conference on Human Settlements, Habitat II, which was held in Istanbul, Turkey, in 1996. There, it was chosen as one of the "100 International Best Practices" by the U.N. Center on Human Settlements for dissemination worldwide.

Other major programs of Beyond Shelter include the Rental Assistance Department, which helps to run the Emergency Housing Assistance Program and the various Rent to Prevent Eviction Programs for Los Angeles County, all of which are dedicated to aiding homeless families and elderly or disabled individuals in obtaining and maintaining permanent housing. The Employment Services Department helps families to obtain and maintain employment by offering access to job listings, the use of computers so that the unemployed can search for work, tutorials in typing and other basic skills, and other job-placement and job-retention support. A Beyond Shelter case manager and employment counselor work together on a client's behalf, a method that was developed and conducted by Beyond Shelter for the U.S. Department of Labor as a Welfare-to-Work Demonstration Project.

The Beyond Shelter Housing Development Corp. develops, manages, and operates affordable housing in low-income neighborhoods, primarily in Central and South Central Los Angeles, and is currently developing neighborhood resource centers within, or adjacent to, many of its new housing projects. In addition, for the past 10 years Tull and Beyond Shelter have led a neighborhood revitalization project in South Central Los Angeles. With the agency's programs in Los Angeles serving as a laboratory for systemic changes, Tull is focusing her efforts on promoting Beyond Shelter's key initiatives, helping homeless people to secure and maintain housing, on a national scale. Beyond- shelter. org reports that the program's methods are being taught to other organizations across the country with the help of Beyond Shelter's Institute for Research, Training and Technical Assistance and the National Alliance to End Homelessness.

Tull has spoken at many national forums and institutions around the country. She is a member of the advisory committees of the Washington, D.C.- based National Alliance to End Homelessness and the Housing Plus Services Committee of the National Low Income Housing Coalition. She is also a member of the Right to Housing Working Group at the National Law Center on Homelessness and Housing, and she sits on the board of directors of the National Housing Conference.

In addition, she is an adjunct professor for research at the University of Southern California School of Social Work.

Tull and her organization have often been recognized for their tireless efforts to help those less fortunate. She received the Jefferson Award from the National Institute of Public Service in 1982 and the Ralph Bunche Peace Award during the "Year of the Homeless" from the United Nations Organization, Pacific Chapter, in 1987. Tull was named one of *Newsweek's* "One Hundred Heroes of Our Time" in 1986. Two years later she received the Founders Award from the National Association of Fundraising Executives. In addition, Beyond Shelter was given the Community Service Excellence Award by the Federal Interagency Council on the Homeless in 1992. That same year Whittier College, in California, awarded Tull an honorary doctorate in social sciences. Tull and Beyond Shelter were honored with the Nonprofit Sector Achievement Award by the National Alliance to End Homelessness in 1996. She was named an "Unsung Hero" in 2000 at the 85th anniversary celebration of the California Community Foundation. In 2002 Tull was selected as one of *Los Angeles Business Journal's* "Women Who Make a Difference" and received the Community Service Award from the Mexican American Legal Defense and Educational Fund.

## PERSONAL LIFE

From her first marriage Tull has a son, Dani, an artist; she has two daughters, Deborah, a social activist, and Rebecca, a special-projects associate with Beyond Shelter, from her second marriage. In 1985 Tull's second husband died of cancer. She informed *Current Biography* that on December 5, 2004 she would marry B. J. Markel and become stepmother to his 14-year-old son. In her speech at the Gleitsman Foundation award ceremony, Tull stated that when she feels "tired and overwhelmed" by her work and all the suffering and hardship she sees in the course of it, she needs only think of "the single mother with three young children living in her car during a cold Fall in Los Angeles,, holding down a job and bringing [her children] home to the car each night because, after taxes, she could not buy food, pay for the car and child care, and still maintain a roof over their heads. And ultimately I accept the fact that, of everything there might be to do in my life today, nothing could be more important than what I have chosen to do." Tull told *Current Biography*, with regard to the artistic aspirations she had in her youth, "I finally found peace in the work that I do, which represents the integration of the right and left sides of my brain! I apply the creative process to social problems in a way that completely fulfills my multiple interests and skills, i.e. deep thinking, problem-solving, integrating existing information in new ways, writing, creating. In this work daily, I get to use words and my mind to both write and speak out about issues/problems/causes/solutions in a way that shares information with others, helps them to view things differently and to understand, and helps to promote systemic change on a national scale. Sometimes I get to apply my artistic side to the affordable housing that I build. My dream in the future is to write more, I actually have a lot more I want to say."

## FURTHER READING

*http://www.epath.org/site/PATHBeyondShelter/ home;http://nationalhomeless.org/*

# DESMOND (MPILO) TUTU

## Anglican Prelate; Social Activist

**Born:** October 7, 1931; Klerksdorp, Transvaal, South Africa
**Primary Field:** Anti-Apartheid Movement
**Affiliation:** Anglican

### INTRODUCTION

*For his "role as a unifying leader in the campaign to resolve the problem of apartheid in South Africa," and "to direct attention to the nonviolent struggle for liberation" of which he is the chief spokesman, the Norwegian Nobel Committee awarded the 1984 Nobel Peace Prize to the Right Reverend Desmond Tutu, now the Anglican bishop of Johannesburg, the first black to hold that post. Throughout his episcopal career, and especially during his term as general secretary of the South African Council of Churches (1978-84), Bishop Tutu has brought outspoken and tireless Christian witness to the plight of the powerless black majority in a country ruled by a white minority with an official system of racial separatism that is, as he describes it, "as evil as Nazism." Under that system, 4.5 million whites have full dominion over 23 million blacks, who are disenfranchised and deprived of freedom of movement. The Afrikaner government views Tutu as a troublemaker, if not a subversive, but concerned observers in the international community generally see him as he sees himself: a peacemaker in a dangerously polarizing society, preaching racial reconciliation, warning against a "blood bath," and hoping that he is heard before time runs out.*

### EARLY LIFE

Desmond Mpilo Tutu was born in the goldmining town of Klerksdorp, Witwatersrand, Transvaal, South Africa, on October 7, 1931. His middle name, meaning "life" in Sotho, a Bantu language, was given him by his grandmother because he was a sickly baby, not expected to survive. "That," he half-jestingly told an interviewer for the *London Observer* (May 8,1983), "was my first commitment to faith." His father was Zachariah Tutu, a schoolteacher from the Bantu tribe known as the Xhosas, and his mother was Aletta Tutu, a domestic servant whose tribal ancestry was Tswana.

Tutu was baptized a Methodist, because at the time of his birth his father was teaching in a Methodist school. Later, when an older sister enrolled in an Anglican school, the entire family switched denominations. When Tutu was twelve the family moved to Johannesburg where the mother found work as a cook at a missionary school for the blind. At that school Tutu was indelibly edified by examples of compassion for and dedication to serving the deprived. It was there that he first came in contact with his chief mentor and role model, the Anglican cleric Father Trevor Huddleston, now Bishop Huddleston, the leading anti-apartheid voice in Great Britain. Then a parish priest in the black Johannesburg slum of Sophiatown, the magnetic Huddleston was on his way to becoming internationally known as the most outspoken and controversial clergyman in South Africa. In the *Observer* interview, Tutu recalled: "I was standing with my mother one day, when this white man in a cassock [Huddleston] walked past and doffed his big black hat to her. I couldn't believe it, a white man raising his hat to a simple black labouring woman." When Tutu was hospitalized for twenty months in his late teens with tuberculosis, Father Huddleston visited him almost daily. As a teenager, Tutu earned pocket money by selling peanuts at suburban railroad stations and caddying at the Killarney golf course in Johannesburg. When he graduated from Western High School in Johannesburg, he wanted to study medicine, but his family could not afford the medical school tuition and he turned to teaching instead. After taking a diploma at the Bantu Normal College in Pretoria and a B.A. degree at the University of Johannesburg, he taught at Madibane High School in Johannesburg (1954-55) and Munsieville High School in Krugersdorp (1955-57). When the government introduced a calculatedly second class state-run system of "Bantu education" in 1957, Tutu, along with many other teachers, resigned in protest.

## Life's Work

Once out of the classroom, Tutu saw the church as "a likely means of service," and in retrospect he views his transition from teaching to religious ministry as his being "grabbed by God by the scruff of the neck in order to spread His word, whether it is convenient or not." When he began his theological studies under priests of the Community of the Resurrection, the high church or Catholic-bent Anglican religious order to which Father Huddleston belonged, he was "not moved by very high ideals," he has admitted, but his spiritual motivation deepened during his religious training, and the community's practices of daily Communion and regular prayer and meditative retreat became essential components of his life.

After taking his licentiate in theology at St. Peter's Theological College in Johannesburg in 1960, Tutu received the Anglican diaconate, in 1960, and was ordained an Anglican priest, in 1961. His first ministerial assignments in South Africa were as curate of St. Alban's Church in Benoni (1960-61) and St. Philip's Church in Alberton (1961-62). While earning his bachelor's degree in divinity and master's in theology at King's College in London, England, he was assigned to St. Alban's parish in London (1962-65) and St. Mary's in Bletchingley, Surrey (1965-66).

From 1967 to 1969 Tutu lectured at the Federal Theological Seminary in the town of Alice in the tribal homeland of Ciskei, and during the following two years he was a lecturer at the National University of Lesotho, then known as the University of Botswana, Lesotho, and Swaziland. A former British protectorate, once known as Basutoland, Lesotho is an independent tribal enclave within South Africa. In 1972 Tutu returned to England as associate director of the Theological Education Fund, a position in which he administered World Council of Churches scholarships for three years. From his base in

Bromley, Kent, he traveled widely, especially in Asia and black Africa.

Tutu returned to South Africa as the Anglican dean of Johannesburg in 1975, and the following year he was consecrated bishop of Lesotho. When he saw violence brewing among angry youths in the sprawling black township of Soweto on the outskirts of Johannesburg in the spring of 1976, he worked with the activist Nhato Motlana in trying to channel it into peaceful demonstrations, and on May 6, 1976 he wrote to Balthazar J. Vorster, then the prime minister of South Africa, warning him of the situation. Vorster dismissed his letter, according to Tutu, "as a political ploy engineered, perhaps, by the political opposition," and "we all know that all hell broke loose on June 16 that year." Six hundred blacks were shot dead in the Soweto riots.

In 1978 Tutu became the first black secretary general of the interdenominational South African Council of Churches, the nation's contact group with the World Council of Churches. The South African Council of Churches represents 13 million Christians, more than 80 percent of them black. Conspicuously absent from membership are the members of the Dutch Reformed Church, the church of the ruling Afrikaners, the descendants of Dutch, German, and French Huguenots who colonized the country from the eighteenth century onward. (Three-fifths of the South African whites are Afrikaners.) Much of the budget of the council is spent in legal and other services for imprisoned blacks and those detained without trial, and for their families.

With the main African nationalist parties banned, the South African Council of Churches under Tutu became an important vehicle of black protest. In 1979 Tutu offended the South African government grievously on two occasions. The first occasion was the enactment of the Group Areas Act, a statute authorizing the government to remove blacks from urban areas to barren tribal lands. After witnessing the pathetic condition in the black squatters' camps, Tutu outraged the government by describing that condition as the government's "final solution" to the black-majority problem. He later retracted his phrasing but continued to insist, "People are starving not because there isn't food but because of deliberate policy, and that in a country that boasts about its maize exports to Zambia!"

More serious in the eyes of the government was Tutu's advocacy of the withdrawal of foreign investments from South Africa. In a television interview in Denmark in the fall of 1979, Tutu called on the Danish government to stop buying coal from South Africa. On his return to South Africa, his passport was confiscated, an action generally interpreted as a warning that he was close to joining the ranks of the 150-odd "subversives" banned from social (beyond family contacts) and political activity in South Africa. Undaunted, Tutu proceeded to exhort parents of mixed ethnic background to support a nationwide school boycott condemned as Communist-inspired by the government; to warn that the arrest and detention of protesters would lead to a resurgence of rioting; and to predict that Nelson R. Mandela, the jailed (from 1964-1990) leader of the outlawed African National Congress (now based in Zambia), or a similar black figure would be prime minister of South Africa within ten years.

After his passport was restored, in January 1981, Tutu toured Europe and the United States, delivering to the international community one constant message: "If you want to see fundamental change in South Africa by peaceful means, you must give assistance by applying pressure on the South African government, political, diplomatic, but above all, economic." When he returned to South Africa in April 1981 his passport was again seized, and since that time his trips abroad have been with "travel documents" on which his nationality is described as "undetermined."

When Columbia University conferred an honorary doctorate of sacred theology on Tutu in August 1982, he was denied permission to go to New York to receive the degree. Because Columbia does not grant degrees in absentia, Michael I. Sovern, the president of the university, traveled to Johannesburg for the ceremony. In his citation, Sovern hailed Bishop Tutu as "a stalwart and fearless advocate of justice, peace, and reconciliation among the peoples of [his] troubled land" and as "the voice of [his] oppressed people, a beacon leading them to peaceful opposition to the injustices of apartheid and a symbol of hope for a unified Africa." Meanwhile, the South African Council of Churches was being investigated by a government appointed judicial commission, known as the Eloff Commission, after its head, Mr. Justice Eloff. In his submission to the commission, Tutu pointed out that "oppression dehumanizes the oppressor as much as, if not more than, the oppressed" and that "whites need to hear and know that their value as persons is intrinsic to who they are by virtue of having been created in God's image." He also declared against "false or cheap reconciliation," the crying of "peace, peace when there is no peace." In its report, published in

February 1984, the Eloff Commission stopped short of banning the South African Council of Churches, declaring that the council is not a tool of foreign manipulators and that, although "the amount of money spent" in the direction of helping "the needy and deserving" is "meagre when compared with that used mainly for political purposes, innocent people will suffer if the S.A.C.C. were to be rendered largely ineffective." On the negative side, the commission criticized the council's financial administration, pointing out the fraud conviction of a former general secretary; recommended that the government pass a law making the advocacy of international disinvestment in South Africa criminally punishable as "economic sabotage"; and denounced Tutu for making public statements attacking military conscription and lending respectability to the African National Congress. Tutu's response was to express his wholehearted support of the African National Congress' struggle for a "truly democratic," non-racial South Africa.

In September 1984 Tutu began a three-month sabbatical at General Theological Seminary in New York City. It was in the midst of his sojourn in Manhattan, on October 16, 1984, that he, along with the world, received the news that the Norwegian Nobel Committee had named him the 1984 Nobel peace laureate. In announcing the award, Egil Aarvik, the chairman of the Nobel committee, noted that the peace prize had been awarded to a South African once before, to Albert John Luthuli, the former president of the African National Congress, in 1960. "This year's award should be seen as a renewed recognition of the courage and heroism shown by black South Africans in their use of peaceful methods in the struggle against apartheid," the Nobel citation read. "It is the committee's wish that the Peace Prize now awarded to Desmond Tutu should be regarded not only as a gesture of support to him and to the South African Council of Churches of which he is leader, but also to all individuals and groups in South Africa who, with their concern for human dignity, fraternity and democracy, incite the admiration of the world."

"Hey, we are winning! Justice is going to win," was Tutu's first reaction to the news of the award. "[It] means we musn't give up." He told reporters that he planned to put much of the $193,000 Nobel cash award into a trust fund for scholarships for indigent South African blacks. In a more negative vein, he expressed scorn for the South African government's recent attempts, including the enfranchisement of Asians and mixed-blood "coloreds" while still excluding blacks, to portray an improvement in social relations. "If things are changing, they are changing for the worse," he said. "So now we have multiracial sports in order to compete on an international level. But they say nothing about realignment of political power and they still control 87 percent of the land when they only have 20 percent of the population." He warned that "this is our very last chance for change, because if that doesn't happen, it seems the bloodbath will be inevitable."

On October 18, 1984 Tutu returned to South Africa to celebrate his award with his people. The joyous welcome he received counterpointed violent confrontations between rioting South African blacks and white security forces, 7,000 of whom raided black townships. In the violence, which had been escalating for two months, eighty blacks were killed; strikes had closed mines and factories; and approximately 200,000 students were boycotting classes. Much of the rioting was precipitated by resentment of rent increases and new utility rates in the townships, along with political frustration. It was in September 1984 that the new constitution giving separate parliamentary representation to all non-whites excepting blacks took effect. The worst violence took place in the township of Sharpeville, where a black deputy mayor was hacked to death on his porch by blacks. The presidents, mayors, and other tribal leaders in the "homelands" were accused by many blacks of legitimizing forcible resettlement.

At the very time that the Norwegian Nobel Committee decided to give Tutu the peace prize, the white and black Anglican diocesan electors in Johannesburg, the South African Anglican church's largest diocese, a predominantly black see, were deadlocked (reportedly along racial lines) over the choice of Tutu as the diocese's new bishop. The national Anglican hierarchy intervened, and on November 3,1984 a synod of eleven white and twelve black bishops, meeting in the Orange Free State, elected Tutu the first Anglican bishop of Johannesburg. Tutu was quoted in the press as welcoming the new position with the words, "The time is just right for me to leave the South African Council of Churches. I am fundamentally a pastor. That is what God ordained me to do."

Sermons, speeches, and other statements by Tutu have been collected in two volumes: *Crying in the Wilderness* (Eerdmans, 1982) and *Hope and Suffering* (Eerdmans, 1984). One of the speeches in *Hope and Suffering* addressed the policy of "constructive engagement" pursued by the United States under the presidency of Ronald Reagan, which leans to impartiality regarding South Africa's internal affairs, for strategic reasons. "To be impartial is indeed to have taken sides already, with the status quo," Tutu pointed out. "How are you to remain impartial when the South African authorities evict helpless mothers and children and let them shiver in the winter rain? At least under [President] Carter our morale was upheld by their encouraging rhetoric of disapproval. They did not talk about the overriding strategic importance of South Africa, with her wealth in key strategic resources more important than human freedom. When we are free, South Africa will still be of strategic importance, and we will remember who helped us to get free." Following a meeting with President Reagan in the White House on December 7,1984, the bishop told reporters, "We are no nearer each other than before." For his part, the president cited South Africa's release of eleven imprisoned labor agitators as an example of the effectiveness of his "quiet diplomacy." Spokesmen for South Africa denied that the pressure of demonstrations at South African government offices in American cities had any influence in the decision to release the labor militants.

International political and economic pressure on South Africa mounted sharply in 1985, and even President Reagan began gesturing in the direction of sanctions, ordering a ban on imports of Krugerrands into the United States. Domestically, world disinvestment in South Africa's economy created a financial crisis at the same time that rioting by blacks escalated, resulting in hundreds of deaths (mostly of alleged black quislings) and mass arrests under a state of virtual martial law declared by President Pieter W. Botha. Among those arrested was Trevor Tutu, the bishop's son, for protesting a police roundup of boycotting schoolchildren. Defying a government ban on "political" funerals, Bishop Tutu on August 6 intervened in a confrontation between a procession of black mourners and government security forces and negotiated with police to provide buses to transport the mourners to the burial site. On another occasion he risked his own life to rescue an alleged police informer from a black mob that was beating and trying to burn the man to death.

## PERSONAL LIFE

As self-confident in bearing as he is diminutive in stature, Desmond Tutu is gregarious and ebullient, emanating a spirit of joy despite his intense sense of mission. His conversation is punctuated with high-pitched chuckles, and his wit invades even his political parables. "We had the land, and they had the Bible," one of the parables goes. "Then they said, 'let us pray,' and we closed our eyes. When we opened them again, they had the land and we had the Bible. Maybe we got the better end of the deal." When conducting the Eucharistic service in the Sotho language in his old parish in Johannesburg's black township of Soweto, he often breaks into yelps and giggles, and sometimes he dances down the aisle, whooping and laughing with the congregation. As retired Bishop of Johannesburg, he has residences in Cape Town and Johannesburg. Tutu and his wife, Leah Nomalizo Shenxane, who were married in 1955, have one son and three daughters. The bishop lists his recreations as music, reading, and jogging. He still sees himself as "a simple pastor, passionately concerned for justice, peace, and reconciliation," and, as he constantly

points out, the number of preachers of reconciliation in South Africa is fast diminishing. "Most of us are not prisoners of the Gospel," Buti Thiagale, a young black Roman Catholic priest and a member of the Black Consciousness movement, has said. "We want to use it for a certain purpose. He [Tutu] will say, 'Love your enemy.' At his age, he should hate a little bit more. [But] he believes in the Gospel literally."

## FURTHER READING

*Crying in the Wilderness; Hope and Suffering; The Words of Desmond Tutu; The Rainbow People of God: The Making of a Peaceful Revolution; Worshipping Church in Africa; The Essential Desmond Tutu; No Future Without Forgiveness; An African Prayerbook; God Has a Dream: A Vision of Hope for Our Time*

# V

## MARY VERDI-FLETCHER

### Dancer; Teacher

**Born:** June 4, 1955; Cleveland, Ohio
**Primary Field:** Equal Rights
**Affiliation:** Cleveland Ballet Dancing Wheels

#### INTRODUCTION

*"Who made up the rule that you have to dance on your two feet? Dance is an expression and an emotion that comes from within. It can be created in many different ways." That is the philosophy of the dancer Mary Verdi-Fletcher, the president and founding director of Cleveland Ballet Dancing Wheels, one of the few dance companies whose members include people in wheelchairs and the first professional troupe of its kind in the United States. By demonstrating the often unrecognized abilities of dancers with disabilities and providing an opportunity for them to collaborate with able-bodied artists, the company, like Verdi-Fletcher herself, has served as a highly effective champion of the disabled since its establishment (as Dancing Wheels), in 1980, as has Professional Flair, the nonprofit organization that she set up nine years later. In addition to presenting innovative lecture performances throughout the United States and in Europe, Cleveland Ballet Dancing Wheels has corn-missioned and premiered critically acclaimed dances, in many of which Verdi-Fletcher has assumed principal roles.*

*Unable to walk or even stand since childhood, Verdi-Fletcher began dancing in a wheelchair in the late 1970s, when she was in her early 20s. Billed as Dancing Wheels, beginning in 1980 she and a series of able-bodied partners performed in their spare time for community groups. For most of the 1980s, she also* *worked full-time for an Ohio organization dedicated to helping people with disabilities live independently, and she became well known as an advocate for the disabled community. On a par with her success as a champion of the disabled is the artistry she herself brings to the stage. "That is a dancer," Dennis Nahat, the artistic director of the Cleveland Ballet, thought to himself when he first saw Verdi-Fletcher perform. "She had the spark, the spirit that makes a dancer. You can't take your eyes off her, whether she's sitting still, or on the floor, or has her head in profile. Rarely do you see an artist that can be standing still and yet hold your attention." In 1992, a reviewer for* Attitude: The Dancers' Magazine, *wrote, "Far from being just another gifted dancer amongst the multitude on the face of this planet, this young woman is a wellspring of spiritual inspiration for all those fortunate enough to be touched by her life and her art." "I firmly, firmly believe that I was born to be a dancer," Verdi-Fletcher told an interviewer in 1993. "I think that I just had it inbred in me. There is nothing in my life that brings me more joy and more excitement than to be involved in dance."*

#### EARLY LIFE

The second of the two children of Sylvio Verdi and Nancy (Baruzzi) Verdi, Mary Verdi-Fletcher was born Mary Regina Verdi on June 4, 1955, in Bratenahl, a suburb of Cleveland, Ohio. She was born with spina bifida, an often disabling neural defect in which part of the spinal cord and/or part of the membranes covering the spinal cord protrudes through the spinal column. Thanks to surgery performed before she was two months old (it was the first of a dozen major operations she has undergone), she gained a little control of her legs. When she was about four, she began wearing metal braces, and, using crutches, she was able to walk, albeit very slowly. While her legs remained feeble, she developed "tremendous upper-body strength," as she was quoted as saying in *Chronicles of Courage: Very Special Artists* (1993), by Jean Kennedy Smith and George Plimpton.

Along with her older brother, Brian, who became a firefighter, Verdi-Fletcher grew up in a 28 room house in Cleveland in which not only her immediate family but also her maternal great-grandparents, grandparents, and some of her aunts, uncles, and cousins lived. "[My family] never cut me any slack because I was disabled," she has recalled. "I was treated normally; there was no element of pity. I grew up not focusing on my disability, but on my ability." In *Dance Movements in Time* (published by Professional Flair in 1995), Melinda Ule-Grohol quoted her as saying that a "friendly yet competitive spirit" existed among the cousins, and she often participated in crawling races and living-room dance contests with them.

Music and dance are an important part of the Verdi family history. For years before becoming a waitress and then a full-time homemaker, Verdi-Fletcher's mother danced professionally; calling themselves the Baruzzi Twins, she and her younger sister performed on the vaudeville circuit. Sylvio Verdi, too, had earned a living in vaudeville, as a pit musician who played clarinet and saxophone; he later became a quality-control technician. From her earliest years Mary dreamed of becoming a dancer, but in those days no dancing school in the Cleveland area would accept a student in a wheelchair. Guided by her mother, she often danced with her brother, who would swing her, braces and all, off the floor. She also danced alone, by pivoting on her heels and moving her hips, so vigorously that her braces repeatedly broke. After she was fitted with stronger braces, it was her legs, not the braces, that bore the brunt of her twists and turns. One of her legs was permanently damaged when it broke for the third time, when she was about 12, and her wheelchair became her sole mode of self-locomotion. "In a way, the wheelchair was a means of freedom for me in terms of movement because it wasn't as binding and cumbersome as the braces," she has said.

As a child, whenever she overheard people expressing pity for her, Verdi-Fletcher told them, as her mother had taught her to do, "I'm not handicapped, I'm Mary!" Even more than her parents, her maternal grandmother served as "an example of strength" for her and played a significant role in her development as a "very directed

person," in her words. She has also attributed her inner strength and determination to the many hospitalizations she endured, including three months that she spent in a body cast; a month during which she was treated for a nearly fatal case of acute bedsores; and weeks following the removal of a kidney, when she almost died from complications. "You see a lot of sickness, a lot of pain around you [in a hospital], she was quoted as saying in *Chronicles of Courage*. "I was around adults a lot more than other children. You gain a lot of understanding of people and of yourself when you're lying in bed and not able to move, you have a lot of time to think. All those elements help you to become much more, not centered, exactly, but to know yourself."

Verdi-Fletcher attended a Roman Catholic grammar school, where her mother became a volunteer so that she would be available to carry Mary up and down stairs. During a trip to Europe when Mary was 10, her mother, hoping for a miraculous cure, took her to see Pope Paul VI and various Roman Catholic shrines. After her graduation from the Villa Angela Academy, a parochial high school, in 1975, Verdi-Fletcher took a course in keypunch operation. She then got a job as a keypunch operator, but she hated it and quit after a few months.

## LIFE'S WORK
In 1978, the year she turned 23, Verdi-Fletcher moved with her parents to the rural community of Perry, Ohio, where she made many new friends. While hanging out with them at a neighborhood gathering place called Dan's Village Inn, she met a man, Terry Michael, who, she has said, taught her "a lot about independence and assertiveness." "He put me in touch with the people and organizations that could help me do many things I'd never even thought of," she told Melinda Ule-Grohol. Those things included learning to drive a car equipped with hand controls, a skill that enabled her to leave her parents' home and move into an apartment with a friend, in 1980, and to matriculate at Lakeland Community College, in Mentor, Ohio, where she studied marketing and public relations. She later took Dale Carnegie courses in public speaking.

When the windows at Dan's Village Inn were open and music from the jukebox could be heard outside, Verdi-Fletcher's friends would dance in the parking lot. One evening, as Verdi-Fletcher sat watching them, a friend began twirling her wheelchair in large circles in time with the music. She was thrilled. "I became hooked on the fact that I could dance in my chair," she has recalled. "I became a believer that I could dance in my chair. " Not long afterward, while at a dance club, she met her best friend from high school and the friend's husband, David Brewster, a dance enthusiast. After guiding her on the dance floor that night, Brewster became Verdi-Fletcher's regular partner. To perfect her head, torso, and arm movements, she would analyze the performances of others, Fred Astaire and Ginger Rogers (on film) and ballroom dancers, for example.

In 1979, Verdi-Fletcher and Brewster danced together in front of an audience of more than 2,000 people at one of the auditions-cum-competitions held around the country by the producer of the Los Angeles-based television show *Dance Fever*. "When I got onstage, there was a major hush," Verdi-Fletcher has recalled. "You could tell people were thinking, 'What is a person in a wheelchair doing in a dance competition?'" In *Northern Ohio Live* (August 1993), Ted Schwarz reported that the couple ended their performance with "a show-stopping maneuver in which Mary halted [and] turned the chair and grabbed the wheels to brace it as her partner leaped onto the armrest [and] then flipped over her head." The audience gave them a standing ovation, and the duo won the chance to enter another *Dance Fever* contest, in Los Angeles, where they were named first runners-up. Verdi-Fletcher has said that those experiences gave her "the competitive edge and the desire to perform" and showed her that, despite her disabilities and lack of formal training, people recognized her abilities as a dancer.

The *Dance Fever* competitions sparked a flurry of publicity in the Cleveland area, which led to many requests for performances at nursing care facilities, conferences, and other such venues. In 1980, Verdi-Fletcher and Brewster made their partnership formal and began appearing as Dancing Wheels. Their association ended in the mid-1980s, when he and his wife got divorced. For the next few years, Verdi-Fletcher danced with a series of male partners. Invacare, a wheelchair manufacturer, sponsored their performances.

Meanwhile, acting upon what she had learned from Terry Michael, Verdi-Fletcher had become an advocate for the disabled. After speaking on a radio talk show, in 1979, she was offered a job by another of the show's guests, the director of Services for Independent Living, an Ohio organization whose mission is to create specially equipped housing for disabled people. As die first attendant care coordinator for the Independent Living

Center and, later, as its director of development, she organized a statewide advocacy group and set up a program for fund-raising that is still in effect, among other accomplishments.

On August 11,1984, Mary Verdi married Robert A. Fletcher. In 1989, her husband's career as a financial consultant having become firmly established, Verdi-Fletcher resigned from her job to devote herself full-time to dance and to finding and creating opportunities for disabled people who were eager to dance professionally or to enter other professions in the arts but were thwarted by obstacles related to their disabilities. In many theaters, for example, backstage areas do not have wheelchair access, so people in wheelchairs cannot serve as actors or wardrobe assistants. Toward that end, she founded Professional Flair, a nonprofit organization with three divisions: Dancing Wheels; Theatrical Expressions, which works with actors; and Career Insight, which helps people develop personal skills.

From September 1989 to March 1990, Verdi-Fletcher worked under contract as a tour director for the Cleveland Ballet, with responsibility for handling such tasks as promotion and making travel arrangements. After learning that the ballet's board and administrators wanted to develop a community outreach program, she proposed to them that, as a joint endeavor, the Cleveland Ballet and Dancing Wheels offer a blend of performance and lectures at schools and other places, to give audiences insights into choreography, dance training, rehearsals, and possibilities for disabled dancers. "I wanted to demonstrate the diversity of dance and that dance can be performed by anyone," Verdi-Fletcher explained to Ule- Grohol. "We would be setting an example." Her proposal was accepted, and, in September 1990, Cleveland Ballet Dancing Wheels came into being, with Verdi-Fletcher as director.

Meanwhile, Verdi-Fletcher had begun dancing with JonCarlo Franchi, a member of the Cleveland Ballet corps, and with Todd Goodman, who had danced with the Fort Worth Ballet and Pacific Northwest Ballet. Goodman became the associate artistic director of Dancing Wheels (as the company is usually called), and he, Franchi, and Daniel Job, a former ballet master with the School of Cleveland Ballet, became its choreographers. Verdi-Fletcher has observed that "the wheelchair out of necessity dictates the creation of an entirely new form and style of dance." Conversely, Verdi-Fletcher's determination to open the world of dance to people with disabilities has led to the development of new kinds of wheelchairs. For a long time she danced in a fairly standard wheelchair that weighed 55 pounds. The specially designed chair that she has used since about 1990 weighs only 24 pounds; it has caster wheels that move and pivot easily, and its low back makes it much easier for her partners to lift her from it and for her to extend her port de bras. Other dancers "enjoy working with me because I'm very strong and lightweight," Verdi-Fletcher, who in 1996 weighed 73 pounds, has said. "Proportionately, Mary's strength to her body weight is phenomenal," Todd Goodman told Melinda Ule for *Dance Magazine* (February 1993).

Supported in part by a grant from the Ohio Arts Council, the Cleveland Ballet Dancing Wheels company began giving lecture demonstrations all across the United States, and in its first 15 months, the troupe performed 108 times before more than 50,000 people. "We educate [audiences] about the fact that Dancing Wheels is not just someone in a wheelchair being moved around," Verdi-Fletcher has explained. "It's dance that involves and works with classical methods and classically trained dancers." The company consists of three men and five women, several of whom are disabled.

In April 1991, Verdi-Fletcher made her first professional "mainstage" appearance, dancing in *Gypsy*, choreographed by Todd Goodman, and in *Above*, by Daniel Job, at the Beck Center, in Cleveland. In *Above* she performed without her wheelchair; she created images and movement by using floorwork and by being lifted and held aloft by her able-bodied partners. "Every time we rehearsed this piece, I felt like crying," Verdi-Fletcher has said. "This piece shows my abilities as a dancer more than others, because people don't single me out as a disabled dancer at all. It was designed as a spiritual piece, a message for us to rise above what is human. I feel as if I've gone inside myself and felt my spirit and my spirituality." In a review of a later performance of *Above*, at the Marymount Manhattan Theater, in New York City, Anna Kisselgoff of the *New York Times* (February 8, 1993) described the work as an "eloquent allegory of human aspiration" and wrote that "Verdi-Fletcher seem[ed] to take flight with impressive naturalness."

On February 27, 1992, in her New York City debut, Verdi-Fletcher danced *Gypsy* with Goodman at the Theatre of the Riverside Church, during the Morningside Dance Festival. "The interplay between the two dancers is that of control and reversal of control," a critic for *Attitude: The Dancers' Magazine* (Spring/Summer

1992) wrote. "The dancer on wheels just as often appears to instigate the movement, leaving the audience to wonder whether it's Mary or her partner who serves as catalyst for each particular swirl, lift, balance, and so forth." In an assessment of the same performance for the *New York City Westsider* (March 5-11, 1992), Hilary Ostlere wrote that Verdi-Fletcher "obviously has the spirit and the soul of a dancer, and her eloquent upper body, expressive arms, and poise of head mark her as a very special artist."

Verdi-Fletcher has also appeared in the two versions of *Heaven?*, by Goodman, who left the company in 1993. Other dances in her repertoire include *Picture Imperfect*, a work by Norman Walker, and *Epitaph for Elizabeth*, *Egress*, *May Ring*, *Koto Vivaldi I, II, and III*, *Dance Energies*, *1420 MHz*, and *Glass Spiral*, all choreographed by Sabatino Verlezza, who was a soloist with the May O'Donnell Dance Company for a dozen years and who has served as Dancing Wheel's co-artistic director and resident choreographer since 1994.

## PERSONAL LIFE

Early in 1994, Verdi-Fletcher became critically ill, when her remaining kidney ceased to function. Three surgical attempts to repair the organ did not succeed, and it was removed. For the next four months, she underwent hemodialysis three times a week, fitting the treatments into her dance and work schedule. Then she had a kidney transplant; the donated kidney came from her husband. Within two days she was conducting business by phone from her hospital bed, and a month later she began dancing again. She also resumed teaching; along with Verlezza, his wife, Barbara Allegra Verlezza, and other members of Dancing Wheels, she gives classes in dance for children and adults with and without disbilities (including people with sensory impairments). Jenny Sikora, a disabled youngster who began taking classes in 1990, when she was four, has often performed with Dancing Wheels.

Verdi-Fletcher's other activities include planning for and participating in "A Celebration of Arts and Access." A month-long event that she herself instigated, it has been held annually in Cleveland since 1992 and focuses on dance and the theater in alternate years. Its aims include bringing together arts professionals and advocates for the disabled as well as educating the public about "what it means to have full and equal access to the arts world," in the words of Ule-Grohol. Verdi-Fletcher helped to set up DanceAbility, Dancing Wheels

Georgia, in Atlanta, and she is working to establish similar dance groups elsewhere.

During the 1994 Celebration of Arts and Access, Verdi-Fletcher received the Invacare Award of Excellence in the Arts, for her "tireless efforts to change social perceptions about the talents and abilities of people with disabilities." Her other honors include the 1990 Outstanding Young Clevelanders Award, the 1991 Oracle Merit Award for Outstanding Educational and Outreach Programming, the 1992 Outstanding Young Clevelanders Award, and the 1996 Ohio Theater Alliance Award for Accessibility in Theater. She is a board member of OhioDance, Very Special Arts Ohio, and the

Ohio Alliance for Arts Education, among other groups. In her home in Sagamore Hills, a suburb of Cleveland, where she lives with her husband, the red-haired Verdi-Fletcher exercises daily in an individualized home fitness center. Her avocational interests include watching football and soccer games.

**FURTHER READING**
*Chronicles of Courage, Dance Movements in Time, 199*

# Kah Walla

## Political Leader; Businesswoman

**Born:** February 28, 1965; Ibadan, Nigeria
**Primary Field:** Politics
**Affiliation:** STRATEGIES!

### Introduction

*Like many women in countries where gender equality is not the norm, the young Kah Walla probably did not anticipate becoming one of her nation's most influential political voices. However, she did exactly that. Since establishing herself as an accomplished entrepreneur, Walla has risen to become one of her native Cameroon's most outspoken political activists and a well-known proponent of reforms aimed at increasing government accountability and reducing corruption. Though she has faced considerable opposition, Walla has never backed down. Long before she ever dreamed of stepping into the political arena, Walla focused her attention on becoming a success in the business world. Realizing that her educational options in Cameroon were limited, she headed to the United States to attend college. She returned home with an MBA and she began working for a consulting agency. Though she rose through the company's ranks in short order, the agency went out of business. Some might ,have seen this as a setback, but Walla perceived it as an opportunity to use what she had learned to start her own business. She founded STRAT-EGIES!, a consulting firm that served a wide variety of both domestic and foreign clients. Although Walla made the firm a success, the difficulties she experienced dealing with government officials while trying to run her business convinced her to take a more serious interest in politics.*

*After beginning her political career as a community organizer, Walla took her first significant step as a government leader when she was elected to the municipal council of the First District of Douala. In that position, she fought aggressively for improved governmental transparency and electoral reform. As her public profile grew, Walla faced increasing resistance to her policies, particularly from her own government, and repeatedly found herself the target of harassment, beatings, and even kidnappings. Unwilling to cave to the intense pressure from her adversaries, she announced her candidacy for the Cameroonian presidential election in 2011. Though she ultimately lost the presidential race, Walla remains an outspoken critic of government corruption and one of Cameroon's leading advocates of reform.*

### Early Life

Born Edith Kabbang Walla on February 28, 1965, Walla spent time growing up in both her native Cameroon and in the Ivory Coast (Cote d'Ivoire). At an early age, Walla developed a keen interest in business and a desire to have a successful professional career. As she grew older, however, it became clear that gender inequality in Cameroon would make it difficult for her to get the education she would need to establish a career in the business world. Determined to see her dreams come to fruition, Walla left Cameroon for the United States, where she studied business and earned an MBA at Howard University in Washington, DC. With degree in hand, she returned to Cameroon in 1989, eager to put what she had learned to good use.

Walla's return to Cameroon coincided with a radical shift in gender equality in the country. Women gained new rights and freedoms that made it much easier for them to run their own businesses. Suddenly, Walla and countless other women like her felt empowered and optimistic about their future. Walla commented in an interview that appeared in the 2008 World Bank report *Doing Business: Women in Africa*, "You got a sense that women felt liberated in a very literal way." Walla's initial entry into the business world came when she landed a position with a local consulting firm. At first, her work with the company went quite well, and she quickly climbed the ranks to the office of managing director. When she finally assumed control, however, Walla learned that business was not doing as well as she thought and, as a result of prior mismanagement, the firm closed.

## LIFE'S WORK

When the firm where she had been working went out of business, Walla decided to start her own company. To that end, she founded STRATEGIES!, a business management consulting firm much like her former employer. STRATEGIES! started small, so small, in fact, that Walla initially had to operate out of her father's dining room. With an equally small staff of dedicated supporters, Walla took her first steps into the local marketplace and began to establish her brand. Her strategy was to bring the high quality consulting services available on the international market to Cameroon; she wanted to focus on the specific needs of businesses in that market, such as team building and recruiting. Before long, STRATEGIES! had become a success in Cameroon.

Having established a firm foothold in the local market, Walla's next move was to begin looking for business opportunities elsewhere. "One of our biggest successes came when one of our consultants, Sophie, asked why we were just working in Cameroun," Walla told Soetan. "She proposed going to Chad to seek out clients, a trip that would cost $3000, money we couldn't afford to waste. We eventually agreed and it turned out to be the best decision we ever made." By 2013, more than 80 percent of the firm's business was being generated from foreign markets.

Achieving and maintaining success proved to be a continual uphill battle for Walla, principally because of the restrictive business environment in Cameroon. Of particular concern was the country's tax system which was poorly regulated and rife with corruption. Complex and frequently changing regulations, as well as a lack of clear communication, made dealing with taxes nearly a full-time job for Walla. "There is no transparency," she said in her *Doing Business: Women in Africa* interview. "Well-qualified tax consultants have a very hard time telling you whether what is being asked of you by the taxation officer is right or wrong. There is an enormous amount of interpretation in the system and it really is extremely arbitrary." To make matters worse, some tax officials expected Walla to offer them bribes because she was a woman. She refused to do so and took legal action against a number of officials. While these and other troubles with corruption in Cameroon made operating STRATEGIES! more difficult for Walla, they also inspired her to start thinking about taking a more active role in local politics.

Frustrated with Cameroon's dysfunctional taxation system and male-dominated political culture, Walla increasingly felt the need to start doing something to help bring about change. Her earliest foray into politics came as an activist and community organizer. Walla became an ardent leader and supporter of several grassroots campaigns aimed at stemming corruption, making it easier to operate businesses, and improving quality of life in Cameroon. One of her most significant grassroots accomplishments was founding Cameroon O'Bosso, a citizenship movement that implemented a number of key electoral reforms, such as instituting a voter registration program. Another of Walla's noteworthy campaigns saw her work with the nongovernmental organization Vital Voices to provide training in business registration, tax procedures, and space management to more than five hundred female traders at Sandaga, which is one of the largest produce markets in Douala, Cameroon's largest city and its leading economic center.

Despite how much she seemed to be accomplishing, however, Walla came to believe she could do more to effect change by becoming directly involved in politics as an elected official. In her interview with Soetan, Walla said that while she had never previously considered taking this step, she knew it was the right choice: "I used to say to myself back when I started my business, anything but politics!'" Walla added: "But it became clear to me as time went on and as I ran my business that at the end of the day,

I always came up against the government. The government was always somehow a stumbling block or obstacle to running my business effectively whether in form of its policies, operations or officials. It became clear that I couldn't make change from the outside."

Walla began her journey into politics in 2007 as a candidate for the Social Democratic Front (SDF). She had been an active supporter of the SDF for many years. Walla successfully campaigned for a seat on the municipal council of the First District of Douala. After winning the election, she quickly became one of the councils most outspoken and progressive members. Walla pursued an agenda that emphasized increased governmental transparency and improved budgetary management while continuing to be a strong proponent of electoral reform. She also became a vocal critic of a constitutional amendment proposed in 2009 that was designed to do away with presidential term limits. In time, Walla became one of Cameroon's most recognized political figures and began to consider taking her political career to the next level.

After establishing herself as a politician, Walla began considering the possibility of running for her nation's highest office in 2011. As she told the *Huffington Post's* Stephenie Foster (February 13, 2012), she believed she had what it took to do the job. "After working for 20 years in the private sector and as a civil society activist, I realized that my country's main problem is one of political leadership and governance)" Walla said. "I [had] the right combination of grassroots experience, knowledge and expertise in a broad range of development issues and the courage and capacity to lead. It was time to demonstrate that Cameroon has innovative, efficient leaders capable of putting the country's best interest at the forefront of their agenda."

After leaving the SDF in October 2010 and aligning herself with the Cameroon People's Party (CPP), Walla announced her candidacy for the office of president. Her biggest opponent was incumbent President Paul Biya, who has served as president of Cameroon since 1982. Though she was well aware that her bid for the presidency was a long shot, Walla and her supporters remained hopeful. Moreover, Walla was steadfast about running a campaign that did not rely on bribery or electoral fraud to succeed. Instead, she focused on generating support among women and young Cameroonians through her platform of change.

When the election returns came in, Biya was ushered into another term as president. Suspecting that there may have been some foul play involved, Walla and several other candidates contested the results but they were eventually forced to concede. Though she garnered relatively few votes in comparison with Biya, Walla was proud of her performance and of her supporters' enthusiasm.

Although she failed to win her the presidency, Walla told Foster that her campaign succeeded in planting the seeds of change in Cameroon. "Our Time Is Now' campaign definitely ignited a new spark all across Cameroon and within the Diaspora," Walla said.

## PERSONAL LIFE

Even after losing the presidential election, Walla continues her work as a leading political activist in Cameroon. Indeed, the exposure the election afforded her allowed Walla to position herself as a major figure in the fight for political and economic reform. Unfortunately, it also made her a highly visible target for those who oppose such reform. Walla has repeatedly been the victim of harassment and violence intended to discourage her from continuing her activism. She has been blasted with chemical-laced water cannons, beaten by police officers, and was even kidnapped by government agents. Despite this, Walla has refused to give in to her tormentors' demand for silence. She views everything that has happened to her as a sign that she is making an impression on the current government. As Alyse Nelson, president and CEO of Vital Voices, pointed out in an interview with Anna Louie Sussman of the *Women in the World Foundation* (September 21, 2011): "[Walla] joked to me that that meant she had a chance at winning." Adding, "to her, getting kidnapped was a sign that the party in power is taking her candidacy seriously."

Regardless of whatever adversity she might have to overcome, Walla has made it clear that she is still determined to bring real, substantive change to Cameroon. Though she is unceasingly optimistic, Walla is acutely aware that achieving real progress will be a daunting challenge, as she made clear to Foster. She said, "Change is such a simple word, and so difficult to actually effect."

## FURTHER READING

*http://venturesafrica.com/unleashing-africas-potential-with-cameroons-kah-walla/; http://www.nebafuh. com/2010/10/the-possible-impact-of-kah-wallas-presidential-bid.html*

# JIM WALLIS

## Evangelical Minister; Social Activist

**Born:** June 4, 1948; Detroit, Michigan
**Primary Field:** Peace and Social Justice
**Affiliation:** Christian Left

### INTRODUCTION

*"Whoever wins the battle over values is going to win the American political future,"* Jim Wallis told Jason White for the Religion News Service *(January 27, 2005). "The Republicans are comfortable with the language of moral values, but then they narrow it to one or two issues, albeit important issues, like abortion and gay marriage and family issues. A serious moral values conversation will challenge an economic agenda that rewards wealth over work and favors the rich over the poor and sees war as the first resort not the last resort." Espousing a mixture of left-leaning politics and conservative values, Wallis is among the few evangelical Christian leaders who speak out about social injustice. He is the founder of the Sojourners Fellowship, a group based in a poor, urban area of Washington, D.C., and serves as the editor in chief of the fellowship's magazine, Sojourners, which focuses on such issues as the environment, nuclear disarmament, poverty, and government policies.*

*Wallis told Wen Stephenson for the* Boston Globe *(January 23, 2005) that he agrees with right-wing Evangelicals that political decisions should be made on the basis of moral and religious values, "but then you've got to make an argument for the common good, you've got to persuade your fellow citizens that this is best for the country, that these are good things for all of us." Nonetheless, Wallis does not completely identify with liberals, who he feels are scared of talking about faith and provide more lip service than action on social issues. "I am from the progressive world, I am from the left but I will say, there is no progressive, economic agenda that will [alleviate] poverty in our neighborhoods unless we begin to reweave the fabric of family and community,"* he said at a conference of social activists, as reported by Bob von Sternberg for the Minneapolis, Minnesota, Star Tribune *(May 2, 1996). He explained to Gayle White for the* Atlanta Journal-Constitution *(January 19, 2002), "What you don't have is a really powerful movement drawn from liberals and conservatives who want to eradicate poverty and help people move out of poverty into dignity and self-sufficiency. We need*

*to change both the structural barriers and the cultural barriers that keep people stuck in poverty." Wallis has attempted to fill that vacuum by forming the ecumenical Call to Renewal, a group of churches and faith-based organizations across the theological spectrum that have agreed to work together to combat poverty. "Most of the world's religions believe in this concept, that the value of each person is the same,"* he told Howard Kohn for the Los Angeles Times *(November 6, 1994). "A rich person's life is no more sacred than a poor person's. If we could only adopt this simple concept in our lives, how might the world be transformed?" In fighting for dramatic social change, Wallis is attempting to revitalize the religiously conservative but socially liberal movements that helped lead to some of the greatest social advancements in American history. "Many of the most progressive social movements in American history, antislavery, women's suffrage, the fight for child labor laws, and the civil rights movement, had overt religious roots and motivations,"* Wallis told Stephenson.

### EARLY LIFE

John Wallis was born on June 4, 1948 in Detroit, Michigan. He is the son of James E. and Phyllis Wallis, members of a Baptist church who raised their children as evangelical Christians. As a teenager Wallis questioned why his church was racially segregated and why the community did not do more to help the poor. As a result of his questioning, he was ostracized; even his parents had difficulty understanding their son. "To them," he told Kohn, "faith was a personal act. They didn't relate it to people's suffering on the larger scale of war or racism. But I kept asking, why do we live in this nice little white, middle-class enclave, while a mile away, black people are living in slums?" Wallis began to attend African-American churches in inner-city Detroit and later became a civil rights activist. As a student at Michigan State University, in East Lansing, he also protested the Vietnam War. He came to the conclusion that no activism could be complete without ministry to the poor. "I was not on drugs or strung out," he told Megan Rosenfeld for the *Washington Post* (August 24, 1980), "it was a spiritual process, a pilgrimage. It was a political and intellectual conversion as well as personal." After earning a B.S. degree, in 1970, he began studies at Trinity Evangelical Divinity School, in Deerfield, Illinois. There, he continued to organize protests as he had in East Lansing, actions that led some of the school's alumni to call for his expulsion. In one memorable exercise while he was in divinity school, Wallis cut out every reference to the poor in a copy of the Bible, leaving dozens of holes in the pages. In 1971 Wallis and several other divinity students created *Sojourners* magazine, which focused on the Christian mission to pursue social justice.

## LIFE'S WORK

Wallis left divinity school in 1972 without a degree. That year, in Chicago, Illinois, he formed the Sojourners Fellowship, an ecumenical, live-in community of Christians devoted to social justice. In 1975 he moved the fellowship to an inner-city neighborhood in Washington, D.C., 20 blocks north of the White House. In their new location the approximately 45 members of the community helped residents of the neighborhood with landlord-tenant issues through the fellowship's Southern Colonial Heights Tenants Union. They also ran a food bank and education programs for adults and teens and operated an all-purpose community center. Each fellowship member received less than $20 a month for personal expenses. "I would like our life style not to make people gasp," Wallis told Rosenfeld. "We don't want people to think we're either crazy or admirable. We're not a commune; this is not a place where people sleep around. Nor do we live a monastic existence; we're not suffering. We're trying to show that you can establish a new way of life. We can live on less than we ever thought we could."

In 1979 Wallis's work with *Sojourners* led the editors of *Time* to name him one of their "50 Faces for America's Future." By 1980 *Sojourners* had a subscription rate of 45,000, and Wallis was spending about half of each year traveling around the country, to provide people with an alternative to such right-wing preachers as Jerry Falwell and Jimmy Swaggart. Wallis frequently discussed the growing gulf between rich and poor and the nuclear-arms race, both of which he found inconsistent with biblical teachings. While he criticized right-wing Evangelicals for not having enough compassion and for believing in God-ordained American power, he also attacked President Jimmy Carter, a Democrat, for not following his moral convictions with regard to nuclear disarmament, human rights, and U.S. support of military dictatorships. In 1981 Wallis, along with the leaders of four other church groups, wrote the New Abolitionist Covenant, which included, among other items, a promise to bear witness against the existence of nuclear weapons. In 1983 he and hundreds of others were jailed for demonstrating against nuclear weapons in the rotunda of the U.S. Capitol. "Opposition [to] nuclear weapons is a matter of obedience to Jesus Christ," he said, as reported by Stan W. Metzler for United Press International (May 29,1983). He also commented that Christians "cannot simultaneously love [their] enemies and plot their annihilation." Wallis was arrested again the following April at the U.S. Defense Department's test-ban site near Las Vegas, Nevada, along with 14 other people who were demonstrating to call attention to continuing underground testing of nuclear weapons. The members of the Sojourners Fellowship also arranged to follow a train that carried nuclear weapons so that it could be greeted with vigils and demonstrations as it reached various locations. In the mid-1980s the fellowship began its Witness for Peace program, in which groups of 15 to 20 activists went to Nicaragua to rebuild schools and hospitals and to help the local populace after U.S.-backed rebel attacks. Ultimately, more than 1,000 people took part in the program. "All life is sacred for us," Wallis told George E. Curry for the *Chicago Tribune* (June 11, 1985). "We want to defend life whenever and wherever it is threatened, from the beginning of the life cycle to the end, whether it be women or the unborn, or those oppressed in Central America, or workers and children in South Africa, or people of Afghanistan, suffering under Soviet invasion or whether it be on death row or whether it be all of us under the shadows of nuclear war."

Wallis's actions often brought him into conflict with conservative Evangelicals. Pat Robertson, according to Curry, has called Wallis a "socialist"; Jerry Falwell deems him and others like him "pseudo-evangelicals." For his part, Wallis told Curry that the right-wing evangelical movement "is more American than Christian. The gospel it preaches is much more an American gospel than it is the message of the Bible. Many leaders of that movement are kind of religious coconspirators with established power, and they've become court chaplains."

During the lead-up to the U.S.-led Gulf War, fought in response to Iraq's occupation of Kuwait in 1990, Wallis vocally opposed the actions of President George H. W. Bush. "Are we finally ready to make the critical choices to opt for energy conservation and the shift to safer, more reliable and renewable sources of fuel for the sake of the Earth and our children? Or are we prepared to bomb the children of Baghdad if necessary to protect 'our oil?'" he wrote in an op-ed piece for the *Washington Post* (October 30, 1990). Although he was cautiously optimistic after Bill Clinton's election to the presidency in 1992, Wallis quickly became discouraged with what he saw as Clinton's failure to follow through fully on his promises. Wallis told Robert Marquand for the *Christian Science Monitor* (January 26, 1995), "Clinton makes good speeches, but it isn't followed with a coherent vision that includes action that means something. We need a new politics with spiritual values." Wallis was later critical of President Clinton's having lied to a grand jury about his extramarital sexual relations with Monica Lewinsky, a former White House intern. He told Cathy Lynn Grossman for *USA Today* (January 26, 1998), "There is a connection between personal morality and social morality, between personal integrity and public trust." He stopped short of completely condemning the president, however. "You can't only focus on someone's personal morality," he told Grossman. "Is he faithful to his spouse, a good parent and all the rest. [You must] look at his public morality, how he treats the poor, how he treats his enemies."

Despite his demanding work with the Sojourners Fellowship and his hectic lecture schedule, Wallis found time to write or edit many books. He had published his first, *Agenda for Biblical People*, in 1976. In *Call to Conversion* (1981), he criticized churches for failing to heed Jesus's call to help all people. Wallis next edited the books *Waging Peace: A Handbook for the Struggle to Abolish Nuclear Weapons* (1982) and *Peacemakers, Christian Voices from the New Abolitionist Movement* (1983). That year he also published *Revive Us Again: A Sojourner's Story*. In 1987 he edited *Rise of Christian Conscience: The Emergence of a Dramatic Renewal Movement in the Church Today*. He co-edited (with Joyce Hollyday) both *Crucible of Fire: The Church Confronts Apartheid* (1989) and *Cloud of Witnesses* (1991). *In Soul of Politics: A Practical and Prophetic Vision for Change* (1994), Wallis wrote of the need for the U.S. to confront the ongoing effects of its racist past. In a review of the book for the *Pittsburgh Post-Gazette* (January 29, 1995), Tony Norman described it as "equal parts political biography and spiritual tract, with Wallis expertly knitting together the disparate skeins of secular and theological thought that make him one of our most fascinating and unlikely political radicals." Other critics praised the book but criticized Wallis for not offering in-depth solutions to the problems he identified. In

the *Washington Post* (January 22, 1995), for example, Jim Naughton wrote that Wallis "offers a romanticized view of the oppressed and an uninformed analysis of the middle-class. He is strident in his denunciation of our 'predatory' economic system but silent when faced with articulating an alternative."

In May 1995 Wallis was instrumental in forming Call to Renewal, a national ecumenical federation of approximately 80 churches and faith-based organizations that put their differences aside to work to overcome poverty. The organization hosts annual Roundtables on Poverty for national religious leaders and meetings about poverty that are attended by hundreds of people from many religious and secular organizations. The group also signed a declaration that stated its disagreement with such right-wing religious groups as the Christian Coalition and Focus on the Family. The declaration, as printed in the *Orlando Sentinel* (May 27, 1995), states, "The almost total identification of the religious right with the new Republican majority in Washington is a dangerous liaison of religion with political power." At the time the group estimated that as many as one-third of the total evangelical population could be considered progressive. "The public perception of a right-wing evangelical juggernaut is a false impression that we would like to correct," Wallis told a reporter for the *Wisconsin State Journal* (May 28, 1995). In December of that year, Wallis and 54 evangelical leaders associated with Call to Renewal were arrested in the Capitol rotunda for protesting Congress's lack of action to help the poor. "The poor don't have a voice here," Wallis told Francis X. Clines for the *New York Times* (December 8, 1995). "The poor don't have clout. They don't have the special interest."

Wallis was highly critical of the welfare-reform law passed by the U.S. Congress in 1996, which made it more difficult for recipients of aid to stay on welfare rolls. He vocally challenged conservative churches to enter into relationships with poor people on more than a symbolic level and for liberal churches to turn their words of compassion into action. In 1999 Call to Renewal sponsored the National Summit on the Church and Welfare Reform. In 2000 Wallis helped spearhead Call to Renewal's "Covenant to Overcome Poverty," a petition signed by a reported one million Christians. The petition stated in part that biblical precepts and Christian obligation demand that all people have access to affordable housing and health care, be able to live in safe neighborhoods and earn a living wage for responsible work, and have equal educational opportunities. "It has become fashionable to deny poverty's existence based on the generalized assumption that we are all in the midst of good economic times," Wallis told Ira J. Hadnot for the *Dallas Morning News* (June 18, 2000). "Only yachts are rising in this tide of economic prosperity. Poor people are being left behind in record numbers." While the presidential candidates George W. Bush and Al Gore focused part of their 2000 campaigns at wooing middle-class "soccer moms," Wallis told Hadnot that no one was talking about the woman working "at the drive-in window of a Burger King" who "keeps running back and forth to a small table in the back. It is 4 p.m., and she is trying to help her children with their homework while working this window. She cannot afford after-school care or health benefits."

In December 2000 Wallis, who had voted for Gore in the previous month's election, and 20 other religious leaders met with then President, Bush. He has since met with Bush on other occasions. In Wallis's view, the president's religious faith is sincere but incomplete. Wallis disagreed with Bush on the need for military action in Afghanistan, and in 2003 he led a delegation of religious leaders to visit with Prime Minister Tony Blair of Great Britain, a proponent of war against Iraq, to try to persuade him to change course. "Any war on terrorism that doesn't fundamentally target the eradication of global poverty is in fact doomed to failure," Wallis told Gayle White. Despite his disagreements with President Bush on military matters, he was enthusiastic about Bush's controversial plan to support faith-based charities with federal funds. In an op-ed piece for the *New York Times* (February 3, 2001), he wrote, "I don't believe such an office [the White House Office of Faith-Based and Com- munity Initiatives] threatens the principle of church-state separation. Why not forge partnerships with the most effective non-profits, whether they are religious or secular? And why discriminate against non-profits just because they are religious?" In 2000 Wallis published *Faith Works: Lessons from the Life of an Activist Preacher*. "With an idealism firmly rooted in practicality," Marilyn Gardner wrote for the *Christian Science Monitor* (March 23, 2000), "Wallis's book, like his life work, serves as an eloquent reminder of the importance of reaching out."

More recently, Wallis wrote in an editorial for *Sojourners* (July/August 2003, on-line) that the faith-based initiative effort "is fast becoming a hollow program that merely provides equal access for religious groups to the crumbs falling from the federal table." Wallis was also disenchanted with other aspects of the Bush administration, and he found the Democrats equally frustrating. "How a candidate deals with poverty is a religious issue, and the Bush administration's failure to support poor working families should be named as a religious failure," he wrote in an op-ed piece for the *New York Times* (December 28, 2003). "Neglect of the environment is a religious issue. Fighting preemptive and unilateral wars based on false claims is a religious issue. Such issues could pose problems for the Bush administration among religious and nonreligious people alike, if someone were to define them in moral terms. The failure of the Democrats to do so is not just a political miscalculation. It shows they do not appreciate the contributions of religion to American life."

During the 2004 presidential campaign, Wallis tried to convince Evangelicals that, contrary to what many of their leaders said, Bush was not the only acceptable candidate for Christians. He helped introduce a petition, signed by more than 40 Christian leaders and 40,000 laypeople, that criticized the belief that Christians could vote in good conscience for Bush only. The petition appeared in a full-page ad in the New York Times that was paid for by supporters of *Sojourners*. "Good Christians can vote for President Bush; I have no problem with that," Wallis said during a sermon, according to Jean Torkelson in the *Rocky Mountain News* (September 13, 2004). "But you can't ordain one candidate as God's candidate and you can't be single-issue voters." Many political observers believed that the Democratic presidential nominee, Senator John F. Kerry of Massachusetts, lost his bid for the presidency because he could not connect to citizens with deep evangelical faith. After the election Wallis became a sought after adviser for the Democratic Party; he has since spoken before the Democratic members of both the House of Representatives and Congress.

In early 2005 Wallis published *God's Politics: Why the Right Gets It Wrong and the Left Doesn't Get It*. The book berates conservatives for not fighting for peace, the environment, and the eradication of poverty and criticizes liberals for failing to take concrete action on those issues and to recognize the importance of faith and moral values in a healthy society. "The real theological problem in America today," he wrote in the book, as quoted by Sandi Dolbee in the *San Diego Union-Tribune* (March 3, 2005), "is no longer the religious right, but the nationalist religion of the Bush administration, one that confuses the identity of the nation with the church, and God's purposes with the mission of American empire." *God's Politics* peaked at number two on the Amazon.com sales chart and reached sixth place and fifth place on the bestseller lists of the *New York Times* and the *Washington Post*, respectively. Wallis's other books include *Who Speaks for God?: An Alternative to the Religious Right—A New Politics of Compassion, Community an d Civility* (1996).

## PERSONAL LIFE

Wallis is married to Joy Carroll Wallis, an Anglican priest who is a native of England. She reportedly served as the inspiration for a British television comedy series called *The Vicar of Dibley*. The couple have two children and live as part of the Sojourners Fellowship. Although their Washington, D.C., neighborhood is slowly gentrifying, it is still plagued by poverty and crime. "For me, living in that kind of place was a spiritual discipline as much as prayer," he told Jason White. "Because it forced me to be conscious of what it means to live in a poor and violent neighborhood, even if in one sense I am never fully a part of it because of my options and choices. So when I am having conversations at these national levels about these issues, I know this stuff at a feeling level, at a friendship level, at a painful level."

From 1998 to 1999 Wallis taught at the John F. Kennedy School of Government at Harvard University, in Cambridge, Massachusetts. He continues to speak at numerous events each year and struggles to find funding for his magazine and his community. "Sojourners falls between the cracks. We are anathema to both sides," he told Howard Kohn. "The Christian Right will not help us because we talk about racial and economic justice and are opposed to war; the liberal-funding world is remarkably biased against religion." Nevertheless, Wallis retains hope. "Whenever we feel helpless and hopeless," he wrote in *The Soul of Politics*, as quoted by Tom Roberts in the *National Catholic Reporter* (November 18, 1994), "we need to understand that our situation is never as static as it may appear to be. Hope always involves the breaking open of new possibilities from seemingly hopeless circumstances. In fact, at the heart of our best spiritual traditions is the wisdom of believing that life will arise out of death." Wallis works as a spiritual adviser to President Barack Obama and as a leader in the Red Letter Christian Movement.

## FURTHER READING

*Agenda for Biblical People; Call to Conversion; Revive Us Again: A Sojourner's Story; Soul of Politics: A Practical and Prophetic Vision for Change; Who Speaks for God?: An Alternative to the Religious Right – A New Politics of Compassion, Community and Civility; Faith Works: Lessons from the Life of an Activist Preacher; God's Politics: Why the Right Gets It Wrong and the Left Doesn't Get It*

---

# FAYE WATTLETON

## Feminist; Activist; Author

**Born:** July 8, 1943; St. Louis, Missouri
**Primary Field:** Reproductive Health
**Affiliation:** Planned Parenthood Federation of America, Inc.

## INTRODUCTION

*"I'm very fortunate to have a career in a field that makes an enormous contribution to the future of the world,"* Faye Wattleton, the president of the Planned Parenthood Federation of America once remarked. From 1978 – 1992 she led the nation's oldest and largest voluntary family planning organization in a crusade to guarantee every person's right to decide if and when to have a child. A professional nurse, Wattleton is committed to alleviating the suffering associated with the three million unintended pregnancies that occur each year in the United States alone, representing half of all pregnancies nationwide in a given year. She became the president of Planned Parenthood in January 1978 in the belief that family planning is the best solution to a host of problems that are exacerbated by the high rate of unintended pregnancies, including child abuse, teenage pregnancy, sexually transmitted diseases, and, especially atrocious in the developing world, poverty, hunger, and an estimated 200,000 deaths a year from illegal, often self-induced abortions.

Ever since Margaret Sanger opened America's first birth control clinic in 1916, Planned Parenthood's *forerunner, in Brooklyn, New York, family planning programs have had to overcome entrenched and powerful resistance to their efforts to provide educational, medical, and counseling services in the highly controversial areas of sexuality and reproductive health. Planned Parenthood offers pregnancy diagnosis, prenatal care, infertility counseling, AIDS testing, and contraceptive services. Only fifty of its 177 affiliates, which are located in forty-six states and the District of Columbia, performed abortions in 1988. That year Planned Parenthood's 30,000 volunteers and staff served 3.8 million Americans; another 4 million people in the developing world were served by Family Planning International Assistance, the international division of Planned Parenthood, which was created in 1971 with funds provided by the United States Agency for International Development. Planned Parenthood's budget for domestic and international services increased nearly threefold during Faye Wattleton's tenure to $303 million in 1988; the nonprofit organization's income included private contributions from approximately 250,000 donors. Planned Parenthood's work is complemented by the research, policy analysis, and public educational efforts undertaken by the Alan Guttmacher Institute, an independent corporation and a special affiliate.*

*Opposition to Planned Parenthood's efforts escalated throughout the 1980s, abetted to an unprecedented degree by the White House of President Ronald Reagan. Attempts to restrict abortion rights in particular proceeded in the courts, the legislatures, and the streets. Faye Wattleton's counter strategy entailed maintaining the offensive while at the same time defending hard-won victories. The weapons at her disposal included litigation, advertising, lobbying both Congress and the public, and frequent appearances on talk shows and news programs.*

*Spurred on by Wattleton's winding combination of enthusiasm and cool rationality, the long complacent pro-choice movement rallied in the wake of the Supreme Court's July 1989 decision in Webster v. Reproductive Health Services that encouraged state legislatures to impose new restrictions on abortion rights. Seizing the momentum created by a newly galvanized movement, Wattleton proposed a Reproductive Rights Amendment to the Constitution and proclaimed her intention to work for the availability to Americans of the French developed "abortion pill" known as RU 486. "Reproductive freedom is critical to a whole range of issues," she said in an interview with Marcia Ann Gillespie. "If*

*we can't take charge of this most personal aspect of our lives, we can't take care of anything. It should not be seen as a privilege or as a benefit, but as a fundamental human right."*

## EARLY LIFE

Alyce Faye Wattleton was born in St. Louis, Missouri on July 8, 1943, the only child of George Wattleton, a factory worker, and Ozie Wattleton, a seamstress and a minister in the fundamentalist Church of God. Describing her upbringing in St. Louis in an interview with Nancy Rubin for Savvy Woman (April 1989), Wattleton disclosed the source of both her altruism and her ability to persevere: "I was raised by my parents to believe that it was my obligation to help those with less than I had. Although we were poor, the value of my family life was that there was a sense of achievement. We were taught to believe that it was possible to succeed, and that if you didn't, you didn't quit." Her drive to succeed became manifest at an early age. She skipped kindergarten and the first grade, entered Ohio State University, in Columbus, Ohio, at sixteen, and obtained her bachelor's degree in nursing in 1964. "Growing up in the 1940s and 1950s," she told Marianne Szegedy-Maszak for the New York Times Magazine (August 6, 1989), "you were either going to be a nurse or a social worker or a teacher. I was always going to be a nurse, a missionary nurse."

But Faye Wattleton's college experiences led her to abandon her fundamentalist beliefs and her goal of becoming a missionary. She was exposed for the first time not only to alternative lifestyles, but also to battered children through her part-time work in a children's hospital, which she performed in exchange for room and board at college. "The doctrinaire approach to religion and life became very frightening to me," she said during an interview with Paula Span for the Washington Post (October 14,1987). "When I saw you had to conduct your life in a certain way or you were unworthy of life hereafter; when I saw people sometimes weren't able to live up to those standards; when I saw that life wasn't always so straightforward, it had a lot of influence on my coming to hold the views I've come to hold."

Nursing reinforced her newly discovered tolerance for diversity, as she made clear in her discussion with Nancy Rubin. "I simply chose a profession that made it difficult for me to see life in such exacting terms," she said. "In a healthcare situation, you see humanity at its most basic and you realize there are no simple yes or no, right or wrong answers." But while she became more accepting of the need to compromise in order to find the most effective solution to a given problem, she did not relinquish all her mother's teachings. The tales of suffering recounted by Ozie Wattleton's fellow missionaries during Faye's childhood "cast a deep impression" on her. In an interview with David Behrens for New York Newsday (October 2, 1989), she said, "I never rejected the foundations of my mother's religion, to want to make the world a better place."

## LIFE'S WORK

After graduating from college, Faye Wattleton taught at the Miami Valley Hospital School of Nursing in Dayton, Ohio for two years. In 1966 she won a full scholarship to Columbia University's master's degree program in maternal and infant health care. Specializing in midwifery during her year at Columbia, Wattleton trained at Harlem Hospital. There, she witnessed the hardship borne by women who tried to terminate their pregnancies during the days of illegal abortion. Many suffered from blood poisoning, a common accompaniment to self-induced abortions. Especially traumatic for Wattleton was watching a seventeen year old in her care die of kidney failure following the injection (by the victim's mother) of a combination of Lysol and bleach into her uterus. "A healthy, beautiful human being died because of the poison," she recalled during an interview with Jesse Green for Seven Days (July 12, 1989). "That was the closest I had come to the desperation that women feel."

Wattleton remained in close contact with the victims of mal-administered, illegal abortions as a public health nurse for two years following the receipt of her master's degree in 1967. As assistant director of the Montgomery County Combined Public Health District in Dayton, she worked to expand local prenatal healthcare services. Her success resulted in her appointment, in 1970, as executive director of the local Planned Parenthood board, which she had been asked to join eighteen months earlier. Asked by a reporter for USA Today (December 28, 1982) what had originally induced her to join Planned Parenthood, she replied, "I had to ask myself, 'Is it better to continue trying to save these children and those people who are injured and vulnerable, or to work for a world in which these conditions don't occur?'"

During Faye Wattleton's seven and a half years at the helm of Planned Parenthood in Dayton, she weathered criticism from all sides of the abortion and birth control debate, for the 1970s were a period of increasing right wing militancy, both in Congress and in American communities. Shortly after the Supreme Court decided in 1977 that states were not required to fund abortions for indigent women, two-thirds of the states enacted laws that deprived poor women of equal access to safe and legal abortions. "It is a reflection of this country's tremendous anger and resentment toward poor people," Wattleton said in her interview with Gillespie. "I see the attacks on abortion and family planning as fundamentally anti-woman, and the attacks on poor women as being primarily anti-poor and anti-black, because poverty conjures up images of black women on welfare."

Ironically, some black activists and some feminists in the 1960s and early 1970s criticized Planned Parenthood itself as racist and anti-woman. In their view, the organization's national image was, respectively, that of a white run agency whose mission was to reduce the black birth rate through population control, or that of a mal-directed effort to control women's reproductive lives at the expense of their health. Wattleton dismissed such charges in an interview with Shawn D. Lewis for Ebony (September 1978): "It would be difficult to label Planned Parenthood as genocidal to minorities when only 30 percent of the women we service are minorities. I believe it is genocidal for black women to have children they don't want. The future and strength of the race is for women to be able to have kids when they want them and to love and provide them with the tools they'll need to get through a hostile world. The image of the black woman bearing child upon child against her will is the real threat to the race."

The appointment of a black woman to the presidency of Planned Parenthood in January 1978 did more to allay fears of genocidal and misogynous intentions than any rational argument. Faye Wattleton was not only the first black and the first woman to lead the agency; she was also, at thirty-four, the youngest president that Planned Parenthood had ever had. When she was asked by Shawn D. Lewis to comment on the organization's reasons for selecting her from among over 200 other applicants who were considered during a nine month search, Wattleton cited her compassion, hard work, and the common sense inherent in appointing a woman to lead an agency whose "primary reason for existence deals with women." She elaborated in the 1982 USA Today interview, which was included in the book And Still We Rise by Barbara Reynolds, a compilation of biographies about black role models. "My appointment," she said, "seemed a very bold step for the organization to take. As a black woman I have a deep and personal concern for the tragedy of unwanted children. I know that the burden of such conditions falls much heavier on blacks that on the white community. Being black and a female adds dimension to my sensitivities as I carry out my work." Other reasons why Faye Wattleton was deemed the best qualified candidate for the presidency of Planned Parenthood included her able leadership of the Dayton affiliate, whose fundraising efforts and outreach programs expanded under her direction. Another factor was her outstanding performance as chairwoman of the National Executive Directors' Council, a liaison office between Planned Parenthood's headquarters in New York City and its affiliates, to which she had been elected in 1975.

While some people were reportedly shocked by Faye Wattleton's appointment to a position previously held only by white men, even more controversy was generated by the decision to change the organization's image, which Wattleton once characterized as "an eastern establishment agency credible, cautious, and conservative." Some organization officials were wary of taking on a strong advocacy role, fearing that corporate sponsors would be driven away. "I know there were people who swore they'd never give us another dime," Wattleton recalled in her 1987 interview with Paula Span. "I figured, for every one we lost we'd get two or three more who'd say, 'I'm glad to see Planned Parenthood standing up.'" By 1989, according to a report published in the July 3 issue of *Business Week,* corporate funding had decreased to half the level of the 1970s; on the other hand, corporate grants accounted for a mere 1.5 percent of Planned Parenthood's fundraising budget, which was $65 million.

Others within Planned Parenthood objected to Wattleton's willingness to confront the opposition head-on by staunchly defending even the most controversial reproductive issues, such as abortion rights. Even while defending the necessity of legal abortion, however, she has taken pains to point out that Planned Parenthood is not pro-abortion, but pro-choice. Moreover, most organization employees share her uncompromising pro-choice position. "I make it very clear," she told Paula Span. "If you're not clear where you stand on the abortion issue, if you're worried that birth control for teenagers encourages promiscuity, or you're not so sure everybody ought to have access to birth control whenever they want it it's probably not the kind of outfit you're

comfortable with." Sixty to 70 percent of the national office staff resigned or was asked to leave during the corporate restructuring that accompanied Wattleton's settling-in period.

For all those who voiced their misgivings about her appointment, there were others who advised her against taking the job for her own sake, as she reported during the *USA Today* interview: "There were plenty who said: 'Planned Parenthood's in a terrible state. It has gone through two presidents in rapid succession. The organization is in turmoil. That's what always happens when an organization is on the skids, they turn around and look for a black to save it.' In retrospect, accepting the position was a very courageous move." At the time, of course, Wattleton did not know that the fire-bombing of abortion clinics would be on the rise during her first year as president or that she would receive death threats. "My instincts were that we were in for a tough time," she told Nancy Rubin, "but I don't think I had an inkling of just how bad it was going to be."

Setting out to transform Planned Parenthood's image, Wattleton hired media consultants and poll-takers. Always equipped with appropriate statistics to bolster her arguments, she gave interviews and made many public appearances in an effort to raise public awareness of family planning issues. She established vice-presidencies for nine separate functional areas and created an office in Washington, DC., for lobbying Congress, monitoring legislation, and gathering and disseminating information. Discussing her emphasis on advocacy at the national level in the interview with David Behrens, Wattleton recalled, "It was prophetic that I felt this was the direction we would have to go, without knowing we were nearing the Reagan years. But I saw the growing political opposition on the local level."

Even before the Reagan administration began to implement its conservative social agenda, the pro-choice movement faced an uphill battle in the courts and in the legislatures. Faye Wattleton's first objective was to restore Medicaid funding of abortions. She also sought to increase funding for contraceptive research and for programs to help reduce the incidence of teenage pregnancies, increased the number of individual donors via a direct mail fundraising appeal, and allocated more resources to litigation advertising and community education programs. "We've allowed right-to-lifers to have center stage," Wattleton said, as quoted by *People* (May 22,1978). "They'd trample on our constitutional rights to push their point of view. But those days are over."

The days of antiabortion protesters' hogging the limelight did indeed seem to be numbered, thanks to Faye Wattleton's willingness to step into the breach. Eve Paul, the vice-president for legal affairs at Planned Parenthood, was quoted by Rubin as saying, "One of Faye's major accomplishments has been to make Planned Parenthood better known to the public, and she's done this because she's been able to capture the interest of the media." The talk show host Phil Donahue, also quoted by Rubin, called Wattleton "a talk show host's dream guest. She gets to the point and doesn't talk too much. She doesn't get into brawls, she's eternally civil, and she's always well informed." Wattleton attributed her eloquence to her mother's influence and to her religious upbringing in the interview with Jesse Green: "While [my mother] is not an educated woman, she is very articulate. I was an only child among adults. And when you grow up in the church, particularly the black church, a lot of time is spent listening to people express their opinions."

Time spent in church enhanced Faye Wattleton's debating skills in yet another way, as she revealed to Rubin: "My religious background has been helpful to me in understanding the mentality of the religious Right. Through that understanding, I've been able to position our argument in a way that is compelling to people, rather than attacking or offending those of the right-wing religious or political persuasion. My approach has been very valuable in positioning the organization and these issues in a straightforward, clear, no nonsense manner. We're not saying abortion is right or wrong or preaching a moral cause, because that is a very personal decision. What we are saying is that government has no right telling women what to do with their lives." One person who remains unpersuaded by the merits of legal abortion is Faye Wattleton's own mother, but their disagreement has not diminished the respect they have for each other, Wattleton has said on more than one occasion.

Despite the publicity and sympathy elicited by Faye Wattleton for the cause of family planning, the opposition was pressing ahead with seemingly irreversible momentum during the Reagan years. Reductions in the major source of federal funding for family planning clinics. Planned Parenthood runs 850 clinic sites worldwide amounted to a 15 percent cut in Title X of the Public Health Service Act from 1980 to 1989. She relentlessly pointed out the irony inherent in the opposition's strategy of undermining the very programs that have been shown to reduce the demand for abortions by averting unwanted pregnancies. In 1981 family planning services funded by Title X grants prevented more than 800,000 unintended pregnancies, over half of which would have afflicted teenagers, according to a federally supported study conducted by the Alan Guttmacher Institute. The same study demonstrated a savings to taxpayers of between two and three dollars in costs associated with unplanned pregnancies in a typical year for every government dollar allotted to family planning services the previous year.

Funding cuts notwithstanding, Wattleton viewed the retention of Title X monies in the budget as a victory. Other successes included her refusal to go along with a 1982 Reagan administration proposal that would have required parental notification by recipients of Title X funds when a minor requested a birth control prescription. That proposal was defeated in court. In 1983 anti-choice forces suffered another setback when the Senate rejected the so-called Human Life Amendment to the Constitution that was proposed in an effort to repeal Roe v. Wade. Yet another tactic employed against family planning organizations was strict auditing in an unsuccessful attempt to uncover misuse of funds.

In 1984 the Reagan administration tried to restrict access to reproductive services in the developing world by making federal funding of foreign nongovernmental family planning organizations conditional upon pledging to abide by the so-called Mexico City policy. Announced in Mexico City at the second United Nations International Conference on Population, in 1984, the Mexico City policy prohibited overseas recipients of federal funds from engaging in abortion counseling, referrals, advocacy, or the actual performance of abortions, regardless of whether the abortion-related activities themselves were funded separately by private means. Planned Parenthood fought the Mexico City policy on behalf of its international division with litigation, lobbying, and a controversial advertising campaign. Referring to the ongoing litigation, Faye Wattleton was quoted by Marianne Szegedy-Maszak as saying, "I felt that I had to lead the organization down that route, because to do otherwise would be to make a mockery of all our principles and all we stood for."

The single largest setback for the pro-choice movement since Medicaid funding was abolished in two-thirds of the states was the Supreme Court's Webster decision in July 1989. Although it did not overturn Roe outright, the Webster ruling referred the issue back to the state legislatures by upholding a Missouri law that mandated several abortion restrictions, the like of which had not passed constitutional muster. Jesse Green reported a typical question asked of Wattleton in anticipation of a reversal of Roe v. Wade. "If the American public is in favor of abortions, as Planned Parenthood is always claiming, why wouldn't you welcome the chance to fight it out in the state legislatures?" an editor asked. Wattleton replied, "The American public believes in free speech, but I'm sure that you, as a member of the press, wouldn't want to see it argued state by state. A woman's right to abortion is similarly a matter of settled constitutional law."

As abortion became a controversial issue in the 1989 gubernatorial campaigns in New Jersey and Virginia, and as lawmakers debated new restrictions on abortions in the Florida and Pennsylvania legislatures, Faye Wattleton argued for an all-out, door-to-door community-organizing campaign. "Block by block," she said in the interview with Marcia Ann Gillespie, "we have to actively educate our friends and neighbors to the issues. We have to take the debate to the people. There needs to be someone at every political meeting, asking politicians, 'What is your position on abortion? What is your position on funding abortions for poor women?' Women must stand up and say that these are bottom line issues for us. There can be no compromise position." In October 1989 she announced the establishment of Planned Parenthood Action Fund to augment her organization's lobbying efforts against abortion restrictions. Reasoning that a purely defensive posture for Planned Parenthood was no longer tenable since the status quo had been challenged by Webster, Wattleton argued, "I want to see us take [the debate] to a higher ground by calling for a Reproductive Rights Amendment to the Constitution. If we, don't prevail in keeping abortions legal and available to all women in all states, then hundreds of thousands of faceless and powerless women will continue to bear the burden."

The Webster decision invigorated not only the pro-choice movement, which subsequently joined together in a coalition that led to cooperation among Planned Parenthood, the National Organization for Women, and other groups; it seemed also to revitalize Faye Wattleton's personal drive. In the interview with Nancy Rubin, which bracketed a four-month sabbatical taken by Wattleton in 1988-89 to begin writing a book on the influence on national politics of American attitudes toward sexuality, she hinted at leaving Planned Parenthood. "We're going to have some very significant battles ahead, whether I'm going to lead them or someone else. Whoever is providing leadership needs to be as fresh and thoughtful and reflective as possible to make the very best fight." But after Webster she was quoted by Mary T. Schmich for the *Chicago Tribune* (July 23, 1989) as saying, "There is no life after Planned Parenthood for the foreseeable future."

## PERSONAL LIFE

Faye Wattleton, who once modeled part-time during her nursing days in Dayton, dresses so stylishly and looks so sophisticated that an image consultant reportedly told her, "You don't need me. You have natural talent." Slender at five feet, eleven inches, Wattleton has been commended on her appearance even by leaders of the anti-choice movement. She has received numerous humanitarian awards and belongs to the board of the United States Committee for UNICEF, the Young Presidents' Organization, and the National Advisory Committee of the Tufts School of Public Service. In 1990 she wrote a history of birth control and abortion, to be published in 1991 by Knopf. She has contributed to the American Humanist Association and has won several prestigious awards for her commitment to reproductive health and justice. She is currently a managing director at Alvarez & Marshal, an international consulting firm.

Divorced since 1981, Faye Wattleton has one daughter Felicia, who studied law at New York University. Her hobbies have included collecting antiques and Oriental art, playing tennis, breeding Afghan dogs, and exercising. Her former husband, Franklin Gordon, was a social worker and a jazz pianist. The date of their marriage has been variously reported as 1969, 1972, or 1973. "Since my divorce," Wattleton revealed to Jesse Green, "I've dated a lot, but I haven't wanted a parade of men coming through my home. I have to think of what's good for Felicia. And ultimately I believe in marriage. I believe in family."

## FURTHER READING

*Contemporary Newsmakers; And Still We Rise; Interviews with 50 Black Role Models; How to Talk with Your Child about Sexuality*

# TOM WICKER

## Journalist; Writer; Novelist; Speaker

**Born:** June 18, 1926; Hamlet, North Carolina
**Died:** November 25, 2011; Rochester, Vermont
**Primary Field:** Freedom & Equality
**Affiliations:** Society of Nieman Fellows; Century Association Club

### INTRODUCTION

*Once praised by a colleague as the "Earl Warren of journalism" Tom Wicker, the columnist and novelist who was an Associate Editor and a columnist of the* New York Times *prior to being the Washington, D.C., Bureau Chief of the paper, had been a perceptive observer of the American scene for more than 20 years. His thrice-weekly "In the Nation" column, which had been called "one of our principal national assets" by Newsweek's Peter S. Prescott, provoked the anger of conservatives and liberals alike.*

*A stubborn idealist and determined Civil Libertarian, Wicker had attacked the omnibus anticrime bill, opposed the Senate's passage of the "no-knock entry" provision in a drug-control bill, and accused the Nixon Administration of creating the "beginnings of a police state." Appalled by Watergate, he had argued that "a prima facie case of neglect of duty" be brought against then President Richard Nixon, and he had denounced the covert bombing in Cambodia as the latest in a "long chronicle of lies" and deceptions. For his outspokenness, Wicker was one of several news reporters named to the so-called "enemies list" that was prepared several years ago by Nixon's aides and submitted to the Senate Select Committee on Presidential Campaign Activities by former White House Counsel John W. Dean, 3rd.*

### EARLY LIFE

The son of Delancey David and Esta (Cameron) Wicker, Thomas Grey Wicker was born on June 18, 1926, in Hamlet, N.C. His father, a freight conductor for the Seaboard Air Line Railway, occasionally rewarded Tom, who stacked firewood, shoveled coal, and he performed other household tasks for his mother, with free train rides. In 1937, the Wicker family traveled overnight on a railroad "trip pass," to visit Washington, D.C. "I never got over it," Wicker wrote years later in his Introduction to a New York Times guidebook to the capital. "I

thought the [Capitol] dome against the sky was the most beautiful sight I had ever seen, and I still do."

After working his way through the University of North Carolina, from which he graduated, in 1948, with a B.A. degree in journalism, Wicker worked briefly as the Executive Director of the Southern Pines (North Carolina) Chamber of Commerce. In 1949, he became Editor of the Sandhill Citizen, a weekly in Aberdeen, N.C. Still dissatisfied, he moved to nearby Lumberton later that year to become the Managing Editor of The Robesonian, a Democratic daily. Temporarily suspending his journalistic career, in 1950, he served as the Public Information Director for the North Carolina Board of Public Welfare. The following year, he joined the staff of the Winston-Salem Journal as its copy editor. Wicker remained with the Journal for the next eight years, serving successively as its sports editor, Sunday feature editor, Washington correspondent, city hall reporter and editorial writer. His career at the Journal was interrupted, in 1952, when he began a two-year tour of duty as a lieutenant (j.g.) in the United States Naval Reserve, and, again, in the 1957 to 1958 academic year, when he attended Harvard University as a Nieman Fellow in Journalism. In 1959, he was named Associate Editor of the Nashville Tennessean, but, he resigned, only six months later, to become a staff reporter for the New York Times's Washington Bureau.

Wicker had first attempted to land a job with the Times, in 1958, but, according to Gay Talese (The Kingdom and the Power, 1969), the clean-shaven, meticulously dressed, and conservative New York editors objected to the bearded Wicker's easygoing manner and casual, almost unkempt appearance. Two years later, on the recommendation of another Times reporter, Wicker applied directly to the Washington Bureau, then headed by James B. ("Scotty") Reston, and was immediately hired. As a Capitol Hill reporter, and, later, as a White House correspondent, Wicker criss crossed the country, covering political campaigns, Presidential public appearances, and Congressional elections. On November 22, 1963, Wicker, who was the only Times reporter with the Presidential party in Dallas, scored a journalistic coup. Relying on his instinct, which he continued to trust more readily than his sources, Wicker sifted through rumors, second-hand reports, tips from other reporters, bits of official information, and his own notes scribbled on the mimeographed Presidential itinerary to piece together a detailed account of the assassination of President John F. Kennedy. His 106-paragraph story, telephoned two pages at a time to the Times home office from a Dallas airport telephone booth, filled two front-page columns, and, the entire second page of the newspaper's November 23rd edition. Despite that only a few paragraphs described events that Wicker had actually witnessed, the article was incredibly accurate.

## LIFE'S WORK

On September 1, 1964, Wicker was named Washington Bureau Chief at the insistence of his mentor James B. Reston, who had asked to be relieved following Times Publisher Arthur Ochs Sulzberger's sweeping reorganization of the newspaper's executive structure. In addition to carrying out his administrative duties as Bureau Chief, Wicker continued to cover out-of-town and out-of-country assignments, to contribute articles to the New York Times Magazine, and to write news analyses and occasional columns. It prompted criticism from the head office that he was devoting too much attention to his own pursuits at the bureau's expense. Several New York editors, among them Harrison Salisbury, A. M. Rosenthal, and Clifton Daniel, complained about aggressive competition from the Washington Post and from the television networks' growing Press Corps, charging that Wicker's bureau was not producing enough front-page exclusives. Backed by Reston, and, by columnist and former Bureau Chief Arthur Krock, both of whom had maintained independent bureaus, Wicker objected to the editors' interference, on the grounds that the continual and, in his view, unjustified rewriting of the frustrated Washington staff's copy was damaging staff morale. When Managing Editor Turner Catledge tried to replace Wicker with Assistant Managing Editor Harrison Salisbury, in the summer of 1966, he placated Wicker by promising him Arthur Krock's column when the older man retired. Wicker reluctantly agreed. The Times's national political correspondent, David Broder, resigned in protest and sent a scathing memo to Publisher Sulzberger, in which he accused the New York office of "'endless bureaucratic frustrations.' The head office relented, Wicker remained in charge of the bureau, and. a few months later, he inherited Krock's column.

With Sulzberger's approval, in February 1968, Managing Editor Daniel and Assistant Managing Editor Rosenthal appointed James Greenfield to succeed Wicker as Chief of the Washington Bureau. Faced with the prospect of resignations from Wicker, Reston, and White House Correspondent Max Frankel in a Presidential election year, Sulzberger once again reversed his decision at a top-level executive meeting in New York. A few months later, Wicker was named an Associate Editor of the New York Times, to be effective on December 1, 1968.

While he was a reporter in the South, Wicker published three thrillers under the pseudonym Paul Connoll: Kingpin (Sloane, 1953); So Fair, So Evil (Fawcett, 1955); and, The Devil Must (Harper, 1957). In Washington, he completed another novel, The Judgment (Sloane, 1961), before turning to political reportage. Kennedy Without Tears: The Man Behind the Myth (Morrow, 1964), a recollection of his coverage of the Kennedy White House, received mixed reviews. Wicker, who had always believed that personality is a more decisive factor in public life than political persuasion, examined the effects of two disparate personalities on the office of the Presidency in JFK and LBJ: The Influence of Personality Upon Politics (Morrow, 1968). Generally well received, the book relied on character analysis to try to explain Kennedy's apparent inability to push domestic programs through an obstinate Congress and Johnson's inevitable "credibility gap" in relation to the Vietnam War (officially known as the Vietnam Conflict).

Because, as he told Thomas Collins in an interview for Newsday (July 16, 1973), "there are things you can do in a novel that you can't do in journalism," Wicker began work on his fifth novel, tentatively called "The Golden Touch," in 1969. The product of three summer vacations, Facing the Lions, as the novel was finally entitled, follows the career of Hunt Anderson, a charismatic Southern Senator, through the eyes of reporter Rich Morgan, a hard-bitten but softhearted Washington Bureau Chief with a background not unlike Wicker's own. Although Wicker conceded a similarity between the fictional Senator Anderson and the late Senator Estes Kefauver (a powerful—and considered honest by his constituents, his peers, and the media—New Deal politician who tried to run for President on the Democratic Party ticket against Eisenhower) in that both men enjoyed "a swift rise and sowed the seeds" of their political defeats, he denied a conscious resemblance between himself and Morgan. "I've never known any Presidential candidates or Senators as well as he does," Wicker told Thomas Collins, "and I don't want to." An instant best seller (it was on The Times best-seller list for 18 weeks), Facing the Lions was widely reviewed after its publication by Viking Press in 1973.

As a member of the Washington Press Corps, Tom Wicker had been upbraided by then Vice-President Spiro T. Agnew for his "irresponsibility and thoughtlessness." Agnew, like Nixon, later resigned. (Nixon resigned in disgrace over the Watergate cover-up; Agnew resigned after pleading no contest to evading taxes on bribes he had taken while he was Governor of Maryland.) Agreeing that the press is often guilty of irresponsible journalism, Wicker maintained that the press should not be censured for over-analyzing the news, as the Vice-President contended, but rather for under-analyzing it. In a speech before Columbia University students, Wicker condemned the media's establishment-oriented approach to the news. The press's "biggest weakness," he argued, "is its reliance on, and acceptance of, official sources—indeed, its 'objectivity' in presenting the news." "Anything that is an institution gets quoted—government, or a corporation, or a university," he had complained, "but it's hard to get the other side." Ever since he became a Washington correspondent, Wicker had been fighting the "press box mentality" that relies on official sources and press releases for information. During the Johnson Administration, he broke established tradition when he asked permission to quote assistant White House Press Secretary Andrew Hatcher directly, insisting his readers had a right to know the source of the story. Hatcher refused and Wicker was forced to attribute the information to the customary "sources close to the President."

As a source of reliable information, Presidential press conferences are, in Wicker's view, equally inadequate. In a New York Times Magazine article (September 8, 1963), he compared reporters at a Presidential press conference to "spear carriers in Cyrano de Bergerac," unable to challenge the President's answers, ask follow-up questions, or request clarification of evasive or contradictory replies. Wicker believed that the skillful news management of the Nixon Administration had made it even more difficult to avoid the "ultimate trap" of official versions. "We feel the general pressure," Wicker told political writer David Wise in an interview for the Atlantic Monthly (April 1973). "There is a constant pattern of pressure intended to inhibit us . . . to make us unconsciously pull in our horns."

At the first A. J. Liebling Counter-Convention ( a conference that was "counter" to the American Newspaper Publishers Association convention) held in honor of the late New Yorker press critic in New York City, in April 1972, Wicker told assembled reporters and journalism students that "spurious objectivity" was as much

a result of reportorial bias as of dependence on official sources. His admiration of Senator George S. McGovern caused Wicker to accept, without question, the 1972 Democratic Presidential candidate's controversial plans for welfare reform and for redistribution of income. On the basis of explanations from McGovern aides, Wicker endorsed the plans in his column of June 4, 1972. A few weeks later, in another column, he apologized for his failure to double check the feasibility of the plan with outside economic experts, and accepted full responsibility for his "journalistic sin." Although as a columnist, Wicker was not bound by the customary mathematical balance accorded both sides of an issue in a news story, he had publicly stated his opposition to advocacy journalism.

Later, Wicker had, with increasing frequency, exchanged the role of impartial observer for that of participant. Addressing an antiwar teach-in at Harvard's Sanders Theatre, on February 22, 1971, he urged his listeners to "engage in civil disobedience" in protesting against the war in Southeast Asia. "We got one President out," he told his cheering audience, "and perhaps we can do it again." His moving extemporaneous speech, partly reprinted in the March 6, 1971, issue of the New Yorker, condemned the Administration's program of Vietnamization that "required the invasion of two countries and the bombing of three to evacuate one" as a policy with "very little future to it and very little profit." Inspired by his address, a group of Boston journalists wired the White House, protesting the war as a "crime against mankind."

Later that year, rioting inmates at the Attica State Correctional Facility, in Upstate New York, named Wicker, who had recently written a sympathetic column after the death of Black militant George Jackson, who was one of the "Soledad Brothers," in San Quentin (California), to the Citizens' Mediating Committee. That group of civilians was selected by the prisoners to inspect prison conditions and to witness negotiations between inmates and prison officials. As a result of his activism, Wicker had suffered a measure of professional ostracism. "There is a mainstream of journalism," he explained to David Wise, "and if you get out of the mainstream . . . off the reservation, you feel it. I feel more support today from the public, and less from among my peers in the Press Corps."

His New York Times obituary, on November 25, 2011, stated about his coverage of the Attica prison riots: "Wicker, in a column, described a night in the yard with the rebels: Flickering oil-drum fires, bull-necked convicts armed with bats and iron pipes, faceless men in hoods or football helmets huddled on mattresses behind wooden barricades. He wrote: 'This is another world — terrifying to the outsider, yet imposing in its strangeness — behind those massive walls, in this murmurous darkness, within the temporary but real power of desperate men.'"

According to the obituary, "After talks broke down, then Gov. Nelson Rockefeller "rejected appeals by the observers to go to Attica, and after a four-day standoff, troopers and guards stormed the prison. Ten hostages and 29 inmates were killed by the authorities' gunfire in what witnesses called a turkey shoot; three inmates were killed by other convicts, who also beat a guard to death. Afterward, many prisoners were beaten and abused in reprisals."

Later, Wicker wrote a book about the uprising, A Time to Die (1975). Most critics hailed it as his best book. Attica, a television movie starring Morgan Freeman as a jailhouse lawyer and George Grizzard as Wicker, was made by ABC in 1980. (See "Tom Wicker, Times Journalist, Dies at 85," http://www.nytimes.com/2011/11/26/us/tom-wicker-journalist-and-author-dies-at-85.html)

The obituary also described Wicker as a hard-hitting Southern liberal journalist. Besides his eyewitness account of the Kennedy assassination (Wicker was riding in the motorcade), which made him a "household name," his opposition to the Vietnam Conflict and the policies of both the Johnson Administration and the Nixon Administration, and, his columns on Watergate, he also wrote hardball commentary about "Jimmy Carter, for 'temporizing' in the face of soaring inflation and the Iranian Hostage Crisis; Ronald Reagan, for dozing through the Iran-Contra Scandal, and the elder George Bush, for letting the Persian Gulf War outweigh educational and health care needs at home."

Besides the books already mentioned, Wicker also wrote: On Press (1978); One of Us: Richard Nixon and the American Dream (1991); Tragic Failure: Racial Integration in America (1996); On the Record: An Insider's Guide to Journalism (2001); Dwight D. Eisenhower (2002); George Herbert Walker Bush (2004); and Shooting Star: The Brief Arc of Joe McCarthy (2006). His later novels were: Unto This Hour (1984), a Civil War story on the best-seller list for 15 weeks; Donovan's Wife (1992); and Easter Lilly (1998). Wicker also wrote short stories and freelance articles that appeared in The Atlantic, Esquire, Harper's, Life, The New Republic, The New York Review of Books, The New Yorker, Playboy, Rolling Stone and Vogue.

He was a member of the Society of Nieman Fellows and the Century Association, an exclusive club of authors, editors, historians, and social critics; he also was the recipient of the St. Augustine Award from Villanova University and an honorary doctor of law's from Dickinson College, in Carlisle, Pa. He received many awards and honorary degrees from a dozen universities.

## PERSONAL LIFE

Tom Wicker was a tall, hefty man, had a ruddy complexion and graying reddish hair. A colleague told Lee Belser, author of a Coronet magazine profile of the columnist (June 1966), "He reminds me of my mother's homemade apple pie, but, believe it or not, the spice is there, too—right underneath that crispy crust." Like many news reporters, Wicker was so devoted to his engrossing career that he had little time for recreational activities, although he occasionally enjoyed tennis, golf, and fishing. Wicker married the former Neva Jewett McLean, on August 20, 1949. They were divorced in 1973. They had two children. In 1974, he married Pamela Hill, a producer of television documentaries. Besides his wife, he is survived by the children of his first marriage, a daughter, Cameron Wicker, and a son, Thomas Grey Wicker, Jr.; two stepdaughters, Kayce Freed Jennings and Lisa Freed; and, a stepson, Christopher Hill.

## FURTHER READING

Esquire 71:95+ Ap '69 por; Newsday A p9 Jl 16 '73; Catledge, Turner. My Life and the Times (1971); Talese, Gay. The Kingdom and the Power (1969); Who's Who in America, 1972-73

# ELIE WIESEL

## Writer; Educator; Activist

**Born:** September 30, 1928; Sighet, Kingdom of Romania
**Died:** July 2, 2016; New York, New York
**Primary Field:** Human Rights
**Affiliation:** Religious Studies; Philosophy

### INTRODUCTION

*Once described as "the spiritual archivist of the holocaust," the writer, educator, and philosopher Elie Wiesel is, in the words of his biographer Robert McAfee Brown, "a messenger to all humanity" whose "themes touch us all." Wiesel achieved one of the greatest honors the United States can bestow upon a civilian when on April 19, 1985 President Ronald Reagan presented him with the Congressional Gold Medal of Achievement in recognition of his leadership as chairman of the United States Holocaust Memorial Council, his work in advancing human rights, and his contributions to literature. The White House ceremony was, however, marred by controversy over the president's announced plan to visit a military cemetery at Bitburg, West Germany, containing graves of members of the Nazi elite, the S.S., among other German war dead. In his comments to the president, Wiesel tried unsuccessfully to dissuade him from making the cemetery visit with the plea: "That place, Mr. President, is not your place. Your place is with the victims of the S.S." At the same time, Wiesel affirmed his support for a reconciliation with the German people and his opposition to the notion of collective guilt.*

*Wiesel, who is said to have been the first to use the term "holocaust" to describe the killing of some 6 million Jews by the Nazis, has also spoken out for the civil rights of such groups as South Africa's black population, the "boat people" of Indochina, the Miskito Indians of Nicaragua, Argentine political prisoners, and Soviet Jewry. He received the ultimate recognition for his commitment to human dignity when he was awarded the 1986 Nobel Peace Prize.*

### EARLY LIFE

Eliezer Wiesel was born to Shlorno and Sarah (Feig) Wiesel on September 30,1928 in the town of Sighet in northern Transylvania, near the Ukrainian border. In 1940 Romania, under German pressure, ceded the area

*Elie Wiesel.*

David Shankbone

to Hungary, but it was returned to Romania in 1945 by the Soviet Union. Wiesel's father, a shopkeeper, instilled in his only son humanist values and encouraged him to learn modern Hebrew and its literature. In the author's view, his father represented reason and his mother stood for faith, since it was she who urged him to study the Torah, the Talmud, and the mystical teachings of Hasidism and the Cabala. His religious studies were further inspired by his maternal grandfather, Dodye Feig, a Hasid and farmer, whose stories about the Hasidic masters charmed the young boy and still provide a source of inspiration to the writer.

Childhood, a recurrent theme in his work, ended for Elie Wiesel in the spring of 1944 when the Nazis ordered the deportation of Sighet's 15,000 Jews. He and his family were transported to Auschwitz concentration camp in Poland, where his mother and his youngest sister, Tzipora, died in the gas chambers. Separated from his two older sisters, Hilda and Batya, he did not learn of their survival until after the war. In 1945 Elie Wiesel and his father were sent to Buchenwald concentration camp in Germany. There, Shlomo Wiesel died from starvation and dysentery.

## LIFE'S WORK

After the liberation of Buchenwald on April 11, 1945 by the United States Third Army, Wiesel wanted to go to Palestine, the hope of many of the Jewish survivors, but was unable to obtain a certificate because of British immigration restrictions. Refusing repatriation to Eastern Europe, he was placed on a train bound for Belgium with some 400 other orphans. En route, the train was diverted to France at the intervention of General Charles de Gaulle. Settling first in Normandy under the care of a Jewish children's aid organization, the Oeuvres du Secours aux Enfants, he later moved to Paris, where from 1948 to 1951 he studied literature, philosophy, and psychology at the Sorbonne while earning his living as a choir director, teacher of Hebrew and the Bible, translator, and summer camp counselor. Meanwhile, under the tutelage of Gustav Wahl, a young French philosopher, Wiesel had mastered the French language by reading its classics, beginning with the works of Jean Racine.

While attending the Sorbonne, Wiesel became a journalist, and in 1948 he traveled to Israel to cover the newly founded state's struggle for survival for the French newspaper *L'Arche*. On a trip to India in 1952 as the Paris correspondent for the Tel Aviv daily *Yedioth Ahronot*, he acquired a working knowledge of English, and though he never completed his studies at the Sorbonne he began writing a long dissertation comparing Jewish, Christian, and Hindu asceticism that remained unfinished. In 1956, while reporting on the United Nations in New York City for the same Israeli newspaper, he was struck by a taxicab in Times Square. Confined to a wheelchair for almost a year, he was persuaded by an American immigration official to apply for United States citizenship after unsuccessful efforts to have his French travel document extended. "Since then I'm grateful to America," he told interviewer Harry James Cargas. "Even when I oppose some of the administration's policies I do it out of a sense of gratitude toward this country." In 1957 Wiesel became a writer of feature articles for the *New York Jewish Daily Forward*.

Wiesel's ambition to become a writer is rooted in the Hasidic storyteller tradition of his childhood, and when he was about twelve, he wrote a book of commentaries on the Bible. In the months following the liberation of Buchenwald, he became convinced that the purpose of his survival was "to give testimony, to bear witness." Nevertheless, he made a vow to remain silent for ten years. "I didn't want to use the wrong words," he explained to John S. Friedman, as quoted in *The Paris Review* (Spring 1984). "I was afraid that words might betray it. I waited."

The journalist's self-imposed silence came to an end in 1954 after he interviewed Frangois Mauriac, the French Roman Catholic writer and Nobel laureate, for *Yedioth Ahronot*. Acknowledging Christian responsibility for the holocaust, Mauriac urged Wiesel to relate his death camp experiences. Two years later, Wiesel published his first book in Yiddish, the language of his childhood, in Buenos Aires under the title *Un di Veit Hot Geshvign* (And the World Has Remained Silent). Unsuccessful in his efforts to have the 800 page manuscript published in France, Wiesel condensed his memoir to 127 pages and translated it into French. It appeared in 1958 as *La Nuit*, with a foreword by Mauriac, who had arranged for its publication by Editions de Minuit. The book is dedicated to the memory of Wiesel's parents and his sister Tzipora. Translated into English by Stella Rodway, it was published in the United States, after several rejections, under the title *Night* (Hill & Wang, 1960). "The holocaust was not something people wanted to know about in those days," Wiesel remembered in a *Time* magazine interview (March 18, 1985). "*The Diary of Anne Frank* was about as far as anyone wanted to venture into the dark."

With the publication of *Night*, Wiesel proceeded to turn from the world of the holocaust to that of the survivor. The result was a series of short semi- autobiographical novels in which the author explored such themes as suicide, madness, killing, political action, hate, friendship, indifference, and faith. *L'Aube* (Editions du Seuil, 1960), translated by Anne Borchardt as *Dawn* (Hill & Wang, 1961), is based on the author's unrealized desire to join the Israeli underground in 1946. Its protagonist is a young holocaust survivor who joins a terrorist group in Palestine and is faced with the moral crisis of having to kill for his country. *Le Jour* (1961), translated as *The Accident* (1962), concerns a survivor recovering from an automobile accident in New York City and his contemplation of suicide because of feelings of guilt for having survived Auschwitz. *La Ville de la Chance* (1964), translated by Stephen Becker as *The Town Beyond the Wall* (Atheneum, 1964) centers on indifference and focuses on a man whom the author remembers watching silently from a window as he and his family were led through the streets of Sighet during the deportation. The survivor in this story returns to his hometown in Hungary to confront just such' a "face in the window."

*Les Portes de la Foret* (1966), translated by Frances Frenaye as *The Gates of the Forest* (Holt, 1966), which examines faith and friendship and the relationship between man and God, is the story of a young Hungarian Jew who survives the German occupation because of the self-sacrifice of others. *Le Mendiant de Jerusalem* (1968), translated by Lily Edelman and the author as *A Beggar in Jerusalem* (Random House, 1970), is a fictionalized treatment of the Israeli-Arab Six-Day War of June 1967, as a turning point in Jewish history. In Wiesel's view, that conflict ended the cycle of despair and marked a renewal of hope and faith in the history of the Jewish people. The book became a leading best seller both in France and in the United States.

Wiesel's concept of the writer as witness made him increasingly sensitive to the conditions of Jews in the Soviet Union, and he is credited with being a pioneer of the movement in behalf of Soviet Jewry. Reports of revived anti-Semitism in the Soviet Union prompted him to make the first of several visits to that country during the High Holy Days in 1965. His account, *The Jews of Silence; A Personal Report on Soviet Jewry* {Holt, 1966), translated by Neal Kozodoy, first appeared in Hebrew as a series of articles for *Yedioth Ahrotiot* and was published in part in the *Saturday Evening Post* (November 19,1966). While refraining from condemning Communism, Wiesel described the fear, suspicion, and courage he encountered on the streets and in the synagogues of the five Soviet cities he visited and criticized what he saw as Jewish indifference in the West to the plight of Soviet Jewry. "What torments me most is not the Jews of silence I met in Russia, " he wrote, "but the silence of the Jews I live among today."

That indifference led Wiesel to write his first play, *Zalmen; ou La Folie de Dieu*, translated by Lily and Nathan Edelman as *Zalmen; or, The Madness of God* (Holt, 1968), on the theme of anti-Semitism in the Soviet Union, In it, an aged rabbi is persuaded by his *shammes*, or beadle, Zalmen, to speak out against the persecution in the presence of visiting foreigners, "If you, our brothers, forsake us," cries the rabbi, "we will be the last Jews in this land, the last witnesses."

An earlier Russia is the setting of Wiesel's three act play *Le Proces de Shamgorod tel qu'il se deroula le 25 Fevrier 1649* (1978), translated by his wife, Marion Wiesel, as *The Trial of God (As It Was Held on February 25; 1649 in Shamgorod)* and published by Random House in 1979, in which he goes beyond man's indifference to that of God. Survivors of a pogrom bring God to trial for forsaking the Jews by allowing the massacres to occur, As in the Book of Job, the question of God's role in the suffering of man is raised.

Returning to the theme of Soviet anti-Semitism, Wiesel wrote *Le Testament d'un Poete Juif Assassin* (1980), translated by Marion Wiesel as *The Testament* (Summit Books, 1981), perhaps the most panoramic of his novels. It tells the story of Paltiel Kossover, an idealistic Jew in the Soviet Union, who is put on trial during the anti-Semitic purges of the Stalin era, As narrated by the protagonist's son Grisha, the novel chronicles Paltiel's rise in Soviet society after he embraces Communism and his eventual downfall because of the religion that he had long since forsaken.

After a twenty-year absence, Wiesel returned to Sighet, Romania for a brief visit in the fall of 1964. He wrote about that experience in *Le Ghant des Morts* (1966), translated by Steven Donadio as *Legends of Our Time* (Holt, 1968), his first collection of short stories, autobiographical fragments, and reflective essays. The importance of Sighet in Wiesel's life and work can be seen in the narrative "The Last Return," in which he wrote, "I began to wander across the world, knowing all the while that to run away was useless: all roads lead home." The holocaust permanently destroyed his birthplace for him, the loss of which is the focus of his second collection of essays, stories, and dialogues, *Entre Deux Soleils*, translated by Lily Edelman and the author as *One Generation After* (Random House, 1970). In the essay "Journey's Beginning," he wrote: "Twenty-five years separate the witness from the object of his testimony. A little town I wanted to enter one last time and leave there all I possess: my memory." And in the story "The Watch," a bar mitzvah gift, unearthed twenty years later by a returning survivor, becomes the symbol of the irrevocable loss of parents and childhood and of the irreversibility of time.

*Un Juif*, Aujourd'hui, translated by Marion Wiesel as *A Jew Today* (Random House, 1978), WieseTs third collection of essays, stories, and dialogues, focuses on a variety of subjects, from a Jewish perspective. His sensitivity to suffering encompasses concern for the people of South Africa, Vietnam, Biafra, and Bangladesh. As in his earlier collections, Wiesel retains an abiding interest in Soviet Jewry. Once again he affirms his belief that the Jew today must bear witness to all suffering, and that to remain silent and indifferent is the greatest sin of all. As he told the interviewer for *Time* (March 18,1985): "If we ignore the suffering, our true literary prophecy will not be *The Trial or The Stranger* but Hitler's *Mein Kampf.* This is what I fight against."

The need to remember and to testify has been the driving force behind Wiesel's literary career, and his writings on the holocaust have been a major factor in increasing public awareness of the near total destruction of European Jewry. Yet Wiesel remains troubled by the "trivialization" in film and literature of the holocaust experience, an event he believes to be unique in human history. Because to him, silence broken by ill-advised words is worse than silence itself, he imposed that vow of silence upon himself at the end of World War II. In his novel *Le Serment* de Kolvillag, translated by Marion Wiesel as *The Oath* (Random House, 1973), Wiesel describes events surrounding a pogrom in Central Europe. Convinced that the telling of their experience would not prevent further atrocities, the survivors decide to take an oath of silence in order not to profane their suffering. That vow is only broken when one of them, in an effort to save a young man from suicide, divulges the secret of the pogrom. By doing so, he convinces the youth that his suicide would be just another in a series of murders.

In the novel *Le Cinquieme Fils* (Editions Bernard Grasset, 1983), translated by Marion Wiesel as *The Fifth Son* (Summit Books, 1985), Wiesel extended his concern for the survivor to include the next generation and its psychological traumas over parental suffering. Its protagonist, the son of holocaust survivors, is desperately searching for the story of his parents' past.

Wiesel's exploration of his past through the study of Hasidic personalities inspired him to publish the volumes *Celebration hassidique; Portraits et legendes,* translated by Marion Wiesel as *Souls on Fire; Portraits and Legends of Hasidic Masters* (Random House, 1972); *Four Hasidic Masters and Their Struggle Against Melancholy* (Univ. of Notre Dame Press, 1978); and *Somewhere a Master* (Summit Books, 1982). For those books he culled the vast lore of folktales relating to the Hasidic masters, beginning with Rabbi Israel Baal Shem-Tov, the enigmatic eighteenth-century founder of Hasidism. More than merely sounding a retreat into elegiac childhood memories, they recreate the living presence of those Hasidic masters as they wrestle with the ultimate questions of God, suffering, and evil.

In *Celebration Biblique; Portraits et Legendes* (1975), translated by Marion Wiesel as *Messengers of God; Biblical Portraits and Legends* (Random House, 1976); *Images from the Bible* (Overlook Press, 1980); and *Five Biblical Portraits* (Univ. of Notre Dame Press, 1981), Wiesel's journey into his past led him to study the relevance of biblical figures for contemporary man. Here, such archetypal personalities as Abraham and Isaac are seen as the first Jewish survivors forced to live through their own personal holocausts. Wiesel's works also include the cantata *Ani Maamin* (Random House, 1973), a "poetic retelling of a Talmudic tale," set to music by Darius Milhaud; and his reconstruction of the medieval Jewish legend *The Golem* (Summit Books, 1983). A three-volume collection of his essays, lectures, interviews, and commentaries was published in 1985 by the Holocaust Library under the title *Against Silence: The Voice and Vision of Elie Wiesel*

Although primarily centered on Jewish themes, Wiesel's work has elicited strong responses from Jewish and non-Jewish observers alike, perhaps because his probing questions are directed not only at the survivor but at the executioner as well. Asserting the primacy of "mystery," Wiesel wrote in *One Generation After*, "I attach more importance to questions than to answers. For only the questions can be shared." The persistence of moral issues, the discursive prose, and the abundant use of paradox in his works have been viewed by critics as a clear indication of the real tradition within which he writes: the Bible, the Midrash, the Haggadah, and Hasidic tales, although some influence of contemporary existentialist philosophy and of the modern European novel can also be observed in his work.

The significance that critics have attached to Wiesel's work can be seen in the scores of literary awards that he has received over the years. Among them are the Prix Rivarol (1963), the Prix Medicis (1968), the Eleanor Roosevelt Award (1972), the Martin Luther King Medallion (1973), the Frank and Ethel Cohen Award (1973), the Jewish Book Council Literary Award (1965, 1973), the Prix Livre-Inter (1980), the Prix des Bibliothequaires (1981), and the Grand Prix de la Litterature de la ville de Paris (1983).

## PERSONAL LIFE

For several years, Wiesel had been considered a leading candidate for the Nobel Peace Prize, and in 1985 some seventy members of the West German Bundestag recommended him for the honor. In awarding him the prize, on October 14, 1986, the Norwegian Nobel Committee cited him as "one of the most important spiritual leaders and guides" in an age characterized by "violence, repression, and racism," and that his message was "one of peace, atonement, and dignity." On receiving the award, Wiesel said that it would permit him to "speak louder" and "reach more people" for the causes that have driven him throughout his adult life. "I dedicate [the prize] to my fellow survivors and their children," Wiesel told a news conference. "The honor is not mine alone." Shortly afterward, he visited the Soviet Union, where he met with old friends and appealed to the authorities in behalf of Jews wising to emigrate.

Elie Wiesel was married on the eve of Passover, 1969 to Marion Erster Rose, who has a daughter, Jennifer Rose, from her previous marriage. With their teenaged son, Shlomo Elisha, they made their home in New York City. Wiesel, a United States citizen since 1963, was distinguished professor of Judaic studies at the City University of New York from 1972 to 1976. He commuted regularly to Boston, where he served from 1976 as Andrew Mellon Professor in the Humanities at Boston University. He enjoyed playing chess, reading, studying the Talmud, listening to classical music, and visiting the Hasidic community in Brooklyn's Crown Heights. He led an austere life, abstained from alcohol, and appeared indifferent to most foods, although he retains a childhood love for chocolate. For years he gave a popular series of lectures on biblical studies at the 92d Street YM & YWHA in New York City. In his later years he placed a greater emphasis on his role as an educator, writing remained an essential element in Wiesel's life. Among his greatest concerns in his last years was the growing threat of nuclear conflict. Wiesel died in Manhattan, New York on July 2, 2016 at the age of 87.

## FURTHER READING

*Elie Wiesel: Messenger to All Humanity (1983); fames, In Conversation With Elie Wiesel (1976); Contemporary Authors new rev vol 8 (1983); Fine, Ellen S. Legacy of Night; the Literary Universe of Elie Wiesel (1982); Stern, Ellen Norman. Elie Wiesel: Witness for Life*

# ROGER WILKINS

## Journalist; Educator; Lawyer

**Born:** March, 25, 1932; Kansas City, Missouri
**Primary Field:** Civil Rights; Academia
**Affiliation:** George Mason University

### INTRODUCTION

*"In a sense," the journalist, educator, lawyer, and former government official Roger Wilkins has written, "I have been an explorer, and I sailed as far out into the white world as a black man of my generation could sail." After practicing law in the late 1950s and early 1960s, Wilkins began his rise to prominence as a government figure in the administration of President Lyndon B. Johnson, eventually becoming an assistant attorney general charged with finding ways to calm the unrest and rioting that shook American inner cities in the 1960s. He later served as an officer of the Ford Foundation before making the transition, in 1972, to journalism, as a member of the editorial staff at the Washington Post. His editorials on the Watergate scandal were cited by the board that awarded the newspaper a Pulitzer Prize in 1973.*

*Wilkins was subsequently an editorial writer and columnist for the* New York Times *and the* Washington Star*, and he has contributed essays, articles, and book reviews to numerous other publications. He is also the author of* A Man's Life: An Autobiography *(1982), a highly personal account of the difficulties he has faced as a successful African-American in a society marred by racism, and the coeditor of* Quiet Riots: Race and Poverty in the United States *(1988). Commenting on the findings published in the latter work, Wilkins told an interviewer, "We've done the easy part, we have made opportunity for the blacks for whom it was easy to provide opportunities. We haven't come close to dealing with the problems of the most burdened legatees of our racist past, the poor and the unemployed." From 1987 to his retirement in 2007, Wilkins was the Clarence J. Robinson Professor of History and American Culture at George Mason University, in Fairfax, Virginia.*

### EARLY LIFE

Roger Wood Wilkins was born on March 25, 1932 in Kansas City, Missouri, the only child of Earl William Wilkins, an advertising manager at the Kansas City Call, a black weekly newspaper, and Helen Natalie (Jackson)

Wilkins, a national board member of the YWCA. His uncle Roy Wilkins was an assistant executive secretary of the NAACP; he went on to become the organization's executive secretary. The Wilkins family, including Roger Wilkins's grandmother, lived in a stucco house in a black section of *Kansas City* called Roundtop. From a very young age, Roger Wilkins was bused every day past several all-white schools to an older, segregated school in another black section of the city. To some extent, as Wilkins suggested in *A Man's Life,* his family internalized the racial stereotypes that lay at the root of the segregation they experienced. Neither African nor African-American history was discussed in the house, and Wilkins has recalled his grandmother's using a hairbrush "to try to insure that [he] didn't have [nappy] hair."

Following Earl Wilkins's death from tuberculosis in 1941, the family moved to the Sugar Hill section of Harlem, in New York City, where they lived in an apartment near Roy Wilkins, his wife, Minnie, and other relatives. "As life in New York settled into a routine," Wilkins wrote in his autobiography, "my life came to be dominated by four women: my mother, her sisters, and her mother. Nobody else had any children, so everybody concentrated on me." His family lived in Harlem until 1943, when Helen Wilkins's work with the YWCA took her to Grand Rapids, Michigan, where she met and married a doctor. Shortly thereafter, Roger traveled by train to Grand Rapids to join his mother and stepfather. Years later Wilkins wrote about that train journey, "[The] train also took me beyond the last point in my life when I would feel totally at peace with my blackness."

In Grand Rapids the Wilkins family moved into what had been an all-white neighborhood. Despite some early exposure to blatant racism, such as his first white friend's being forbidden by his father to associate with the black youngster, Wilkins found acceptance among his white peers; that acceptance, however, came at an emotional cost. Because he felt his blackness set him apart from his new friends, he was painfully conscious of anything that might draw attention to it. "I carried my race around with me like an open basket of rotten eggs. I knew I could drop one at any moment, and it would explode with a stench over everything," he wrote in his autobiography. "It seemed to me that my tenuous purchase in this larger white world depended on the maintenance between me and my friends of our unspoken bargain to ignore my difference, my shame, and their embarrassment. If none of us had to deal with it, I thought, we

could all handle it. My white friends behaved as if they perceived the bargain exactly as I did."

If Wilkins was inwardly uncomfortable around whites, then he was outwardly ill at ease in the presence of the blacks he met in Grand Rapids. "Black street language had evolved since my Harlem days, and I had not kept pace," he explained in *A Man's Life.* "Customs, attitudes, and the other common social currencies of everyday black life had evolved away from me. I didn't know how to talk, to banter, to move my body." He recalled trying, "probably at [his] mother's urging," to strike up an acquaintance at a black church function. "Because the language [of the church members] was so foreign to me, I understood little of what was being said, but I did know that the word used for a white was paddy. Then a boy, whom my mother particularly wanted me to be friends with, inclined his head slightly toward me and said, to whoops of laughter, 'technicolor *paddy.*' My feet felt rooted in stone, and my head was aflame. I never forgot that phrase."

Following his graduation from Creston High School, where he had been elected student council president, in 1949, Wilkins enrolled at the University of Michigan, in Ann Arbor. He became president of his graduating class and received his A.B. degree in 1953. After earning his law degree three years later from the same institution, he practiced international law in the New York City legal firm of Delson, Levin & Gordon. During the early years of his employment with that firm, he took a leave of absence for nine months to serve as a welfare caseworker in Cleveland, Ohio.

## LIFE'S WORK

In 1962 Fowler Hamilton, the administrator of the Agency for International Development, in Washington, D.C., recruited Wilkins as a special assistant. Two years later, LeRoy Collins, the director of the Community Relations Service (CRS), which had been established under the guidelines of the Civil Rights Act of 1964 to combat racial discrimination at the local level, tapped Wilkins to run the branch of that organization designed to defuse and prevent urban riots. In the summer of 1965, a year plagued by rioting, looting, and arson in several urban areas, most notably the largely black Watts section of Los Angeles, Wilkins headed a study group that focused on the problems of nine cities. Later in the year, President Johnson promoted Wilkins, who was not yet thirty-four, to the post of director of the Community Relations Service. At about the same time,

Johnson made the decision to move the CRS from the Commerce Department to the Justice Department, with the result that Wilkins received the rank of assistant United States attorney general. As the *New York Times* (January 10, 1966) reported, in his new capacity Wilkins soon "emerged as the [Johnson] administration's chief troubleshooter on racial problems" in American inner cities. Summarizing Wilkins's approach to the problem, the *Times* correspondent said that his "idea of how to prevent riots [was] not to put a damper on an explosive situation but to correct the causes of the conflict."

Despite the efforts of Wilkins and others, in the mid and late 1960s violence continued to erupt in various cities across the country. In an interview broadcast worldwide by the Voice of America, Wilkins described the unrest as merely a symptom of a larger problem, "The real threat to American life," he said, as quoted in a *New York Times* (June 25, 1967) synopsis of the program, "is our inattention to the really depressed and anguished conditions of the minority-group people who live in the ghettos of this country, whether they are Puerto Rican or Chinese or Mexican-Americans. Those are the conditions that cause the riots."

When President Johnson's successor, Richard Nixon, took office in early 1969, Wilkins left government service to join the Ford Foundation, in New York City. As the director of one of the organization's domestic divisions, Wilkings oversaw the funding of programs for job training, drug rehabilitation, education for the poor, and other projects. During his three years at the foundation, he became increasingly unhappy and disillusioned. He has written that the black-power movement of the late 1960s, which emphasized the importance of African-Americans' history and achievements and their need to purge themselves of notions of white people's innate superiority, had a profound effect on him. As he noted in his biography, he had spent much of his personal as well as his professional life learning "how white people operated in the world" and seeking "to emulate them." Even the Ford Foundation, as he came to view it, was for him "another way station in the white establishment," one run entirely by "middle-aged white males," where he found himself powerless to fund many of the projects he considered worthy. Before resigning from his post, Wilkins attended a meeting of the Ford Foundation's trustees, at which he read aloud a memorandum deploring the lack of "young, nonwhite, female" input at the organization.

In the period immediately following his resignation from the Ford Foundation, Wilkins found himself at a crossroads in his life. Having left behind the trappings and prestige associated with his high profile jobs (while working at the Ford Foundation, he had socialized with such luminaries as the writer Norman Mailer and the conductor and composer Leonard Bernstein), he faced the challenge of "getting to something more basic, myself confronting myself, alone, without props," as he put it. His groping for his identity involved searching for an occupation he would find spiritually nourishing; it also meant dealing with his guilt over his estrangement from his two children and his wife, Eve (Tyler) Wilkins, whom he had met at the University of Michigan and married in 1956. He became so depressed that he even considered suicide.

Wilkins's outlook brightened when, in 1972, he took a job as an editorial writer on the staff of the *Washington Post*. In *A Man's Life*, Wilkins recalled, "I was excited. I was going into the kind of work my father had done. I would sit at a machine and work there. At the end of a day something would exist that I had made." His new career in journalism, together with his exposure to the black-power movement, afforded him the opportunity to "gradually [abandon] the desperate search for white approval" and take on "a role as an advocate for all blacks," as Joel Dreyfuss phrased it in the *New York Times Book Review* (June 20, 1982).

After two years with the *Post*, Wilkins left that newspaper to join the staff of the *New York Times*, as a member of the editorial board. He became a regular *Times* columnist in 1977. At the Times, his being an "advocate for blacks" went beyond his professional duties. During his years there, a lawsuit was brought under Title VII of the Civil Rights Act of 1964 against the newspaper on behalf of its minority employees. "After some hesitation," Wilkins reported in his autobiography, "I got into it with fervor. Apart from the encouragement that I gave to others, my most significant participation in the case was the day-long pretrial testimony I gave to the *Times* lawyers about what I saw as the paper's deficiencies in its coverage of minority issues and its handling of black talent." Realizing that his future at the *New York Times* would be, to use his word, "difficult" after his testimony, he left the newspaper in 1979.

Returning to Washington, Wilkins served as associate editor of the now-defunct *Washington Star* from 1980 to 1981. In 1982 he became a senior fellow at the Institute for Policy Studies, a Washington based nonprofit organization that examines various aspects of international affairs and domestic public policy. In the same year, he published *A Man's Life: An Autobiography*, in which he reflected on his status as a black man working in white-dominated institutions and on his Personal Life, including his depression and his bout with alcohol dependency. "I was a man living in a never-never land somewhere far beyond the constraints my grandparents had known but far short of true freedom," he wrote. "I knew no black people-young or old, rich or poor, who didn't feel injured by the experience of being black in America. Though some went mad, most coped with the special problems that race presented to them. I had coped by translating my anguish into words, by trying to change the minds and hearts of people."

*A Man's Life* received generally good notices. The celebrated novelist and essayist James Baldwin wrote in the *Washington Post Book World*, "Wilkins has written a most beautiful book, has delivered an impeccable testimony out of that implacable private place where a man either lives or dies." Evaluating the book in the *New York Times Book Review* (June 20,1982), Joel Dreyfuss praised Wilkins's "devastating thumbnail sketches" of a number of prominent, ostensibly liberal whites and noted that the "tales of slights and intolerance" in the autobiography represent "more than personal affronts to Roger Wilkins. They are evidence that the race issue has been shunted aside rather than resolved." Although Dreyfuss objected to Wilkins's "kiss and tell" accounts of his romantic involvements and drinking binges and his "facile" accounts of some complex issues, he concluded, "This is an important, groundbreaking work." Among those who found fault with the book was a writer for the *National Review* (August 20, 1982), who complained that Wilkins "confuse[d] his own status problems with the ills that afflict poor blacks." Wilkins answered that charge and others in an October 17, 1982 essay in the *Washington Post*. "After a while," he wrote, "I became philosophical about the blows I was taking from some white writers because I understood they were killing the messenger." He was especially critical of those reviewers who "seemed to think that [he] couldn't be middle class and care for the plight of black poor at the same time."

In 1988 Wilkins co-chaired, along with former senator Fred R. Harris, a national conference on urban affairs, whose main focus was the state of American race relations twenty years after the 1968 Kerner commission report had declared the nation to be on the way to becoming two separate and unequal societies, one black, one white. The Kerner commission, the informal name given to the National Advisory Commission on Civil Disorders, was established by President Johnson in 1967, in the wake of the urban riots of the mid-1960s, to look into race relations and the possible causes of violence in inner-city neighborhoods. Wilkins and Harris subsequently collected the papers presented at the follow-up conference in the book *Quiet Riots: Race and Poverty in the United States* (1988). Identifying the contemporary "riots" as "unemployment, poverty, social disorganization, segregation, family disintegration, housing and school deterioration, and crime," the editors observed, "These 'quiet riots' are not as alarming as the violent riots of twenty years ago, or as noticeable to outsiders. But they are even more destructive of human life." In a review for the *Washington Post* (November 27, 1988), Jonathan Yardley described *Quiet Riots* as "a slender but pointed and depressing volume that confirms nothing so much as the inability of this country's political, economic, and social institutions to respond to the urgent messages that were sent out of the ghettos in the uprisings of the 1960s."

In addition to his work for the Institute for Policy Studies and his teaching duties at George Mason University, where was a faculty member from 1987-2007, Wilkins continued to contribute regularly to such publications as *Mother Jones*, the *Progressive*, the *Nation*, the *New York Times*, and the *Washington Post*, commenting on a variety of issues but making race relations and poverty in America his most frequent topics. He has occasionally come under attack for "harping" on racism. Wilkins responded to such criticism in a December 1989 column in *Mother Jones*, in which he contended that whites did not want to face the fact that America continued to be a racist society. "I don't write and talk about racism to make whites feel guilty," he said, "but because I believe that to solve a problem, we must first admit it exists."

One race-related issue to which Wilkins has frequently turned his attention is affirmative action. In a piece published in *Mother Jones* (July/August 1990), he addressed blacks who worry that being the beneficiaries of preferential treatment causes others to doubt their abilities: "White folks were looking at black folks funny long before affirmative action was invented." He also rejected the notion that the controversial method of remedying racial injustice was no longer necessary. "Anyone who thinks there are no more battles to be fought, even on the highest battlements of the ivoriest of the ivory towers," he wrote, "simply doesn't understand America."

Wilkins has also attacked race-baiting, or the tendency of some politicians to exploit whites' fear of blacks and other minorities for the purpose of getting votes. In particular he found George Bush Sr. and his advisers to have been guilty of that practice during the 1988 presidential campaign. "Race-baiting," as Wilkins explained in another essay in *Mother Jones* (November 1988), is ultimately harmful to whites and minorities alike: "[Racial politics] obscures the nation's real needs, its gut, core value issues. All over the country our urban life is deteriorating. Business executives are deeply worried about the quality of our work force. Human beings are falling out of the economy. Our debt-ridden national economy is being pounded by fierce international competition. The scapegoats [of racial politics] get hurt, of course, but while the supposed beneficiaries are watching, they too usually get taken."

Among Wilkins's numerous awards and honors is the Roger Baldwin Civil Liberties Award, which was given to him in 1987 by the New York Civil Liberties Union. He has also received honorary degrees from institutions including the University of Michigan, Georgetown University Law School, Central Michigan University, Wilberforce University, and the Union of Experimenting Universities. In 1980 he became one of the first two blacks (with the columnist William Raspberry) to sit on the Pulitzer Prize board; eight years later he served as its chairman. In the 1980s Wilkins was a radio commentator for CBS, in New York City, and for the Mutual Broadcasting network, in Alexandria, Virginia, and since 1990 he has served in that capacity for National Public Radio. In addition, he has written and narrated two PBS Frontline documentaries: *Keeping the Faith* (1987), about the changing role of black churches, and *Throwaway People* (1990), which focused on poor black men. From 1984 to 1986 Wilkins was a member of the steering committee of the Free South Africa Movement, and in 1990, after the African National Congress leader and political prisoner Nelson Mandela was released from prison in South Africa, Wilkins was the coordinator of Mandela's visit to the United States. He served as a trustee of the University of the District of Columbia for five years beginning in 1989, and he is chairman of the board of trustees of the African-American Institute, the largest organization currently performing human-resources development in Africa.

## PERSONAL LIFE

Roger Wilkins has been described as "lean and intense" and as "soft-voiced." His marriage to Eve Wilkins ended in divorce in 1976; his children from that union are Amy Tyler and David Earl. A second marriage, to Mary Myers, ended in divorce in 1978. Wilkins lives in Washington, D.C., with his third wife, Patricia A. King, a law professor, whom he married on February 21, 1981. The couple have a daughter, Elizabeth. Wilkins and his family live "on a street in Washington, D.C., where the Speaker of the House, senators, congressmen, and a couple of Supreme Court justices also live," he wrote in *Mother Jones* (November/December 1992). "A few blocks away are two large public-housing projects. The Safeway where we all shop may be the most racially and economically integrated supermarket in America. Public servants with big titles shop alongside people who buy their staples with food stamps." He lives where he does, he explained, in part because he wanted his daughter Elizabeth "to grow up in a truly integrated neighborhood."

## FURTHER READING

*A Man's Life: An Autobiography; Quiet Riots: Race and Poverty in the United States; Jefferson's Pillow: The Founding Fathers and the Dilemma of Black Patriotism*

# JODY WILLIAMS

## Peace Activist

**Born:** October 9, 1950;
**Primary Field:** Human Rights
**Affiliation:** Peace and Conflict Studies

## INTRODUCTION

*For countries at war, minefields are a relatively inexpensive way of defending territory. The cheapest land mines cost as little as $3, and unlike soldiers, they need neither lodging nor sustenance. Ever ready to discharge, they are ever vigilant, unfeeling, unthinking sentries, so unthinking, in fact, that they often kill and maim long after hostilities have ended. In the North African desert, people still occasionally find active mines that were planted during World War II. In areas where more recent conflicts have been waged, Laos, Cambodia, Afghanistan, Iraq, Bosnia and Herzegovina, Somalia, Nicaragua, to name a few, land mines represent an even greater threat. Many a farmer plowing a former battlefield has unwittingly triggered a forgotten mine. The result, half the time, is shredded limbs; other times, the result is death.*

*The United Nations has estimated that about 100 million land mines are currently deployed across the globe, one for every 60 people, and more are laid each day. There are two types of land mines. One of them, the antitank land mine, normally explodes only when exposed to the pressure of very heavy objects, such as tanks or automobiles. As little as six pounds of pressure can set off the second type, the antipersonnel mine. Land mines kill or maim approximately 26,000 people a year, and most of these victims are not soldiers at war but civilians in peacetime. Indeed, some observers claim that land mines have inflicted more damage than certain weapons associated with mass destruction. "People were rightly outraged when Saddam Hussein used chemical weapons against the Kurds," Senator Patrick J. Leahy of Vermont told the* Washington Post *(August 8, 1993). "But how many people realize that all the deaths from chemical, biological and even nuclear weapons are only a fraction of the number who have been killed or maimed by land mines?"*

*Recently, a global drive was launched to ban the use of land mines. Perhaps the best known leader of this movement is Jody Williams. As the coordinator, since 1991, of the International Campaign to Ban Landmines*

*(ICBL), and co-author, with Shawn Roberts, of the book* After the Guns Fall Silent: The Enduring Legacy of Landmines *(1995), she has led a vigorous effort to clear the world of this scourge, and by most accounts, she and her fellow activists have made great strides in their mission. In October 1997, Williams and the ICBL were awarded the Nobel Peace Prize for instigating talks that led representatives of some 90 countries to draft a treaty aimed at stopping the production, deployment, stockpiling, and sale of antipersonnel land mines. That December, more than 120 countries signed the treaty.*

*The treaty is historic not only in its intent but also because never before has a group of small, nongovernmental organizations successfully pressured the worldwide community to enact such a global ban so quickly. Indeed, Williams and her fellow activists have been surprised at their own success. In part coordinated via the Internet, the ICBL may prove to be an excellent model for social movements in the information age. At the Nobel Peace Prize acceptance ceremony in Oslo, the Norwegian Nobel Committee stated, "As a model for similar process in the future, it could prove of decisive importance to the international effort for disarmament and peace."*

## LIFE'S WORK

Jody Williams became involved with the anti-landmine coalition through her work as an international activist. For 11 years after her graduation from the Johns Hopkins School of Advanced International Studies, in Baltimore, Maryland, she worked on issues related to the United States' policy toward Latin America. She coordinated the Nicaragua-Honduras Education Project, which led fact-finding delegations in Central America, and later, she became the associate director of Medical Aid to El Salvador, an organization based in Los Angeles. During her many trips to Central America, Williams witnessed firsthand the devastating effects of land mines on civilian populations.

On a Sunday afternoon in November 1991, Bobby Muller, the president of the Vietnam Veterans of America Foundation, called a meeting of a small group of activists, including Williams, to discuss the problem of land mines. The foundation subsequently hired Williams to coordinate a campaign against the use of land mines. "For sure, none of us thought we would ever ban land mines," she recalled to Raymond Bonner of the *New York Times* (September 20, 1997).

In addition to the Vietnam Veterans of America Foundation, the ICBL initially included such groups as Human Rights Watch, which is based in New York City; Physicians for Human Rights (Boston); Medico International (Germany); Handicap International (France); and the Mines Advisory Group (England). One of their earliest supporters was Lloyd Axworthy, the foreign minister of Canada, and he proved to be influential in lobbying other nations to ban land mines. The first U.S. politician to join the ICBL's cause was Senator Leahy, who, in 1992, persuaded the U.S. Congress to pass a bill prohibiting the United States from exporting land mines for one year. George Bush, who was then the president, signed the bill into law. A year later, Leahy successfully engineered a three-year extension of the moratorium. Another influential voice was the International Committee of the Red Cross. "It was the first time that the Red Cross, [traditionally] fearful of offending governments lest it lose its neutrality and effectiveness in the field, had engaged in vigorous advocacy," Raymond Bonner wrote in the *New York Times*.

By 1997, over a thousand organizations from 60 countries had aligned themselves with the coalition. Celebrities, among them Princess Diana of Great Britain, also publicly supported the cause. Williams kept in touch with her fellow activists largely through email, thereby demonstrating the usefulness of the internet for social activism. "From day one, we recognized that instant communication was critical," she told the *Washington Post* (October 11, 1997). "It made people feel they were part of it."

In September 1997, the movement to ban land mines took a giant leap forward. That month, approximately 90 countries drafted a treaty to ban antipersonnel land mines completely, and on December 3, 1997, in Ottawa, Canada, more than 120 countries signed the treaty. Signatories to the treaty, which will go into effect after 40 countries have ratified it, must destroy stockpiles of land mines within four years of ratification and remove all deployed land mines within 10 years of ratification. The cost of finding, deactivating, and discarding a single deployed land mine has been estimated at between $300 and $1,000. If, as the United Nations has estimated, 100 million land mines remain deployed, getting rid of every one of them would cost at least $30 billion.

The ICBL considers the treaty a stunning achievement but by no means the complete answer to the problem of land mines. That is because some of the world's biggest producers of land mines, Russia, China, and the United States, were conspicuously absent from the signing in Ottawa. President Bill Clinton opted against having the United States sign the treaty because he believes that so-called smart mines, which are designed to self-destruct after a predetermined period of time, pose no threat to civilians after a war is concluded. Moreover, in his opinion, the land-mine ban should not include South Korea, whose border with North Korea is one of the most heavily militarized regions on the planet. While experts generally agree that South Korean and U.S. forces would be able to defeat a North Korean invasion of South Korea, they believe that the allied troops would incur greater casualties if the nearly one million land mines that the U.S. has deployed along the border were not in place.

Williams has dismissed such arguments and has accused Clinton of being against "the tide of history." "France, United Kingdom, Germany have decided that they do not need this weapon and they can destroy it now. Why does the one remaining superpower with the most advanced war weapons in the world still need to rely on the land mine?" she asked in her interview with Phil Ponce for the *Online Newshour* (October 10, 1997). Williams's position has been endorsed by 14 retired American generals (including General H. Norman Schwarzkopf, the leader of the coalition forces against Iraq in the 1991 Persian Gulf War), who in 1996 signed a statement expressing their opposition to the continued use of land mines.

Perhaps influenced by the efforts of the ICBL, former President Clinton announced his own timetable for the elimination of land mines. In May 1996, he announced that the U.S. would stop using "dumb" mines (mines that remain live for years, or even decades). Recently, he stated that by 2003, the U.S. would stop using antipersonnel mines except in South Korea. He has also directed the Pentagon to investigate alternatives to land mines so that by 2006, they can be eliminated in South Korea as well.

When Phil Ponce asked Jody Williams what receiving the Nobel Peace Prize meant to her, she responded, "Very few people are allowed the luxury to decide that they want to do something out of the mainstream. Most people tend to pretty much go to college and get a job and buy a house and pay the mortgage. For whatever reason, I've had the luxury of deciding to do things a little bit differently. And I consider much of my life to be a privilege, and this is sort of the most amazing part."

## PERSONAL LIFE

The second of five children, Williams was born on October 9, 1950, and raised in Brattleboro, Vermont. Her father was a Vermont county judge, and her mother oversaw housing projects. Her brother Stephen is deaf, and it was from defending him from the taunts of other children that she learned to speak out on behalf of others. "Anybody who didn't know how to speak for themselves, I thought, 'I know how. I'll speak for you,'" she told *People* (October 27, 1997). Later, at the signing of the anti-landmine treaty, she made the point that many voices speaking out together can successfully challenge not only schoolyard bullies but also the governments of the world's most powerful nations. "Together we are a superpower," she said. "It's a new definition of superpower. It is not one, it's everybody." Williams lives in a farmhouse in Putney, Vermont.

## FURTHER READING

*After the Guns Fall Silent: The Enduring Legacy of Landmines; Banning Landmines: Disarmament, Citizen Diplomacy and Human Security; My Name Is Jody Williams: A Vermont Girl's Winding Path to the Nobel Peace Prize*

---

# BETTY (SMYTH) WILLIAMS

## Irish Peace Activist; Speaker

**Born:** May 22, 1943; Belfast, Northern Ireland
**Primary Field:** Peace & Justice Movement

## INTRODUCTION

*At the Nobel Prize ceremonies in Oslo, Norway, in December 1977, almost 40 years ago, an impassioned Betty Williams recalled in her address the chain of events that that began, in mid-August 1976, which led to her selection as co-winner with Mairead Corrigan Maguire (she has since married) of the 1976 Nobel Peace Prize: "We are for life and creation and we are against war and destruction, and in our rage in that terrible week, we screamed that the violence had to stop." Shock over the accidental killing of three children in the clash between Provisional IRA and British forces in Northern Ireland drove the two young Irish women, Ms. Williams and Ms. Corrigan, to join Ciaran McKeown, a journalist, in founding the Peace People, or Community of Peace People, a movement that captured world attention.*

*The Peace People leaders did not expect to solve Northern Ireland's complex political problems, but, wanted to end the fighting and killing, which had been severe since 1969. After staging a series of peace marches and demonstrations in Northern Irish and English cities, in 1976, they focused their efforts on a variety of social projects. Betty Williams had said that perhaps 30 years of change may be required to achieve what she wanted for Northern Ireland: A unification of Catholics and Protestants in setting up their own government. On April 15, 1978, Ms. Williams, Ms. Corrigan, and McKeown announced that in order to promote democracy within the Community of Peace People, they were resigning as leaders to give others a chance to run the government, with which they would continue to work.*

*According to Norwegian Noble Institute, "The Northern Irish peace movement disintegrated in the course of 1978. This was due both to internal disagreements and to the spreading of malicious rumors by Catholic and Protestant extremists"*

*Since then, the Community of Peace People dissolved, and Ms. Williams left the organization in the early 80s. Now in her 70s, she advocates for global peace.*

## EARLY LIFE

Betty Smyth Williams was born on May 22, 1943, in Andersonstown, a Catholic section of Belfast, Northern Ireland, the first child of a Catholic mother and a Protestant father, in the type of mixed marriage often regarded as akin to treason in Northern Ireland, where Protestants and Roman Catholics have been in conflict for centuries. When Betty was 13 her mother, who had been a waitress, was paralyzed by a stroke, and Betty assumed much of the responsibility for caring for her sister, Margaret, five years younger, and for running the home. Their father worked in a butcher shop. He tried to raise his daughters to be free of prejudice in a country and city where prejudice was a way of life. Ms. Williams recalls that her father once scolded her because she identified a little girl she had met as being a Protestant. Another force against bigotry in her Early Life was her love for her maternal grandfather, a Polish Jew who had lost much of his family in Europe, during World War II, but did not show bitterness.

## LIFE'S WORK

One of the goals that Betty Williams had for Northern Ireland was the mingling of Catholic and Protestant children in educational and social activities. When she was growing up, few persons ever discussed the possibility of integration of schools in Belfast. The Catholic schools that she attended were St. Teresa's Primary School and St. Dominic's Grammar School. She then took secretarial courses at Orange Academy. On June 14, 1961, she married Ralph Edward Williams, an engineer in the merchant marine, an Englishman, and a Protestant. She traveled for a while with her first husband, living in Bermuda in 1964 to 1965, and visiting New York City on several occasions. Because of her lively interest in what was going on in the world and her desire to keep mentally active, Betty Williams wanted to go on working after her marriage. She would move from job to job, enjoying the change, and, at the time that she helped to launch the peace movement, she held a clerical post in a firm of technical consultants and moonlighted as a waitress.

In 1968, the Catholic minority in Northern Ireland (about half a million to a million Protestants), inspired in part by the Civil Rights protesters in the United States, began demonstrating against Protestant discrimination, demanding greater job opportunities, an end to housing restrictions, and electoral reform that would increase their political power. A new militant faction of the Irish Republican Army (IRA), which has always stood for union with the Irish Republic to the south, was organized to help the Catholics in their campaign and to cut the ties between Britain and Northern Ireland. The members of the Provisional IRA, as it was called, resorted to bombings, shooting, and other types of violence to gain its ends, chief of which was the expulsion of the British. Opposing the Provisionals ("Provos" or "Provies") was the pro-British Protestant Ulster Defense League. To maintain control over their respective Catholic and Protestant areas in Belfast, and throughout Northern Ireland, those two paramilitary organizations engaged in extensive guerrilla warfare. From 1969

through 1975, the fighting resulted in over 1,400 deaths and injuries, of which more than 1,000 were among the general population.

Like many others in the Andersonstown ghetto, Betty Williams had observed the harassment of Republican demonstrators by the British troops, and for some years her sympathies lay with the IRA. However, she came to realize, she had explained, that violence only generated more violence through vengeance, and that brutality and terrorism victimized the innocent. In 1972, when the Reverend Joseph Parker, a Protestant clergyman, organized Witness for Peace in an effort to bring Catholics and Protestants together, she joined his unsuccessful protest against violence. Privately, she urged Provos among her acquaintances to abandon their cause. One day, in 1973, when a young British soldier was shot down in a Belfast street almost at her feet, she tried to comfort him as he lay dying on the sidewalk. Other women nearby upbraided her for that gesture of compassion. Recounting the incident to Richard Deutsch, who interviewed her for his book *Mairead Corrigan/ Betty Williams* (1977), she said, "I learned that people had obviously lost their sense of value of human life."

During the eighth year of the Catholic-Protestant civil war, on August 10, 1976, an event occurred in Belfast that led to the meeting of Betty Williams, Mairead Corrigan, and Ciaran McKeown and to their resolution to march together for peace. While they walked along the sidewalk, a Catholic mother, Anne Maguire, and her three children were struck by a getaway car when the driver, an IRA member, was shot dead at the wheel by British pursuers. Two of the children were killed instantly; the third died the next day; and the mother was seriously injured.

Mairead Corrigan, aunt of the Maguire children, appeared on local television the next day, pleading for an end to violence and slaughter, and blaming the IRA for the accident. Betty Williams had seen the accident, and impelled by an anger that overrode her fear, she began canvassing the streets within a few hours with her first peace petition. She herself went on television two days after the children's deaths and called on all women, Protestants and Catholic, to help her bring pressure on the Provisional IRA to end military operations. She also announced plans for a peace march in the Andersonstown area where the children had been killed. Approximately 10,000 women, responding to the call, convened on Saturday August 14, to pray and sing hymns. With Betty Williams and Mairead Corrigan, they marched to the Maguires' gravesites, undeterred by the verbal and physical opposition of IRA members and sympathizers, who struck out at the peace demonstrators, singling out the known Protestants and tearing placards from their hands.

Determined to see to it that their movement would endure beyond the emotional climate of the moment, Ms. Williams and Mairead Corrigan met the next day with Ciaran McKeown, a reporter for the *Irish Press,* who had offered his help to the two women. His newspaper background and his knowledge of politics in Northern Ireland were valuable in helping the organization to get started, and he eventually planned the overall strategy for the movement and formulated its philosophy in the Declaration of Peace, which summed up his own ideas on peace and nonviolence, as did his pamphlet *The Price of Peace.* It was McKeown, also, who suggested the name "Peace People" for the movement.

The Peace People leaders planned a series of marches to be held once a week in different places in Northern Ireland and Great Britain, with either Betty Williams or Mairead Corrigan attending each meeting, until December 4, 1976, a date chosen to be the culmination of the first phase of the peace movement. The August 28, 1976, march from a Catholic area of Belfast into a Protestant sector drew an estimated 35,000 supporters, and, as Deutsch reported in his book, "It demonstrated to those Protestants who were still hanging back that the peace movement was not an exclusively Catholic phenomenon; that it was nonsectarian." Although the Provisional IRA charged that the movement sought "peace at any price" instead of "peace with justice," recruits by the thousands joined the marchers throughout Northern Ireland. "We had tapped into something that must have been there for a long time. Suddenly it broke out in the open," Betty Williams said during an interview for *Family Circle* (March 27, 1978).

By the fall of 1976, as the courageous leadership of Ms. Williams and Ms. Corrigan was stirring worldwide sympathy for their cause, the two women became the popular choice for that year's Nobel Peace Prize. But since their movement had begun six months after the February deadline for acceptance of nominations, the Nobel committee could not consider them as candidates. The sentiment for honoring their work, however, was so strong that the Norwegian press and a group of civic organizations collected private donations of $340,000. In late November 1976, the two women traveled to Oslo, where the money was presented to them as

a special Norwegian People's Peace Prize. The following year, the 1976 Nobel Peace Prize of $140,000 was awarded to them retroactively. The citation read in part: "Their initiative paved the way for the strong resistance against violence and misuse of power which was present in broad circles of the people." Both award winners have said in interviews that they regretted that Ciaran McKeown had not been named to share in the prize that they accepted on behalf of their movement in Oslo on December 10, 1977, but they insisted that he be given part of the cash award.

Because of having to give up their regular jobs when the campaign against violence demanded their full time, Betty Williams and Mairead Corrigan had received a stipend from the Peace People organization. Money from their prizes enabled them to become volunteers in the movement and to pay their own expenses. The prize money also made possible the purchase of a headquarters building and some small community-center buildings, and helped to start up a number of local Peace People chapters. As reported in *Newsweek* (March 27, 1978), within a year and a half after its founding, the Peace People had become occupied with projects totaling some $5,000,000. To help fund the projects, the Peace Women, as Betty Williams and Mairead Corrigan had come to be called, often traveled abroad in pursuit of financial aid, as well as moral support.

On one such trip, in the fall of 1977, Ms. Williams met with members of the West German government, industrialists, and financiers, trying to interest them in investing in the economy of Northern Ireland, where there is 40 percent unemployment among the adult population. She was well aware of the link between poverty and the type of discontent that sought outlets in shootings and bombings, as she had made clear in an interview a few months earlier for *Christian Century* (August 21-September 7, 1977). In that interview, she also discussed the shift of the peace movement from its "charismatic phase" of the great rallies to an emphasis on hard work at the grass roots level, getting people involved in their local communities as they bridge their religious and political divisions.

Through the project Lifeline, for example, the Peace People aided the survivors of those killed in terrorist attacks. They distributed pamphlets to let Ulstermen know their rights when arrested, and to instruct victims of violence in claiming compensation. By March 1978, they had assisted over 150 repentant activists in getting out of the country to avoid retaliation.

"People need defending," Ms. Williams said, as quoted in *Newsweek* (March 27, 1978). "And if the police or the soldiers are violent, we'll say so. We don't want to be a nice, comfortable peace movement."

Along with threats of physical violence, including the slogan "Shoot Betty" painted on Belfast walls, the movement's leaders were the targets of continuing criticism. They were often accused of naïveté because of failure to offer political solutions for the troubles of Northern Ireland. Andrew Boyd contended in the *Nation* (April 16, 1977) that the movement began to founder early in 1977, because of Protestant suspicion of its three Catholic leaders. He pessimistically concluded that, like all of the peace groups active in Northern Ireland since 1969, the group founded by Betty Williams and her associates was doomed to fail because an agreement on peace can be reached only by the IRA, the British army, and the other factions that are making war.

Ms. Williams admitted that the movement had not brought peace, but she insisted that it had "created a climate for peace to become respectable." Although violence continued in Northern Ireland, the first eight months of 1977, compared to the same period in 1976, showed a decline in killings from 222 to 96, and, in bombings from 464 to 225. Some observers linked the decline to United States condemnation of terrorist activities and calls by American political leaders for peace coupled with requests to cease all aid to groups involved in fighting in Northern Ireland. British authorities, however, give the Peace People some credit for the reduction in violence, saying that more people are cooperating with the police and the army.

Rejecting the image of the Community of the Peace People as a "petticoat brigade," Betty Williams emphasized that the movement was not feminist, despite the preponderance of women who were active in it. She told Claude Servan-Schreiber in an interview for *Ms.* (December 1976) that men were wanted in the movement because they were the ones who were doing the fighting; hence, they were the ones who must stop. She knows, however, that one reason that men fight is that society makes a "hero of the man who carries a gun." In her Nobel address she acknowledged the importance of women in the peace effort: "The voice of women has a special role and a special soul-force in the struggle for a nonviolent world."

In addition to the Nobel Prize and the prize from the Norwegian people, Ms. Williams received the Carl von Ossietzky Medal for Courage from the Berlin section of the International League of Human Rights, in 1976, and an honorary Doctor of Law degree from Yale University, in 1977. She also received the Martin Luther King, Jr., Award, the Eleanor Roosevelt Award, in 1984, the International Platform Association's Speaker of the Year award, also in 1984; and the Frank Foundation Child Care International Oliver Award. In 1995, she was awarded the Rotary Club International "Paul Harris Fellowship" and the Together for Peace Building Award.

Williams, after divorcing her first husband, Ralph Williams, married James T. Perkins, in 1982, and they moved to Florida. She lectured extensively in the United States. She then taught at Sam Houston State University, in Huntsville, Texas, as Visiting Professor in Political Science and History, where she worked to unite ethnic and cultural groups on campus and in the local community. In Huntsville, she headed the Global Children's Foundation, and became a co-founder of The Center for Partnership Studies (CPS) through its initiative, the Spiritual Alliance to Stop Intimate Violence (SAIV), in Pacific Grove, Calif. In 1997, Ms. Williams founded The World Centers of Compassion for Children International (W.C.C.C.I.), with world headquarters in Galloway, Republic of Ireland, where Ms. Williams now lives. According to the website, W.C.C.C.I. advocates for disadvantaged children, especially refugees, world wide. By providing education, nurturing, and legal protections for the world's children, the group believes W.C.C.C.I programs will help create a new world view. It plans to undertake Three Pillars of Actions: First, to develop Centers of Compassion for Children (a model center is being created in the Region Basilicata of Italy) that would provide appropriate medical care (mind and body), education with specific emphasis on a 'peace curriculum,' and, job training to become functioning and productive world citizens—focusing on training for "green economy;" second, peace education; and, third, the adoption and implementation of the Universal Declaration of Rights for Children.

Williams also has been a speaker for the PeaceJam Foundation, an international organization whose mission statement is "to create young leaders committed to positive change in themselves, their communities, and the world through the inspiration of Nobel Peace Laureates who pass on the spirit, skills, and wisdom they embody."

In 2006 she joined Mairead Corrigan Maguire and fellow Nobel Peace Prize winners Shirin Ebadi, Jody Williams, Wangari Maathai, and Rigoberta Menchú to found the Nobel Women's Initiative. In 2014, Williams participated in the 14th World Summit of Nobel Peace Laureates, in Rome, with other Nobel Peace Prize winners and prominent global figures, who are "active in social, scientific, political and cultural areas."

## PERSONAL LIFE

Betty Williams' first marriage was to Richard Williams, whom she married on June 14, 1961, in Bermuda. They had two children, Deborah and Paul. After the first marriage ended in divorce, she married James T. Perkins, in 1982.

## FURTHER READING

*Christian Century 94:746+ Ag 31-S 7 '77; Family Circle 91:38+ Mr 27 ' '78 por; Ms. 5:62+ D '76; N Y Daily News p80 My 25 '78 por; N Y Times pl4 O 11 '77, Cpl + D 8'77 por; N Y Times Mag p29+ D 19 '76 pors; Deutsch, Richard. Mairead Corrigan/Betty Williams (1977); Les Prix Nobel 1977 (1978)*

---

# MARIE C. WILSON
## Feminist; Author; Political Organizer; Entrepreneur

**Born:** September 6, 1940; Atlanta, Georgia
**Primary Field:** Feminist Politics
**Affiliation:** Ms. Foundation for Women

## INTRODUCTION

*"In a democracy, a group with over half your population deserves to be represented at the highest levels," the women's advocate Marie C. Wilson wrote in response to a Des Moines Business Record (October 5,1998) questionnaire. "In over 20 countries, there has been a woman prime minister or president. We're the leading democracy, so others wonder why we haven't had a woman leader." Since the 1970s, when she directed women's programs at a mid-western college, Wilson has worked to achieve gender equity in all spheres of society.*

*For two decades, from early 1985 to mid-2004, she led the Ms. Foundation for Women, which describes itself as the country's "only national multi-issue women's fund." "The mission [that its founders] put in place has basically held: to make sure women have the resources to influence their own lives and the world around them," Wilson told AAUW Outlook (Fall/Winter 2002, online), a publication of the American Association of University Women. According to the Ms. Foundation's Web site, "Through its leadership, expertise and financial support, the Foundation champions an equitable society by effecting change in public consciousness, law, philanthropy and social policy." Under Wilson's direction the foundation provided training, technical assistance, and millions of dollars in grants to grassroots orga-nizations striving to improve the health and safety of women and girls; enable women to gain economic self-sufficiency; and help women gain the skills, and develop the desire and confidence, to hold leadership positions in the public and private sectors of American society. It did so through such groundbreaking programs as the Institute for Women's Economic EmPOWERment (an annual event launched in 1986); the Reproductive Rights Coalition and Organizing Fund (set up in 1989); the Collaborative Fund for Women's Economic Development (1990); Take Our Daughters to Work Day (1993), now called Take Our Daughters and Sons to Work Day; the Collaborative Fund for Healthy Girls/ Healthy Women, the Women and AIDS Fund, and the Democracy Funding Circle (all 1996), the last of which, according to the foundation's website, aims "to combat the growing influence of conservatism" by supporting "organizations working toward a progressive vision of democracy"; and the Collaborative Fund for Youth-Led Social Change (2002).*

*Wilson stepped down from the presidency of the Ms. Foundation for Women to concentrate on her work with the White House Project, a national, nonpartisan organization that she co-founded in 1997. The White House Project seeks to increase the number of female political leaders; one of the group's principal goals is the election of a female U.S. president or vice president. A poll conducted four years ago indicated that "79 percent of the public feel that women's leadership in America is not truly going to be accepted until women hold one of these high offices," as Wilson told an interviewer for the* Women's Review of Books *(July 2000). "So one of the most important things that we can do is to intensify our efforts to educate people about possible women candidates." As of June 30, 2004, according to the Inter-Parliamentary Union (online), women made up 14.8 percent of the delegates in the U.S. House of Representatives; thus, in terms of the percentage of women serving in their countries' lower or single legislative body, the U.S. ranked 58th (along with Andorra) among the world's nations, behind Rwanda and Sweden (which ranked first and second, respectively, with 48.8 and 45.3 percent) and such countries as Cuba (36.0 percent), Bulgaria (26.2), China (20.2), and Peru (18.3). Keenly aware of that fact, Wilson and her colleagues have encouraged American women to run for office at all levels of government and have tried to create an environment in which their election will become a reality. Wilson believes that the day a woman will occupy the White House is not far off. "This is our time," she told Lynda Richardson for the* New York Times *(February 17, 2004). "I think by 2008, we're going to see several women in the race." She added, "And that's the point, to get enough women running so they are seen and they're evaluated on their agenda, not just gender."*

## EARLY LIFE

The daughter of a typesetter and a dental hygienist, Marie C. Wilson was born on September 6, 1940 in Georgia and raised in Atlanta, the state capital. She has recalled that once, when she was a child, a bus driver dragged her, weeping, from the back of the bus, where she had been sitting next to her black babysitter, to the front section, reserved for whites. Her memory of that incident contributed to her later involvement, in the early 1960s, in the civil rights movement. Earlier, in high school, she was a cheerleader and, one year, homecoming queen. In about 1963 she earned a bachelor's degree in philosophy from Vanderbilt University, in Nashville, Tennessee. Some years later, when she was a full-time homemaker with four children, she and her husband adopted a baby boy who, they later learned, suffered from cerebral palsy. "I worked with the school system to help him get what he needed," she told Judith Stone for *O, the Oprah Magazine* (March 2004). "I lobbied for affordable childcare. Then I realized, Oh, my God, politics is about me! '" Wilson's husband was a minister of music (a person who plans services and oversees the choir and various other congregational activities in a place of worship), and she and their children accompanied him each time he got a job with a different church, in Delaware, Pennsylvania, and Iowa. In Des Moines, Iowa, Wilson earned a master's degree in education

from Drake University in 1980. Subsequently, she was appointed director of women's programs at Drake; in that position she assisted in career-development efforts and instituted such workplace innovations as flextime and job sharing. In 1983 she became the first woman to be elected as an at-large member of the Des Moines City Council.

In the mid-1980s a representative of the Ms. Foundation for Women "came to Des Moines and asked a group of us what was happening for women in Iowa," as Wilson recalled for *AA UW Outlook*. "Right then I swore I would work for that organization. No one had ever asked us what was happening for women in Iowa. No one had ever told women in local communities that we mattered." In 1985 Wilson was named president of the foundation, which was organized in 1972 as a conduit for transferring some of the profits generated by *Ms. Magazine* to the grassroots women's movement. *Ms.*, launched earlier that year by Gloria Steinem, Patricia Carbine, Letty Cottin Pogrebin, and Mario Thomas, was an instant popular, though not financial, success. The foundation has raised funds independently of the magazine since 1974. When Wilson arrived, the foundation had four staff members and an annual budget of $500,000; currently, it has 40 employees, a budget of over $10 million, and an endowment fund of over $20 million.

Under Wilson's leadership, the Collaborative Fund for Women's Economic Development, a preeminent model of collaborative grant making by individual, family, and institutional donors, began operating in 1990. Since 1991 that fund has committed over $10 million to support local programs that create jobs for low-income women. The Ms. Foundation's most recent venture of this sort is the Collaborative Fund for Youth-Led Social Change, which supports programs that develop new ways for adolescent and teenage boys and girls to work together and explore nontraditional gender roles, among other activities. In addition to the Ms. Foundation, the 19 donors or sponsors of that fund include the Diana, Princess of Wales Memorial Fund (U.S.); the Women's Foundation of Colorado; the Girl's Best Friend Foundation, in Chicago, Illinois; and Polly Howells, a Brooklyn, New York-based psychotherapist. The 12 grantees include the Appalachian Women's Leadership Project, in Hamlin, West Virginia; Asian Immigrant Women Advocates, in Oakland, California; Sista II Sista, in Brooklyn, New York; and Sisters in Action for Power, in Portland, Oregon.

In 1993, along with Gloria Steinem, Wilson created Take Our Daughters to Work Day, a public-education campaign that, according to the Ms. Foundation's Web site, "focused on making girls visible, valued, and heard." The event was also designed to expose girls to the variety of careers open to them and to foster dialogue about women's changing roles in the workplace. In 2003 the project was renamed Take Our Daughters and Sons to Work Day. "The new program," the foundation's Web site states, "encourages both girls and boys to share their expectations for the future and think about how they can participate fully in family, work, and community"; it also "challenges workplaces to consider policies that will help their female and male employees better integrate these multiple demands." Wilson also regarded the event as a way to decrease, with time, the reluctance of many men to take advantage of family-leave benefits; studies have shown that men who take family leave assume more responsibilities at home than men who do not. In recent years an estimated 15 million adults have brought one or more children to their jobs on Take Our Daughters and Sons to Work Day; about 30 percent of U.S. businesses take part.

One of Wilson's top concerns is obtaining paid family leave, in which, when member of their families need special care, employees can take up to six weeks of leave while earning 50 to 60 percent of their salaries (after first using their vacation time), in arrangements similar to those that provide disability benefits. "Studies show when employees can take some time away from work to handle crises, they're happier and more productive," Wilson told Geoff Williams for *Entrepreneur* (May 1, 2003). "This isn't full paid leave, so employees aren't going to make this decision lightly. But it's a safety net, and if it's not there, [employers are] going to pay full price for a lot of lost productivity." In a commentary for the Spokane, Washington, *Spokesman-Review* (October 27, 2003, online), Wilson noted, "Of the industrialized nations, only Australia and the United States do not provide paid family leave." While the federal Family Medical Leave Act, passed in 1993, allows workers to take off six weeks without pay, millions of people cannot afford to forgo their salaries for so long. In addition, many employees do not take needed leave for fear of being labeled disloyal or worse by their employers. "One of the best things about paid family leave is that it could help change the corporate culture," Wilson told Williams. "By letting your employees know you support paid family leave, you can send the message to your employees that their family lives and personal growth matter to you. Ultimately, that's going to make your company stronger and attract more qualified people." In 1997, along with Laura Liswood, who then taught at the Kennedy School of Government at Harvard University, Wilson launched the White House Project (WHP), a national, nonpartisan organization dedicated to fostering the entry of women into leadership positions, among them the U.S. presidency. In July 2004 the WHP's home page noted that of the 12,000 people who have served in the U.S. Congress since its inception, only 215 have been women. Wilson is endeavoring to increase the number of women at all levels of government. "We make up 52 percent of the population but only 14 percent of Congress," she told Stone in 2004. "And men are 86 percent of elected officials under the age of 35, from whose ranks come half of our presidents, governors, and members of Congress." She contends that women bring valuable assets to public service that are rare in men. "Research shows that women legislators look at issues more broadly, are more open, and bring more people into the [legislative] process," she told Stone. "If leading by consensus-building weren't devalued because it's something women do, it would already have transformed the world."

The WHP is focusing on three major projects. The first is a study called "Framing Gender on the Campaign Trail," which examines how the media's treatment of female and male candidates for public office differs. In the second, called "Six to Sixty," WHP is attempting to educate and train females ages six to 60 for activities or careers in politics. The third project involves analyzing barriers to and opportunities for women's leadership in public life and defining what is meant by the phrase "qualified woman." Wilson has observed that the expectations regarding female candidates are much higher than those for males. "When we did focus groups I could hardly believe the stress on perfection, the feeling that 'whoever does this has to be the perfect person,'" she told the *Women's Review of Books*. "If the first woman to be, say, president has to represent this perfect standard, she will not be able to bring her whole self into the process; most likely, she'll be a woman who fits a more masculine model. We want a woman who can be her whole self, all her masculine self, all her feminine self, her whole self. That will not happen if she's forced into being the first token [female president]. She'll have to meet standards that are really about gender. That's why we have to keep pushing numbers, so we get beyond gender. Because this project, electing a woman to the White House, is about having a democracy and moving beyond gender." The White House Project recently teamed up with V-Day, an organization founded by the playwright Eve Ensler with the goal of eradicating violence against women, on Women Elect the Future, a national effort to mobilize women to vote and to develop leadership skills. According to various polls, a far greater percentage of the public than ever before professes willingness to vote for qualified female candidates. Indeed, many people perceive women as having special expertise and even "more credibility," in Wilson's words, on issues connected with family, health care, education, and the workplace, and view women as generally more trustworthy than men. "For better or worse, the growing dissatisfaction with politicians has really been pushing people to think differently about leadership," she told the *Des Moines Business Record*. "Our polls show that people think women provide more integrity in leadership." Wilson has maintained that popular culture should not be ignored as a means of changing perceptions about gender and power. The film *Air Force One*, for example, in which the actress Glenn Close played the U.S. vice president, may have led many people to consider the idea of a woman in a powerful position, according to Wilson. In 2000, at Wilson's suggestion, the giant toy manufacturer Mattel introduced a President Barbie doll. Wilson had learned that in 1994, according to Mattel, American girls ages three to 10 owned an average of eight Barbie dolls each. President Barbie is available as a Caucasian, an African-American, and a Latina (but not an Asian or a Native American). "I almost lost my feminist credentials for suggesting the doll," Wilson told Stone, referring to Barbie as a target of feminists who criticize the doll as an example of a highly unrealistic female body image, a symbol of materialism, and the epitome of an unhealthy emphasis on fashion and appearance. "But to make change, you've got to go where the people are. And more and more girls think they're going to grow up to be president and call a joint session of Congress because their dolls can." Other feminists have noted with approval that Barbie holds a job outside the home and is self-supporting. Included with every President Barbie is the WHP's Girls' Action Agenda for children and parents and a Girls' Bill of Rights, prepared by Girls Inc. (which, its Web site states, is a nonprofit organization "dedicated to inspiring all girls to be strong, smart, and bold").

After a WHP study found that between January 1, 2000 and June 30, 2001, only 11 percent of guests on the five major Sunday-morning television news shows were women, WHP created a database of the names of female experts in various fields, in the so-called Visibility Project. With Elizabeth Debold and Idelisse Malave, Wilson wrote *Mother Daughter Revolution: from Betrayal to Power* (1993), which, as Catherine Hunter wrote for *Herizons* (Summer 1994), "places the problematic relationship between mothers and daughters in its wider political context." Her second book, written solo, is *Closing the Leadership Gap: Why Women Can and Must Help Run the World* (2004). She co-wrote the preface to *Girls Seen and Heard: 52 Life Lessons for Our Daughters* (1999), by Sondra Forsyth and Ms. Foundation staff members. Wilson and her successor as president of the Ms. Foundation, Sara K. Gould, wrote the preface to *Kitchen Table Entrepreneurs: How Eleven Women Escaped Poverty and Became Their Own Bosses* (2002), in which Martha Shirk and Anna S. Wadia wrote about 11 women who received grants bom the Ms. Foundation to start their own businesses. Wilson also wrote the forewords to *Woman: A Celebration to Benefit the Ms. Foundation for Women* (2002), a compendium of essays and photographs of and by women, and to *If Women Ruled the World* (2004), another compilation of essays by women, edited by Sheila Ellison.

## PERSONAL LIFE

Wilson has received the Robert W. Scrivner Award for Creative Grantmaking, the Leadership for Equity and Diversity (LEAD) Award bom Women & Philanthropy, and an honorary doctorate of public service from Drake University. In 2004 the Ms. Foundation established the Marie C. Wilson Leadership Fund in her honor. She is a sought-after speaker at local, state, national, and international events; her topics include a variety of women's, philanthropic, and political issues. Wilson served as an official U.S. delegate to the United Nations' Fourth World Conference on Women, held in Beijing, China, in 1995. Although the Ms. Foundation and the White House Project are nonpartisan, she has identified herself as a Democrat.

Wilson, who is divorced, has five children and several grandchildren. She and her partner of 15 years, Nancy A. Lee, a New York Times vice president for business development, live in New York City.

**FURTHER READING**
*Mother Daughter Revolution: from Betrayal to Power; Closing the Leadership Gap: Why Women Can and Must Help Run the World*

---

# EVAN WOLFSON

## Attorney; Civil Rights Advocate

**Born:** February 4, 1957; Brooklyn, New York
**Primary Field:** Civil Rights
**Affiliation:** Freedom to Marry

### INTRODUCTION

*Evan Wolfson, the founder (in 2001) and executive director of the organization Freedom to Marry, eschews the term "gay marriage." He believes that the term creates artificial distinctions and reinforces false perceptions regarding the marriages of men and women, on the one hand, and same-sex couples on the other. For the same reasons he does not accept the concept of civil unions, which offer same-sex couples only some of the rights that marriage confers. "Gay marriage is not what we're looking for," Wolfson explained to Robert Finn for the* New York Times *(February 18, 2007). "We're looking for the legal right for gays to marry. You don't ask for half a loaf. We don't need two lines at the clerk's office when there's already an institution that works in this country, and it's called marriage. One of the main protections that come with marriage is inherent in the word: certainly in times of crisis any other word than marriage would not bring the same clarity or impart the same dignity." Wolfson considers the fight for same-sex marriage to be the most important civil rights battle at present. He also views it as the latest in a series of steps that have served not only to define marriage in contemporary society but also to determine the reach and limits of the law regarding marriage. Among those steps are the Supreme Court decision in 1967 to legalize interracial marriage and the ruling in 1984 that rapes that occur within marriage are illegal, that in the eyes of the law, the rape of a wife by a husband is no different from any other rape. "When we ended that legal subordination of women, we transformed marriage," Wolfson told Gary E. Nelson for* Masthead *(Winter 2005), "from a union based on domination to one based on love, commitment, and the choice of two equal partners." Wolf-*

*son, who revealed his homosexuality to his family when he was in his early 20s, has fought for equal rights for lesbians, gay men, bisexuals, and transgender people both as a lawyer and as a volunteer and then staff member of the Lambda Defense and Education Fund. In his book,* Why Marriage Matters *(2004), he offered a point-by-point argument for the legalization of same-sex marriage. As of October 2009 same-sex marriage was legal in four states, Massachusetts, Vermont, Connecticut, and Iowa, and it will become legal in New Hampshire on January 1, 2010. "The classic pattern for civil rights advancement in America is patchwork, but I see equal marriage rights for gays becoming a nationwide reality over the next 15 to 20 years," Wolfson told Finn. "I really believe it will happen in my lifetime."*

### EARLY LIFE

One of the four children of Jerome H. "Jerry" Wolfson and Joan Wolfson, Evan Wolfson was born into a civic-minded Jewish family on February 4, 1957 in the New York City borough of Brooklyn. His father is a pediatrician; his mother was a full-time homemaker who later became a social worker. He has two brothers, David, a pediatrician, and Michael, a film producer and internet entrepreneur, and one sister, Alison, a non-practicing lawyer, who is gay. Wolfson was raised in the Squirrel Hill neighborhood of Pittsburgh, Pennsylvania, where his family attended a synagogue aligned with the Conservative branch of Judaism. He was a member of the Cub Scouts and then, briefly, the Boy Scouts. He attended Taylor Allderdice High School, the largest of Pittsburgh's public high schools, where his main interests were history, politics, and reading; the school's principal predicted to him that he would become the nation's first Jewish president. After his graduation, in 1974, Wolfson entered Yale University, in New Haven, Connecticut. "When he went to college, my husband and I couldn't get over how quiet the dinner table was," his mother told Mark S. Warnick for the *Pittsburgh Post-Gazette* (March 11, 1997). "He evoked a lot of ideas. He would often take the opposite side of something, just to get the discussion going."

## LIFE'S WORK

At Yale, Wolfson was elected speaker of the school's political union and was the campus coordinator for the 1976 campaign of the Democratic presidential and vice-presidential nominees, Governor Jimmy Carter of Georgia and U.S, senator Walter Mondale of Minnesota. During those years Wolfson had a couple of "intense crushes" on male classmates, as he told Joseph Hanania for the *Los Angeles Times* (August 26, 1996), and he came to the realization that he was gay. After he earned a B.A. degree in history, in 1978, Wolfson was accepted at Harvard Law School, in Cambridge, Massachusetts, but he did not enroll. Feeling that he needed a break from academia, he joined the Peace Corps. He spent two years in the tiny West African country of Togo, in the village of Pagouda, where he taught English and established the Pittsburgh-Pagouda Friendship Library. Wolfson told Hanania that in Togo he had a chance to "explore life free from everything that had gone on before. It was the feeling of always being an alien, being alone. That made me think about sexual orientation. I realized that people can be gay on the inside, but how they build their life around that is shaped by society. I made [gay] friends in Africa who will undoubtedly marry women. They will never be as happy or as fulfilled as they would be were they able to do what their true heart wants."

When Wolfson returned from the Peace Corps, he told his parents that he was gay. "I think their main reaction was sadness," he told Warnick, "that I was not going to have the kind of life they expected and were familiar with. But they were always loving and supportive. They're very proud of what I do and they've always been there for me." Wolfson also reapplied to Harvard Law School, and when he was accepted again, he concluded that he was meant to be a lawyer. While at Harvard he read John Boswell's book *Christianity, Social Tolerance, and Homosexuality: Gay People in Western Europe from the Beginning of the Christian Era to the Fourteenth Century* (1980). "This book opened my eyes to the fact that being gay wasn't just about me personally," he told L. A. Johnson for the *Pittsburgh Post-Gazette* (July 26, 2004), "but had a political context that could change the way in which gay people are excluded from very important participation in society." In his last year at law school, Wolfson wrote a paper arguing in favor of the legalization of gay marriage, a subject not widely discussed at that time. After he earned a J.D. degree, in 1983, he taught political philosophy at Harvard College. He turned down lucrative job offers from law firms to work, from 1984 to 1988, as an assistant district attorney in Brooklyn.

Concurrently, beginning in 1985, Wolfson performed pro-bono work for the Lambda Defense and Education Fund; founded in 1973, Lambda is the nation's oldest and largest organization working to expand civil rights for lesbians, gay men, bisexuals, transgender people, and people infected with HIV (the virus that causes AIDS), through litigation, education, and public policy efforts. In 1985 Wolfson wrote an amicus brief presented to the U.S. Supreme Court regarding *National Gay Task Force v. the Board of Education of Oklahoma City.* "Amicus" means "friend" in Latin; an amicus brief is a document written by an individual or group not directly involved in the case at hand, filed to support the argument of the plaintiff or the defendant. In his brief, which he filed as a "friend" of the National Gay Task Force, Wolfson argued against an Oklahoma state law that permitted the firing of teachers who "promote or support homosexuality." The National Gay Task Force won that case, and the law was overturned. Wolfson wrote another amicus brief for Michael Hardwick, the defendant in the closely watched 1986 Supreme Court case *Bowers v. Hardwick.* The plaintiff was Michael Bowers, the attorney general of Georgia. Hardwick and a gay friend of his had been arrested in their bedroom in Georgia on charges of sodomy; the police officer who made the arrest had been admitted into their home by another friend to deliver a summons for a lesser crime that Hardwick had committed. The case hinged on the notion of privacy, which is nowhere defined in the Constitution, as well as that of free association, which is protected by the Bill of Rights; the defense argued that the policeman had invaded Hardwick's privacy and that Georgia's anti-sodomy statute was unconstitutional. The Supreme Court ruled, 5-4, in favor of the state, arguing that historically, sodomy has long been reviled and forbidden, and therefore, in the words of Justice Byron White, who wrote the majority opinion, "to claim that a right to engage in such conduct is 'deeply rooted in this Nation's history and tradition' or 'implicit in the concept of ordered liberty' is, at best, facetious." Chief Justice Warren Burger, in a concurring opinion, wrote, "To hold that the act of homosexual sodomy is somehow protected as a fundamental right would be to cast aside millennia of moral teaching." Justice Lewis Powell, who cast the deciding vote, later said that his reasoning had been erroneous. The Supreme Court struck down that ruling in 2003, in the case *Lawrence v. Texas*.

Impressed by Wolfson's work with Lambda, his supervisor, Elizabeth Holtzman, the Brooklyn district attorney, asked him to write an amicus brief for *Batson v. Kentucky* (1986), which concerned racial discrimination in jury selection. In that case the U.S. Supreme Court ruled that it is illegal for prosecutors to exclude potential jurors based solely on their race. Wolfson also wrote a brief for a case, *People v. Liberia*, tried in 1984 in the New York State Court of Appeals that helped to eliminate the so-called marital-rape exemption, according to which who practiced in Hawaii. In 1993 the Hawaii Supreme Court ruled that legal barriers to same-sex marriage are discriminatory under the "equal protection" clause of the state constitution. Though the ruling did not technically strike down the law, it required Hawaii to show "compelling interest," the strictest level of scrutiny required under judicial review, for the state to restrict same-sex marriage. If the state could not demonstrate compelling interest, the restriction would be overturned. The ruling sparked a national debate and led opponents of same-sex marriage to propose bills in state legislatures across the country that would ban it. Congress passed the Defense of Marriage Act, outlawing the federal recognition of gay marriage and allowing states to refuse to recognize same-sex marriages performed in other states. In September 1996 President Bill Clinton signed it into law.

At Foley's request Wolfson joined him as co-counsel in *Baehr v. Miike*, as the case was now known. At the trial hearing, in 1996, the state's witnesses relied on arguments related to parenting, presenting evidence that children were better off when raised by a married man and woman. The court found those arguments insufficient; it concluded that the key to good parenting was parents' ability to nurture, not their sexual orientation. That decision made Hawaii the first state to allow same-sex couples to marry. Much credit was given to Wolfson for his successful efforts to portray homosexual couples as no different from heterosexual couples. The landmark decision galvanized people on both sides of the argument; in subsequent years lawyers from the organization Gay and Lesbian Advocates and Defenders (GLAD) began to challenge laws in other states excluding gays from marriage, filing lawsuits in Vermont and Massachusetts, and state legislatures passed laws

banning same-sex marriage. Hawaii was among the latter group; in 1998 the state's legislature amended the state's constitution to prohibit same-sex couples from marrying.

In 2000 Wolfson became the first Lambda attorney to argue before the U.S. Supreme Court. He represented James Dale, who in 1990, at 19 years of age, was dismissed from his position as assistant scoutmaster of a Boy Scout troop in Matawan, New Jersey, after being identified in a newspaper as the co-president of a campus lesbian and gay student group at Rutgers University (the state university of New Jersey). The Boy Scouts' Monmouth Council revoked Dale's registration as an adult leader, on the grounds that the organization did not allow openly gay members to lead troops. Dale sued, arguing that his ouster was illegal under New Jersey's antidiscrimination law. The New Jersey Supreme Court agreed with Dale and unanimously struck down the law. The Boy Scouts of America appealed, and the case eventually reached the U.S. Supreme Court. Among the issues the court considered were the right of public organizations to determine their own membership criteria and the right of individuals to join public organizations

The law in New York defined rape as forcible sexual intercourse with a female "who was not a spouse." In *People v. Liberta* the New York court ruled that marital rape is illegal. Nebraska became the first state to abolish the marital-rape exemption, in 1976, Although marital rape is now illegal in every state, in some states the punishments for marital rape and other aspects of the law differ from those for other types of rape.

In 1988 Wolfson was hired by Lawrence E. Walsh, the independent counsel, also known as the special prosecutor, appointed to investigate the Iran-Contra scandal, which involved weapons sold to Iran by members of the administration of President Ronald Reagan; those who participated in the sales then illegally directed the profits to anticommunist rebels in Nicaragua. Walsh recalled to Hanania that Wolfson was "completely unafraid" when he drafted a brief challenging the refusal of the FBI and the CIA (backed by Attorney General Richard Thornburgh) to provide information about those activities.

In 1989 Wolfson took on a new job, as one of Lambda's four full-time attorneys and head of its marriage-equality division. The next year Lambda was approached by two women, Ninia Baehr and Genora Dancel, who had been denied a marriage license in Hawaii and wanted help in challenging legal restrictions to same-sex marriage in that state. Wolfson wanted to take on the case, but Lambda turned it down, sensing that the issue of same-sex marriage was not yet "ripe enough" for successful litigation. Wolfson provided Baehr and Dancel, along with two other same-sex couples who wanted to file a joint lawsuit, with informal advice and referred them to a civil rights lawyer, Dan Foley, without being discriminated against. Wolfson argued that because the Scouts were not primarily an "anti-gay organization," Dale's sexual orientation did not interfere with the group's message. In June 2000 the Supreme Court ruled that the Boy Scouts could legally refuse to admit gay troop leaders under the First Amendment right of "expressive association." Although the ruling was a disappointment, Wolfson was pleased with the public attention that the case brought to the issue of discrimination against gay people. "We may have lost the case five to four, but we're winning the cause," he told John Tanasychuk for the Fort Lauderdale, Florida, *Sun-Sentinel* (October 30, 2000). "Nongay people are now taking up their moral responsibility to speak out against discrimination and protect all kids, including gay kids. And their opinions are much more important than what five justices had to say."

Also in 2000 Wolfson submitted a brief to the Vermont Supreme Court arguing against the state's Defense of Marriage Act, which restricted marriage to one man and one woman. The court ruled that the act illegally discriminated against same-sex couples. In an effort to abide by the ruling, the Vermont legislature created the new category of "civil union," which provides gay and lesbian couples with the full range of legal rights and responsibilities awarded by the state to married couples, provided that they obtain a license and exchange vows in a civil-union ceremony. In no state do civil unions guarantee all of the federal benefits provided to married couples. Because the decision to legally recognize civil unions performed in other states is decided on a state-by-state basis, civil unions are not necessarily respected in states outside the ones in which they were performed.

Over the years other states, including Connecticut, New Jersey, and New Hampshire, allowed gay couples to form legally recognized civil unions. While Wolfson has acknowledged that the rights afforded by civil unions indicate progress, he has maintained that because civil unions, or domestic partnerships, another legal status, represent a separate status for gay couples, they are not sufficient. One reason stems from the use of language. "When you say, 'I'm married,' everyone knows who you are in relation to the primary person you're building your life with," Wolfson explained to Bill Hammond for the *New York Daily News* (April 21, 2009). "'Civil union' doesn't offer that clarity, that immediately understood respect." Wolfson told Hammond that opponents of same-sex marriage "can't have it both ways. Either civil union is the same as marriage, in which case, why do we need two lines at the clerk's office? Or it's not the same, in which case, what is the government withholding?"

In 2001 Wolfson left Lambda and founded Freedom to Marry, "a gay and non-gay partnership working to win marriage equality nationwide," according to the group's Web site. He spent much of his time delivering lectures, engaging in interviews and debates, and writing articles in support of the cause. In November 2003 the Massachusetts Supreme Court ruled that the state's constitution guaranteed equal marriage rights for gay couples, thereby legalizing same-sex marriage in that state. In many towns and cities across the country, mayors and county clerks began accepting marriage- license applications from same-sex couples illegally, prompting the launching of legal processes to challenge existing marriage laws. On January 20, 2004, in his State of the Union address, President George W. Bush declared that the U.S. needed to "defend the sanctity of marriage." By April 2005 18 states had approved amendments to their state constitutions banning same-sex marriage. In September 2005 the California legislature became the first state lawmaking body in the U.S. to pass a bill legalizing same-sex marriage without being forced to do so by court order, but Governor Arnold Schwarzenegger vetoed the bill.

Wolfson presented his case for legalizing same-sex marriage in his book, *Why Marriage Matters: America, Equality, and Gay People's Right to Marry*, published in 2004. Organized as a series of responses to the main arguments advanced by opponents of same-sex marriage, its chapters bear such titles as "Why Now?," "Isn't Marriage for Procreation?," and "Why Not Use Another Word?" Wolfson pointed out the areas in which only people who are legally married enjoy certain rights and privileges, among them family leave (which enables a spouse to take time off from work for particular family-related reasons, such as a spouse's illness), job-related health benefits, retirement benefits, adoption of children, visitation in hospital intensive-care units, and benefits related to death and inheritance. Wolfson responded to what he considers to be his opposition's weakest argument, that marriage be restricted to males and females in order to encourage childbearing, by noting that "no state requires that non-gay couples prove that they can procreate, or promise that they will procreate, before issuing them a marriage license." Wolfson also wrote, "There are at least a million kids being raised by gay and lesbian parents in this country who are indisputably disadvantaged by their families' inability to secure the legal protections and benefits that automatically accrue to heterosexual parents." He presented the finding of scientific studies that children raised by same-sex couples experienced no detectable disadvantages, countering the often repeated claim that a male-female household is the optimal setting for child rearing.

Wolfson's book was well received by gay-rights supporters, who judged it to be an important, lucidly written primer on the issue. In a representative review for the *Sunday Oregonian* (August 1, 2004), Kimberly Marlowe Hartnett wrote, "Wolfson adopts a patient tone and explains that marriage is a basic right and one that protects committed couples and their children without threatening heterosexual marriage or so-called traditional family values. He does so by reviewing the history of marriage, gathering points from relevant court cases at all levels and excerpting thoughtful commentators' work, then gluing it all together with common sense." Hartnett further noted: "Armed with Wolfson's arguments, you could sell anyone with an IQ over room temperature on the wisdom and humanity of marriage equality." The *Slate.com* columnist William Saletan, who has described himself as a liberal Republican and who supports same-sex marriage, nevertheless questioned some of Wolfson's reasoning; in an assessment of *Why Marriage Matters* for the *New York Times Book Review* (September 26, 2004), he took issue with Wolfson's argument that it is wrong to discriminate against those who are "different," noting that the term "different" "would apply even more clearly to polygamist and incestuous couples. Wolfson dismisses the idea that gay marriage will lead down this slippery slope, but his do your own thing rationale invites it." The author, Saletan complained, had "fail[ed] to clarify how gays can be admitted to this institution [i.e., marriage] without spreading chaos."

Same-sex marriage continues to be a prime topic of national debate. During the 2008 presidential campaign, Wolfson commended the Democratic candidates' unanimous support for equal rights for committed gay and lesbian couples but criticized the failure of all of them, except Congressman Dennis Kucinich, to support the rights of gays and lesbians to marry. In May 2008 gay-rights advocates won a big victory in California, when that state's Supreme Court ruled that banning same-sex marriage was unconstitutional. That decision was overturned in November 2008, when California voters passed Proposition 8, amending the constitution to define marriage as between one man and one woman; in May 2009 the state Supreme Court upheld the legality of that vote. Earlier, in October 2008, same-sex marriage was made legal in Connecticut by that state's Supreme Court. In April 2009 two more states, Iowa and Vermont, legalized same-sex marriage; in Vermont, the first state in which a legislature did so, the law went into effect on September 1, 2009. In addition to those states where same-sex marriage is legal, three states, New York, Rhode Island, and California, as well as the District of Columbia, officially recognize same-sex marriage performed in other states. According to the California bill signed into law in October 2009, the state will also recognize those marriages performed in California before the passage of Proposition 8. On June 3, 2009 the governor of New Hampshire, John Lynch, signed into law a bill approving same-sex marriage, effective on January 1, 2010. On May 6, 2009 Maine's governor, John Baldacci, signed into law a bill allowing same-sex couples to marry. Before the law was to take effect, in mid-September, anti-same-sex-marriage protestors gathered more than the requisite 55,087 signatures to postpone the law's implementation and submit the matter to voters on Election Day, November 3, 2009. Supporters of same- sex marriage organized, under the name "No on 1/Protect Maine Equality," to mobilize voters to support the new law. Nonetheless, a majority of Maine's voters, 53 percent, came out against same-sex marriage.

Still, Wolfson has credited the discriminatory rhetoric of anti-same-sex marriage movements for spurring many people to support his side. "Any time people are prompted to push past their discomfort, the more fair minded people move to our side," he told Ruth Horowitz for the Burlington, Vermont, newspaper *Seven Days* (June 21-28, 2006). Polls have shown that the percentage of Americans who favor the legalization of same-sex marriage has grown from 20 to more than 30 in the last five years. Internationally same-sex marriage is legal in countries including the Netherlands, Spain, Norway, Sweden, Belgium, Canada, and South Africa.

## PERSONAL LIFE

Wolfson, who described himself to Finn as "portly, short, and baldish," has taught at Columbia Law School and Rutgers University and is a senior fellow at the Erwin and Rose Wolfson Center for National Affairs, a division of the New School, in New York City. Erwin and Rose were not his grandparents. He was named one of the most influential attorneys in America by the *National Law Journal* in 2000, one of the 100 most influential people in the world by *Time* magazine in 2004, and among the 100 most influential gay men and women in

America by *Out* Magazine in 2008. A resident of New York City, he is in a long-term relationship with Cheng He, a Canadian who has a doctorate degree in molecular/cellular biology, whom he met online. The couple reportedly have no plans to marry, but Wolfson told Finn, "We would love the opportunity to have that choice."

## FURTHER READING

*Why Marriage Matters: America, Equality; and Gay People's Right to Marry*

---

# DONALD WOODS

## Journalist; Social Activist

**Born:** December 15, 1933; Elliotdale, Transkei, South Africa
**Died:** August 19, 2001; London, England
**Primary Field:** Human Rights
**Affiliation:** Anti-apartheid Movement

## INTRODUCTION

*The South African journalist Donald Woods made international headlines in December 1977, when he fled his native country in a dramatic escape from a five-year "banning" imposed upon him by the Afrikaner Nationalist government. The crusading editor of the East London Daily Dispatch and a widely read syndicated columnist, Woods was long recognized in his country as a relentless foe of apartheid, the official policy of racial segregation. Since leaving South Africa, Woods has informed millions on every continent about his country's injustice through the mass media and his two books:* Biko *(1978), a biography of Stephen Biko, who headed the Black Consciousness Movement until his death in prison in 1977; and* Asking for Trouble *(1981), a candid, provocative autobiography that traces his own gradual radicalization. Still a loyal South African, Woods, who lived in England until his death, called repeatedly for international sanctions against his country, for legal procedures against its political leaders, and for an end to apartheid.*

## EARLY LIFE

Donald Woods was a fifth-generation South African, descended, on his father's side, from an early

nineteenth-century settler who bad come from Cornwall, England. He was born on December 15, 1933 in Elliotdale, a small town in the southeastern Transkei, in the Eastern Cape of South Africa, the third child of Walter John and Edna (Lawlor) Woods. His mother, whose ancestry was Irish, brought up her children in her Roman Catholic faith. Woods has a sister, Joan (Mrs. Jim Inglis), and a brother, Harland. Like his maternal grandfather, his father was a white trader, assigned a sector of tribal reserve where he exchanged such basic goods as tools, farm implements, blankets, and medicines with tribesmen for hides, wool, grain, and tobacco. Woods grew up near the Indian Ocean at Hobeni, in what he described in his autobiography as "a lovely, sunny region of green hills and valleys, rivers, forests, and beaches." The only white child among thousands of Bonvana tribesmen, regarded as the most primitive people in the nation's remotest area, Woods spoke their language, the Xhosa, as naturally as English. Unlike other white boys, therefore, he had "two distinctly separate childhoods,"

As a boy, Woods, in his own words, "regarded blacks as inferior and easily accepted the general white attitude that color and race were the determinants of the chasms in cultures," He inherited his family's conservative political allegiance to the predominantly English United party of Prime Minister Jan Smuts, who shared a belief with Dutch opposition Afrikaner Nationalists that some 5,000,000 whites should rule over 20,000,000 blacks but unlike most Afrikaners staunchly supported the Allied cause in World War II. Woods attended parochial hoarding school beyond his home territory and received his preparatory education at the Holy Cross Convent School in Umtata, seventy miles from Hobeni.

At eleven he transferred to the De La Salle College in the seaport city of East London, and in 1946 he entered secondary school at Christian Brothers College in Kimberley. In his free time he studied piano, read voraciously, and excelled as a cricketer.

When in 1952 Woods went to study law at the University of Cape Town, he was still virtually untouched by political concerns and by the increasingly harsh apartheid laws passed by the Afrikaner Nationalist government that had assumed power in 1948, In *Asking for Trouble* Woods described his five years of law study, three at the University of Cape Town and two as a law clerk in Elliotdale, as "a period of inner turmoil." Uncertain about his vocation, Woods also underwent major adjustments in his thinking as his "confident bigotry" was challenged from various quarters. One law professor, Harold Levy, was dismayed by his views on white superiority. His studies made him aware of historical principles of legal equity that contradicted ideas of white South African justice. Formerly passive blacks, organized by the moderate African National Congress, were becoming more defiant. And when Woods met his first visiting black American student, his manner of speaking led him to conclude that culture is a factor of environment, not of race and color. Those views were reinforced in his mind by his extensive reading of works by figures like Abraham Lincoln and the British abolitionist William Wilberforoe, as well as courageous new voices of South African protest such as those of the writers Alan Paton and Nadine Gordimer.

## LIFE'S WORK
In the early 1950's, spurred by parliamentary debates he had heard in Cape Town, Woods decided that the "great obscene lie" of apartheid should be fought by political action. He first joined ranks with the United party, which represented the principal opposition to the Afrikaner government. In 1953 he left it for the newly formed Federal party, which espoused a nonracial franchise and a federal structure of government resembling that of the United States. At the time, Woods still opposed immediate black majority rule but favored the franchise for those who met certain educational and economic qualifications and the removal of "all unfair obstacles" that prevented blacks from taking part in the political process.

During his clerkship in Elliotdale, Woods became a Federal party organizer for the Transkei and wrote articles about federalism for the *East London Daily Dispatch*, the major opposition newspaper of the region. In 1957 Woods was asked by leaders of both the United and Federal parties to run for Parliament in an East London by election. Choosing to run on the Federal ticket, he drew concentrated fire from spokesmen for the powerful United party for shattering "white unity." Polling only 728 votes, Woods lost the election by over 6,000.

Although that experience ended Woods's political ambitions, his vocation had meanwhile taken another turn when he accepted a position as a cub reporter that' had been offered by Vernon Barber, veteran editor of the *Daily Dispatch*. Woods look the job, as he later recalled, "because the idea of journalism excited me, and because the practice of law was boring me beyond further endurance. To become a journalist for an anti-government newspaper in South Africa in 1957 was to begin an experience that promised to be anything but dull."

For a year Woods studied the fundamentals of journalism, first as a junior reporter and then as a junior subeditor of the *Dispatch*. In June 1958 he and a journalist friend set out for England, hoping to widen their experience on London's hallowed Fleet Street. Woods worked briefly for a local West London weekly before landing a job as a subeditor at the *Western Mail* in Cardiff, Wales. After resigning the Gardiff post to travel by van through Western Europe, Woods returned to Fleet Street, this time finding two jobs, as a reporter for the *London Daily Herald* and as assistant editor of a trade journal. As his planned two years overseas neared their end, Woods negotiated a Herald assignment to compare South African apartheid with segregation in the American South. He sailed for New York City, with Little Rock, Arkansas as his final destination, where Governor Orval Faubus was offering diehard resistance to integration. Woods concluded in his report that although in South Africa racism was more entrenched, in the American South it often took on more crude and violent manifestations. On completing that assignment, Woods worked briefly for the *Toronto Daily Star,* writing several articles on South Africa. He returned to the *East London Daily Dispatch* just after the "Sharpeville massacre" of March 1960, when white policemen fired on black demonstrators who were protesting against restrictive pass laws. The incident resulted in the killing of scores of blacks and the wounding of many more.

By the 1961 Parliamentary sessions in Cape Town, which Woods covered for the *Dispatch*, the regime of Prime Minister H. F. Verwoerd, who had taken office in 1958, had on the books more than twenty stringent laws governing the press, with penalties varying from suspension of publication to personal bannings or jail sentences imposed on offending journalists. Supported by the *Dispatch's* long tradition of independence, Woods demonstrated his acumen as a leader writer, columnist, and political correspondent. Among his most challenging assignments was one in South West Africa, later known as Namibia, on the eve of a United Nations Commission inspection there in 1961 to determine the territory's future. He arranged interviews with Chiefs Clemens Kapuuo and Hosea Kotako, black leaders of the underground South West Africa People's Organization (SWAPO), which was fighting for independence against South African administration. Woods also initiated the first of a series of exclusive interviews with Balthazar Johannes Verster, Verwoerd's Minister of Justice and Police, who later became Prime Minister.

Woods's advancement on the staff of the *Daily Dispatch* was spectacularly rapid. At the beginning of 1963 he was appointed deputy editor. After becoming editor and a member of the board of directors in early 1965, he embarked immediately on a more forceful editorial condemnation of apartheid and a radical reorganization of the staff. Woods was one of the first editors in South Africa to recruit black journalists, and he regularly featured articles about the black community. In time, half of the *Dispatch* journalists were non-whites, and the paper carried weekly supplements of black news, printed half in English, half in Xhosa. Despite the fact that East London was one of the most conservative white communities in South Africa, the paper flourished under Woods's editorship, gaining more advertisers and readers among the black population than it lost among the white. With the help of his law training, Woods managed to circumvent governmental restrictions against the *Dispatch* and defended himself against attacks by agencies such as the state-controlled South African Broadcasting Corporation, which charged the *Dispatch* with fomenting unrest.

During Verwoerd's regime the *Dispatch* was increasingly pressured by government officials looking for violations of laws. When Verwoerd was assassinated in 1966 by a white South African, his successor, Vorster, promised Woods even harsher measures if the Dispatch continued to "betray South Africa." Talks between Prime Minister Vorster and Woods were generally cordial, but at times heated. Explaining during one interview why he kept talking to Woods while refusing to see less outspoken English language editors, Vorster

said, "It's because I like to know what the real enemy is thinking."

By 1977, when Vorster's government finally moved against Woods, Afrikaner Nationalist governments had for almost three decades imposed oppressive apartheid prohibitions on blacks regarding voting, labor conditions, social and sexual relations, travel, public accommodation, and hundreds of other matters. Moreover, the Afrikaner "homelands" policy, which divided the nation into nine autonomous regions based on black ethnic subgroups, militated against black unity without depriving the white-dominated economy of needed black labor. Resistance to such measures was met with increasingly severe retaliation directed by James I. Kruger, Minister of Justice, and General Mike Geldenhuys, head of the Security Police. Imprisonment without trial was introduced, the number of "bannings" multiplied, and periodic crackdowns were launched against individuals and organizations opposing official racial policies.

"When I took over the editorship of the *Dispatch*," Woods wrote in *Biko*, "I prayed for three years of immunity from arrest, detention, or banning. I was to have twelve." Week after week throughout those years, Woods attacked the government in the *Dispatch* and in a nationally syndicated column that ran in six newspapers. Wherever possible, he tried to use certain aspects of the system to his own advantage. For example, under the "law of defamation" he filed suits against Cabinet members, government officials, and poison-pen letter writers and won twenty of them. He also tried to make his influence felt in local and national politics, and he helped to enhance South Africa's international standing through his partly successful efforts to eliminate racial segregation in cricket, rugby, and tournament chess.

Although he was vehemently opposed to the Afrikaner government and its apartheid policies, Woods considered himself a moderate liberal until 1973, when he first met Stephen Biko. As honorary vice-president of the National Union of South African Students (NUSAS), a liberal body of English-speaking students, Woods had attacked Biko for what he considered the retrogressively racist policies of the South African Students Organization (SASO), the all-black movement that Biko headed after it split from NUSAS. To clear up what he considered Woods's misunderstanding of SASO's purposes, Biko arranged a meeting in King William's Town, where he lived under a government banning.

Woods found Biko an impressive young man of vigor, courage, and imagination, "the personification of an immense new force at the forefront of black politics in South Africa." The two became close friends despite Biko's conviction that black South Africans should invest no hope in white liberals. Woods assigned a black columnist to cover Biko's Black Consciousness movement for the *Dispatch* and tried to convince government officials that since such organizations as the Black African Congress were outlawed, they should negotiate with new leaders like Biko rather than persecute them.

It was largely because of his close association with Stephen Biko that Woods became internationally known. In 1975, after Biko's offices at King William's Town were broken into, Woods pressed legal charges against the policemen he believed to be responsible. When he refused to name his informant in court, he was sentenced to six months imprisonment, suspended only after he filed an immediate appeal. On August 18, 1977 Biko was jailed for the fourth time by security police and reportedly subjected to hours of interrogation, torture, and beatings, which were believed to have resulted in his death on September 12, at the age of thirty. Amid conflicting accounts of circumstances surrounding his death, some 10,000 blacks staged a protest rally at Biko's funeral. In his writings, and at many public meetings, Woods led an outcry against the atrocity, demanding a public inquest and refuting Justice Minister Kruger's suggestion that Biko died of self-starvation.

Woods was among the fifty persons arrested or placed under ban on October 19, 1977 when Minister Kruger carried out a sweeping crackdown against opponents to the government, closing two black newspapers, outlawing eighteen civil rights organizations, and jailing black leaders, among them Percy Qoboza, editor of the *Johannesburg World*. A protest by the United States State Department under President Jimmy Carter was met by Prime Minister Vorster's reply: "We are not governed from overseas." Under the conditions of his five-year ban, Woods was forbidden to write or to speak publicly, to be with more than one person-other than members of his family, at a time, to travel, or to engage in any "common social purpose." He was banned from the Dispatch offices and was required to report weekly to the police. Within ten days of his house arrest, Woods secretly began to write his biography of Biko, aided by research undertaken by his wife. Originally he had planned to publish it abroad anonymously, but as threats against his family made life in South Africa increasingly

precarious, fie realized that he would have to leave the country before the book could be published.

In December 1977 two small t-shirts picturing Biko arrived in the mail, apparently a present to Woods's children from a friend. As was later revealed, the package seemed to have been intercepted by security police, who treated the shirts with a mace-like chemical that scorched Woods's five-year old daughter, Mary, when she put one of them on, fortunately with no lasting effects. That act of harassment, coming on the heels of the sweeping victory of Vorster's Nationalists in the November parliamentary elections, clinched the family's determination to escape South Africa as soon as possible.

Disguised as a priest, Woods fled South Africa on December 29, 1977 with the help of friends and went overland to the black independent nation of Lesotho, where he was joined by his wife and children. The family then flew to Botswana, from there to Zambia, and finally to London where, to protect those who helped him, Woods told the reporters a false escape story. Soon thereafter he launched an international antiapartheid campaign, traveling many thousands of miles and addressing an estimated 3,000,000 people. Invited as the first private citizen to speak before the United Nations Security Council, on January 26, 1978 he called for "positive, constructive, and nonviolent" action against apartheid by the world body, including economic sanctions, ostracism of the Pretoria regime, and a register of international criminals that would include the "arch-culprits" who perpetrate apartheid in South Africa. In 1978 Woods also testified before a United States Congressional subcommittee and met with Secretary of State Cyrus Vance, Vice-President Walter F. Mondale, and President Jimmy Carter, urging them to set a timetable for an end of apartheid, with effective sanctions if it should not be met. Later that year, Woods served at Harvard University as a Nieman Fellow in journalism, which represents one of that profession's greatest achievements. Donald Woods's honors also include an Overseas Press Club Award.

In his articles and his two books, Woods tried to counteract the propaganda from Africa intended to convince the world that race relations there improved after Prime Minister P. W. Botha succeeded Vorster in September 1978. Written in haste and under harrowing conditions, the book *Biko* (Paddington Press, 1978) was applauded both as "an annotated sourcebook" on his friend's life and as a "devastating indictment of the

South African government." *Asking for Trouble: The Autobiography of a Banned Journalist* (Gollancz, 1980; Atheneum, 1981), an engaging, good-humored account of Woods's life, is in addition a searing expose of South African injustice. After reading it, the South African novelist Nadine Gordimer concluded: "There has never been a book like this one. Woods has laid his life on the line for what he believes, without a trace of self-righteousness." In the fall of 1981 Woods was working with the American film producer Carl Foreman in preparing a motion picture version of Asking for Trouble. Eventually, the film was retitled *Cry Freedom* and released in 1987. Directed by Richard Attenborough, it received critical acclaim and won numerous awards.

On February 11, 1990, Nelson Mandela was released from prison after serving twenty-seven years on Robben Island. That Easter, Mandela came to London to attend a concert at Wembley Stadium to thank the anti-apartheid Movement and the British people for all their years of campaigning against apartheid. Woods gave Mandela a tie in the black, green and gold colours of the African National Congress to celebrate the event. On Easter Sunday, Mandela phoned to thank Woods' family for the tie and said that he would wear it at the concert the next day, which he did.

Woods returned to South Africa in 1994 to support the fundraising efforts for the ANC election fund. His son Dillon was one of the organizers of the fundraising appeal in the United Kingdom. On April 27, 1994, Woods went to vote at the City Hall in Johannesburg. A cheering crowd took him to the head of the queue, giving him the place of honor so that he could be one of the first to vote in the new South Africa. Following the election, Donald worked for the Institute for the Advancement of Journalism in Johannesburg.

On September 9, 1997, on the twentieth anniversary of the death of Steve Biko, Woods was present in East London when a statue of Biko was unveiled by Nelson Mandela and the bridge across the Buffalo River was renamed the "Biko Bridge." Woods also gave his support to the Action for Southern Africa event in Islington, London honoring Biko, helping to secure messages from Ntsiki Biko, Mamphela Ramphele (then the Vice Chancellor of the University of Cape Town), and Mandela.

## PERSONAL LIFE

Donald Woods was married in 1963 at the Roman Catholic cathedral in Umtata to Wendy Bruce, a librarian, whom he has described as his front-runner "in the race away from rigid conservatism." The couple had five children, Jane, Dillon, Duncan, Gavin, and Mary, who lived in what they regard as temporary exile in England. Woods was a tall, bespectacled, distinguished looking man with graying hair, whose gadfly role seems at odds with his outgoing personality and his patience in trying to understand his opponents. He was a gifted amateur pianist and composer, an avid golfer, and an international tournament chess player who once carried Soviet grand master Viktor Korchnoi to a draw in Switzerland. A family man and a committed Christian, Woods was governed by the belief that "Man must be persuaded to get on with other men, regardless of race or color." In the last year of his life, Woods gave his name to support an appeal to erect a statue of Nelson Mandela in Trafalgar Square outside the South African High Commission, where anti-apartheid campaigners had demonstrated during the period of the apartheid regime. He died of cancer in London on August 19, 2001.

## FURTHER READING

*Biko; Asking for Trouble: The Autobiography of a Banned Journalist*

# Y

## MOLLY YARD
### Feminist; Social Activist

**Born:** July 6, 1912; Chengdu, Sichuan, China
**Died:** September 21, 2005; Pittsburgh, Pennsylvania
**Primary Field:** Gender Equality; Human Rights
**Affiliation:** Second-wave Feminism

### INTRODUCTION

*Molly Yard, who was elected to a three-year term as president of the 150,000-member National Organization for Women (NOW) in July 1987, was an activist in the cause of social justice for over half a century, from the student and labor movements of the 1930s and 1940s, through the civil rights struggles of the 1950s and 1960s, to feminist activism in the 1970s and 1980s. The first grandmother to head the national feminist group, Molly Yard, adamantly refused to divulge her exact age because of her unyielding conviction that "what matters is who you are and what you are capable of doing." Her longtime friends insist that she lost none of her intensity and zeal over the years, and she maintained that her abiding optimism and faith in the liberal agenda reflect the lessons that she learned from Eleanor Roosevelt, whom she called "almost a second mother to me."*

*For Molly Yard, according to Jacqueline Trescott of the* Washington Post *(September 23, 1987), "the new agenda is the old agenda." The journalist quotes her as saying: "Some of our friends on the Right tried to make 'liberal' a dirty word. [But] some things never change. The belief in social justice is a continuing concern. It comes right out of the Judeo-Christian ethic. That does not change."*

### EARLY LIFE

Molly Yard liked to declare: "I was born a feminist." Her father, James Maxon Yard, a Methodist missionary in Chengdu, the capital of Szechuan Province in China, received a brass bowl from his Chinese friends when his wife, Mabelle Merriam (Hickcox) Yard, gave birth to their third child and third daughter, Molly, in 1912. The gift symbolized their consolation that James Yard was still without a son. Growing up in China, Molly Yard heard at night the terrified, pained cries of young girls whose feet were being bound and unbound. She told Jacqueline Trescott, "I can still hear [those cries]." She remembers vividly, too, the sight of people dying in the streets from cholera. It was her parents, she says, who taught her to have a social conscience and not to surrender, no matter how great the obstacles.

James Yard's entire family suffered as a result of his outspokenness on behalf of the powerless. On one speaking tour back in the United States, he pressed for all the missions' in China to be turned over to the Chinese themselves. Such a radical proposal, at a time when every university in China started by the missions had a white president, was too audacious for Yard's superiors, and he was forced out of his mission job. Molly Yard was thirteen years old when the family returned to the United States and, as she told Marilyn Goldstein of *Newsday* (July 31, 1987), she had "an idealized view of America," concerning treatment of women and girls. She soon received a rude awakening in the American school system, where both academic and athletic preference were still being given to boys.

James Yard continued to reconcile the Christian religion with social activism and, as director of religious activities at Northwestern University, his efforts on behalf of race relations, union organizing, and the peace movement led to his firing. That took place during the lean Depression years, and Molly Yard remembers that it was her mother who supported the family by running a mail-order business for goods that she imported from China. "It was my mother who kept us going," she told Jacqueline Trescott, adding that, since her mother had been denied a college education by her own father, who had said that college was not for girls, she was determined that her own four daughters would have that chance.

Molly Yard attended Swarthmore College in Swarthmore, Pennsylvania, where she majored in political science. She established a reputation on campus as a political activist when she campaigned, successfully, for the abolition of the fraternity and sorority systems, after a Jewish friend was refused admittance to those enclaves of snobbism and elitism. Her Swarthmore yearbook wrote of her: "Molly, with the help of smiling blue eyes, manages to escape even the slightest hint of disheveled radicalism. But by temperament she is an authentic agitator. No abuse is too well-established, no precedent too accepted, no majority too overwhelming to silence her." Following her graduation, with an A.B. degree with honors, in 1933, she turned to social work, but soon found that avenue too frustrating for her militant inclinations.

## LIFE'S WORK

Becoming active in the American Student Union (ASU), Molly Yard served first as its national organization secretary and then as its chairperson. She first came to the attention of Eleanor Roosevelt because of the ASU's criticisms of the New Deal: there were still no jobs for students coming out of school. After Mrs. Roosevelt met with Molly Yard and offered her a sympathetic ear, the two women developed a warm friendship as well as a working relationship, and the ASU, which had become one of the major forces for social change during the Great Depression, later strongly backed Franklin D. Roosevelt and the New Deal. Joseph Lash, Eleanor Roosevelt's biographer and a colleague of Molly Yard's in the ASU in the 1930s, described her in those years as "a very spirited girl and very passionate about the causes we were involved in. She quickly showed she had the ability to serve people by her oratory and that she was a good organizer."

The president of NOW retains a living memory of Eleanor Roosevelt, to whom she refers in conversation as "E.R." She recalled for Jacqueline Trescott: "She was the one who in my youth, anytime you were defeated, down in the dumps, she could say, 'Don't worry, you can't always win; keep at what you believe in, and you will see that there are many times in life when you do win.'" When, in 1984, the Reagan White House hosted a celebration of the centennial of Eleanor Roosevelt's birth, Molly Yard joined a small group of demonstrators outside, carrying a "Retire Ronald Reagan" sign and sporting her t-shirt supporting the Equal Rights Amendment, which Reagan opposed. In her view, that the Reagans should "honor" Eleanor Roosevelt was an affront to "E.R.'s" memory.

In the 1940s Molly Yard became actively involved in Democratic party politics, a passionate interest that lasted some twenty-five years. While organizing for Democratic candidates in Philadelphia in the late 1940s, she was accused by one Republican political opponent of being a Communist. Unintimidated, she fought back with a lawsuit, and Eleanor Roosevelt testified on her behalf that "this is a grave injustice to a fine American and completely the reverse of the truth. As a sincere believer in and a fighter for democracy, she was never content to sit on the sidelines but met and fought the Communists in liberal organizations where they were attempting to infiltrate and take over." Molly Yard won $1,500 from the local Republicans, in addition to an apology on the front page of the local newspapers.

By 1950 Molly Yard had moved to California, together with her husband, the labor arbitrator Sylvester Garrett, who was then teaching on the law faculty of Stanford University. Because the couple, married in 1938, had three children, she took what she has described as a "domestic" break, though she has admitted that she "was not a genius as a mother." Discovering that she was unable to stay out of politics, she actively campaigned in the 1950 Senate race, supporting Helen Gahagan Douglas against Richard M. Nixon. Returning to Pennsylvania, she worked for the successful 1956 and 1962 senatorial campaigns of Joseph Clark, as well as the 1960 Citizens for Kennedy presidential campaign. In 1964 Molly Yard finally entered the political fray directly, running for a seat in the state legislature of Pennsylvania, but she was defeated in the effort.

Molly Yard's activities in the civil rights movement paralleled her activism elsewhere. She was the organizer in western Pennsylvania for the 1963 March on Washington, and she was heavily involved in the 1960s and early 1970s in the campaign to pass civil rights legislation nationally. As chairperson of the Pittsburgh YWCA, she worked to end racism at all levels, especially in housing, employment and education. In 1964 she led a massive march on the Pittsburgh Post Office, taking thousands of letters to senators and members of the House of Representatives, urging passage of the 1964 Civil Rights Act. In the same year she began working with the Leadership Conference on Civil Rights, a relationship she has maintained continuously since that time.

Molly Yard's consciousness of society's discrimination against women, which had begun in her childhood, gradually deepened through the years. When she married Sylvester Garrett, for example, she decided to keep her own name, but found that she could not open a joint bank account with two names, unless, she was told, she was Garrett's mistress, not his wife. But it was, surprisingly, in the American Progressive movement, as well as in society at large, that she encountered sexism. As a staff member of the VISTA program in the 1960s, she and the one other woman on the senior staff were never invited to the senior staff meetings. One day, they simply walked in to the meeting uninvited, feeling, as she recalled years later, "They couldn't throw us out." When, by the 1970s, she encountered no more than lip service to the principle of women delegates on the part of the Pennsylvania State Democratic Committee, she decided it was time to contact NOW.

Eleanor Smeal then headed the Pennsylvania NOW organization, and a political partnership began between Molly Yard and and Miss Smeal when the former became active in the Pittsburgh NOW chapter. In 1977 Eleanor Smeal was elected president of the national NOW, and in the following year, when the organization began an outreach campaign to obtain an extension of the deadline for the ratification of the Equal Rights Amendment passed by Congress in 1972, Molly Yard called Eleanor Smeal and, with her usual aplomb, said, "Hey, I think I know how to do this." She moved to Washington, D.C., to head that campaign, and after the ratification deadline was extended to June 1982, she joined NOW's national strike force for the ERA countdown campaign in Illinois, Florida, Oklahoma, North Carolina, and Virginia.

The final showdown came in Illinois, and Molly Yard traversed the marble halls of that state's legislature so much that she permanently injured the nerve endings in her feet. The Illinois, and national campaign lost, but she insisted that a "defeat" was no time for retrenchment, and within a month of the ERA setback, in June

1982, she organized a rally of 12,000 people to march on the Republican National Convention. She also served on the NOW Political Action Committee's (PAC) senior staff, from 1978 to 1984, and as NOW's political director, from 1985 to 1987. In 1986 she was responsible for the successful recruitment of over 350 co-sponsoring organizations for the National March for Women's Lives, and she acted as mistress of ceremonies at the massive rally following the march, in Washington, D.C. She was the senior staff person for NOW/Equality/PAC activities for 1986, during which NOW was a key factor in the defeat of four anti-abortion referenda. Her most severe loss also came in 1986, when she was the national NOW coordinator in the campaign for a state ERA in Vermont, a case, she herself has conceded, of defeat being snatched from the jaws of victory.

Despite her long experience and tireless energy, Molly Yard admits that she did have a moment's hesitation at the thought of running for the NOW presidency, after Eleanor Smeal announced she would not be seeking reelection in 1987. But then, she told Marilyn Goldstein, she thought about the nineteenth-century feminist pioneers Elizabeth Cady Stanton and Susan B. Anthony, who were active in that cause into their late eighties. "And I said sure I'd do it," she recounted, "I have a lot of years in front of me." She was backed by Eleanor Smeal for the top post, but though a vote for Molly Yard was viewed at the July 1987 NOW convention in Philadelphia as an endorsement of Eleanor Smeal's "back to the streets" visibility approach, the then incumbent made certain to emphasize that Molly Yard was not just her "extension." Referring to the fact that Molly Yard had opened the Philadelphia convention by running the last mile of the torch relay that had begun in Washington, she commented: "You want to know the differences between Molly and me, she ran a mile; I ran a block."

Also running for the post was forty-year-old Noreen Connell, the New York State NOW president, who maintained that Eleanor Smeal's high-profile style, with its emphasis on mass demonstrations and marches, detracted from a needed emphasis on local chapter-building and the steady, ongoing work of lobbying government officials. Molly Yard won, by a vote of 940 to 629, after a final campaign speech in which she pledged to organize a demonstration of a million marchers for the ERA and against toxic waste and prodigal defense spending. "The only war we seek is the war to end poverty, ignorance, and disease," she proclaimed in her booming orator's voice. As supporters sang out "Hello,

Molly," she stepped to the podium when her victory was announced, and there embraced her daughter, Joan Garrett-Goodyear, a professor of English at Smith College. "This is for all our daughters," she said.

In her typical go-getter fashion, Molly Yard was up early the next day, ready to "hit the decks running," garnering support for a possible run for the presidency of the United States by Representative Patricia Schroeder of Colorado. The "feminization of power" had become NOW's slogan, working toward the 1988 elections and a hoped-for field flooded with women candidates. Not one to mince words, Molly Yard publicly called for the impeachment of President Reagan and labeled his nominee for the United States Supreme Court, Robert H. Bork, "a Neanderthal." In addition to fighting Bork's nomination and encouraging Pat Schroeder's candidacy, her agenda for the first month in office included a protest outside the Vatican Embassy, during the Pope's American tour. A group of women, armed with a purple and yellow banner reading "A Message to the Pope: Women's Rights Are Human Rights," placed a "last lunch" at the Embassy door. As Molly Yard explained to the press, "The last supper was about betrayal. The last lunch is about [the] betrayal of women's rights by the Roman Catholic Church." She and her press secretary, Jeanne Clark, were arrested, handcuffed, and taken away in a waiting police van.

NOW's concentration on getting women to run for office at all levels in the 1988 elections was tied to its determination to renew the fight for the ERA. On June 30,1988 Molly Yard brought to the Capitol steps petitions with 100,000 signatures, calling for passage of the ERA. Representatives Pat Schroeder and Don Edwards stated they would reintroduce the amendment in the House of Representatives in January 1989, and Senator Edward M. Kennedy sent word that he would do the same in the Senate.

## PERSONAL LIFE

On Yard's attitude, "She's never discouraged in the conventional sense," her husband of some fifty years, Sylvester Garrett, has remarked. "She believes there's enough good in all human beings that our problems can be solved if people keep working on it." Leo Rifkin, a California history professor who first knew Molly Yard back in her ASU days, commented that when he saw her again in the 1980s, "The only difference is she's older. Basically, she's the same kind of person, very socially motivated, interested in making a better world. She said if she had to do it all over again, she'd do it the same way." A short, stocky, and athletic woman who wore her grey hair in a prim bun, Molly Yard lived with her husband on a sixty-acre farm in Ligonier, outside Pittsburgh, and commuted to a townhouse in Washington, D.C. They have three children and five grandchildren, and she enjoyed mountain climbing and skiing. She died in her sleep in a nursing home just outside Pittsburgh in on September 20, 2005.

## FURTHER READING

*http://now.org/*

# LENNOX YEARWOOD

## Minister; Activist

**Born:** 1969; Shreveport, Louisiana
**Primary Field:** Political Hip-Hop
**Affiliation:** Christian

## INTRODUCTION

*Most often seen publically clad in clerical clothing (black pants and shirt with a white collar) and a black baseball cap resting slightly askew atop his head, activist Lennox Yearwood Jr. embodies the seemingly incongruent intermingling of religion and hip-hop. An ordained minister with a master of divinity degree, Yearwood has embraced hip-hop as not only an expression of cultural identity, but also as a tool to raise social and political awareness among young people. As president of the Hip Hop Caucus, a nonprofit organization that focuses on increasing political involvement by integrating hip-hop music and culture into its public campaigns, Yearwood promotes an agenda that encompasses racial, environmental, and social issues through the lens of peaceful nonviolence.*

*Yearwood's purpose is twofold: to attract a young voting base that may feel like the political process is out of its hands, and to influence those in power to account for the young, primarily urban, voting bloc. "We're non-partisan," he told Arielle Loren for BET. com (September 17, 2012). "We want people to make [a voting] decision. We want an educated voter." On the other hand, he encourages politicians to engage young, specifically minority, voters. "[Do not] disregard a base of people because the numbers don't show they voted in the past, but figure out what we have to do to make sure they can vote." As a civil rights leader, Yearwood sees an increasing encroachment on basic rights, and his message is essentially that for freedom to be protected, people must understand the issues confronting policy makers and engage in the process of policy making by voting.*

## EARLY LIFE

Yearwood was born in 1969 in Shreveport, Louisiana, and was the first of his family, who mostly hail from Trinidad and Tobago, to be born in the United States. As an African American from a family of immigrants, he had a unique perspective on race relations that has informed his career arc.

*Lennox Yearwood.*

In 1990, as a student at the University of the District of Columbia (UDC), in his first foray into activism, Yearwood organized a student sit-in that lasted ten days. He and the other students were protesting both budget cuts and a proposed relocation of the campus; the school did eventually close its downtown campus, moving to the North Cleveland Park area of the capital city. Yearwood graduated from UDC in 1998. Four years later, he earned a master of divinity degree from Howard University. He also spent time in the US Air Force Reserve, joining in 2000 in order to help pay for his education. He entered the Chaplain Candidates program, finishing in 2003, at which point he decided not to become an Air Force chaplain, though he remained a reservist.

## LIFE'S WORK

Yearwood came to prominence as an advocate for the importance of youth culture. Though he has been described by many as a radical, he has spent more than a decade as a political activist focused on empowering African Americans and other minorities, as well as exposing what he deems to be the political corruption of the federal government. In 2004, Yearwood partnered with rap superstar Sean Combs to create the "Vote or Die" campaign, encouraging young people and minorities to play a part in the political process. "We have to grow our power within politics to be able to break down barriers," Combs said at the time (*NBCNews.com* October 29, 2004). "Vote or Die" was one of several campaigns in 2004 that focused on the youth vote, which accounted for 18.4 percent of the total vote and set a precedent for future voter campaigns.

Yearwood began the Hip Flop Caucus nonprofit organization in 2004; his goal was to integrate hip-hop culture and political campaigns to increase public involvement. He linked his agenda with that of Combs and rap mogul Russell Simmons, who, with Yearwood, embarked on the Hip Hop Team Vote Bus Tour. Yearwood's work with rap luminaries coincided with the general mission of the Hip Hop Caucus. Addressing the reason for his involvement with the hip-hop generation, in an interview with Martha van Gelder for *Green America* (Jan./Feb. 2013), Yearwood said, "I think that there's an idealistic viewpoint that this world can be something better. I think there's a hope, there's an energy. But most importantly, for students everywhere, it's about their future."

Continuing what he started in 2004, Yearwood initiated "Respect My Vote!" for the 2008 election cycle to target young adults between the ages of eighteen and. twenty-nine without college experience. The "One Day Vote" campaign headed by the Hip Hop Caucus registered more than thirty thousand people on September 30, 2008, and featured performers such as Nelly, "This one day event proves that we can make an impact in this election, and that working together to get out the vote is the only way to see results," Yearwood said at the time (*Common Dreams* October 3, 2008). Because of its success in 2008, Yearwood insists that the hip-hop generation was a primary force behind the election of President Barack Obama. "Respect My Vote" resurfaced for the midterm elections of 2010. Registering young people to vote has been a much publicized aspect of the Flip Flop Caucus's mission, but its overarching goal has been to help young people identify the connections between poverty, racism, and the environment, among other issues.

As a minister of Church of God in Christ, a Pentecostal and largely African-American denomination, Yearwood has been a spokesman for peace; he was particularly outspoken about the US invasion of Iraq in 2003, at which time he was training to be a chaplain in the Air Force. A February 2003 sermon that he delivered at Andrews Air Force Base (entitled "Who Would Jesus Bomb?") aligned him with the interpretation of the biblical Jesus as a promoter of peace. Over the following years, Yearwood began a vociferous campaign against the Iraq War, one that pitted him against the establishment in which he was entrenched; he conflated events such as the federal government's handling of Hurricane Katrina in New Orleans with military action in the Middle East and the country's history of oppressing minorities. In a July 2, 2007, press release from the Hip Flop Caucus, Yearwood insisted, "This moment in history is our generation's lunch-counter moment, Iraq is our Vietnam and New Orleans is our Birmingham. Our generation could be the generation to defeat racism, poverty and war, but only if we come together as people of conscience."

Soon after launching the "Make Hip Flop Not War" tour in 2007, Yearwood received notice that he was to be discharged from the Air Force, ostensibly because of his antiwar stance. He issued the July 2007 press release to inform the general public of the campaign being waged against him. Because of Yearwood's resistance to being discharged, the Air Force reportedly considered deploying him to Iraq or sentencing him to jail With pressure from the public, the Air Force eventually decided to grant him an honorable discharge. "I will end my service with the honorable discharge that I earned," Yearwood stated, as quoted by Ken Butigan on the website *Waging Nonviolence* (February 7, 2013). "I am eternally grateful, and evermore committed to taking on the powers that be for the powers that ought to be."

Only months after his letter, in September 2007, Yearwood was at the center of another controversy when he was arrested while trying to enter the hearing room where General David Petraeus was testifying about the Iraq War. A widely circulated online video shows Yearwood trying to regain his place in line after exiting to conduct an interview (according to him, with permission from the police) and then being denied entrance to the hearing. After he and the officer who denied him access spoke for a brief period, a group of officers surrounded him, handcuffed him, and dragged him to the ground. On September 12, after his arraignment for charges that included assaulting an officer and disorderly conduct, he released, a statement via the Flip Hop Caucus (and quoted on the website *Common Dreams*) in response to his arrest: "My role is to make government more transparent to the people, especially people of color. How am I supposed to convince other African-Americans to come to Capitol Hill to participate in democracy, when Capitol Police will go so far as to jump me when I question my exclusion from a hearing that is open to the public?" His arrest only served to affirm his belief in an unjust system that sought to exclude minorities and those who questioned the machinations of the federal government.

Yearwood has used hip-hop to connect to a young generation that is increasingly politically aware, a development for which he is at least partially responsible, and as he has gained more political footing within the community, he has begun to shift his focus to environmental issues, specifically climate change. Yearwood was a key participant in the "Forward on Climate" rally held in Washington, DC, in February 2013; he also served as the host of the event. Yearwood has established himself as a unique personality in the environmental movement, lending a perspective to a cause that has been primarily a white middle to upper class undertaking.

"This year is the 150th anniversary of the Emancipation Proclamation, and were celebrating that from the standpoint that slavery was an institution, just like Big Oil, that we were able to get rid of. It took a lot, but we were able to get rid of that," Yearwood explained to Van Gelder for *Green America*. By conflating race issues with the environment, Yearwood hopes both to expose what he perceives to be the establishment's resistance to change even in the face of overwhelming evidence and to remind the public, specifically minority communities, that institutions can be altered. To push his environmental agenda, he and the Hip Hop Caucus have reached out to black colleges, where issues concerning the environment have not always been at the forefront, and to others in minority communities that usually set issues of race, poverty, and education above environmentalism. He told Van Gelder: "They need to understand that while there is clearly a need to address poverty and education and issues of imbalance, if we don't correct the situation involving our planet, all those problems will cease to exist."

Yearwood first began to see how climate issues impact underprivileged communities during Hurricane Katrina, creating the Gulf Coast Renewal Campaign, and he continues to focus on the role young people can play in the debate over climate change and its effects. "[They] have always been at the core of every single movement that has created change in this country, and

it cannot stop now," he said to Van Gelder. As he told Alexander Zaitchik for *Rolling Stone*, "What we're seeing now, young people willing to get arrested, is what we need, because the situation is critical. For me, if that means literally putting my body against the gears of the machine to stop the madness, that's what I'll do." Yearwood's radicalism, sparked by both the power imbalance he experienced as an African American youth and his understanding of the Christian gospel as a mechanism for peaceful change, has made him a key figure in the environmental movement, one of the most pressing ongoing political issues.

Yearwood has garnered comparisons to Martin Luther King Jr., a spokesman for justice and peace at a critical juncture in the history of the United States. The underlying connections are obvious: like King, Yearwood is a minister and civil rights leader who employs nonviolent resistance to engender political change. Though King and his ideas entered the mainstream long ago, Yearwood insists that the radical nature of King's mission is often glossed over. "His message was neutered," Yearwood claimed in an interview with Michael Cooper Jr. for *Generation Progress* (January 23, 2013). "In his last speech he linked up with the striking sanitation workers in Memphis. He was against the [Vietnam] war, and even called out his country as one of the greatest purveyors of violence in this world. It is almost intentional to neutralize his message." Despite feeling that King's radicalism has been neutralized, however, Yearwood is emboldened by the stances taken by King and. is clearly influenced by him. He points to King as an early purveyor of the intermingling of politics and culture, which is the foundation of the Hip Hop Caucus, "Culture comes before politics," he told Cooper. "Using artists like 2 Chainz or Immortal Technique allows us to create a drum beat to march to, which makes our work easier, Even Dr. King worked with Harry Belafonte, Every movement needs cultural game changers to make a difference." To Yearwood, linking entertainment and politics is not counterintuitive, but, contrarily, is essential to provoking change, and he uses King as an example of the ways religion, culture, and politics can mingle to incite people to think about broad issues that affect entire communities.

## PERSONAL LIFE

Named in 2010 as one of *Ebony* magazine's one hundred most powerful African Americans, Yearwood, through the Hip Hop Caucus, has promoted politics as cool, collaborating with Combs, Jay-Z, and many others in the hip-hop community to raise awareness in schools and among youth in general. "I believe that we are the most important generation this country has ever had," he said to Cooper, "If we fight for justice, and equality, and fairness, we can change this country and the world." Saint Paul's College in Virginia granted him an

honorary doctorate degree in 2011. Yearwood is the father of two boys and lives in the Washington, DC, area.

### FURTHER READING
*http://www.hiphopcaucus.org/; http://www.huffington-post.com/rev-lennox-yearwood/*

---

# ANDREW YOUNG (JACKSON, JR.)

## United States Ambassador to the United Nations

**Born:** Mar. 12, 1932, New Orleans, Louisiana
**Primary Field:** Civil Rights

### INTRODUCTION

*Andrew Jackson Young, Jr., now in his 80's, has dedicated his entire life to the Civil Rights Movement. The former Mayor of Atlanta, American Ambassador to the United Nations (U.N.), and U.S. House of Representative from Georgia's Fifth Congressional District, now retired from politics, continues to share his knowledge of the Civil Rights Movement and his memories of Rev. Dr. Martin Luther King, Jr.*

*When U.S. Representative Andrew Young accepted then President Jimmy Carter's nomination to become United States Ambassador to the United Nations, he exchanged a promising and secure political future that almost certainly included eventual succession to the Chairmanship of the influential House Rules Committee, for a precarious and, in the eyes of many of his Black colleagues, no longer prestigious position. Young, a clergyman and deputy to the slain Civil Rights leader, Dr. Martin Luther King, Jr., entered politics as a liberal Democrat to continue the struggle for human rights. Elected to the House of Representatives from Georgia's Fifth Congressional District, in 1972, he was the state's first Black Congressman since Reconstruction. Because Young was a close friend of, and political adviser to, President Carter, most political observers saw the U.N. appointment as a sign of a moral regeneration in American foreign policy. In her syndicated column of December 14, 1976, Mary McGrory added that the "symbolism of a Black American speaking for this country to all the nations of the world will not be lost."*

*Unfortunately, his tenure in that office was cut short on August 14, 1979, when the President asked him*

*to resign due to the "Andy Young Affair," when Young met with a Zehdi Terzi, the U.N. representative of the Palestine Liberation Organization (P.L.O) at the apartment of the U.N. Ambassador from Kuwait. On August 10, news of this meeting became public when Mossad (the intelligence arm of the Israeli government) leaked its illegally acquired transcript of the meeting first to Prime Minister Menachem Begin, and then through his office to Newsweek. The meeting was highly controversial, since the United States had already promised Israel that it would not meet directly with the P.L.O. until the PLO recognized Israel's right to exist.*

*Young stated to* Time *magazine: "It is very difficult to do the things that I think are in the interest of the country and maintain the standards of protocol and diplomacy. . . I really don't feel a bit sorry for anything that I have done." Later he stated that Israel was 'stubborn and intransigent.'"Despite this setback, Young began speaking on the university lecture circuit and successfully ran as Mayor of Atlanta.*

### EARLY LIFE

The grandson of a prosperous "bayou entrepreneur," Andrew Jackson Young, Jr., was born in New Orleans, La., on March 12, 1932. His father, Andrew J. Young, was a well-to-do dentist; his mother, Daisy (Fuller) Young, a teacher. Reared in what he has described as a "black bourgeois" environment, he and his younger brother Walter grew up as the only Black children in a middle-class, predominantly Irish and Italian neighborhood. According to Young, his parents went "to great lengths" to shield him from racism and taught him to be proud of his heritage. "I was taught to fight when people called me nigger," he said, as quoted in *Time* (October 5, 1970) magazine. "That's when I learned that negotiating was better than fighting."

Young learned to read and write before he reached school age and began his formal education in the third grade of a segregated Black elementary school. Following his graduation from Gilbert Academy, a private high school, in 1947, he enrolled at Dillard University in New Orleans.

## LIFE'S WORK

The following year, he transferred to Howard University in Washington, D.C., as a pre-med student. Young had intended to become a dentist, but, after obtaining his B.S. degree in 1951, began to have second thoughts about his career. Inspired by a dedicated clergyman, he finally decided to enter the ministry. At the Hartford Theological Seminary in Hartford, Conn., he studied, among other things, the teachings of Mohandas Gandhi and became convinced that he could, in his words, "change this country without violence."

Graduated in 1955 with a B.D. degree, Young was ordained a minister in the United Church of Christ, a largely White denomination with a demonstrated interest in social action. Denied permission to establish a mission in Angola, then a Portuguese colony, he returned to the South, where he became a pastor of churches in Marion, Ala., and in Thomasville and Beachton, Ga. "I wanted to be around plain, wise, Black folk," he explained to Orde Coombs in an interview for *New York* (July 19, 1976) magazine. "I thought, then, that poor people who knew suffering and love and God could save the world." As the Civil Rights Movement gained momentum, Young organized his church members into community action groups and, despite repeated threats from the Ku Klux Klan, spearheaded a voter registration drive in his district.

Hired by the National Council of Churches, in 1957, Young spent the next four years in New York City, working almost exclusively with White youths. As the Associate Director of the Department of Youth Work, Young was in charge of the council's athletics and media programs. Eager to take part in the accelerating effort to end segregation, he readily accepted when United Church of Christ officials asked him to administer a voter education and registration project funded by the Field Foundation. In the course of his work, Young often collaborated with Dr. Martin Luther King, Jr., the leader of the Southern Christian Leadership Conference (S.C.L.C.), the largest and most influential of the Civil Rights groups. He eventually joined that organization late in 1961, rising to the post of Executive Director in 1964.

Along with other black spokesmen, Young helped to draft the Civil Rights Act of 1964 and the Voting Rights Act of 1965. As the S.C.L.C.'s top strategist, he developed training programs for local Black leaders, many of whom have since become sheriffs or mayors, and led the behind-the-scenes negotiations with White businessmen and politicians that resulted in phased programs of desegregation in many Southern cities. Often marching in the front lines of Dr. King's nonviolent protest demonstrations, he directed the massive campaign against segregation in Birmingham, Ala., and was in charge of the demonstration on May 3, 1963, when Police Commissioner Eugene ("Bull") Connor used dogs and high-pressure fire hoses to repulse the marchers. He later walked at Dr. King's side through threatening and jeering crowds in a demonstration for open occupancy in Chicago.

After Dr. King's assassination in April 1968, Rev. Ralph David Abernathy, King's trusted lieutenant, took over the leadership of the S.C.L.C. and immediately named Young his Executive Vice-President. Together, the two men mapped out their strategy for a Poor People's Campaign, climaxing in a mass march on Washington, D.C., in May 1968, to pressure Congress to enact antipoverty legislation. At first, the S.C.L.C. was strengthened by a tremendous influx of funds and volunteers following King's death, but it lost both contributions and volunteer help to the growing Peace Movement in the late 1960s. Recognizing that the S.C.L.C. was no longer strong enough to take on any national issues, Young outlined a conservative new course for the organization in mid-1969, in which he stressed voter registration and political action campaigns.

Convinced that the "power in America is in the political structure," Andrew Young resigned from the S.C.L.C. in 1970 to run for the United States House of Representatives from Georgia's predominantly White Fifth Congressional District. "The whole movement now has to move to more active political participation," he explained to Earl Caldwell in an interview for the *New York Times* (August 9, 1970). "If a White majority elects a Black man to Congress, it will say that the American dream is still possible and it will restore faith in this country and in the political process for a lot of people—the young and the poor and the Black—those groups that are most alienated."

With the support of Abernathy, Coretta Scott King, Martin Luther King's widow, and Julian Bond, the Black Georgia State Legislator who attracted national attention at the Democratic National Convention, in Chicago, in 1968, Young put together a biracial political organization of hard-working volunteers, many of them veterans of the Civil Rights wars. Preaching conciliation and moderation, he easily defeated Lonnie King, a Black, and two White contenders for the Democratic nomination in the primary, in September 1970. His opponent in the general election was the two-term incumbent Fletcher Thompson, a conservative Republican and Nixon supporter, who contended that Young's election would lead to the collapse of Western civilization. Aided by the votes of nervous, middle-class Whites, Thompson defeated Young by more than 20,000 votes.

After his defeat, Young took a job as Chairman of the Atlanta Community Relations Commission. Two years later, he resigned to make a second run for Congress. Since his first attempt, the Fifth Congressional District had been redistricted by court order to reflect the state's changing demography. Consequently, the proportion of registered Black voters increased from less than 30 percent to about 44 percent. Running on a progressive platform symbolized by such catchy slogans as "Think Young" and "Young Ideas for Atlanta," Young appealed to Blacks and to White liberals. In the November general election, he took virtually the entire Black vote and about 25 percent of the White vote, defeating his moderate Republican opponent, Rodney M. Cook by 72,289 votes to 64,495 votes. He was returned to Congress in landslide victories of 72 percent in 1974 and 80 percent in 1976.

During his freshman term in office, Young established a reputation as a conscientious, hard-working Representative, attuned to the needs and desires of his constituents. Despite the pressure of legislative duties and his work on the House Banking and Currency Committee, he made frequent weekend visits to his district. "That's doubly important where Black people are concerned," he explained to Hamilton Bims in an interview for *Ebony* magazine (February 1973). "We're terribly cynical about people we don't see. We don't read too much about our men in the paper, so it's their physical presence and accessibility that counts."

On the House floor, Young repeatedly rejected attempts to cut domestic appropriations for the poor. He voted to increase the minimum wage, and, to extend its coverage to domestic workers; to broaden the food stamp program; to establish a federal day-care program; and, to create federally funded public service jobs for the unemployed. Young also approved legislation authorizing the use of government subsidies to help out-of-work homeowners meet mortgage payments; the expansion of the Medicaid program to include coverage for abortions; the creation of a consumer protection agency; and, federal aid to New York City. Appalled at the rising cost of medical care, Young introduced a bill outlining a comprehensive national health care plan. He also took stands to support busing to end racial segregation in the schools; tax reform; simplified voter registration; and, the public financing of Congressional elections. An ardent conservationist, he voted for the establishment of minimum federal standards for surface mining and land reclamation, and, for the creation of a national land use program.

Long opposed to the war in Vietnam (officially known as the Vietnam Conflict), Young joined his colleagues in the House and Senate in overriding Nixon's veto of the War Powers Bill limiting Executive warmaking powers. He refused to approve military aid to the South Vietnamese regime headed by President Nguyen Van Thieu but, after the fall of the Saigon government, in April 1975, agreed to supply emergency humanitarian and evacuation aid. The U.S. Representative, who admitted to a deep-seated "fear of the power of the military," repeatedly denied Department of Defense requests for increased military expenditures, and disapproved the appropriation of funds for antiballistic missiles, nerve gas, and the controversial B-l bomber. Committed to majority rule in Africa, he introduced legislation prohibiting aid to Portuguese military factions in Angola, Mozambique, and Guinea-Bissau—all former Portuguese colonies.

In assessing Young's voting behavior, the liberal Americans for Democratic Action consistently rated him at 95 percent, or higher, while the Conservative Americans for Constitutional Action regularly assigned him ratings of 7 percent, or lower. Despite his decidedly liberal bent, Young occasionally took surprising positions. In October 1973, for example, he shocked his colleagues in the Congressional Black Caucus when he made a speech in the House supporting President Nixon's nomination of Gerald R. Ford as Vice-President. "Gerald Ford had voted against everything I had been for, yet, I found being around him a good experience," he explained to Phil Gamer in an interview for the *Atlanta Journal* (March 24, 1974). "I decided that here was a guy I wanted to give a chance. He was certainly better than a Reagan or any of the other alternatives at the time. Besides, Atlanta was going to need to work very closely with the next Administration." The following year, he was the only Black legislator who defended President Ford's "full, free, and absolute" pardon of Richard Nixon.

Young first met Jimmy Carter when the latter was campaigning for the governorship of Georgia, in 1970. Impressed by his ability and political expertise, Governor Carter openly sought the younger man's advice and frequently conferred with him on matters of special interest to Blacks. Although he originally preferred a more liberal Democratic aspirant to the Presidency, Young eventually concluded that Carter, because of his "great understanding and sympathy for Blacks and poor people," was the only candidate who could deliver the South and ensure a Democratic victory in 1976. In general, Young was delighted with Carter's folksy campaign style, but objected to the candidate's off-the-cuff remark about the right of individuals to resist "Black intrusion" and "alien groups," and to preserve the "ethnic purity of [their] neighborhoods." Although Young conceded that Carter's position was "as American as apple pie," he deplored his choice of words in that instance as "awful" and "loaded with Hitlerian connotations." Acting on Young's advice, Carter issued a public apology.

Generally credited with mustering Black support for Carter, Young delivered one of the seconding speeches placing the Governor's name in nomination at the Democratic National Convention in New York City, in July 1976. "I'm ready to lay down the burden of race," he told the assembled delegates, "and Jimmy Carter comes from a part of the country which, whether you know it or not, has done just that." To counteract Republican gains in the public opinion polls, Young mobilized a massive door-to- door voter registration drive in the inner cities, netting 3,104,000 new, predominantly Democratic voters. His efforts paid off on Election Day, when Carter defeated Ford by slightly more than 1,744,000 votes. Young is the only person to whom Carter has openly acknowledged a political debt.

In mid-November, President-elect Carter chose Young to represent the new Administration at a meeting of American and African leaders in Lesotho, South Africa. Young's grasp of the situation on the troubled continent led Carter to nominate him for the post of American Ambassador to the United Nations on December 16, 1976. At first Young hesitated, but, he finally accepted,

after receiving assurances from Carter that he would have a role in the formulation of foreign policy. At his confirmation hearings before the Senate Foreign Relations Committee on January 25, 1977, Young replied to the Senators' probing questions with characteristic frankness. Among other measures, he recommended that the United States "move forthrightly" to establish a normal diplomatic relationship with the Socialist Republic of Vietnam, and, that Congress repeal the Byrd amendment permitting the importation of chrome in defiance of United Nations sanctions as an indication of American commitment to majority rule in Rhodesia and South Africa. Unanimously endorsed by the Committee, Young was quickly approved by the full Senate.

On January 31, 1977, Ambassador Young presented his credentials to Kurt Waldheim, then the Secretary General of the United Nations, and, after making a round of courtesy calls, set to work housecleaning the United States Mission. Distrustful of Foreign Service professionals, he brought his own staff to the mission and hired women, and, Hispanics and other minorities, for diversity. Young envisioned an international system of "five worlds," in which the United States was no longer a dominant power—the industrial nations; the oil-rich and mineral-rich emerging nations; developing countries, (such as the People's

Republic of China); and then, last, the multinational corporations. Young believed that to survive in that new world, the United States must "get on the right side of the moral issues."

Underscoring the Carter Administrations support for a peaceful transition to majority rule in Rhodesia (now Zimbabwe), Young left on a second ten-day fact-finding mission to Africa, shortly after he took office. There he attended the Second World Black and African Festival of Arts and Culture in Lagos, Nigeria, and met with several Black African leaders, including Julius Nyerere, the President of Tanzania, Kenneth Kaunda, the President of Zambia, and President Agostinho Neto of Angola. He also conferred with Ivor Richard, the British chairman of the disbanded talks on Rhodesia. Young's outspoken analyses of the explosive political situation in Rhodesia and other trouble spots was repudiated by the State Department three times. "To preserve the right to say what I really believe," Young said in an interview, "I'd be willing to take whatever flak came, and I'd be willing to be repudiated . . . whenever it was officially necessary."

During his tenure as Ambassador, Young continued to be controversial, which led to his resignation in August 1979. During a July 1978 interview with French newspaper *Le Matin de Paris*, while discussing the Soviet Union and its treatment of political dissidents, he said, "We still have hundreds of people that I would categorize as political prisoners in our prisons," in reference to jailed civil-rights and anti-war protestors. U.S. Representative Larry McDonald (D-GA) sponsored a resolution to impeach Young, which failed, 293 to 82. Carter called it an "unfortunate statement."

In another controversy, Young played a leading role in advancing a settlement in Rhodesia with Robert Mugabe and Joshua Nkomo, who had been two of the military leaders in the Rhodesian Bush War, which had ended in 1979. The settlement paved the way for Mugabe to take power as Prime Minister of the newly formed Republic of Zimbabwe. This negated a general election, in 1979, which brought Bishop Abel Muzorewa to power as leader of the United African National Council, and the formation of the short-lived country of Zimbabwe Rhodesia. Young refused to accept the elections results, and described the election as "neofascist," a sentiment echoed by United Nations Security Council Resolution 445 and 448. The situation was resolved the next year with the Lancaster House Agreement and the establishment of Zimbabwe.

The controversy that led his resignation in August 1979 resulted because Young felt that an upcoming report by the United Nations Division for Palestinian Rights, which called for the creation of a Palestinian State, needed to be delayed. He wanted to delay the report because the Carter Administration was dealing with too many other issues at the time. He met with U.N. representatives of several Arab countries to try to convince them the report should be delayed; but they insisted that the P.L.O. also had to agree, which in turn led to the furor over Young's meeting with the P.L.O. At the time, the P.L.O. was considered a terrorist organization and Young had committed a serious breach of protocol in U.S. foreign relations.

Andrew Young went on to successfully run for Mayor of Atlanta, in 1981, at the urging of Coretta Scott King. He was elected later that year with 55 percent of the vote, succeeding Maynard Jackson. As Mayor of Atlanta, Young brought in $70 billion of new private investment. He continued and expanded Jackson's programs for including minority and female-owned businesses in all city contracts. Young was re-elected

as Mayor in 1985 with more than 80 percent of the vote. During Young's tenure, Atlanta hosted the 1988 Democratic National Convention. He was barred from running for a third term, so in 1990, Young launched a failed bid for the Democratic nomination for Governor in 1990. Young, however, was successful in his campaign for Atlanta to host the Olympic Games in 1996.

Since that time, Young has been active mostly in the private, not-for-profit sector. He was a director of the Drum Major Institute for Public Policy; is also the Chairman of the Board for the Global Initiative for the Advancement of Nutritional Therapy; again served as President of the National Council of Churches, from 2000 to 2001; founded the Andrew Young Foundation, in 2003 (an organization meant to support and promote education, health, leadership and human rights in the United States, Africa and the Caribbean); and, served as the public spokesman for Working Families for Wal-Mart, an advocacy group for the retail chain Wal-Mart, from February to August 2006 (he resigned after a controversial interview with the *Los Angeles Sentinel*, in which, when asked about Wal-Mart hurting independent businesses, he replied, "You see those are the people who have been overcharging us, and they sold out and moved to Florida. I think they've ripped off our communities enough. First it was Jews, then it was Koreans and now . . . Arabs.")

Young, in 2007, served as the narrator of the film, *Rwanda Rising*, which in turn led to *Andrew Young Presents*, a series of quarterly, hour-long specials airing on nationally syndicated television. Young appeared as a guest on the television show *The Colbert Report*, on January 22, 2008, and again on November 5, 2008.

Young has received several acoledes: The Presidential Medal of Freedom; the National Association for the Advancement of Colored People's Springarn Medalin; the Golden Plate Award from the American Academy of Achievement, which website has a fascinating interview about his life (see http://www.achievement.org/autodoc/page/you0int-1); Morehouse College in Atlanta established the Center for International Studies, in 1993, which was renamed the Andrew Young Center for International Studies, in March 1998; he also became a professor at the Georgia State University's school named for him: the Andrew Young School of Policy Studies, where he can still be spotted by students in the halls.

He has written several books, including *A Way Out of No Way* (1994); *An Easy Burden: The Civil Rights*

*Movement and the Transformation of America* (1996); and, *Walk in My Shoes: Conversations Between a Civil Rights Legend and His Godson on the Journey Ahead* (2010).

## PERSONAL LIFE

On June 7, 1954, he married Jean Childs Young, a teacher. They had four children, Andrea, Lisa Dow, Paula Jean, and Andrew "Bo" Young 3rd. His first wife died of cancer in 1994. He married his second wife, Carolyn, in 1996.

## FURTHER READING

*Biog N p605 + My '74 pors Ebony 28:83+ F '73 pors London Observer pl3 N 21 '76 por N Y Times B p5 D 17 '76 por; Mag pl7 + F 6 '77 pors Sat Rev 4:6+ O 16 '76 pors Washington Post H pl+ Jl 25 '76 pors Who's Who in America, 1976-77 Who's Who in American Politics*

---

# MALALA YOUSAFZAI

## Activist

**Born:** July 12, 1997; Pakistan
**Primary Field:** Human Rights
**Affiliation:** Humanitarianism; Education

## INTRODUCTION

*Malala Yousafzai had been a thorn in the side of the Pakistani Taliban since at least the age of eleven when she began publicly blogging for the BBC about life in her town under the Taliban's oppressive rule. A bright and inquisitive student, she was especially distressed that their rigid interpretation of Islamic law called for banning education for girls. With schools being shuttered and often destroyed, Yousafzai also appeared in a series of documentaries made by the New York Times to bring attention to the issue. Taliban leaders found the attention unwelcome, and on October 9, 2012, a gunman boarded the school bus on which Yousafzai was riding and shot her in the head.*

*Although gravely injured, Yousafzai survived and subsequently continued her activism on an even wider stage. "In trying, and failing, to kill Malala, the Taliban appear to have made a crucial mistake," Aryn Baker wrote for Time (December 19, 2012), "they wanted to silence her. Instead, they amplified her voice." Since October her message has been heard around the world, from cramped classrooms where girls scratch out lessons in the dirt to the halls of the UN and national governments and NGOs, where legions of activists argue ever more vehemently that the key to raising living standards throughout the developing world is the empowerment of women and girls. Yousafzai was already a spokesperson; the Taliban made her a symbol.*

*So powerful a symbol did Yousafzai become, in fact, that in 2014 she garnered a Nobel Peace Prize, the first Pakistani person ever to do so, and at seventeen, she also became the youngest ever recipient of the prize. "I tell my story, not because it is unique, but because it is not, she said at the Nobel ceremony in Oslo. I am Malala. But I am also Shazia. I am Kainat. I am those 66 million girls who are deprived of education. And today I am not raising my voice, it is the voice of those 66 million girls."*

## EARLY LIFE

Malala Yousafzai was born on July 12, 1997, in the Swat District of Pakistan, an area known for its abundant natural beauty and as a tourist destination. Yousafzai was named for Malalai of Maiwand, a famous female Pashtun poet; the name means "grief-stricken." Yousafzai was raised in the town of Mingora, and her father, Ziauddin, is a poet and former student activist who sat on Mingora's Qaumi Jirga (community council). Believing strongly in education for all, he ran the private Khushal School, named for Khushal Khan Khattak, a seventeenth-century Pashtun warrior and poet celebrated for standing up to the Mongols. There the classes included English, physics, biology, and math, among other topics.

Yousafzai's mother, Tor Pekai, never attended school and is rarely seen in public. The family is Sunni, and Tor Pekai adheres to the traditional practice of 'Purdah' or separation from unrelated men. Still, she is widely described as a source of quiet strength and support for her daughter and husband. Yousafzai has two brothers, Khushal and Atal, and during her Nobel acceptance speech she quipped, "I am pretty certain that I am the first recipient of the Nobel Peace Prize who still fights with her younger brothers. I want there to be peace everywhere, but my brothers and I are still working on that."

When Yousafzai was very young, the family lived in a two-room apartment connected to the school. They later moved to a larger home with a garden. Even as a toddler, Yousafzai regularly accompanied her father to work at the school and often sat with the older children and absorbed all she could. "Right from the beginning, Malala was my pet," Ziauddin told Marie Brenner for *Vanity Fair* (April 2013). "She was always in the school and always very curious." Yousafzai was soon writing long essays, reciting Urdu poetry, and winning debate contests. Among her favorite books was Paulo Coelho's *The Alchemist*, and when other young girls were decorating their hands with henna drawings of flowers and swirls, she adorned hers with mathematical equations. In other ways, Yousafzai was a typical preadolescent girl, watching a reality show called *My Dream Boy Will Come to Marry Me* and rooting for her favorite cricket players.

## LIFE'S WORK

In mid-2008, the Pakistani Taliban, formally known as Tehrik-i-Taliban Pakistan (TTP) and closely linked to the Afghan Taliban and al-Qaeda began gaining control in the Swat Valley and imposing strict Sharia law. They banned the sale of DVDs, ordered beauty shops to shut down, and announced their intention to close girls' schools. At the age of eleven, Yousafzai accompanied her father to the press club in Peshawar and gave a speech titled "How Dare the Taliban Take Away My Basic Right to Education?" While many in attendance criticized Ziauddin for allowing her to give a speech that was sure to anger members of the militant Islamist group, he asserted that his daughter knew her own mind and wanted to speak out.

Foreign journalists were drawn to the events taking place in the Swat Valley, and the BBC approached Ziauddin to help them find a schoolgirl to blog for them. After the first candidate declined because of her fear of the TTP, Yousafzai stepped in and corresponded with the British media outlet under a pseudonym. In early January 2009 she wrote, "I was afraid going to school because the Taliban had issued an edict banning all girls from attending schools. Only 11 students attended the class out of 27. On my way from school to home I heard a man saying 'I will kill you.' I hastened my pace [but] to my utter relief he was talking on his mobile and must have been threatening someone else over the phone." In

all, she wrote almost forty entries using the pen name Gul Makai. She rarely hesitated to make her opinions known in person, and proclaimed on a televised show hosted by anti-Taliban broadcaster Hamid Mir, "All I want is an education, and I am afraid of no one."

When the *New York Times* sent a documentary team to film the final days of school for girls in the Swat Valley, Ziauddin somewhat reluctantly allowed his family to be the focus of the project. A close friend said, "'This documentary will do more for Swat than you could do in 100 years.' I could not imagine the bad consequences," he told Brenner, explaining that no one believed that the Taliban would attempt to assassinate a schoolgirl.

By the time the Taliban were driven from Swat, some four hundred schools had been destroyed, the vast majority of them girls' schools. Yousafzai used her increased profile to campaign to raise government spending on education and encourage parents to allow their daughters to attend classes. Several rebuilt schools were named in her honor.

Yousafzai's high profile and willingness to speak out continued to enrage Taliban leaders, and on October 9, 2012, two men stopped her school bus, which held about a dozen girls and a handful of teachers. They boarded the bus, and while one began conversing with the driver, the other approached the girls and asked, "Which one of you is Malala?" Uneasy, some glanced quickly at her, and the gunman fired, shooting her in the head. Her friend, Shazia, screamed, and the man reacted by shooting her and a third girl.

The bullet that had been aimed at Yousafzai grazed the exterior of her skull, hit her jawbone, traveled through her neck and lodged in the muscle above her left shoulder blade. Pakistani doctors worked feverishly to remove the bullet, and within days she was flown to Queen Elizabeth Hospital in Birmingham, England, for further treatment. In a series of lengthy surgeries, British doctors inserted a titanium plate in her skull and provided her with a cochlear implant. Photos of Yousafzai in her hospital bed looking weak but gazing unflinchingly at the photographer, galvanized public outrage. Cards and gifts flooded into the facility, and Yousafzai had several well-known visitors, including the president of Pakistan, Asif Ali Zardari.

Maulana Fazlullah, the leader of the Taliban in Swat during that time, publicly admitted to ordering the assassination attempt. "We did not want to kill her, as we knew it would cause us a bad name in the media," Sirajuddin Ahmad, a spokesman for the group, told

Baker a few months after the failed attempt. "But there was no other option."

Yousafzai garnered several notable international prizes before and after being shot. In 2011 she won Pakistan's National Youth Peace Prize, which has since been renamed the National Malala Peace Prize. She was in the running as *Time's* Person of the Year in 2012, and the following year she was named by the editors of the magazine as one of the one hundred most influential people in the world. She won a Mother Teresa Memorial Award for Social Justice in 2012, and in 2013 she was awarded the Simone de Beauvoir Prize for Women's Freedom for her international human rights work.

In 2014, Yousafzai received one of the most prestigious awards in the world: the Nobel Peace Prize. She shared the prize with Indian Kailash Satyarthi, a fellow children's rights activist. In a press release, the Nobel Committee announced that it "regards it as an important point for a Hindu and a Muslim, an Indian and a Pakistani, to join in a common struggle for education and against extremism."

Later in the year, Yousafzai won the $50,000 World Children's Prize, which she ultimately donated to the United Nations Relief and Works Agency for Palestine Refugees for the purpose of rebuilding schools in the Gaza Strip that were damaged in the Israel-Hamas conflict.

## PERSONAL LIFE

The Yousafzai family remained in England after Malala recuperated. Ziauddin was appointed the United Nations Special Advisor on Global Education and the educational attaché to the Pakistani Consulate in Birmingham. He also chairs the board of the Malala Fund, a nonprofit group dedicated to promoting education for all girls worldwide and helping them to stand up for their right to education.

In 2013, Yousafzai's memoir, *I Am Malala*, cowritten by journalist Christina Lamb, was published to near-universal acclaim. She now attends Birmingham's Edgbaston High School for Girls, and she told a reporter for *BBC News* (March 19, 2013), "I think it is the happiest moment that I'm going back to school, this is what I dreamed, that all children should be able to go to school because it is their basic right." She continues to speak out on issues of importance to her, including the kidnapping of Nigerian schoolgirls by Boko Haram and the plight of Syrian refugees.

## FURTHER READING

*I Am Malala; The Girl Who Was Shot for Going to School*

# Appendixes

# UNIVERSAL DECLARATION OF HUMAN RIGHTS

*The Universal Declaration of Human Rights (UDHR) is a milestone document in the history of human rights. Drafted by representatives with different legal and cultural backgrounds from all regions of the world, the Declaration was proclaimed by the United Nations General Assembly in Paris on December 10, 1948.*

*A common standard of achievements for all peoples and all nations, General Assembly resolution 217(III) sets out, for the first time, fundamental human rights to be universally protected.*

## Preamble

Whereas recognition of the inherent dignity and of the equal and inalienable rights of all members of the human family is the foundation of freedom, justice and peace in the world,

Whereas disregard and contempt for human rights have resulted in barbarous acts which have outraged the conscience of mankind, and the advent of a world in which human beings shall enjoy freedom of speech and belief and freedom from fear and want has been proclaimed as the highest aspiration of the common people,

Whereas it is essential, if man is not to be compelled to have recourse, as a last resort, to rebellion against tyranny and oppression, that human rights should be protected by the rule of law,

Whereas it is essential to promote the development of friendly relations between nations,

Whereas the peoples of the United Nations have in the Charter reaffirmed their faith in fundamental human rights, in the dignity and worth of the human person and in the equal rights of men and women and have determined to promote social progress and better standards of life in larger freedom,

Whereas Member States have pledged themselves to achieve, in cooperation with the United Nations, the promotion of universal respect for and observance of human rights and fundamental freedoms,

Whereas a common understanding of these rights and freedoms is of the greatest importance for the full realization of this pledge,

Now, therefore,
The General Assembly,

Proclaims this Universal Declaration of Human Rights as a common standard of achievement for all peoples and all nations, to the end that every individual and every organ of society, keeping this Declaration constantly in mind, shall strive by teaching and education to promote respect for these rights and freedoms and by progressive measures, national and international, to secure their universal and effective recognition and observance, both among the peoples of Member States themselves and among the peoples of territories under their jurisdiction.

## Article I

All human beings are born free and equal in dignity and rights. They are endowed with reason and conscience and should act towards one another in a spirit of brotherhood.

## Article 2

Everyone is entitled to all the rights and freedoms set forth in this Declaration, without distinction of any kind, such as race, colour, sex, language, religion, political or other opinion, national or social origin, property, birth or other status.

Furthermore, no distinction shall be made on the basis of the political, jurisdictional or international status of the country or territory to which a person belongs, whether it be independent, trust, non-self-governing or under any other limitation of sovereignty.

## Article 3

Everyone has the right to life, liberty and security of person.

## Article 4

No one shall be held in slavery or servitude; slavery and the slave trade shall be prohibited in all their forms.

## Article 5

No one shall be subjected to torture or to cruel, inhuman or degrading treatment or punishment.

## Article 6

Everyone has the right to recognition everywhere as a person before the law.

## Article 7

All are equal before the law and are entitled without any discrimination to equal protection of the law. All are entitled to equal protection against any discrimination in violation of this Declaration and against any incitement to such discrimination.

## Article 8

Everyone has the right to an effective remedy by the competent national tribunals for acts violating the fundamental rights granted him by the constitution or by law.

## Article 9

No one shall be subjected to arbitrary arrest, detention or exile.

## Article 10

Everyone is entitled in full equality to a fair and public hearing by an independent and impartial tribunal, in the determination of his rights and obligations and of any criminal charge against him.

## Article 11

1. Everyone charged with a penal offence has the right to be presumed innocent until proved guilty according to law in a public trial at which he has had all the guarantees necessary for his defence.
2. No one shall be held guilty of any penal offence on account of any act or omission which did not constitute a penal offence, under national or international law, at the time when it was committed. Nor shall a heavier penalty be imposed than the one that was applicable at the time the penal offence was committed.

## Article 12

No one shall be subjected to arbitrary interference with his privacy, family, home or correspondence, nor to attacks upon his honour and reputation. Everyone has the right to the protection of the law against such interference or attacks.

## Article 13

1. Everyone has the right to freedom of movement and residence within the borders of each State.

2. Everyone has the right to leave any country, including his own, and to return to his country.

## Article 14

1. Everyone has the right to seek and to enjoy in other countries asylum from persecution.
2. This right may not be invoked in the case of prosecutions genuinely arising from non-political crimes or from acts contrary to the purposes and principles of the United Nations.

## Article 15

1. Everyone has the right to a nationality.
2. No one shall be arbitrarily deprived of his nationality nor denied the right to change his nationality.

## Article 16

1. Men and women of full age, without any limitation due to race, nationality or religion, have the right to marry and to found a family. They are entitled to equal rights as to marriage, during marriage and at its dissolution.
2. Marriage shall be entered into only with the free and full consent of the intending spouses.
3. The family is the natural and fundamental group unit of society and is entitled to protection by society and the State.

## Article 17

1. Everyone has the right to own property alone as well as in association with others.
2. No one shall be arbitrarily deprived of his property.

## Article 18

Everyone has the right to freedom of thought, conscience and religion; this right includes freedom to change his religion or belief, and freedom, either alone or in community with others and in public or private, to manifest his religion or belief in teaching, practice, worship and observance.

## Article 19

Everyone has the right to freedom of opinion and expression; this right includes freedom to hold opinions without interference and to seek, receive and impart information and ideas through any media and regardless of frontiers.

## Article 20

1. Everyone has the right to freedom of peaceful assembly and association.

2. No one may be compelled to belong to an association.

### Article 21

1. Everyone has the right to take part in the government of his country, directly or through freely chosen representatives.

2. Everyone has the right to equal access to public service in his country.

3. The will of the people shall be the basis of the authority of government; this will shall be expressed in periodic and genuine elections which shall be by universal and equal suffrage and shall be held by secret vote or by equivalent free voting procedures.

### Article 22

Everyone, as a member of society, has the right to social security and is entitled to realization, through national effort and international co-operation and in accordance with the organization and resources of each State, of the economic, social and cultural rights indispensable for his dignity and the free development of his personality.

### Article 23

1. Everyone has the right to work, to free choice of employment, to just and favourable conditions of work and to protection against unemployment.

2. Everyone, without any discrimination, has the right to equal pay for equal work.

3. Everyone who works has the right to just and favourable remuneration ensuring for himself and his family an existence worthy of human dignity, and supplemented, if necessary, by other means of social protection.

4. Everyone has the right to form and to join trade unions for the protection of his interests.

### Article 24

Everyone has the right to rest and leisure, including reasonable limitation of working hours and periodic holidays with pay.

### Article 25

1. Everyone has the right to a standard of living adequate for the health and well-being of himself and of his family, including food, clothing, housing and medical care and necessary social services, and the right to security in the event of unemployment, sickness, disability, widowhood, old age or other lack of livelihood in circumstances beyond his control.

2. Motherhood and childhood are entitled to special care and assistance. All children, whether born in or out of wedlock, shall enjoy the same social protection.

### Article 26

1. Everyone has the right to education. Education shall be free, at least in the elementary and fundamental stages. Elementary education shall be compulsory. Technical and professional education shall be made generally available and higher education shall be equally accessible to all on the basis of merit.

2. Education shall be directed to the full development of the human personality and to the strengthening of respect for human rights and fundamental freedoms. It shall promote understanding, tolerance and friendship among all nations, racial or religious groups, and shall further the activities of the United Nations for the maintenance of peace.

3. Parents have a prior right to choose the kind of education that shall be given to their children.

### Article 27

1. Everyone has the right freely to participate in the cultural life of the community, to enjoy the arts and to share in scientific advancement and its benefits.

2. Everyone has the right to the protection of the moral and material interests resulting from any scientific, literary or artistic production of which he is the author.

### Article 28

Everyone is entitled to a social and international order in which the rights and freedoms set forth in this Declaration can be fully realized.

### Article 29

1. Everyone has duties to the community in which alone the free and full development of his personality is possible.

2. In the exercise of his rights and freedoms, everyone shall be subject only to such limitations as are determined by law solely for the purpose of securing due recognition and respect for the rights and freedoms of others and of meeting the just requirements of morality, public order and the general welfare in a democratic society.

3. These rights and freedoms may in no case be exercised contrary to the purposes and principles of the United Nations.

**Article 30**

Nothing in this Declaration may be interpreted as implying for any State, group or person any right to engage in any activity or to perform any act aimed at the destruction of any of the rights and freedoms set forth herein.

# Chronology of Human Rights
## 1946-2016

**1946**    The Economic and Social Council (ECOSOC) of the U.N. establishes the Commission of Human Rights, whose initial objective is to draft an international statement defining human rights.

Following the Nuremberg trials, an international conference is held in Paris to establish an international criminal code, from which was born the International Criminal Court.

**1947**    India receives its independence after years of non-violent protests led by Mahatma Gandhi.

Universal Declaration of Human Rights is adopted by the U.N. General Assembly.

The UN adopts the Convention of the Prevention and Punishment of the Crime of Genocide.

The Organization of American States adopts the Declaration of the Rights of Man.

**1949**    The Diplomatic Conference for the Establishment of International Conventions for the Protection of Victims of War (Geneva Convention) approves standards for more humane treatment for prisoners of war, the wounded, and civilians.

The Statute of the Council of Europe asserts that human rights and fundamental freedoms are the basis of the emerging European system.

**1952**    U.S. Congress passes the Immigration and Nationality Act (aka the McCarran-Walter Act), ending the last racial and ethnic barriers to naturalization of aliens living in the U.S., but reduces U.S. immigration quotas from eastern and southeastern Europe.

**1954**    The U.S. Supreme Court rules in *Brown v. Board of Education* that racial segregation in public schools is unconstitutional.

**1955**    The Montgomery, Alabama bus boycott begins when African American Rosa Parks refuses to give up her seat on the bus.

The U.S. adopts the Standard Minimum Rules for the Treatment of Prisoners.

**1957**    The Civil Rights Act of 1957 is passed by Congress.

Great Britain decriminalizes homosexual behavior between two consenting adults but bans gays in the military.

**1961**    President John F. Kennedy appoints Eleanor Roosevelt to head the first Presidential Commission on the Status of Women.

**1963**    200,000 Americans gather in Washington, D.C., for the March on Washington for Jobs and Freedom, designed to illuminate challenges faced by African Americans.

**1964**        Civil Rights Act of 1964, protecting individuals against racial or sexual discrimination, is passed by Congress.

**1965**        The Voting Rights Act of 1965, aimed to overcome legal barriers preventing African Americans from voting, is passed by Congress.

President Lyndon B. Johnson signs the Immigration Act of 1965, eliminating the ethnic quotas established under the McCarran-Walter Act of 1952.

**1966**        In *Miranda v Arizona*, the U.S. Supreme Court rules that law enforcement must give individuals suspected of committing a crime certain protections under the law.

**1967**        Congress passes Age Discrimination Act of 1967, aimed to protect those Americans 40 years of age and older from employment discrimination.

**1968**        First International Conference on Human Rights convenes in the capital of Iran.

**1969**        The Stonewall Riots in New York City begin a movement for gay rights.

**1972**        *Furman v Georgia* decision by the U.S. Supreme Court requires consistency in death penalty determination, resulting in a national moratorium on capital punishment.

Title IX passes, guaranteeing that "No person in the United States shall, on the basis of sex, be excluded from participation in, be denied the benefits of, or be subjected to discrimination under any program or activity receiving Federal financial assistance."

**1973**        In *Roe v Wade*, the Supreme Court's decision states that bans on abortion are unconstitutional, and protects a woman's right to privacy.

**1976**        Executions resume in the U.S. when the U.S. Supreme Court decides *Gregg v Georgia*, finding state death penalties constitutional when additional criteria is met.

**1977**        A human rights bureau is created within the U.S. Department of State, issuing its first reports on human rights the same year.

U.S. President Jimmy Carter begins to institutionalize human rights agendas into American foreign policy.

**1980**        Convention on Elimination of Discrimination of Women is signed by the U.S.

**1981**        Declaration on the Elimination of All Forms of Intolerance Based on Religion or Belief is adopted by the U.N.

**1982**        The U.N. adopts the Principles of Medical Ethics.

**1985**        The Committee on Economic, Social, and Cultural Rights is established within the U.N.
U.N. adopts the Nairobi Forward-looking Strategies for the Advancement of Women.

**1986**        U.N. adopts the Declaration on the Right to Development.

**1989**         In *Sanford v Kentucky*, the U.S. Supreme Court rules constitutional capital punishment of children who are 16 and over when their crime was committed.

The Berlin Wall is dismantled.

**1990**         The Americans with Disabilities Act is signed into law, establishing "a clear and comprehensive prohibition of discrimination on the basis of disability."

**1992**         U.N. Security Council resolution condemns "ethnic cleansing" in Bosnia and Herzegovina. A second resolution demands that all detention camps in Bosnia and Herzegovina be closed.

**1993**         Office of the High Commissioner for Human Rights is established by the U.N. General Assembly.

The U.S. adopts the policy "Don't Ask, Don't Tell, Don't Pursue" which gives the government the right to remove open homosexuals from military service.

U.N. adopts the Declaration on the Elimination of Violence against Women.

**1994**         An emergency session of the Commission on Human Rights convenes in response to genocide in Rwanda.

The first U.N. High Commissioner for Human Rights, Jose Ayala Lasso, takes his post.

The U.N. declares a Decade for Human Rights Education on December 23, 1994.

**1995**         Fourth World Conference on Women, aimed at empowering women around the world, takes place in Beijing.

The Truth and Reconciliation Commission is created by the South African Government to address human rights violations under apartheid.

**1997**         Mary Robinson, former President of the Republic of Ireland, becomes the second U.N. High Commissioner for Human Rights.

**1998**         The International Religious Freedom Act is passed by Congress.

**2001**         "War on Terror" is declared by President George W. Bush following terrorist attacks in New York and Washington, D.C.

Congress passes the Patriot Act, aimed to unite and strengthen the U.S. by providing appropriate tools to intercept and obstruct terrorism.

**2002**         Capital punishment of mentally ill persons is deemed unconstitutional following the U.S. Supreme Court's decision in *Atkins v Virginia*.

Guantánamo Bay Detention Camp is opened to house suspected terrorists.

**2004**          U.S. Supreme Court rules in Rasul v Bush that U.S. District Courts have jurisdiction to determine legality of detention of Guantánamo "enemy combatant" detainees.

U.N. Security Council adopts resolution referring Sudan to the International Criminal Court for human rights crimes in Darfur.

Two years after the invasion of Iraq by Coalition Forces to remove Saddam Hussein, the Iraqi people hold their first free election.

**2006**          In *Hamdan v Rumsfeld*, the U.S. Supreme Court rules that the military commission set up to try Guantánamo detainees lacked authority.

**2009**          U.S. issues "Human Rights Pledge" and is elected a member of the U.N. Human Rights Council.

Convention on the Rights of Persons with Disabilities is signed by the U.S.

**2010**          Human Rights Policy is announced by President Barack Obama's administration.

Patient Protection and Affordable Care Act is passed by Congress.

**2011**          U.S. completes Universal Periodic Review procedure by U.N. Human Rights Council, who adopts final Outcome Report.

The U.S. Department of Justice issues final standards under the Prison Rape Elimination Act (PREA), for the detection, prevention, reduction, and punishment of rape in prison facilities.

The U.S. Supreme Court upholds the Affordable Care Act, intended to expand access to health insurance and medical care.

**2013**          Congress renews the Violence Against Women Act (VAWA), which provides legal protection and services to victims of domestic and sexual violence and stalking, and enhances the law to include protections for immigrants and LGBT victims.

**2014**          The U.S. Supreme Court rules in *Burwell v. Hobby Lobby Stores, Inc.* that certain corporations can refuse to cover contraception in employee health insurance plans based on the owner's religious views.

**2015**          The National Defense Authorization Act (NDAA) is signed into law by President Obama, tightening restrictions on the transfer of detainees out of Guantanamo.

U.S. Supreme Court issues the landmark decision that grants same-sex couples the right to marry.

**2016**          A federal judge temporarily rules that the University of North Carolina can't block transgender students from using bathrooms that match their gender identity.

# WEBSITE DIRECTORY

**American Civil Liberties Union**
www.aclu.org

**Amnesty International USA**
www.amnestyusa.org

**Human Rights Campaign**
www.hrc.org

**Human Rights Watch**
http://www.hrw.org

**International Justice Mission**
www.ijm.org

**International Labour Organization**
www.ilo.org

**Lawyers Committee for Human Rights**
www.lchr.org

**National Youth Rights Organization**
www.youthrights.org

**Office of the High Commissioner for Human Rights**
www.unhchr.ch

**United Nations Foundation**
www.unfoundation.org

**United Nations International Children's Emergency Fund (UNICEF)**
www.unicef.org

**United Nations Development Programme**
www.undp.org

**United Nations Population Fund**
www.unfpa.org

**World Health Organization**
www.who.int

# Indexes

# HUMAN RIGHTS CATEGORY INDEX

**Homelessness Reform**
Robert M(ichael) Hayes

**Human Rights**
Adolfo Perez Esquivel
Ai-jen Poo
John Prendergast
David Protess
Bruce Ritter
Randall Robinson
Paul Rusesabagina
Eunice Kennedy Shriver
Joe Solmonese
Jacobo Timerman
Elie Wiesel
Jody Williams
Donald Woods
Molly Yard
Malala Yousafzai

**Literacy Reform**
Jonathan Kozol
Rueben Martinez

**Native American Activism**
Wilma P. Mankiller

**Peace Movement**
Daniel Berrigan
Philip Francis Berrigan
Joan Blades & Wes Boyd
Paul Chan
Mairead Corrigan Maguire
Daniel Ellsberg
Leymah Gbowee
Linus C. Pauling
Joseph Rotblat
Jim Wallis

**Peace & Justice Movement**
William Sloane Coffin, Jr.
Pope Paul VI
Albert Schweitzer
Betty (Smyth) Williams

**Political Dissident**
William Blum
Adam Michnik
Mihajlo Mihajlov

Anatoly Shcharansky

**Population Control**
Werner H. Fornos

**Pro-Choice Abortion Rights**
Ellen R. Malcolm

**Public Health**
Frederica Perera
Elizabeth Pisani
Nafis Sadik

**Race Equality**
Allan (Aubrey) Boesak
Kimberlé Williams Crenshaw
Morris S. Dees, Jr.
Emory Douglas
Deadria Farmer-Paellmann
Bell Hooks
Rick Lowe
Eleanor Holmes Norton
Tavis Smiley

**Religious Freedom**
W. Deen Mohammed

**Reproductive Health**
Faye Wattleton

**Social Equality & Reform**
Dennis Banks
Judianne Densen-Gerber
Mahasweta Devi
John Doerr
Amitai Etzioni
Sam Harris
Hazel Henderson
Dolores Huerta
Howard (Arnold) Jarvis
Maggie Kuhn
Rigoberta Menchu

**Social Justice**
Susan George
Thuli Madonsela
Mahmood Mamdani
Rigoberta Menchu
Jim Wallis

# INDEX